HP-UX
Virtual Partitions

ISBN 0-13-035212-8

90000

Hewlett-Packard® Professional Books

Hewlett-Packard Professional Books

MORE BOOKS FROM MARTY PONIATOWSKI

HP-UX Virtual Partitions

◆

UNIX User's Handbook, Second Edition

◆

HP-UX 11i System Administration Handbook and Toolkit

◆

HP-UX 11.x System Administration Handbook and Toolkit

◆

HP-UX 11.x System Administration "How To" Book,
Second Edition

◆

HP-UX System Administration Handbook and Toolkit

◆

HP-UX 10.x System Administration "How To" Book

◆

Learning the HP-UX Operating System

HP-UX
Virtual Partitions

Marty Poniatowski

Hewlett-Packard Company

www.hp.com/hpbooks

Prentice Hall PTR
Upper Saddle River, New Jersey 07458
www.phptr.com

Library of Congress Cataloging-in-Publication Data

A CIP catalogue record for this book can be obtained from the Library of Congress.

Editorial/production supervision: *Patti Guerrieri*
Cover design director: *Jerry Votta*
Cover design: *Talar Boorujy*
Manufacturing manager: *Maura Zaldivar*
Acquisitions editor: *Jill Harry*
Editorial assistant: *Sarah Hand*
Marketing manager: *Dan DePasquale*

Publisher, Hewlett-Packard Books: *Patricia Pekary*

Published by Prentice Hall PTR
A division of Pearson Education, Inc.
Upper Saddle River, New Jersey 07458

Prentice Hall books are widely used by corporations and government agencies for training, marketing, and resale.

The publisher offers discounts on this book when ordered in bulk quantities. For more information, contact Corporate Sales Department, Phone: 800-382-3419; FAX: 201-236-7141;
E-mail: corpsales@prenhall.com
Or write: Prentice Hall PTR, Corporate Sales Dept., One Lake Street, Upper Saddle River, NJ 07458.

Printed in the United States of America
10   9   8   7   6   5   4   3   2   1

ISBN 0-13-035212-8

Pearson Education LTD.
Pearson Education Australia PTY, Limited
Pearson Education Singapore, Pte. Ltd.
Pearson Education North Asia Ltd.
Pearson Education Canada, Ltd.
Pearson Educación de Mexico, S.A. de C.V.
Pearson Education — Japan
Pearson Education Malaysia, Pte. Ltd.

Chapter 13 Networking. 815

PREFACE

About Virtual Partitions

With Virtual Partitions (vPars) you can take almost any HP 9000 server and turn it into many "virtual" computers. These virtual computers can each be running their own instance of HP-UX and associated applications. The virtual computers are isolated from one another at the software level. Software running on one Virtual Partition will not affect software running in any other Virtual Partition. In the Virtual Partitions you can run different revisions of HP-UX, different patch levels of HP-UX, different applications, or any software you want and not affect other partitions.

There are some base requirements that must be met in order to run vPars on your system. At the time of this writing, the following requirements minimum requirements must be met for each vPar on your system:

- Minimum of one CPU.

- Sufficient memory to run HP-UX and any other software that will be present in the vPar.

- A boot disk off of which HP-UX can be booted. At the time of this writing it is not possible to share bus adapters between vPars. Therefore, a separate bus adapter is required for each of the vPars. This requirement may have been removed by the time you read this book.

• A console for managing the system. The console can be either physical or virtual. We'll cover the console in detail in the book.

• An HP 9000 system supported by HP-UX 11i. At the time of this writing only HP-UX 11i is supported in vPars. With systems based on Itanium Processor Family (IPF) processors, there are plans to support numerous operating systems in vPars in the future.

The system we'll use in most of the examples throughout this book is an L-Class system that meets all of the requirements in the previous list. You may also want to have additional disks and a separate LAN card in each of your vPars. I strongly recommend the LAN card so that you can establish TELNET, or other, sessions to your vPars rather than connect to them only from the console. The LAN card is also required to perform backup and Ignite-UX related work.

If you have Instant Capacity on Demand (iCOD) employed on your server, all CPUs must be activitated in order for vPars to work. When employing Processor Sets (psets) in a vPar, use only bound CPUs.

There is a vPars product bundled with HP-UX 11i as well as a full, or add-on product. There are very few limitations with the add-on product. The bundled product has a limitation of a maximum of two vPars and one of the vPars can have only one CPU.

This book was written with Virtual Partitions software that had not yet been released. There have been many enhancements to Virtual Partitions since the writing of this book. There is a Graphical User Interface being considered for vPars that I haven't covered in this book. There is something to be said for working with a product when it is new. You really get a good understanding of the functionality of the product by using the command line only and performing a lot of manual procedures. In addition, Superdome vPars software in covered in Appendix A had just become available as early access software. The vPars software for Superdome operates identically to that on the L-Class and N-Class systems covered in the earlier examples in the book. Although the Virtual Partitions product has been streamlined since the writing of this book you'll gain a good understanding of Virtual Partitions by the procedures I cover herein.

I hope you enjoy reading the book and learning the material as much as I did writing it.

Marty Poniatowski

marty_poniatowski@hp.com

Virtual Partitions (vPars) Background

HP-UX Virtual Partitions (vPars) allow you to run multiple instances of HP-UX on the same HP 9000 server. From a hardware perspective a vPar consists of CPU, memory, and I/O that is a subset of the overall hardware on the computer. From a software perspective a vPar consists of the HP-UX 11i Operating Environment and all application-related software to successfully run your workload. Figure P-1 shows a conceptual diagram of the way in whcih HP 9000 computer system resources can be allocated to support multiple vPars.

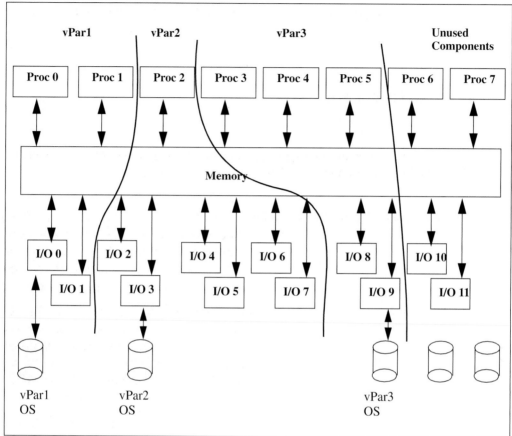

Figure P-1 Example of HP System Resource Allocation with vPars

The components of which your HP 9000 is comprised can be allocated in a variety of ways. You can see that the eight-way system shown has a different number of processors, different amount of memory, and different number of I/O cards allocated to each vPar. The unused components can be added to any of the vPars or be the basis for yet another vPar. In addition, components can be moved from one vPar to another (with some restrictions described later in the book).

Uses of Virtual Partitions

I have worked on many vPars installations that have a variety of uses for vPars. The following are a sampling of the reasons to use vPars:

Increased System Utilization - Many servers are underutilized. With vPars you can devote a subset of system resources to each vPar. With each vPar running its own instance of HP-UX 11i and associated applications, you'll get higher overall system utilization.

Flexibility -   Many applications have resource needs that change. With vPars you can devote fewer system components when application needs are low and additional resources when an application needs them. An increased end-of-the-month workload, for instance, can be given more system resources to complete faster.

Server Consolidation - Running multiple instances of HP-UX 11i and their assoicated applications on one HP server reduces the overall number of servers required. Web servers that had run on different servers can now be run in different vPars on the same computer.

Application Isolation - HP vPars are fully software-isolated from one another. A software failure in one vPar does not affect other vPars.

Mixed Production, Test, and Development - Production and testing can take place on the same server with vPars. When testing is complete, the test vPar can become the production vPar. Similarly, development usually takes place on a separate system. With the software isolation of vPars, however; development can take place on the same system with other applications.

These are just a sampling of the uses I've seen for vPars. Many others will emerge as vPars become widely used and systems experts implement them in more computing environments.

Organization of the Book

I did not restrict this book to covering only Virtual Partitions (vPars) related material. I cover many HP-UX 11i system administration topics and the way in which they are affected by vPars. This is, however, not a complete HP-UX 11i system administration book. *The HP-UX 11i System Administration Handbook and Toolkit* is a complete system administration guide that you may want to consider as a companion to this book. It also contains a UNIX® section as well as an HP-UX and Windows® interoperabilty section.

Each chapter starts with partition-specific information and later in the chapter contains background information on the topic. In the chapter covering booting partitions, for instance, I first cover topics specifically related to booting partitions. Later in the chapter I cover booting in general. Covering both the partition-specific information related to a topic and then background information on the same topic gives you most of what you need to know to successfully deal with partitions.

Relevant URLs

There are many Web sites that can assist you in your Virtual Partition-related work and HP-UX system administration in general. The following are some of the more prominent HP-UX-related Web sites as they existed at the time of this writing:

IT Resource Center
(This is essential for every HP-UX administrator):
http://www.itrc.com

Technical documentation, including most HP-UX documents:
http://www.docs.hp.com

Software depot home page:
http://www.software.hp.com

vPar product information:
http://www.hp.com/go/servicecontrol

vPar Systems Administrator's Guide:
http://docs.hp.com/hpux

Instant Capacity on Demand (iCOD):
http://www.hp.com/go/icod

The International Association of HP Computing Professionals:
http://www.interex.org

Configurable kernel parameters:
http://docs.hp.com/hpux/onlinedocs/os/KCparams.OverviewAll.html

Index of HP-UX online documents:
http://docs.hp.com/hpux/onlinedocs/os

Information on HP's new architecture Itanium processor family:
http://www.IA64.hp.com

Register name servers at:
http://www.icann.org/registrars/accredited-list.html.

Excellent unsupported system administration scripts at:
ftp://contrib:9unsupp8@hprc.external.hp.com/sysadmin/

Software used for UNIX and Windows interoperability at:
http://www.hummingbird.com/products/evals/index.html

Information on Perl, including sites to download Perl:

http://www.perl.com

The Perl Journal:

http://www.tpj.com

Information about the GNOME desktop environment:

http://www.gnome.org

Public-domain software that has been ported to HP-UX:

http://hpux.connect.org.uk

Site devoted to managing and promoting open source:

http://www.opensource.org

Linux documentation site:

http://www.linuxdoc.org

Information on Java running on HP:

http://www.hp.com/go/java

Manual Pages Supplied with the Book

I am most grateful to Hewlett-Packard Company for having allowed me to include vPars manual pages and a few other select manual pages in this book. I have received a great deal of positive feedback on the inclusion of manual pages in my previous books. Many readers find it helpful to have the manual pages in the book to refer to when reading it when there is no system available to check on a command (apparently, a lot of people are reading my books while not at the office).

When a command is used for which there is an online manual page included in the book, the following information appears in the margin:

This is a "man page" block, which includes the man page icon, the command name, in this case **vparstatus**, and the chapter number in which the online manual page appears, in this case Appendix A.

Acknowledgments

There were too many people involved in helping me with this book to list each and every one. I have, therefore, decided to formally thank those who wrote sections of the book and those who took time to review it. I'm still not sure whether it takes more time to write something or review something that has been written to ensure that it is correct.

Duane Zitzner

Duane Zitzner is President Computing Systems and Vice President Hewlett-Packard Company. Duane acted as the executive champion and sponsor of this book. His support was invaluable in helping get the resources necessary to complete this book.

The Author - Marty Poniatowski

Marty has been a System Engineer with Hewlett-Packard Company for fifteen years in the New York area. He has worked with hundreds of Hewlett Packard customers in many industries, including Internet startups, financial services, and manufacturing. Marty has been widely published in computer industry trade publications. He has published over 50 articles on various computer-related topics. In addition to this book, he is the author of nine other Prentice Hall books: Marty holds an M.S. in Information Systems from Polytechnic University (Brooklyn, NY), an M.S. in Management Engineering from the University of Bridgeport (Bridgeport, CT), and a B.S. in Electrical Engineering from Roger Williams University (Bristol, RI).

Francis Huang - vPars Expert and Reviewer

My sincere thanks to Francis Huang of Hewlett-Packard Company in Cupertino, CA. Mr. Huang wrote the official HP manuals for vPars and generously devoted a great deal of time to reviewing the vPars sections of all chapters in this book.

Francis was formerly an HP-UX systems administrator and a MPE applications programmer. He is currently a technical writer at Hewlett-Packard in the San Francisco Bay area. He holds a B.S. in Computer Science, is a licensed esthetician for the State of California, and will soon begin his first paid assign-ment as a professional home-office organizer.

Geff Blaha - vPars Expert and Reviewer

Mr. Blaha has worked on a number of activities related to vPars software includ-ing: development of web-based training; field review of the product as part of the early access program when only select group of HP installations were using the product; and Ignite-UX-related work including the procedure for using Ignite-UX and vPars that appears in the book.

Geff reviewed the entire vPars-specific part of this book and contributed the vPars Ignite-UX procedure. Geff is a UNIX Support Knowledge engineer, devel-oping training for the HP-UX operating system and kernel subsystems. Geff started his career at Hewlett-Packard more than 23 years ago in Los Angeles, working as a Customer Engineer and Senior Customer Engineer supporting Real-Time and HP-UX systems. His contributions to support include working in the San Francisco Bay area as a Response Center Engineer and WorldWide Technol-ogy Expert Center (WTEC) Engineer, providing solutions for RTE, HP-RT, and HP-UX customers. Geff holds a B.S. in Engineering Technology from California State Polytechnic University, Pomona.

Hayden Brown - vPars Expert

Hayden Brown is a vPars expert who was my primary contact in all of the work I performed with vPars before the release of the product. He helped me through many of the initial hurdles I had to overcome when working with a new product and his help was invaluable.

Hayden brought his UNIX expertise to Hewlett-Packard over eleven years ago. He has worked in a variety of rolls from account support engineer, technical consultant and customer education instructor teaching courses on networking, HP-UX administration and HP-UX internals. For the past four years he has been a member of the E-Commerce Data Center Lab's Advance Technology Center. He was chartered with developing and training both HP technical consultants and customers on Systems Consolidation strategy. Part of the strategy is the HP Parti-tioning Continuum which includes technologies such as Process Resource Man-ager, Workload Manager, Processor Sets, and Virtual Partitions. Hayden has presented papers on these technologies at HPWorld and InterWorks over the last several years. In a supporting roll for the vPar Lab, Hayden wrote the first technical white paper on vPars, and managed the Early Access Program for HP customers on vPars. Through his interactions with customers and HP technologists he is helping to shape the future of partitioning technologies within Hewlett-Packard.

Conventions Used in the Book

I don't use a lot of complex notations in the book. Here are a few simple conventions I've used to make the examples clear and the text easy to follow:

$ and #	The HP-UX command prompt. Every command issued in the book is preceded by a command prompt. Either one of these two will be used or a system name are usually used as prompts.
italics	Italics are used for variable values and when referring to functional areas and menu picks in the System Administration Manager (SAM).
bold and " "	Bold text is the information you would type, such as the command you issue after a prompt or the information you type when running a script. Sometimes information you would type is also referred to in the text explaining it, and the typed information may appear in quotes.
<----	When selections have to be made, this convention indicates the one chosen for the purposes of the example.
[ ]	Brackets indicate optional items and command descriptions.
{ }	Curly braces indicate a list from which you must choose.
|	A vertical bar separates items in a list of choices.
<Enter>	Indicates that the "Enter" key has been pressed on the keyboard. Sometimes <Return> is used to indicate that the return key has been pressed.

One additional convention is that used for command formats. I don't use command formats more than I have to because I could never do as thorough a job describing commands as the HP-UX manual pages. The manual pages go into detail on all HP-UX commands. Here is the format I use when I cover commands:

    form 1   command [option(s)] [arg(s)]
    form 2   command [option(s)] [arg(s)]
    form n   command [option(s)] [arg(s)]

I try not to get carried away with detail when covering a command, but there are sometimes many components that must be covered in order to understand a command. Here is a brief description of the components listed above:

form # -There are sometimes many forms of a command. If there is more than one form of a command that requires explanation, then I will show more than one form.

command - The name of the executable.

option(s) - Several options may appear across a command line.

cmd_arg(s) - Command arguments such as path name.

CHAPTER 1

Installing HP-UX 11i and Virtual Partitions Software

Introduction to Virtual Partitions

I want to cover only loading software in this chapter but I can't do it. Even though loading software is the first step to creating Virtual Partitions (vPars) we'll have to go over some background in order to understand the concept of vPars and select the devices off which our vPars will boot.

HP-UX Virtual Partitions allow you to run multiple instances of HP-UX on the same HP 9000 server. From a hardware perspective a vPar consists of CPU, memory, and I/O that is a subset of the overall hardware on the computer. From a software perspective a vPar consists of the HP-UX 11i Operating Environment and all application-related software to successfully run your workload. Figure 1-1, which appears in other places throughout this book, shows a conceptual diagram of the way in which HP 9000 computer system resources can be allocated to support multiple vPars.

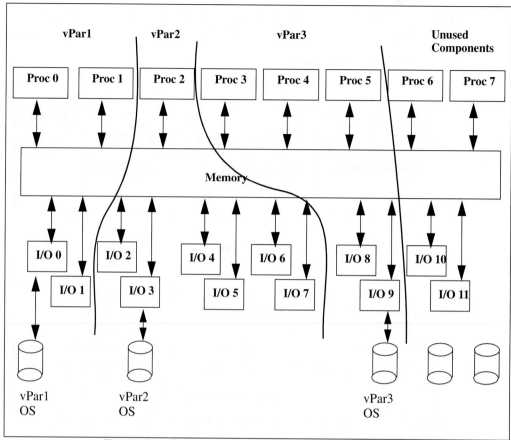

Figure 1-1 Example of HP System Resource Allocation with vPars

The components of which your HP 9000 is comprised can be allocated in a variety of ways. You can see that the eight-way system shown has a different number of processors, different amount of memory, and different number of I/O cards allocated to each vPar. The unused components can be added to any of the vPars or be the basis for yet another vPar. In addition, components can be moved from one vPar to another (with some restrictions described later in the book.)

In this chapter we're most concerned about the software included in each vPar. We want to end up with both HP-UX 11i and the Virtual Partitions software on every disk that will host a Virtual Partition. This means that if you have a system on which you want to run two vPars, you'll have to load all of the software necessary to support completely independent instances of HP-UX 11i. We'll end up with a system that looks like that shown in Figure 1-2.

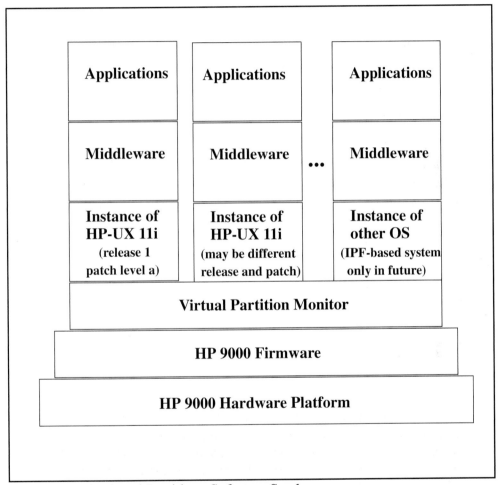

Figure 1-2 Virtual Partitions Software Stack

There are many components in Figure 1-2. Starting from the bottom we have the hardware, firmware, and Virtual Partition Monitor (covered as part of the boot process in Chapter 3.) Next, we move up to the software components, which include HP-UX 11i installed on two different disks. There are two HP-UX 11i instances shown in the leftmost two stacks of Figure 1-2. These operating systems will have to be loaded on every disk that will act as the boot disk of a Virtual Partition.

The Virtual Partition Monitor is a component of the Virtual Partition application. Without this application the two HP-UX 11i instances can't run simultaneously on this system. We cover loading the Virtual Partitions application in this chapter.

Without Virtual Partitions created we can boot HP-UX off one *or* the other of these disks, but we can't run both. Creating our Virtual Partitions is covered in Chapter 2. Once this is done, we can indeed have two instances of HP-UX 11i running simultaneously. After Virtual Partitions have been created, you can proceed to load the middleware and applications shown on top of HP-UX 11i in Figure 1-2.

Although we're covering running multiple instances of HP-UX 11i in the Virtual Partitions we create, we won't be restricted to only HP-UX 11i in the future. On systems based on the Itanium Processor Family (IPF) CPUs we'll be able to run additional operating systems. The rightmost Virtual Partition on Figure 1-2 depicts this future capability. This capability does not exist at the time of this writing, so it is not covered. Look for an updated revision of this book in the future to cover this capability once it exists, and keep an eye on *www.hp.com* for both IPF and Virtual Partition enhancements.

We need to select the devices on which we'll install software before beginning our software load. The next section covers this topic.

Selecting the Disks on Which to the Load Software

There are some restrictions related to the devices on which we can load the operating system and other software used by Virtual Partitions. You'll want to read two upcoming chapters that cover hardware in detail when you get to the point of creating and working with vPars: Chapter 2 covers working with vPars and Chapter 5 covers vPars and devices. In this section, however; we do need to cover the basics of selecting disks on which to load software so that you meet the restrictions at the time of this writing and load the software on disks that meet the requirements of vPars.

Let's take a look at an **ioscan** output that shows the disks on a system (**ioscan** and issues related to hardware and vPars in general are covered in detail in Chapters 2 and 5 as mentioned earlier.)

At the time of this writing, components that are at or below the Local Bus Adapter (LBA) level are devoted to a partition. This means that the disks on which you load the software for two different vPars must be on two different LBAs. Let's take a brief look at the LBAs and disks on a system in order to select the disks on which we'll load software. If you need more detail than is covered here, please refer to the chapters that cover this topic in more detail. Also please keep in mind that the layout of systems varies depending on the model and that you need to become familiar with the layout of your system to the extent that you can determine the location of components in your system relative to the LBA level.

Let's take a look at an L-Class system to view the System Bus Adapter (SBA) and multiple LBAs.

```
# ioscan -f | grep ba
```
                                                                          L-Class

```
cvhdcon3:/ # ioscan -f | grep ba
ioa        0   0      sba    CLAIMED   BUS_NEXUS System Bus Adapter (803)
ba         0   0/0    lba    CLAIMED   BUS_NEXUS Local PCI Bus Adapter (782)
ba         1   0/1    lba    CLAIMED   BUS_NEXUS Local PCI Bus Adapter (782)
ba         2   0/2    lba    CLAIMED   BUS_NEXUS Local PCI Bus Adapter (782)
ba         3   0/3    lba    CLAIMED   BUS_NEXUS Local PCI Bus Adapter (782)
ba         4   0/4    lba    CLAIMED   BUS_NEXUS Local PCI Bus Adapter (782)
ba         5   0/5    lba    CLAIMED   BUS_NEXUS Local PCI Bus Adapter (782)
ba         6   0/8    lba    CLAIMED   BUS_NEXUS Local PCI Bus Adapter (782)
ba         7   0/9    lba    CLAIMED   BUS_NEXUS Local PCI Bus Adapter (782)
ba         8   0/10   lba    CLAIMED   BUS_NEXUS Local PCI Bus Adapter (782)
ba         9   0/12   lba    CLAIMED   BUS_NEXUS Local PCI Bus Adapter (782)
cvhdcon3:/ #
```

This L-Class has only one SBA, as indicated by the leading *0* on all of the buses in the previous listing, and it has two SCSI buses on LBA *0/0*. The internal disks are normally mirrored across these two different SCSI buses. There are then many additional LBAs. Let's now see what disks are connected to this system and determine with what LBA they are associated.

```
cvhdcon3:/ # ioscan -f | grep disk
disk       0   0/0/1/0.1.0     sdisk    CLAIMED   DEVICE          HP       DVD-ROM 304
disk       1   0/0/1/1.0.0     sdisk    CLAIMED   DEVICE          SEAGATE ST173404LC
disk       2   0/0/1/1.2.0     sdisk    CLAIMED   DEVICE          SEAGATE ST173404LC
disk       3   0/0/2/0.0.0     sdisk    CLAIMED   DEVICE          SEAGATE ST173404LC
disk       4   0/0/2/0.2.0     sdisk    CLAIMED   DEVICE          SEAGATE ST173404LC
disk       7   0/8/0/0.8.0.5.0.0.0   sdisk   CLAIMED   DEVICE   HP   A5277A
disk      10   0/8/0/0.8.0.5.0.0.1   sdisk   CLAIMED   DEVICE   HP   A5277A
disk      11   0/8/0/0.8.0.5.0.0.2   sdisk   CLAIMED   DEVICE   HP   A5277A
disk      12   0/8/0/0.8.0.5.0.0.3   sdisk   CLAIMED   DEVICE   HP   A5277A
disk      15   0/8/0/0.8.0.5.0.1.0   sdisk   CLAIMED   DEVICE   HP   A5277A
disk      17   0/8/0/0.8.0.5.0.2.0   sdisk   CLAIMED   DEVICE   HP   A5277A
```

```
disk         18    0/8/0/0.8.0.5.0.3.0    sdisk    CLAIMED    DEVICE    HP    A5277A
disk          5    0/9/0/0.8.0.4.0.0.0    sdisk    CLAIMED    DEVICE    HP    A5277A
disk          6    0/9/0/0.8.0.4.0.0.1    sdisk    CLAIMED    DEVICE    HP    A5277A
disk          8    0/9/0/0.8.0.4.0.0.2    sdisk    CLAIMED    DEVICE    HP    A5277A
disk          9    0/9/0/0.8.0.4.0.0.3    sdisk    CLAIMED    DEVICE    HP    A5277A
disk         13    0/9/0/0.8.0.4.0.1.0    sdisk    CLAIMED    DEVICE    HP    A5277A
disk         14    0/9/0/0.8.0.4.0.2.0    sdisk    CLAIMED    DEVICE    HP    A5277A
disk         16    0/9/0/0.8.0.4.0.3.0    sdisk    CLAIMED    DEVICE    HP    A5277A
cvhdcon3:/ #
```

This listing shows first the DVD-ROM, then the four internal disks, and finally, the 14 Logical UNits (LUNs) configured on our external storage enclosure.

The internal disks are all on the same LBA as indicated by the leading *0/0*. The first *0* is for the SBA and the second *0* is for LBA *0*. These disks must all be part of the same vPar since they are associated with the same LBA. We have many LUNs connected to two other LBAs at *8* and *9*. This means that we could have as many as three vPars on this system since there are potential boot volumes connected to three different LBAs.

An example of two devices on which we might load our operating system and vPars software would be the internal disk at path *0/0/1/1.2.0* and the device at path *0/8/0/0.8.0.5.0.0.0*. Using these devices, which meet the separate LBA requirement, we can now proceed to loading software.

Loading the Software

The non-vPars-specific part of this chapter covers loading HP-UX 11i in detail. If you haven't before loaded HP-UX 11,i that portion of the chapter will help you complete the task of loading 11i on all of the disks that you will use for your vPars. Based on our previous discussion of disks, we might load HP-UX 11i on the internal disk at path *0/0/1/1.2.0* and the device at path *0/8/0/0.8.0.5.0.0.0*. The non-vPars-specific portion of this chapter will walk you through the process of selecting a target device on which to load HP-UX 11i as well as the process of loading 11i. The following is a bullet list of steps you would perform on every disk that will act as a vPar boot device:

- Install the HP-UX 11i *Operating Environment.*

- Set system parameters at the time of first boot after loading HP-UX 11i with **set_parms**.

- Download and install select patches on your system (at the time of this writing there are many patches required to support vPars.)

- Install vPars software.

- Configure vPars.

- Install additional software.

You would typically load software in the order shown above: Install the base *Operating Environment*; boot your system and use **set_parms**; load patches; install vPars software; configure vPars; and then install and configure all other software. You may want to view Chapter 10, which covers Ignite-UX. Among the material covered is an Ignite-UX procedure to load vPars written by an HP lab expert on vPars. If you're setting up many vPars systems, this procedure may save you some time.

Since there is extensive background on loading HP-UX 11i in the non-vPars-specific section of the chapter, let's jump to loading vPars software in the next section.

Loading the Software Required for Virtual Partitions

We cover installing Virtual Partitions software in this section. I assume that you already have HP-UX 11i installed on your system or know how to do so. If you have not yet installed HP-UX 11i on your system, please jump ahead to the non-vPars-specific section, which covers installing HP-UX 11i. We also earlier covered selecting devices on which to base your vPars and install HP-UX 11i.

Keep in mind that HP-UX must be loaded for each Virtual Partition you wish to run. If, for instance, you want to run two Virtual Partitions, as we do in our examples in this book, HP-UX 11i will need to be loaded for both Virtual Partitions. The procedure covered for loading HP-UX 11i needs to be performed for every Virtual Partition you want to run. HP-UX 11i can be loaded from media, such as your HP-UX 11i distribution on a CD-ROM or from an Ignite/UX server. You can use any method to load HP-UX 11i and the Virtual Partitions software for every Virtual Partition you want to run.

At the time of this writing there are two vPars products: a product with the full functionality covered throughout the book and a free product that has a subset of the full product. The free product has a limitation of a maximum of two vPars ,and one of the vPars can have only one CPU.

When you buy the full product, product number T1335AC, a CD-ROM is provided that has on it the following components:

- vPars software
- patches
- vPars administration guide
- booklet
- WINSTALL files used for booting

At some point the full product will be on standard distribution rather than a separate CD-ROM. The free product, called VPARSBASE at the time of this writing, can be downloaded from *www.software.hp.com.*

Figure 1-3 shows an example of the software components that appear below the full product T1335AC.

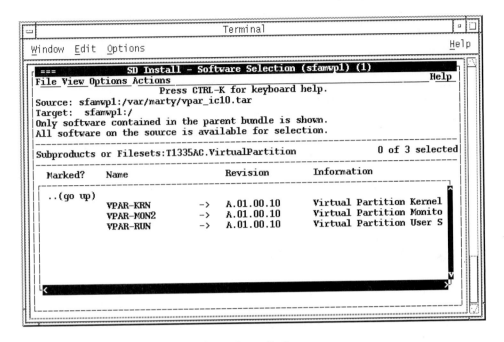

Figure 1-3 Example of Loading vPars Software

Figure 1-3 shows the three components of which T1355AC is comprised: the kernel, monitor, and run environment. The additional components listed earlier, patches and WINSTALL, will also have to be loaded for vPars to be fully operational.

Please keep in mind that because the vPars software used in this chapter has not yet been released, you may see some different product numbers.

After loading this software, a reboot takes place to build the kernel. This is done for you automatically, however; vPars kernel-related background is covered in both Chapters 2 and 4.

All of the vPars software must be loaded on every HP-UX 11i volume that will be used on your vPars server. The loading of this software will take place for every HP-UX 11i instance that you wish to run simultaneously on your vPars server. There are two ways to load the HP-UX 11i operating system and vPars software on all of the volumes used for vPars. The first, which is the method used throughout this book, is to load HP-UX 11i and vPars software on all vPars volumes prior to creating Virtual Partitions. The second is to load only the volume of the first vPar with all software, create as many vPars as you want, and then use **vparboot -p** *vp_name* **-I** *ignite_kernel* to boot and load HP-UX 11i on the other disks. In this chapter, I first load HP-UX 11i and vPars software on all disks before creating vPars.

A lot of software has been loaded as a result of loading the vPars software. The **/sbin** directory has in it the *vpar* commands we'll use in upcoming chapters. The following is a long listing of the *vpar* commands in **/sbin**.

```
# ll /sbin/vpar*
-r-xr-xr-x   1 bin        bin         128760 Oct 18 22:08 /sbin/vparboot
-r-xr-xr-x   1 bin        bin         161216 Oct 18 22:07 /sbin/vparcreate
-r-xr-xr-x   1 bin        bin         101040 Oct 18 22:04 /sbin/vpard
-r-xr-xr-x   1 bin        bin          59592 Oct 18 22:04 /sbin/vpardump
-r-xr-xr-x   1 bin        bin          30520 Oct 18 22:04 /sbin/vparextract
-r-xr-xr-x   1 bin        bin         140072 Oct 18 22:08 /sbin/vparmodify
-r-xr-xr-x   1 bin        bin          47232 Oct 18 22:04 /sbin/vparreloc
-r-xr-xr-x   1 bin        bin         127808 Oct 18 22:08 /sbin/vparremove
-r-xr-xr-x   1 bin        bin         132008 Oct 18 22:08 /sbin/vparreset
-r-xr-xr-x   1 bin        bin         152040 Oct 18 22:08 /sbin/vparstatus
-r-xr-xr-x   1 bin        bin          26152 Oct 18 22:04 /sbin/vparutil
#
```

These are the commands that you'll use to create, view, modify, and work with vPars in general. Chapter 2 is devoted to describing these commands and giving examples of using most of them in their various forms. In addition, the tear-out card included with the book summarizes many of these commands.

There are several files in **/stand** related to the vPars kernel. The following listing shows some of these:

```
# ll /stand/vp*
-rw-------   1 root       root          8232 Nov 16 07:09 /stand/vpdb
-r-xr-xr-x   1 bin        bin         849992 Oct 18 22:02 /stand/vpmon
#
```

vpmon is loaded at the time of system startup and is the basis for running vPars. Chapter 3 covers booting in detail, including bringing up **vpmon**. **vpdb** is the vPars database that contains all information related to all of the vPars running on your system. This file is automatically synchronized by the vPars application to ensure that all vPars have the same information about all vPars on your system.

There are several startup-related files, including those shown below, which are covered in more detail in Chapter 8 covering startup.

```
/etc/rc.config.d/vpard
/etc/rc.config.d/vparhb
/etc/rc.config.d/vparinit

/sbin/init.d/vpard
/sbin/init.d/vparhb
/sbin/init.d/vparinit
```

These files are covered in detail in Chapter 8, which covers vPars startup in detail. Of particular interest is **vparhp**, which is the *heartbeat* daemon related to keeping **vpdb** synchronized on all of your vPars.

Very important to your work related to vPars are the online man pages. The following listing shows the man pages loaded on my system at the time of this writing.

```
# man -k vpar
vparboot(1M)       - boot a virtual partition
vparcreate(1M)     - create a virtual partition
vpardump(1M)       - manage monitor dump files
vparextract(1M)    - extract memory images from a running virtual
                     partition system
vparmodify(1M)     - modify the attributes of a virtual partition
vparreloc(1M)      - relocate the load address of a vmunix file,
                     determine if a vmunix file is relocatable,
                     or promote the scope of symbols in a
                     relocatable vmunix file
vparremove(1M)     - remove a virtual partition
vparreset(1M)      - reset a virtual partition
vparresources(5)   - description of virtual partition resources
                     and their requirements
vparstatus(1M)     - display information about one or more
                     virtual partitions
vpartition(1)      - display information about the Virtual
                     Partition Command Line Interface
vparutil(1M)       - get and set SCSI parameters for SCSI
                     controllers from a virtual partition
#
```

Many of these man pages appear in Appendix A, so you can refer to them as you read the chapters in this book.

At this point we have HP-UX 11i and the Virtual Partitions software loaded on the system. In the next chapter we'll configure Virtual Partitions which will allow us to run multiple instances of HP-UX 11i simultaneously on the same server.

The remainder of this chapter covers background related to loading HP-UX 11i. This will need to be done on a volume for every HP-UX 11i you wish to run simultaneously on your vPars server. This is a step-by-step procedure so if you've never loaded HP-UX 11i, this procedure will walk you through the process start to finish.

Non-vPars-Specific Section of Chapter - Install HP-UX 11i Operating Environment

Installing HP-UX means installing one of the 11i *Operating Environments* and later building your complete fully functional HP-UX system by installing both HP and non-HP applications. The initial system is loaded from the 11i media, or from another system on the network using Ignite-UX. This chapter covers installing from media. The Ignite-UX chapter covers installing from a server. If you don't now have HP-UX 11i loaded on your system you would complete this procedure and then load the Virtual Partitions software covered earlier.

You can have your system delivered with instant ignition, which means that HP-UX has been loaded on your system and you'll only have to add to it the application software you'll need. I cover the complete installation process from media so you can see the process from start to finish. If you have instant ignition on your system, you may need to install additional software on your system in the future and can, therefore, use some of the techniques described in this section to load that software.

One of the features of moving any version of the 11.x operating system (including 11i) is the option of taking advantage of 64-bit computing. Whereas previous versions of HP-UX supported only the 32-bit processor, with 11.x, you have the option of running either the 32-bit or the 64-bit version. Which version of the operating system you choose is dependent on two things: what hardware you are using and your application requirements. The 64-bit version is not supported on some Series 700 workstations and many of the low-end Series 800s, but it is required for the L-Class, N-Class, V-Class, and Superdome servers. With other Series 800s, most notably the K Class and T Class servers, you have the option to install either the 32-bit or the 64-bit version. But don't worry too much if you are unsure whether your hardware supports 64-bit or not. If your hardware doesn't support the 64-bit version, you won't be prompted as to which version to install. The 32-bit version will be installed automatically. If you have the option to install the 32-bit or 64-bit version, then your hardware supports either.

Your application requirements will also help determine whether you will install the 32-bit or 64-bit operating system. If your applications are 32-bit, then you really have no reason to run the 64-bit version. If, however, you will be running a 64-bit application, then you obviously will need to install the 64-bit operating system. The good news is that if you install the 32-bit operating system and then find that an application you want to install is 64-

bit, you can upgrade to the 64-bit operating system, assuming, of course, that your hardware also supports it.

Booting the System and "Advanced Installation"

In order to install HP-UX software, place the core operating system media for HP-UX 11i into the DVD-ROM or CD-ROM drive. At the time of this writing, the CD-ROM was labeled *HP-UX Release 11.11*. There were two CD-ROMs as part of the core operating system I was working with because I was loading the *Mission Critical Operating Environment* which was on two CD-ROMs (more about the *Operating Environments later.)* Be sure to insert the CD-ROM Install media before you begin the installation. As your HP 9000 unit boots, you will see a variety of messages fly by, including information about your processors, buses, boot paths, and so on. See Chapter 3, which covers the boot process, to get more information about booting.

The following example shows several steps that were taken. The example begins at the end of early boot. The early boot is the first part of the load process from media. There were many early boot-related messages that appeared before the point where our example begins. We discontinued the boot process by pressing a key. After discontinuing the boot we run *SEArch* to find bootable devices. Among the devices shown is the DVD-ROM drive containing our operating system media. We select *p0* to boot off of with the **bo p0** command. We then choose not to interact with IPL.

```
************ EARLY BOOT VFP *************
End of early boot detected
*****************************************

Firmware Version  39.46

Duplex Console IO Dependent Code (IODC) revision 1

--------------------------------------------------------------------------------
   (c) Copyright 1995-1998, Hewlett-Packard Company, All rights reserved
--------------------------------------------------------------------------------

   Processor    Speed            State          CoProcessor State  Cache Size
   Number                                       State              Inst    Data
   ---------    --------    ---------------------    ------------------    -----------
       0        440  MHz    Active                   Functional           512 KB   1 MB
       3        440  MHz    Idle                     Functional           512 KB   1 MB

   Central Bus Speed (in MHz)  :        82
   Available Memory            :   2097152  KB
   Good Memory Required        :     16908  KB

    Primary boot path:     0/0/1/1.2
    Alternate boot path:   0/0/2/0.2
    Console path:          0/0/4/0.0
```

```
      Keyboard path:         0/0/4/0.0

   WARNING:  The non-destructive test bit was set, so memory was not tested
             destructively.  Information only, no action required.


   Processor is booting from first available device.

   To discontinue, press any key within 10 seconds.

   Boot terminated.


   ---- Main Menu -------------------------------------------------------------

        Command                        Description
        -------                        -----------
        BOot [PRI|ALT|<path>]          Boot from specified path
        PAth [PRI|ALT] [<path>]        Display or modify a path
        SEArch [DIsplay|IPL] [<path>]  Search for boot devices

        COnfiguration menu             Displays or sets boot values
        INformation menu               Displays hardware information
        SERvice menu                   Displays service commands

        DIsplay                        Redisplay the current menu
        HElp [<menu>|<command>]        Display help for menu or command
        RESET                          Restart the system
   ----
   Main Menu: Enter command or menu > search

   Searching for potential boot device(s)
   This may take several minutes.

   To discontinue search, press any key (termination may not be immediate).


        Path#  Device Path (dec)   Device Path (mnem)   Device Type
        -----  -----------------   ------------------   -----------
        P0     0/0/1/0.3           extscsi.3            Random access media
        P1     0/0/1/1.2           intscsib.2           Random access media
        P2     0/0/2/0.2           intscsia.2           Random access media


   Main Menu: Enter command or menu > bo P0
   Interact with IPL (Y, N, or Cancel)?> n

   Booting...
```

The *SEArch* command in the previous listing showed us the bootable devices. There are three possible boot devices. The second two are in the internal disks, one of which would normally be the primary boot device and the other which is normally the alternate boot device. These two disks are on two different SCSI buses internal to the L-Class. The first device was the external DVD-ROM that contains the HP-UX 11i CD-ROM, which is operating system media off of which we want to boot.

In order to boot off of the media and not interact with IPL (for more information on IPL, see Chapter 3), we issued the following command:

```
Main Menu: Enter command or menu > bo p0
Interact with IPL (Y or N)?> N
```

After booting off of *P0*, we are given the *Welcome to the HP-UX instal-lation/recovery process!* menu shown in the following example:

```
          Welcome to the HP-UX installation/recovery process!

Use the <tab> key to navigate between fields, and the arrow keys
within fields.  Use the <return/enter> key to select an item.
Use the <return> or <space-bar> to pop-up a choices list.  If the
menus are not clear, select the "Help" item for more information.

Hardware Summary:          System Model: 9000/800/L2000-44
+--------------------+----------------+--------------------+ [ Scan Again  ]
| Disks: 2  ( 33.9GB)| Floppies: 0    | LAN cards:    2    |
| CD/DVDs:        1  | Tapes:    0    | Memory:   2048Mb   |
| Graphics Ports: 0  | IO Buses: 8    | CPUs:         2    | [ H/W Details ]
+--------------------+----------------+--------------------+

                 [     Install HP-UX      ]

                 [  Run a Recovery Shell  ]

                 [   Advanced Options     ]

         [ Reboot  ]                        [ Help  ]
```

The *Welcome to the HP-UX installation/recovery process!* menu is the first menu displayed. It gives a summary of the hardware on your system. If you want to see more detail, select the *H/W Details* option on the right side of the screen. This takes you to a detailed listing of your hardware. It includes items such as hardware paths, disk drive capacities, and LAN addresses. We won't perform any other functions in this example other than our selection of *Install HP-UX*.

When we select *Install HP-UX,* we get the *User Interface and Media Options* menu shown in the following example:

```
                           User Interface and Media Options


    This screen lets you pick from options that will determine if an
    Ignite-UX server is used, and your user interface preference.


Source Location Options:
    [ * ]   Media only installation
    [   ]   Media with Network enabled (allows use of SD depots)
    [   ]   Ignite-UX server based installation


User Interface Options:
    [   ]   Guided Installation   (recommended for basic installs)
    [ * ]   Advanced Installation (recommended for disk and filesystem management)
    [   ]   No user interface - use all the defaults and go



    Hint: If you need to make LVM size changes, or want to set the
          final networking parameters during the install, you will
          need to use the Advanced mode (or remote graphical interface).



    [   OK   ]                  [ Cancel ]                    [  Help  ]
```

This menu gives you the option of installing from the media only, installing from the media combined with the software depots on your network, or the Ignite-UX product. We'll be installing from the media only in our example.

We next select *Advanced Installation* because this gives us the greatest level of flexibility when installing. *Guided Installation* leads you through a basic system configuration setup. It allows for only a few system-specific options. *Advanced Installation* is much more flexible and allows for extensive system-specific parameters to be set. We'll walk through the *Advanced Installation* steps.

The display that now appears is similar to that used by Ignite-UX. In fact, it is the same except that Ignite-UX uses a graphical user interface (GUI) versus the terminal user interface (TUI.) Figure 1-4 shows this display.

```
                    /opt/ignite/bin/itool


/-------\/----------\/--------\/-------------\/----------\
| Basic || Software|| System || File System || Advanced |
\        \----------:---------------------------------/
 Configurations:  [ HP-UX B.11.11 Default    ->] [ Description...  ]

 Environments:    [ Mission Critical OE-64bit  ->] (HP-UX B.11.11)

 [ Root Disk...  ] SEAGATE ST318203LC, 0/0/1/1.2.0, 17366 M

 File System:     [ Logical Volume Manager (LVM) with VxFS  ->]

 [ Root Swap (MB)... ] 1024   Physical Memory (RAM) =  2048 MB
        [  Languages...  ] English  [ Keyboards...  ] [ Additional...  ]

 -------------------------------------------------------------------

 [ Show Summary...  ]                        [ Reset Configuration ]

 -------------------------------------------------------------------

     [  Go!   ]                 [ Cancel ]              [Help]
```

Figure 1-4 Ignite/UX Display *Basic* Tab Area Using TUI

        The *Advanced Installation* menu lets you choose from among the menu
tab areas with the ability of going back and forth among them until you are
satisfied with your choices.
        Across the top of the menu display are five tab areas: *Basic*, *Software*,
System, *File System*, and *Advanced*. By pressing the tab key, each Tab area
can be highlighted. To select the highlighted tab area, press the Enter/Return
key. This will cause that tab area's screen to be displayed. Within each of
these areas are several parameters that can be modified for your specific system. Listed below are the main features of each tab area:

- *Basic* - configuration and environment information.

- *Software* - ability to choose optional software to be installed. Mostly the same options that appear under *Guided Installation.*

- *System* - networking parameters. Also configurable via the **set_parms** command.

- *File System* - disk space allocation.

- *Advanced* - advanced disk, file system, logical volume, and volume group parameters.

We configure our system beginning with the *Basic* screen as shown in Figure 1-4.

Items of particular importance are discussed below:

- Configuration - we use *HP-UX B.11.11 Default.* HP-UX 11i is called by its original name, 11.11, in some cases.

- Environments - there are four 11i environments to select from at the time of this writing. This is a major change in the software distribution method for HP-UX 11i. The *Operating Environments* are bundles of software that make installing 11i easier. We'll select the first of the four, which is the top level, or most elaborate, of the *Operating Environments* as shown in the following example:

```
Mission Critical OE-64bit .>] (HP-UX B.11.11)
                   Enterprise OE-64bit
                   HP-UX 11i OE-64bit
                   HP-UX 11i Base OS-64bit
```

- Root Disk - the default selection for the root disk is the first internal disk drive, which is the disk with a path of 0/0/1/1.2.0 in our example.

- File System - we are given the option of choosing wholedisk (not LVM) with HFS, Logical Volume Manager with HFS, or Logical Volume Manager with VxFS. If you have not reviewed the Logical

Volume Manager section of this chapter, you will want to do so before you make this selection (LVM is Logical Volume Manager.) I am a strong advocate of using Logical Volume Manager with VxFS whenever possible.

- Root Swap - The system automatically selects an amount twice the size of your main memory, or a maximum of 1024 MB. You will want to consider your primary swap space very carefully. The L-Class system in our example has 2GBytes of memory and we'll go with the default of 1 GByte of swap as shown.

- Languages - We'll install English on our system; however, there are many languages available for 11i systems.

- Additional - This is the pick at the bottom right corner of the screen, not the tab area. Here is where you can configure such things as a second swap area, adding a second disk drive to the root volume, and disabling DHCP. With 11i, DHCP, Dynamic Host Configuration Protocol, works with an Ignite-UX server that automatically assigns system name, IP address, and so on.

The major difference between the selections just discussed for 11i and earlier releases of 11.x are the *Operating Environments*. 11i is the first HP-UX release for which *Operating Environments* are available.

Moving to the *Software* tab area, we find software on the installation CD-ROM for 11i that has been marked for installation. Since we have selected the *Mission Critical Operating Environment* there is a lot of software automatically selected as part of this installation.

Figure 1-5 shows some of the software we have selected in the *Software* tab area. We have selected *All* so that we can see all of the software that has been selected as part of the *Mission Critical Operating Environment*. We could scroll down to see additional software.

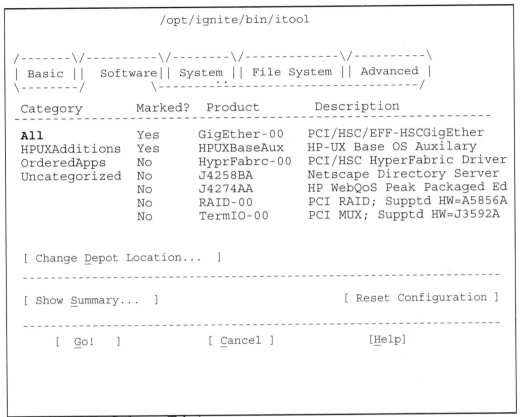

```
                    /opt/ignite/bin/itool


/-------\/----------\/--------\/-------------\/----------\
| Basic ||  Software|| System || File System || Advanced |
\--------/          \-------------------------------------/

Category        Marked?   Product        Description
-----------------------------------------------------------
All             Yes       GigEther-00    PCI/HSC/EFF-HSCGigEther
HPUXAdditions   Yes       HPUXBaseAux    HP-UX Base OS Auxilary
OrderedApps     No        HyprFabrc-00   PCI/HSC HyperFabric Driver
Uncategorized   No        J4258BA        Netscape Directory Server
                No        J4274AA        HP WebQoS Peak Packaged Ed
                No        RAID-00        PCI RAID; Supptd HW=A5856A
                No        TermIO-00      PCI MUX; Supptd HW=J3592A



[ Change Depot Location...  ]
-----------------------------------------------------------------

[ Show Summary... ]                       [ Reset Configuration ]

-----------------------------------------------------------------
    [ Go! ]                [ Cancel ]           [Help]
```

Figure 1-5 *Software* Tab Area

Other software you may want to install can be selected from the installation CD. In the example the first two items have automaticallly been selected as part of the *Mission Critical Operating Environment*. At this point, we could select additional software such as *Hyperfabric* and *Netscape Directory Server* in this window. Keep in mind that the software shown in this window is on the core operating system CD-ROM for 11i. You may later want to install application software from the HP-UX Applications CD set. This is done using Software Distributor. An overview of the Software Distributor product used for installing all HP-UX 11i software appears later in this chapter. You may want to take a look at this overview to get a feel for the

man page

"sw" - 2

type of functionality that Software Distributor offers. The **swinstall** program is the Software Distributor program used to install software. If you have application software to be installed, you will interact with **swinstall,** and possibly be asked for codeword information for some of the software to be installed. If your software is protected, you will have to enter the codeword information. If you need a codeword, it should be printed on the CD-ROM certificate you received with your software. This codeword is tied to the ID number of a hardware device in your system.

With the software we wish to load on our system having been selected we can move on to the next area.

The *System* tab area, shown in Figure 1-6, is where system identification-related configuration information can be found. Since we want to configure networking and other related information after the installation is complete, we have changed only the first item on this screen. The options for the first item are:

Final system parameters: [Set parameters now]
                         [Ask at first boot]

We selected *Ask at first boot.*

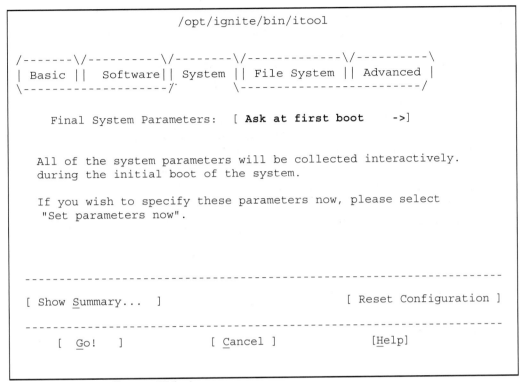

Figure 1-6 *System* Tab Area

When the system first boots, we'll be asked to enter system identification-related information.

The *File System* tab area, shown in Figure 1-7, is of particular importance. Here is where you can change file system sizes. You will not normally be satisfied with the default sizes of some of the logical volumes. I normally spend some time in this tab area increasing the sizes of some of the logical volumes. Figure 1-7 also shows the layout of the *File System* screen and the values of three of the logical volumes with their updated sizes. Root is highlighted in this example, so the parameters related to it appear under *Usage, Size,* and so on.

```
                      /opt/ignite/bin/itool

/-------\/-----------\/--------\/-------------\/----------\
| Basic || Software|| System || File System || Advanced |
\---------------------------------/          \----------/

Mount Dir      Usage    Size(MB)  % Used  Group    S
/stand         HFS      300       7       vg00     F ^ [ Add      ]
primary        SWAP+D   1024      0       vg00     R   [ Modify   ]
/              VxFS     400       9       vg00     F v [ Remove   ]

Usage:  [ VxFS       ->]  Group:  [ vg ->]  Mount Dir:  /_____

Size:   [ Fixed MB      ->]  400     Avail: 13360 MB

[ Add/Remove Disks... ]    [ ---- Additional Tasks ----    ->]


---------------------------------------------------------------
[ Show Summary... ]                       [ Reset Configuration ]
---------------------------------------------------------------
     [  Go!  ]            [ Cancel ]            [Help]
```

Figure 1-7 *File System* Tab Area

To make logical volume size changes, you select the mount directory of the logical volume, tab down to *Size,* and enter the desired new size. In addition to *Size,* there are several other parameters related to the logical volume that you can change.

You will notice that *Avail* shows you how much disk space is left to be allocated on your disk drive. It is perfectly all right to leave some disk space unallocated. This will give you a cushion for when you need to increase disk space down the road.

After making all the volume size-related modifications, we are ready to go ahead and install the system. However, first we want to choose the *Show Summary* option toward the bottom of the screen. This option will show us a summary of all the changes we made. This gives us a chance to make sure that we didn't forget something. Figure 1-8 shows the *General Summary* screen.

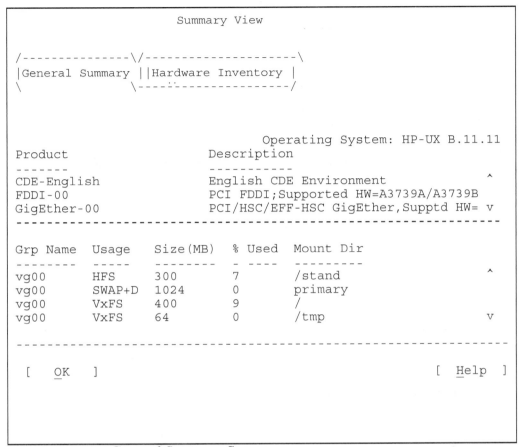

Figure 1-8 *General Summary* Screen

This screen provides information on the software we have selected to load and information on our logical volumes.

Figure 1-9 shows the *Hardware Inventory Summary* screen.

```
                        Summary View


/--------------\/--------------------\
|General Summary ||Hardware  Inventory |
\-------------/\      ··                \

Hardware Summary:          System Model: 9000/800/L2000-44       ^
+--------------------+----------------+-------------------+
| Disks: 2  ( 33.9GB) | Floppies: 0   | LAN cards:   2      |
| CD/DVDs:          1 | Tapes:    0   | Memory:    2048Mb   |
| Graphics Ports: 0   | IO Buses: 8   | CPUs:        2      |
+--------------------+----------------+-------------------+

Disk Drives:
H/W Path                Capacity(Mb)     Model
0/0/1/1.2.0               17366          SEAGATE_ST318203LC
0/0/2/0.2.0               17366          SEAGATE_ST318203LC
                                                              v
F<                                                        >G




-----------------------------------------------------------------

[   OK   ]                                            [  Help  ]

```

Figure 1-9 *Hardware Inventory Summary* Screen

The *Hardware Inventory Summary* screen information provides a short summary of system hardware.

Since we are satisfied with all of the modifications we have made, we are ready to load the operating system. We choose *Go!* which appears at the bottom of all the tab area screens and the screen in Figure 1-10 appears:

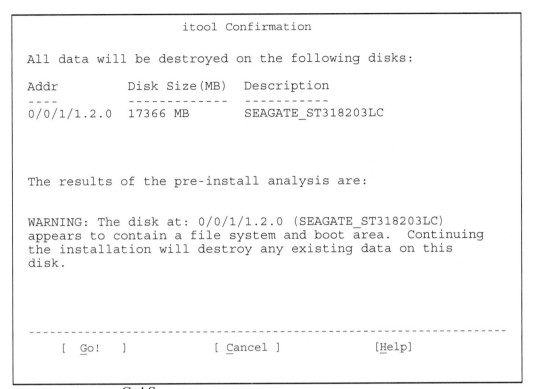

```
                    itool Confirmation

All data will be destroyed on the following disks:

Addr            Disk Size(MB)   Description
----            -------------   -----------
0/0/1/1.2.0   17366 MB          SEAGATE_ST318203LC




The results of the pre-install analysis are:


WARNING: The disk at: 0/0/1/1.2.0 (SEAGATE_ST318203LC)
appears to contain a file system and boot area.  Continuing
the installation will destroy any existing data on this
disk.




-----------------------------------------------------------------

    [  Go!  ]              [ Cancel ]              [Help]
```

Figure 1-10 *Go!* Screen

This screen warns us that there is an operating system already present
on our target disk, but we want to proceed with the installation anyway and
select *Go!*. The load of the HP-UX is automatic at this point and you can
come back in an hour or so to check the log file and see if loading the operating system completed successfully.

It may be that your HP-UX 11i *Operating Environment* requires a second CD-ROM to complete the installation, as is the case with our *Mission
Critical Operating Environment*. As shown in the upcoming listing, you'll
be prompted to load the second CD-ROM:

```
========================================================================
                    USER INTERACTION REQUIRED:
To complete the installation you must now insert the
"MC_OE" CD.

Once this is done, press the <Return> key to continue:

        * Starting swinstall of the source (MC_OE).
        * Running command: "/usr/sbin/swinstall -s/tmp/ign_configure/SD_CDROM
          -f/tmp/ign_configure/software_file  -x os_release=B.11.11 -x
          os_name=HP-UX:64 "
```

When the operating system load is complete, we're asked for the system identification-related information we did not earlier enter. The following listing shows the first of these screens:

```
─────────────────────────────────────────────────────────────────
                    Welcome to HP-UX!

Before using your system, you will need to answer a few questions.

The first question is whether you plan to use this system on a network.

Answer "yes" if you have connected the system to a network and are ready
to link with a network.

Answer "no" if you:

        * Plan to set up this system as a standalone (no networking).

        * Want to use the system now as a standalone and connect to a
          network later.
─────────────────────────────────────────────────────────────────
Are you ready to link this system to a network?

Press [y] for yes or [n] for no, then press [Enter]
```

If you choose to connect your system network, you'll be asked a variety of questions about the networking configuration. You don't have to enter this information now because there is a command called **set_parms** that we'll cover in the next section which is an alternative way of entering system identification-related information. We'll cover this command in the next section.

Now that our *Mission Critical Operating Environment* installation is complete, we'll check the operating system revision with **uname -a** and software bundles that have been loaded on the system with **swlist** in the following listing:

```
# uname -a
HP-UX l3 B.11.11 U 9000/800 143901527 unlimited-user license
# swlist
# Initializing...
# Contacting target "l3"...
#
# Target:  l3:/
#


#
# Bundle(s):
#

  CDE-English            B.11.11.%20A    English CDE Environment
  FDDI-00                B.11.11.%20     PCI FDDI;Supported HW=A3739A/A3739B;SW=J3 626AA
  GigEther-00            B.11.11.11.08   PCI/HSC/EFF-HSC GigEther,Supptd HW=A4926A
                                         ,A4929A,A4924A,A4925A;SW=J1642AA
  HPUX11i-OE-MC          B.11.11.%20A    HP-UX Mission Critical Operating
                                         Environment Component
  HPUXBase64             B.11.11.%20A    HP-UX 64-bit Base OS
  HPUXBaseAux            B.11.11.%20A    HP-UX Base OS Auxilary
      #
```

This listing shows that HP-UX 11i has indeed been loaded, shown as 11.11 in the listing, and that several software bundles have been loaded as well, including the *Mission Critical Operating Environment.*

Let's now move to the next section, in which we'll specify the system-related information we have put off during our installation.

Setting the System Parameters after Booting

When the system comes up after installation, a series of windows appear that allow you to configure your system name, time zone, root password, Internet Protocol (IP) address, subnet mask, and other networking settings (IP address and subnet mask background is provided in Chapter 13 covering Networking.) One of the first questions you will be asked is whether or not you wish to use DHCP to obtain networking information. Dynamic host configuration protocol works with an Ignite-UX server that automatically assigns system name, IP address, and so on. Since our installation does not use this, I answered "no" which means we'll have to enter all of our information manually.

The system-specific information to be entered next can also be entered, after your system boots, by running **/sbin/set_parms**. This program can be used to set an individual system parameter or all the system parameters that would be set at boot time. **/sbin/set_parms** uses one of the arguments in Table 1-1, depending on what you would like to configure.

TABLE 1-1　/sbin/set_parms Arguments

set_parms Argument	Comments
hostname	Set hostname.
timezone	Set time zone.
date_time	Set date and time.
root_passwd	Set root password.
ip_address	Set Internet Protocol address (see Chapter 2 for networking background).
addl_network	Configure subnet mask, Domain Name System, and Network Information Service.
initial	Go through the entire question-and-answer session you would experience at boot time.

If you use the **initial** argument, you'll interact with a variety of dialog boxes asking you for information. The System Hostname dialog box is shown in Figure 1-11.

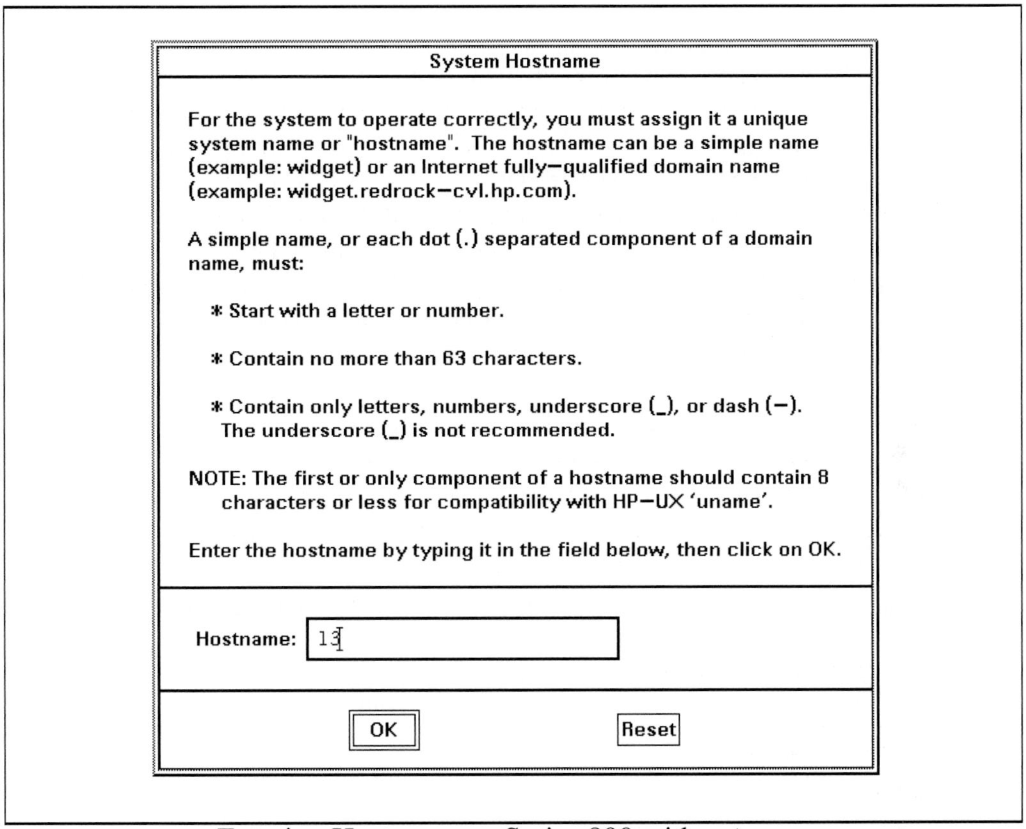

Figure 1-11 Entering Hostname on Series 800 with **set_parms**

You'll then be asked for your time zone and root password. Figure 1-12 shows the dialog box for entering your IP address:

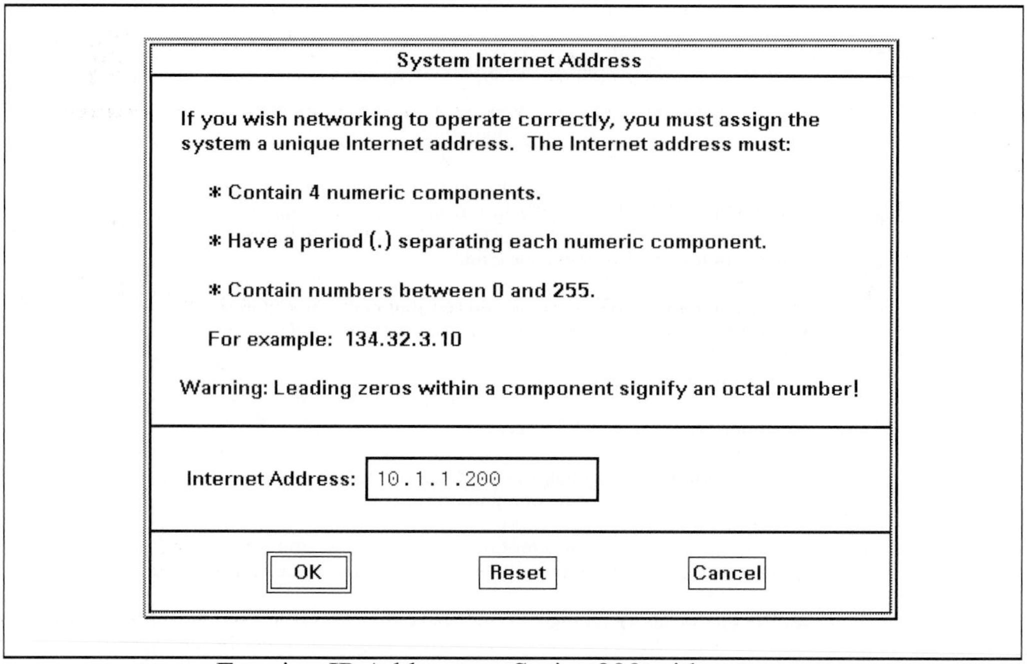

System Internet Address

If you wish networking to operate correctly, you must assign the system a unique Internet address. The Internet address must:

* Contain 4 numeric components.

* Have a period (.) separating each numeric component.

* Contain numbers between 0 and 255.

For example: 134.32.3.10

Warning: Leading zeros within a component signify an octal number!

Internet Address: `10.1.1.200`

| OK | Reset | Cancel |

Figure 1-12 Entering IP Address on Series 800 with **set_parms**

You can then configure your subnet mask and other networking parameters.

Configuration includes the items shown in Figure 1-13:

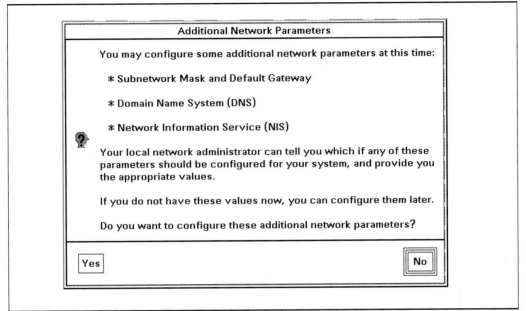

Figure 1-13 Additional Configuration with **set_parms setparms3.bmp**

Running **set_parms initial** or **set_parms** with other options allows you to specify all of the initial information related to your system setup. This saves you the trouble of finding all of the relevant files in which you'd have to place the information you provide to **set_parms**.

Software Distributor Example

man page

"sw" - 2

Software Distributor-HP-UX (I'll call this Software Distributor throughout the book; HP documentation typically uses SD-UX) is the program used in HP-UX 11i to perform all tasks related to software management. Software Distributor will be used in an example to install software on the same system we loaded our operating system on earlier in this chapter. Software Distributor is a standards-based way to perform software management. It conforms to the Portable Operating System Interface (POSIX) standard for packaging software and utilities related to software managment. The Software Distributor product described in this section comes with your HP-UX system. Additional functionality can be obtained by buying the OpenView Software Distributor (SD-OV) product. SD-OV provides support for additional platforms, allows you to push software out to target systems, features centralized monitoring, and provides a job browser to assist in managing software on target systems. In this section, I won't cover SD-OV, but will make some comments about SD-OV functionality where appropriate.

Software Distributor can be invoked using the commands described in this section, by using SAM (covered in Chapter 11), or by installing software for the first time as described earlier in this chapter.

The following are the four phases of software installation performed with Software Distributor:

- Selection(1) - You can select the source and software you wish to load during this phase. In the upcoming example, the graphical user interface of Software Distributor is used and you'll see how easily you can select these.

- Analysis(2) - All kinds of checks are performed for you, including free disk space; dependencies; compatibility; mounted volumes; and others. One of the very useful outputs of this phase is the amount of space the software you wish to load will consume on each logical volume. This will be shown in the example.

- Load(3) - After you are satisfied with the analysis, you may proceed with loading the software.

- Configuration(4) - The software you load may require kernel rebuilding and a system reboot. Startup and shutdown scripts may also need to be modified.

man page

"sw" - 2

There is some terminology associated with Software Distributor that I tend to use somewhat loosely. I have nothing but good things to say about Software Distributor, but I don't tend to conform to the official Software Distributor terminology as much as I should. I tend, for instance, to use the word "*system*" a lot, which could mean many different things in the Software Distributor world. For instance, Software Distributor uses "*local host*" (a system on which Software Distributor is running or software is to be installed or managed by Software Distributor), "*distribution depot*" (a directory that is used as a place for software products), and "*development system*" (a place where software is prepared for distribution). I will use the word *system* to mean the system on which we are working in the examples, because software is loaded onto the system from media.

The example of Software Distributor in this section describes the process of loading software from CD-ROM or DVD to the local system. What I show here only begins to scratch the surface of functionality you have with Software Distributor, but since I want to get you up and running quickly, this overview should be helpful. You can load software from a variety of media as well as across the network. You can run **swinstall** through the graphical interface used throughout this section, the character user interface, or the command line. You can use the **swinstall** command from the command line specifying source, options, target, etc. I would recommend using the character or graphical user interface because they are so much easier. If, however, you like to do things the "traditional UNIX" way, you can issue the **swinstall** command with arguments. You can look at the manual page for **swinstall** to understand its arguments and options and use this command from the command line. The graphical user interface of Software Distributor works with the **sd** (this is an SD-OV command and may also be invoked with **swjob -i**), **swcopy**, **swremove**, **swlist**, and **swinstall** commands. There is also an interactive terminal user interface for these commands if you don't have a graphics display.

On the L-Class system used in the upcoming example, there wasn't much to do in order to load software from a CD-ROM. I just physically put the CD-ROM in the DVD drive and typed **swinstall** at the command line. To mount the DVD-ROM device manually, I issued the command **mount /dev/dsk/c0t3d0 /cdrom**. To find the disk devices on your system, including DVD-ROMs and CD-ROMs, you issue the command **ioscan -funC disk**. I was given the screen shown in Figure 1-14 after invoking **swinstall** which shows the source for the software installation:

```
┌─────────────────────────────────────────────────────────────────────┐
│ ┌───┐                    Specify Source (I3)                    ┌─┐  │
│ └───┘                                                           └─┘  │
│                                                                      │
│  Specify the source type, then host name, then path on that host.    │
│                                                                      │
│  Source Depot Type:  ┌─────────────────────────────┐  ┌────────────┐ │
│                      │Network Directory/CDROM  ▭    │  │Find Local CD│ │
│                      └─────────────────────────────┘  └────────────┘ │
│                                                                      │
│     ┌───────────────────────────┐  ┌───────────────────────────────┐ │
│     │   Source Host Name...     │  │13                             │ │
│     └───────────────────────────┘  └───────────────────────────────┘ │
│                                                                      │
│     ┌───────────────────────────┐  ┌───────────────────────────────┐ │
│     │   Source Depot Path...    │  │/cdrom                         │ │
│     └───────────────────────────┘  └───────────────────────────────┘ │
│                                                                      │
│ ┌──────────┐         ┌──────────────┐              ┌──────────────┐  │
│ │   OK     │         │   Cancel     │              │    Help      │  │
│ └──────────┘         └──────────────┘              └──────────────┘  │
└─────────────────────────────────────────────────────────────────────┘
```

Figure 1-14 *Specify Source* Software Distributor Screen

man page

"sw" - 2

swinstall filled in the information shown in the dialog box. I did not have to create the directory **/cdrom** or issue the **mount** command at the command line as I often had to do in past releases of HP-UX. **swinstall** filled in all of the information shown in Figure 1-15. The applications CD-ROM from which we'll be loading applications in this example was labeled *HP-UX Release 11.11 and Application Products.*

After accepting the information shown in the figure, I proceeded to select (Step 1 - Selection) the software from the list that I wanted to load by "marking" it.

When selecting software to load you may receive a "Yes" in the "Marked?" column or a "Partial." "Yes" means all of the filesets associated with your selection will be loaded and "Partial" means only some will be loaded. Figure 1-15 shows "Yes" in the "Marked?" column for software that has been selected.

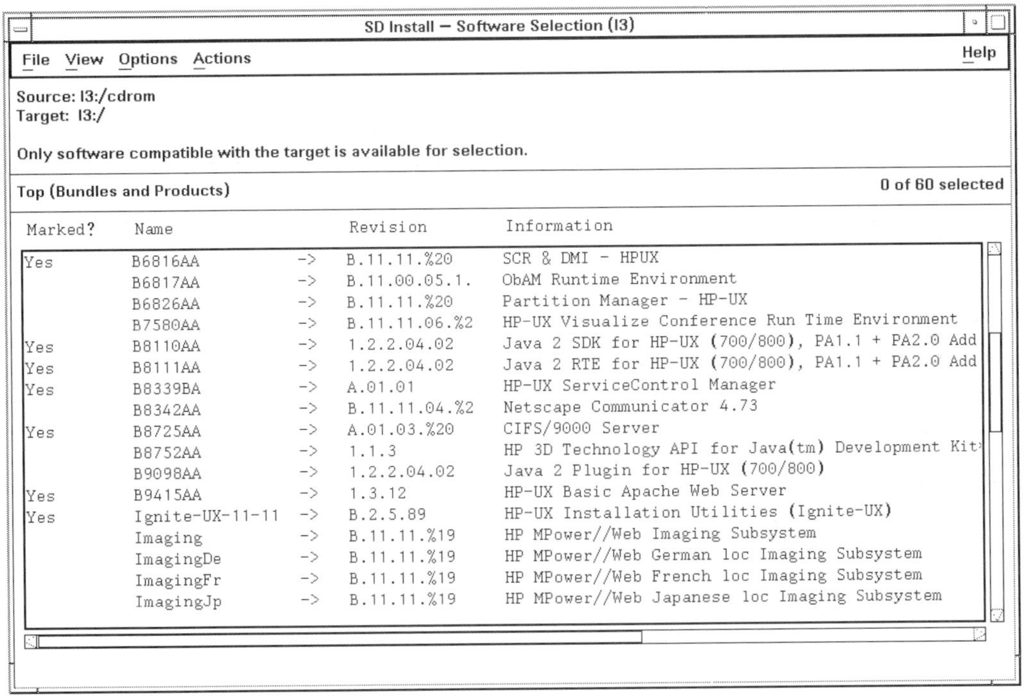

```
┌──────────────────────────────────────────────────────────────────────────────┐
│ ─                    SD Install — Software Selection (I3)              ◦ ▢ │
├──────────────────────────────────────────────────────────────────────────────┤
│  File  View  Options  Actions                                          Help  │
├──────────────────────────────────────────────────────────────────────────────┤
│ Source: I3:/cdrom                                                              │
│ Target: I3:/                                                                   │
│                                                                                │
│ Only software compatible with the target is available for selection.          │
├──────────────────────────────────────────────────────────────────────────────┤
│ Top (Bundles and Products)                                      0 of 60 selected │
│                                                                                │
│  Marked?   Name            Revision        Information                         │
│ ┌────────────────────────────────────────────────────────────────────────┐   │
│ │Yes       B6816AA     ->  B.11.11.%20     SCR & DMI - HPUX              ▲│   │
│ │          B6817AA     ->  B.11.00.05.1.   ObAM Runtime Environment       │   │
│ │          B6826AA     ->  B.11.11.%20     Partition Manager - HP-UX      │   │
│ │          B7580AA     ->  B.11.11.06.%2   HP-UX Visualize Conference Run Time Environment │
│ │Yes       B8110AA     ->  1.2.2.04.02     Java 2 SDK for HP-UX (700/800), PA1.1 + PA2.0 Add│
│ │Yes       B8111AA     ->  1.2.2.04.02     Java 2 RTE for HP-UX (700/800), PA1.1 + PA2.0 Add│
│ │Yes       B8339BA     ->  A.01.01         HP-UX ServiceControl Manager   │   │
│ │          B8342AA     ->  B.11.11.04.%2   Netscape Communicator 4.73     │   │
│ │Yes       B8725AA     ->  A.01.03.%20     CIFS/9000 Server               │   │
│ │          B8752AA     ->  1.1.3           HP 3D Technology API for Java(tm) Development Kit│
│ │          B9098AA     ->  1.2.2.04.02     Java 2 Plugin for HP-UX (700/800) │ │
│ │Yes       B9415AA     ->  1.3.12          HP-UX Basic Apache Web Server  │   │
│ │Yes       Ignite-UX-11-11 -> B.2.5.89     HP-UX Installation Utilities (Ignite-UX) │
│ │          Imaging     ->  B.11.11.%19     HP MPower//Web Imaging Subsystem │  │
│ │          ImagingDe   ->  B.11.11.%19     HP MPower//Web German loc Imaging Subsystem │
│ │          ImagingFr   ->  B.11.11.%19     HP MPower//Web French loc Imaging Subsystem │
│ │          ImagingJp   ->  B.11.11.%19     HP MPower//Web Japanese loc Imaging Subsystem ▼│
│ └────────────────────────────────────────────────────────────────────────┘   │
└──────────────────────────────────────────────────────────────────────────────┘
```

Figure 1-15 *Software Selection* Software Distributor Screen

A bundle of software that you select to install may be composed of products, subproducts, and filesets. You can select any item you have "Marked" for loading to see of what filesets it is comprised. I have done this for a Java products for 11i. I selected this *bundle* to see the software of which it is comprised in Figure 1-16:

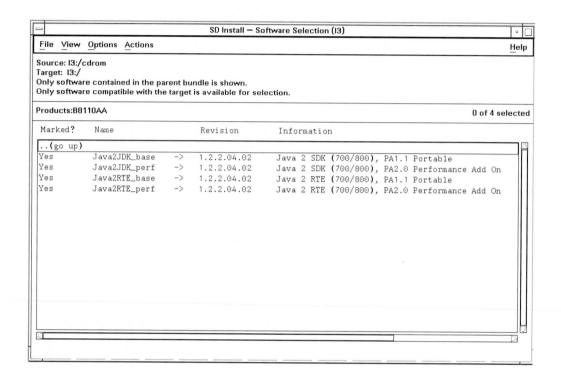

Figure 1-16 *Components of a Software Product*

Figure 1-16 shows that the Java software is indeed composed of many components. To go back to the top, we select *(go up)*.

Selecting *Install* runs analysis (Step 2 - Analysis) on the software you have selected to load. After the analysis has been completed, you can take a look at the logfile, view the disk space analysis, and perform other tasks. I normally take a look at the disk space analysis just to see the impact the software I am loading is having on free disk space, as shown in Figure 1-17:

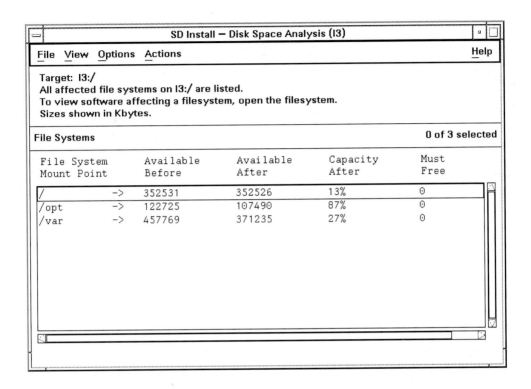

Figure 1-17 *Disk Space Analysis* Software Distributor Screen

I also look at the products to ensure that I'm loading the software I expect to load, as shown in Figure 1-18 for the products earlier marked for installation:

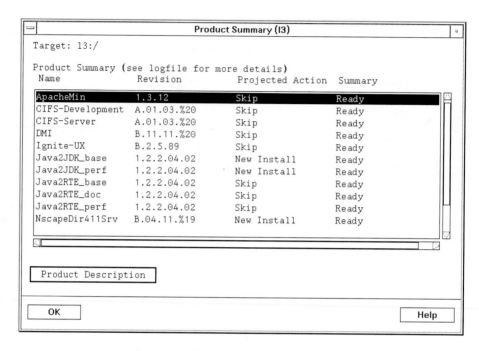

Figure 1-18 *Product Summary* Software Distributor Screen

After you are satisfied with the analysis, you can proceed with the installation (Step 3 - Load.) Figure 1-19 shows the type of status you are provided as software is loaded on the system:

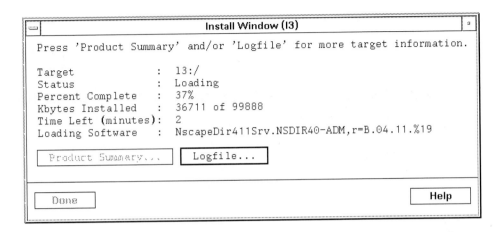

Figure 1-19 *Install Window* Software Distributor Screen Showing Status

In this case we have loaded about *37%* of the total software we have selected. The software currently being loaded is *Netscape Directory Server.* We could view the logfile to see the status of what has been loaded thus far.

After the load of your software is complete, you can either exit the session or you will be given a message indicating that a reboot will be required to complete the configuration (Step 4 - Configuration). Not all software requires a reboot in order for configuration to take place. Most software will run configuration routines after the software is loaded without the need for a reboot. If a reboot is required, you will be asked if you wish to reboot; but it could be a bad time to reboot, so you may want to wait, or delay the reboot.

The process of loading software from media using Software Distributor is easy and thorough. The user interface to Software Distributor makes it easy to select and load software from media.

Loading Patches

HP-UX patches can be obtained from a variety of sources. Most people start at *IT Resource Center (us-support.external.hp.com)* because a variety of useful HP-UX information can be found there using your browser.

When you set up your account with *IT Resource Center* initially, you will want to enter your system handle, and the serial number of one of your systems if you have it to get full access to all of the information on the site.

The process of viewing individual patches on *IT Resource Center* is self-explanatory when you log in to the site. Selecting *Individual Patches* and *HP-UX Patches* will allow you to select a specific release of HP-UX, such as 11.11 for HP-UX 11i, and select the patch(es) you wish to load on your system. You can then add the patches to your *Shopping Cart* and download them.

When you search *IT Resource Center* for a patch, you will be told if the patch has been replaced by a more recent patch. After selecting the patch you wish to view, a lot of useful information related to the patch will be available, including:

- Patch Files
- Dependencies
- Supersedes
- Size
- Critical
- Symptoms
- Defect Description
- Installation Instructions

I always view the installation instructions for a patch while on the Web site to see if any special work is required to load the patch. The following are the installation instructions for installing a patch we'll download and install in our example:

```
1. Back up your system before installing a patch.

            2. Login as root.

            3. Copy the patch to the /tmp directory.

            4. Move to the /tmp directory and unshar the patch:

            cd /tmp
            sh PHCO_21187

            5. Run swinstall to install the patch:

            swinstall -x autoreboot=true -x patch_match_target=true \
              -s /tmp/PHCO_21187.depot

            By default swinstall will archive the original software in
            /var/adm/sw/save/PHCO_21187.  If you do not wish to retain a
            copy of the original software, use the patch_save_files option:

            swinstall -x autoreboot=true -x patch_match_target=true \
              -x patch_save_files=false -s /tmp/PHCO_21187.depot

            WARNING: If patch_save_files is false when a patch is installed,
             the patch cannot be deinstalled.  Please be careful
             when using this feature.

            For future reference, the contents of the PHCO_21187.text file is
            available in the product readme:

            swlist -l product -a readme -d @ /tmp/PHCO_21187.depot

            To put this patch on a magnetic tape and install from the
            tape drive, use the command:

            dd if=/tmp/PHCO_21187.depot of=/dev/rmt/0m bs=2k

Special Installation Instructions: None
```

In the installation procedure for many patches, a reboot is required. This patch has the *autoreboot* option equal to *true,* meaning that a reboot will automatically take place if indeed a reboot is required. With HP-UX 11i, there are many more *Dynamic Patches* being introduced, which means that a reboot is not required when the patch is installed. You will see more and more patches for which a reboot is not required. Combined with *Dynamically Loadable Kernel Modules* and *Dynamically Tunable Kernel Parameters,* there will be fewer and fewer reboots required of 11i systems.

After reviewing the information related to the patch, we'll download it using a browser by selecting the patch and *Add to Cart*. Figure 1-20 shows a patch that has been placed in the *Shopping Cart* and is ready for download:

Figure 1-20   Patch in *Shopping Cart* Ready to Download

Note at the bottom of the figure that you can select to download the patch(es) with FTP instead of through the browser.

Figure 1-21 shows a patch that is in the process of being downloaded through the browser:

Figure 1-21 Patch Download

Once the patch is downloaded, you simply follow the instructions for installing the patch, such as those that were shown earlier for the patch in our example. You normally download a patch into the **/tmp** directory and run **sh** against the downloaded file, which produces *patchname*.**depot**. You can then run *Software Distributor* commands on the command line, as shown in the instructions.

man page

"sw" - 2

For the patch in our example, I've run **sh** against the file downloaded which produced a **.depot** file. We'll run **swinstall** to invoke the user interface. Figure 1-22 shows specifying the source as a *Local Directory* rather than a *Network Directory/CDROM,* as in the earlier example in this chapter, and the *Source Depot Path* of our **.depot** file in the **/tmp** directory:

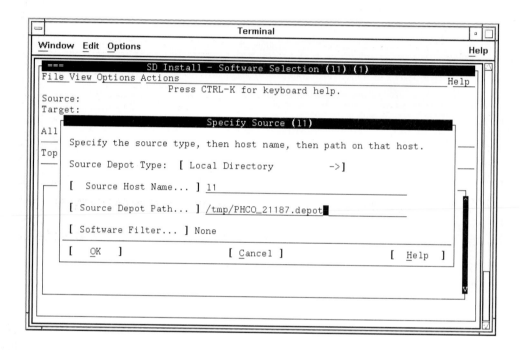

Figure 1-22 *Specify Source* of Patch

We would then mark the patch for installation as shown in Figure 1-23:

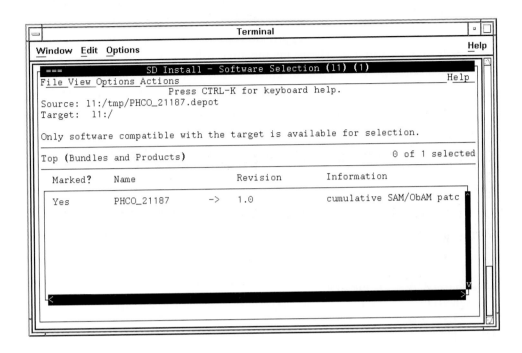

Figure 1-23 Patch Marked for Installation

You can load patches using **swinstall** interactively as I have done in this example, or following the instructions embedded in the patch and running **swinstall** from the command line.

Software Distributor Background

You need to have some background on the way software is organized in Software Distributor. There are the four following types of objects into which software is grouped in Software Distributor; bundle, product, sub-product, and fileset. Figure 1-24 shows the hierarchy of Software Distributor objects.

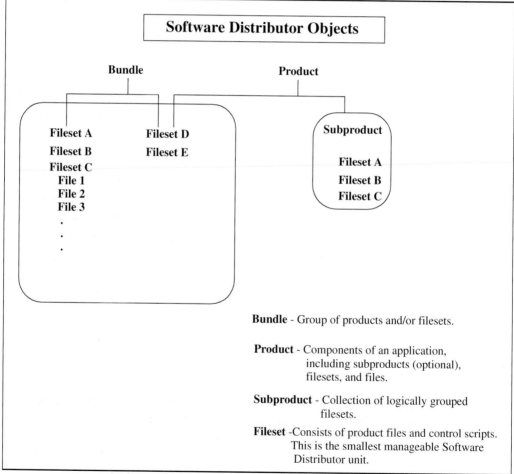

Figure 1-24   Software Distributor Objects

You can look at the bundle in Figure 1-24 as a group of software. This can be products, subproducts, and filesets, as shown in the diagram. The concept here is to organize software in such a way that it is easy to manage. The diagram shows that some filesets are shared between different bundles and products. This hierarchical organization and sharing makes managing software with Software Distributor flexible.

Next, we'll cover some of the common software management-related tasks you can perform with Software Distributor.

Installing and Updating Software (Command Line or GUI)

man page

"sw" - 2

The **swinstall** command is used to install and update software. The source of the software you are loading can come from a variety of places, including CD-ROM, magnetic tape, or a "depot" directory from which software can be distributed. Using the depot, you can load software into a directory and then install and update software on other nodes from this directory. Software loaded from CD-ROM with Software Distributor must be loaded onto the local system; this technique is used in the upcoming example. You have a lot of flexibility with SD-OV when selecting the target system onto which you want to load software and the source from which you will load the software. You can, for instance, load software from a depot that is on another system on your network. This command can be run at the command line or with the graphical user interface.

Copying Software to a Depot (Command Line or GUI)

The **swcopy** command is used to copy software from one depot to another. The depot used in the upcoming examples is a CD-ROM. By setting up depots, you can quickly install or update software to other nodes simultaneously with SD-OV. This command can be run at the command line or with the graphical user interface.

Removing Software from a System (Command Line or GUI)

The **swremove** command is used to remove software from a system that has had software loaded with Software Distributor. This includes removing installed and configured software from a system or removing software from a depot. This command can be run at the command line or with the graphical user interface.

List Information about Installation Software

The **swlist** command provides information about the depots that exist on a system, the contents of a depot, or information about installed software. Examples of using this command are provided shortly. This command can be run at the command line or with the graphical user interface.

Configure Installed Software

The **swconfig** command configures or unconfigures installed software. Configuration of software normally takes place as part of **swinstall,** but configuration can be deferred until a later time.

Verify Software

The **swverify** command confirms the integrity of installed software or software stored in a depot.

Package Software That Can Later Be Installed (Local Sys Only)

You may want to produce "packages" of software that you can later put on tape or in a depot with the **swpackage** command. This packaged software

can then be used as a source for **swinstall** and be managed by other Software
Distributor commands.

Control Access to Software Distributor Objects

You may want to apply restricted access to Software Distributor objects such
as packaged software. Using the **swacl** command, you can view and change
the Access Control List (ACL) for objects.

Modify Information about Loaded Software (Local System Only)

The Installed Products Database (IPD) and associated files are used to maintain information about software products you have loaded. **swmodify** can be
run at the command line to modify these files.

Register or Unregister a Depot

A software depot can be registered or unregistered with **swreg**. This means
you don't have to remove a depot; if you temporarily don't want it used, you
can unregister it.

Manage Jobs (Command Line or GUI, this is SD-OV only)

Software Distributor jobs can be viewed and removed with **swjob**. The
graphical user interface version of this command can be invoked with **sd** or
swjob -i.

Listing the Software

man page

"sw" - 2

Although I like the graphical user interface of **swinstall,** you can also issue Software Distributor commands at the command line. One example is the **swlist** command. The **swlist** command is useful for viewing the software you have loaded on your system, viewing the software you have loaded in a depot, or producing a list of depots. A graphical user interface to the **swlist** command can be invoked with the *-i* option and is also available in SAM. With the **swlist** command, you perform many functions, including the following:

- List the software you have at the specified level with the *-l* option. I will show several examples shortly. The levels you can specify are:

  root
  depot
  bundle
  product
  subproduct
  fileset
  file

Levels are delineated by "." so you will see *bundle.[product].[subproduct].[fileset]*. You can get all kinds of useful information out of **swlist** and use this for other purposes. Some of the things you can do with **swlist** are:

- Display the table of contents from a software source.

- Specify which attributes you wish to see for a level of software such as name, size, revision, and so on.

- Create a list of products that can be used as input to other Software Distributor commands, such as **swinstall** and **swremove**.

When you run **swlist** with no options, you get a list of the software products installed on your system. Let's try a few **swlist** commands with the *-l* option to view software installed on a system (by default, **swlist** will list installed products; you can use the **-s** option to specify a software depot or other source). The following example shows listing software at the *bundle* level.

```
$ swlist -l bundle

# various header information
#              .
B2491BA        B.11.00 MirrorDisk/UX
B3701AA_TRY    B 11.00.31 Trial HP GlancePlus/UX Pak s800
B3929BA        B11.00  HP   OnLineJFS (Advanced VxFS)
B3947BA        B.11.00 HP Process Resource Manager
B5725AA        B.1.4   HP-UX Installation Utilities (Ignite-UX)
HPUXEng32RT    B 11.00 English HP-UX 32-bit Runtime Environment
```

This system has the HP-UX runtime environment, GlancePlus/UX trial software, HP OnLineJFS, and MirrorDisk/UX.

If we run **swlist** at the product level, the following is produced for GlancePlus/UX trial software:

```
$ swlist -l product B3701AA_TRY

# various header information
#              .
#              .
#              .
B3701AA_TRY                   B.11.00.31  Trial HP GlancePlus/UX Pak for s800 11.00
B3701AA_TRY.MeasurementInt    B.11.00.31  HP-UX Measurement Interface for 11.00
B3701AA_TRY.MeasureWare       B.11.00.31  MeasureWare Software/UX
B3701AA_TRY.Glance            B.11.00.31  HP GlancePlus/UX

 (bundle)   (product)
```

GlancePlus/UX is comprised of the two products shown in this example. Are there any subproducts of which GlancePlus/UX is comprised? The following example will help us determine the answer.

```
$ swlist -l subproduct B3701AA_TRY

# various header information
#              .
#              .
#              .
B3701AA_TRY                   B.11.00.31  Trial HP GlancePlus/UX Pak for s800 11.00
B3701AA_TRY.MeasurementInt    B.11.00.31  HP-UX Measurement Interface for 11.00
B3701AA_TRY.MeasureWare       B.11.00.31  MeasureWare Software/UX
B3701AA_TRY.Glance            B.11.00.31  HP GlancePlus/UX

 (bundle)   (product)
```

The output of the products and subproducts levels is the same; therefore, there are no subproducts in GlancePlus/UX. We can go one step further and take this to the fileset level, as shown in the following example:

```
$ swlist -l fileset B3701AA_TRY

# various header information
#           .
#           .
#           .
B3701AA_TRY                       B.11.00.31  Trial HP GlancePlus/UX Pak for s800 11.00
B3701AA_TRY.MeasurementInt         B.11.00.31  HP-UX Measurement Interface for 11.00
B3701AA_TRY.MeasurementInt.ARM     B.11.00.31  HP-UX Application Response Measurement
for 11.00
B3701AA_TRY.MeasurementInt.MI      B.11.00.31 HP-UX Measurement Interface for 11.00
B3701AA_TRY.MeasureWare            B.11.00.31 MeasureWare Software/UX
B3701AA_TRY.MeasureWare.MWA        B.11.00.31 MeasureWare Software files
B3701AA_TRY.MeasureWare.MWANO      B.11.00.31 MeasureWare NOS Connectivity Module
Software files
B3701AA_TRY.MeasureWare.PERFDSI    B.11.00.31 HP PCS Data Source Integration
B3701AA_TRY.Glance                 B.11.00.31 HP GlancePlus/UX
B3701AA_TRY.Glance.GLANC           B.11.00.31 HP GlancePlus files
B3701AA_TRY.Glance.GPM             B.11.00.31     HP GlancePlus Motif interface files

(bundle)    (product) (fileset)
```

man page

"sw" - 2

With the **swlist** command and the *-l* option, we have worked our way down the hierarchy of HP GlancePlus/UX. Going down to the file level with the *-l file* option produces a long list of files associated with this product.

Table 1-2 shows some of the *-l* options to **swlist** that I use:

TABLE 1-2   List of Some swlist -l Options

Command	Explanation
swlist -l root	Shows the root level.
swlist -l shroot	Shows the shared roots.
swlist -l prroot	Shows the private roots.
swlist -l bundle	Shows bundles only.
swlist -l product	Shows products only.
swlist -l subproduct	Shows both products and subproducts.
swlist -l fileset	Shows products, subproducts, and filesets.
swlist -l file	Shows products, subproducts, filesets, files and numbers.
swlist -l category	Shows all categories of available patches if they have category in their definition.
swlist -l patch	Shows all applied patches.

Command	Explanation
swlist -l depot	Shows all depots on the local host.
swlist -l depot @ sys	Shows all depots on *sys*.

I also like to use the *-a* option with **swlist.** *-a* specifies that you would like see a specific attribute associated with the software you are listing. You can look at the **sd** manual page on your HP-UX system to get a complete list of attributes. One attribute I often look at is *size*. To get a list of the *subproducts* in *NETWORKING* and their *size* in KBytes, you would issue the following command:

```
$ swlist -l subproduct -a size NETWORKING
```

Another attribute I often view is *revision,* which you can view with the following command:

```
$ swlist -l subproduct -a revision NETWORKING
```

man page

"sw" - 2

Sometimes, the brief descriptions of filesets that are given are insufficient to really understand the fileset. The *title* attribute provides a descriptive title, which you can see with the following command for the fileset level:

```
$ swlist -l fileset -a title NETWORKING
```

Table 1-3 is a list of some attributes that you may find of interest.

TABLE 1-3   List of Some Attributes of Interest

Attribute	Explanation
architecture	Shows the target systems supported by the software.
category	Shows the type of software.
description	Shows more detailed description of software.
title	Shows the official name of the software.

Attribute	Explanation
owner	Shows the owner of the file.
path	Shows the full pathname of the file.
revision	Shows the revision number of the software object.
size	Shows the size of all filesets.
state	Shows the state of the fileset.

The other Software Distributor commands listed earlier can also be issued at the command line. You may want to look at the manual pages for these commands as you prepare to do more advanced Software Distributor work than loading software from DVD, CD-ROM, or tape.

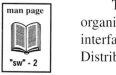

To system administrators familiar with HP-UX 9.x, there is a different organization of software in HP-UX 10.x and 11.x, but the graphical user interface of **swinstall** combined with the better organization of Software Distributor makes this an advantage of HP-UX 11.x.

Manual Pages for Commands Used in Chapter 1

The following section contains copies of the manual pages for commands used in Chapter 1. This makes a quick reference for you to use when issuing the commands commonly used throughout your system administration day. The manual pages, more commonly referred to as man pages, are listed in detail with the exception of the Software Distributor (SD-UX). Because Software Distributor is commonly used from the GUI, only a summary of the command-line version of these commands is given. These commands are listed under "sw command summaries."

"sw" command summaries

man page

"sw" - 2

"sw" commands - Command summaries related to software distribution.

---

swacl(1M)   **Hewlett-Packard Company**   **swacl(1M)**

NAME

swacl - View or modify the Access Control Lists (ACLs) which protect
software products

SYNOPSIS

swacl -l level [-M acl_entryl -D acl_entryl -F acl_file] [-x
option=value]
[-X option_file] [-f software_file] [-t target_file]
[software_selections] [@ target_selections]

swagentd(1M)   **Hewlett-Packard Company**   **swagentd(1M)**
swagent(1M)   swagent(1M)

NAME

swagentd - Serve local or remote SD software management tasks,
including invoking a swagent command.

swagent - Perform SD software management tasks as the agent of an SD
command.

   SWAGENTD.EXE - Perform HP OpenView Software Distributor PC
software management tasks, or serve local PC software for distribution. See
"Remarks:" below.

SYNOPSIS

swagentd [-k] [-n] [-r] [-x option=value] [-X option_file]

SWAGENTD.EXE (HP OpenView Software Distributor only)

swcluster(1M)   **swcluster(1M)**

NAME
  swcluster - Install or remove software from diskless server

SYNOPSIS

  swcluster [XToolkit Options] [-v][v] [-i] [-p] [-f] [-r] [-b] [-l
  list_class] [-n] [-s source]
  [-C session_file] [-S session_file] [-x option=value] [-X option_file]
  [software_selections] [@ target_selections]

swconfig(1M)   **Hewlett-Packard Company**   **swconfig(1M)**

NAME
  swconfig - Configure, unconfigure, or reconfigure installed software

SYNOPSIS

  swconfig [-p] [-v] [-u] [-x option=value] [-X option_file] [-f
  software_file] [-t target_file]
  [-C session_file] [-S session_file] [-Q date] [-J jobid]
  [software_selections] [@ target_selections]

swgettools(1M)   **Hewlett-Packard Company**   **swgettools(1M)**

NAME
  swgettools - Utility for retrieving the SD product from new SD media

SYNOPSIS

swgettools -s <source_media_location> [-t <temp_dir_location>]

swinstall(1M)   **Hewlett-Packard Company**   **swinstall(1M)**
swcopy(1M)   **swcopy(1M)**

NAME
swinstall - Install and configure software products

swcopy - Copy software products for subsequent installation or
distribution

SYNOPSIS

swinstall [XToolkit Options] [-i] [-p] [-v] [-r] [-s source] [-x
option=value] [-X option_file]
[-f software_file] [-t target_file] [-C session_file] [-S session_file]
[-Q date] [-J jobid]
[software_selections] [@ target_selections]

swcopy [XToolkit Options] [-i] [-p] [-v] [-s source] [-x option=value]
[-X option_file]
[-f software_file] [-t target_file] [-C session_file] [-S session_file]
[-Q date] [-J jobid]
[software_selections] [@ target_selections]

swjob(1M)   **Hewlett-Packard Company**   **swjob(1M)**
sd(1M)   **sd(1M)**

NAME
swjob - Display job information and remove jobs.

sd - Interactive interface for creating and monitoring jobs.

For a description of the HP OpenView Software Distributor objects,
attributes and data formats, see the sd(4) manual page by typing:
    man 4 sd

    For an overview of all HP OpenView Software Distributor commands,
see
    the sd(5) manual page by typing:
    man 5 sd

SYNOPSIS

    swjob [-i] [-u] [-v] [-R] [-a attribute] [-x option=value] [-X
    option_file] [-f jobid_file]
    [-t target_file] [-C session_file] [-S session_file] [jobid(s)] [
    @ target_selections]

    sd [-x option=value] [-X option_file]

swlist(1M)   **Hewlett-Packard Company**   **swlist(1M)**

NAME
    swlist - Display information about software products

SYNOPSIS

    swlist [-d|-r] [-l level] [-v] [-a attribute] [-R] [-s source] [-x
    option=value] [-X option_file]
    [-f software_file] [-t target_file] [-C session_file] [-S session_file]
    [software_selections] [@ target_selections]

swmodify(1M)   **Hewlett-Packard Company**   **swmodify(1M)**

NAME
    swmodify - Modify software products in a target root or depot

SYNOPSIS

    swmodify [-d|-r] [-p] [-P pathname_file] [-v[v]] [-V] [-u]
    [-s product_specification_file| -a attribute=[value]] [-x option=value]
    [-X option_file]
    [-f software_file] [-C session_file] [-S session_file]
    [software_selections] [@ target_selection]

swpackage(1M)   **Hewlett-Packard Company**   **swpackage(1M)**

NAME
    swpackage - Package software products into a target depot or tape

    For a description of the Product Specification File used as input to
    the swpackage command, see the swpackage(4) manual page by typing:
        man 4 swpackage

SYNOPSIS

    swpackage [-p] [-v[v]] [-V] [-s product_specification_file|directory]
    [-d directory|device]
    [-x option=value] [-X option_file] [-f software_file] [-C session_file]
    [-S session_file]
    [software_selections] [@ target_selection]

swreg(1M)   **Hewlett-Packard Company**   **swreg(1M)**

NAME
    swreg - Register or unregister depots and roots

SYNOPSIS

swreg -l level [-u] [-v] [-x option=value] [-X option_file] [-f object_file] [-t target_file]
[-C session_file] [-S session_file] [objects_to_(un)register] [@ target_selections]

swremove(1M)   **Hewlett-Packard Company**   **swre-move(1M)**

NAME
swremove - Unconfigure and remove software products

SYNOPSIS

swremove [XToolkit Options] [-i] [-p] [-v] [-d|-r] [-x option=value]
[-X option_file] [-f software_file] [-t target_file] [-C session_file]
[-S session_file] [-Q date] [-J jobid] [software_selections] [@ target_selections]

swverify(1M)   **Hewlett-Packard Company**   **swverify(1M)**

NAME
swverify - Verify software products

SYNOPSIS

swverify [-v] [-d|-r] [-x option=value] [-X option_file] [-f software_file] [-t target_file]
[-C session_file] [-S session_file] [-Q date] [-J jobid]
[software_selections] [@ target_selections]

CHAPTER 2

Working With vPars

Preparing to Create Virtual Partitions

In Chapter 1 we loaded HP-UX 11i and Virtual Partitions software. Now we're ready to create Virtual Partitions. After we create Virtual Partitions in this chapter we have to boot the partitions we've created. Although we will boot the partitions in this chapter, the details of booting Virtual Partitions, and HP 9000 booting in general, are covered in detail in Chapter 3.

With both HP-UX 11i and the Virtual Partitions software on our disk, we can begin the process of creating partitions. Our goal is to have a system that looks like that in Figure 2-1:

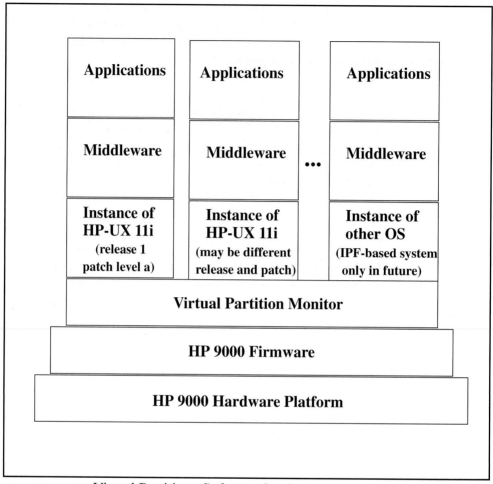

Figure 2-1 Virtual Partitions Software Stack

There are many components in Figure 2-1. We already have many of the components in this diagram on our system. Starting from the bottom we have the hardware, firmware, Virtual Partition Monitor (covered as part of the boot process in Chapter 3), and HP-UX 11i installed on two different disks. There are two HP-UX 11i instances shown in the leftmost two stacks of Figure 2-1. These are the operating systems we already have loaded.

The two HP-UX 11i instances can't run simultaneously on our L-Class system because we have not yet created our Virtual Partitions. Without Virtual Partitions created, we can boot HP-UX off of one *or* the other of these disks but we can't run both. Let's now create our Virtual Partitions so we can indeed have two instances of HP-UX 11i running simultaneously. After Virtual Partitions have been created, you can proceed to load the middleware and applications shown on top of HP-UX 11i in Figure 2-1.

Although we're covering running multiple instances of HP-UX 11i in the Virtual Partitions we create, we won't be restricted to only HP-UX 11i in the future. On systems based on the Itanium Processor Family (IPF) CPUs, we'll be able to run additional operating systems. The rightmost Virtual Partition In Figure 2-1 depicts this future capability. This capability does not exist at the time of this writing, so it is not covered. Look for an updated revision of this book in the future to cover this capability once it exists and keep an eye on *www.hp.com* for both IPF and Virtual Partition enhancements.

Although the examples in this chapter take place on four-way (four-processor) L-Class systems, vPars run on most HP servers. The more components of which your HP server is comprised, the more vPars you can have on the server and the more options you have for crafting vPars. Figure 2-2 shows an example of an eight-way HP server and the way vPars can be configured:

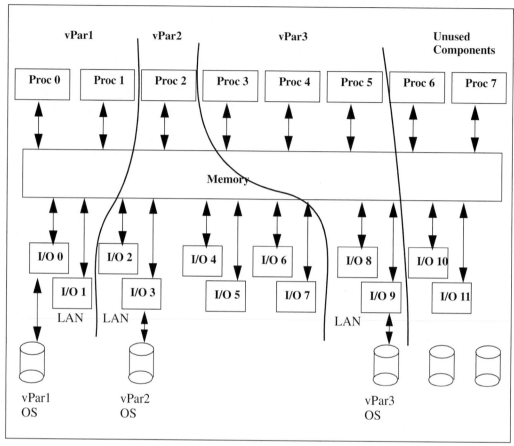

Figure 2-2 Example of HP Server Resource Allocation with vPars

You can see that the eight-way system shown has a different number of processors, different amount of memory, and different number of I/O cards allocated to each Virtual Partition. The unused components can be added to any of the vPars or be the basis for yet another vPar. In addition, components can be moved from one vPar to another (with some restrictions described later in this chapter.)

In the examples in this chapter we'll end up with a four-way L-Class with two fully configured Virtual Partitions. Before we proceed with the examples, let's first take a look at the commands we'll be using throughout the chapter in the next section.

Virtual Partitions Command Summary

There are several commands used to create and work with Virtual Partitions in Figure 2-1 that we have not yet covered. Table 2-1 is provides an overview of many commonly used Virtual Partitions-related commands. This is the same information that is on the tear-out Overture Partitions Command Summary.

Table 2-1   Virtual Partition Command Summary

Command	Description
ISL> Initial System Load prompt.	Virtual Partitions Monitor is loaded from *ISL>* with: ISL> **hpux /stand/vpmon** MON> To load Virtual Partitions directly from *ISL>*, use: ISL> **hpux /stand/vpmon vparload -p** *vPar_name*
MON> Virtual Partitions Monitor prompt. (Also see **vparload** command.)	This is loaded from *ISL* with: ISL> **hpux /stand/vpmon** MON> To load an alternate database from *ISL,* use: ISL> **hpux /stand/vpmon -D** *db_file* To load one vPar from *MON* , use: MON> **vparload** *vPar_name* Many other commands can be issued from *MON*. Type **help** or **?** to list. (Commands include: **scan, vparinfo, ls, log, getauto, lifls, cbuf, cat.**)

Command	Description
vparload Load Virtual Partitions from *MON>* prompt only.	form1: vparload -all form2: vparload -auto form3: vparload -p vp_name [-b kernelpath] [-o "boot_options"] [-B hardware_path] To boot a Virtual Partition from *MON>*: MON> **vparload -p** *vPar_name* To boot all Virtual Partitions from *MON>*: MON> **vparload -all** To boot a Virtual Partition in single-user mode from *MON>*: MON> **vparload -p** *vPar_name* **-o "-is"** Some other options to issue at *MON>* include: **"-lq"** (low quorum,) **"-lm"** (maintenance mode)
vparboot Boot a Virtual Partition from the command line only.	form1: vparboot -p vp_name [-b kernel_path] [-o boot_opts] [-B boot_addr] form2: vparboot -p vp_name -I ignite_kernel To boot a Virtual Partition from the command line: # **vparboot -p** *vPar_name* To boot a Virtual Partition from the command line in single-user mode: # **vparboot -p** *vPar_name* **-o -"is"**

Command	Description
vparcreate Create a Virtual Partition.	form: vparcreate -p vp_name [-B boot_attr] [-D db_file] [-S static_attr] [-b kernel_path] [-o boot_opts] [-a rsrc] [-a...] To create a Virtual Partition with three processors (*num*) total, two bound (*min*), 2048MB RAM, all components on 0/0, boot disk at 0/0/1/1.2.0, with a kernel of **/stand/vmunix**, autoboot on, and console at 0/0/4/0: `# vparcreate -p vPar_name -a cpu::3 -a cpu:::2:4 -a mem::2048 -a io:0/0 -a io:0/0/1/1.2.0:boot -b /stand/vmunix -B auto` Notes: - HP-UX 11i must be loaded on volume before or after Virtual Partition is created. If HP-UX 11i is loaded after vPar is created, `vparboot -p vp_name -I ignite_kernel` is used to load 11i. - **/stand/vmunix** is default and does not need to be specified. - vPar was not set to *static,* meaning that it can be modified later. - CPUs are three total (*num*), two bound (*min*), and as many as two unbound (*max*).

vparmodify
 	
Modify the attributes of a Virtual Partition.
 	
(Note that CPUs are added relative to the current number with *-a. -a cpu::2* adds two CPUs to the current number of CPUs. *-m cpu::3* specifies an absolute number of CPUs of three.)
	vparmodify -p vp_name [-B boot_attr] [-D db_file] [-S static_attr] [-b kernel_path] [-o boot_opts] [-P new_vp_name]
	[-a rsrc] [-a...]
	[-m rsrc] [-m...]
	[-d rsrc] [-d...]
	
	To add processor at path *109* (adds this proc to those already assigned):
	`# vparmodify -p vPar_name -a cpu:109`
	To specify an absolute number of three processors:
	`# vparmodify -p vPar_name -m cpu::3`

vparremove Delete a Virtual Partition.	vparremove -p vp_name [-D db_file] [-f] To delete a Virtual Partition in the currently running database: `# vparremove -p vPar_name`

Command	Description
vparreset Reset a Virtual Partition.	vparreset -p vp_name [-h|-t] [-q] [-f] To reset a Virtual Partition simulating the TOC operations at the *Ctrl-B* prompt. Without the *-h* option the default command simulates only a TOC. # **vparreset -p** *vPar_name* To force a hard reset of a Virtual Partition: # **vparreset -p** *vPar_name* **-h -f**
vparresources(5) man page Provides description of Virtual Partitions and their resources.	This is a manual page that describes Virtual Partition resources in general and how resources are specified in other commands, such as **vparmodify**.
vparstatus Display the status of Virtual Partitions.	form1: vparstatus [-v	-M] [-p vp_name] [-p...] [-D db_file] form2: vparstatus -A [-M] (available resources) form3: vparstatus -w (name of current vPar) form4: vparstatus -e (event log of Virtual Partition Monitor) fomr5: vparstatus -R [-p vp_name] (PIM data from most recent reset) To display the status of a Virtual Partition in verbose mode: # **vparstatus -v -p** *vPar_name* To display the status of all Virtual Partitions in verbose mode: # **vparstatus -v** To display the available or unused resources: # **vparstatus -A**
vpartition man page Display information about the Virtual Partition Command Line Interface.	Provides the following brief description of Virtual Partitions commands: **vparboot** Boot (start) a virtual partition. **vparcreate** Create a new virtual partition. **vparmodify** Modify an existing virtual partition. **vparremove** Remove (delete) an existing virtual partition. **vparreset** Simulate a TOC or hard reset to a virtual partition. **vparstatus** Display virtual partition and available resources information.

Command	Description
Specify CPU Resources by:	Number of bound and unbound CPUs: *cpu::num* CPU hardware path(s): *cpu:path* Minimum and maximum number: *cpu:::[min][:[max]]*
Types of CPUs: (See vparresources man page for more detail on all types of resources.)	*Bound*: CPU is tied to a Virtual Partition when vPar is active. Allocation is done at the time of vPar creation. Lowest number bound CPU is *monarch* for the vPar. Interrupts are handled by *bound* CPUs. *Unbound*: CPU that can be dynamically reassigned. Do not handle interrupts.
Specify Memory by:	Size *mem::size* Base and range: *mem:::base:range* combination of both above.
Specify I/O:	Use path: *io:path[:attr1[,attr2[...]]]* (see man page **vparresources** for details).
To add resources use: (This adds component relative to what already exists if running **vparmodify**.)	*-a cpu:path* *-a cpu::num* (can be done with vPar running) *[-a cpu::num] [-a cpu:::[min]:[max]] -[a cpu:path]* (*:::* is **vparcreate** only) *-a io:path[:attr1[,attr2[...]]]* *-a mem::size* *-a mem:::base:range*
To delete resources use (This deletes component relative to what already exists if running **vparmodify**.)	*-d cpu:path* *-d cpu::num* (can be done with vPar running) *-d io:path[:attr1[,attr2[...]]]* *-d mem::size* *-d mem:::base:range*
To modify resources use: (This modifies to absolute number rather than relative.)	*-m cpu::num* (can be done with vPar running) *-m cpu:::[min][:max]]* *-m io:path[:attr1[,attr2[...]]]* *-m mem::size*

Command	Description

vPars **setboot** Options:
-*a*
-*b*
-*p*
-*s*
no options
	Changes the alternate boot path of the Virtual Partition.
	Sets the autoboot attribute of the Virtual Partition.
	Changes the primary boot path of the Virtual Partition.
	No effect.
	Displays information about boot attributes.
	
	To set Autoboot *on*:
	`# setboot -b on`
	To set the primary boot path:
	`# setboot -p 0/0/1/1.2.0`
	To set the alternate boot path:
	`# setboot -a 0/8/0/0.8.0.5.0.0.0`

vPars States: *load* *boot* *up* *shut* *down* *crash* *hung*	The kernel image of a Virtual Partition is being loaded into memory. This is done by the Virtual Partition monitor. The Virtual Partition is in the process of booting. The kernel image has been successfully loaded by the Virtual Partition monitor. The Virtual Partition has been successfully booted and is running. The Virtual Partition is in the process of shutting down. The Virtual Partition is not running and is down. The Virtual Partition has experienced a panic and is crashing. The Virtual Partition is not responding and is hung.

We'll use some of the commands shown in Table 2-1 in the upcoming section on creating virtual partitions. There is more detail on the Virtual Partition commands in Appendix A, which contains the online manual pages for the commands.

Let's now move on to creating our virtual partitions.

Steps to Create Virtual Partitions

In this section we'll cover the steps to create Virtual Partitions. These are steps I performed while working with vPars with some of the very first installations. This list should serve as a framework for working with vPars. You may chose not to perform some of the steps and to add others. It is only a framework for getting vPars working on your system.

In our upcoming examples to create our Virtual Partitions, we'll execute the steps shown in Figure 2-3.

1) Load HP-UX 11i onto the disks on which you want to run a Virtual Partition* (media or Ignite/UX server.)

2) Load Virtual Partitions software onto the disk(s) on which you want to run a Virtual Partition.

3) Gather information on system components and hardware paths using **ioscan**, **dmesg**, and other commands.

4) List components of which Virtual Partitions will be comprised.

5) Build new HP-UX 11i kernels on all volumes on which Virtual Partitions will run* with **mk_kernel** and **kmupdate** (done automatically, done for all 11i instances that will run vPars.)

6) Create first Virtual Partition with **vparcreate**.

7) Boot first Virtual Partition with **vparload** at *MON>* prompt. Use **vparstatus -v** to see running vPar and **vparstatus -A** to see available components.

8) Create second Virtual Partition with **vparcreate** (can also be done before booting any vPars.)

9) Boot second Virtual Partition with **vparboot** from the first vPar and monitor it booting with **vparstatus**. After it has booted, view remaining available components with **vparstatus -A**.

10) Modify Virtual Partition(s) as required with **vparmodify** and view modifications with **vparstatus -v** and **vparstatus -A**. Modifications can be any type, such as adding CPUs, changing attributes, and so on.

Other tasks and comments:

- Many other tasks can be performed. Commands **vparremove** and **vparreset** were not used in steps above.

- A typical list of components of which a vPar would be comprised looks like the following:

```
name            cable1
processors      min of 1 (bound) max of 3 (1 bound 2 unbound) with num equal to 1
memory          1024 MB
LAN           0/0/0/0 (not specified explicity)
boot disk     0/0/1/1.2.0
kernel        /stand/vmunix
autoboot       off (manual)
console       0/0/4/0 (not specified explicity)
```

* HP-UX 11i must be loaded on volume before or after Virtual Partition is created. If HP-UX 11i is loaded after vPar is created, then `vparboot -p vp_name -I ignite_kernel` is used to load 11i.

Figure 2-3 Steps to Create Virtual Partitions

1) Load HP-UX 11i

HP-UX 11i must be loaded on the volumes that will be used to host all vPars. The method you use to install 11i, either media, Ignite-UX, or some other technique, are all acceptable provided that HP-UX 11i is present on all of the disks. HP-UX 11i must be present on the first disk before you begin the vPar creation. You can create vPars on other disks before HP-UX 11i is loaded on them and then use **vparboot -p** *vp_name* **-I** *ignite_kernel* to boot and load HP-UX 11i on the other disks. In this chapter I first load HP-UX 11i on all disks before creating vPars. Chapter 1 covers loading HP-UX 11i and vPars software. In our upcoming example the first Virtual Partition will be created on the internal disk on an L-Class system. The second Virtual Partition will be created on an external disk. After loading HP-UX 11i on one of the root volumes, I issued **uname**, which resulted in the following output:

```
# uname -a
HP-UX cvhdcon3 B.11.11 U 9000/800 136414696 unlimited-user license
#
```

The hostname of *cvhdcon3* and HP-UX revision *11.11*, which is the latest HP-UX 11i available at the time of this writing, are shown.

An interesting nuance to working with vPars is the naming of hosts and vPars. There is a hostname section in Chapter 1 that you may want to review. In a nutshell, you supply hostnames when installing 11i and Virtual Partition names when creating vPars. It reduces confusion if both the hostname and vPar name are the same for an instance of HP-UX 11i. In some cases, however, organizations require hostnames to conform to conventions that result in names that are difficult to remember. In this case some system administrators pick easy-to-remember vPar names. In the upcoming example we used different names for the vPars and hostnames.

Our upcoming examples have hostnames of *cvhdcon3* and *cvhdcon4*. The respective vPar names used are *cable1* and *cable2*.

2) Load the Virtual Partitions Application Software

The Virtual Partitions software must also be loaded on the volumes that will
be used to host all vPars. At the time of this writing there are *base* and *full*
versions of the software. The restrictions of the *base* software is a maximum
of two vPars and a maximum of one CPU in one of the vPars. After loading
the vPars software on one of the root volumes I ran **swlist** which resulted in
the following output:

```
# swlist
# Initializing...
# Contacting target "cvhdcon3"...
#
# Target:  cvhdcon3:/
#

#
# Bundle(s):
#

  BUNDLE11i            B.11.11.0102.2 Required Patch Bundle for HP-UX 11i, Febr
uary 2001
  CDE-English          B.11.11        English CDE Environment
  FDDI-00              B.11.11.01     PCI FDDI;Supptd HW=A3739A/A3739B;SW=J3626
AA
  FibrChanl-00         B.11.11.06     PCI/HSC FibreChannel;Supptd HW=A6684A,A66
85A,A5158A
  GigEther-00          B.11.11.14     PCI/HSC GigEther;Supptd HW=A4926A/A4929A/
A4924A/A4925A;SW=J1642AA
  HPUX11i-OE-MC        B.11.11.0106   HP-UX Mission Critical Operating Environm
ent Component
  HPUXBase64           B.11.11        HP-UX 64-bit Base OS
  HPUXBaseAux          B.11.11.0106   HP-UX Base OS Auxiliary
  HWEnable11i          B.11.11.0106.8 Hardware Enablement Patches for HP-UX 11i
, June 2001
  OnlineDiag           B.11.11.03.08  HPUX 11.11 Support Tools Bundle, Jun 2001

  RAID-00              B.11.11.01     PCI RAID; Supptd HW=A5856A
  VPARSBASE            A.01.00.03     HP-UX Virtual Partitions
#
```

The *HP-UX Virtual Partitions* software is the last entry shown in this
listing.

3) Gather the System Component and Hardware Paths

You get to know your hardware at an intimate level when working with vPars. You not only need to know the components of which your system is comprised, you also need to know the paths of much of the hardware. Some system components, such as *System Bus Adapters* and the *memory controller*, are shared among vPars, so you don't specify those components as part of individual Virtual Partitions. Most other components in your system, such as processors, I/O cards, disks, and others, are fixed to specific vPars.

   In order to see the components of which our example system is comprised, we'll run **ioscan -f** and **dmesg** in the following listing:

```
# ioscan -f
Class       I   H/W Path       Driver    S/W State   H/W Type      Description
===================================================================================
root        0                  root      CLAIMED     BUS_NEXUS
ioa         0   0              sba       CLAIMED     BUS_NEXUS     System Bus
                                                                   Adapter (803)
ba          0   0/0            lba       CLAIMED     BUS_NEXUS     Local PCI Bus
                                                                   Adapter (782)
lan         0   0/0/0/0        btlan     CLAIMED     INTERFACE     HP PCI 10/100
                                                                   Base-TX Core
ext_bus     0   0/0/1/0        c720      CLAIMED     INTERFACE     SCSI C896
                                                     Ultra Wide Single-Ended
target      0   0/0/1/0.1      tgt       CLAIMED     DEVICE
disk        0   0/0/1/0.1.0    sdisk     CLAIMED     DEVICE        HP DVD-ROM 304
target      1   0/0/1/0.3      tgt       CLAIMED     DEVICE
tape        0   0/0/1/0.3.0    stape     CLAIMED     DEVICE        HP      C1537A
target      2   0/0/1/0.7      tgt       CLAIMED     DEVICE
ctl         0   0/0/1/0.7.0    sctl      CLAIMED     DEVICE        Initiator
ext_bus     1   0/0/1/1        c720      CLAIMED     INTERFACE     SCSI C896
                                                     Ultra Wide Single-Ended
target      3   0/0/1/1.0      tgt       CLAIMED     DEVICE
disk        1   0/0/1/1.0.0    sdisk     CLAIMED     DEVICE        SEAGATE ST17340 4LC
target      4   0/0/1/1.2      tgt       CLAIMED     DEVICE
disk        2   0/0/1/1.2.0    sdisk     CLAIMED     DEVICE        SEAGATE ST17340 4LC
target      5   0/0/1/1.7      tgt       CLAIMED     DEVICE
ctl         1   0/0/1/1.7.0    sctl      CLAIMED     DEVICE        Initiator
ext_bus     2   0/0/2/0        c720      CLAIMED     INTERFACE     SCSI C87x
                                                     Ultra Wide Single-Ended
target      6   0/0/2/0.0      tgt       CLAIMED     DEVICE
disk        3   0/0/2/0.0.0    sdisk     CLAIMED     DEVICE        SEAGATE ST17340 4LC
target      7   0/0/2/0.2      tgt       CLAIMED     DEVICE
disk        4   0/0/2/0.2.0    sdisk     CLAIMED     DEVICE        SEAGATE ST17340 4lc
target      8   0/0/2/0.7      tgt       CLAIMED     DEVICE
ctl         2   0/0/2/0.7.0    sctl      CLAIMED     DEVICE        Initiator
ext_bus     3   0/0/2/1        c720      CLAIMED     INTERFACE     SCSI C87x
                                                     Ultra Wide Single-Ended
target      9   0/0/2/1.7      tgt       CLAIMED     DEVICE
ctl         3   0/0/2/1.7.0    sctl      CLAIMED     DEVICE        Initiator
tty         0   0/0/4/0        asio0     CLAIMED     INTERFACE     PCI Serial
tty         1   0/0/5/0        asio0     CLAIMED     INTERFACE     PCI Serial
ba          1   0/1            lba       CLAIMED     BUS_NEXUS     Local PCI Bus
                                                                   Adapter (782)
ba          2   0/2            lba       CLAIMED     BUS_NEXUS     Local PCI Bus
                                                                   Adapter (782)
ba          3   0/3            lba       CLAIMED     BUS_NEXUS     Local PCI Bus
                                                                   Adapter (782)
ba          4   0/4            lba       CLAIMED     BUS_NEXUS     Local PCI Bus
```

```
ba          5   0/5                   lba      CLAIMED    BUS_NEXUS   Local PCI Bus
                                                                     Adapter (782)
ba          6   0/8                   lba      CLAIMED    BUS_NEXUS   Local PCI Bus
                                                                     Adapter (782)
fc          0   0/8/0/0               td       CLAIMED    INTERFACE   HP Tachyon TL/TS
                                                          Fibre Channel Mass Storage Adapter
fcp         0   0/8/0/0.8             fcp      CLAIMED    INTERFACE   FCP Protocol
                                                                     Adapter
ext_bus     4   0/8/0/0.8.0.5.0       fcparray CLAIMED    INTERFACE     FCP
                                                                     Array Interface
target     10   0/8/0/0.8.0.5.0.0     tgt      CLAIMED    DEVICE
disk        5   0/8/0/0.8.0.5.0.0.0   sdisk    CLAIMED    DEVICE   HP A5277A
disk        6   0/8/0/0.8.0.5.0.0.1   sdisk    CLAIMED    DEVICE   HP A5277A
disk        7   0/8/0/0.8.0.5.0.0.2   sdisk    CLAIMED    DEVICE   HP A5277A
disk        8   0/8/0/0.8.0.5.0.0.3   sdisk    CLAIMED    DEVICE   HP A5277A
target     11   0/8/0/0.8.0.5.0.1     tgt      CLAIMED    DEVICE
disk        9   0/8/0/0.8.0.5.0.1.0   sdisk    CLAIMED    DEVICE   HP A5277A
target     12   0/8/0/0.8.0.5.0.2     tgt      CLAIMED    DEVICE
disk       10   0/8/0/0.8.0.5.0.2.0   sdisk    CLAIMED    DEVICE   HP A5277A
target     13   0/8/0/0.8.0.5.0.3     tgt      CLAIMED    DEVICE
disk       11   0/8/0/0.8.0.5.0.3.0   sdisk    CLAIMED    DEVICE   HP A5277A
ext_bus     5   0/8/0/0.8.0.255.0     fcpdev   CLAIMED    INTERFACE     FCP
                                                                     Device Interface
target     14   0/8/0/0.8.0.255.0.5   tgt      CLAIMED    DEVICE
ctl         4   0/8/0/0.8.0.255.0.5.0 sctl     CLAIMED    DEVICE   HP A5277A
ba          7   0/9                   lba      CLAIMED    BUS_NEXUS Local PCI
                                                          Bus Adapter (782)
fc          1   0/9/0/0               td       CLAIMED    INTERFACE HP Tachyon
                                                          TL/TS Fibre Channel Mass Storage Adapter
fcp         1   0/9/0/0.8             fcp      CLAIMED    INTERFACE FCP Protocol
                                                                     Adapter
ext_bus     6   0/9/0/0.8.0.4.0       fcparray CLAIMED    INTERFACE FCP Array
                                                          Interface
target     15   0/9/0/0.8.0.4.0.0     tgt      CLAIMED    DEVICE
disk       12   0/9/0/0.8.0.4.0.0.0   sdisk    CLAIMED    DEVICE HP A5277A
disk       13   0/9/0/0.8.0.4.0.0.1   sdisk    CLAIMED    DEVICE HP A5277A
disk       14   0/9/0/0.8.0.4.0.0.2   sdisk    CLAIMED    DEVICE HP A5277A
disk       15   0/9/0/0.8.0.4.0.0.3   sdisk    CLAIMED    DEVICE HP A5277A
target     16   0/9/0/0.8.0.4.0.1     tgt      CLAIMED    DEVICE
disk       16   0/9/0/0.8.0.4.0.1.0   sdisk    CLAIMED    DEVICE HP A5277A
target     17   0/9/0/0.8.0.4.0.2     tgt      CLAIMED    DEVICE
disk       17   0/9/0/0.8.0.4.0.2.0   sdisk    CLAIMED    DEVICE HP A5277A
target     18   0/9/0/0.8.0.4.0.3     tgt      CLAIMED    DEVICE
disk       18   0/9/0/0.8.0.4.0.3.0   sdisk    CLAIMED    DEVICE HP A5277A
ext_bus     7   0/9/0/0.8.0.255.0     fcpdev   CLAIMED    INTERFACE FCP
                                                          Device Interface
target     19   0/9/0/0.8.0.255.0.4   tgt      CLAIMED    DEVICE
ctl         5   0/9/0/0.8.0.255.0.4.0 sctl     CLAIMED    DEVICE HP A5277A
ba          8   0/10                  lba      CLAIMED    BUS_NEXUS Local PCI
                                                          Bus Adapter (782)
lan         1   0/10/0/0              btlan    CLAIMED    INTERFACE HP A5230A/
                                                          B5509BA PCI 10/100Base-TX Addon
ba          9   0/12                  lba      CLAIMED    BUS_NEXUS Local PCI
                                                          Bus Adapter (782)
lan         2   0/12/0/0              btlan    CLAIMED    INTERFACE   HP A5230A/
                                                          B5509BA PCI 10/100Base-TX Addon
pbc         0   32                    pbc      CLAIMED    BUS_NEXUS   Bus Converter
processor   0   33                    processor CLAIMED   PROCESSOR   Processor
pbc         1   36                    pbc      CLAIMED    BUS_NEXUS   Bus Converter
processor   1   37                    processor CLAIMED   PROCESSOR   Processor
pbc         2   96                    pbc      CLAIMED    BUS_NEXUS   Bus Converter
processor   2   97                    processor CLAIMED   PROCESSOR   Processor
pbc         3   100                   pbc      CLAIMED    BUS_NEXUS   Bus Converter
processor   3   101                   processor CLAIMED   PROCESSOR   Processor
memory      0   192                   memory   CLAIMED    MEMORY      Memory
#
```

```
# dmesg

Jul 31 20:03
gate64: sysvec_vaddr = 0xc0002000 for 2 pages
NOTICE: nfs3_link(): File system was registered at index 3.
NOTICE: autofs_link(): File system was registered at index 6.
NOTICE: cachefs_link(): File system was registered at index 7.
0 sba
0/0 lba
0/0/0/0 btlan
0/0/1/0 c720
0/0/1/0.1 tgt
0/0/1/0.1.0 sdisk
0/0/1/0.3 tgt
0/0/1/0.3.0 stape
0/0/1/0.7 tgt
0/0/1/0.7.0 sctl
0/0/1/1 c720
0/0/1/1.0 tgt
0/0/1/1.0.0 sdisk
0/0/1/1.2 tgt
0/0/1/1.2.0 sdisk
0/0/1/1.7 tgt
0/0/1/1.7.0 sctl
0/0/2/0 c720
0/0/2/0.0 tgt
0/0/2/0.0.0 sdisk
0/0/2/0.2 tgt
0/0/2/0.2.0 sdisk
0/0/2/0.7 tgt
0/0/2/0.7.0 sctl
0/0/2/1 c720
0/0/2/1.7 tgt
0/0/2/1.7.0 sctl
0/0/4/0 asio0
0/0/5/0 asio0
0/1 lba
0/2 lba
0/3 lba
0/4 lba
0/5 lba
0/8 lba
0/8/0/0 td
td: claimed Tachyon TL/TS Fibre Channel Mass Storage card at 0/8/0/0
0/8/0/0.8 fcp
0/8/0/0.8.0.5.0 fcparray
0/8/0/0.8.0.5.0.0 tgt
0/8/0/0.8.0.5.0.0.0 sdisk
0/8/0/0.8.0.5.0.0.1 sdisk
0/8/0/0.8.0.5.0.0.2 sdisk
0/8/0/0.8.0.5.0.0.3 sdisk
0/8/0/0.8.0.5.0.1 tgt
0/8/0/0.8.0.5.0.1.0 sdisk
0/8/0/0.8.0.5.0.2 tgt
0/8/0/0.8.0.5.0.2.0 sdisk
0/8/0/0.8.0.5.0.3 tgt
0/8/0/0.8.0.5.0.3.0 sdisk
0/8/0/0.8.0.255.0 fcpdev
0/8/0/0.8.0.255.0.5 tgt
0/8/0/0.8.0.255.0.5.0 sctl
0/9 lba
0/9/0/0 td
td: claimed Tachyon TL/TS Fibre Channel Mass Storage card at 0/9/0/0
0/9/0/0.8 fcp
0/9/0/0.8.0.4.0 fcparray
0/9/0/0.8.0.4.0.0 tgt
0/9/0/0.8.0.4.0.0.0 sdisk
0/9/0/0.8.0.4.0.0.1 sdisk
0/9/0/0.8.0.4.0.0.2 sdisk
0/9/0/0.8.0.4.0.0.3 sdisk
0/9/0/0.8.0.4.0.1 tgt
0/9/0/0.8.0.4.0.1.0 sdisk
0/9/0/0.8.0.4.0.2 tgt
0/9/0/0.8.0.4.0.2.0 sdisk
0/9/0/0.8.0.4.0.3 tgt
```

```
0/9/0/0.8.0.4.0.3.0 sdisk
0/9/0/0.8.0.255.0 fcpdev
0/9/0/0.8.0.255.0.4 tgt
0/9/0/0.8.0.255.0.4.0 sctl
0/10 lba
0/10/0/0 btlan
0/12 lba
0/12/0/0 btlan
32 pbc
33 processor
36 pbc
37 processor
96 pbc
97 processor
100 pbc
101 processor
192 memory
btlan: Initializing 10/100BASE-TX card at 0/0/0/0....

    System Console is on the Built-In Serial Interface
btlan: Initializing 10/100BASE-TX card at 0/10/0/0....
btlan: Initializing 10/100BASE-TX card at 0/12/0/0....
Entering cifs_init...
Initialization finished successfully... slot is 9
Logical volume 64, 0x3 configured as ROOT
Logical volume 64, 0x2 configured as SWAP
Logical volume 64, 0x2 configured as DUMP
    Swap device table:  (start & size given in 512-byte blocks)
        entry 0 - major is 64, minor is 0x2; start = 0, size = 8388608
    Dump device table:  (start & size given in 1-Kbyte blocks)
        entry 0000000000000000 - major is 31, minor is 0x12000; start = 117600,
size = 4194304
Starting the STREAMS daemons-phase 1
Create STCP device files
Starting the STREAMS daemons-phase 2
        $Revision: vmunix:    vw: -proj    selectors: CUPI80_BL2000_1108 -c 'Vw
for CUPI80_BL2000_1108 build' -- cupi80_bl2000_1108 'CUPI80_BL2000_1108'   Wed
Nov  8 19:24:56 PST 2000 $
Memory Information:
  physical page size = 4096 bytes, logical page size = 4096 bytes
  Physical: 4194304 Kbytes, lockable: 3231756 Kbytes, available: 3711728 Kbytes

#
```

The output of **ioscan -f** and **dmesg** provide a lot of useful information about our system. We'll use the components and paths in **ioscan** output and the memory information in **dmesg** to create a list of components for the respective vPars in the upcoming step. We now know, for instance, that the paths of two of the LAN cards are at *0/0/0/0* and *0/10/0/0*. We know the paths of all four processors of *33, 37, 97,* and *101*. The console is located at *0/0/4/0*. From the **dmesg** output we know that we have a total of four GBytes of RAM that can be spread among the vPars.

From these two outputs we have the information we need to create the Virtual Partitions in the next step.

4) List the Components of the Virtual Partitions

From the **ioscan** and **dmesg** messages we can select the components of our first Virtual Partition. The following is a list of components we'll include in this partition:

First vPar *cable1*

```
name            cable1
processors      min of one (bound) max of three (two unbound)
                with num (bound + unbound) equal to one
memory          1024 MB
LBA Core I/O    0/0 (all components on 0/0 are implied)
LAN             0/0/0/0 (not specified explicitly, on 0/0)
boot disk       0/0/1/1.2.0
kernel          /stand/vmunix (this is default)
autoboot        off (manual)
console         0/0/4/0 (not specified explicitly, on 0/0)
```

You may want to set *autoboot* to *auto* during installation and set to *manual* after installation. This makes booting easier during installation.

Some of the components require some explanation concerning the way in which they are implemented with vPars. The following is a more detailed discussion of some of these components, including CPU, memory, and LAN, bootdisk, setboot, kernel, and console.

CPU

The CPUs used in both this partition (*cable1*) and the one we will define shortly (*cable2*) are specified with *min*, *max*, and *num*. We will have *min bound* CPUs that have I/O interrupts assigned to them and are therefore ideal for I/O-intensive applications. The additional CPUs assigned to the vPars are *unbound*, which do not process I/O interrupts. Therefore, *unbound* CPUs are ideal for processor-intensive applications as opposed to I/O-intensive applications. *unbound* CPUs can be freely moved from one vPar to another while vPars are running, so having *min* bound CPUs gives us the freedom to move around the *unbound* CPUs. *Bound* CPUs can also be added to and deleted from Virtual Partitions only when the partition is down.

On machines that employ Non-Uniform Memory Access (NUMA) you would use hardware paths (*path*) to specify CPUs. This is to ensure that you minimize the distance between CPUs and memory. On systems such as the N-Class and L-Class that do not employ NUMA, *min* is recommended to define *bound* CPUs.

There is detailed information on working with CPUs in Chapter 5. For our work on *cable1* and *cable2* and for my work with vPars in general, the most common desire is to have a *min* number of *bound* CPUs in all vPars and then move around *unbound* CPUs as the applications in vPars need them. For instance, when **vparcreate** is run we would specify the following:

man page

vparcreate
appendix a

vparcreate -p cable1 -a cpu:::1:3 -a cpu::1

At the time of creation *cable1* will have one *bound* CPU only because we specified a *min* of one and a *num* of one. *num* is the total *bound* + *unbound* CPUs and since we specified one for *num*, we'll get one *bound* CPU (I have seen some vPars material use *num* and some use *total* so *num* and *total* are interchangeable in this book.) Since *max* is three we have left the door open to add as many as two additional *unbound* CPUs. If we have two *unbound* CPUs on our system, we can move them among the vPars as required with **vparmodify**. To remove the two *unbound* CPUs from *cable2* and add them to *cable1*, we would issue the two following **vparmodify** commands:

man page

vparmodify
appendix a

vparmodify -p cable2 -m cpu::1   <-- reduces cable2 from 3 to 1

vparmodify -p cable1 -m cpu::3   <-- increases cable1 from 1 to 3

We first removed the two *unbound* CPUs from *cable2* and then added them to *cable1*. If the two *unbound* CPUs were not assigned to a vPar, we would not have to remove them from *cable2* prior to adding them to *cable1*.

There are many ways to work with CPUs, some of which are described in Chapter 5, so by characterizing your applications and understanding the options for using *bound* and *unbound* CPUs, you can use the processor mix that best meets you needs.

Memory

We have identified one GByte of memory for *cable1*. Memory can be specified by *range* or *size*.

To add one GByte of memory to *cable1* using *size* we would use the following **vparcreate** command:

```
vparcreate -p cable1 -a mem::1024
```

man page

vparcreate
appendix a

This **vparcreate** command specifies only the memory for use in *cable1*. The full **vparcreate** command for creating *cable1* will be shown in an upcoming section.

The memory is specified in MBytes (1024 MBytes = 1 GByte) in multiples of 64 MBytes. At the time of this writing, the Virtual Partition Monitor consumes roughly 128 MBytes of RAM, so this will not be available to allocate to a Virtual Partition. Modifying memory allocation requires that the Virtual Partition be down at the time of this writing.

On machines that employ Non-Uniform Memory Access (NUMA) you would use the *range*. *Range* is a subset of *size*. On systems such as the N-Class and L-Class that do not employ NUMA, the *size* is recommended to define memory. The syntax for specifying memory by range is as follows:

```
mem:::base:range
```

None of the examples in this book were prepared using NUMA systems so you won't see any examples using the *range* syntax; all examples use the *size* syntax.

LAN

The LAN interface used for this first Virtual Partition is on Local Bus Adapter (LBA) zero. This means that any other components on LBA zero would have to be in this Virtual Partition as well. At the time of this writing, components on an LBA can't be shared between vPars.

Note that we have decided not to use the hostname as our Virtual Partition name. As mentioned earlier, it is desirable to use the same name for the hostname and vPar. Because our hostnames are a little hard to remember the system administrator decided to use simple vPar names. When we loaded HP-UX 11i on the system we selected the hostnames (you can also run **set_parms** after loading 11i to set the system name and other parameters) of *cvhdcon3* and *cvhdcon4*. We then chose the simple vPar names of *cable1* and *cable2*, respectively.

Boot Disk

The **ioscan** issued earlier in this chapter showed many disk devices. The boot device for our first Virtual Partition is the internal disk with the hardware path *0/0/1/1.2.0*.

At the time of this writing, components that are at or below the Local Bus Adapter (LBA) level are devoted to a single Virtual Partition. This means that although the output of our earlier **ioscan** command shows four internal disks, all four of these disks must be in the same Virtual Partition because they are on the same LBA. Chapter 5 covers LBAs and hardware in more detail.

Kernel

man page

vparcreate
appendix a

We'll use the default HP-UX kernel of **/stand/vmunix** for the kernel in this Virtual Partition. Since we're using the default kernel, we don't have to specify this as part of the **vparcreate** command, however; we'll include it in the **vparcreate** command for completeness purposes. Chapter 4 covers the HP-UX kernel.

setboot Command

In our example we have *autoboot* set to *off* for our Virtual Partition. The **setboot** command on a non-vPars system reads from and writes to stable storage. On a vPars system the **setboot** command interacts with the Virtual Partition database. In our upcoming example we'll set the *autoboot* to *off* when we create *cable1* with **vparcreate**. Running **setboot** on a vPars system has the effects shown in Table 2-2:

Table 2-2   setboot and Virtual Partitions

vPars setboot Option	Description
-a	Changes the alternate boot path of the Virtual Partition. To set the alternate boot path: `# setboot -a 0/8/0/0.8.0.5.0.0.0`
-b	Sets the autoboot attribute of the Virtual Partition. To set Autoboot *on*: `# setboot -b on`
-p	Changes the primary boot path of the Virtual Partition. To set the primary boot path: `# setboot -p 0/0/1/1.2.0`
-s	Has no effect.
no options	Displays information about boot attributes.

The **setboot** command is one of the aspects of working with vPars that is different from a non-vPars system.

Console

Chapter 5 contains a description of the way in which the console is implemented with vPars. In our first partition we have specified LBA *0/0* as a component of vPar *cable1*. Since the physical console at *0/0/4/0* is on the Core I/O card at *0/0*, it is an implied component of *cable1* and we do not have to specify the physical console in this partition. The other Virtual Partitions on this system will use the virtual console functionality of vPars whereby issuing *Ctrl-A* cycles between virtual console displays.

Database

The Virtual Partition database that contains all vPar-related information is **/stand/vpdb**. This is managed, and synchronized for you (as described in Chapter 8) so you don't need to pay too much attention to it if you don't want to. You can, however; create an alternate database if you wish. You may want to do this in order to create a completely different Virtual Partition configuration for your system without affecting your currently running database.

man page

vparcreate
appendix a

When creating Virtual Partitions with **vparcreate** you can use the *-D* option and specify an alternate database name that is a file in the **/stand** directory, such as **/stand/vpdb.app2**. When you boot vPars from this database (with ISL> **hpux /stand/vpmon -D** *db_file*) it is the default, so all modifications made to vPars defined in this database are made to it rather than the default.

Second vPar *cable2*

We'll list the same categories of components for *cable2* as we did for *cable1* in the following list:

```
name          cable2
processors    min of one (bound) max of three (two unbound)
              with num (bound + unbound) equal to one
memory        1024 MB
LAN           0/10/0/0
boot disk     0/8/0/0.8.0.5.0.0.0
kernel        /stand/vmunix (this is the default)
autoboot      off (manual)
console       virtual console to be created
```

We now have a list of components for two vPars. The result is that our L-Class system has been divided into two vPars that look like Figure 2-4:

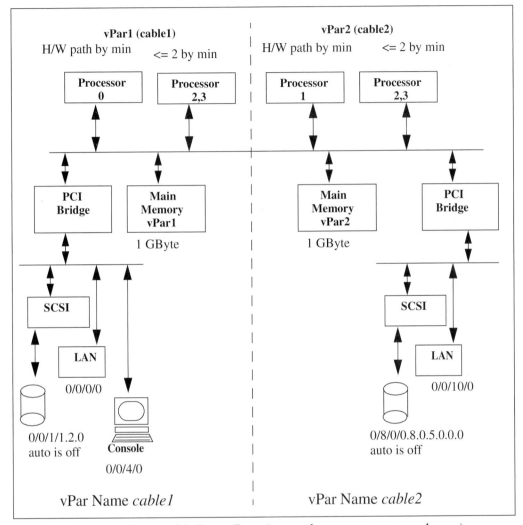

Figure 2-4 L-Class with Two vPars (unused components not shown)

Figure 2-4 reflects what our system will look like when we perform the upcoming steps to create our two vPars. Note that two *unbound* processors, shown as *2,3* in Figure 2-4, can be assigned to *cable1* and *cable2* as required.

5) Virtual Partition Kernel-Related Work

Each Virtual Partition has its own instance of HP-UX 11i, which has its own HP-UX kernel. It is likely that you'll customize these kernels in a variety of ways to suit the applications you have running in the respective vPars. When you install the vPars software, it automatically reconfigures the kernel to include the vPar drivers and make the kernel relocatable. You do not have to perform the kernel-related steps in this section because they are performed for you when vPars software is loaded. It is still informative; however, to see the steps that were manually performed in this section to get better insight concerning the way vPars operate. In this step we'll investigate the files that have been updated by the vPars application and build the new kernel. Keep in mind that the new kernel needs to be built on every volume that has HP-UX 11i on it and will run a vPar.

Because memory is shared among multiple vPars, the kernel must be relocatable in memory. At the time of this writing, there are patches that allow the kernel to be built as a relocatable kernel. We won't perform any checks related to patches.

The file **/sbin/vecheck** is a vPar file that is required on the system. The following listing is a portion of **/usr/conf/gen/config.sys** that checks to see if **/sbin/vecheck** has been loaded on the system:

```
# Determine whether the linker supports kernel relocation.  If it does,
# link the kernel using the relocation options.
LOADOPTS_ADDL=` \
        if [ -f /sbin/vecheck ]; then \
                ${WHAT} ${LD} | \
                ${AWK} '$$0 ~ /92453-07 linker/ { \
                        split($$7, vers, "."); \
                        if ( vers[1] == "B" && \
                        ( vers[2] == 11 && vers[3] >= 25 ) || vers[2] > 11 ) \
                                print "${LOADOPTS_RELOC}"; \
                        else print "${LOADOPTS_STATIC}"; }'; \
        else \
                echo "${LOADOPTS_STATIC}"; \
        fi; \
        `
```

The following is a long listing of **/sbin/vecheck** which was loaded with the vPar software:

```
# ll /sbin/vecheck
-r-xr-xr-x   1 bin        bin          20533 Mar  5 19:01 /sbin/vecheck
#
```

Next let's take a look at **/stand/system** to see the *vpar* driver that has been added to the file:

```
# cat /stand/system
****************************************
* Source: /ux/core/kern/filesets.info/CORE-KRN/generic
* @(#)B.11.11_LR
*
****************************************
* Additional drivers required in every machine-type to
* create a complete
* system file during cold install. This list is every driver that the
* master.d/ files do not force on the system or is not identifiable by
* ioscan.
* Other CPU-type specific files can exist for their special cases.
* see create_sysfile (1m).
****************************************
*
* Drivers/Subsystems
sba
lba
c720
sctl
sdisk
asio0
cdfs
cxperf
olar_psm
olar_psm_if
dev_olar
diag0
diag1
diag2
dmem
dev_config
iomem
nfs_core
nfs_client
nfs_server
btlan
maclan
dlpi
token_arp
inet
uipc
tun
telm
tels
netdiag1
nms
```

```
        hpstreams
        clone
        strlog
        sad
        echo
        sc
        timod
        tirdwr
        pipedev
        pipemod
        ffs
        ldterm
        ptem
        pts
        ptm
        pckt
        td
        fddi4
        gelan
        GSCtoPCI
        iop_drv
        bs_osm
        vxfs
        vxportal
        lvm
        lv
        nfsm
        rpcmod
        autofsc
        cachefsc
        cifs
        prm
        vpar                                   <--- vpar driver added here
        STRMSGSZ             65535
        nstrpty             60
        dump lvol
        maxswapchunks       2048
        #
```

The *vpar* driver is a master driver described in **/usr/conf/master.d** as shown below:

```
# pwd
/usr/conf/master.d
# cat vpar
$CDIO
vpar        0
$$$

$DRIVER_INSTALL
vcn             -1              209
vcs             -1              -1
```

```
vpar_driver     -1              -1
$$$

$DRIVER_DEPENDENCY
vcn             vpar
vcs             vpar
vpar            vcs vcn vpar_driver
vpar_driver     vpar
$$$

$DRIVER_LIBRARY
*
* The driver/library table.  This table defines which libraries a given
* driver depends on.  If the driver is included in the dfile, then the
* libraries that driver depends on will be included on the ld(1) command
* line.  Only optional libraries *need* to be specified in this table,
* (but required ones can be included, as well).
*
* Driver handle    <libraries>
*
* subsystems first
vcn             libvpar-pdk.a
vcs             libvpar-pdk.a
vpar            libvpar-pdk.a
vpar_driver     libvpar-pdk.a
$$$

$LIBRARY
*
* The library table.  Each element in the library table describes
* one unique library.  The flag member is a boolean value, it is
* initialized to 1 if the library should *always* be included on
* the ld(1) command line, or 0 if the library is optional (i.e. it
* is only included when one or more drivers require it).  The order
* of the library table determines the order of the libraries on the
* ld(1) command line, (i.e. defines an implicit load order).  New
* libraries must be added to this table.
* Note: libhp-ux.a must be the last entry, do not place
* anything after it.
*
* Library     <required>
*
libvpar-pdk.a       0
$$$
#
```

You can see in this file there are multiple drivers present. The *vcn* and *vcs* drivers are used to support the console in a vPars environment. Since you'll probably only have one physical console for multiple partitions, you need a way to share the physical device. The use of these drivers is described in Chapter 4 in which kernel configuration is covered. For now it is sufficient to know that these drivers exist as part of the vPars installation and must be built into the kernel.

Now that the kernel has what it needs to be built relocatable and the drivers are present for vPars, we can run **mk_kernel** to build the new kernel and **kmupdate** to move the new kernel-related files into place. This is done automatically for you but the following commands show how you would perform this process:

```
# mk_kernel
Generating module: krm...
Compiling /stand/build/conf.c...
Loading the kernel...
Generating kernel symbol table...
# kmupdate

  Kernel update request is scheduled.

  Default kernel /stand/vmunix will be updated by
  newly built kernel /stand/build/vmunix_test
  at next system shutdown or startup time.

#
```

Keep in mind that this procedure needs to be performed for all HP-UX 11i operating systems that will run a Virtual Partition. Kernel creation and modification can also be done in SAM, as described in Chapter 11.

6) Create the First Virtual Partition

man page

vparcreate
appendix a

The **vparcreate** command is used to create a vPar. The summary of this command is shown in Table 2-1 and its man page appears in Appendix A. The general form of the command is as follows:

```
vparcreate -p vp_name [-B boot_attr] [-D db_file] [-S static_attr]
[-b kernel_path] [-o boot_opts] [-a rsrc] [-a...]
```

When creating this vPar, I placed the **vparcreate** command in a file so that I could modify it for the second vPar and execute it. The **vparcreate** command is shown below:

```
# cat /tmp/cable1
vparcreate -p cable1 -B manual -b /stand/vmunix -a cpu::1
-a cpu:::1:3 -a mem::1024 -a io:0/0 -a io:0/0/1/1.2.0:boot
#
```

After changing the permissions on this file and running it, the vPar *cable1* was successfully created. Next we'll boot the vPar we just created.

7) Boot the First Virtual Partition

Now that the first vPar has been created and the kernel automatically rebuilt to support vPars, we can boot the first vPar which we named *cable1*.

We'll both boot off the first vPar and check its status. Booting is covered in detail in Chapter 3; however, we need to load the Virtual Partition Monitor (**vpmon**) at the *ISL>* prompt. **vpmon** is a *ramdisk* kernel, similar to *vmunix*, that needs to be loaded at the time of boot. From the *ISL>* prompt we are going to run **vpmon** to get the *MON>* prompt. From the *MON>* prompt we boot our Virtual Partition with **vparload,** as shown in the following example:

```
ISL> hpux /stand/vpmon

Boot
: disk(0/0/1/1.2.0.0.0.0;0)/stand/vpmon
421888 + 142056 + 4247112 start 0x23000
cable1: WARNING: No boot device specified

Welcome to VPMON (type '?' for a list of commands)

MON> vparload -p cable1

[MON] Console client set to cable1

[MON] cable1 loaded
```

.
.
.

You may see messages different that those shown in the example after the **vparload** command was issued. In any event, the system progressed through the remainder of the boot process and booted the one Virtual Partition *cable1* that we created. We now have a subset of the system components dedicated to this Virtual Partition.

man page

vparload
appendix a

The **vparload** command has the following three forms:

```
form1: vparload -all

form2: vparload -auto

form3: vparload -p vp_name [-b kernelpath] [-o boot_options]
[-B hardware_path]
```

We issued the third form shown above. Please see Chapter 3 for a detailed description of all *MON>* commands.

Now that the partition has booted, let's first obtain the status of the one Virtual Partition we created, called *cable1*, that we have running:

man page

vparstatus
appendix a

```
# vparstatus -p cable1 -v

[Virtual Partition Details]
Name:         cable1
State:        Up
Attributes:   Dynamic,Manual
Kernel Path:  /stand/vmunix
Boot Opts:

[CPU Details]
Min/Max:  1/3
Bound by User [Path]:
Bound by Monitor [Path]:   33
Unbound [Path]:

[IO Details]
    0.0
    0.0.1.1.2.0   BOOT

[Memory Details]
```

```
Specified [Base   /Range]:
          (bytes)  (MB)
Total Memory (MB):    1024
#
```

man page

vparstatus
appendix a

The output of **vparstatus** shows that *cable1* is *up*. The *-v* option is used to obtain a verbose output. You can see from this listing that the bound CPU at hardware path *33* (the *bound* CPU we specified with the *min*) is part of the partition, that there is one GByte of memory in the partition, and that the I/O components we specified are in the partition. Had there been other partitions configured, we would have seen their output as well.

Note that the console at *0/0/4/0* is an implied component of this vPar. So too is the LAN interface at *0/0/0/0*. Both of these components are part of the Core I/O card that we specified as part of *cable1* with the *-a io:0/0* argument to the **vparcreate** command.

man page

vparcreate
appendix a

We can now run **vparstatus -A** to view the available components of our system. Since we created a first partition with only one CPU, we should see three CPUs and many other system components available, as shown in the following listing:

```
# vparstatus -A

[Unbound CPUs (path)]:    37
                          97
                          101
[Available CPUs]:   3

[Available I/O devices (path)]:    0.1
                                   0.2
                                   0.3
                                   0.4
                                   0.5
                                   0.8
                                   0.9
                                   0.10
                                   0.12
                                   32
                                   36
                                   96
                                   100

[Unbound memory (Base   /Range)]:    0x0/128
                 (bytes)  (MB)        0xc000000/1856
                                      0x180000000/1088
[Available memory (MB)]:    3072
#
```

This output shows many components available for our second partition. Based on our earlier planning exercise, we know the components that we wish to include in the second vPar and this **vparstatus -A** command confirms that they are indeed available.

For *cable2* we want one CPU initially, and there are three available. We want the I/O cards for boot and LAN at *0/8* and *0/10* respectively We want one GByte of memory and there are now roughly three GBytes available. We have all of the components we need to proceed to our next step of creating *cable2*.

8) Create the Second Virtual Partition

man page

vparstatus
appendix a

We earlier listed all of the components of which our second partition is to be comprised and confirmed that these components are still available with the **vparstatus -A** command. HP-UX 11i has already been loaded on a second disk on the same system used to create our first Virtual Partition *cable1*. We can create our second Virtual Partition, which we'll call *cable2*. We'll create the second while the first is running and boot the second vPar from the first.

Here are the components we earlier listed for our second vPar:

```
name          cable2
processors    min of one (bound) max of three (two unbound)
              with num (bound + unbound) equal to one
memory        1024 MB
LAN           0/10
LBA           0/8
boot disk     0/8/0/0.8.0.5.0.0.0
kernel        /stand/vmunix (this is the default)
autoboot      off (manual)
console       virtual console to be created
```

There are several differences between the list of components for the two vPars. We have devoted a different LAN card and boot disk. We have specified the CPUs in the same manner in both vPars with *min* (this will be *bound*) of one and *max* of three, *num* of one, and let the vPars software identify the one *bound* processor. These two Virtual Partitions will use different I/O paths for their devices. Let's now run the **vparcreate** command to create *cable2*:

We can now proceed to create the second partition with the command shown in the following file:

man page

vparcreate
appendix a

```
# cat /tmp/cable2
vparcreate -p cable2 -B manual -b /stand/vmunix -a cpu::1
-a cpu:::1:3 -a mem::1024 -a io:0/8
-a io:0/8/0/0.8.0.5.0.0.0:boot -a io:0/10
#
```

After executing this file we can determine if the second vPar has been created and the components of which it is comprised by running **vparstatus**:

man page

vparstatus
appendix a

```
# vparstatus -v
[Virtual Partition Details]
Name:          cable1
State:         Up
Attributes:    Dynamic,Manual
Kernel Path:   /stand/vmunix
Boot Opts:

[CPU Details]
Min/Max:  1/3
Bound by User [Path]:
Bound by Monitor [Path]:   33
Unbound [Path]:

[IO Details]
   0.0
   0.0.1.1.2.0   BOOT

[Memory Details]
Specified [Base  /Range]:
         (bytes) (MB)
Total Memory (MB):   1024

[Virtual Partition Details]
Name:          cable2
State:         Down
Attributes:    Dynamic,Manual
Kernel Path:   /stand/vmunix
Boot Opts:
```

```
[CPU Details]
Min/Max:   1/3
Bound by User [Path]:
Bound by Monitor [Path]:   37
Unbound [Path]:

[IO Details]
   0.8
   0.8.0.0.8.0.5.0.0.0, BOOT
   0.10

[Memory Details]
Specified [Base   /Range]:
          (bytes) (MB)
Total Memory (MB):   1024
#
```

This output shows that the first vPar is intact and that the second has been successfully created with the name, kernel file, CPU, I/O, and memory components we specified. Note that each vPar has one bound CPU assigned to it. The LAN card assigned to *cable2* appears in the output because we specifed LBA *0/10* as one of the components of *cable2*. The console at *0/0/4/0* and the LAN interface at *0/0/0/0* are implied components of *cable1* and do not appear in the **vparstatus -v** output.

man page

vparstatus
appendix a

With the second vPar created, we can proceed to the next step and boot it.

9) Boot the Second Virtual Partition

man page

vparboot
appendix a

Since we already have the first vPar running, called *cable1*, and the second vPar created, called *cable2*, we can boot the second vPar from the first. There are many options to boot vPars. Since we already have the first vPar running, we'll simply boot the second from the first with **vparboot** and then run **vparstatus -v** as shown in the following example. If we type subsequent **vparstatus** commands we can see the status of vPar *cable2* progress from *Load*, to *Boot* in the next output, and finally *Up* when the vPar is running, as shown in the following listing:

```
# vparboot -p cable2
vparboot: Booting cable2.  Please wait...

# vparstatus
[Virtual Partition]
                                                                    Boot
                                                                    Opts
Virtual Partition Name         State Attributes Kernel Path
============================== ===== ========== ========================= =====
cable1                         Up    Dyn,Manl   /stand/vmunix
cable2                         Load  Dyn,Manl   /stand/vmunix

[Virtual Partition Resource Summary]
                                         CPU    Num        Memory (MB)
                                CPU    Bound/  IO   # Ranges/
Virtual Partition Name         Min/Max Unbound devs Total MB    Total MB
============================== =============== ==== ====================
cable1                          1/ 3    1   0    4    0/ 0        1024
cable2                          1/ 3    1   0    4    0/ 0        1024

# vparstatus
[Virtual Partition]
                                                                    Boot
                                                                    Opts
Virtual Partition Name         State Attributes Kernel Path
============================== ===== ========== ========================= =====
cable1                         Up    Dyn,Manl   /stand/vmunix
cable2                         Boot  Dyn,Manl   /stand/vmunix

[Virtual Partition Resource Summary]
                                         CPU    Num        Memory (MB)
                                CPU    Bound/  IO   # Ranges/
Virtual Partition Name         Min/Max Unbound devs Total MB    Total MB
============================== =============== ==== ====================
cable1                          1/ 3    1   0    4    0/ 0        1024
cable2                          1/ 3    1   0    4    0/ 0        1024

# vparstatus
[Virtual Partition]
                                                                    Boot
                                                                    Opts
Virtual Partition Name         State Attributes Kernel Path
============================== ===== ========== ========================= =====
cable1                         Up    Dyn,Manl   /stand/vmunix
cable2                         Up    Dyn,Manl   /stand/vmunix

[Virtual Partition Resource Summary]
                                         CPU    Num        Memory (MB)
                                CPU    Bound/  IO   # Ranges/
Virtual Partition Name         Min/Max Unbound devs Total MB    Total MB
============================== =============== ==== ====================
cable1                          1/ 3    1   0    4    0/ 0        1024
cable2                          1/ 3    1   0    4    0/ 0        1024

#
```

This progression of states of *cable2* reflects the time it takes to boot the operating system from the second volume on which this vPar is run.

In addition to *load*, *boot*, and *up*, there are other states in which you may find a Virtual Partition as well. Table 2-3 summarizes the states of Virtual Partitions at the time of this writing:

Table 2-3   Virtual Partitions States

vPars State	Description
load	The kernel image of a Virtual Partition is being loaded into memory. This is done by the Virtual Partition monitor.
boot	The Virtual Partition is in the process of booting. The kernel image has been successfully loaded by the Virtual Partition monitor.
up	The Virtual Partition has been successfully booted and is running.
shut	The Virtual Partition is in the process of shutting down.
down	The Virtual Partition is not running and is down.
crash	The Virtual Partition has experienced a panic and is crashing.
hung	The Virtual Partition is not responding and is hung.

With more than one vPar running, you would use the built-in vPars drivers to toggle the console between any number of Virtual Partitions using *Ctrl-A*. Figure 2-5 shows using the console to view *cable1* with a hostname of *cvhdcon3*. Issuing *Ctrl-A* connects to vPar *cable2* with a hostname of *cvhdcon4*. When you issue *Ctrl-A* to switch to the next vPar in the console you are supplied with the name of the vPar to which you have connected in brackets, such as *[cable1]*.

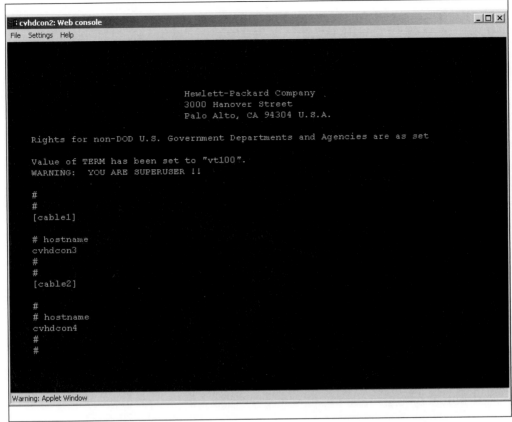

Figure 2-5 Console Shown Using *Ctrl-A* to Toggle Between vPars

In addition to using the console to switch between vPars, you can also use the LAN cards configured into the respective vPars to open a *TELNET* or other type of session to the vPars. This is the same technique you would use to connect to any system over the network and is one of the primary reasons you always want to have a LAN card configured as part of every vPar.

We did not cover the configuration of the two LAN cards, one in each vPar, in this chapter. The LAN configuration would have to be completed for both vPars in order to use the networking cards for such operations as a *TELNET* session. Chapter 13 covers many networking topics, including the **/etc/hosts** file; **/etc/rc.config.d/netconf** file, which must be configured on each vPar; and many others.

10) Modify the Virtual Partition

It is likely that you'll want to modify your Virtual Partitions in a variety of ways. You may want to add or remove a CPU, for instance. Let's take a look at an example of adding a CPU to a Virtual Partition.

man page

**vparstatus
appendix a**

In the upcoming example there is a four-processor system on which there are the two Virtual Partitions we just created: *cable1* and *cable2*. Each vPar has one *bound* CPU that was assigned by *min* when the vPars were created. Let's run **vparstatus** to see the components of which these two Virtual Partitions are comprised and confirm that each has one bound CPU:

```
# vparstatus -p cable1 -v

[Virtual Partition Details]
Name:          cable1
State:         Up
Attributes:    Dynamic,Manual
Kernel Path:   /stand/vmunix
Boot Opts:

[CPU Details]
Min/Max:  1/3
Bound by User [Path]:
Bound by Monitor [Path]:  33      <-- one bound CPU @ 33
Unbound [Path]:

[IO Details]
   0.0
   0.0.1.1.2.0   BOOT

[Memory Details]
Specified [Base  /Range]:
          (bytes) (MB)
Total Memory (MB):  1024
#


# vparstatus -p cable2 -v


[Virtual Partition Details]
Name:          cable2
State:         Up
Attributes:    Dynamic,Manual
Kernel Path:   /stand/vmunix
```

```
Boot Opts:

[CPU Details]
Min/Max:  1/3
Bound by User [Path]:
Bound by Monitor [Path]:  37     <-- one CPU in use at 37
Unbound [Path]:

[IO Details]
    0.8.0.0.8.0.5.0.0.0  BOOT
    0.10.0.0

[Memory Details]
Specified [Base   /Range]:
          (bytes) (MB)
Total Memory (MB):  1024
#
```

man page

vparstatus
appendix a

     The output of these two **vparstatus** commands shows that *cable1* has one *bound* CPU and *cable2* has one *bound* CPU. On the L-Class system on which these vPars were created there are a total of four CPUs. This means that two CPUs should be available. Let's run **vparstatus -A** to view the available components on a system:

```
# vparstatus -A

[Unbound CPUs (path)]:  97
                       101
[Available CPUs]:  2

[Available I/O devices (path)]:  0.1
                                 0.2
                                 0.3
                                 0.4
                                 0.5
                                 0.9
                                 0.12
                                 32
                                 36
                                 96
                                 100

[Unbound memory (Base   /Range)]:  0x0/64
               (bytes) (MB)        0xc000000/1856
                                   0x180000000/128
[Available memory (MB)]:  2048
#
```

man page

vparmodify
appendix a

       This output confirms that there are two CPUs available at hardware paths *97* and *101*. We can add these CPUs in a variety of ways. Let's use the **vparmodify** command to change the *num* of CPUs in *cable1* to two CPUs. We do this by *adding* one to the current number of CPUs with -*a*. This is a relative operation in that one CPU will be added to the current number of CPUs. You can use **vparmodify -m** if you want to specify the absolute number of CPUs for the vPar rather than the relative number. The following shows this **vparmodify** command:

```
# vparmodify -p cable1 -a cpu::1
#
```

man page

vparstatus
appendix a

       We can now run **vparstatus -p cable1 -v** to confirm that the CPU has been added, shown in the following listing:

```
# vparstatus -p cable1 -v
```

```
[Virtual Partition Details]
Name:           cable1
State:          Up
Attributes:     Dynamic,Manual
Kernel Path:    /stand/vmunix
Boot Opts:

[CPU Details]
Min/Max:  1/3
Bound by User [Path]:
Bound by Monitor [Path]:  33      <-- original CPU @ 33
Unbound [Path]:  97               <-- unbound CPU @ 97

[IO Details]
   0.0
   0.0.1.1.2.0  BOOT

[Memory Details]
Specified [Base  /Range]:
         (bytes) (MB)
Total Memory (MB):  1024
#
```

       The **vparstatus** output shows that the CPU at hardware path *97* has indeed been added to *cable1* with the **vparmodify** command as *unbound*.

In addition, we can run GlancePlus or **top** to confirm that there are two CPUs in use on *cable2*. The following is a **top** output run on *cable2*:

```
# top

System: cvhdcon3                               Thu Oct  4 15:30:42 2001
Load averages: 0.19, 0.51, 0.62
124 processes: 110 sleeping, 14 running
Cpu states:
CPU  LOAD   USER  NICE   SYS  IDLE BLOCK  SWAIT  INTR  SSYS
 0   0.37   0.0%  0.2%  0.0% 99.8%  0.0%   0.0%  0.0%  0.0%
 1   0.02   0.0%  0.0%  0.8% 99.2%  0.0%   0.0%  0.0%  0.0%
---  ----   ----- ----- ----- ----- -----  -----  ----- -----
avg  0.19   0.0%  0.2%  0.4% 99.4%  0.0%   0.0%  0.0%  0.0%

Memory: 93636K (57816K) real, 322124K (239536K) virtual, 746284K free  Page# 1/4

CPU TTY         PID USERNAME PRI NI   SIZE    RES STATE   TIME %WCPU %CPU COMMAND
 0   ?          36 root     152 20     0K   832K run     0:00  0.33 0.33 vxfsd
 1   ?        1342 root     158 10    80K   212K sleep   0:10  0.28 0.28 cclogd
 0   ?        1149 root     152 20  4644K  7260K run     0:06  0.21 0.21 prm3d
 1   ?         922 root     154 24   540K   808K sleep   0:00  0.15 0.15 hpterm
 0 pty/ttyp1  3114 root     186 24   596K   528K run     0:00  0.17 0.15 top
 1   ?        1146 root     -16 20  7788K  7240K run     0:03  0.14 0.13 midaemon
 1   ?           3 root     128 20     0K    32K sleep   0:04  0.11 0.11 statdaemon
 0   ?        2018 root     154 20  3908K  1908K sleep   0:00  0.05 0.04 alarmgen
 1   ?        1272 root     152 20   856K   960K run     0:00  0.04 0.04 opcmona
 1   ?        1372 root     152 20  1076K  2356K run     0:00  0.04 0.04 samd
 0   ?           0 root     128 20     0K     0K sleep   0:11  0.02 0.02 swapper
 1   ?           1 root     168 20   448K   204K sleep   0:00  0.02 0.02 init
 0   ?           2 root     128 20     0K    32K sleep   0:00  0.02 0.02 vhand
 0   ?           4 root     128 20     0K    32K sleep   0:00  0.02 0.02 unhashdaemo
 1   ?          20 root     147 20     0K    32K sleep   0:00  0.02 0.02 lvmkd
 0   ?          22 root     147 20     0K    32K sleep   0:00  0.02 0.02 lvmkd
 1   ?          24 root     147 20     0K    32K sleep   0:00  0.02 0.02 lvmkd
 0   ?         339 root     154 20   152K   204K sleep   0:00  0.02 0.02 syncer
 0   ?         342 root     168 20    76K   192K sleep   0:00  0.02 0.02 vphbd
 0   ?         345 root     168 20   156K   216K sleep   0:00  0.02 0.02 vpard
 0   ?         410 root     154 20    80K   224K sleep   0:00  0.02 0.02 syslogd
 0   ?         446 root     127 20   156K   424K sleep   0:00  0.02 0.02 netfmt
 0   ?         552 root     154 20   740K   816K sleep   0:00  0.02 0.02 rpc.statd
 0   ?         558 root     154 20  1004K  1032K sleep   0:00  0.02 0.02 rpc.lockd
 0   ?         586 root     154 20   180K   316K sleep   0:00  0.02 0.02 inetd
 0   ?         855 root     154 20  1064K   472K sleep   0:00  0.02 0.02 sendmail:
 0   ?         863 root     154 20   772K   712K sleep   0:00  0.02 0.02 snmpdm
 0   ?         896 root     154 20   620K   552K sleep   0:00  0.02 0.02 mib2agt
 0   ?         914 root     154 20  1332K   444K sleep   0:00  0.02 0.02 cmsnmpd
 1   ?         951 root     154 20  4044K  1840K sleep   0:00  0.02 0.02 rpcd
 1 pty/ttyp1   952 root     158 24   512K   180K sleep   0:00  0.02 0.02 sh
 0   ?         974 root     168 20   152K   304K sleep   0:04  0.02 0.02 scrdaemon
 0   ?         996 root     154 20   200K   336K sleep   0:00  0.02 0.02 pwgrd
 0   ?        1039 root     154 10   308K   428K sleep   0:00  0.02 0.02 diagmond
 0   ?        1093 root     154 20  1224K   816K sleep   0:00  0.02 0.02 ttd
 1   ?        1135 root     154 20  2588K  1624K sleep   0:00  0.02 0.02 perflbd
 0   ?        1156 root     154 20  2952K  1572K sleep   0:00  0.02 0.02 swagentd
 0   ?        1167 root     154 20   224K   252K sleep   0:00  0.02 0.02 emsagent
 0   ?        1168 root     127 20  2380K  2204K sleep   0:00  0.02 0.02 scopeux
```

This output show two CPUs, labeled *0* and *1*, in *cable1*. The *System* name of *cvhdcon3* is shown at the output because the hostname for *cable1* is *cvhdcon3*.

Although this is a simple example showing how a Virtual Partition can be modified, it also demonstrates the power of vPars. While both vPars on the system are running, a processor can be added to one or both without interruption of the programs running in the vPars.

Note that the *-a* option to **vparmodify** changed the number of CPUs *relative* to the current number. In our case the current number of CPUs was one and using *-a cpu::1* added one CPU to the current number of one resulting in two CPUs. This is true also when we use the *-d* option to **vparmodify** to remove processors. The following example shows running **vparstatus** to see the two CPUs, using **vparmodify** to change the number of CPUs back to one (this is also relative to the current number of CPUs, which is two,) and a **vparstatus** to confirm that this change has taken place:

```
# vparstatus -p cable1 -v

# vparstatus -p cable1 -v

[Virtual Partition Details]
Name:          cable1
State:         Up
Attributes:    Dynamic,Manual
Kernel Path:   /stand/vmunix
Boot Opts:

[CPU Details]
Min/Max:  1/3
Bound by User [Path]:
Bound by Monitor [Path]:   33       <-- bound CPU @ 33
Unbound [Path]:  97                 <-- unbound CPU @ 97

[IO Details]
    0.0
    0.0.0.0
    0.0.1.1.2.0  BOOT
    0.0.4.0  CONSOLE

[Memory Details]
Specified [Base  /Range]:
          (bytes) (MB)
Total Memory (MB):  1024
# vparmodify -p cable1 -d cpu::1
# vparstatus -p cable1 -v

[Virtual Partition Details]
Name:          cable1
State:         Up
Attributes:    Dynamic,Manual
Kernel Path:   /stand/vmunix
Boot Opts:

[CPU Details]
Min/Max:  1/3
```

```
Bound by User [Path]:
Bound by Monitor [Path]:  33          <-- original CPU @ 33
Unbound [Path]:                       <-- no unbound CPUs

[IO Details]
    0.0
    0.0.0.0
    0.0.1.1.2.0  BOOT
    0.0.4.0  CONSOLE

[Memory Details]
Specified [Base  /Range]:
           (bytes) (MB)
Total Memory (MB):  1024
#
```

We could perform many other modifications to the vPars with the two *unbound* CPUs that are available, such as adding two CPUs to one of the vPars or one CPU to each vPar.

Please keep in mind the relative nature of components when using **vparmodify** and that some changes, such as modifying memory or adding I/O components require the vPar to be down at the time of this writing. This is covered in detail in Chapter 5.

man page

vparmodify
appendix a

Virtual Partition Dump Files

When a Virtual Partition crashes, a dump file is created in **/stand/vmpon.dmp**. When the Virtual Partition boots, files are created in **/var/adm/crash/vpar**. The files have an extension with a number indicating the number of the dump that occurred. For instance, **vpmon.1**, **vpmon.dmp.1**, and **summary.1** indicate the first set of files that are saved in **/var/adm/crash/vpar**.

An example of what you might see in **/stand** and **/var/adm/crash/vpar** related to dumps are shown in the following listing:

```
VPARNAME = extraq1

# ll /stand
total 100400
-rw-r--r--   1 root       sys           19 Jul 13 15:04 bootconf
drwxr-xr-x   4 root       sys         2048 Oct 18 11:43 build
drwxrwxrwx   5 root       sys         1024 Oct 18 13:06 dlkm
drwxrwxrwx   5 root       root        1024 Oct 18 11:21 dlkm.vmunix.prev
-rw-r--r--   1 root       sys         3388 Oct 18 13:16 ioconfig
-r--r--r--   1 root       sys           82 Jul 13 15:34 kernrel
drwxr-xr-x   2 root       sys         1024 Oct 18 13:18 krs
```

```
drwxr-xr-x   2 root       root          1024 Oct 18 13:16 krs_lkg
drwxr-xr-x   2 root       root          1024 Oct 18 13:18 krs_tmp
drwxr-xr-x   2 root       root          8192 Jul 13 15:04 lost+found
-rw-------   1 root       root            12 Oct 18 13:16 rootconf
-r--r--r--   1 root       sys           2035 Oct 18 11:42 system
-r--r--r--   1 root       sys            994 Jul 13 15:28 system.01
-r--r--r--   1 root       sys            999 Jul 13 15:56 system.02
-r--r--r--   1 root       sys            994 Jul 13 15:28 system.base
drwxr-xr-x   2 root       sys           1024 Jul 13 15:37 system.d
-r--r--r--   1 root       sys           2035 Oct 18 10:55 system.prev
-rwxr-xr-x   1 root       root      22682568 Oct 18 13:16 vmunix
-rwxr-xr-x   1 root       root      22682568 Oct 18 11:04 vmunix.prev
-rw-------   1 root       sys           8232 Oct 18 13:36 vpdb
-rw-------   1 root       root          8232 Jul 17 14:11 vpdb.OLD
-r-xr-xr-x   1 bin        bin         837616 Aug 31 18:59 vpmon
-rw-------   1 root       root       5078504 Oct 10 10:43 vpmon.dmp  <-- vPar dump

# ll /var/adm/crash/vpar                                <-- vPar dump directory
total 46464
-rw-r--r--   1 root       root             2 Oct 10 10:43 count
-rw-r--r--   1 root       root         16794 Jul 17 13:26 summary.0
-rw-r--r--   1 root       root         17953 Jul 18 10:35 summary.1
-rw-r--r--   1 root       root         19538 Jul 18 11:36 summary.2
-rw-r--r--   1 root       root         10012 Oct 10 10:43 summary.3
-r-xr-xr-x   1 root       root        855928 Jul 17 13:26 vpmon.0
-r-xr-xr-x   1 root       root        855928 Jul 18 10:35 vpmon.1
-r-xr-xr-x   1 root       root        855928 Jul 18 11:36 vpmon.2
-r-xr-xr-x   1 root       root        837616 Oct 10 10:43 vpmon.3
-rw-------   1 root       root       5078504 Jul 17 13:26 vpmon.dmp.0
-rw-------   1 root       root       5078504 Jul 18 10:35 vpmon.dmp.1
-rw-------   1 root       root       5078504 Jul 18 11:36 vpmon.dmp.2
-rw-------   1 root       root       5078504 Oct 10 10:43 vpmon.dmp.3
```

man page

vparreset
appendix a

The **/var/adm/crash/vpar** directory has in it the vPar dump-related files for four (*0-3*) crashes.

The dump file created in **/stand** is saved in **/var/adm/crash/vpar** and and extended with the crash number. The dump file in **/stand** is overwritten with each crash, but you have a history with all of the dump files and related information in **/var/adm/crash/vpar**. Please leave in place the **/stand/vpmon.dmp** file.

Summary

man page

vparremove
appendix a

The **vparreset** and **vparremove** commands summarized in Table 2-1 were not issued at all for instance. The **vparremove** command can be run on any vPar provided that it is in the *down* state. The general steps to get vPars up and running and to perform some modification was performed to give you a simple framework from which to work. There are some other commands that were not covered, for which there are manual pages in Appendix A as well.

More detail in specific areas appears in other chapters of the book and I encourage you to review the online man pages for all of the vPars in Appendix A.

There are also some considerations related to server technology that we did not cover. If you have Instant Capacity on Demand (iCOD) employed on your server, all CPUs must be activated in order for vPars to work. When employing Processor Sets (psets) in a vPar, use only bound CPUs.

CHAPTER 3

Booting and vPars

vpmon, vparload, vparboot, PDC, ISL, hpux, Secure Web Console, GSP Configuration

Background

We have already done a lot of work on our system in previous chapters to load and configure HP-UX 11i and Virtual Partitions (vPars.) Now let's take a step back and examine the details of booting an HP 9000. After having loaded vPars onto a system there are some modifications in the boot process. Let's cover booting with vPars and then examine booting in general later in the chapter. First we'll cover booting after vPars have been installed on a system to see the impact that vPars have on the boot process. And then in the non-vPars-specific portion of this chapter you'll get an overview of: the low-level boot and configuration of an HP 9000; setting up HP Secure Web Console; and configuring the Guardian Service Processor (GSP).

Most of the systems used in the examples in this chapter for both the vPars-specific and non-vPars-specific sections are L-Class systems. I intentionally used a simple system so that we could concentrate on the boot process with a minimum amount of hardware-related messages. Since booting varies from system to system, even within the HP 9000 family, this is not a comprehensive study, but rather, an overview.

Virtual Partition Boot Process Overview

Booting partitions is similar to booting without partitions. The primary difference is the *Virtual Partition Monitor* - what I'll call **vpmon** in this chapter. **vpmon** is loaded at the time of boot and is located in **/stand/vpmon**.

The **vpmon** sits between the firmware and operating system on your HP 9000. Figure 3-1 depicts the position of the **vpmon** relative to other HP 9000 components.

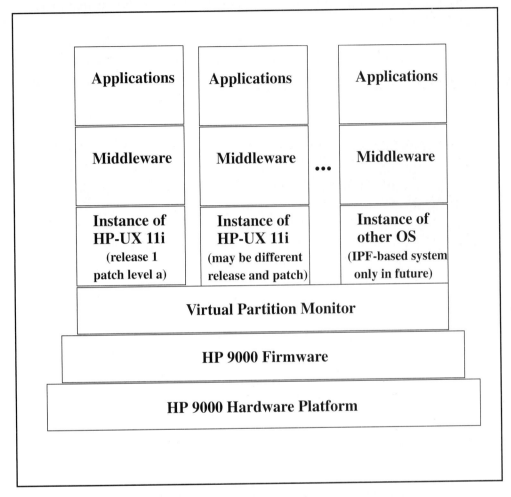

Figure 3-1 Virtual Partitions Software Stack

Notice in the figure that different versions and patch levels of HP-UX 11i may be running in vPars. On Itanium Processor Family (IPF) systems, operating systems other than HP-UX may be running in vPars. This functionality was not available at the time of this writing, so only HP-UX 11i-based vPars are covered in this book.

In the process of creating vPars, a partition database is produced that tracks the resources associated with vPars. The **vpmon** manages these resources, loads kernels, and performs other functions that make it look as though each virtual partition is its own system.

Rather than booting a kernel directly from the ISL (see the non-vPars-specific portion of this chapter for detailed information on all aspects of booting including ISL), you boot the **vpmon**. The **vpmon** then loads the partition database **/stand/vpdb** and creates the vPars based on the resources allocated to the vPars in the database. **vpdb** is the default database which contains partition-related information. A copy of **vpdb** is kept on the disk for every partition and is automatically kept synchronized. When a change is made to any partition, the master **vpdb** is updated and then the local copies on other vPars are automatically updated. This synchronization occurs every few seconds and ensures that **vpdb** on all running partitions remains synchronized. If a partition is not running its **vpdb** cannot be updated.

Without vPars you would boot the HP-UX kernel directly from ISL as shown below:

man page

hpux - 3

```
ISL> hpux /stand/vmunix
```

You can boot the **vpmon** from ISL with the command below:

```
ISL> hpux /stand/vpmon
```

The **vpmon** is invoked with this command and the **vpmon** prompt appears from which you can load vPars.

From the **vpmon** prompt we could issue the **vparload** command to load one or more Virtual Partitions. There are many options to the **vparload** command. There is no man page for **vparload** in Appendix A because it is a **vpmon** command. **vparboot** is a shell command so there is a man page in Appendix A for it. The following are the three forms of **vparboot** at the time of this writing:

```
form1: vparload -all

form2: vparload -auto

form3: vparload -p vp_name [-b kernelpath] [-o boot_options]
[-B hardware_path]
```

form1 boots all vPars. *form2* boots all vPars that have the *autoboot* attribute set. *form3* allows you to specify options such as: the *kernelpath* to boot; the *boot_options,* such as *"is"* for single user mode; or *hardware_path,* which specifies the boot device to be used for the vPar.

Issuing the **/stand/vpmon** command at the *ISL>* prompt gives us the *MON>* prompt. To use **vparload** to boot all Virtual Partitions on a server we would issue the following command:

man page

vparload
appendix a

```
MON> vparload -all
```

To use **vparload** to boot Virtual Partition *symbol1*, we would issue the following command:

```
MON> vparload -p symbol1
```

You could perform the steps to load both the **vpmon** and virtual partition *symbol1* from ISL with the command below at the ISL prompt:

man page

hpux - 3

```
ISL> hpux /stand/vpmon vparload -p symbol1
```

This command boots both **vpmon** and then *symbol1*. You may perform experimentation with the kernels of the vPars on your system and have to boot different kernels. The following example shows booting from a kernel called **vmunix_test1**:

```
MON> vparload -p symbol1 -b /stand/vmunix_test1
```

As a side note, the kernel path above is loaded with this **vparload**, but no permanent changes were made. To make a permanent change to the vPars database you would issue the following command:

```
# vparmodify -p symbol1 -b "stand/vmunix_test1"
```

The vPar database has now been modified to have a default kernel of **/stand/vmunix_test1**.

You can boot a vPar in single-user mode with the following command:

```
MON> vparload -p symbol1 -o "is"
```

There are a variety of other options that you can use for booting vPars. As you can see from this discussion, the options are similar to options you would use on a non-vPars system.

There are a variety of other commands that you can issue from *MON>*. The following shows some of the more common commands:

help   Displays all of the commands available in *MON>* as shown below (**?** produces the same results:)

```
MON> help

Supported Commands:

?              Print list of commands
cat            Dump contents of file to screen
cbuf           Dump contents of console buffer
getauto        Print the AUTO file
help           Print list of commands
lifls          List files in LIF directory
log            View the event log
```

```
ls                List files in a directory
readdb            Read a partition DB
reboot            Reboot system
scan              Scan the system
toddriftreset     Reset the TOD drift of all vpars
vparload          Load vPar
vparinfo          Display vPar info
```

scan   Displays all hardware discovered by the Virtual Partition monitor and indicates which vPar, if any, owns the device. Note in the following listing that some components, such as the System Bus Adapters (SBAs) at *0* and *1* and the memory controller at *192,* are owned by the Virtual Partition monitor and are therefore owned by *VPAR-ALL.* Other components are owned by vPar *uhnjlvp1/2.* This is an informative listing of all components and the vPar that owns them, as shown below:

```
MON> scan
0          BUSCONV      sv_model= 12   HPA=0xfffffffffed00000   VPAR=ALL
0/0        BUS_BRIDGE   sv_model= 10   HPA=0xfffffffffbffe0000   VPAR=uhnjlvp1
0/1        BUS_BRIDGE   sv_model= 10   HPA=0xfffffffffbffe2000   VPAR=NONE
0/2        BUS_BRIDGE   sv_model= 10   HPA=0xfffffffffbffe4000   VPAR=NONE
0/4        BUS_BRIDGE   sv_model= 10   HPA=0xfffffffffbffe8000   VPAR=NONE
0/5        BUS_BRIDGE   sv_model= 10   HPA=0xfffffffffbffea000   VPAR=NONE
0/8        BUS_BRIDGE   sv_model= 10   HPA=0xfffffffffbfff0000   VPAR=uhnjlvp2
0/10       BUS_BRIDGE   sv_model= 10   HPA=0xfffffffffbfff4000   VPAR=NONE
0/12       BUS_BRIDGE   sv_model= 10   HPA=0xfffffffffbfff8000   VPAR=uhnjlvp1
1          BUSCONV      sv_model= 12   HPA=0xfffffffffed40000   VPAR=ALL
1/0        BUS_BRIDGE   sv_model= 10   HPA=0xfffffffffece0000   VPAR=NONE
1/2        BUS_BRIDGE   sv_model= 10   HPA=0xfffffffffece4000   VPAR=NONE
1/4        BUS_BRIDGE   sv_model= 10   HPA=0xfffffffffece8000   VPAR=NONE
1/8        BUS_BRIDGE   sv_model= 10   HPA=0xfffffffffecf0000   VPAR=NONE
1/10       BUS_BRIDGE   sv_model= 10   HPA=0xfffffffffecf4000   VPAR=NONE
1/12       BUS_BRIDGE   sv_model= 10   HPA=0xfffffffffecf8000   VPAR=uhnjlvp2
36         BUSCONV      sv_model= 12   HPA=0xfffffffffed24000   VPAR=NONE
37         NPROC        sv_model=  4   HPA=0xfffffffffed25000   VPAR=uhnjlvp1
44         BUSCONV      sv_model= 12   HPA=0xfffffffffed2c000   VPAR=NONE
45         NPROC        sv_model=  4   HPA=0xfffffffffed2d000   VPAR=uhnjlvp2
192        MEMORY       sv_model=  9   HPA=0xfffffffffedc0000   VPAR=ALL
MON> vparinfo uhnjlvp1

Resources assigned to partition 0 (uhnjlvp1)...
---------------------------------------
0          0xfffffffffed00000      1      0   TYPE= 7   SV_MODEL= 12
0/0        0xfffffffffbffe0000     1      0   TYPE=13   SV_MODEL= 10
0/12       0xfffffffffbfff8000     1      0   TYPE=13   SV_MODEL= 10
```

```
1               0xfffffffffed40000      1      0  TYPE= 7  SV_MODEL= 12
37              0xfffffffffed25000      1      0  TYPE= 0  SV_MODEL=  4
192             0xfffffffffedc0000      1      0  TYPE= 1  SV_MODEL=  9

Effective Size: 1572864 kb

Boot: 0/0/2/0.6.0
Console: 0/0/4/0
Boot Image: (0/0/2/0.6.0;)/stand/vmunix
Boot Options:
AUTOBOOT:off
DYNAMIC
```

vparinfo *[partition_name]* Displays resources assigned to the specified vPar or those resources that are unassigned if the vPar name is not specified. The following listing shows the resources assigned to vPar *uhnjlvp2*:

```
MON> vparinfo uhnjlvp2

Resources assigned to partition 1 (uhnjlvp2)...
----------------------------------------
0               0xfffffffffed00000      1      0  TYPE= 7  SV_MODEL= 12
0/8             0xfffffffffbfff0000      1      0  TYPE=13  SV_MODEL= 10
1               0xfffffffffed40000      1      0  TYPE= 7  SV_MODEL= 12
1/12            0xfffffffffecf8000      1      0  TYPE=13  SV_MODEL= 10
45              0xfffffffffed2d000      1      0  TYPE= 0  SV_MODEL=  4
192             0xfffffffffedc0000      1      0  TYPE= 1  SV_MODEL=  9

Effective Size: 524288 kb

Boot: 1/12/0/0.12.0
Console: Default
Boot Image: (1/12/0/0.12.0;)/stand/vmunix
Boot Options:
AUTOBOOT:off
DYNAMIC
```

vparload The three forms of this command are listed below. The example after the three forms shows the beginning of loading all vPars with **vparload -all**:

```
form1: vparload -all

form2: vparload -auto

form3: vparload -p vp_name [-b kernelpath] [-o boot_options]
[-B hardware_path]
```

```
MON> vparload -all
[MON] Booting uhnjlvp2...
[MON] Booting uhnjlvp1...
[MON] Console client set to uhnjlvp2

[MON] uhnjlvp2 loaded

[MON] uhnjlvp1 loaded
```

     .
     .
     .

lifls   Displays the files in the LIF area as shown
                             below:

```
MON> lifls
volume ISL10 data size 7802 directory size 8
filename     type    start    size       implement   created
==========================================================
ODE          -12960 584       848
MAPFILE      -12277 1432      128
SYSLIB       -12280 1560      353
CONFIGDATA   -12278 1920      218
SLMOD2       -12276 2144      140
SLDEV2       -12276 2288      134
SLDRV2       -12276 2424      168
SLSCSI2      -12276 2592      116
MAPPER2      -12279 2712      142
IOTEST2      -12279 2856      89
PERFVER2     -12279 2952      125
PVCU         -12801 3080      64
SSINFO       -12286 3144      2
ISL          -12800 3152      306
AUTO         -12289 3464      1
HPUX         -12928 3472      848
LABEL        -23951 4320      8
```

getauto   Displays the contents of the LIF area auto
                             file as shown below:

```
MON> getauto
hpux
```

log   Displays all information in the Virtual Partition monitor log. The information is displayed in chronological order as shown below:

```
MON> log
INFO:CPU0:MON:[20:16:31 10/1/2001 GMT] VPAR Monitor ver-
sion 0.2 started
INFO:CPU0:MON:Version  string:  @(#)  $Revision:  vpmon:
vw: --     selectors: CUP
11.11_BL2001_0616            'cup_cvinod_vpar_ncf_trial'
'cup_shep_r11.11'  Tue Sep 25 18:2
1:12 PDT 2001 $
INFO:CPU0:MON:Partition uhnjlvp1 monarch set to 37
INFO:CPU0:MON:Partition uhnjlvp2 monarch set to 45
```

ls *directory*   Lists the contents of a directory in much the same way as UNIX **ls** command. At the time of this writing, the *directory* must be HFS. The **/stand** directory is used by default. You can also add *-a* for all entries, *-l* for long listing, *-n* for numerical entries, *-i* for inode, and *-F* for file type appended to the output, such as a slash (*/*) after directories, as shown below using the *-l* option:

```
MON> ls -l /stand
drwxr-xr-x    2 0      0           8192 lost+found
-rw-rw-rw-    1 0      3           5416 ioconfig
drwxr-xr-x    4 0      3           2048 build
-rwxr-xr-x    1 0      0       15273152 vmunix
drwxrwxrwx    5 0      3           1024 dlkm.vmunix.prev
-rw-r--r--    1 0      3             19 bootconf
-r--r--r--    1 0      3             82 kernrel
-rw-------    1 0      0             12 rootconf
-r--r--r--    1 0      3           1040 system
-r--r--r--    1 0      3           1035 system.prev
-rwxr-xr-x    1 0      3       14488016 vmunix.prev
drwxrwxrwx    5 0      0           1024 dlkm
drwxr-xr-x    2 0      3           1024 system.d
drwxr-xr-x    2 0      3           1024 krs
drwxr-xr-x    2 0      0           1024 krs_tmp
drwxr-xr-x    2 0      0           1024 krs_lkg
```

```
-r-xr-xr-x    1 2      2           845680 vpmon
-rw-------    1 0      0           102640 vpmon.dmp
-rw-------    2 0      0             8232 vpdb
```

cbuf *partition_name*   Displays the information in the console buffer for the specified Virtual Partition. If no information is present in the buffer you'll receive the following message:

```
MON> cbuf uhnjlvp1
      Buffer is empty
```

Many of these commands at *MON>* are informative. Let's now move on to vPars states.

Virtual Partition Boot States

We've seen many examples of vPars in a variety of different boot states in Chapter 2 when we were creating and modifying vPars. When we boot a Virtual Partition, it progresses through *load*, then *boot*, and finally, *up*. There are other states in which you may find a Virtual Partition as well. Table 3-1 summarizes the states of Virtual Partitions at the time of this writing:

Table 3-1 Virtual Partitions States

vPars State	Description
load	The kernel image of a Virtual Partition is being loaded into memory. This is done by the Virtual Partition monitor.
boot	The Virtual Partition is in the process of booting. The kernel image has been successfully loaded by the Virtual Partition monitor.
up	The Virtual Partition has been successfully booted and is running.
shut	The Virtual Partition is in the process of shutting down.
down	The Virtual Partition is not running and is down.
crash	The Virtual Partition has experienced a panic and is crashing.
hung	The Virtual Partition is not responding and is hung.

We have seen several of these states in Chapter 2 when we created Virtual Partitions and watched them boot by issuing successive **vparstatus** commands. The following example shows the process of the Virtual Partition *cable2* booting:

```
# vparboot -p cable2
# vparstatus
[Virtual Partition]                                                   Boot
Virtual Partition Name          State Attributes Kernel Path          Opts
============================== ===== ========== ======================= =====
cable1                          Up    Dyn,Manl   /stand/vmunix
cable2                          Load  Dyn,Manl   /stand/vmunix

[Virtual Partition Resource                    CPU    Num     Memory (MB)
 Summary]                        CPU       Bound/  IO   # Ranges/
Virtual Partition Name          Min/Max  Unbound  devs  Total MB   Total MB
============================== =============== ========== ==== ====================
cable1                          2/  4      2     0      4    0/  0        2048
cable2                          2/  2      2     0      4    0/  0        1024
# vparstatus
[Virtual Partition]                                                   Boot
Virtual Partition Name          State Attributes Kernel Path          Opts
============================== ===== ========== ======================= =====
cable1                          Up    Dyn,Manl   /stand/vmunix
cable2                          Boot  Dyn,Manl   /stand/vmunix

[Virtual Partition Resource                    CPU    Num     Memory (MB)
 Summary]                        CPU       Bound/  IO   # Ranges/
Virtual Partition Name          Min/Max  Unbound  devs  Total MB   Total MB
============================== =============== ========== ==== ====================
cable1                          2/  4      2     0      4    0/  0        2048
cable2                          2/  2      2     0      4    0/  0        1024
# vparstatus
[Virtual Partition]                                                   Boot
Virtual Partition Name          State Attributes Kernel Path          Opts
============================== ===== ========== ======================= =====
cable1                          Up    Dyn,Manl   /stand/vmunix
```

```
cable2                            Up     Dyn,Manl   /stand/vmunix

[Virtual Partition Resource              CPU    Num       Memory (MB)
 Summary]                          CPU   Bound/  IO   # Ranges/
Virtual Partition Name           Min/Max Unbound devs Total MB    Total MB
============================== =============== ==== ==================
cable1                            2/ 4    2   0     4    0/ 0         2048
cable2                            2/ 2    2   0     4    0/ 0         1024
#
```

This example shows *cable2* progressing through the *load*, then *boot*, and finally, *up*. *cable2* was booted from *cable1* running on the same hardware. The system had already gone through the boot process when *cable1* booted. The boot time for *cable2* is very quick since most of the hardware is already running. The boot time for the first Virtual Partition is comparable to the boot time of a non-Virtual Partition system, but the subsequent vPars boot much more quickly.

setboot Command and vPars

In our example vPars in Chapter 2, we had *autoboot* set to *off* for our Virtual Partition. The **setboot** command on a non-vPars system reads from and writes to stable storage. On a vPars system the **setboot** command interacts with the Virtual Partition database. Running **setboot** on a vPars system has the effects shown in Table 3-2:

Table 3-2   setboot and Virtual Partitions

vPars setboot Option	Description
-a	Changes the alternate boot path of the Virtual Partition. To set the alternate boot path: # **setboot -a 0/8/0/0.8.0.5.0.0.0**

vPars setboot Option	Description
-b	Sets the autoboot attribute of the Virtual Partition. To set Autoboot *on*: `# setboot -b on`
-p	Changes the primary boot path of the Virtual Partition. To set the primary boot path: `# setboot -p 0/0/1/1.2.0`
-s	Has no effect.
no options	Displays information about boot attributes.

man page

vparmodify
appendix a

The **setboot** command is one of the aspects of working with vPars that is different from a non-vPars system.

You can also set the primary and alternate boot paths with **vparmodify**.

Other Boot Topics

Virtual Partition and HP-UX startup is covered in Chapter 8. Startup and boot are related, so you may want to take a look at Chapter 8. To see how LAN cards are configured with vPars (i.e. *lan0* and *lan1*) please see Chapter 13. The remainder of this chapter provides extensive background information on booting.

Non-vPars-Specific Section of Chapter: Boot Process Overview

man page

boot - 3

The boot process on an HP 9000 system can be reduced in its simplest form to three steps. I'll provide a quick description of the three steps and then we'll take a look at some example boot processes so we can see these three steps in action. The following is a description of the three steps:

man page

pdc - 3

PDC   HP 9000 systems come with firmware installed called Processor Dependent Code (PDC - man page pdc). After the system is powered on or the processor is RESET, the PDC runs self test operations and initializes the processor. PDC also identifies the console path so it can provide messages and accept input. PDC would then begin the "autoboot" process unless you were to interrupt it during the 10-second interval that is supplied. If you interrupt the "autoboot" process, you can issue a variety of commands. The interface to PDC commands is called the Boot Console Handler (BCH.) This is sometimes a point of confusion; that is, are we issuing PDC commands or BCH commands? The commands are normally described as PDC commands and the interface through which you execute them is the BCH.

man page

isl - 3

ISL   The Initial System Loader (ISL - man page isl) is run after PDC. You would normally just run an "autoboot" sequence from ISL; however, there are a number of commands that you could run from the ISL prompt.

man page
hpux - 3

hpux

The hpux utility manages loading the HP-UX kernel and gives control to the kernel. ISL can have hpux run an "autoexecute" file, or commands can be given interactively. In most situations, you would just want to automatically boot the system; however, we'll take a look at some of the hpux commands you can execute. This is sometimes called the Secondary System Loader (SSL.)

I find that there is a lot of confusion related to the boot process for new system administrators. To begin with, there is not much documentation that comes with new systems related to HP 9000 boot. Secondly, without any background on the boot process, it is difficult to determine at which phase of the boot your system is at any given time. Table 3-3 shows some system states and the corresponding prompts you can expect for each state in roughly the order you might see them at the time of system boot:

TABLE 3-3   /sbin/set_parms Arguments

Boot State of System	Prompt
Boot Console Handler (BCH) Seen when you discontinue boot within 10 seconds. Used to perform PDC-related work.	`Main Menu: Enter command or menu >`
Initial System Loader (ISL) Seen after PDC-related work.	`ISL> ?`
hpux Prompt varies. You usually issue **hpux** command at ISL prompt to boot. This is sometimes called the Secondary System Loader (SSL).	Varies depending on the state of the system.

Boot State of System	Prompt
Guardian Service Processor (GSP) Seen when you type ^b (control b) to get access to GSP.	GSP>

man page

boot - 3

There is only one way to describe the boot process and that is through example. The boot of a system with minimal hardware will be covered in the upcoming sections. I choose the boot of a system with minimal hardware so as not to get bogged down in hardware-related details, but to instead focus on the boot process. The messages supplied as a result of booting this modest system will allow us to focus on the boot process rather than on the many hardware components. The boot process consists of mostly the same steps for any HP 9000, so you can apply this information to your system. It may be, however, that you have a much larger system with more components that will produce more lengthy boot messages.

Boot Console Handler (BCH) & Processor Dependent Code (PDC)

man page

pdc - 3

As mentioned earlier, HP 9000 systems come with firmware installed called Processor Dependent Code (PDC.) After the system is powered on or the processor is RESET, the PDC runs self-test operations and initializes the processor. PDC also identifies the console path so it can provide messages and accept input. PDC would then begin the "auto-boot" process, unless you were to interrupt it during the 10-second interval that is supplied. If you interrupt the "autoboot" process, you can issue a variety of commands.

The following example shows booting an L-Class system and the PDC-related messages we receive on the system. The first messages you see are a variety of self-test-related messages. The processor, memory, I/O, and other components are run through a variety of tests. I abbreviated the list of messages in the example, wherever you see three dots, because the complete list of test results was too long to include in this book:

```
Value of TERM has been set to "vt100".
WARNING:  YOU ARE SUPERUSER !!1.00] (see /etc/issue)
Console Login: root
# reboot -h...checking for disk quotas
Shutdown at 17:41 (in 0 minutes) ckard Co.,  All Rights Reserved.
(c)Copyright 1979, 1980, 1983, 1985-1993 The Regents of the Univ. of California
(c)C*** FINAL System shutdown message from root@hp.serviceengine.com ***
(c)Copyright 1986-1992 Sun Microsystems, Inc.
System going down IMMEDIATELY Massachusetts Institute of Technology
(c)Copyright 1989-1993  The Open Software Foundation, Inc.
System shutdown time has arrivedent Corp.
(c)Copyright 1990 Motorola, Inc.
(c)Copyright 1990, 1991, 1992 Cornell University
(c)Copyright 1989-1991 The University of Maryland
Console reset done.arnegie Mellon University
(c)Copyright 1991-1997 Mentat, Inc.
Boot device reset done.ng Star Technologies, Inc.
(c)Copyright 1996 Progressive Systems, Inc.
(c)Copyright 1997 Isogon Corporation

System has halted
OK to turn off power or reset systemD RIGHTS LEGEND
UNLESS "WAIT for UPS to turn off power" message was printed above to
restrictions as set forth in sub-paragraph (c)(1)(ii) of the Rights in
********** VIRTUAL FRONT PANEL **********se in DFARS 252.227-7013.
System Boot detected
*****************************************
LEDs:  RUN       ATTENTION     FAULT     REMOTE     POWER
       ON        FLASH         OFF       OFF        ON
                            Palo Alto, CA 94304 U.S.A.
       platform             config                  626F
       processor            slave rendezvous        1C17ies are as set
       processor            test                    1142
       processor            test                    1100
       processor            test                    1100
       processor            test                    1100
       processor            test                    1100
       processor            test                    1100
       processor            test                    1100
       processor            test                    1100
       processor            test                    1100
       processor            test                    1100
       PDH                  config                  322F
       PDH                  test                    3149
       PDH                  test                    3160
       platform             test                    616A
       processor            test                    1146
       processor            INIT                    1701
       processor            INIT                    1701
       processor            test                    1110
       .
       .
       .
       processor            test                    111C
       processor            test                    111D
       processor            test                    111D
       processor cache      test                    2111
       processor cache      test                    2111
       processor cache      test                    2112
       processor cache      test                    2112
       processor cache      test                    2113
```

```
processor cache           test                        2113
processor cache           test                        2121
processor cache           test                        2121
  .
  .
  .
memory                    test                        71A4
memory                    test                        71A5
memory                    test                        71A5
memory                    test                        71A6
memory                    test                        71A6
memory                    config                      7210
I/O                       INIT                        8701
I/O                       test                        8118
I/O                       test                        8118
I/O                       INIT                        8701
I/O                       INIT                        8701
I/O                       INIT                        8701
I/O                       INIT                        8701
I/O                       INIT                        8701
I/O                       INIT                        8701
I/O                       INIT                        8701
I/O                       INIT                        8701
I/O                       INIT                        8701
memory                    config                      7240
memory                    INIT                        7702
memory                    config                      7241
memory                    config                      7243
memory                    config                      72A0
memory                    test                        71A1
memory                    test                        71A2
  .
  .
processor                 test                        1120
processor                 slave rendezvous            1C40
processor                 test                        1142
processor                 test                        113B
platform                  test                        612A
I/O                       config                      8238


*******************************************

************ EARLY BOOT VFP *************
End of early boot detected
*******************************************

Firmware Version  39.46

Duplex Console IO Dependent Code (IODC) revision 1


-----------------------------------------------------------------------
    (c) Copyright 1995-1998, Hewlett-Packard Company, All rights reserved
-----------------------------------------------------------------------

Processor   Speed          State          CoProcessor State  Cache Size
Number                                     State              Inst   Data
---------   --------   -------------------  -----------------  ------------
    0       440  MHz   Active             Functional         512 KB  1 MB
    3       440  MHz   Idle               Functional         512 KB  1 MB

Central Bus Speed (in MHz)  :          82
Available Memory            :     2097152  KB
Good Memory Required        :       11468  KB

  Primary boot path:     0/0/1/1.2
  Alternate boot path:   0/0/2/0.2
  Console path:          0/0/4/0.0
  Keyboard path:         0/0/4/0.0
```

Processor is booting from first available device.

To discontinue, press any key within 10 seconds.

man page

pdc - 3

After the "early" boot is complete, we get a brief system summary, including the firmware revision on our system, and are then given the option to automatically boot off of the primary path or press any key to stop the boot process. Under normal system operation, you would autoboot; however, in our case, we'll interrupt the boot process to see what commands are available in the PDC. When we interrupt the boot process, the following menu appears:

```
Boot terminated.

---- Main Menu ----------------------------------------------------------

     Command                          Description
     -------                          -----------
     BOot [PRI|ALT|<path>]            Boot from specified path
     PAth [PRI|ALT] [<path>]          Display or modify a path
     SEArch [DIsplay|IPL] [<path>]    Search for boot devices

     COnfiguration menu               Displays or sets boot values
     INformation menu                 Displays hardware information
     SERvice menu                     Displays service commands

     DIsplay                          Redisplay the current menu
     HElp [<menu>|<command>]          Display help for menu or command
     RESET                            Restart the system
----
Main Menu: Enter command or menu >
```

The interface to the PDC is called the Boot Console Handler (BCH.) In our discussion the commands we are issuing are PDC commands and the interface through which we issue them is the BCH. Many of the commands in this menu are helpful to system administrators, but are sometimes ignored because they are pre-operating system and therefore usually overlooked.

We'll skip the first three commands for the time being and start by looking at the *COnfiguration* menu command by typing *co*. The uppercase "*CO*" in *COnfiguration* means that you could type just *co* as an abbeviation for configuration:

```
Main Menu: Enter command or menu > co

---- Configuration Menu -----------------------------------------------------

     Command                       Description
     -------                       -----------
     AUto [BOot|SEArch|STart] [ON|OFF] Display or set specified flag
     BootID [<proc>] [<bootid>]    Display or set Boot Identifier
     BootINfo                      Display boot-related information
     BootTimer [0 - 200]           Seconds allowed for boot attempt
     CPUconfig [<proc>] [ON|OFF]   Config/Deconfig processor
     DEfault                       Set the system to predefined values
     FAn [HI|NORmal]               Display or change fan speed
     FastBoot [ON|OFF]             Display or set boot tests execution
     PAth [PRI|ALT] [<path>]       Display or modify a path
     SEArch [DIsplay|IPL] [<path>] Search for boot devices
     TIme [c:y:m:d:h:m:[s]]        Read or set the real time clock in GMT

     BOot [PRI|ALT|<path>]         Boot from specified path
     DIsplay                       Redisplay the current menu
     HElp [<command>]              Display help for specified command
     RESET                         Restart the system
     MAin                          Return to Main Menu
----
Configuration Menu: Enter command >
```

Under the *COnfiguration* menu are several useful commands. You can, for example, enable *FastBoot*, which gives control over tests run at boot time. We'll issue the **FastBoot** command to see how our system is currently set but not change the value of *FastBoot*:

```
Configuration Menu: Enter command > FastBoot

     Fastboot:            OFF

Configuration Menu: Enter command >
```

Our system has *FastBoot off*, meaning we'll run all available tests at boot time. If you would like to reduce system boot time and are willing to bypass boot tests, you would turn *on* FastBoot.

There are a variety of other commands under the *COnfiguration* menu that you may want to issue, depending on your needs, such as *CPUconfig* to configure and deconfigure processors.

Let's now issue the *Main* command to get back to the *Main* menu and then *IN* to get access to the *INformation* menu:

```
Configuration Menu: Enter command > main

---- Main Menu ----------------------------------------------------------

     Command                           Description
     -------                           -----------
     BOot [PRI|ALT|<path>]             Boot from specified path
     PAth [PRI|ALT] [<path>]           Display or modify a path
     SEArch [DIsplay|IPL] [<path>]     Search for boot devices

     COnfiguration menu                Displays or sets boot values
     INformation menu                  Displays hardware information
     SERvice menu                      Displays service commands

     DIsplay                           Redisplay the current menu
     HElp [<menu>|<command>]           Display help for menu or command
     RESET                             Restart the system
----
Main Menu: Enter command or menu > IN

---- Information Menu --------------------------------------------------

     Command                           Description
     -------                           -----------
     ALL                               Display all system information
     BootINfo                          Display boot-related information
     CAche                             Display cache information
     ChipRevisions                     Display revisions of major VLSI
     COprocessor                       Display coprocessor information
     FRU                               Display FRU information
     FwrVersion                        Display firmware version
     IO                                Display I/O interface information
     LanAddress                        Display Core LAN station address
     MEmory                            Display memory information
     PRocessor                         Display processor information
     WArnings                          Display selftest warning messages

     BOot [PRI|ALT|<path>]             Boot from specified path
     DIsplay                           Redisplay the current menu
     HElp [<command>]                  Display help for specified command
     RESET                             Restart the system
     MAin                              Return to Main Menu
----
Information Menu: Enter command >
```

The *INformation* menu is a hidden gem for system administrators. Among the menu selections is one to display *ALL* system information, which produces the following report for our L-Class system. I abbreviated this report at the point where you see the three dots near the end of the report:

```
Information Menu: Enter command > all

    Model:                   9000/800/L2000-44

PROCESSOR INFORMATION

                   HVERSION  SVERSION              Processor
  Processor  Speed  Model   Model/Op  CVERSION       State
  ---------  -----  ------  --------  --------   -------------
      0    440 MHz  0x05c4   0x0491    2.  4     Active
      3    440 MHz  0x05c4   0x0491    2.  4     Idle
```

```
        Central Bus Speed (in MHz)  :        82
        Software ID (dec)           :  143901527
        Software ID (hex)           :  0x0893c357
        Software Capability         :  0x01f0
```

```
COPROCESSOR INFORMATION

                    Coprocessor    Coprocessor      Coprocessor
        Processor      Model        Revision          State
        -----------  -----------   -----------    -----------------
            0        0x00000010          1          Functional
            3        0x00000010          1          Functional
```

```
CACHE INFORMATION

        Processor    Instruction Cache Size    Data Cache Size
        -----------  -----------------------   ---------------
            0               512 KB                  1 MB
            3               512 KB                  1 MB
```

```
MEMORY INFORMATION

        MEMORY STATUS TABLE (MB)  (Current Boot Status)

    Slot 0a   512M   Active
    Slot 0b   512M   Active
    Slot 1a   512M   Active
    Slot 1b   512M   Active

    Slot 2a    -
    Slot 2b    -
    Slot 3a    -
    Slot 3b    -

    Slot 4a    -
    Slot 4b    -
    Slot 5a    -
    Slot 5b    -

    Slot 6a    -
    Slot 6b    -
    Slot 7a    -
    Slot 7b    -

    Subtotal 2048M

       TOTAL =  2048 MB
             ---------
```

```
                    Memory Installation Guidelines
                    ------------------------------

  - For DIMMs to work, both DIMMs in a slot pair (a/b) must be the same type.
      (Same part number = same type)

  - For proper cooling, install DIMMs in the following order:
      0a/b 1a/b 2a/b 3a/b 4a/b 5a/b 6a/b 7a/b.
```

```
        Active, Installed Memory      :     2048  MB of SDRAM
        Deallocated Pages             :        0  Pages
                                            -----------
        Available Memory              :     2048  MB

        Good Memory Required by OS    :       12  MB

              Memory
        HVERSION  SVERSION
        --------  ----------
         0x0950  0x00000900

    I/O MODULE INFORMATION
```

```
                          Path   Slot                           IODC
Type                      (dec)  Number  HVERSION  SVERSION     Vers
----                      -----  ------  --------  --------     ----
System bus adapter        0              0x5820    0xb10        0x0
Local bus adapter         0/0    1       0x7820    0xa00        0x0
Local bus adapter         0/1    6       0x7820    0xa00        0x0
Local bus adapter         0/2    8       0x7820    0xa00        0x0
Local bus adapter         0/3    10      0x7820    0xa00        0x0
Local bus adapter         0/4    12      0x7820    0xa00        0x0
Local bus adapter         0/5    7       0x7820    0xa00        0x0
Local bus adapter         0/6    9       0x7820    0xa00        0x0
Local bus adapter         0/7    11      0x7820    0xa00        0x0

PCI DEVICE INFORMATION

                          Path           Vendor  Device  Bus   Slot
Description               (dec)          Id      Id      #     #
-----------               -----          ----    ----    ---   ---
Ethernet cntlr            0/0/0/0        0x1011  0x19    0     1
SCSI bus cntlr            0/0/1/0        0x1000  0xb     0     1
SCSI bus cntlr            0/0/1/1        0x1000  0xb     0     1
SCSI bus cntlr            0/0/2/0        0x1000  0xf     0     1
SCSI bus cntlr            0/0/2/1        0x1000  0xf     0     1
Comp. ser cntlr           0/0/4/0        0x103c  0x1048  0     2
Comp. ser cntlr           0/0/5/0        0x103c  0x1048  0     2
Ethernet cntlr            0/3/0/0        0x1011  0x19    24    10
SCSI bus cntlr            0/4/0/0        0x1000  0xf     32    12
SCSI bus cntlr            0/4/0/1        0x1000  0xf     32    12
SCSI bus cntlr            0/7/0/0        0x1000  0xf     56    11
SCSI bus cntlr            0/7/0/1        0x1000  0xf     56    11

BOOT INFORMATION

      Processor           Boot ID
      ---------           -------
          0                  2
          3                  2

   Autoboot:               ON
   Autosearch:             ON
   Autostart:              ON
   Fastboot:               OFF

   Primary boot path:      intscsib.2
                           0/0/1/1.2
                           0/0/01/01.2    (hex)
   Alternate boot path:    intscsia.2
                           0/0/2/0.2
                           0/0/02/0.2     (hex)
   Console path:           0/0/4/0.0
                           0/0/04/0.0     (hex)
   Keyboard path:          0/0/4/0.0
                           0/0/04/0.0     (hex)

   LAN Station Address:    001083-fc9288

   Wed Apr  19 22:02:46 GMT 2000     (20:00:04:19:22:02:46)

FIRMWARE INFORMATION

   Firmware Version:          39.46

          Module              Revision
          ------              --------
          System Board        A443938
          PA 8500 CPU Module  2.4
          PA 8500 CPU Module  2.4

FRU INFORMATION

FRU Name:               SYS_BD
Part Number:            A5191-60001
Serial Number:          A56405282277
Physical Location:      00ffff0001ffff69
Engineering Date Code:  3938
```

```
Art Work Revision:      A4
Scan Revision:
FRU Specific Info:      USS40130E3

FRU Name:               IO_BP
Part Number:            A5191-60002
Serial Number:          52SCFK23WX
Physical Location:      00ffff0002ffff69
Engineering Date Code: 3942
Art Work Revision:      A2
Scan Revision:
FRU Specific Info:

FRU Name:               LAN_SCSI_CORE_IO
Part Number:            A5191-60011
Serial Number:            52SCFK28DE
Physical Location:      000000ffff01ff85
Engineering Date Code: 3933
Art Work Revision:      A5
Scan Revision:
FRU Specific Info:

   .
   .
   .

FRU Name:               DIMM_512
Part Number:            A5798-60001
Serial Number:          A56E02093896
Physical Location:      0000ff00001bff74
Engineering Date Code: 3938
Art Work Revision:      A4
Scan Revision:
FRU Specific Info:

Information Menu: Enter command >
```

This report would be an excellent addition to a system administration notebook. Knowing such information as the firmware revision levels and the settings of the boot flags is valuable.

man page

pdc - 3

In the previous example, we used the BCH to issue the PDC commands *INformation* and then *ALL*. Both *INformation* and *ALL* are PDC commands issued through the BCH interface. Sometimes PDC and BCH are used interchangeably in documentation, however, knowing that BCH is the interface through which PDC commands are issued will usually serve you well when looking for information on specific commands.

Let's now go back to the *Main* menu and then look at the *SERvice* menu:

```
Service Menu: Enter command > main

---- Main Menu ------------------------------------------------------

      Command                        Description
      -------                        -----------
      BOot [PRI|ALT|<path>]          Boot from specified path
```

```
          PAth [PRI|ALT] [<path>]              Display or modify a path
          SEArch [DIsplay|IPL] [<path>]        Search for boot devices

          COnfiguration menu                   Displays or sets boot values
          INformation menu                     Displays hardware information
          SERvice menu                         Displays service commands

          DIsplay                              Redisplay the current menu
          HElp [<menu>|<command>]              Display help for menu or command
          RESET                                Restart the system
    ----
    Main Menu: Enter command or menu > ser

    ---- Service Menu ----------------------------------------------------------

          Command                              Description
          -------                              -----------
          CLEARPIM                             Clear (zero) the contents of PIM
          SCSI [option] [<path>] [<val>]       Display or set SCSI controller values
          MemRead <address> [<len>]            Read memory and I/O locations
          PDT [CLEAR]                          Display or clear the PDT
          PIM [<proc>] [HPMC|LPMC|TOC]         Display PIM information
          ProductNum <O|C> [<number>]          Display or set Product Number
          SELftests [ON|OFF]                   Enable/disable self test execution

          BOot [PRI|ALT|<path>]                Boot from specified path
          DIsplay                              Redisplay the current menu
          HElp [<command>]                     Display help for specified command
          RESET                                Restart the system
          MAin                                 Return to Main Menu
    ----
    Service Menu: Enter command >
```

Among the options you have in *SERvice* menu is to manipulate the Processor Internal Memory, display SCSI controller values, and enable and disable self-tests. In the following example, we run *SCSI* to get information on our SCSI interfaces and then return to the *Main* menu:

```
Service Menu: Enter command > SCSI

Path (dec)       Initiator ID    SCSI Rate    Auto Term
-----------      ------------    ---------    ---------------
0/0/1/0          7               Fast         Unknown
0/0/1/1          7               Ultra        Unknown
0/0/2/0          7               Ultra        Unknown
0/0/2/1          7               Ultra        Unknown

Service Menu: Enter command > main

---- Main Menu -------------------------------------------------------------

      Command                          Description
      -------                          -----------
      BOot [PRI|ALT|<path>]            Boot from specified path
      PAth [PRI|ALT] [<path>]          Display or modify a path
      SEArch [DIsplay|IPL] [<path>]    Search for boot devices
```

```
            COnfiguration menu          Displays or sets boot values
            INformation menu            Displays hardware information
            SERvice menu                Displays service commands

            DIsplay                     Redisplay the current menu
            HElp [<menu>|<command>]     Display help for menu or command
            RESET                       Restart the system
      ----
      Main Menu: Enter command or menu >
```

man page

pdc - 3

Now that we've looked at some of the PDC commands, let's get back to the process of booting by looking at the first three commands under *Main* menu.

BOot allows you to specify the path from which you'll boot your system. *PAth* allows you to display or modify the boot paths. *SEArch* will display boot paths. In the following example we'll *SEArch* to show all potential boot devices on our L-Class system, run *PAth* to display our existing boot path, and then specify the device from which we want to boot our system:

```
Service Menu: Enter command > main

---- Main Menu ----------------------------------------------------------------

      Command                     Description
      -------                     -----------
      BOot [PRI|ALT|<path>]       Boot from specified path
      PAth [PRI|ALT] [<path>]     Display or modify a path
      SEArch [DIsplay|IPL] [<path>]  Search for boot devices

      COnfiguration menu          Displays or sets boot values
      INformation menu            Displays hardware information
      SERvice menu                Displays service commands

      DIsplay                     Redisplay the current menu
      HElp [<menu>|<command>]     Display help for menu or command
      RESET                       Restart the system
   ----
Main Menu: Enter command or menu >
Main Menu: Enter command or menu > sea

Searching for potential boot device(s)
This may take several minutes.

To discontinue search, press any key (termination may not be immediate).


      Path#  Device Path (dec)   Device Path (mnem)  Device Type
      -----  -----------------   ------------------  -----------
      P0     0/0/1/1.2           intscsib.2          Random access media
      P1     0/0/2/0.2           intscsia.2          Random access media


Main Menu: Enter command or menu > pa

      Primary boot path:    intscsib.2
```

```
                              0/0/1/1.2
                              0/0/01/01.2    (hex)

         Alternate boot path:  intscsia.2
                              0/0/2/0.2
                              0/0/02/0.2     (hex)

         Console path:         0/0/4/0.0
                              0/0/04/0.0     (hex)

         Keyboard path:        0/0/4/0.0
                              0/0/04/0.0     (hex)

      Main Menu: Enter command or menu > bo p0
      Interact with IPL (Y, N, or Cancel)?> y
```

The *SEArch* command shows two potential boot devices; in this case, our two internal disks on two different SCSI buses. The path of the two boot devices is composed of numbers separated by slashes (/), which indicate bus converters, and dots (.), which indicate cards, slot numbers, and addresses. You sometimes end up decoding these paths to figure out what boot devices map to what hardware devices on your system. In our case we have only the two internal disks, one on bus 1 and the other on bus 2.

The *PAth* command shows that the primary boot device is the disk on internal bus 1, and the alternate boot device is the disk on internal bus 2.

When I issued the *BOot* command in the preceding example, I specified a device of *p0,* which corresponds to the disk on internal bus1 shown in the *SEArch* command results. I responded that I did indeed want to interact with IPL, which would normally not be the case when booting the system; however, I want to look briefly at IPL in the upcoming IPL section.

PDC commands issued through BCH are a mystery to many new system administrators. I covered enough in this section to get you comfortable enough on your system to look at the non-intrusive commands, that is, those that supply useful information without changing the settings on your system. Please be careful if you issue commands that change your configuration. Under

man page

pdc - 3

MAIN-CON-CPU

for instance, you can configure and reconfigure processors. You would not want to experiment with this command unless your system is unused and you are free to modify your CPUs.

PDC Commands

man page

pdc - 3

The following is a list of PDC commands available on an N-Class system at the time of this writing. Although an L-Class system was used in the examples in this chapter, the PDC for the L-Class and N-Class are similar. Keep in mind that the PDC commands for your system may be somewhat different than those listed. The PDC is updated occasionally, so the list for the N-Class may also be somewhat different than what is shown in Table 3-4.

TABLE 3-4   List of PDC Commands for N-Class

Command	Explanation
ALL	Display the collection of all information provided by other display commands typically resident in INFORMATION menu.
AUTO	Used to display or set status of AUTOBOOT, AUTOSEARCH, or AUTOSTART flags.
BOOT	Initiate boot sequence.
BOOTID	Display or modify boot *id* for the processors present.
BOOTINFO	Display PDC-level information about the configured parameters used for system boot.
BOOTTIMER	Sets a delay value in the system to wait for external mass storage devices to come on-line.
CACHE	Displays information about the cache memory portion of all installed processors.
CHASSISCODES	Displays a queue of the most recent chassis codes.
CHIPREVISIONS	Used to display the revisions of major Very Large Scale Integration (VLSI) in the system.
CLEARPIM	Used to clear (zero) the contents of the Processor Internal Memory (PIM).
CONFIGURATION	Used to enter the Configuration sub-menu.

Command	Explanation
COPROCESSOR	Displays information about all installed coprocessors.
CPUCONFIG	Allows the user to configure or deconfigure processors in the system.
DEFAULT	Used to set the system to pre-defined defaults.
DISPLAY	Used to redisplay the current menu.
FAN	Used to display or set the speed of system internal fans.
FASTBOOT	Used to display or set the fastboot flag.
FWRVERSION	Displays the revision of currently installed firmware.
HELP	Returns help information for the specified command, menu, or the system itself.
INFORMATION	Used to acess the Information menu.
IO	Displays I/O interface on all I/O modules in the system.
LANADDRESS	Allows the user to display station address.
LANCONFIG	Used to configure the LAN card.
MAIN	User interface for PDC.
MEMORY	Displays memory information for total amount of physical memory as well as configured memory in a system.
MEMREAD	Used to read memory locations.
MONITOR	Allows the user to view and change the monitor type for graphic cards.
PATH	Used to set and/or display the system paths from Stable Storage.
PDT	Display or clear the Page Deallocation Table (PDT).
PIM	Displays Processor Internal Memory (PIM) Information.
PROCESSOR	Displays information about the processor(s) in the system.
RESET	Resets the machine state.
SEARCH	Search for boot devices in the system.
SECURE	Used to display or set the secure mode flag.
SERVICE	Allows the user to go to the Service menu.
TIME	Read or set the real time clock in GMT.
WARNINGS	Display any warning messages that may have resulted from the previous PDC selftest execution.

Initial System Load

man page

isl - 3

As mentioned earlier, the Initial System Loader (ISL) is run after the PDC. You would normally just run an "autoboot" sequence from ISL, however, there are a number of commands you could run from the ISL prompt.

Picking up where we left off in the preceding example, we have chosen to *BOot* off of device *p0* and interact with IPL as shown in the following example:

```
Main Menu: Enter command or menu > bo p0
Interact with IPL (Y, N, or Cancel)?> y

Booting...
Boot IO Dependent Code (IODC) revision 1

HARD Booted.

ISL Revision A.00.38  OCT 26, 1994

ISL> ?
        HELP           Help Facility
        LS             List ISL utilities
        AUTOBOOT       Set or clear autoboot flag in stable storage
        AUTOSEARCH     Set or clear autosearch flag in stable storage
        PRIMPATH       Modify primary boot path in stable storage
        ALTPATH        Modify alternate boot path in stable storage
        CONSPATH       Modify system console path in stable storage
        DISPLAY        Display boot and console paths in stable storage
        LSAUTOFL       List contents of autoboot file
        FASTSIZE       Sets or displays FASTSIZE
        800SUPPORT     Boots the s800 Support Kernel from the boot device
        700SUPPORT     Boot the s700 Support Kernel from the boot device
        READNVM        Displays contents of one word of NVM
        READSS         Displays contents of one word of stable storage
        LSBATCH        List contents of batch file
        BATCH          Execute commands in batch file
        LSEST          List contents of EST (Extended Self Test) file
        EST            Execute commands in EST (Extended Self Test) file

Enter 'LS' to see a list of the ISL utilities.

ISL>
```

Issuing a *?* produces a list of ISL commands that we could issue. Issuing the *DISPLAY* command shows the boot and console paths and *LS* lists the ISL utilities available, as shown in the following example:

```
ISL> display

    Fastsize value is 0000000F

    Autoboot is ON (enabled)

    Autosearch is ON (enabled)

    Primary boot path is 0/0/1/1.2.0.0.0.0.0
    Primary boot path is (hex) 0/0/1/1.2.0.0.0.0.0

    Alternate boot path is 0/0/2/0.2.0.0.0.0.0
    Alternate boot path is (hex) 0/0/2/0.2.0.0.0.0.0

    System console path is 0/0/4/0.0.0.0.0.0.0
    System console path is (hex) 0/0/4/0.0.0.0.0.0.0

ISL> ls

    Utilities on this system are:

filename    type    start    size    created
====================================================
ODE        -12960   584      1216    00/01/21 16:45:48
HPUX       -12928   3480     800     99/10/28 15:23:53

ISL>
```

DISPLAY produced the information we expected based on what we had seen in the preceding section produced by PDC. *LS* produced two utilities available to us: *ODE* and *HPUX*. *ODE* is the Offline Diagnostics Environment. The following example shows listing the *ODE* utilities available on the system by running *ODE*, the *HELP* command to see what commands are available, and *LS* to list the *ODE* utilities:

```
ISL> ode

*****************************************************************
******                                                     ******
******          Offline Diagnostic Environment             ******
******                                                     ******
******   (C) Copyright Hewlett-Packard Co 1993-2000        ******
******              All Rights Reserved                    ******
******                                                     ******
******   HP shall not be liable for any damages resulting from the  ******
******   use of this program.                              ******
******                                                     ******
******              TC  Version A.02.20                    ******
******            SysLib Version A.00.74                   ******
******            Loader Version A.00.59                   ******
******            Mapfile Version A.01.23                  ******
******                                                     ******
*****************************************************************
```

```
Type HELP for command information.
ODE> help

ODE Help

    Basic Commands
    --------------
    HELP -- Prints detailed information to the screen, when "help <command>"
            or "help <var>" is typed
    LS -- List modules available on boot medium
    <Module_Name> -- Load and initialize a module by typing its name
                     (For more help, type "help module_name")
    MENU -- Launch ODE's ease-of-use interface
    RUN -- Run a module (after setting desired environment variables)
    Control-Y|Control-C -- Abort an ODE command; pause a module run
    RESUME -- Restart a paused module
    DISPLOG -- After running a module, display contents of a log
    EXIT -- Return to next higher level prompt

    Environmental Variables
    -----------------------
    SHOWSTATE -- Display the value of the following environment variables:
        LOOP -- Run a test this many times
        ERRPRINT [ON|OFF] -- Print low-level error messages to console
                             (primarily for manufacturing use)
        ERRNUM [ON|OFF] -- Print one-line, numbered errors to the console

Continue ([y]/n)? y

        ERRPAUSE [ON|OFF] -- Pause module upon error detection
        ERRONLY [ON|OFF] -- Print ONLY error messages; disable non-error
                            and isolation message printing
        INFOPRINT [ON|OFF] -- Print informational messages to the console
        ISOPRINT [ON|OFF] -- Print fault isolation messages to the console
        ISOPAUSE [ON|OFF] -- Pause module when isolation message is generated
    LOGSIZE -- Set the size of a message log
    DEFAULT -- Reset environment variables to default state

ODE> ls

        Modules on this boot media are:

filename   type   size   created   description
----------------------------------------------------------------------------
MAPPER2    TM     126    00/01/21  64 bit version of the system mapping ut
IOTEST2    TM     88     00/01/21  64 bit version that runs ROM-based self
PERFVER2   TM     124    00/01/21  64 bit version that runs ROM-based self

ODE>
```

When we ran *ODE* in this example and issued *LS* the three utilities at the end of the example were listed. I always load *ODE* as a part of system installations to help in the event of a possible system hardware problem that an HP CE may need to diagnose.

Next, we'll proceed with the boot process by running the *HPUX* utility:

HPUX Secondary System Loader (hpux)

man page

hpux - 3

man page

isl - 3

As mentioned earlier, the *hpux* utility manages loading the HP-UX kernel and gives control to the kernel. ISL can have hpux run an "autoexecute" file or commands can be given interactively. In most situations you would just want to automatically boot the system, however, in our example so far, we have decided to interact with IPL in the interest of looking at some of the functionality in ISL. We proceed with the boot process by simply issuing the *HPUX* utility name as shown in the following example:

```
ISL> hpux

Boot
: disk(0/0/1/1.2.0.0.0.0.0;0)/stand/vmunix
7094272 + 849200 + 724128 start 0x241068


alloc_pdc_pages: Relocating PDC from 0xf0f0000000 to 0x7f9ab000.
gate64: sysvec_vaddr = 0xc0002000 for 1 pages
NOTICE: nfs3_link(): File system was registered at index 4.
NOTICE: autofs_link(): File system was registered at index 6.

    System Console is on the Built-In Serial Interface
Entering cifs_init...
Initialization finished successfully... slot is 8
Logical volume 64, 0x3 configured as ROOT
Logical volume 64, 0x2 configured as SWAP
Logical volume 64, 0x2 configured as DUMP
    Swap device table:  (start & size given in 512-byte blocks)
        entry 0 - major is 64, minor is 0x2; start = 0, size = 2097152
Starting the STREAMS daemons-phase 1
Checking root file system.
file system is clean - log replay is not required
Root check done.
Create STCP device files
Starting the STREAMS daemons-phase 2
    B2352B/9245XB HP-UX (B.11.00) #1: Wed Nov  5 22:38:19 PST 1997

Memory Information:
    physical page size = 4096 bytes, logical page size = 4096 bytes
    Physical: 2097152 Kbytes, lockable: 1574352 Kbytes, available: 1815496 Kbytes

/sbin/ioinitrc:

/sbin/bcheckrc:
Checking for LVM volume groups and Activating (if any exist)
Volume group "/dev/vg00" has been successfully changed.
vxfs fsck: sanity check: root file system OK (mounted read/write)
Checking hfs file systems
/sbin/fsclean: /dev/vg00/lvol1 (mounted) ok
HFS file systems are OK, not running fsck
Checking vxfs file systems
/dev/vg00/lvol8 :
vxfs fsck: sanity check: /dev/vg00/lvol8 OK
/dev/vg00/lvol3 :
vxfs fsck: sanity check: root file system OK (mounted read/write)
/dev/vg00/lvol4 :
```

```
vxfs fsck: sanity check: /dev/vg00/lvol4 OK
/dev/vg00/lvol5 :
vxfs fsck: sanity check: /dev/vg00/lvol5 OK
/dev/vg00/lvol6 :
vxfs fsck: sanity check: /dev/vg00/lvol6 OK
/dev/vg00/lvol7 :
vxfs fsck: sanity check: /dev/vg00/lvol7 OK


(c)Copyright 1983-1997 Hewlett-Packard Co.,  All Rights Reserved.
(c)Copyright 1979, 1980, 1983, 1985-1993 The Regents of the Univ. of California
(c)Copyright 1980, 1984, 1986 Novell, Inc.
(c)Copyright 1986-1992 Sun Microsystems, Inc.
(c)Copyright 1985, 1986, 1988 Massachusetts Institute of Technology
(c)Copyright 1989-1993  The Open Software Foundation, Inc.
(c)Copyright 1986 Digital Equipment Corp.
(c)Copyright 1990 Motorola, Inc.
(c)Copyright 1990, 1991, 1992 Cornell University
(c)Copyright 1989-1991 The University of Maryland
(c)Copyright 1988 Carnegie Mellon University
(c)Copyright 1991-1997 Mentat, Inc.
(c)Copyright 1996 Morning Star Technologies, Inc.
(c)Copyright 1996 Progressive Systems, Inc.
(c)Copyright 1997 Isogon Corporation


                     RESTRICTED RIGHTS LEGEND
Use, duplication, or disclosure by the U.S. Government is subject to
restrictions as set forth in sub-paragraph (c)(1)(ii) of the Rights in
Technical Data and Computer Software clause in DFARS 252.227-7013.


                 Hewlett-Packard Company
                 3000 Hanover Street
                 Palo Alto, CA 94304 U.S.A.

Rights for non-DOD U.S. Government Departments and Agencies are as set
forth in FAR 52.227-19(c)(1,2).

     .
     .
     .
Console Login:
```

I abbreviated this listing where the three dots appear before the *Console Login:* prompt.

man page

hpux - 3

We have a number of options we can issue with the *HPUX* utility. The manual page at the end of this chapter describes several options in detail. Table 3-5 is a list of examples of some common *HPUX* utility booting options, some of which are from the man page:

TABLE 3-5   hpux Examples

Command (all at *ISL>* prompt)	Comments
Automatic Boot	No interaction - autoboot sequence.
hpux -is	Bring up system at run level *s* for single-user mode.
hpux	Default boot sequence from **autoexecute** normally object file is **/stand/vmuinx**.
hpux vmunix.test	Boot object file **vmunix.test**.
hpux (52.5.0.0) /stand/vmunix	Boot from **/stand/vmunix** on the disk at the path *52.5.0.0*.
hpux lan(32) /stand/vmunix	Boot from LAN.
hpux -v	Get HP-UX version numbers..
hp-ux ll /stand	List contents of **/stand** on root disk.

man page

hpux - 3

The part of the boot that takes place after the **hpux** command is issued is in the four following parts:

1. HP-UX initializes the system hardware and devices - The HP-UX kernel locates and initializes system hardware such as memory, I/O busses and devices, and so on. Kernel device drivers are associated with I/O devices at this time. You see many messages fly-by on the system console as this process is taking place.

2. HP-UX kernel data structures are created and initialized - There are many tables for system processes and memory, file systems, and so on, that are created. You also see the status of this part of the boot on the system console.

3. HP-UX searches for the root file system - The base file system contains critical system files and is usually found on the disk from which HP-UX boots. Many commands are run as part of this process.

4. HP-UX starts the init process called **/sbin/init** - The init process, which has an ID of one, starts all other processes on the system. The init process reads **/etc/inittab** for direction. There is a detailed description of the contents of **/etc/inittab** in Chapter 7.

I encourage you to issue some of the PDC, ISL, and hpux utility commands covered earlier, especially those that do not modify your system in any way but only provide information about the system.

The next section covers configuring the Secure Web Console.

Secure Web Console

You have a choice concerning the type of console to use with your HP 9000. You can connect a terminal to the console port or use a browser and the Secure Web Console (there is also a LAN console port available on systems as another alternative). There is also a console consolidation solution that supports up to 224 consoles that I won't cover here. The Secure Web Console is a device that connects to the HP 9000 console port that has a built-in Web server that allows you to use your browser as a console. This means that from one system running a browser, you can open up several windows that are the console screens for different HP 9000 systems. This obviates the need to walk from console to console when you want to perform system administration functions - you can sit at one system running a browser and administrate many systems.

In this section, I'll cover configuring a Secure Web Console and include several screen shots so that you can decide whether you prefer the Secure Web Console or a dedicated terminal as a console.

You can download the document that describes the procedure of installing and configuring the Secure Web Console from http://docs.hp.com/hpux/content/swc_inst/config.html at the time of this writing. I'll provide an example of a configuration in this section.

Connecting and Configuring the Secure Web Console

The Secure Web Console is a device that is connected to the console port on your HP 9000 and to your LAN. On an L-Class system, for instance, slot 2 has in it a Core I/O card that includes a LAN console port and a connector for the UPS and console - the serial port on the Secure Web Console is plugged into this console cable. There is also a networking port on the Secure Web Console so that you can connect it to your LAN. Figure 3-2 depicts the general setup of the Secure Web Console:

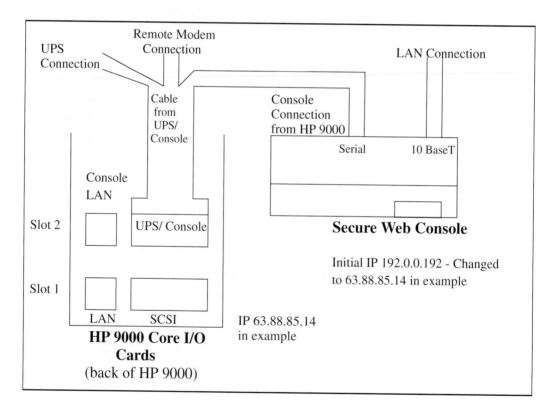

Figure 3-2 Secure Web Console Connectivity on L-Class Used in Upcoming Example

Keep in mind that the HP 9000 connections on your system may differ from what is shown in the figure. The cable connected to the UPS/Console port turns into the three connections shown in Figure 1-1. The Secure Web Console connects to the rightmost of the three connectors when facing the back of the computer on my system. Its other connection is a networking connection to the LAN. The Secure Web Console also has its own power source so that you can connect to it from your browser even when the computer is powered off.

The Secure Web Console has a default IP address of 192.0.0.192. This address is assigned so that you can connect to the Secure Web Console upon installation and reconfigure it.

With the hardware connections complete, we'll proceed to set up the system running a browser and connect to the Secure Web Console using the following steps:

Disable Proxies   Assuming that you are running a supported version of a browser, you want to "Disable Proxies" or use "No Proxies" until the Secure Web Console configuration is complete.

Add a Route   Use the following command to add a route from the computer where your browser is running to the Secure Web Console:

route add 192.0.0.192 63.88.95.15

In this example the computer on which I'm running my browser has an IP address of 63.88.95.15.

Check Connection Use the **ping** command to check the connection between the computer running the browser and the default IP address of the Secure Web Console:

ping 192.0.0.192

Use **arp**

If you did not receive a response using **ping** you may have to use **arp** as shown below for a PC and UNIX system:

PC: **arp -s 192.0.0.192 00-10-83-fa-3f-11**

UNIX: **arp -s 192.0.0.192 00: 10: 83: fa: 3f: 11**

I have not had to use the **arp** command in my configurations, however, the document at the URL earlier mentioned recommends the **arp** command if indeed your **ping** fails. Re-issue the **ping** command after using **arp** to check your connection. The -*s* option is for a static **arp**.

Web Browser

With a successful **ping** you can now access the Secure Web Console through your browser.

Figure 3-3 shows the steps I performed. You can see **route** and **ping** on my PC at the command line to get access to the Secure Web Console:

```
Command Prompt                                                    _ □ ✕
Microsoft(R) Windows NT(TM)
(C) Copyright 1985-1996 Microsoft Corp.

D:\>ping 192.0.0.192

Pinging 192.0.0.192 with 32 bytes of data:

Destination host unreachable.
Destination host unreachable.
Destination host unreachable.
Destination host unreachable.

D:\>route add 192.0.0.192 63.88.85.15

D:\>ping 192.0.0.192

Pinging 192.0.0.192 with 32 bytes of data:

Reply from 192.0.0.192: bytes=32 time=10ms TTL=255
Reply from 192.0.0.192: bytes=32 time<10ms TTL=255
Reply from 192.0.0.192: bytes=32 time<10ms TTL=255
Reply from 192.0.0.192: bytes=32 time<10ms TTL=255

D:\>
```

Figure 3-3 **route** and **ping** with Secure Web Console

This screen shot does not show the "disable proxies" step I performed prior to the commands issued at the prompt.

Note: I sometimes configure the Secure Web Console by connecting a crossover LAN cable from the Secure Web Console directly to my laptop computer. After I have completed the initial configuration steps, I connect the Secure Web Console to the LAN and use a desktop system to access it with a browser. The connection to my portable is only a temporary connection in order to configure the Secure Web Console with its final IP address.

With a connection having been established and the browser properly configured on my computer (proxy server was earlier disabled), I can use the browser to connect to the Web server on the Secure Web Console. You must be on the same subnet for this to work in most situations. Figure 3-4 is a screen shot showing that I specified the preconfigured IP address of the Secure Web Console with http:// 192.0.0.192:

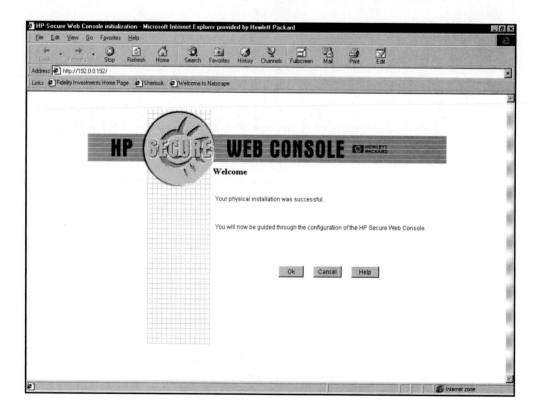

Figure 3-4 Initial Secure Web Console Screen

The "Welcome" screen confirms that we performed the necessary configuration to make our initial connection to the Secure Web Console. After you select "OK" on this screen, you can proceed with the configuration of the Secure Web Console.

The next screen (Figure 3-5) shows the initial information related to the Secure Web Console for which you will be prompted when you select "OK". This information is for an administrator of the Secure Web Console, not for the HP 9000. In the upcoming examples, I zoom in so you that can see the Secure Web Console information more clearly. The browser information is not shown in the figures, but it is insignificant as far as the Secure Web Console configuration is concerned from this point foward.

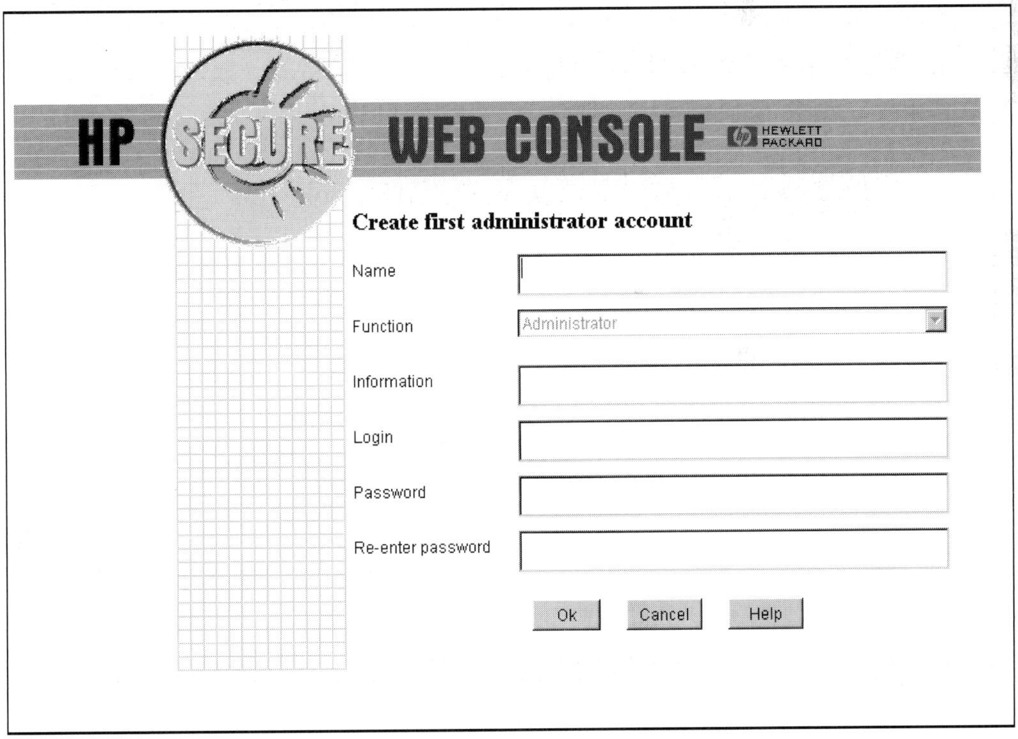

Figure 3-5 Secure Web Console Screen for First Administrator Account

After adding all of this information, you have configured the initial administrator account. As we'll see later, you can add subsequent administrator and operator accounts to the Secure Web Console.

The next screen (Figure 3-6) shows the network-related configuration we'll make to the Secure Web Console. Since it came with a pre-configured IP address, we'll now assign the dedicated IP address for the device.

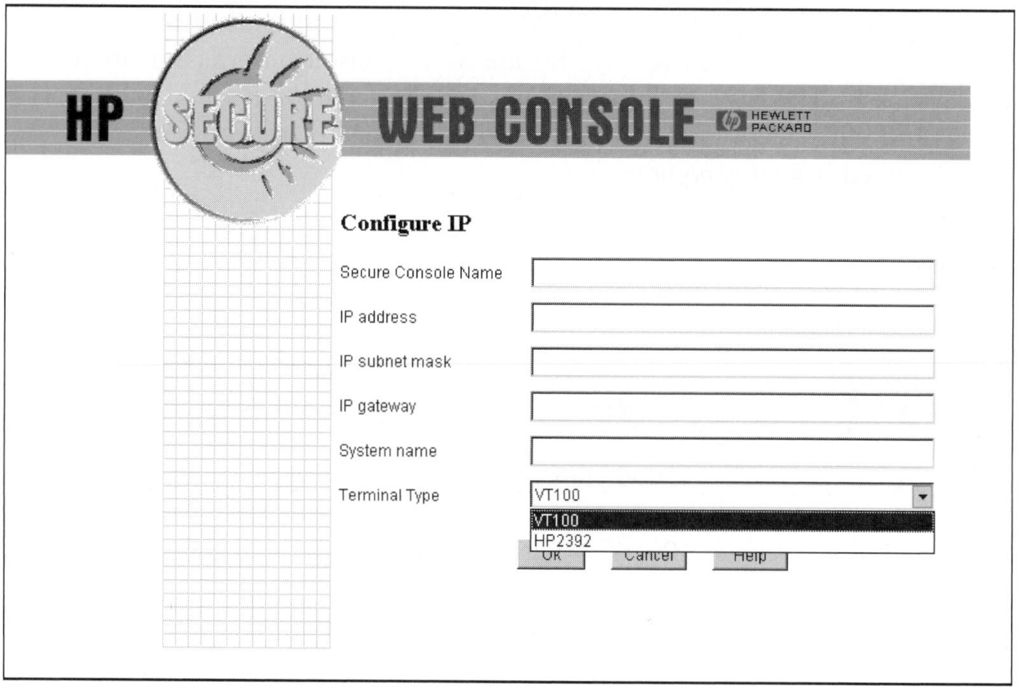

Figure 3-6   Secure Web Console Screen to Configure Final IP Address

In Figure 3-6 I show the two types of terminals that you can select. In this "Configure IP" screen, you'll enter both a name for the Secure Web Console and the computer to which it is connected. All of the IP-related information is entered in this screen as well. The Secure Web Console requires a dedicated IP address because you connect directly to it to make a console connection to the HP 9000.

When all of the information has been added, we select "OK" on this screen and are shown the following message in Figure 3-7:

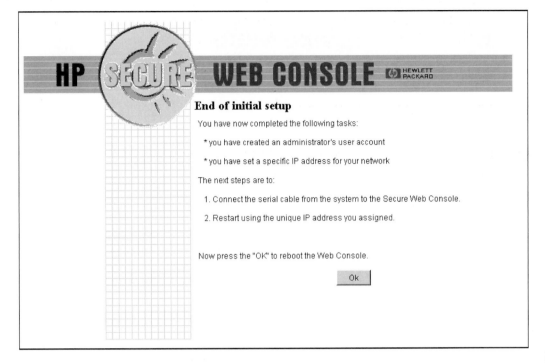

Figure 3-7   Initial Secure Web Console Setup Complete

After we select "OK" in Figure 1-6, we can reconnect to the Secure Web Console using the IP address we assigned to it during the configuration. In our case, we would use http://15.88.85.14 to reconnect ,as shown in Figure 3-8:

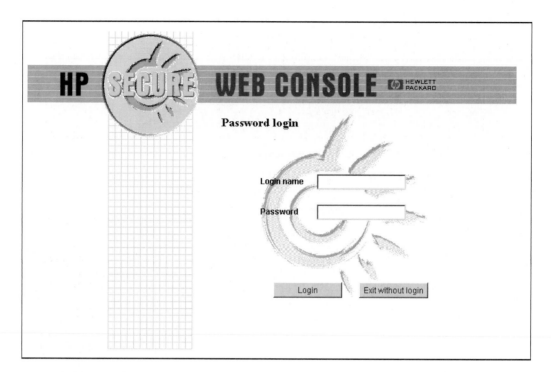

Figure 3-8   Secure Web Console Login Screen

We log in with the name and password we earlier defined for the Secure Web Console administrator and are then connected as shown in Figure 3-9:

Figure 3-9 Secure Web Console Menu

At this point, you can select from a number of Secure Web Console-related functions to perform, such as configuring additional users, or you can access the console on your HP 9000, which is the purpose of connecting the device. The *Access console* selection gives us the console of the HP 9000, as shown in Figure 3-10:

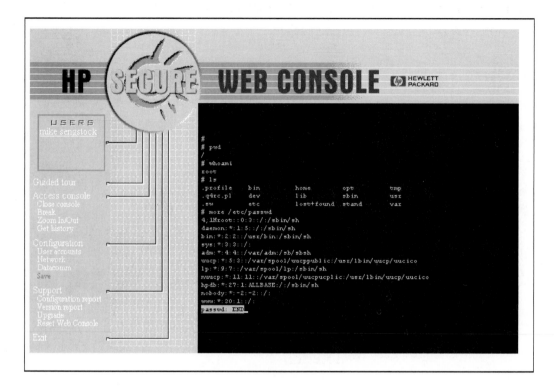

Figure 3-10   Initial Secure Web Console Screen

Notice that we are logged in as root when we select *Access console*. You could use the Secure Web Console menu to configure additional administrators and operators (we configured only one administrator in our example and no operators) to give multiple users access to your HP 9000 through the Secure Web Console.

The Secure Web Console can be a good alternative to using a dedicated console on each HP 9000. I wanted to provide you with the basic information for configuring the Secure Web Console, the URL for the configuration document, and an overview of the product to help you determine if it is right for your environment.

Configuring the Guardian Service Processor (GSP)

The Guardian Service Processor (GSP) is a built-in processor on most HP 9000 systems, such as the L-Class and N-Class, that can be used for either local or remote system administration functions. I won't cover the use of the GSP, but I will cover its initial configuration. The initial configuration is important because the first person to gain access to the GSP before it has been configured is a GSP administrator by default.

You gain access to the GSP with ^b (control b). If the GSP has not been configured, anyone who gets access to the console can type ^b and gain access to the system. I recommend that you perform GSP configuration as soon as possible after installing your system.

The following example shows issuing a ^b, which results in the *GSP>* prompt, and issuing **he** for help:

```
Service Processor login:
Service Processor password:



        Hewlett-Packard Guardian Service Processor

        9000/800/L2000-44 System Name: uninitialized

GSP Host Name:  uninitialized
GSP>



GSP Host Name:  uninitialized
GSP> he


HE
        Hardware Revision 8  Firmware Revision  A.01.06  Aug  2 1999,11:38:47
AC : Alert Display Configuration        PC : Remote Power Control
AR : Config. Automatic System Restart   PS : Power Management Module status
CA : Configure serial port parameters   RP : Reset password configuration
CE : Log repair info in history buffer  RS : System reset through RST signal
CL : Display console history            SDM: Set Display Mode (hex or text)
CO : Return to Console Mode             SE : Activate a system session
DC : Default configuration              SL : Display SPU status logs
DI : Disconnect remote or LAN console   SO : Security options & access control
DR : Disable remote or LAN console      SS : System's processor status
ER : Enable remote or LAN console       TC : System reset through INIT signal
HE : Display the available commands     TE : Sends a message to other terminals
IT : Modify GSP inactivity timeouts     VFP: Activates Alert Log Display
LC : Configure LAN console              WHO: Display list of GSP connected users
LS : Display LAN console status         XD : GSP Diagnostics and Reset
```

```
MR : Modem Reset                    XU : Upgrade the GSP Firmware
MS : Display the status of the Modem

GSP Host Name:  uninitialized
GSP>
```

You can see that in order to log in after the ^b was issued, neither a login name nor a password were required. This is because GSP users have not yet been configured, so anyone can get access to this menu with ^b at the system console.

There are several commands here to which you don't want unauthorized users to have access, so the first step we'll take is to set up security with **SO**:

```
GSP> so


SO

This command allow you to modify the security options and access control.

GSP wide parameters are:
  . Login Timeout: 1  minutes.
  . Number of Password Faults allowed: 3
  . Flow Control Timeout: 5  minutes.

Do you want to modify the GSP wide parameters? (Y/[N])


User number 1 parameters are:
  . User's Name:
  . User's Login:
  . Organization's Name:
  . Dial-back configuration: Disabled
  . Access Level: Operator
  . Mode: Single
  . User's state: Disabled

Do you want to modify the user number 1 parameters? (Y/[N]/Q to quit) :
```

From this menu you can change GSP-wide parameters and establish GSP users. The first user added the first time you enter this screen will be the GSP system administrator. This is the user you want to set initially so your system is secure. You can add one administrator and 19 users. This is an important step since users will now have to add a username and password to gain access to GSP. The user information you add is shown in the preceding listing and is self-explanatory.

In addition to configuring users, there are many useful features of GSP, so I encourage you to experiment with it. One feature I often use is to issue **CL** to display a console history as shown in the following listing for the L-Class system used throughout the examples in this chapter:

```
GSP> cl

CL


Firmware Version  39.46

Duplex Console IO Dependent Code (IODC) revision 1

-------------------------------------------------------------------------------
     (c) Copyright 1995-1998, Hewlett-Packard Company, All rights reserved
-------------------------------------------------------------------------------

   Processor   Speed              State       CoProcessor State  Cache Size
   Number                                     State             Inst    Data
   ---------   --------   ------------------- -----------------  ------------
       0       440  MHz   Active              Functional         512 KB   1 MB
       3       440  MHz   Idle                Functional         512 KB   1 MB

   Central Bus Speed (in MHz)   :        82
   Available Memory             :   2097152  KB
   Good Memory Required         :     11468  KB

Press Q/q to quit, Enter to continue:

   Primary boot path:     0/0/1/1.2
   Alternate boot path:   0/0/2/0.2
   Console path:          0/0/4/0.0
   Keyboard path:         0/0/4/0.0

WARNING:  The non-destructive test bit was set, so memory was not tested
          destructively.  Information only, no action required.


Processor is booting from first available device.

To discontinue, press any key within 10 seconds.

10 seconds expired.
Proceeding...

Trying Primary Boot Path
------------------------
Booting...
Boot IO Dependent Code (IODC) revision 1


Press Q/q to quit, Enter to continue:

HARD Booted.

ISL Revision A.00.38  OCT 26, 1994

ISL booting  hpux

Boot
: disk(0/0/1/1.2.0.0.0.0.0;0)/stand/vmunix
6340608 + 821576 + 695024 start 0x210ce8
```

```
alloc_pdc_pages: Relocating PDC from 0xf0f0000000 to 0x7f9ab000.
gate64: sysvec_vaddr = 0xc0002000 for 1 pages
Unexpected interrupt on EIRR bit 32
NOTICE: autofs_link(): File system was registered at index 3.
NOTICE: nfs3_link(): File system was registered at index 5.


    System Console is on the Built-In Serial Interface
Logical volume 64, 0x3 configured as ROOT
Logical volume 64, 0x2 configured as SWAP
Logical volume 64, 0x2 configured as DUMP
    Swap device table:  (start & size given in 512-byte blocks)
        entry 0 - major is 64, minor is 0x2; start = 0, size = 2097152
Starting the STREAMS daemons-phase 1
Checking root file system.
log replay in progress
replay complete - marking super-block as CLEAN
Root check done.
Create STCP device files
Starting the STREAMS daemons-phase 2
    B2352B/9245XB HP-UX (B.11.00) #1: Wed Nov  5 22:38:19 PST 1997

Memory Information:
    physical page size = 4096 bytes, logical page size = 4096 bytes

    Physical: 2097152 Kbytes, lockable: 1575156 Kbytes, available: 1816368 Kbyts

/sbin/ioinitrc:
/dev/vg00/lvol1: 34 files, 0 icont, 25716 used, 173665 free (81 frags, 21698 bl)

/sbin/bcheckrc:
Checking for LVM volume groups and Activating (if any exist)
Volume group "/dev/vg00" has been successfully changed.
Activated volume group
Volume group "/dev/vg01" has been successfully changed.
Resynchronized volume group /dev/vg00
Resynchronized volume group /dev/vg01
vxfs fsck: sanity check: root file system OK (mounted read/write)
Checking hfs file systems
/sbin/fsclean: /dev/vg00/lvol1 (mounted) ok
HFS file systems are OK, not running fsck

Checking vxfs file systems
/dev/vg00/lvol8 :
vxfs fsck: sanity check: /dev/vg00/lvol8 needs checking
log replay in progress
replay complete - marking super-block as CLEAN
/dev/vg01/lvol09 :
vxfs fsck: sanity check: /dev/vg01/lvol09 needs checking
log replay in progress
replay complete - marking super-block as CLEAN
/dev/vg00/lvol3 :
vxfs fsck: sanity check: root file system OK (mounted read/write)
/dev/vg00/lvol4 :
vxfs fsck: sanity check: /dev/vg00/lvol4 needs checking
log replay in progress
replay complete - marking super-block as CLEAN
/dev/vg00/lvol5 :
vxfs fsck: sanity check: /dev/vg00/lvol5 needs checking
log replay in progress
replay complete - marking super-block as CLEAN
/dev/vg00/lvol6 :
vxfs fsck: sanity check: /dev/vg00/lvol6 needs checking
log replay in progress
replay complete - marking super-block as CLEAN
/dev/vg00/lvol7 :
vxfs fsck: sanity check: /dev/vg00/lvol7 needs checking
log replay in progress
replay complete - marking super-block as CLEAN
```

```
/sbin/auto_parms: DHCP access is disabled (see /etc/auto_parms.log)

/sbin/rc: failed to read row and column info from screen

    HP-UX Start-up in progress
    ─────────────────────────

    Configure system crash dumps ............................. OK
    Mount file systems ....................................... OK
    Update kernel and loadable modules ....................... N/A
    Initialize loadable modules .............................. N/A
    Setting hostname ......................................... OK
    Set privilege group ...................................... N/A
    Display date ............................................. N/A
    Save system crash dump if needed ......................... N/A
    Enable auxiliary swap space .............................. OK
    Start syncer daemon ...................................... OK
    Configure HP Fibre Channel interfaces .................... OK
    Configure Loopback interfaces (lo0) ...................... OK
    Start Software Distributor agent daemon .................. OK
    Configuring all unconfigured software filesets ........... OK
    Recover editor crash files ............................... OK
    Clean UUCP ............................................... OK
    List and/or clear temporary files ........................ N/A
    Clean up old log files ................................... OK
    Start system message logging daemon ...................... OK
    Start pty allocator daemon ............................... OK
    Start network tracing and logging daemon ................. OK
    Configure HP Ethernet interfaces ......................... OK
    Configure HP 100BT interfaces ............................ OK
    Configure HP SPP 100BT interfaces ........................ N/A
    Configure LAN interfaces ................................. OK
    Start name server daemon ................................. N/A
    Start NFS core subsystem ................................. OK
    Start NIS+ server subsystem .............................. OK
    Start NIS+ client subsystem .............................. OK
    Start NIS server subsystem ............................... OK
    Start NIS client subsystem ............................... OK
    Start NFS client subsystem ............................... OK
    Start the Trusted Mode with Nis+ subsystem ............... N/A
    Configure pseudo devices for MAC/LLA access .............. OK
    Start multicast routing daemon ........................... N/A
    Start Internet services daemon ........................... OK
    Start dynamic routing daemon ............................. N/A
    Start router discover protocol daemon .................... N/A
    Configuring PPP Interface ................................ OK
    Start RARP protocol daemon ............................... N/A
    Start remote system status daemon ........................ N/A
```

```
Configuring man pages for Internet Services ............... OK
Starting mail daemon ....................................... OK
Starting outbound connection daemons for DDFA software .... N/A
Start SNMP Master Network Management daemon ............... OK
Start OSPF MIB Network Management subAgent ................ N/A
Start SNMP HP-UNIX Network Management subAgent ............ OK
Start SNMP MIB-2 Network Management subAgent .............. OK
Start SNMP Trap Dest Network Management subAgent .......... OK
Start DCE daemons ......................................... N/A
Start RPC daemon if needed ................................ OK
Start the Isogon License Server daemon .................... N/A
Start remote boot daemon .................................. OK
Starting X Font Server at TCP port 7000 ................... OK
Start vt daemon ........................................... OK
Start time synchronization ................................ N/A
Start accounting .......................................... N/A
Starting the password/group assist subsystem ............. OK
Starting HP Disk Array Manager daemons. .................. OK
Starting disk array monitor daemons. ..................... OK
Start print spooler ....................................... N/A
Starting HP Distributed Print Service .................... OK
Start clock daemon ........................................ OK
Support Tools Informational Fileset ....................... OK
Start environment monitoring daemon ...................... OK
Start auditing subsystem .................................. N/A
Start audio server daemon ................................. N/A
Start Distributed Single Logical Screen daemon ........... OK
SAM System administration configuration .................. OK
Reinitialize Software Distributor agent daemon ........... OK
Configure HP Fibre Channel Mass Storage interfaces ....... OK
Start NFS server subsystem ................................ OK
Start X print server(s) ................................... N/A
Starting ColdFusion Application Server ................... OK
Start CDE login server .................................... OK


The system is ready.

GenericSysName [HP Release B.11.00] (see /etc/issue)
Console Login:
************************10/100 Mb/s LAN/9000 Networking********************@#%
Fri May 26 EDT 2000 15:43:26.401827  DISASTER      Subsys:BASE100     Loc:00000
<6001> HPCORE 10/100BASE-T driver detected bad cable connection between
     the adapter in slot 0 and the hub or switch.
~~~~~~~~~~~~~~~~~~~~~~~~~~~~~~~~~~~~~~~~~~~~~~~~~~~~~~~~~~~~~~~~~~~~~~~~~~~~~~~~~

************************10/100 Mb/s LAN/9000 Networking********************@#%
Fri May 26 EDT 2000 17:18:31.401884  DISASTER      Subsys:BASE100     Loc:00000
<6001> HPCORE 10/100BASE-T driver detected bad cable connection between
     the adapter in slot 0 and the hub or switch.
~~~~~~~~~~~~~~~~~~~~~~~~~~~~~~~~~~~~~~~~~~~~~~~~~~~~~~~~~~~~~~~~~~~~~~~~~~~~~~~~~

GenericSysName [HP Release B.11.00] (see /etc/issue)
Console Login: root
Password:
```

This listing shows a smooth boot; however, there are often boot-related problems you may encounter and you can produce this listing with ^b anytime to review the sequence of events that took place at the time of boot.

You can obtain the status of power modules with **ps** as shown in the following listing:

```
GSP> ps
```

```
PS

Power Monitor Status:
Temperature      : Normal     Over temperature: Enable
Power Switch     : ON         Soft power       : Disable
Global fan state: Normal      System power state: On

              Power supplies      | Fan
  #   State          Type         | States
-----------------------------------------------------------------
  0   Normal         1220 Watt    | Normal
  1   Normal         1220 Watt    | Normal
  2   Not Installed    -          | Normal
  3     -              -          | Normal
  4     -              -          | Normal
  5     -              -          | Normal
  6     -              -          | Normal
  7     -              -          | Normal


GSP Host Name:  uninitialized
GSP>
```

This shows that we have two power supplies installed and a third
is not installed.

You can view processor status with **ss** as shown in the following
listing:

```
GSP> ss

SS

System Processor Status:

    Monarch Processor: 0

    Processor 0 is : Installed and Configured
    Processor 1 is : Not Installed
    Processor 2 is : Not Installed
    Processor 3 is : Installed and Configured


GSP Host Name:  uninitialized
GSP>
```

After you have completed your GSP-related work you can return
to console mode from the GSP prompt simply by issuing **co** as shown
in the following listing:

```
GSP> co


CO

Leaving Guardian Service Processor Command Interface and entering
Console mode. Type Ctrl-B to reactivate the GSP Command Interface.


GenericSysName [HP Release B.11.00] (see /etc/issue)
Console Login:
```

Anytime you are on the console, you can issue ^b and get access to GSP to issue any GSP commands and then get back to console mode with **co**.

The following is a list of GSP commands available on an N-Class system at the time of this writing. Although an L-Class system was used in the examples in this chapter, the GSP for the L-Class and N-Class are similar. Keep in mind that the GSP commands for your system may be somewhat different than those listed. GSP is updated occassionally, so the list for the N-Class may also be somewhat different than what is shown in Table 3-6.

TABLE 3-6   List of GSP Commands for N-Class

Command (Function)	Explanation
AR (Config)	Configure the Automatic System Restart.
CA (Config)	Configure Asynchronous and Modem parameters.
CE (Chassis Codes)	Log a chassis code in the SAS chassis code history.
CL (Console)	Display console history.
CO (Console)	Return to console mode.

Command (Function)	Explanation
DC (Config)	Default configuration.
DI (Remote)	Disconnect remote or LAN console.
DR (Remote)	Disable remote or LAN console access.
ER (Remote)	Enable remote or LAN console access.
HE (Help)	Display the list of available commands.
IT (Admin)	Modify SAS inactivity timeouts.
LC (Config)	Configure LAN connected and PPP console.
LR (Paging)	Reserve modem for paging.
LS (Console)	Display LAN connected and PPP console status.
MR (Remote)	Modem Reset.
MS (Remote)	Display the status of the modem.
PC (Remote)	Remote power control.
PG (Paging)	Configure Paging.
PS (Status)	Display the status of the power.
RP (Reset)	System reset through RST signal.
SE (Session)	Activate a system session on local or remote port. (One session/remote and local console.)
SL (Status)	Display SPU status logs.
SO (Admin)	Configure security options and access control.
SS (Reset)	Display the status of the system processors.

Command (Function)	Explanation
TC (Session)	System reset through INIT signal.
TE (Admin)	Sends a message to other terminals.
TN (Session)	Start a Telnet session on local or remote port.
UR (Remote)	Unlock remote support modem access.
VSC (Config)	Configure the Virtual Front Panel display.
VFD (Chassis Codes)	Activates the immediate display of the Virtual Front Panel.
WHO (Admin)	Display a list of SAS connected users.
XD	SAS Diagnostics and Reset.
XU	Upgrade the GSP firmware.
ZTOGCCD (Chassis Codes)	DEBUG feature: Change the way the chassis codes are displayed by SL command and VFPD.

Manual Pages for Commands Used in Chapter 3

The following section contains copies of the manual pages for commands used in Chapter 3. This makes a quick reference for you to use when issuing the commands commonly used during your system administration day. The manual pages, more commonly referred to as man pages, are listed in full detail.

boot

boot - Bootstrap process overview.

```
boot(1M)                        Series 700/800 Only                    boot(1M)

NAME
     boot - bootstrap process

DESCRIPTION
     The Series 700 and 800 bootstrap process involves the execution of
     three software components:

          -  pdc (see pdc(1M),

          -  isl (see isl(1M), and

          -  hpux (see hpux_800(1M)).

     After the processor is RESET, pdc, the processor-dependent code
     (firmware), performs a self-test and initializes the processor.  It
     then loads and transfers control to isl, the operating-system-
     independent initial system loader.  isl, in turn, loads and transfers
     control to the hpux utility, the HP-UX-specific bootstrap loader.
     hpux then downloads the HP-UX kernel object file from an HP-UX file
     system and transfers control to the loaded kernel image.

SEE ALSO
     hpux(1M), hpux_800(1M), isl(1M), pdc(1M).
```

hpux

hpux - Boot HP-UX operating system.

hpux(1M)   hpux(1M)

NAME
     hpux - HP-UX bootstrap

SYNOPSIS
     hpux [-F] [-lm] [-a[C|R|S|D] devicefile] [-fnumber] [-istring] [boot]
     [devicefile]
     hpux ll [devicefile] (same as hpux ls -aFln)
     hpux ls [-aFiln] [devicefile]
     hpux set autofile devicefile string
     hpux show autofile [devicefile]
     hpux -v
     hpux restore devicefile (Series 700 only; see DEPENDENCIES.)

DESCRIPTION
     hpux is the HP-UX specific secondary system loader (SSL) utility for
     bootstrap (see isl(1M) for the initial system loader). It supports
     the operations summarized below, as shown in the SYNOPSIS and detailed
     later in this DESCRIPTION.

         boot   Loads an object file from an HP-UX file
                                 system or raw device and transfers control
                                 to the loaded image. (Note, the boot
                                 operation is position dependent).

         ll   Lists the contents of HP-UX directories in
                                 a format similar to ls -aFln. (See ls(1);
                                 ls only works on a local disk with a HFS
                                 file system).

         ls   Lists the contents of HP-UX directories.
                                 (See ls(1); ls only works on a local disk
                                 with a HFS file system).

         show autofile   Displays the contents of the autoexecute
                                 file.

         set autofile   Changes the contents of the autoexecute
                                 file to that specified by string.

         -v   Displays the release and version numbers of
                                 the hpux utility.

         restore   Recovers the system from a properly
                                 formatted bootable tape. (Series 700
                                 specific; see DEPENDENCIES.)

     hpux commands can be given interactively from the keyboard, or
     provided in an isl autoexecute file.

     hpux is limited to operations on the interface initialized by pdc(1M).
     In most cases, operations are limited to the boot device interface.

Notation
    hpux accepts numbers (numeric constants) in many of its options.
    Numbers follow the C language notation for decimal, octal, and
    hexadecimal constants. A leading 0 (zero) implies octal and a leading
    0x or 0X implies hexadecimal. For example, 037, 0x1F, 0X1f, and 31
    all represent the same number, decimal 31.

    hpux boot, ll, ls, set autofile, show autofile, and restore operations
    accept devicefile specifications, which have the following format:

        manager(w/x.y.z;n)filename

    The devicefiles specification is comprised of a device name and a file
    name. The device name (manager(w/x.y.z;n)), consists of a generic
    name of an I/O system manager (device or interface driver) such as
    disc, a hardware path to the device, and minor number. The manager
    name can be omitted entirely if the default is used. w/x.y.z is the
    physical hardware path to the device, identifying bus converters, slot
    numbers, and hardware addresses. For Series 700 machines, there are a
    set of mnemonics that can be used instead of the hardware paths. The
    n is the minor number that controls manager-dependent functionality.
    The file name part, filename, is a standard HP-UX path name. Some
    hpux operations have defaults for particular components. A devicefile
    specification containing a device part only specifies a raw device. A
    devicefile specification containing a file name implies that the
    device contains an HP-UX file system, and that the filename resides in
    that file system.

    A typical boot devicefile specification is

        disc(2/4.0.0;0)/stand/vmunix

    The manager is disc, the hardware path to the disk device is 2/4.0.0,
    the minor number shown as 0 by default, and the /stand/vmunix is the
    filename for the boot device.

    hpux now supports a consolidated list of managers: disc, tape, and
    lan. The manager disc manages all CS/80 disks connected via HP-IB
    (formerly disc0); CS/80 disks connected via the HP27111 interface
    (formerly disc2); CS/80 disks connected via NIO HP-IB (formerly
    disc1); all disks connected via SCSI, (formerly disc3), and all
    autochanger disk devices (formerly disc30). The manager lan manages
    remote boot through the HP28652A NIO based LAN interface (formerly
    lan1). Remote boot is currently supported on this card only and not
    on any CIO-based LAN card. The manager tape manages the HP7974,
    HP7978, and HP7980 tape drives via HP-IB (formerly tape1) and tape
    drives via SCSI (formerly tape2).

    The hardware path in a devicefile specification is a string of
    numbers, each suffixed by slash, (/), followed by a string of numbers
    separated by dots (.), each number identifying a hardware component
    notated sequentially from the bus address to the device address. A
    hardware component suffixed by a slash indicates a bus converter and
    may not be necessary on your machine. For example, in w/x.y.z w is
    the address of the bus converter, x is the address of the MID-BUS
    module, y is the CIO slot number, and z is the HP-IB address or
    HP27111 bus address.

    The minor number, n, in a devicefile specification controls driver-
    dependent functionality. (See the manual, Configuring HP-UX for
    Peripherals, for minor-number bit assignments of specific drivers).

    File names are standard HP-UX path names. No preceding slash (/) is
    necessary and specifying one will not cause problems.

Defaults

Default values chosen by hpux to complete a command are obtained through a sequence of steps. First, any components of the command specified explicitly are used. If the command is not complete, hpux attempts to construct defaults from information maintained by pdc (see pdc(1M)). If sufficient information to complete the command is unavailable, the autoexecute file is searched. If the search fails, any remaining unresolved components of the command are satisfied by hard-coded defaults.

There is no hard-coded default choice for a manager; if none can be chosen, hpux reports an error.

When the hardware path to the boot device is not specified, hpux defaults to information maintained by pdc. The hardware path element has no hard-coded default.

If the minor number element is not supplied, hpux takes its default from the autoexecute file. Failing that, the hard-coded default of 0 is used.

For the boot command, a devicefile specification without a file name indicates that the boot device does not contain an HP-UX file system. hpux interprets this as a NULL (instead of missing) file name and does not search for a default. If the entire devicefile specification is missing, hpux searches for a default; either the autoexecute file contents or the hard-coded default is chosen.

There are two possible hard-coded default devicefile specifications. One hard-coded default devicefile specification is /vmunix. The other hard-coded default devicefile specification is /stand/vmunix.

If you have a LVM system where the boot volume and the root volume are on different logical volumes, the kernel would be /vmunix. This is because the boot volume will be mounted under /stand when the system is up.

For all other configurations, the kernel would be /stand/vmunix.

The search order for the hard-coded defaults is /stand/vmunix and then /vmunix.

boot Operation

The boot operation loads an object file from an HP-UX file system or raw device as specified by the optional devicefile. It then transfers control to the loaded image.

Any missing components in a specified devicefile are supplied with a default. For example, a devicefile of vmunix.new would actually yield:

        disc(8.0.0;0)vmunix.new

and a devicefile of (8.0.1)/stand/vmunix, for booting from the disk at HP-IB address 1, would yield

        disc(8.0.1;0)/stand/vmunix

Regardless of how incomplete the specified devicefile may be, boot announces the complete devicefile specification used to find the object file. Along with this information, boot gives the sizes of the TEXT, DATA, and BSS, segments and the entry offset of the loaded image, before transferring control to it.

The boot operation accepts several options. Note that boot options must be specified positionally as shown in the syntax statement in the

SYNOPSIS. Options for the boot operations are as follows:

-a[C|R|S|D] devicefile
    Accept a new location (as specified by devicefile) and pass it to the loaded image. If that image is an HP-UX kernel, the kernel will erase its predefined I/O configuration, and configure in the specified devicefile. If the C, R, S, or D option is specified, the kernel configures the devicefile as the console, root, swap, or dump device, respectively. Note that -a can be repeated multiple times.

-fnumber
    Use the number and pass it as the flags word to the loaded image.

-istring
    Set the initial run-level for init (see init(1M)) when booting the system. The run-level specified will override any run-level specified in an initdefault entry in /etc/inittab (see inittab(4)).

-lm
    Boot the system in LVM maintenance mode, configure only the root volume, and then initiate single user mode.

-F
    Use with SwitchOver/UX software. Ignore any locks on the boot disk. The -F option should be used only when it is known that the processor holding the lock is no longer running. (If this option is not specified and a disk is locked by another processor, the kernel will not boot from it, to avoid the corruption that would result if the other processor were still using the disk).

boot places some restrictions on object files it can load. It accepts only the HP-UX magic numbers EXECMAGIC (0407), SHAREMAGIC (0410), and DEMANDMAGIC (0413). See magic(4). The object file must contain an Auxiliary Header of the HPUX_AUX_ID type and it must be the first Auxiliary Header (see a.out(4)).

ll and ls Operations
    The ll and ls operations list the contents of the HP-UX directory specified by the optional devicefile. The output is similar to that of ls -aFl command, except the date information is not printed.

    The default devicefile is generated just as for boot, defaulting to the current directory.

set autofile Operation
    The set autofile operation overwrites the contents of the autoexecute file, autofile, with the string specified (see autoexecute in the EXAMPLES section).

show autofile Operation
    The show autofile operation displays the contents of the autoexecute file, autofile (see autoexecute in the EXAMPLES section).

DIAGNOSTICS
    If an error is encountered, hpux prints diagnostic messages to

indicate the cause of the error. These messages fall into the
General, Boot, Copy, Configuration, and System Call categories.
System Call error messages are described in errno(2). The remaining
messages are listed below.

General
  bad minor number in devicefile spec
       The minor number in the devicefile specification is not
       recognized.

  bad path in devicefile spec
       The hardware path in the devicefile specification is not
       recognized.

  command too complex for parsing
       The command line contains too many arguments.

  no path in devicefile spec
       The devicefile specification requires (but does not contain) a
       hardware path component.

  panic (in hpuxboot): (display==number, flags==number) string
       A severe internal hpux error has occurred. Report to your
       nearest HP Field Representative.

Boot
  bad magic
       The specified object file does not have a recognizable magic
       number.

  bad number in flags spec
       The flags specification in the -f option is not recognized.

  Exec failed: Cannot find /stand/vmunix or /vmunix.
       Neither /stand/vmunix or /vmunix could be found.

  booting from raw character device
       In booting from a raw device, the manager specified only has a
       character interface, which might cause problems if the block size
       is incorrect.

  isl not present, please hit system RESET button to continue
       An unsuccessful boot operation has overlaid isl in memory. It is
       impossible to return control to isl.

  short read
       The specified object file is internally inconsistent; it is not
       long enough.

  would overlay
       Loading the specified object file would overlay hpux.

Configuration
  cannot add path, error number
       An unknown error has occurred in adding the hardware path to the
       I/O tree. The internal error number is given. Contact your HP
       Field Representative.

  driver does not exist
       The manager specified is not configured into hpux.

  driver is not a logical device manager
       The manager named is not that of a logical device manager and
       cannot be used for direct I/O operations.

  error rewinding device"

An error was encountered attempting to rewind a device.

error skipping file
> An error was encountered attempting to forward-space a tape device.

negative skip count
> The skip count, if specified, must be greater than or equal to zero.

no major number
> The specified manager has no entry in the block or character device switch tables.

path incompatible with another path
> Multiple incompatible hardware paths have been specified.

path long
> The hardware path specified contains too many components for the specified manager.

path short
> The hardware path specified contains too few components for the specified manager.

table full
> Too many devices have been specified to hpux.

EXAMPLES
> As a preface to the examples which follow, here is a brief overview of HP-UX system boot-up sequences.

Automatic Boot
> Automatic boot processes on various HP-UX systems follow similar general sequences. When power is applied to the HP-UX system processor, or the system Reset button is pressed, processor-dependent code (firmware) is executed to verify hardware and general system integrity (see pdc(1M)). After checking the hardware, pdc gives the user the option to override the autoboot sequence by pressing the Esc key. At that point, a message resembling the following usually appears on the console.

> > (c) Copyright. Hewlett-Packard Company. 1994.
> > All rights reserved.
> >
> > PDC ROM rev. 130.0
> > 32 MB of memory configured and tested.
> >
> > Selecting a system to boot.
> > To stop selection process, press and hold the ESCAPE key...

> If no keyboard activity is detected, pdc commences the autoboot sequence by loading isl (see isl(1M)) and transferring control to it. Since an autoboot sequence is occurring, isl finds and executes the autoexecute file which, on an HP-UX system, requests that hpux be run with appropriate arguments. Messages similar to the following are displayed by isl on the console:

> > Booting from: scsi.6 HP 2213A
> > Hard booted.
> > ISL Revision A.00.09 March 27, 1990
> > ISL booting hpux boot disk(;0)/stand/vmunix

> hpux, the secondary system loader, then announces the operation it is performing, in this case boot, the devicefile from which the load image comes, and the TEXT size, DATA size, BSS size, and start address

of the load image, as shown below, before control is passed to the
image.

```
Booting disk(scsi.6;0)/stand/vmunix
966616+397312+409688 start 0x6c50
```

The loaded image then displays numerous configuration and status
messages.

Interactive Boot

To use hpux interactively, isl must be brought up in interactive mode
by pressing the Esc key during the interval allowed by pdc. pdc then
searches for and displays all bootable devices and presents a set of
boot options. If the appropriate option is chosen, pdc loads isl and
isl interactively prompts for commands. Information similar to the
following is displayed:

```
Selection process stopped.

Searching for Potential Boot Devices.
To terminate search, press and hold the ESCAPE key.

Device Selection   Device Path              Device Type
-----------------------------------------------------------
P0                 scsi.6.0                 QUANTUM PD210S
P1                 scsi.1.0                 HP      2213A
p2                 lan.ffffff-ffffff.f.f    hpfoobar

b)   Boot from specified device
s)   Search for bootable devices
a)   Enter Boot Administration mode
x)   Exit and continue boot sequence

Select from menu: b p0 isl

Trying scsi.6.0
Boot path initialized.
Attempting to load IPL.

Hard booted.
ISL Revision A.00.2G  Mar  27, 1994
ISL>
```

Although all of the operations and options of hpux can be used from
isl interactively, they can also be executed from an autoexecute file.
In the examples below, user input is the remainder of the line after
each ISL> prompt shown. The remainder of each example is text
displayed by the system. Before going over specific examples of the
various options and operations of hpux, here is an outline of the
steps taken in the automatic boot process. Although the hardware
configuration and boot paths shown are for a single Series 800
machine, the user interfaces are consistent across all models. When
the system Reset button is depressed, pdc executes self-test, and
assuming the hardware tests pass, pdc announces itself, sends a BELL
character to the controlling terminal, and gives the user 10 seconds
to override the autoboot sequence by entering any character. Text
resembling the following is displayed on the console:

```
Processor Dependent Code (PDC) revision 1.2
Duplex Console IO Dependent Code (IODC) revision 3

Console path        = 56.0.0.0.0.0.0   (dec)
                      38.0.0.0.0.0.0    (hex)

Primary boot path   = 44.3.0.0.0.0.0   (dec)
                      2c.00000003.0.0.0.0.0  (hex)
```

```
Alternate boot path = 52.0.0.0.0.0.0.0   (dec)
                      34.0.0.0.0.0.0.0   (hex)

32 MB of memory configured and tested.

Autosearch for boot path enabled

To override, press any key within 10 seconds.
```

If no keyboard character is pressed within 10 seconds, pdc commences the autoboot sequence by loading isl and transferring control to it. Because an autoboot sequence is occurring, isl merely announces itself, finds and executes the autoexecute file which, on an HP-UX system, requests that hpux be run with appropriate arguments. The following is displayed on the console.

```
10 seconds expired.
Proceeding with autoboot.

Trying Primary Boot Path
------------------------
Booting...
Boot IO Dependent Code (IODC) revision 2

HARD Booted.

ISL Revision A.00.2G Mar  20, 1994

ISL booting  hpux
```

hpux then announces the operation it is performing, in this case boot, the devicefile from which the load image comes, and the TEXT size, DATA size, BSS size, and start address of the load image. The following is displayed before control is passed to the image.

```
Boot
: disc3(44.3.0;0)/stand/vmunix
3288076 + 323584 + 405312 start 0x11f3e8
```

Finally, the loaded image displays numerous configuration and status messages, then proceeds to init run-level 2 for multiuser mode of operation.

isl must be brought up in interactive mode to use the operations and options of hpux. To do this, simply enter a character during the 10 second interval allowed by pdc. pdc then asks if the primary boot path is acceptable. Answering yes (Y) is usually appropriate. pdc then loads isl and isl interactively prompts for commands. The following lines show the boot prompt, the Y response, subsequent boot messages, and finally the Initial System Loader (ISL) prompt that are sent to the display terminal:

```
Boot from primary boot path (Y or N)?> y
Interact with IPL (Y or N)?> y

Booting...
Boot IO Dependent Code (IODC) revision 2

HARD Booted.

ISL Revision A.00.2G Mar  20, 1994

ISL>
```

Although all of the operations and options of hpux can be used from

isl interactively, they can also be executed from an autoexecute file.
In the examples below, all user input follows the ISL> prompt on the
same line. Subsequent text is resultant messages from the ISL.

Default Boot
   Entering hpux initiates the default boot sequence. The boot path read
   from pdc is 8.0.0, the manager associated with the device at that path
   is disc, the minor number, in this case derived from the autoexecute
   file, is 4 specifying section 4 of the disk, and the object file name
   is /stand/vmunix.

        ISL> hpux

        Boot
        : disc3(44.3.0;0)/stand/vmunix
        3288076 + 323584 + 405312 start 0x11f3e8

Booting Another Kernel
   In this example, hpux initiates a boot operation where the name of the
   object file is vmunix.new.

        ISL> hpux vmunix.new

        Boot
        : disc3(44.3.0;0)/stand/vmunix.new
        3288076 + 323584 + 405312 start 0x11f3e8

Booting From Another Section
   In this example (shown for backward compatibility), a kernel is booted
   from another section of the root disk. For example, suppose kernel
   development takes place under /mnt/azure/root.port which happens to
   reside in its own section, section 3 of the root disk. By specifying
   a minor number of 3 in the above example, the object file
   sys.azure/S800/vmunix is loaded from /mnt/azure/root.port.

        ISL> hpux (;3)sys.azure/S800/vmunix

        Boot
        : disc(8.0.0;0x3)sys.azure/S800/vmunix
        966616+397312+409688 start 0x6c50

Booting From Another Disk
   Only the hardware path and file name are specified in this example.
   All other values are boot defaults. The object file comes from the
   file system on another disk.

        ISL> hpux (52.5.0.0)/stand/vmunix

        Boot
        : disc(52.5.0.0)/stand/vmunix
        966616+397312+409688 start 0x6c50

Booting From LAN
   This example shows how to boot a cluster client from the LAN. Though
   this example specifies a devicefile, you can also use default boot, as
   shown in a previous example. For a boot operation other than default
   boot, the file name must be specified and can be no longer than 11
   characters. Booting to isl from a local disk then requesting an image
   to be loaded from the LAN is not supported.

        ISL> hpux lan(32)/stand/vmunix

        Boot
        : lan(32;0x0)/stand/vmunix
        966616+397312+409688 start 0x6c50

Booting To Single User Mode

In this example, the -i option is used to make the system come up in run-level s, for single user mode of operation.

```
ISL> hpux -is

Boot
: disc(8.0.0;0x0)/stand/vmunix
966616+397312+409688 start 0x6c50

    Kernel Startup Messages Omitted

INIT: Overriding default level with level 's'

INIT: SINGLE USER MODE
WARNING:  YOU ARE SUPERUSER !!
#
```

Booting With A Modified I/O Configuration

Here, a tape driver is configured in at CIO slot 2, HP-IB address 0. Regardless of what was present in the kernel's original I/O configuration, the driver tape is now configured at that hardware path. Similarly, mux0 is configured in at CIO slot 1 which is to be the console. The only other devices configured are the console and root device, which boot derived from pdc.

```
ISL> hpux -aC mux0(8.1) -a tape(8.2.0)

Boot
: disc(8.0.0;0x0)/stand/vmunix
: Adding mux0(8.1;0x0)...
: Adding tape(8.2.0;0x0)...
966616+397312+409688 start 0x6c50
Beginning I/O System Configuration.
cio_ca0 address = 8
   hpib0 address = 0
        disc0 lu = 0 address = 0
   mux0 lu = 0 address = 1
   hpib0 address = 2
        tape1 lu = 0 address = 0
I/O System Configuration complete.

    Additional Kernel Startup Messages Omitted
```

Booting From A Raw Device

This example shows booting from a raw device (that is, a device containing no file system). Note that no file name is specified in the devicefile. The device is an HP7974 tape drive, and therefore tape is the manager used. The tape drive is at CIO slot 2, HP-IB address 3. The first file on the tape will be skipped. The minor number specifies a tape density of 1600 BPI with no rewind on close. Depending on the minor number, tape requires the tape be written with 512 or 1024 byte blocks.

```
ISL> hpux tape(8.2.3;0xa0000)

Boot
: tape(8.2.3;0xa0000)
966616+397312+409688 start 0x6c50
```

Displaying The Autoexecute File

In this example, show autofile is used to print the contents of the autoexecute file residing in the boot LIF, on the device from which hpux was booted. Optionally, a devicefile can be specified in order to read the autoexecute file from the boot LIF of another boot device.

```
ISL> hpux show autofile
Show autofile
: AUTO file contains (hpux)
```

Changing The Autoexecute File
This example shows how to change the contents of the autoexecute file.
Once done, the system can be reset, and the new command will be used
during any unattended boot.

```
ISL> hpux set autofile "hpux /stand/vmunix.std"
Set autofile
: disk(2/0/1.3.0.0.0.0.0;0)
: AUTO file now contains "(hpux /stand/vmunix.std)"
```

Listing Directory Contents
The contents of the directory (/stand) on the root disk are listed.
The format shows the file protections, number of links, user id, group
id, and size in bytes for each file in the directory. There are three
available kernels to boot: vmunix, vmunix.test, and vmunix.prev.
Listing the files over the LAN is not supported.

```
ISL> hpux ll /stand

Ls
: disk(2/0/1.3.0.0.0.0.0;0)/stand
dr-xr-xr-x   3 2      2              1024 ./
drwxr-xr-x  17 0      0              1024 ../
-rw-r--r--   1 0      3               191 bootconf
drwxr-xr-x   2 0      0              1024 build/
-rw-r--r--   1 0      0               632 ioconfig
-rw-r--r--   1 0      3                82 kernrel
-r--r--r--   1 0      3               426 system
-rw-r--r--   1 0      3               437 system.prev
-rwxr-xr-x   1 0      3           7771408 vmunix*
-rwxr-xr-x   1 0      3           7771408 vmunix.prev*
```

Getting The Version
The -v option is used to get the version numbers of hpux.

```
ISL> hpux -v

Release: 10.00
Release Version:
@(#) X10.20.B HP-UX() #1: Dec  4 1995 16:55:08
```

DEPENDENCIES
Series 700 Only
The restore operation is provided as a recovery mechanism in the event
that a disk becomes totally corrupted. It copies data from a properly
formatted bootable tape to disk. When this tape contains a backup
image of the disk, the entire disk is restored. To create a properly
formatted tape (DDS ONLY), the following commands should be executed:

```
dd if=/usr/lib/uxbootlf of=/dev/rmt/0mn bs=2k
dd if=/dev/rdsk/1ss of=/dev/rmt/0m bs=64k
```

The first dd puts a boot area on the tape, making it a bootable image
(see dd(1)). Once the boot image is on tape, the tape is not rewound.
The next dd appends an image of the disk to the tape. The entire
process takes about one hour for a 660 MB HP2213 disk. To avoid later
problems with fsck after the disk is restored, bring the system to
single user mode and type sync a few times before doing the second dd
(see fsck(1M)). Once created, the tape can be used to completely
restore the disk:

1. Insert the tape into the tape drive.

2. Instruct the machine to boot to ISL from the tape. This is usually done by specifying scsi.3 as the boot path.

3. Enter the following in response to the ISL prompt:

       ISL> hpux restore disk(scsi.1;0)

This restores the disk image from the tape to the actual disk at scsi.1. Any existing data on the disk will be lost. This command destroys the contents of the device specified by devicefile. The restoration process takes about one hour for a 660 MB drive.

NOTE: There is a 2 GB limit on the amount of data that can be restored. The tape and disk must be on the boot device interface.

Also, this command may be replaced in the future by superior installation and recovery mechanisms. At that time, this command will be removed.

SEE ALSO
    boot(1M), fsck(1M), init(1M), isl(1M), pdc(1M), errno(2), a.out(4), inittab(4), magic(4).

isl

isl - Initial System Loader (isl) overview.

```
isl(1M)                          Series 800 Only                      isl(1M)

NAME
     isl - initial system loader

DESCRIPTION
     isl implements the operating system independent portion of the
     bootstrap process.  It is loaded and executed after self-test and
     initialization have completed successfully.

     The processor contains special purpose memory for maintaining critical
     configuration related parameters (e.g. Primary Boot, Alternate Boot,
     and Console Paths).  Two forms of memory are supported: Stable Storage
     and Non-Volatile Memory (NVM).

     Typically, when control is transferred to isl, an autoboot sequence
     takes place.  An autoboot sequence allows a complete bootstrap
     operation to occur with no intervention from an operator.  isl
     executes commands from the autoexecute file in a script-like fashion.
     autoboot is enabled by a flag in Stable Storage.

     autosearch is a mechanism that automatically locates the boot and
     console devices.  For further information, see pdc(1M).

     During an autoboot sequence, isl displays its revision and the name of
     any utility it executes.  However, if autoboot is disabled, after isl
     displays its revision, it then prompts for input from the console
     device.  Acceptable input is any isl command name or the name of any
     utility available on the system.  If a non-fatal error occurs or the
     executed utility returns, isl again prompts for input.

   Commands
     There are several commands available in isl. The following is a list
     with a short description.  Parameters may be entered on the command
     line following the command name.  They must be separated by spaces.
     isl prompts for any necessary parameters that are not entered on the
     command line.

          ?
          help            Help - List commands and available utilities

          listf
          ls              List available utilities

          autoboot        Enable or disable the autoboot sequence
                          Parameter - on or off

          autosearch      Enable or disable the autosearch sequence
                          Parameter - on or off

          primpath        Modify the Primary Boot Path
                          Parameter - Primary Boot Path in decimal
```

```
        altpath         Modify the Alternate Boot Path
                        Parameter - Alternate Boot Path in decimal

        conspath        Modify the Console Path
                        Parameter - Console Path in decimal

        lsautofl
        listautofl      List contents of the autoexecute file

        display         Display the Primary Boot, Alternate Boot, and
                        Console Paths

        readnvm         Display the contents of one word of NVM in
                        hexadecimal
                        Parameter - NVM address in decimal or standard
                        hexadecimal notation

        readss          Display the contents of one word of Stable Storage
                        in hexadecimal
                        Parameter - Stable Storage address in decimal or
                        standard hexadecimal notation
```

DIAGNOSTICS

isl displays diagnostic information through error messages written on the console and display codes on the LED display.

For the display codes, CE0x are informative only. CE1x and CE2x indicate errors, some of which are fatal and cause the system to halt. Other errors merely cause isl to display a message.

Non-fatal errors during an autoboot sequence cause the autoboot sequence to be aborted and isl to prompt for input. After non-fatal errors during an interactive isl session, isl merely prompts for input.

Fatal errors cause the system to halt. The problem must be corrected and the system RESET to recover.

```
        CE00   isl is executing.
        CE01   isl is autobooting from the autoexecute file.
        CE02   Cannot find an autoexecute file.  autoboot aborted.
        CE03   No console found, isl can only autoboot.
        CE05   Directory of utilities is too big, isl reads only 2K bytes.
        CE06   autoexecute file is inconsistent.  autoboot aborted.
        CE07   Utility file header inconsistent: SOM values invalid.
         CE08    autoexecute file input string exceeds 2048 characters.    autoboot
aborted.
        CE09   isl command or utility name exceeds 10 characters.
        CE0F   isl has transferred control to the utility.
        CE10   Internal inconsistency: Volume label - FATAL.
        CE11   Internal inconsistency: Directory - FATAL.
        CE12   Error reading autoexecute file.
        CE13   Error reading from console - FATAL.
        CE14   Error writing to console - FATAL.
        CE15   Not an isl command or utility.
        CE16   Utility file header inconsistent: Invalid System ID.
        CE17   Error reading utility file header.
        CE18   Utility file header inconsistent: Bad magic number.
        CE19   Utility would overlay isl in memory.
        CE1A   Utility requires more memory than is configured.
        CE1B   Error reading utility into memory.
        CE1C   Incorrect checksum: Reading utility into memory.
        CE1D   Console needed - FATAL.
        CE1E   Internal inconsistency: Boot device class - FATAL.
        CE21   Destination memory address of utility is invalid.
```

CE22   Utility file header inconsistent: pdc_cache entry.
CE23   Internal inconsistency: iodc_entry_init - FATAL.
CE24   Internal inconsistency: iodc_entry_init - console - FATAL.
CE25   Internal inconsistency: iodc_entry_init - boot device - FATAL.
CE26   Utility file header inconsistent: Bad aux_id.
CE27   Bad utility file type.

SEE ALSO
     boot(1M), hpux_800(1M), pdc(1M).

pdc

man page

pdc - 3

pdc - Processor Dependent Code (pdc) overview.

```
pdc(1M)                                                                pdc(1M)

NAME
     pdc - processor-dependent code (firmware)

DESCRIPTION
     pdc is the firmware that implements all processor-dependent
     functionality, including initialization and self-test of the
     processor.  Upon completion, it loads and transfers control to the
     initial system loader (isl(1M)).  Firmware behavior varies somewhat,
     depending on the hardware series as described below.

     Series 800 Behavior
        To load isl from an external medium, pdc must know the particular
        device on which isl resides.  Typically the device is identified by
        the Primary Boot Path that is maintained by pdc in Stable Storage.  A
        path specification is a series of decimal numbers each suffixed by
        '/', indicating bus converters, followed by a series of decimal
        numbers separated by '.', indicating the various card and slot numbers
        and addresses.  The first number, not specifying a bus converter, is
        the MID-BUS module number (that is, slot number times four) and
        followed by the CIO slot number.  If the CIO slot contains an HP-IB
        card, the next number is the HP-IB address, followed by the unit
        number of the device if the device supports units.  If the CIO slot
        contains a terminal card, the next number is the port number, which
        must be zero for the console.

        When the processor is reset after initialization and self-test
        complete, pdc reads the Console Path from Stable Storage, and attempts
        to initialize the console device.  If the initialization fails, pdc
        attempts to find and initialize a console device.  Algorithms used to
        find a console device are model-dependent.  pdc then announces the
        Primary Boot, Alternate Boot, and Console Paths.

        If autoboot (see isl(1M)) is enabled, pdc provides a 10-second delay,
        during which time the operator can override the autoboot sequence by
        typing any character on the console.  If the operator does not
        interrupt this process, pdc initializes and reads isl from the Primary
        Boot Path.  On models that support autosearch, if this path is not
        valid and autosearch (see isl(1M)) is enabled, pdc then searches
        through the MID-BUS modules and CIO slots to find a bootable medium.
        Currently, autosearch is only implemented on the model 825.

        If the autoboot sequence is unsuccessful, overridden by the operator,
        or not enabled in the first place, pdc interactively prompts the
        operator for the Boot Path to use.  Any required path components that
        are not supplied default to zero.

        The Primary Boot, Alternate Boot, and Console Paths as well as
        autoboot and autosearch enable can be modified via isl.

     Series 700 Behavior
        To load isl from an external medium, pdc must know the particular
```

device on which isl resides. Typically the device is identified by
the Primary Boot Path that is maintained by pdc in Stable Storage. A
path specification is an I/O subsystem mnemonic that varies according
to hardware model.

When the processor is reset after initialization and self-test
complete, pdc reads the Console Path from Stable Storage, and attempts
to initialize the console device. If the initialization fails, pdc
attempts to find and initialize a console device. Algorithms used to
find a console device vary according to hardware model.

If autoboot and autosearch (see isl(1M)) are enabled, pdc waits for
approximately 10 seconds during which time the operator can override
the autoboot sequence pressing and holding the ESC (escape) key on the
console.

The system then begins a search for potentially bootable devices. If
allowed to complete, a list of potentially bootable devices is
displayed, labeled with abbreviated path identifiers (P0, P1, etc). A
simple menu is then displayed where the user can:

- Boot a specific device, using the abbreviated path identifier,
  or the full mnenomic.

- Start a device search where the contents are searched for IPL
  images (note the first search only identified devices and did
  not check the contents).

- Enter the boot administration level.

- Exit the menu and return to autobooting

- Get help on choices

The search of potentially bootable devices can be aborted by pressing
and holding the escape key. The search for device contents can also
be aborted by pressing and holding the escape key.

If the operator does not interrupt the search process, pdc initializes
and reads isl from the Primary Boot Path.

If the autoboot sequence is unsuccessful, overridden by the operator,
or not enabled in the first place, pdc executes the device search and
enters the menu described above.

The Primary Boot, Alternate Boot, and Console Paths as well as
autoboot and autosearch enable can be modified via isl or at the pdc
boot administration level.

SEE ALSO
          boot(1M), hpuxboot(1M), isl(1M).

CHAPTER 4

Building an HP-UX Kernel

Virtual Partitions and the Kernel

As covered in Chapter 3, booting with vPars is different from booting without vPars, in that booting with vPars is managed through the Virtual Partition Monitor (**vpmon**). You still boot an HP-UX kernel, just as you normally would without vPars, however; **vpmon** manages the Virtual Partitions that allow you to run multiple instances of HP-UX on the same computer.

Every Virtual Partition has its own HP-UX 11i operating system running, including a unique kernel. You can customize the operating system and kernel in each Virtual Partition to suit your needs.

man page

vparcreate
appendix a

In the examples earlier in this book, the **vparcreate** command specified a kernel of **/stand/vmunix**, which is the default kernel. It is likely that you will modify this kernel in some way(s) in order to optimize it for the applications you'll be running in each Virtual Partition. You may end up with radically different kernels for each of your Virtual Partitions, depending on the application(s) and specific requirements for each vPar.

In Chapter 3, covering booting vPars, we covered and example of specifying a kernel path. Your default kernel in HP-UX is **/stand/vmunix**. You may perform experimentation with the kernels of the vPars on your system and have to boot these experimental kernels other than **/stand/vmunix**. The following example shows booting from a kernel called **vmunix_test1** with the -*b* option to **vparload**:

```
MON> vparload -p symbol1 -b /stand/vmunix_test1
```

The kernel path above is loaded with this **vparload**, but no permanent changes were made. To make a permanent change to the vPars database file to update the kernel path, you would issue the following command:

```
# vparmodify -p symbol1 -b "stand/vmunix_test1"
```

The vPar has now been modified to have a default kernel of **/stand/vmunix_test1**.

We'll first cover the procedure used in Chapter 2 to perform Virtual Partition kernel-related work. Next we'll cover device drivers in general and an example of using a tape device and its device driver in a Virtual Partition. Later in this chapter, where background is provided on the HP-UX kernel, there is extensive coverage of modifying kernel parameters and a detailed description of HP-UX 11i kernel parameters.

Virtual Partition Kernel-Related Work

Each Virtual Partition has its own instance of HP-UX 11i, which has its own HP-UX kernel. It is likely that you'll customize these kernels in a variety of ways to suit the applications you have running in the respective vPars. The kernel is automatically built for you when you install vPars software. Several drivers are included in the kernel, and the kernel is configured so that it can be relocated in memory. Relocation is required because you'll have multiple HP-UX kernels in memory and they must be resident in different locations. In this section, in order to get vPars running, you have to reconfigure the kernel to include the vPar drivers and make the kernel relocatable. Creating the new kernels takes place for you on every volume that has HP-UX 11i on it and will run a vPar. Let's take a look at some of the kernel-related work that is taking place for you behind the scenes.

Because memory is shared among multiple vPars, the kernel must be relocatable in memory. At the time of this writing there are patches that allow the kernel to be built as a relocatable kernel. We won't peform any checks related to patches.

The file **/sbin/vecheck** is a vPar file that is required on the system. The following listing is a portion of **/usr/conf/gen/config.sys** that checks to see if **/sbin/vecheck** has been loaded on the system:

```
# Determine whether the linker supports kernel relocation.  If it does,
# link the kernel using the relocation options.
LOADOPTS_ADDL=` \
        if [ -f /sbin/vecheck ]; then \
                ${WHAT} ${LD} | \
                ${AWK} '$$0 ~ /92453-07 linker/ { \
                        split($$7, vers, "."); \
                        if ( vers[1] == "B" && \
                        ( vers[2] == 11 && vers[3] >= 25 ) || vers[2] > 11 ) \
                                print "${LOADOPTS_RELOC}"; \
                        else print "${LOADOPTS_STATIC}"; }'; \
        else \
                echo "${LOADOPTS_STATIC}"; \
        fi; \
`
```

The following is a long listing of **/sbin/vecheck** that was loaded with the vPar software:

```
# ll /sbin/vecheck
-r-xr-xr-x   1 bin        bin         20533 Mar  5 19:01 /sbin/vecheck
#
```

Next, let's take a look at **/stand/system** to see the *vpar* driver that has been added to the file:

```
# cat /stand/system
****************************************
* Source: /ux/core/kern/filesets.info/CORE-KRN/generic
* @(#)B.11.11_LR
*
****************************************
* Additional drivers required in every machine-type to
* create a complete
* system file during cold install.  This list is every driver that the
* master.d/ files do not force on the system or is not identifiable by
* ioscan.
* Other CPU-type specific files can exist for their special cases.
* see create_sysfile (1m).
```

```
*****************************************
*
* Drivers/Subsystems
sba
lba
c720
sctl
sdisk
asio0
cdfs
cxperf
olar_psm
olar_psm_if
dev_olar
diag0
diag1
diag2
dmem
dev_config
iomem
nfs_core
nfs_client
nfs_server
btlan
maclan
dlpi
token_arp
inet
uipc
tun
telm
tels
netdiag1
nms
hpstreams
clone
strlog
sad
echo
sc
timod
tirdwr
pipedev
pipemod
ffs
ldterm
ptem
pts
ptm
pckt
td
fddi4
gelan
GSCtoPCI
iop_drv
bs_osm
vxfs
vxportal
```

```
           lvm
           lv
           nfsm
           rpcmod
           autofsc
           cachefsc
           cifs
           prm
           vpar                                  <--- vpar driver added here
           STRMSGSZ           65535
           nstrpty            60
           dump lvol
           maxswapchunks      2048
           #
```

The *vpar* driver is a master driver described in **/usr/conf/master.d** as shown below:

```
# pwd
/usr/conf/master.d
# cat vpar
$CDIO
vpar        0
$$$

$DRIVER_INSTALL
vcn            -1              209
vcs            -1              -1
vpar_driver    -1              -1
$$$

$DRIVER_DEPENDENCY
vcn            vpar
vcs            vpar
vpar           vcs vcn vpar_driver
vpar_driver    vpar
$$$

$DRIVER_LIBRARY
*
* The driver/library table.  This table defines which libraries a given
* driver depends on.  If the driver is included in the dfile, then the
* libraries that driver depends on will be included on the ld(1) command
* line.  Only optional libraries *need* to be specified in this table,
* (but required ones can be included, as well).
*
* Driver handle    <libraries>
*
* subsystems first
vcn            libvpar-pdk.a
vcs            libvpar-pdk.a
vpar           libvpar-pdk.a
vpar_driver    libvpar-pdk.a
```

```
$$$

$LIBRARY
*
* The library table.  Each element in the library table describes
* one unique library.  The flag member is a boolean value, it is
* initialized to 1 if the library should *always* be included on
* the ld(1) command line, or 0 if the library is optional (i.e. it
* is only included when one or more drivers require it).  The order
* of the library table determines the order of the libraries on the
* ld(1) command line, (i.e. defines an implicit load order).  New
* libraries must be added to this table.
* Note: libhp-ux.a must be the last entry, do not place
* anything after it.
*
* Library    <required>
*
libvpar-pdk.a      0
$$$
#
```

You can see in this file that there are multiple drivers present. The *vcn* and *vcs* drivers are used to support the console in a vPars environment. Since you'll probably only have one physical console for multiple partitions, you need a way to share the physical device.

The following is a description of these two drivers:

vcn	This is a Virtual CoNsole for use by vPars. Since only one physical console exists on a system, *vcn* is used as a virtual console. Console information is sent by *vcn* to **vpmon**, where it is buffered. The buffered information is sent to the *vcs* driver (see the next item), where it can be viewed.
vcs	This is the Virtual Console Slave driver. This driver is the focal point for all Virtual Consoles. Information stored by **vpmon** is sent to *vcs* when a connection is established.

Figure 4-1 shows the relationship between *vcs, vcn,* and **vpmon**.

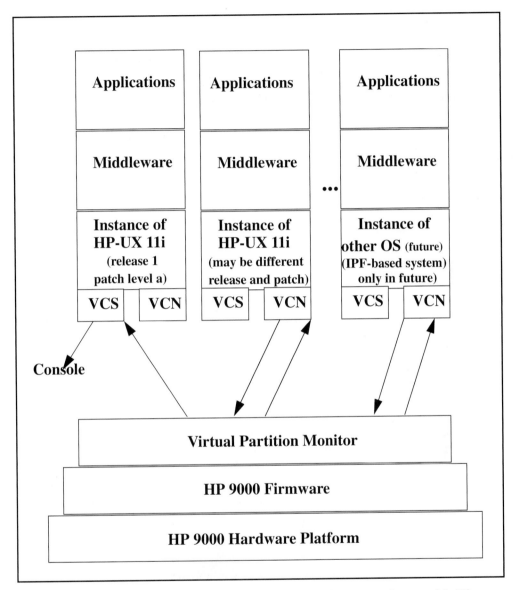

Figure 4-1 Virtual Consoles Implemented with *vcn* and *vcs* with First vPar Running

If the partition that owns the physical console is not running, in Figure 4-1 this is the leftmost partition, then **vpmon** emulates the *vcs* driver and manages the physical console. This ensures that the physical console will be available even if the vPar that owns it is not running.

We can also use SAM to view all aspects of the kernel and make changes to the kernel for vPars. Keep in mind that running SAM in different vPars is like running SAM on different systems. Figure 4-2 shows a screen shot of SAM displaying drivers for vPar *cable1* (hostname of *cvhdcon4* shown in the top of all of the SAM windows):

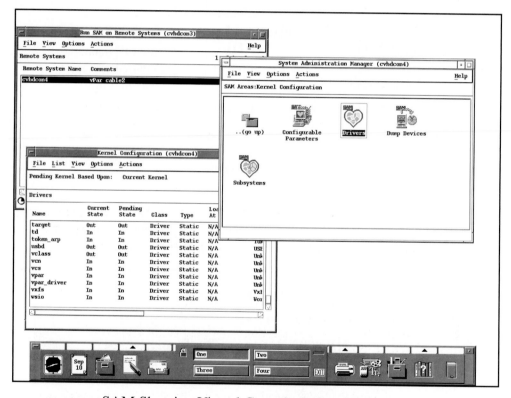

Figure 4-2 SAM Showing Virtual Console-Related Drivers

Note in the lower left window of Figure 4-2 that *vcn*, *vcs*, and *vpar_driver* have a *Current State* of *In*, indicating that the kernel has these three drivers present in it.

Chapter 11 covers SAM and vPars. Suffice it to say for the purposes of our kernel discussion that all of the work we've been performing on vPars at the command line can be performed in SAM as well.

Although we didn't have to manually build the kernel to include these drivers, we could have done so at the command line with **mk_kernel** to build the new kernel and **kmupdate** to move the new kernel-related files into place, as shown in the following listing:

```
# mk_kernel
Generating module: krm...
Compiling /stand/build/conf.c...
Loading the kernel...
Generating kernel symbol table...
# kmupdate

  Kernel update request is scheduled.

  Default kernel /stand/vmunix will be updated by
  newly built kernel /stand/build/vmunix_test
  at next system shutdown or startup time.

#
```

kmupdate is moving numerous kernel-related new files into place and saving a copy of your old files. Although **kmupdate** saves you some typing, it is important to know that it is peforming the following moves for you:

```
# mv /stand/vmunix /stand/vmunix.prev
# mv /stand/dlkm /stand/dlkm.prev
# mv /stand/build/vmunix_test /stand/vmunix
# mv /stand/build/dlkm.vmunix_test /stand/dlkm
```

Keep in mind that this procedure for rebuilding the kernel is performed for you when vPars software is loaded and configured. It is important to know what is taking place in the background, however; in the event that you have to troubleshoot a problem related to your updated kernel. Kernel creation and modification can also be done in SAM as described in Chapter 11.

Since you will have more than one kernel to maintain on your system when using vPars you'll want to become familar with this process so you can customize your kernel for each vPar to ensure that it is optimized for the application(s) running in each vPar.

You may want to review the background portion of this chapter that describes rebuilding the kernel if you don't have much experience doing so.

Devices and Virtual Partitions

You may be moving various devices on your HP 9000 from one Virtual Partition to another. This means that the kernels in the respective Virtual Partitions will need to have in them the drivers of hardware devices which will be used by the Virtual Partition. Let's take a look at all of the hardware on our system and then see if there is a component we'll want to move from one Virtual Partition to another.

To begin with, let's take a look at the *full* hardware on a system with **ioscan -f** in the following example:

```
cvhdcon3:/ # ioscan -fn


Class      I  H/W Path      Driver   S/W State  H/W Type    Description
=======================================================================
root       0                root     CLAIMED    BUS_NEXUS
ioa        0  0             sba      CLAIMED    BUS_NEXUS   System Bus Adap
ter (803)
ba         0  0/0           lba      CLAIMED    BUS_NEXUS   Local PCI Bus A
dapter (782)
lan        0  0/0/0/0       btlan    CLAIMED    INTERFACE   HP PCI 10/100Ba
se-TX Core
                            /dev/diag/lan0   /dev/ether0      /dev/lan0
ext_bus    0  0/0/1/0       c720     CLAIMED    INTERFACE   SCSI C896 Ultra
  Wide Single-Ended
target     0  0/0/1/0.1     tgt      CLAIMED    DEVICE
disk       0  0/0/1/0.1.0   sdisk    CLAIMED    DEVICE      HP       DVD-ROM
  304
                            /dev/dsk/c0t1d0   /dev/rdsk/c0t1d0
target     1  0/0/1/0.3     tgt      CLAIMED    DEVICE
tape       0  0/0/1/0.3.0   stape    CLAIMED    DEVICE      HP       C1537A
                            /dev/rmt/0m          /dev/rmt/c0t3d0BESTn
                            /dev/rmt/0mb         /dev/rmt/c0t3d0BESTnb
                            /dev/rmt/0mn         /dev/rmt/c0t3d0DDS
                            /dev/rmt/0mnb        /dev/rmt/c0t3d0DDSb
                            /dev/rmt/c0t3d0BEST  /dev/rmt/c0t3d0DDSn
                            /dev/rmt/c0t3d0BESTb /dev/rmt/c0t3d0DDSnb
target     2  0/0/1/0.7     tgt      CLAIMED    DEVICE
ctl        0  0/0/1/0.7.0   sctl     CLAIMED    DEVICE      Initiator
                            /dev/rscsi/c0t7d0
ext_bus    1  0/0/1/1       c720     CLAIMED    INTERFACE   SCSI C896 Ultra
  Wide Single-Ended
target     3  0/0/1/1.0     tgt      CLAIMED    DEVICE
```

```
disk        1   0/0/1/1.0.0     sdisk   CLAIMED     DEVICE      SEAGATE ST17340
4LC
                                /dev/dsk/c1t0d0   /dev/rdsk/c1t0d0
target      4   0/0/1/1.2       tgt     CLAIMED     DEVICE
disk        2   0/0/1/1.2.0     sdisk   CLAIMED     DEVICE      SEAGATE ST17340
4LC
                                /dev/dsk/c1t2d0   /dev/rdsk/c1t2d0
target      5   0/0/1/1.7       tgt     CLAIMED     DEVICE
ctl         1   0/0/1/1.7.0     sctl    CLAIMED     DEVICE      Initiator
                                /dev/rscsi/c1t7d0
ext_bus     2   0/0/2/0         c720    CLAIMED     INTERFACE   SCSI C87x Ultra
 Wide Single-Ended
target      6   0/0/2/0.0       tgt     CLAIMED     DEVICE
disk        3   0/0/2/0.0.0     sdisk   CLAIMED     DEVICE      SEAGATE ST17340
4LC
                                /dev/dsk/c2t0d0   /dev/rdsk/c2t0d0
target      7   0/0/2/0.2       tgt     CLAIMED     DEVICE
disk        4   0/0/2/0.2.0     sdisk   CLAIMED     DEVICE      SEAGATE ST17340
4LC
                                /dev/dsk/c2t2d0   /dev/rdsk/c2t2d0
target      8   0/0/2/0.7       tgt     CLAIMED     DEVICE
ctl         2   0/0/2/0.7.0     sctl    CLAIMED     DEVICE      Initiator
                                /dev/rscsi/c2t7d0
ext_bus     3   0/0/2/1         c720    CLAIMED     INTERFACE   SCSI C87x Ultra
 Wide Single-Ended
target      9   0/0/2/1.7       tgt     CLAIMED     DEVICE
ctl         3   0/0/2/1.7.0     sctl    CLAIMED     DEVICE      Initiator
                                /dev/rscsi/c3t7d0
tty         0   0/0/4/0         asio0   CLAIMED     INTERFACE   PCI Serial (103
c1048)
                                /dev/GSPdiag1   /dev/mux0      /dev/tty0p1
                                /dev/diag/mux0  /dev/tty0p0    /dev/tty0p2
tty         1   0/0/5/0         asio0   CLAIMED     INTERFACE   PCI Serial (103
c1048)
                                /dev/GSPdiag2   /dev/mux1
                                /dev/diag/mux1  /dev/tty1p1
ba          1   0/1            lba      CLAIMED     BUS_NEXUS   Local PCI Bus A
dapter (782)
ba          2   0/2            lba      CLAIMED     BUS_NEXUS   Local PCI Bus A
dapter (782)
ba          3   0/3            lba      CLAIMED     BUS_NEXUS   Local PCI Bus A
dapter (782)
ba          4   0/4            lba      CLAIMED     BUS_NEXUS   Local PCI Bus A
dapter (782)
ba          5   0/5            lba      CLAIMED     BUS_NEXUS   Local PCI Bus A
dapter (782)
ba          6   0/8            lba      CLAIMED     BUS_NEXUS   Local PCI Bus A
dapter (782)
fc          0   0/8/0/0         td      CLAIMED     INTERFACE   HP Tachyon TL/T
S Fibre Channel Mass Storage Adapter
                                /dev/td0
fcp         0   0/8/0/0.8       fcp     CLAIMED     INTERFACE   FCP Protocol Ad
apter
ext_bus     7   0/8/0/0.8.0.5.0          fcparray  CLAIMED     INTERFACE   FCP Arr
ay Interface
target     10   0/8/0/0.8.0.5.0.0        tgt       CLAIMED     DEVICE
disk        7   0/8/0/0.8.0.5.0.0.0      sdisk     CLAIMED     DEVICE      HP
 A5277A
                                /dev/dsk/c7t0d0   /dev/rdsk/c7t0d0
disk       10   0/8/0/0.8.0.5.0.0.1      sdisk     CLAIMED     DEVICE      HP
 A5277A
                                /dev/dsk/c7t0d1   /dev/rdsk/c7t0d1
disk       11   0/8/0/0.8.0.5.0.0.2      sdisk     CLAIMED     DEVICE      HP
 A5277A
                                /dev/dsk/c7t0d2   /dev/rdsk/c7t0d2
disk       12   0/8/0/0.8.0.5.0.0.3      sdisk     CLAIMED     DEVICE      HP
 A5277A
                                /dev/dsk/c7t0d3   /dev/rdsk/c7t0d3
target     11   0/8/0/0.8.0.5.0.1        tgt       CLAIMED     DEVICE
disk       15   0/8/0/0.8.0.5.0.1.0      sdisk     CLAIMED     DEVICE      HP
 A5277A
                                /dev/dsk/c7t1d0   /dev/rdsk/c7t1d0
target     12   0/8/0/0.8.0.5.0.2        tgt       CLAIMED     DEVICE
disk       17   0/8/0/0.8.0.5.0.2.0      sdisk     CLAIMED     DEVICE      HP
 A5277A
```

```
                                    /dev/dsk/c7t2d0   /dev/rdsk/c7t2d0
target      13   0/8/0/0.8.0.5.0.3      tgt       CLAIMED      DEVICE
disk        18   0/8/0/0.8.0.5.0.3.0    sdisk     CLAIMED      DEVICE           HP
  A5277A
                                    /dev/dsk/c7t3d0   /dev/rdsk/c7t3d0
ext_bus      4   0/8/0/0.8.0.255.0      fcpdev    CLAIMED      INTERFACE    FCP Dev
ice Interface
target      14   0/8/0/0.8.0.255.0.5    tgt       CLAIMED      DEVICE
ctl          4   0/8/0/0.8.0.255.0.5.0  sctl      CLAIMED      DEVICE           HP
  A5277A
                                    /dev/rscsi/c4t5d0
ba           7   0/9                    lba       CLAIMED      BUS_NEXUS    Local PCI Bus A
dapter (782)
fc           1   0/9/0/0                td        CLAIMED      INTERFACE    HP Tachyon TL/T
S Fibre Channel Mass Storage Adapter
                                    /dev/td1
fcp          1   0/9/0/0.8              fcp       CLAIMED      INTERFACE    FCP Protocol Ad
apter
ext_bus      6   0/9/0/0.8.0.4.0                  fcparray  CLAIMED    INTERFACE    FCP Arr
ay Interface
target      15   0/9/0/0.8.0.4.0.0      tgt       CLAIMED      DEVICE
disk         5   0/9/0/0.8.0.4.0.0.0    sdisk     CLAIMED      DEVICE           HP
  A5277A
                                    /dev/dsk/c6t0d0   /dev/rdsk/c6t0d0
disk         6   0/9/0/0.8.0.4.0.0.1    sdisk     CLAIMED      DEVICE           HP
  A5277A
                                    /dev/dsk/c6t0d1   /dev/rdsk/c6t0d1
disk         8   0/9/0/0.8.0.4.0.0.2    sdisk     CLAIMED      DEVICE           HP
  A5277A
                                    /dev/dsk/c6t0d2   /dev/rdsk/c6t0d2
disk         9   0/9/0/0.8.0.4.0.0.3    sdisk     CLAIMED      DEVICE           HP
  A5277A
                                    /dev/dsk/c6t0d3   /dev/rdsk/c6t0d3
target      16   0/9/0/0.8.0.4.0.1      tgt       CLAIMED      DEVICE
disk        13   0/9/0/0.8.0.4.0.1.0    sdisk     CLAIMED      DEVICE           HP
  A5277A
                                    /dev/dsk/c6t1d0   /dev/rdsk/c6t1d0
target      17   0/9/0/0.8.0.4.0.2      tgt       CLAIMED      DEVICE
disk        14   0/9/0/0.8.0.4.0.2.0    sdisk     CLAIMED      DEVICE           HP
  A5277A
                                    /dev/dsk/c6t2d0   /dev/rdsk/c6t2d0
target      18   0/9/0/0.8.0.4.0.3      tgt       CLAIMED      DEVICE
disk        16   0/9/0/0.8.0.4.0.3.0    sdisk     CLAIMED      DEVICE           HP
  A5277A
                                    /dev/dsk/c6t3d0   /dev/rdsk/c6t3d0
ext_bus      5   0/9/0/0.8.0.255.0      fcpdev    CLAIMED      INTERFACE    FCP Dev
ice Interface
target      19   0/9/0/0.8.0.255.0.4    tgt       CLAIMED      DEVICE
ctl          5   0/9/0/0.8.0.255.0.4.0  sctl      CLAIMED      DEVICE           HP
  A5277A
                                    /dev/rscsi/c5t4d0
ba           8   0/10                   lba       CLAIMED      BUS_NEXUS    Local PCI Bus A
dapter (782)
lan          1   0/10/0/0               btlan     CLAIMED      INTERFACE    HP A5230A/B5509
BA PCI 10/100Base-TX Addon
                                    /dev/diag/lan1   /dev/ether1      /dev/lan1
ba           9   0/12                   lba       CLAIMED      BUS_NEXUS    Local PCI Bus A
dapter (782)
lan          2   0/12/0/0               btlan     CLAIMED      INTERFACE    HP A5230A/B5509
BA PCI 10/100Base-TX Addon
                                    /dev/diag/lan2   /dev/ether2      /dev/lan2
pbc          0   32                     pbc       CLAIMED      BUS_NEXUS    Bus Converter
processor    0   33                     processor CLAIMED      PROCESSOR    Processor
pbc          1   36                     pbc       CLAIMED      BUS_NEXUS    Bus Converter
processor    1   37                     processor CLAIMED      PROCESSOR    Processor
pbc          2   96                     pbc       CLAIMED      BUS_NEXUS    Bus Converter
processor    2   97                     processor CLAIMED      PROCESSOR    Processor
pbc          3   100                    pbc       CLAIMED      BUS_NEXUS    Bus Converter
processor    3   101                    processor CLAIMED      PROCESSOR    Processor
memory       0   192                    memory    CLAIMED      MEMORY       Memory
virtbus      0   es                     sdm       CLAIMED      VIRTBUS      Enhanced-SCSI v
irtual bus
cvhdcon3:/ #
```

I used the -*f* option because it produces a full listing of all I/O. I omitted the -*u* option, which produces a list of usable I/O devices. For a device to be usable, there must be a driver for the device in the kernel and an instance number. I often find devices on a system for which no driver exists in the kernel. I like to know about these devices so I can add a driver and use them if none exists.

Going back to our earlier **ioscan -f** example, there was a DDS drive present in the listing. The tape drive is assigned to vPar *cable1* but not *cable2*, as shown in the following listing:

man page

vparstatus
appendix a

```
# vparstatus -p cable1 -v

[Virtual Partition Details]
Name:          cable1
State:         Up
Attributes:    Dynamic,Manual
Kernel Path:   /stand/vmunix
Boot Opts:

[CPU Details]
Min/Max:   2/3
Bound [Path]:    33
                 37
Unbound [Path]:

[IO Details]
   0.0.1.1.2.0   BOOT
   0.0.4.0   CONSOLE
   0.0.0.0
   0.0.1.0.3.0                      <-- tape drive in cable1

[Memory Details]
Specified [Base   /Range]:
          (bytes) (MB)
Total Memory (MB):   2048
#



# vparstatus -p cable2 -v

[Virtual Partition Details]
Name:          cable2
State:         Up
Attributes:    Dynamic,Manual
Kernel Path:   /stand/vmunix
Boot Opts:

[CPU Details]
Min/Max:   1/2
Bound [Path]:    97
```

```
Unbound [Path]:   101

[IO Details]
   0.8.0.0.8.0.5.0.0.0   BOOT
   0.10.0.0                              <-- no tape drive present

[Memory Details]
Specified [Base  /Range]:
        (bytes) (MB)
Total Memory (MB):   1024
#
```

The **vmunix** for *cable1* should have in it the device driver necessary to support the tape drive, in this case *stape*. We know that *stape* is the driver by issuing an **ioscan** as shown below:

```
cvhdcon3:/ # ioscan -fun | grep tape
tape     0  0/0/1/0.3.0   stape   CLAIMED     DEVICE      HP      C1537A
cvhdcon3:/ #
```

The driver for the tape drive should be present in every Virtual Partition that will use it. If your tape drive interface is in a PCI slot that you can move from one vPar to another, you want to have the driver for it in the kernel of every Virtual Partition that will use it. Keep in mind that in order to move the tape drive, its interface will have to be on an LBA that can be moved from one vPar to another. At the time of this writing an LBA can't be shared between vPars. In our case the tape drive is connected to the Core I/O card and won't be moved from *cable1* to *cable2*.

The following listing of **/stand/system** shows that the *stape* driver we need for the tape is present:

```
cvhdcon3:/ # cat /stand/system
* Drivers and Subsystems

DlkmDrv
GSCtoPCI
PCItoPCI
arp
asio0
asp
autofsc
autox0
bs_osm
btlan
btlan1
```

```
c720
cachefsc
cb
cdfs
cifs
clone
core
cxperf
dev_config
dev_olar
devkrs
diag0
diag1
diag2
disc3
dlkm
dlpi
dmem
echo
esctl
esdisk
fcT1
fcT1_cntl
fcT1_fcp
fcms
fcp
fcp_cdio
fcparray
fcpdev
fcpmux
fdc
fddi4
ffs
gelan
hpstreams
i2o_cdio
inet
iomem
iop_drv
ip
kepd
klog
krio
krs
lasi
lba
ldterm
lv
lvm
maclan
netdiag1
netqa
nfs_client
nfs_core
nfs_server
nfsm
nms
nuls
```

```
olar_psm
olar_psm_if
pa_generic_psm
pa_psm
pat_psm
pci
pckt
pflop
pipedev
pipemod
prm
ptem
ptm
pts
rawip
rpcmod
sad
sapic
sba
sc
schgr
scsi1
scsi3
sctl
sdisk
sdm
sio
spt
spt0
ssrfc
stape
stcpmap
strlog
strpty_included
strtelnet_included
target
tcp
td
telm
tels
timod
tirdwr
tlclts
tlcots
tlcotsod
token_arp
tun
udp
ufs
uipc
vcn
vcs
ve_psm
ve_psm_driver
vxfs
vxportal
wsio
```

```
* Kernel Device info

dump lvol


* Tunable parameters

STRMSGSZ         65535
dnlc_hash_locks  512
maxdsiz_64bit    0X40000000
maxssiz          0X800000
maxssiz_64bit    0X800000
maxswapchunks    2048
maxtsiz          0X4000000
maxtsiz_64bit    0X40000000
nstrpty          60
shmmax           0X4000000
cvhdcon3:/ #
```

We could now use the tape drive to perform a backup of *cable1*. There is detailed information on backup in Chapter 7, including performing a backup using a remote tape drive. The following example shows the **fbackup** command issued:

```
fbackup -0u -f /dev/rmt/0m -g /tmp/backupgraph -I
       /tmp/backupindex.`date '+%y%m%d.%H:M'` 2>
       /tmp/backup.`date '+%y%m%d.%H:%M'`
```

This produces an *index* file of the backup of **/var** on *cable1* that contains the following entries:

```
1024              1 /
1024              1 /var
1024              1 /var/tmp
200               1 /var/tmp/..fmt
0                 1 /var/tmp/aaaa01664
0                 1 /var/tmp/aaaa01745
0                 1 /var/tmp/aaaa01806
0                 1 /var/tmp/aaaa02391
0                 1 /var/tmp/cmd_res3036
0                 1 /var/tmp/cmd_res4403
1560              1 /var/tmp/disk_em.fmt
324               1 /var/tmp/dm_TL_adapter.fmt
1392              1 /var/tmp/dm_stape.fmt
1241              1 /var/tmp/ems_inittab.old
28                1 /var/tmp/envd.action2
28                1 /var/tmp/envd.action5
200               1 /var/tmp/fc60mon.fmt
4106              1 /var/tmp/inetd.conf.old
```

```
0                          1  /var/tmp/lpmc_em.fmt
96                         1  /var/tmp/ntp
0                          1  /var/tmp/oe.config.4525
0                          1  /var/tmp/rdskACAa01881
0                          1  /var/tmp/rdskQBAa01841
0                          1  /var/tmp/rdskSDCa06262
0                          1  /var/tmp/rdskSJAa01574
0                          1  /var/tmp/rdskUBAa01853
7184                       1  /var/tmp/swagent.log
```

If the tape interface were not on the Core I/O card, which is devoted to *cable1*, we could move the interface from *cable1* to *cable2*, confirm that the driver is in **/stand/system**, and then backup *cable2*

Since there are many devices that you may want to move among the vPars running on your system, you want to make sure you have all of the device drivers required to support these devices in your kernel.

Non-vPar Specific Section of Chapter - Modify and Build an HP-UX Kernel

You may need to modify your HP-UX 11i kernel in some way, such as changing a kernel parameter, and then rebuild your kernel. You may need to create a new HP-UX kernel in order to add device drivers or subsystems, to tune the kernel to get improved performance, to alter configurable parameters, or to change the dump and swap devices. If you update or modify a dynamic element of your kernel, as shown in the example in this chapter, a reboot is not required. Updating or modifying a static element requires a reboot and may also require some additional steps.

With HP-UX 11i it is not necessary to rebuild your kernel for all changes that take place to it. In 11i, there are many *Dynamically Tunable Kernel Parameters* and *Dynamically Loadable Kernel Modules* that will modify your kernel but not require a reboot. Combined with many *Dynamic Patches* that are available in 11i, you will need to reboot your system less often.

In the next section, we'll modify a *Dynamically Tunable Kernel Parameter*, thereby modifying the kernel, and do not have to reboot the system in order for the change to take place. We'll then make a change to the kernel and fully rebuild it so that you can see the process of a complete rebuild, including a reboot. I normally use the System Administration Manager (SAM) covered in Chapter 11 to make kernel modifications. There is, however, no substitute for understanding the process by which you would manually build an HP-UX kernel and, therefore, be more informed when you have SAM do this for you in the future. In this chapter, I discuss various commands related to kernel generation and cover the process by which you would manually create a kernel.

Dynamically Loadable Kernel Modules

New with 11.0 was the introduction of dynamically loadable kernel modules. In 11.x, the infrastructure for this feature was put into place, providing a separate system file for each module. With 11.0 is provided the ability of specially created modules to be loaded or unloaded into the kernel without having to reboot the system as long as the module is not being used. HP-UX 11i continues to support all of this dynamic functionality. This new mechanism provides great flexibility and improved system uptime. Detailed information about this advanced feature can be reviewed in the *HP-UX 11.x Release Notes*. Most of the dynamically loadable kernel modules available at the time of this writing are third party. The *IT Resource Center* Web site (*itrc.hp.com*) contains information on this topic, including a developer's guide.

Building a Kernel

To begin, let's take a look at an existing kernel running on an HP-UX 11i L-Class system used in many of the examples throughout this book. The **sysdef** command is used to analyze and report tunable parameters of a currently running system. You can specify a particular file to analyze if you don't wish to use the currently running system. The following is a *partial* listing of having run **sysdef** on an 11i L-Class system:

```
# /usr/sbin/sysdef
NAME                    VALUE       BOOT        MIN-MAX         UNITS     FLAGS
acctresume                  4         -        -100-100                     -
acctsuspend                 2         -        -100-100                     -
allocate_fs_swapmap         0         -           -                         -
bufpages                32074         -           0-            Pages        -
create_fastlinks            0         -           -                         -
dbc_max_pct                50         -           -                         -
dbc_min_pct                 5         -           -                         -
default_disk_ir             0         -           -                         -
dskless_node                0         -           0-1                       -
eisa_io_estimate          768         -           -                         -
eqmemsize                  23         -           -                         -
file_pad                   10         -           0-                        -
fs_async                    0         -           0-1                       -
hpux_aes_override           0         -           -                         -
maxdsiz                     2         -        0-655360         Pages        -
maxdsiz_64bit           16384         -        256-1048576      Pages        -
maxfiles                   60         -         30-2048                     -
maxfiles_lim             1024         -         30-2048                     -
maxssiz                 65536         -        0-655360         Pages        -
maxssiz_64bit          262144         -        256-1048576      Pages        -
maxswapchunks             512         -         1-16384                     -
maxtsiz                  2048         -        0-655360         Pages        -
maxtsiz_64bit            2048         -        256-1048576      Pages        -
maxuprc                    75         -           3-                        -
maxvgs                     10         -           -                         -
msgmap                2555904         -           3-                        -
nbuf                    18720         -           0-                        -
ncallout                  515         -           6-                        -
ncdnode                   150         -           -                         -
ndilbuffers                30         -           1-                        -
netisr_priority            -1         -         -1-127                      -
netmemmax                   0         -           -                         -
nfile                     920         -          14-                        -
nflocks                   200         -           2-                        -
```

```
ninode             476        -      14-                      -
no_lvm_disks         0        -       -                       -
nproc              400        -      10-                      -
npty                60        -       1-                      -
nstrpty             60        -       -                       -
nswapdev            10        -       1-25                    -
nswapfs             10        -       1-25                    -
public_shlibs        1        -       -                       -
remote_nfs_swap      0        -       -                       -
rtsched_numpri      32        -       -                       -
sema                 0        -       0-1                     -
semmap         4128768        -       4-                      -
shmem                0        -       0-1                     -
shmmni             200        -       3-1024                  -
streampipes          0        -       0-                      -
swapmem_on           1        -       -                       -
swchunk           2048        -    2048-16384      kBytes     -
timeslice           10        -      -1-2147483648 Ticks      -
unlockable_mem    1800        -       0-            Pages      -
#
```

In addition to the tunable parameters, you may want to see a report of all the hardware found on your system. The **ioscan** command does this for you. Using **sysdef** and **ioscan,** you can see what your tunable parameters are set to and what hardware exists on your system. You will then know how your system is set up and can then make changes to your kernel. The following is an **ioscan** output of the same HP-UX 11i L-Class system for which **sysdef** was run:

```
# /usr/sbin/ioscan -f
Class     I  H/W Path    Driver   S/W State   H/W Type    Description
==========================================================================
root      0              root     CLAIMED     BUS_NEXUS
ioa       0  0           sba      CLAIMED     BUS_NEXUS   System Bus Adapter (582)
ba        0  0/0         lba      CLAIMED     BUS_NEXUS   Local PCI Bus Adapter (782)
lan       0  0/0/0/0     btlan    CLAIMED     INTERFACE   HP PCI 10/100Base-TX Core
ext_bus   0  0/0/1/0     c720     CLAIMED     INTERFACE   SCSI C896 Fast Wide LVD
target    0  0/0/1/0.7   tgt      CLAIMED     DEVICE
ctl       0  0/0/1/0.7.0 sctl     CLAIMED     DEVICE      Initiator
ext_bus   1  0/0/1/1     c720     CLAIMED     INTERFACE
                                                          SCSI C896 Ultra Wide Single-Ended
target    1  0/0/1/1.2   tgt      CLAIMED     DEVICE
disk      1  0/0/1/1.2.0 sdisk    CLAIMED     DEVICE      SEAGATE ST318203LC
target    2  0/0/1/1.7   tgt      CLAIMED     DEVICE
ctl       1  0/0/1/1.7.0 sctl     CLAIMED     DEVICE      Initiator
ext_bus   2  0/0/2/0     c720     CLAIMED     INTERFACE   SCSI C875 Ultra
Wide Single-Ended
target    3  0/0/2/0.2   tgt      CLAIMED     DEVICE
disk      2  0/0/2/0.2.0 sdisk    CLAIMED     DEVICE      SEAGATE ST318203LC
target    4  0/0/2/0.7   tgt      CLAIMED     DEVICE
ctl       2  0/0/2/0.7.0 sctl     CLAIMED     DEVICE      Initiator
ext_bus   3  0/0/2/1     c720     CLAIMED     INTERFACE
                                                          SCSI C875 Ultra Wide Single-Ended
target    5  0/0/2/1.4   tgt      CLAIMED     DEVICE
disk      3  0/0/2/1.4.0 sdisk    CLAIMED     DEVICE      TOSHIBA CD-ROM XM-6201TA
target    6  0/0/2/1.7   tgt      CLAIMED     DEVICE
ctl       3  0/0/2/1.7.0 sctl     CLAIMED     DEVICE      Initiator
tty       0  0/0/4/0     asio0    CLAIMED     INTERFACE   PCI Serial (103c1048)
```

```
tty         1   0/0/5/0        asio0     CLAIMED     INTERFACE    PCI Serial (103c1048)
ba          1   0/1           lba       CLAIMED     BUS_NEXUS    Local PCI Bus Adapter (782)
ba          2   0/2           lba       CLAIMED     BUS_NEXUS    Local PCI Bus Adapter (782)
ba          3   0/3           lba       CLAIMED     BUS_NEXUS    Local PCI Bus Adapter (782)
lan         1   0/3/0/0       btlan     CLAIMED     INTERFACE
                                                                 HP A5230A/B5509BA PCI 10/100Base-TX Addon
ba          4   0/4           lba       CLAIMED     BUS_NEXUS    Local PCI Bus Adapter (782)
ext_bus     4   0/4/0/0       c720      CLAIMED     INTERFACE
                                                                 C875 Fast Wide Differential
target      7   0/4/0/0.7     tgt       CLAIMED     DEVICE
ctl         4   0/4/0/0.7.0   sctl      CLAIMED     DEVICE       Initiator
ext_bus     5   0/4/0/1       c720      CLAIMED     INTERFACE    SCSI C875 Fast
Wide Differential
target      8   0/4/0/1.7     tgt       CLAIMED     DEVICE
ctl         5   0/4/0/1.7.0   sctl      CLAIMED     DEVICE       Initiator
ba          5   0/5           lba       CLAIMED     BUS_NEXUS    Local PCI Bus Adapter (782)
ba          6   0/6           lba       CLAIMED     BUS_NEXUS    Local PCI Bus Adapter (782)
ba          7   0/7           lba       CLAIMED     BUS_NEXUS    Local PCI Bus Adapter (782)
ext_bus     6   0/7/0/0       c720      CLAIMED     INTERFACE
                                                                 SCSI C875 Fast Wide Differential
target      9   0/7/0/0.7     tgt       CLAIMED     DEVICE
ctl         6   0/7/0/0.7.0   sctl      CLAIMED     DEVICE       Initiator
ext_bus     7   0/7/0/1       c720      CLAIMED     INTERFACE
                                                                 SCSI C875 Fast Wide Differential
target     10   0/7/0/1.7     tgt       CLAIMED     DEVICE
ctl         7   0/7/0/1.7.0   sctl      CLAIMED     DEVICE       Initiator
memory      0   8             memory    CLAIMED     MEMORY       Memory
processor   0   160           processor CLAIMED     PROCESSOR    Processor
processor   1   166           processor CLAIMED     PROCESSOR    Processor
#
```

I normally run **ioscan** with the *-f* option because it includes the *Driver, S/W State,* and *H/W Type* columns. I am interested in the driver associated with the hardware in the system that the *-f* option produces.

The **ioscan** output shows all of the hardware that comprises the system, including the two processors in the system.

The file **/stand/vmunix** is the currently running kernel. Here is a long listing of the directory **/stand** on the L-Class system, which shows the file **/stand/vmunix**:

```
# ls -l
total 74274
-rw-r--r--   1 root     sys            19 Aug  4 11:37 bootconf
drwxr-xr-x   4 root     sys          2048 Aug 25 11:24 build
drwxr-xr-x   5 root     sys          1024 Aug 24 13:00 dlkm
drwxr-xr-x   5 root     sys          1024 Aug  4 12:45 dlkm.vmunix.prev
-rw-r--r--   1 root     sys          3024 Aug  4 12:26 ioconfig
-r--r--r--   1 root     sys            82 Aug  4 12:27 kernrel
drwxr-xr-x   2 root     sys          1024 Aug 29 11:39 krs
drwxr-xr-x   2 root     root         1024 Aug 29 11:33 krs_lkg
drwxr-xr-x   2 root     root         1024 Aug 29 11:39 krs_tmp
drwxr-xr-x   2 root     root         8192 Aug  4 11:36 lost+found
-rw-------   1 root     root           12 Aug 29 11:33 rootconf
-rw-rw-rw-   1 root     sys          1180 Aug 24 12:52 system
-r--r--r--   1 root     sys          1026 Aug  4 12:21 system.prev
-rwxr-xr-x   1 root     sys      14774416 Aug 24 12:53 vmunix
```

```
-rwxr-xr-x   1 root     sys     23184584 Aug  4 12:22 vmunix.prev
#
```

Notice that among the directories shown are two related to Dynamically Loadable Kernel Modules (DLKMs.) These are kernel modules that can be included in the kernel without having to reboot the system.

In order to make a change to the kernel, we would change to the **/stand/build** directory, where all work in creating a new kernel is performed, and issue the **system_prep** command as shown below:

```
# cd /stand/build
# /usr/lbin/sysadm/system_prep  -s  system
```

We can now proceed to make the desired changes to the kernel, including adding a driver or subsystem such as cdfs for a CD-ROM file system. With the dynamically loadable kernel module (DLKM) structure in place with 11i, we must use **kmsystem** and **kmtune** to make changes in the kernel system and system description files.

You can use **kmtune** to view the value and parameters related to existing kernel parameters as well as to make proposed modifications to the kernel. The following listing shows issuing **kmtune** (without the *-l* option to view details) to view a summary of the currently running kernel:

```
# kmtune

Parameter               Current Dyn Planned                          Module     Version
==============================================================================
NSTRBLKSCHED                -   -  2
NSTREVENT                  50   -  50
NSTRPUSH                   16   -  16
NSTRSCHED                   0   -  0
STRCTLSZ                 1024   -  1024
STRMSGSZ                65535   -  65535
acctresume                  4   -  4
acctsuspend                 2   -  2
aio_listio_max            256   -  256
aio_max_ops              2048   -  2048
aio_physmem_pct            10   -  10
aio_prio_delta_max         20   -  20
allocate_fs_swapmap         0   -  0
alwaysdump                  1   -  1
bootspinlocks               -   -  256
bufcache_hash_locks       128   -  128
bufpages                    0   -  0
```

```
chanq_hash_locks          256   -  256
create_fastlinks            0   -  0
dbc_max_pct                50   -  50
dbc_min_pct                 5   -  5
default_disk_ir             0   -  0
desfree                     -   -  0
disksort_seconds            0   -  0
dnlc_hash_locks           512   -  512
dontdump                    0   -  0
dskless_node                -   -  0
dst                         1   -  1
effective_maxpid            -   -  ((NPROC<22500)?30000:(NPROC*5/4))
eisa_io_estimate            -   -  0x300
enable_idds                 0   -  0
eqmemsize                  15   -  15
executable_stack            1   -  1
fcp_large_config            0   -  0
file_pad                    -   -  10
fs_async                    0   -  0
ftable_hash_locks          64   -  64
hdlpreg_hash_locks        128   -  128
hfs_max_ra_blocks           8   -  8
hfs_max_revra_blocks        8   -  8
hfs_ra_per_disk            64   -  64
hfs_revra_per_disk         64   -  64
hp_hfs_mtra_enabled         1   -  1
hpux_aes_override           -   -  0
initmodmax                 50   -  50
io_ports_hash_locks        64   -  64
iomemsize                   -   -  40000
ksi_alloc_max            2208   -  2208
ksi_send_max               32   -  32
lotsfree                    -   -  0
max_async_ports            50   -  50
max_fcp_reqs              512   -  512
max_mem_window              0   -  0
max_thread_proc            64   -  64
maxdsiz            0x10000000   -  0x10000000
maxdsiz_64bit     0x40000000   -  0X40000000
maxfiles                   60   -  60
maxfiles_lim             1024   Y  1024
maxqueuetime                -   -  0
maxssiz            0x800000   -  0X800000
maxssiz_64bit      0x800000   -  0X800000
maxswapchunks             512   -  512
maxtsiz           0x4000000    Y  0X4000000
maxtsiz_64bit    0x40000000    Y  0x40000000
maxuprc                    77   Y  77
maxusers                   32   -  32
maxvgs                     10   -  10
mesg                        1   -  1
minfree                     -   -  0
modstrmax                 500   -  500
msgmap                     42   -  42
msgmax                   8192   Y  8192
msgmnb                  16384   Y  16384
msgmni                     50   -  50
msgseg                   2048   -  2048
msgssz                      8   -  8
msgtql                     40   -  40
nbuf                        0   -  0
ncallout                  515   -  515
ncdnode                   150   -  150
nclist                    612   -  612
ncsize                   5596   -  5596
ndilbuffers                30   -  30
netisr_priority             -   -  -1
netmemmax                   -   -  0
nfile                     910   -  910
nflocks                   200   -  200
nhtbl_scale                 0   -  0
ninode                    476   -  476
nkthread                  499   -  499
nni                         -   -  2
no_lvm_disks                0   -  0
```

```
    nproc                     400   -   500
    npty                       60   -    60
    nstrpty                    60   -    60
    nstrtel                    60   -    60
    nswapdev                   10   -    10
    nswapfs                    10   -    10
    nsysmap                   800   -   800
    nsysmap64                 800   -   800
    num_tachyon_adapters        0   -     0
    o_sync_is_o_dsync           0   -     0
    page_text_to_local          -   -     0
    pfdat_hash_locks          128   -   128
    public_shlibs               1   -     1
    region_hash_locks         128   -   128
    remote_nfs_swap             0   -     0
    rtsched_numpri             32   -    32
    scroll_lines              100   -   100
    scsi_maxphys          1048576   -   1048576
    sema                        1   -     1
    semaem                  16384   -   16384
    semmap                     66   -    66
    semmni                     64   -    64
    semmns                    128   -   128
    semmnu                     30   -    30
    semume                     10   -    10
    semvmx                  32767   -   32767
    sendfile_max                0   -     0
    shmem                       1   -     1
    shmmax              0x4000000   Y   0X4000000
    shmmni                    200   -   200
    shmseg                    120   Y   120
    st_ats_enabled              1   -     1
    st_fail_overruns            0   -     0
    st_large_recs               0   -     0
    streampipes                 0   -     0
    swapmem_on                  1   -     1
    swchunk                  2048   -   2048
    sysv_hash_locks           128   -   128
    tcphashsz                   0   -     0
    timeslice                  10   -    10
    timezone                  420   -   420
    unlockable_mem              0   -     0
    vas_hash_locks            128   -   128
    vnode_cd_hash_locks       128   -   128
    vnode_hash_locks          128   -   128
    vps_ceiling                16   -    16
    vps_chatr_ceiling     1048576   -   1048576
    vps_pagesize                4   -     4
    vx_fancyra_enable           0   -     0
    vx_maxlink              32767   -   32767
    vx_ncsize                1024   -   1024
    vxfs_max_ra_kbytes       1024   -   1024
    vxfs_ra_per_disk         1024   -   1024
    #
```

Issuing **kmtune** with the *-l* option produces a detailed listing of the kernel. The following shows just the output for one of the parameters:

```
# kmtune -l
Parameter:      maxuprc
Current:        77
Planned:        77
Default:        75
Minimum:        -
```

```
Module:          -
Version:         -
Dynamic:         Yes
#
```

This parameter is *Dynamic* (*Yes*), meaning that the kernel can be dynamically updated. After having viewed this output, we can now modify the value of this dynamic parameter. The following command changes the value of the following parameter from *77*, which is the existing value, to *80*:

```
# kmtune -s maxuprc=80
#
```

We can now issue the **kmtune** to again view the existing and proposed value of the *maxuprc* parameter:

```
# kmtune
Parameter                 Current Dyn Planned                    Module      Version
========================================================================================
NSTRBLKSCHED                  -    -  2
NSTREVENT                    50    -  50
NSTRPUSH                     16    -  16
NSTRSCHED                     0    -  0
STRCTLSZ                   1024    -  1024
STRMSGSZ                  65535    -  65535
acctresume                    4    -  4
acctsuspend                   2    -  2
aio_listio_max              256    -  256
aio_max_ops                2048    -  2048
aio_physmem_pct              10    -  10
aio_prio_delta_max           20    -  20
allocate_fs_swapmap           0    -  0
alwaysdump                    1    -  1
bootspinlocks                 -    -  256
bufcache_hash_locks         128    -  128
bufpages                      0    -  0
chanq_hash_locks            256    -  256
create_fastlinks              0    -  0
dbc_max_pct                  50    -  50
dbc_min_pct                   5    -  5
default_disk_ir               0    -  0
desfree                       -    -  0
disksort_seconds              0    -  0
dnlc_hash_locks             512    -  512
dontdump                      0    -  0
dskless_node                  -    -  0
dst                           1    -  1
effective_maxpid              -    -  ((NPROC<22500)?30000:(NPROC*5/4))
eisa_io_estimate              -    -  0x300
enable_idds                   0    -  0
eqmemsize                    15    -  15
executable_stack              1    -  1
fcp_large_config              0    -  0
```

```
file_pad                    -    -  10
fs_async                    0    -  0
ftable_hash_locks          64    -  64
hdlpreg_hash_locks        128    -  128
hfs_max_ra_blocks           8    -  8
hfs_max_revra_blocks        8    -  8
hfs_ra_per_disk            64    -  64
hfs_revra_per_disk         64    -  64
hp_hfs_mtra_enabled         1    -  1
hpux_aes_override           -    -  0
initmodmax                 50    -  50
io_ports_hash_locks        64    -  64
iomemsize                   -    -  40000
ksi_alloc_max            2208    -  2208
ksi_send_max               32    -  32
lotsfree                    -    -  0
max_async_ports            50    -  50
max_fcp_reqs              512    -  512
max_mem_window              0    -  0
max_thread_proc            64    -  64
maxdsiz            0x10000000    -  0x10000000
maxdsiz_64bit     0x40000000    -  0X40000000
maxfiles                   60    -  60
maxfiles_lim             1024    Y  1200
maxqueuetime                -    -  0
maxssiz            0x800000    -  0X800000
maxssiz_64bit      0x800000    -  0X800000
maxswapchunks             512    -  512
maxtsiz            0x4000000    Y  0X4000000
maxtsiz_64bit     0x40000000    Y  0X40000000
maxuprc                    77    Y  80
maxusers                   32    -  32
maxvgs                     10    -  10
mesg                        1    -  1
minfree                     -    -  0
modstrmax                 500    -  500
msgmap                     42    -  42
msgmax                   8192    Y  8192
msgmnb                  16384    Y  16384
msgmni                     50    -  50
msgseg                   2048    -  2048
msgssz                      8    -  8
msgtql                     40    -  40
nbuf                        0    -  0
ncallout                  515    -  515
ncdnode                   150    -  150
nclist                    612    -  612
ncsize                   5596    -  5596
ndilbuffers                30    -  30
netisr_priority             -    -  -1
netmemmax                   -    -  0
nfile                     910    -  910
nflocks                   200    -  200
nhtbl_scale                 0    -  0
ninode                    476    -  476
nkthread                  499    -  499
nni                         -    -  2
no_lvm_disks                0    -  0
nproc                     400    -  400
npty                       60    -  60
nstrpty                    60    -  60
nstrtel                    60    -  60
nswapdev                   10    -  10
nswapfs                    10    -  10
nsysmap                   800    -  800
nsysmap64                 800    -  800
num_tachyon_adapters        0    -  0
o_sync_is_o_dsync           0    -  0
page_text_to_local          -    -  0
pfdat_hash_locks          128    -  128
public_shlibs               1    -  1
region_hash_locks         128    -  128
remote_nfs_swap             0    -  0
rtsched_numpri             32    -  32
scroll_lines              100    -  100
```

```
scsi_maxphys           1048576    -   1048576
sema                         1    -   1
semaem                   16384    -   16384
semmap                      66    -   66
semmni                      64    -   64
semmns                     128    -   128
semmnu                      30    -   30
semume                      10    -   10
semvmx                   32767    -   32767
sendfile_max                 0    -   0
shmem                        1    -   1
shmmax              0x4000000    Y   0X4000000
shmmni                     200    -   200
shmseg                     120    Y   120
st_ats_enabled               1    -   1
st_fail_overruns             0    -   0
st_large_recs                0    -   0
streampipes                  0    -   0
swapmem_on                   1    -   1
swchunk                   2048    -   2048
sysv_hash_locks            128    -   128
tcphashsz                    0    -   0
timeslice                   10    -   10
timezone                   420    -   420
unlockable_mem               0    -   0
vas_hash_locks             128    -   128
vnode_cd_hash_locks        128    -   128
vnode_hash_locks           128    -   128
vps_ceiling                 16    -   16
vps_chatr_ceiling      1048576    -   1048576
vps_pagesize                 4    -   4
vx_fancyra_enable            0    -   0
vx_maxlink               32767    -   32767
vx_ncsize                 1024    -   1024
vxfs_max_ra_kbytes        1024    -   1024
vxfs_ra_per_disk          1024    -   1024
#
```

This output shows that the change to our parameter is pending.

We can apply the change to the dynamic parameter *maxuprc* from *77* to *80* by issuing **kmtune** with the *-u* option:

```
# kmtune -u
The kernel's value of maxuprc has been set to 80 (0x50).
#
```

This output shows that the change we wanted made to the kernel has been made. We can confirm this by running **kmtune** again and searching for *maxuprc*:

```
# kmtune | grep maxuprc
maxuprc                         80   Y   80
#
```

Both the *Current* and *Planned* values have been updated to *80*. This dynamic update can be done using **kmsystem** to add dynamic drivers to your kernel.

There are many other procedures for which you would have to perform additional steps to include modifications in the kernel and rebuild it. With these non-dynamic changes you would create a new kernel, which will be generated as **/stand/build/vmunix_test,** using the command shown below:

```
# mk_kernel -s system
Compiling conf.c...
Loading the kernel...
Generating kernel symbol table...
#
```

At this point, the new kernel exists in the **/stand/build** directory. The existing kernel is updated with the newly generated kernel with **kmupdate**. **kmupdate** moves the new kernel files into the **/stand** directory. I would first recommend moving the existing **/stand/system** kernel file to a backup file, and then updating the new kernel as shown below:

```
# mv /stand/system /stand/system.prev      (may want to move additional
# kmupdate /stand/build/vmunix_test         files shown in Figure 4-3)

   Kernel update request is scheduled.

   Default kernel /stand/vmunix will be updated by
   newly built kernel /stand/build/vmunix_test
   at next system shutdown or startup time.
#
```

kmupdate will automatically create backup copies of **/stand/vmunix** and **/stand/dlkm** for you. These will be created as **/stand/vmunix.prev** and **/stand/dlkm.vmunix.prev,** respectively.

You can now shut down the system and automatically boot from the new kernel if your update did not take place dynamically and requires a reboot.

Figure 4-3 summarizes the process of building a new kernel in HP-UX 11i.

Step	Comments
1) run **sysdef** and **ioscan -f**	Analyzes and reports tunable parameters of currently running kernel.
2) perform long listing of **/stand** directory	The file **vmunix** is the existing kernel, and **system** is used to build a new kernel.
3) **cd /stand/build**	This is the directory where the new kernel will be built.
4) **/usr/lbin/sysadm/system_prep -s system**	This extracts the **system** file from the currently running kernel.
5) use **kmsystem** and **kmtune** to make changes	Takes place in the **/stand/build** directory. Dyamic update complete here.
6) **mk_kernel -s system**	Makes a new kernel in the **/stand/build** directory called **vmunix_test**. DLKM files are produced in **dlkm.vmunix_test/***.
7) **mv /stand/system /stand/system.prev** **mv /stand/vmunix /stand/vmunix.prev** **mv /stand/dlkm /stand/dlkm.vmunix.prev**	Saves the existing files as **.prev**.
8) **mv /stand/build/system /stand/system** **kmupdate /stand/build/vmunix_test**	Updates the kernel with the newly generated kernel. Automatically saves the old versions in **/stand** as follows: **vmunix** as **/stand/vmunix.prev** **dlkm** as **/dlkm.vmunix.prev**
9) **cd /** **shutdown -r 0**	Changes directory to **/** and shuts down the sytem so that it comes up with the new kernel. This may not be required if your change could be implemented dynamically.

Figure 4-3 Creating a Kernel in HP-UX 11i

There are really two different procedures for generating your kernel - one for dynamic elements, such as the parameter *maxuprc* shown in the earlier example, and one for static elements. The static procedure consists of several additional steps and a reboot. With HP-UX 11i, more and more kernel objects will be updated dynamically, resulting in fewer reboots when modifying your kernel.

Description of Kernel Parameters

The following is a description of kernel parameters in HP-UX 11i at the time of this writing. The first section is a list of and description of each kernel parameter. The second section is an overview of kernel parameters. The full and most recent descriptions can be found at the following URL:

http://docs.hp.com/hpux/onlinedocs/os/KCparams.OverviewAll.html

I encourage you to use the online help of SAM and the URL above to access the most recent and complete information on kernel parameters. Due to limitations of the amount of material I can include in the book, I eliminated much of the background information related to kernel parameters in order to save space. This information is available in the SAM online help and the URL at the time of this writing.

I performed minimal formatting on this material. It is close to the form in which I received it from my HP associates in the lab. I think it is most effective in this somewhat "raw" form because, after all, we're dealing with kernel-related information.

Kernel Parameters

aio_listio_max specifies the maximum number of POSIX asynchronous I/O operations that can be specified in a "listio()" call.

Acceptable Values:

Minimum 2
Maximum 0x10000
Default 256

This parameter places a limit on the system resources that can be consumed if a large number of POSIX asynchronous I/O operations are requested in a single "listio()" call. The value should be set large enough to meet system programming needs while protecting the system against excessive asynchronous I/O operations initiated by a malfunctioning process.

The value specified must not exceed the value of aio_max_ops.

aio_max_ops specifies the system-wide maximum number of POSIX asynchronous I/O operations that can be queued simultaneously at any given time.

Acceptable Values:

Minimum 1
Maximum 0x100000
Default 2048

Specify integer value.

Description

This parameter places a limit on the system resources that can be consumed if a large number of POSIX asynchronous I/O operations are queued on the system at the same time. This parameter limits the ability of competing processes to overwhelm the system with large numbers of asynchronous I/O operations and the memory they require.

Each enqueued asynchronous operation requires allocation of system memory for its internal control structure, thus making this limit necessary. In addition to the system-wide limit, there is a per-process limit that is controlled using the argument "RLIMIT_AIO_OPS" to "getrlimit()" and "setrlimit()" calls.

aio_physmem_pct specifies the maximum percentage of the total physical memory in the system that can be locked for use in POSIX asynchronous I/O operations.

Acceptable Values:

Minimum 5
Maximum 50
Default 10

Specify integer value.

Description

This parameter places a limit on how much system memory can be locked by the combined total number of POSIX asynchronous I/O operations that are in progess at any given time. It is also important to be aware that an operation remains on the active queue and memory is not released, even if the operation is complete, until it is properly terminated by an "aio_return()" call for that operation.

Asynchronous I/O operations that use a request-and-callback mechanism for I/O must be able to lock the memory they are using. The request-and-callback mechanism is used only if the device drivers involved support it. Memory is locked only while the I/O transfer is in progress. On a large server it is better to increase "aio_physmem_pct" to higher values (up to 50).

"aio_physmem_pct" imposes a system-wide limit on lockable physical memory. A per-process lockable-memory limit can also be self-imposed by using the "setrlimit()" system call within the application program.

Remember too that the total amount of memory that can be locked at any given time for any reason, not just for asynchronous I/O, is controlled by the system-wide limit "lockable_mem". Other system activity, including explicit memory locking with plock() and/or mlock() interfaces can also affect the amount of lockable memory at any given time.

There is no kernel parameter named "lockable_mem", but there is a parameter named "unlockable_mem" which affects it. The value of "lockable_mem" is determined by subtracting the value of "unlockable_mem" from the amount of system memory available after system startup. During startup, the system displays on the system console the amount of its lockable memory (along with available memory and physical memory). These values can be retrieved while the system is running by using the "/sbin/dmesg" command.

aio_prio_delta_max specifies the maximum slow-down factor (priority offset) for POSIX asynchronous I/O operations. This is the maximum priority-offset value allowed in the "aio_reqprio" field in the asynchronous I/O control block ("aiocb" structure).

Acceptable values:

Minimum 0
Maximum 20
Default 20
lablist

Specify integer value

Description

This parameter places a limit on how much the priority of a POSIX
asynchronous I/O operation can be reduced to slow down it down.
This limits the value allowed for "int aio_reqprio" in the
asynchronous-I/O control block structure "aiocb".

acctresume

Resume accounting when sufficient free file-system space becomes
available.

Acceptable Values:

Minimum -100
Maximum 101
Default 4

Specify integer value.

Description

This parameter is of interest only if process accounting is being used
on the system.

"acctresume" specifies the minimum amount of free space that must be
available in the file system before the system can resume process
accounting if it is suspended due to insufficient free space. The
threshold at which accounting is suspended is defined by "acctsuspend".

Related Parameters

"acctsuspend" and "acctresume" are interrelated. To prevent
suspend-resume conflicts, the signed, integer value of "acctresume"
must always be greater than the signed, integer value of "acctsuspend".

acctsuspend

Suspend accounting when available free file-system space drops below
specified amount.

Acceptable Values:

Minimum -100
Maximum 100
Default 2

Specify integer value.

Description

This parameter is of interest only if process accounting is being used on the system.

"acctsuspend" prevents accounting files from invading file system free space by specifying the minimum amount of available file system space that must be kept available for other uses while process accounting is running. If the available space drops below that value, accounting is suspended until sufficient file space becomes available again so accounting can resume.

Selecting a Value for "acctsuspend"

Related Parameters

"acctsuspend" and "acctresume" are interrelated. To prevent suspend-resume conflicts, the signed, integer value of "acctsuspend" must always be less than the signed, integer value of "acctresume".

allocate_fs_swapmap

Preallocate sufficient kernel data structures for file-system swap use.

Acceptable Values:

Minimum 0 (allocate swap data structures as needed)
Maximum 1 (preallocate necessary kernel data structures)
Default 0

Specify integer value of "0" or "1".

Description

"allocate_fs_swapmap" determines whether kernel data structures for file-system swap are allocated only when needed or reserved in advance (does not apply to device swap). Only two values are recognized as valid:

"allocate_fs_swapmap" = 0   (default value) System allocates data
                             structures as they are needed in order
                             to conserve system memory. Under

certain conditions, the system could
deny swap requests because it lacks
available data structures, even though
the file system has space available for
swapping.

"allocate_fs_swapmap" = 1   System allocates sufficient data
structures to accommodate the maximum
file system swap limit specified by the
the "swapon()" system call or
"swapon" command. This ensures that
space in memory will support swap
requests as long as the file systems
have swap space available. This mode is
most commonly used on high availability
systems where prevention of process
failures due to unavailable resources is
more important than reduced system
efficiency caused by reserving resources
before they are needed.

alwaysdump

"alwaysdump" is a bit-map value that defines which classes of kernel
memory pages are to be dumped if a kernel panic occurs.

Acceptable Values:

Minimum 0
Maximum none
Default 0

Specify integer value.

Description

On large systems, the time required to dump system memory when a kernel
panic occurs can be excessive or even prohibitive, depending on how much
physical memory is installed in the system. Fast-dump capabilities
controlled by the "dontdump" and "alwaysdump" parameters provides
a means for restricting kernel dumps to specific types of information:

* Unused Physical Memory
* Kernel Static Data
* Kernel Dynamic Data

* File-System Metadata
* Kernel Code
* Buffer Cache
* Process Stack
* User Process

The bit-map value stored in "alwaysdump" specifies which of these memory classes are to be included in the memory dumps associated with a kernel panic.

Related Parameters

"alwaysdump" and "dontdump" have opposite effects. If the bit corresponding to a particular memory-page class is set in one parameter, it should not be set in the other parameter; otherwise a conflict occurs and the actual kernel behavior based on parameter values is undefined. These conflicts do not occur when SAM is used to set the values ([[Modify Page-Class Configuration]] in the [[Actions]] menu, SAM "Dump Devices" subarea in the kernel-configuration area).

bufpages

Define number of 4096-byte memory pages in the file system buffer cache.

Acceptable Values:

Minimum: "0 or 6" ("Nbuf*2" or 64 pages)
Maximum: Memory limited
Default: "0"

Specify integer value or use integer formula expression. Use non-zero value !!only!! if dynamic buffer cache is !!not!! being used.

Description

"bufpages" specifies how many 4096-byte memory pages are allocated for the file system buffer cache. These buffers are used for all file system I/O operations, as well as all other block I/O operations in the system ("exec", "mount", inode reading, and some device drivers.)

Specifying a Value for "bufpages"

To enable dynamic buffer cache allocation, set "bufpages" to zero. Otherwise, set "bufpages" to the desired number of 4-Kbyte pages to be allocated for buffer cache. If the value specified for "bufpages" is non-zero but less than 64, the number is increased at boot time and a message is printed, announcing the change. If "bufpages" is larger than the maximum supported by the system, the number is decreased at boot time and a message is printed.

Related Parameters and System Values

"bufpages" controls how much actual memory is allocated to the buffer pool.

If "bufpages" is zero at system boot time, the system allocates two pages for every buffer header defined by "nbuf". If "bufpages" and "nbuf" are both zero, the system enables dynamic buffer cache allocation and allocates a percentage of available memory.

The maximum amount of memory that can be allocated to the buffer pool is also affected by the amount of memory allocated to the system for other purposes. Thus, modifying parameters that affect system memory may also affect the maximum amount of memory can be made available to the buffer pool.

clicreservedmem

"clicreservedmem" specifies how many bytes of system memory are to be reserved for I/O-mapping use by user processes in high-speed, distributed-server environments such as those used for running large database-processing programs.

Acceptable Values:

Minimum: "0"
Maximum: none
Default: "0"

Specify integer value.

Description

Normal HP-UX systems reserve a relatively small amount of system memory for I/O mapping. However, some specialized applications (such as large database-processing programs) often run on clusters of high-speed servers that are interconnected by specialized high-speed, wideband communication networks. Because of the intense demands on system resources, these applications often communicate by means of memory-mapped I/O where large blocks of memory are shared by the application and the corresponding I/O or networking software.

The configurable parameter "clicreservedmem" provides a means for setting aside as much as 15/16 (approximately 93%) of total system memory for use by applications that perform large-volume, memory-mapped, network I/O. While this value could be as much as 512 Gbytes or even 1 Tbyte, it more commonly ranges from about 1 Gbyte to perhaps 64 Gbytes. Regardless of the value chosen within SAM, the actual memory reserved by the system cannot exceed 15/16 or total system memory.

create_fastlinks

Use fast symbolic links.
Acceptable Values:

Minimum: "0"
Maximum: "1"
Default: "0"

Specify integer value.

Description

When "create_fastlinks" is non-zero, it causes the system to create HFS symbolic links in a manner that reduces the number of disk-block accesses by one for each symbolic link in a pathname lookup. This involves a slight change in the HFS disk format, which makes any disk formatted for fast symbolic links unusable on Series 700 systems prior to HP-UX Release 9.0 and Series 800 systems prior to HP-UX Release 10.0 (this configurable parameter was present on Series 700 Release 9.0 systems, but not on Series 800 HP-UX 9.0 systems).

To provide backward compatibility, the default setting for "create_fastlinks" is zero, which does not create the newer, faster format. However, all HP-UX 10.0 kernels (and all Series 700 HP-UX 9.0 kernels) understand both disk formats, whether "create_fastlinks" is set to zero or non-zero.

dbc_max_pct

Define maximum percentage of memory to be used by dynamic buffer cache.
Acceptable Values:

Minimum: " 2"
Maximum: "90"
Default: "50"

Specify integer value.

Description

When the parameters"bufpages" "nbuf" are both set to their default value of 0, the size of the buffer cache grows or shrinks dynamically, depending on competing requests for system memory.

The value of "dbc_max_pct" sets the maximum percentage of physical memory that can be allocated to the dynamic buffer cache.

dbc_min_pct

Define minimum percentage of memory to be used by dynamic buffer cache.

Acceptable Values:

Minimum: " 2"
Maximum: "90"
Default: " 5"

Specify integer value.
Description

During file-system I/O operations, data is stored in a buffer cache, the size of which can be fixed or dynamically allocated. When the parameters "bufpages" "nbuf" are both set to their default value of 0, the size of the buffer cache grows or shrinks dynamically, depending on competing requests for system memory.

The value of "dbc_min_pct" specifies the minimum percentage of physical memory that is reserved for use by the dynamic buffer cache.

Selecting an Appropriate Value

If "dbc_min_pct" is set to too low a value, very high demand on the buffer cache can effectively hang the system. The is also true when using fixed buffer cache. To determine a reasonable (and conservative) value for the minimum cache size in Mbytes, use the following formula:

(number of system processes) × (largest file-system block size) / 1024

To determine the value for "dbc_min_pct", divide the result by the number of Mbytes of physical memory installed in the computer and multiply that value by 100 to obtain the correct value in percent.

Only those processes that actively use disk I/O should be included in the calculation. All others can be excluded. Here are some examples what processes should be included in or excluded from the calculation:

Include: NFS daemons, text formatters such as "nroff",
            database management applications, text editors,
            compilers, etc. that access or use source and/or
            output files stored in one or more file systems
            mounted on the system.

Exclude: X-display applications, "hpterm", "rlogin",
            login shells, system daemons, "telnet" or
            "uucp" connections, etc. These process use
            very little, if any, disk I/O.

dst

Enable or disable daylight-savings-time conversion and specify
conversion schedule.

Acceptable Values:

Specify one of the following integer values:

"0"   Disable daylight-saving time
"1"   Set daylight-saving time to USA style (this is the default)
"2"   Set daylight-saving time to Australian style
"3"   Set daylight-saving time to Western-Europe style
"4"   Set daylight-saving time to Middle-Europe style
"5"   Set daylight-saving time to Eastern-Europe style

Description

"dst" specifies whether to convert to daylight savings time, and which
schedule to use when converting between daylight-savings and standard
time.

A zero value disables conversion to daylight-savings time. Non-zero
values enable conversion and select a conversion schedule according to
the following definitions in the file "usr/include/sys/time.h":

```
#define DST_NONE    0   /* not on dst */
#define DST_USA     1   /* USA style dst */
#define DST_AUST    2   /* Australian style dst */
#define DST_WET     3   /* Western European dst */
#define DST_MET     4   /* Middle European dst */
#define DST_EET     5   /* Eastern European dst */
```

default_disk_ir

Enable Immediate Reporting on disk I/O.

Acceptable Values:

Minimum: "0" (off)
Maximum: "1" (on)
Default: "0" (off)

Set to "0" (disable immediate reporting) or "1" (enable immediate reporting).

Description

"default_disk_ir" enables or disables immediate reporting.

With Immediate Reporting ON, disk drives that have data caches return from a "write()" system call when the data is cached, rather than returning after the data is written on the media. This sometimes enhances write performance, especially for sequential transfers, but cached data can be lost if a device power failure or reset occurs before the device writes the cached data to media. The recommended value for this parameter on Series 800 systems is zero (OFF).

Although not an option to the "mount" command, the configurable parameter, "default_disk_ir", has a profound effect upon filesystem (and raw) disk performance and, conversely, data integrity through resets. It may either be turned ON (set to 1) or OFF (set to 0).

If this configurable parameter is omitted from the kernel configuration file used to create the kernel ("/stand/system"), it is assumed to be OFF (0). Thus, the default behavior for Immediate Reporting (also known as Write Cache Enable, WCE) is OFF (disabled).

"default_disk_ir" also affects delayed-write versus write-through-filesystem behavior.

dontdump

"dontdump" is a bit-map value that defines which classes of kernel memory pages are to be dumped if a kernel panic occurs.

Acceptable Values:

Minimum: "0"
Maximum: none
Default: "0"

Specify integer value.

Description

On large systems, the time required to dump system memory when a kernel panic occurs can be excessive or even prohibitive, depending on how much physical memory is installed in the system. Fast-dump capabilities controlled by the "dontdump" and "alwaysdump" parameters provide a means for restricting kernel dumps to specific types of information:

* Unused Physical Memory
* Kernel Static Data
* Kernel Dynamic Data
* File-System Metadata
* Kernel Code
* Buffer Cache
* Process Stack
* User Process

The bit-map value stored in "alwaysdump" specifies which of these memory classes are to be included in the memory dumps associated with a kernel panic.

Related Parameters

"alwaysdump" and "dontdump" have opposite effects. If the bit corresponding to a particular memory-page class is set in one parameter, it should not be set in the other parameter; otherwise a coflict occurs and the actual kernel behavior based on parameter values is undefined. These conflicts do not occur when SAM is used to set the values ([[Modify Page-Class Configuration]] in the [[Actions]] menu, SAM "Dump Devices" subarea in the kernel-configration area).

enable_idds

enable_idds is reserved for future use.

Acceptable Values:

Default: "0 (off)"

Specify boolean value.

Description

enable_idds is reserved for future use in an optional product.

Customers should not attempt to change this parameter. Enabling this parameter without the optional product provides no benefit and will lower system performance by a few percentage points.

IDDS = Intrusion Detection Data Source

eqmemsize

Specify size, in pages, of the equivalently mapped memory reserve pool.

Acceptable Values:

Minimum:	" 0"
Maximum:	Memory limited
Default:	"15" pages

Specify integer value or use integer formula expression.

Description

"eqmemsize" specifies the minimum amount of memory space, in pages, that is to be reserved as a pool of space for use by drivers and subsystems that require allocated memory where addressing is the same in real and virtual mode. At boot time, the system may increase the actual space reserved, based upon how much physical memory is installed.

Drivers use these pages to transfer information between hardware interfaces. The driver places data on the page, using virtual mode. The hardware then transfers the data, using DMA (Direct Memory Access) in real mode, bypassing the addressing translation. Since the virtual and real addresses are the same, no special address processing is needed. The space is also used to support address aliasing requests issued on behalf of "EXEC_MAGIC" processes.

Normally, the system handles requests for equivalently mapped memory dynamically by trying to obtain a free page with a matching virtual address from the system-wide memory pool. If the system cannot dynamically obtain an equivalently mapped page, it resorts to its reserve pool. Normally this reserve pool should never be exhausted because the system can usually dynamically allocate an equivalently mapped page. However, systems with a relatively high load and/or a physical memory configuration that exceeds 1 Gbyte could potentially deplete this reserve pool.

Depending on the exact nature of applications running on the system, system load, memory and I/O configurations, and other factors, the reserve pool could still become exhausted. If this happens, the system prints a message to the console indicating that the reserve pool has been exhausted and that "eqmemsize" should be increased.

executable_stack

Allows or denies program execution on the stack (security feature).

Acceptable Values:

Minimum: "   0"
Maximum: "   2"
Default: "   1"

Specify integer value. "0" is disable, "1" is enable, "2" is enable with warning.

Description

executable_stack provides protection against commonly attempted security breaches. It sets the system-wide default for whether to use system memory-mapping hardware to help protect against one of the most common classes of security breaches, commonly known as 'stack buffer overflow attacks.'

Unless you have a proven need to do otherwise, HP strongly recommends that you set this parameter to a value of '0' (zero). This is the most secure of the settings, incurs no performance penalty, and will very rarely interfere with legitimate applications.

Note that, for compatibility reasons, the default setting of this parameter in this release is '1' (one), which is the most compatible but least secure setting. It is equivalent to system behavior on HP-UX 11.00 and earlier, and does not provide protection against this type of attack.

Refer to the description of the '+es' option in the manual page for chatr(1) for a detailed description of the effects of this parameter, the meanings of the possible settings, how to recognize if a different setting may be needed on your system, and how to combine system-wide and per-application settings for the best tradeoffs between security and compatibility for your system.

fs_async

Select synchronous or asynchronous writes of file-system data structures to disk.

Acceptable Values:

Minimum: "0" (Use synchronous disk writes only)
Maximum: "1" (Allow asynchronous disk writes)
Default: "0"

Specify integer value of "0" or "1".

Description

"fs_async" specifies whether or not asychronous writing of file-system data structures to disk is allowed. If no value for "fs_async" is specified, synchronous writes are used.

Synchronous writes to disk make it easier to restore file system integrity if a system crash occurs while file system data structures are being updated on the file system.

If asynchronous writes are selected, HP-UX file system semantics for NFS cluster environments are preserved. In addition, files opened using "open()" with the "0_SYNC" flag (synchronous writing) will continue to be written synchronously when the asynchronous-writes feature has been configured into the kernel.

Asynchronous writes to disk can improve file system performance significantly. However, asynchronous writes can leave file system data structures in an inconsistent state in the event of a system crash. For more information about when to select synchronous or asynchronous writing, refer to the explanatory text later in this help page.

What are Synchronous and Asynchronous Writes?

If a file is open for writing and data is being written to a file, the data is accumulated in buffers and periodically written to disk. When an end-of-file condition occurs and the file is to be closed, any remaining buffer contents are written to the disk, the inode is updated with file size and block pointer information, and the file system's list of free disk blocks is updated. To ensure maximum protection of file system integrity, these operations are handled in a specific sequence that minimizes the risk of file system corruption on the disk if a system crash or power failure occurs while writing to the disk. This sequential update process is called is called !!synchronous writing!!.

HP-UX file systems store free space lists, blocks, inodes, and other file components at random and widely separate locations on disk devices. This means that writing file information blocks in a particular sequence requires additional time to move to the desired location on the disk before performing the write operation. If a power failure or system crash occurs during this sequence, one or more blocks may not be properly updated, leaving a potentially inconsistent file system. The "fsck" command is used to repair such inconsistencies.

Asynchronous writing as it relates to the "fs_async" kernel parameter allows the system to update file system information on the disk in a more convenient (hence faster) sequence rather than in a more secure (safer but slower) sequence, thus reducing search and move delays between writes. However, if a system crash occurs while these operations are being performed, the risk of an inconsistent file system that cannot be automatically repaired by fsck is significantly greater than with synchronous writes.

Consequences of a Crash

If only synchronous writing is used, all updates to directories, file inodes, free space lists, etc. are handled in a sequence that is known to "fsck". If a crash occurs while updating any disk block in the sequence, "fsck" can readily determine where the crash occurred and repair the missing update information, probably without assistance from the system administrator.

If "fs_async" is set to allow asynchronous writes and a crash occurs, "fsck" does not know what sequence was used, and thus will probably require interactive assistance from the administrator while fixing inconsistent file system information, repairing directory and inode entries, etc.

Why Allow Asynchronous Writes?

Waiting for synchronous writing and updating of disk blocks when closing files after writing to them degrades the performance of programs and applications that require frequent file and directory write and close operations. Allowing asynchronous writing significantly reduces those delays, producing a corresponding improvement in performance. However, when applications are CPU intensive with relatively little disk I/O, performance improvements are much lower.

When Should I Use Asynchronous Writes?

Asynchronous writing is advisable for improving system performance if:

* Risk of power failure is low (very dependable power source and/or
uninterruptible power sources).

* Precautions have been taken to enhance data security (sophisticated
file system backup or redundancy strategies), or potential loss of
data due to a system crash is less important than system performance.

* User applications require frequent opening, writing, and closing of
disk files and directories.

* Elimination of synchronous writing would improve system performance
sufficiently to offset any associated risks.

To enable asynchronous writing, set the "fs_async" kernel parameter to
"1" instead of the default value of "0").

hfs_max_ra_blocks

Set the maximum number of read-ahead blocks that the kernel may have
outstanding for a single HFS filesystem.

Acceptable Values:

Minimum: " 0"
Maximum: "128"
Default: " 8"

Specify integer value or use integer formula expression.

Description

When data is read from a disk drive, the system may read additional data
beyond that requested by the operation. This "read-ahead" speeds up sequential
disk accesses, by anticipating that additional data will be read, and
having it available in system buffers before it is requested.
This parameter limits the number of read-ahead blocks that the kernel
is allowed to have outstanding for any given HFS filesystem. The
limit applies to each individual HFS filesystem, !!not!! to the
system-wide total.

"hfs_max_ra_blocks" and "hfs_ra_per_disk"should be adjusted according to
the characteristics of the workload on the system.

Note

To determine the block size of the filesystem containing the current directory, use the command:

df -g

EXAMPLE ONE

A software development environment typically consists of small or
medium sized I/Os with a fair number of disk seeks. Therefore,
"hfs_max_ra_blocks" should be set to 8-to-16 blocks and "hfs_ra_per_disk"
should be set to 32-to-64 kilobytes.

EXAMPLE TWO

An out-of-core solver for an MCAE application has a significant sequential
I/O component, so "hfs_max_ra_blocks" should be set to 64-to-128 blocks and
"hfs_ra_per_disk" to 128-to-256 kilobytes.

hfs_ra_per_disk

Set the amount of HFS filesystem read-ahead per disk drive, in Kbytes.

Acceptable Values:

Minimum: " 0"
Maximim: "8192"
Default: " 64"

Specify an integer value or use an integer formula expression.

Description

When data is read from a disk drive, the system may read additional data
beyond that requested by the operation. This "read-ahead" speeds up sequential
disk accesses, by anticipating that additional data will be read, and
having it available in system buffers before it is requested.
This parameter specifies the amount of read-ahead permitted per disk drive.

The total amount of read-ahead is determined by multiplying
"hfs_ra_per_disk" by the number of drives in the logical volume.
If the filesystem does not reside in a logical volume, then the
number of drives is effectively one.

hfs_revra_blocks

This parameter sets the maximum blocks read with each HFS reverse read-ahead operation.

Acceptable Values:

Minimum: 0''
Maximum: 128''
Default;   8''

Specify integer value.

Description

This tunable defines the maximum number of Kbytes to be read in a read-ahead operation when sequentially reading backwards.

Only HP Field Engineers should modify the hfs_revra_per_disk kernel parameter. Customers should not change this parameter from its default value.

Purpose

This value should be raised when the workload is known to include frequent reverse-order sequential reading of files. This value should be lowered back to its default value if raising the value does not provide noteworthy performance improvement. Increasing this value has potential additional disk contention and performance penalty due to excess read-ahead.

Interactions

The following additional tunable parameters may also need to be modified when changing the value of "hfs_revra_per_disk":

hfs_max_revra_blocks; hfs_ra_per_disk; hfs_max_ra_blocks

hfs_revra_per_disk

This parameter sets the maximum HFS file system blocks read with each reverse read-ahead operation.

Minimum:"0''
Maximum:"8192''
Default:"64''

Specify integer value.

Description

This tunable defines the maximum number of file system blocks to be read in a read-ahead operation when sequentially reading backwards.

Only HP Field Engineers should modify the hfs_revra_per_disk kernel parameter. Customers should not change this parameter from its default value.

Purpose

An increase in the value of this parameter is indicated when there are a large number of reverse sequential file I/Os on file systems with small file system block sizes. Raising the value of this parameter will mean that more memory is used in the buffer cache.

A decrease in the value of this parameter is indicated when there are a small number of reverse sequential file I/Os on files systems with large file system block sizes. Decreasing the value of this parameter can cause a decreased file throughput rate.

Interactions

The following additional tunable parameters may also need to be modified when changing the value of "hfs_revra_per_disk":

hfs_max_revra_blocks; hfs_ra_per_disk; hfs_max_ra_blocks

initmodmax

"initmodmax" specifies the maximum number of kernel modules that the "savecrash" command will handle when a kernel panic causes a system-memory dump.

Acceptable Values:

Minimum: "0"
Maximum: none
Default: "50"

Specify integer value.

Description

When a kernel panic (system crash) occurs, specified areas of system memory are copied to the dump devices before the system shuts down. The "savecrash" command can then be used to copy the dump area into a directory in a file system (requires !!lots!! of space, depending on system size and what memory classes were dumped).

When the kernel includes dynamically loadable kernel modules (drivers
that are not statically installed in the kernel), "savecrash" must
allocate space in one of its structures to hold information about
those modules. Since there is no means to predict how many modules
might be loaded at any given time, this parameter provides an upper
limit that "savecrash" is prepared to deal with.

If "initmodmax" is set to less than the number of loaded kernel
modules, only the first modules encountered up to the limit are
processed by "savecrash". It is therefore important that
system administrators keep track of how many kernel modules are
being loaded during system operation to ensure that "initmodmax"
has a value sufficient to properly handle them in case of a kernel
panic and dump.

Note that this parameter only affects the operation of the "savecrash"
command. It does not limit the number of modules that can be loaded
into the kernel during normal system operation.

ksi_alloc_max

"ksi_alloc_max" specifies the system-wide maximum number of queued
signals that can be allocated.

Acceptable Values:

Minimum: "32"
Maximum: (memory limited)
Default: "nproc * 8"

Specify integer value.

Description

The kernel allocates storage space for the data structures required to
support queued signals that are sent by processes using the
"sigqueue()" system call. This parameter is used to determine how much space
should be allocated. At any given time during normal system operation,
if the combined total number of queued signals sent by existing
processes and still pending at receivers are enough to fill the
available data-structure space, no new queued signals can be sent.

Note that queued signals are different than traditional HP-UX/UNIX
signals. Traditional signals (such as kill or hangup signals) were sent
to the receiving process. If multiple identical signals were sent to a

single process, there was no way for the process to determine that more
than one signal had been sent. Queued signals eliminate that ambiguity
because a process can handle a queued signal, then examine the queue
again to discover another signal on the queue.

"ksi_alloc_max" specifies the maximum number of queued signals that
can be queued at any given time, system wide, by controlling how much
data-structure space is allocated in the kernel for handling queued
signals. The limit value of "SIGQUEUE_MAX" and
"_POSIX_SIGQUEUE_MAX" defined in "/usr/include/limits.h" are
affected by the value of this parameter.

The default value of this parameter is set to "nproc * 8" which allows
a total large enough to accommodate eight signals pending for every
process running on the system, assuming that the system is running at
full capacity. This should be adequate for nearly all systems unless
system software requirements dictate that a more are needed.

ksi_send_max

"ksi_send_max" specifies the maximum number of queued signals that a
single process can send and have pending at one or more receivers.

Acceptable Values:

Minimum: "32"
Maximum: (memory limited)
Default: "32"

Specify integer value.

Description

The kernel allocates storage space for the data structures required to
support queued signals that are sent by processes using the
"sigqueue()" system call. This parameter is used to determine how much space
should be allocated. At any given time during normal system operation,
if the combined total number of queued signals sent by existing
processes and still pending at receivers are enough to fill the
available data-structure space, no new queued signals can be sent.

Note that queued signals are different than traditional HP-UX/UNIX
signals. Traditional signals (such as kill or hangup signals) were sent
to the receiving process. If multiple identical signals were sent to a
single process, there was no way for the process to determine that more
than one signal had been sent. Queued signals eliminate that ambiguity
because a process can handle a queued signal, then examine the queue

again to discover another signal on the queue.

"ksi_send_max" places a limit on the number of queued signals that a
single process can send and/or have pending at one or more receivers.
It provides a mechanism for preventing a single process from
monopolizing the signals data-structure space by issuing too many
signals and thereby preventing other processes from being able to send
and receive signals due to insufficient kernel resources.

The default value of "32" is adequate for most common HP-UX
applications. If you have specialized applications that require more
than that number ("sigqueue()" returns "EAGAIN"), the number should
be increased sufficiently to prevent the error unless the "EAGAIN"
error returned by "sigqueue()" is due to a run-away process generating
signals when it should not.

> **maxvgs**   Maximum number of volume groups configured by the
> Logical Volume Manager on the system.

> **no_lvm_disks**   Flag that notifies the kernel when no logical
> volumes exist on the system. If set, all file
> systems coincide with physical disks on the system
> and physical disk boundaries. The only exception to
> this is when disks are configured for partitions or
> part of the disk is reserved for swap and other
> non-file-system uses.

max_async_ports

Specify the system-wide maximum number of ports to the asynchronous disk
I/O driver that processes can have open at any given time.

Acceptable Values:

Minimum: "1"
Maximum: " "
Default: "50"

Specify integer value.

Description

"max_async_ports" limits the total number of open ports to the
ansynchronous disk-I/O driver that processes on the system can have at
any given time (this has nothing to do with any RS-232 asynchronous

data-communications interfaces). The system allocates an array of port structures for each port when it is opened that is used for all communication between the process and the asynchronous disk driver. The number of asynchronous ports required by a given application is usually specified in the documentation for that application (such as database applications software, video management software, etc.).

To determine a suitable value for "max_async_ports":

* Determine how many ports are required for each application and/or process that uses asynchronous disk I/O.

* Determine which of these applications will be running simultaneously as separate processes. Also determine whether multiple copies of an application will be running at the same time as separate processes.

* Based on these numbers, determine the maximum number of open ports to the asynchronous disk driver that will be needed by all processes at any given time to obtain a reasonable total.

* Set "max_async_ports" to a value that is not less than this number.

maxdsiz and maxdsiz_64bit

Specify the maximum data segment size, in bytes, for an executing process.

Acceptable Values:

"maxdsiz" for 32-bit processes:

Minimum: "0x400000" (4 Mbytes)
Maximum: "0x7B03A000" (approx 2 Gbytes)
Default: "0x4000000" (64 Mbytes)

"maxdsiz_64bit" for 64-bit processes:

Minimum: "0x400000" (4 Mbytes)
Maximum: "4396972769279"
Default: "0x4000000" (64 Mbytes)

Specify integer value.

Description

Enter the value in bytes.

"maxdsiz" and "maxdsiz_64bit" define the maximum size of the
data storage segment of an executing process for 32-bit and 64-bit
processes, respectively.
The data storage segment contains fixed data storage such
as statics and strings, as well as dynamic data space allocated
using "sbrk()" and "malloc()".

Increase the value of "maxdsiz" or "maxdsiz_64bit" only if you have
one or more processes that use large amounts of data storage
space.

Whenever the system loads a process, or an executing process attempts to
expand its data storage segment, the system checks the size of the
process's data storage segment.

If the process' requirements exceed "maxdsiz" or "maxdsiz_64bit",
the system returns an error to the calling process, possibly causing the
process to terminate.

max_fcp_reqs

Define the maximum number of concurrent Fiber-Channel FCP requests that
are to be allowed on any FCP adapter installed in the machine.
Acceptable Values:

Minimum: "   0"
Maximum: "1024"
Default: " 512"

Specify integer value or use integer formula expression.

Description

"max_fcp_reqs" specifies the maximum number of concurrent FCP requests
that are allowed on an FCP adapter. The default value specified when
the system is shipped is 512 requests. To raise or lower the limit,
specify the desired value for this parameter. The optimal limit on
concurrent requests depends on several different factors such as
configuration, device characteristics, I/O load, host memory, and other
values that FCP software cannot easily determine.

Related Parameters and System Values

The system allocates memory for use by Tachyon FCP adapters based on the comination of values specified for "num_tachyon_adapters" and "max_fcp_reqs".

maxssiz and maxssiz_64bit

Set the maximum dynamic storage segment (DSS) size in bytes. Acceptable Values:

"maxssiz" for 32-bit processes:

Minimum: "0x4000 (16" Kbytes)
Maximum: "0x17F00000" (approx 200 Mbytes)
Default: "0x800000" (8 Mbytes)

"maxssiz_64bit" for 64-bit processes:

Minimum: "0x4000 (16" Kbytes)
Maximum: "1073741824"
Default: "0x800000" (8 Mbytes)

Specify integer value.

Description

Enter the value in bytes.

"maxssiz" and "maxssiz_64bit" define, for 32-bit and 64-bit processes respectively, the maximum size of the dynamic storage segment (DSS), also called the user-stack segment, or an executing process's run-time stack. This segment contains stack and register storage space, generally used for local variables.

The default DSS size meets the needs of most processes. Increase the value of "maxssiz" or "maxssiz_64bit" only if you have one or more processes that need large amounts of dynamic storage.

The stack grows dynamically. As it grows, the system checks the size of the process' stack segment. If the stack size requirement exceeds "maxssiz" or "maxssiz_64bit", the system terminates the process.

maxswapchunks

Set the maximum amount of swap space configurable on the system.

Acceptable Values:

Minimum: " 1"
Maximum: "16384"
Default: " 256"

Specify integer value.

Description

"maxswapchunks" specifies the maximum amount of configurable swap space
on the system. The maximum swap space limit is calculated as follows:

* Disk blocks contain "DEV_BSIZE" (1024) bytes each. "DEV_BSIZE" is
  the system-wide mass storage block size and is not configurable.

* Swap space is allocated from device to device in chunks, each chunk
  containing "swchunk" blocks. Selecting an appropriate value for
  "swchunk" requires extensive knowledge of system internals.
  Without such knowledge, the value of "swchunk" should not be
  changed from the standard default value.

* The maximum number of chunks of swap space allowed system-wide is
  "maxswapchunks" chunks.

* The maximum swap space in bytes is:

  "maxswapchunks" × "swchunk" × "DEV_BSIZE"

  For example, using default values for "swchunk" (2048) and
  "maxswapchunks" (256), and assuming "DEV_BSIZE" is 1024 bytes, the
  total configurable swap space equals 537 Mbytes.

Selecting Values

The amount of swap space available on system disk devices is determined
by the contents of file "/etc/fstab", and is not affected by kernel
configuration.

On a stand-alone system or on a cluster client with local swap space,
"maxswapchunks" should be set to support sufficient swap space to
accommodate all swap anticipated. Set the parameter large enough to
avoid having to reconfigure the kernel.

For a server node, set the parameter to include not only the server's
local swap needs, but also sufficient swap for each client node that
will use the swap. At a minimum, allot swap space equal to the amounts

of memory used by each client.

max_thread_proc

Specify the maximum number of threads a single process is allowed
to have.

Acceptable Values:

Minimum: "64"
Maximum: "30000"
Default: "64"

Specify integer value.

Description

"max_thread_proc" limits the number of threads a single process is
allowed to create. This protects the system from excessive use of
system resources if a run-away process creates more threads than it
should in normal operation. The value assigned to this parameter is the
limit value assigned to the limit variables "PTHREAD_THREADS_MAX" and
"_SC_THREAD_THREADS_MAX" defined in "/usr/include/limits.h".

When a process is broken into multiple threads, certain portions of the
process space are replicated for each thread, requiring additional
memory and other system resources. If a run-away process creates too
many processes, or if a user is attacking the system by intentionally
creating a large number of threads, system performance can be seriously
degraded or other malfunctions can be introduced.

Selecting a value for "max_thread_proc" should be based on evaluating
the most complex threaded applications the system will be running and
determine how many threads will be required or created by such
applications under worst-case normal use. The value should be at least
that large but not enough larger that it could compromise other system
needs if something goes wrong.

maxtsiz

Set maximum shared-text segment size in bytes.

Acceptable Values:

"maxtsiz" for 32-bit processes:

Minimum: " 262144'' (256 kbytes)
Maximum: "1073741824'' (1 Gbyte)
Default:" 0x4000000'' (64 Mbytes)

"maxtsiz_64bit'' for 64-bit processess:

Minimum: " 262144'' (256 kbytes)
Maximum: "4398046507008'' (approx 4 Tbytes)
Default: " 0x4000000'' (64 Mbytes)

Specify integer value.

Description

"maxtsiz'' and "maxtsiz_64bit'' define, for 32-bit and 64-bit
processes respectively, the maximum size of the shared text segment
(program storage space) of an executing process. Program executable
object code is stored as read-only, and thus can be shared by multiple
processes if two or more processes are executing the same program
simultaneously, for example.

The normal default value accommodates the text segments of most
processes. Unless you plan to execute a process with a text segment
larger than 64 Mbytes, do not modify "maxtsiz'' or "maxtsiz_64bit''.

Each time the system loads a process with shared text, the system checks
the size of its shared text segment. The system issues an error message
and aborts the process if the process' text segment exceeds "maxtsiz''
or "maxtsiz_64bit''.

"maxtsiz'' and "maxtsiz_64bit'' can be set by rebuilding the kernel
or be set in the running kernel with "settune()''. "SAM'' and
"kmtune'' use "settune()''. Dynamic changes to "maxtsiz'' and
"maxtsiz_64bit'' only affect future calls to "exec()''.
Dynamically lowering these parameters will not affect any running
processes, until they call "exec()''.

maxuprc

Set maximum number of simultaneous user processes.

Acceptable Values:

Minimum: " 3''
Maximum: "Nproc-5''
Default:"50''

Specify integer value.

Description

"maxuprc" establishes the maximum number of simultaneous processes available to each user on the system. A user is identified by the user ID number, not by a login instance. Each user requires at least one process for the login shell, and additional processes for all other processes spawned in that process group. (the default is usually adequate).

The super-user is exempt from this limit.

Pipelines need at least one simultaneous process for each side of a "|". Some commands, such as cc, fc, and pc, use more than one process per invocation.

If a user attempts to start a new process that would cause the total number of processes for that user to exceed "maxuprc", the system issues an error message to the user:

no more processes

If a user process executes a "fork()" system call to create a new process, causing the total number of processes for the user to exceed "maxuprc", "fork()" returns −1 and sets "errno" to "EAGAIN".

"maxuprc" can be set by rebuilding the kernel or be set in the running kernel with "settune()". "SAM" and "kmtune" use "settune()". Dynamic changes to "maxuprc" only affect future calls to "fork()". Lowering "maxuprc" below a user's current number of processes will not affect any running processes. The user's processes will not be able to "fork()" until enough of the current processes exit that the user is below the new limit.

maxusers

Allocate system resources according to the expected number of simultaneous users on the system.

Acceptable Values:

Minimum: "0"
Maximum: Memory limited
Default: "32"

Specify integer value.

Description

"maxusers" limits system resource allocation, not the actual number of users on the system. "maxusers" does not itself determine the size of any structures in the system; instead, the default value of other global system parameters depend on the value of "maxusers". When other configurable parameter values are defined in terms of "maxusers", the kernel is made smaller and more efficient by minimizing wasted space due to improperly balanced resource allocations.

"maxusers" defines the C-language macro MaxUsers (for example, "#define MaxUsers 8"). It determines the size of system tables. The actual limit of the number of users depends on the version of the HP-UX license that was purchased. To determine the actual limit, use the "uname -a" command.

Rather than varying each configurable parameter individually, it is easier to specify certain parameters using a formula based on the maximum number of expected users (for example, "nproc" "(20+8*MaxUsers)"). Thus, if you increase the maximum number of users on your system, you only need to change the "maxusers" parameter.

"maxvgs"

Specify maximum number of volume groups on the system.

Acceptable Values:

Minimum: " 1"
Maximum: "256"
Default: " 10"

Specify integer value.

Description

"maxvgs" specifies the maximum number of volume groups on the system. A set of data structures is created in the kernel for each logical volume group on the system. Setting this parameter to match the number of volume groups on the system conserves kernel storage space by creating only enough data structures to meet actual system needs.

"maxvgs" is set for to ten volume groups by default. To allow more or fewer, change "maxvgs" to reflect a new maximum number.

Related Parameters

None.

maxfiles

Set soft limit for the number of files a process is allowed to have open simultaneously.

Acceptable Values:

Minimum: " 30''
Maximum: "60000''
Default: " 60''

Specify integer value.

Description

"maxfiles'' specifies the system default soft limit for the number of files a process is allowed to have open at any given time. It is possible for a process to increase its soft limit and therefore open more than "maxfiles'' files.

Non-superuser processes can increase their soft limit until they reach the hard limit"maxfiles_lim''.

maxfiles_lim

Set hard limit for number of files a process is allowed to have open simultaneously.

Acceptable Values:

Minimum: " 30''
Maximum: "nfile''
Default: " 1024''

Specify integer value.

Description

"maxfiles_lim'' specifies the system default hard limit for the number of open files a process may have. It is possible for a non-superuser process to increase its soft limit up to this hard limit.

"maxfiles_lim'' can be set by rebuilding the kernel or be set in the running kernel with "settune()''. "SAM'' and "kmtune'' use "settune()''. Dynamic changes affect all existing processes in the system with two classes of exceptions: Process that are already over the new limit will be unaffected. Process that have specifically set their limits through a call to "setrlimit()" (or "ulimit") will be unaffected.

mesg

Enable or disable System V IPC message support in kernel at system boot time (Series 700 only).

Acceptable Values:

Minimum: "0" (Exclude System V IPC message parameters from kernel)
Maximum: "1" (Include System V IPC message parameters in kernel)
Default: "1"

Specify integer value of "0" or "1".

Description

"mesg" specifies whether the code for System V IPC message parameters is to be included in the kernel at system boot time (Series 700 systems only).

"mesg" = 1 Code is included in the kernel (enable IPC messages).

"mesg" = 0 Code is not included in the kernel (disable IPC messages).

Series 800 systems: IPC messages are always enabled in the kernel.

Series 700 systems: If "mesg" is set to zero, all other IPC message parameters are ignored.

modstrmax

"modstrmax" specifies the maximum size of the "savecrash" kernel-module table that contains module names and their location in the file system.

Acceptable Values:

Minimum: "500"
Maximum: none
Default: "500"

Specify integer value.

Description

When a kernel panic (system crash) occurs, specified areas of system
memory are copied to the dump devices before the system shuts down.
The "savecrash" command can then be used to copy the dump area into
a directory in a file system (requires !!lots!! of space, depending
on system size and what memory classes were dumped).

When the kernel includes dynamically loadable kernel modules (drivers
that are not statically installed in the kernel), "savecrash"
allocates space to keep track of module names and their locations on the
file system. The space stores full path names to directories containing
modules, and also module names. Space usage has been optimized by
keeping only one copy of a directory path, even if more than one module
is found there.

As more modules are added to the system, and if module names tend to be
long, or if modules are scattered around the file system, "modstrmax"
will need to be increased to accommodate the extra data.

Note that this parameter only affects the operation of the "savecrash"
command. It does not limit the number of modules that can be loaded
into the kernel during normal system operation.

msgmap

Specify size of the free-space resource map used for assigning locations
for new messages in shared memory.

Acceptable Values:

Minimum: "3"
Maximum: Memory limited
Default: "msgtql+2"

Specify integer value or use integer formula expression.

Description

Message queues are implemented as linked lists in shared memory, each
message consisting of one or more contiguous slots in the message queue.
As messages are allocated and deallocated, the shared memory area
reserved for messages may become fragmented.

"msgmap" specifies the size of a resource map used for allocating
space for new messages. This map shows the free holes in the shared
memory message space used by all message queues. Each entry in the map
contains a pointer to a corresponding set of contiguous unallocated
slots, and includes a pointer to the set plus the size of (number of

segments in) the set.

Free-space fragmentation increases as message size variation increases. Since the resource map requires an entry for each fragment of free space, excessive fragmentation can cause the free-space map array to fill up and overflow. If an overflow occurs when the kernel requests space for a new message or releases space used by a received message, the system issues the message:

DANGER: mfree map overflow

If this error message occurs, regenerate the kernel using a larger value for "msgmap".

msgmax

Specify the maximum individual messages size allowed, in bytes.

Acceptable Values:

Minimum: " 0"
Maximum: "min(msgmnb, msgseg * msgssz, 65535) bytes"
Default: " 8192 bytes"

Specify integer value.

Description

"msgmax" defines the maximum allowable size, in bytes, of individual messages in a queue.

Increase the value of "msgmax" only if applications being used on the system require larger messages. This parameter prevents malicious or poorly written programs from consuming excessive message buffer space.

msgmnb

Specify maximum total size, in bytes, of all messages that can be queued simultaneously on a message queue.

Acceptable Values:

Minimum: " 0"
Maximum: "min(msgseg * msgssz, 65535) bytes"
Default: "16384 bytes"

Specify integer value.

Description

"msgmnb" specifies the maximum total combined size, in bytes, of all messages queued in a given message queue at any one time.

Any "msgsnd()" system call that attempts to exceed this limit returns the error:

"EAGAIN"   If "IPC_NOWAIT" is set.
"EINTR"   If "IPC_NOWAIT" is not set.

"msgmnb" can be set by rebuilding the kernel or be set in the running kernel with "settune()". "SAM" and "kmtune" use "settune()". Dynamically changing this parameter will affect only new message queues as they are created. Existing message queues will be unaffected.

msgmni

Specify maximum number of message queues that can exist simultaneously on the system.

Acceptable Values:

Minimum: " 1"
Maximum: Memory limited
Default: "50"

Specify integer value.

Description

"msgmni" defines the maximum number of message queue identifiers allowed on the system at any given time.

One message queue identifier is needed for each message queue created on the system.

msgseg

"msgseg" specifies the system-wide maximum total number of message segments that can exist in all message queues at any given time.

Acceptable Values:

Minimum: " 1"
Maximum: "32767"
Default: " 2048"

Specify integer value.

Description

"msgseg", multiplied by "msgssz", defines the total amount of shared-memory
message space that can exist for all message queues, system-wide (not
including message header space).

The related parameter, "msgssz" (message segment size in bytes),
defines the number of bytes that are reserved for each message segment
in any queue. When a message is placed in the queue, the length of the
message determines how many "msgssz" segments are used for that
message. Space consumed by each message in the queue is always an
integer multiple of "msgssz".

"msgseg" (message segments) defines the number of these units that are
available for all queues, system-wide.

"msgssz"

Specify message segment size to be used when allocating message space in
message queues.

Acceptable Values:

Minimum: "1"
Maximum: Memory limited
Default: "8 bytes"

Specify integer value.

Description

"msgssz", multiplied by "msgseg", defines the total amount of
shared-memory message space that can exist for all message queues,
system-wide (not including message header space).

"msgssz" specifies the size, in bytes, of the segments of memory space
to be allocated for storing IPC messages. Space for new messages is
created by allocating one or more message segments containing "msgssz"
bytes each as required to hold the entire message.

msgtql

Specify maximum number of messages allowed to exist on the system at
any given time.

Acceptable Values:

Minimum: "1"
Maximum: Memory limited
Default: "40"

Specify integer value.

Description

"msgtql" dimensions an area for message header storage. One message
header is created for each message queued in the system. Thus, the size
of the message header space defines the maximum total number of messages
that can be queued system-wide at any given time. Message headers are
stored in shared (swappable) memory.

If a "msgsnd()" system call attempts to exceed the limit imposed by
"msgtql", it:

  * Blocks waiting for a free header if the "IPC_NOWAIT" flag is
    !!not!! set, or it

  * returns "EAGAIN" if "IPC_NOWAIT" is set.

ndilbuffers

Set maximum number of Device I/O Library device files that can be open
simultaneously at any given time.

Acceptable Values:

Minimum: " 1"
Maximum: Memory limited
Default: "30"

Specify integer value.

Description

"ndilbuffers" defines the maximum number of Device I/O Library (DIL)
device files that can be open, system-wide, at any given time.

"ndilbuffers" is used exclusively by the Device I/O Library. If DIL
is not used, no DIL buffers are necessary.

nbuf

Set system-wide number of file-system buffer and cache buffer headers
(determines maximum total number of buffers on system). See note below.

Acceptable Values:

Minimum: "0 or 16"
Maximum: Memory limited
Default: "0"

Specify integer value of zero (see below).

Description

This parameter is for backwards compatibility and should be set to zero
because dynamic buffer cache is preferred.

If set to a non-zero value, "nbuf" specifies the number of buffer
headers to be allocated for the file system buffer-cache. Each buffer
is allocated 4096 bytes of memory unless overridden by a conflicting
value for "bufpages".

If "nbuf" is set to a non-zero value that is less than 16 or greater
than the maximum supported by the system, or to a value that is
inconsistent with the value of "bufpages", the number will be
increased or decreased as appropriate, and a message printed at boot
time.

Related Parameters

"nbuf" interacts with "bufpages" as follows:

 * "bufpages" = 0, "nbuf" = 0: Enables dynamic buffer cache.

 * "bufpages" not zero, "nbuf" = zero: Creates "BufPages/2"
   buffer headers and allocates "bufpages" times 4 Kbytes of buffer
   pool space at system boot time.

 * "bufpages" = 0, "nbuf" not zero: Allocates "Nbuf*2" pages of
   buffer pool space and creates "Nbuf" headers at boot time.

 * "bufpages" not zero, "nbuf" not zero: Allocates "BufPages"
   pages of buffer pool space and creates "Nbuf" buffer headers at

boot time. If the two values conflict such that it is impossible to configure a system using both of them, "bufpages" takes precedence.

"ncallout"

Specify the maximum number of timeouts that can be scheduled by the kernel at any given time.

Acceptable Values:

Minimum: "6"
Maximum: Memory limited
Default: "16+nproc"

Specify integer value or use integer formula expression.

Description

"ncallout" specifies the maximum number of timeouts that can be scheduled by the kernel at any given time. Timeouts are used by:

* "alarm()" system call,

* "setitimer()" system call,

* "select()" system call,

* drivers,

* "uucp" processes,

* process scheduling.

When the system exceeds the timeout limit, it prints the following fatal error to the system console:

panic: timeout table overflow

Related Parameters

If the value of "nproc" is increased, "ncallout" should be increased proportionately. A general rule is that one callout per process should be allowed unless you have processes that use multiple callouts.

ncdnode

Maximum number of open CD-ROM file-system nodes that can be in memory.

Acceptable Values:

Minimum: "14"
Maximum: Memory limited
Default: "150"

Specify integer value or use integer formula expression.

Description

"ncdnode" specifies the maximum number of CD-ROM file-system nodes
that can be in memory (in the vnode table) at any given time. It is
functionally similar to "ninode" but applies only to CD-ROM file
systems. Behavior is identical on Series 700 and Series 800 systems.

Each node consumes 288 bytes which means, for example, that if
"ncdnodes" is set to 10&sigspace;000, nearly 3 Mbytes of memory is
reserved exclusively for CD-ROM file-system node tables.

nclist

Specify number of cblocks for pty and tty data transfers.

Acceptable Values:

Minimum: "132"
Maximum: Limited by available memory
Default: "(100 + 16 * MAXUSERS)"

Specify integer value or use integer formula expression.

Description

"nclist" specifies how many cblocks are allocated in the system. Data
traffic is stored in cblocks as it passes through tty and pty devices.

The default value for "nclist", "(100 + 16 * MAXUSERS)", is based on
a formula of 100 cblocks for system use in handling traffic to the
console, etc., plus an average of 16 cblocks per user session. Note
that cblocks are also used for serial connections other than login
sessions, such as as SLIP connections, UUCP transfers, terminal
emulators, and such. If your system is using these other kinds of
connections, "nclist" should be increased accordingly.

If the cblock pool is exhausted, data being passed through a tty or pty
device might be lost because no cblock was available when it was needed.

nfile

Set maximum number of files that can be open simultaneously on the system
at any given time.

Acceptable Values:

Minimum: ``14"
Maximum: Memory limited
Default:
``((16*(NPROC+16+MAXUSERS)/10)+32+2*(NPTY+NSTRPTY+NSTRTEL)"

Specify integer value or use integer formula expression.

Description

``nfile" defines the maximum number files that can be open at any one
time, system-wide.

It is the number of slots in the file descriptor table. Be generous
with this number because the required memory is minimal, and not having
enough slots restricts system processing capacity.

nflocks

Specify the maximum combined total number of file locks that are
available system-wide to all processes at any given time.

Acceptable Values:

Minimum: ``2"
Maximum: Memory limited
Default: ``200"

Specify integer value or use integer formula expression.

Description

``nflocks" gives the maximum number of file/record locks that are
available system-wide. When choosing this number, note that one file

may have several locks and databases that use ``lockf()'' may need an exceptionally large number of locks.

Open and locked files consume memory and other system resources. These resources must be balanced against other system needs to maintain optimum overall system performance. Achieving an optimum balance can be quite complex, especially on large systems, because of wide variation in the kinds of applications being used on each system and the number and types of applications that might be running simultaneously, the number of local and/or remote users on the system, and many other factors.

ninode

Specify the maximum number of open inodes that can be in memory.

Acceptable Values:

Minimum: ``14''
Maximum: Memory limited
Default: ``nproc+48+maxusers+(2*npty)''

Specify integer value or use integer formula expression.

Description

``ninode'' defines the number of slots in the inode table, and thus the maximum number of open inodes that can be in memory. The inode table is used as a cache memory. For efficiency reasons, the most recent ``Ninode'' (number of) open inodes is kept in main memory. The table is hashed.

Each unique open file has an open inode associated with it. Therefore, the larger the number of unique open files, the larger ``ninode'' should be.

nkthread

Specify the maximum number of threads that all processes combined can run, system-wide, at any given time.

Acceptable Values:

Minimum ``   50''
Maximum ``30000''
Default ``(nproc*2)+16''

Specify integer or formula value.

Description

Processes that use threads for improved performance create multiple copies of certain portions of their process space, which requires memory space for thread storage as well as processor and system overhead related to managing the threads. On systems running large threaded applications, a large number of threads may be required. The kernel parameter ``max_thread_proc'' limits the number of threads that a single process can create, but there may be other threaded applications on the system that also use a large number of threads or they may have more modest requirements.

``nkthread'' limits the combined total number of threads that can be running on the system at any given time from all processes on the system. This value protects the system against being overwhelmed by a large number of threads that exceeds normal, reasonable operation. It protects the system against overload if multiple large applications are running, and also protects the system from users who might maliciously attempt to sabotage system operation by launching a large number of threaded programs, causing resources to become unavailable for normal system needs.

The default value allows an average of two threads per process plus an additional system allowance. If you need to use a larger value:

* Determine the total number of threads required by each threaded application on the system; especially any large applications.

* Determine how many and which of these will be running simultaneously at any given time.

* Add these together and combine with a reasonable allowance for other users or processes that might run occasionally using threads (``nproc*2'' might be a useful number).

* Select a value for ``nkthread'' that is large enough to accommodate the total, but not so large that it compromises system integrity.

no_lvm_disk

Tell the kernel that no logical volume groups exist on the system (Series 700 only).

Acceptable Values:

Minimum: ``0'' (check for LVM disks)
Maximum: ``1'' (system has no LVM disks)
Default: ``0''

Specify integer value of ``0'' or ``1''.

Description

By default at boot time, the system checks for LVM data structures on
the configured root, swap, and dump disks. If no LVM disks exist on the
system, setting ``no_lvm_disks'' to 1 speeds up the boot process by
omitting the check for LVM data structures.

Setting this parameter to a non-zero value on systems where LVM is
being used causes kernel panics because the kernel does not obtain
the necessary information about logical volumes on the system during
the normal boot process.

``nproc''

number of processes

Minimum: ``10''
Maximum: Memory limited
Default: ``20+(8 * maxusers)''

Specify integer value or use integer formula expression.

Description

``nproc'' specifies the maximum total number of processes that can exist
simultaneously in the system.

There are at least four system overhead processes at all times, and
one entry is always reserved for the super-user.

When the total number of processes in the system is larger than
``nproc'', the system issues these messages:

At the system console:

proc: table is full

Also, if a user tries to start a new process from a shell, the following
message prints on the user's terminal:

no more processes

If a user is executing ``fork()'' to create a new process, ``fork()''
returns −1 and sets ``errno'' to ``EAGAIN''.

npty

Specifies the maximum number of pseudo-tty data structures available
on the system.

Acceptable Values:

Minimum: `` 1''
Maximum: Memory limited
Default: ``60''

Specify integer value.

Description

``npty'' limits the number of the following structures that can be used
by the pseudo-teletype driver:

```
struct tty       pt_tty[npty];
struct tty       *pt_line[npty];
struct pty_info  pty_info[npty];
```

NSTREVENT'

Set the maximum number of outstanding streams bufcalls that are allowed
to exist on the system at any given time.

Acceptable Values:

Minimum: none
Maximum: none
Default: ``50''

Specify integer value.

Description

This parameter limits the maximum number of outstanding bufcalls that
are allowed to exist in a stream at any given time. The number of
bufcalls that exist in a given stream is determined by the number and
nature of the streams modules that have been pushed into that stream.

This parameter is intended to protect the system against resource
overload caused if the combination of modules running in all streams
issue an excessive number of bufcalls. The value selected should be
equal to or greater than the combined maximum number of bufcalls that
can be reasonably expected during normal operation from all streams on
the system. This value depends on the behavior and structure of each
available streams module as well as the number and combinations of
modules that can be pushed onto all streams in the system at any
given time.

nstrpty

Set the system-wide maximum number of streams-based PTYs that are
allowed on the system.

Acceptable Values:

Minimum: ``0"
Maximum: Memory limited
Default: ``0"

Specify integer value.

Description

This parameter limits the number of streams-based PTYs that are allowed
system-wide. When sending data to PTY devices (such as windows), a PTY
device must exist for every window that is open at any given time.

This parameter should be set to a value that is equal to or greater than
the number of PTY devices on the system that will be using streams-based
I/O pipes. Using a parameter value significantly larger than the number
of PTYs is not recommended. ``nstrpty" is used when creating data
structures in the kernel to support those streams-based PTYs, and an
excessively large value wastes kernel memory space.

NSTRPUSH

Set the maximum number of streams modules that are allowed to exist in
any single stream at any given time on the system.

Acceptable Values:

Minimum: none
Maximum: none

Default: ``16''

Specify integer value.

Description

This parameter defines the maximum number of streams modules that can be
pushed onto any given stream. This provides some protection against
run-away processes that might automatically select modules to push onto
a stream, but it is not intended as a defense against malicious use of
streams modules by system users.

Most systems do not require more than about three or four modules in any
given stream. However, there may be some unusual cases where more
modules are needed. The default value for this parameter allows as many
as 16 modules in a stream, which should be sufficient for even the most
demanding installations.

If your system needs more than 16 modules in a stream, the need should
be carefully evaluated, and the demands on other system resources such
as outstanding bufcalls and other factors should also be carefully
evaluated.

NSTRSCHED

Set the maximum number of streams scheduler daemons (``smpsched'') that
are allowed to run at any given time on the system.

Acceptable Values:

Minimum: ``0''
Maximum: ``32''
Default: ``0''

Specify integer value.

Description

This parameter defines the maximum number of multi-processor (MP)
streams-scheduler daemons to run on systems containing more than one
processer. Note that uni-processor (UP) systems do not use an MP
scheduler daemon, but both MP and UP systems always have one UP streams
scheduler (``supsched'').

If the parameter value is set to zero, the system determines how many
daemons to run, based on the number of processors in the system. The
value selected is ``1'' for 2-4 processors, ``2'' for 5-8 processors,

``3'' for 9-16 processors, and ``4'' for more than 16 processors.

If the parameter value is set to a positive, non-zero value, that is the number of ``smpsched'' daemons that will be created on an MP system.

nstrtel

Specifies the number of telnet device files that the kernel can support for incoming ``telnet'' sessions.

Acceptable Values:

Minimum: ``60''
Maximum: `` ''
Default: ``60''

Specify integer value.

Description

``nstrtel'' specifies the number of kernel data structures that are created at system boot time that are required to support the device files used by incoming telnet sessions on a server. This number should match the number of device files that exist on the system. If the ``insf'' command or SAM is used to create more telnet device files, the value of ``nstrtel'' must be increased accordingly or the device files cannot be used because there are no kernel data structures available for communicating with the system.

Select a value for ``nstrtel'' that is equal to or greater than the number of telnet device files on the system. Selecting a value that exceeds the number of device files actually existing on the system wastes the memory consumed by extra data structures, but it may be justified if you are planning to add more device files.

nswapdev

Specify number of disk devices that can be enabled for device swap.

Acceptable Values:

Minimum: `` 1''
Maximum: ``25''
Default: ``10''

Specify an integer value equal to the number of physical disk devices that have been configured for device swap up to the maximum limit of 25. Only an integer value is allowed (formula values do not work for this parameter).

Description

``nswapdev'' defines the maximum number of devices that can be used for device swap.

At system boot time, the kernel creates enough internal data structures to support device swap to the specified number of physical devices that have reserved system swap areas. If the specified value is greater than the number of available devices, the extra data structure space is never used, thus wasting a little bit of memory (<50 bytes per structure). If the value is less than the number of available devices, some devices cannot be used for swap due to lack of supporting data structures in the kernel.

Related Parameters

None.

nswapfs

Specify number of file systems that can be enabled for file-system swap.

Acceptable Values:

Minimum: `` 1"
Maximum: ``25"
Default: ``10"

Specify an integer value equal to the number of file systems that are available for file-system swap up to the maximum limit of 25.

Description

``nswapfs'' defines the maximum number of file systems that can be used for file system swap.

At system boot time, the kernel creates enough internal data structures (about 300 bytes per structure) to support file system swap to the specified number of file systems. If the specified value is greater than the number of available file systems, the extra data structure space is never used, thus wasting that much memory. If the value is less than the number of available file systems, some file systems cannot be used for swap due to lack of supporting data structures.

Related Parameters

nsysmap

Set the number of entries in the kernel dynamic memory virtual address space resource map.

Acceptable Values:

Minimum: `` 800"
Maximum: Memory Limited
Default: `` 2 * nproc"

Specify integer value.

Description

nsysmap and it's 64-bit equivalent, nsysmap64, sets the size of the kernel dynamic memory resource map, an array of address/length pairs that describe the free virtual space in the kernel's dynamic address space. There are different tunables for the 32-bit and 64-bit kernel because the 64-bit kernel has more virtual address space.

Previously, the kernel dynamic memory resource map was set by the system solely, and not easily changed. Certain workloads, which fragmented the kernel address space significantly, resulted in too many entries in the resource map. When this happened, the last entry in the resource map was thrown away, resulting in "leaked" kernel virtual address space. If this overflow happened often enough, virtual space was exhausted.

The system uses an algorithm to automatically scale the map size, at boot time, according to the system workload. If the value is still not set high enough to avoid the problem of overflowing the memory resource map array, you can tune this parameter to fit a particular workload.

Note that even when you override the default value, the kernel may increase the value beyond that value depending on the system size.

Purpose

This tunable was added to address the problem of ``kalloc: out of virtual space" system panics. Only systems that experience the resource map overflow will need to modify this tunable parameter.

The following message will appear on the console when the resource map overflow occurs:

sysmap32: rmap ovflo, lost [X,Y] *
or
sysmap64: rmap ovflo, lost [X,Y]

* Where X and Y are hexadecimal numbers.

If this happens rarely, no action is necessary. If this happens frequently, (for example, several times a day on a system which the user does not intend to reboot for a long time (a year of more), the tunable should be increased. If the tunable is not increased, the following panic may occur:

kalloc: out of kernel virtual space

When increasing nsysmap{32|64}, doubling the tunable value is a reasonable rule of thumb. If the problem persists after doubling the tunable several times from the default, there is likely another kernel problem, and the customer should go through their normal HP support channels to investigate.

Side-Effects

If the value of this parameter is increased, kernel memory use increases very slightly. Depending on the workload, if the tunable is quite large, the performance of kernel memory allocation may be negatively affected.

Lowering the value of this parameter from the default is risky and increases the probability of resource map overflows, eventually leading to a kernel panic. Consult your HP support representative prior to decreasing the value of nsysmap.

num_tachyon_adapters

Define number of Fiber-Channel Tachyon adapters in the system if system does not support I/O virtual addressing.

Acceptable Values:

Minimum: ``0"
Maximum: ``5"

Default: ``0''

Specify integer value or use integer formula expression. A non-zero
value is !!required!! if the system does not provide I/O virtual
addressing. Choose a value equal to the number of Tachyon FCP adapters
installed in the system.

Description

``num_tachyon_adapters'' specifies how many Tachyon FCP adapters are
installed in the system so that an appropriate amount of memory can be
allocated for them at system start-up if the system does not provide
I/O virtual addressing.

Specifying a Value for ``num_tachyon_adapters''

If your system does not provide I/0 virtual addressing, set
``num_tachyon_adapters'' equal to the number of Tachyon FCP adapters
actually installed in the machine. During boot-up, the system then
reserves a corresponding amount of memory for use by those adapters,
varying that amount according to the value of ``max_fcp_reqs''.

If the system supports I/O virtual addressing, set this parameter to
zero. The system then automatically allocates memory as needed.

If you do not know whether your system provides I/O virtual addressing,
setting this parameter to a non-zero value is harmless, provided the
value does not exceed the number of Tachyon FCP adapters actually
installed in the system. If the value exceeds the number of installed
adapters, a corresponding amount of memory is wasted because it cannot
be used for other purposes.

Related Parameters and System Values

The system allocates memory for use by Tachyon FCP adapters based on the
comination of values specified for ``num_tachyon_adapters'' and
``max_fcp_reqs''.

o_sync_is_o_dsync

``o_sync_is_o_dsync'' specifies whether the system is allowed to
translate the ``O_SYNC'' flag in an ``open()'' or ``fcntl()'' call
into an ``O_DSYNC'' flag.

Acceptable Values:

Minimum: ``0''

Maximum: ``1"
Default: ``0"

Specify integer value.

Description

In an ``open()" or ``fcntl()" call, the ``O_SYNC" and ``O_DSYNC"
flags are used to ensure that data is properly written to disk before
the call returns. If these flags are not set, the function returns as
soon as the disk-access request is initiated, and assumes that the write
operation will be successfully completed by the system software and
hardware.

Setting the ``O_SYNC" or ``O_DSYNC" flag prevents the function from
returning to the calling process until the requested disk I/O operation
is complete, thus ensuring that the data in the write operation has been
successfully written on the disk. Both flags are equivalent in this
regard except for one important difference: if ``O_SYNC" is set, the
function does not return until the disk operation is complete !!and!!
until all all file attributes changed by the write operation (including
access time, modification time, and status change time) are also written
to the disk. Only then does it return to the calling process.

Setting ``o_sync_is_o_dsync" to ``1" allows the system to convert any
``open()" or ``fcntl()" calls containing an ``O_SYNC" flag into the
same call using the ``O_DSYNC" flag instead. This means that the
function returns to the calling process before the file attributes are
updated on the disk, thus introducing the risk that this information
might not be on the disk if a system failure occurs.

Setting this parameter to a non-zero value allows the function to
return before file time-stamp attributes are updated, but still ensures
that actual file data has been committed to disk before the calling
process can continue. This is useful in installations that perform
large volumes of disk I/O and require file data integrity, but which can
gain some performance advantages by not forcing the updating of time
stamps before proceeding. When the benefits of performance improvement
exceeds the risks associated with having incorrect file-access timing
information if a system or disk crash occurs, this parameter can be set
to ``1". If that is not the case, it should remain set to its default
value of zero.

The setting of this parameter does not affect disk I/O operations
where ``O_SYNC" is not used.

page_text_to_local

Enable or disable swapping of program text segments to local swap device
on NFS cluster client.

Acceptable Values:

Minimum: ``0" (stand-alone, or client uses file-system server)
Maximum: ``1" (use client local swap)
Default: ``1" (use client local swap)

Specify integer value of ``0" or ``1".

Description

Programs usually contain three segments:

Text segment Unchanging executable-code part of the program.
Data segment Arrays and other fixed data structures
DSS segment   Dynamic storage, stack space, etc.

To minimize unnecessary network traffic, NFS cluster clients that have
no local swap device discard the text segment of programs when it
becomes necessary to swap memory in order to make space available for
another program or application. Text segments are discarded because
swapping to swap space on the server when no local disk is available
then later retrieving the same data that exists in the original program
file wastes server disk space and increases network data traffic.

However, when adequate swap space is available on a local disk device
that is connected to the client machine, it is more efficient to write
the text segment to local swap and retrieve it later. This eliminates
two separate text-segment data transfers to and from the server, thus
improving cluster performance (depending on the particular applications
and programs being used). To use local swap this way, the available
swap space must be greater than the !!maximum!! total swap space
required by !!all!! processes running on the system at any time. If
this condition is not met, system memory-allocation errors occur
when space conflicts arise.

``page_text_to_local" is the configurable kernel parameter that
determines whether text segments are discarded or swapped to the local
device to save network traffic.

``0"   Do not use local client swap device. Client either has no
       local swap device, or sufficient space is not available for
       full text swap support. Discard text segment if memory space

is needed, then retrieve original file from server when ready
to execute again.

``1''   Swap text pages to local swap device when memory space is
        needed for other purposes, then retrieve from swap device when
        the segment is required. This usually improves client
        performance and decreases cluster network data traffic. If
        you use this value, local swap !!must!! be enabled, and the
        available device-swap space on the client's local disk must be
        sufficient for the maximum required virtual memory for !!all!!
        programs that may be running on the client at any given time.
        Otherwise, processes may fail due to insufficient memory.

On stand-alone, non-cluster systems, set ``page_text_to_local'' to ``0''.

pfail_enabled

Disable or enable system power-failure routines (Series 800 only).

Acceptable Values:

Minimum: ``0''
Maximum: ``1''
Default: ``0''

Specify integer value.

Description

``pfail_enabled'' determines whether a Series 800 system can recognize a
local power failure (that halts the computer by affecting its central
bus). The value can be set to zero or ``1'' as follows:

``0''   Disable powerfail detect. This prevents the system from
        running the ``/sbin/powerfail'' command (started from
        ``/etc/inittab'') so that it can provide for recovery when a
        power failure occurs. Programs running when power fails
        cannot resume execution when power is restored.

``1''   Enable powerfail detection. This causes the system to recognize
        a power failure and employ recovery mechanisms related to the
        ``/sbin/powerfail'' command (started from ``/etc/inittab'') so
        that when a power failure occurs, programs running when power
        fails can resume execution when power is restored.

Be sure to follow guidelines for correct shutdown and start-up of a system necessitated by powerfail. These guidelines are discussed in the <book|System Administration Tasks| manual.

Note that although powerfail appears in all ``/etc/inittab'' files, the entry is only recognized and used by systems that support powerfail.

public_shlibs

Enable "public" protection IDs on shared libraries.

Acceptable Values:

Minimum: ``0''
Maximum: ``1'' (or non-zero)
Default: ``1''

Specify integer value.

Description

``public_shlibs'' enables the use of "public" protection IDs on shared libraries.

Shared libraries are implemented using ``mmap()'', and each individual ``mmap()'' is given a unique protection ID. Processes have four protection ID registers of which two are hard-coded to text/data. The remaining two are shared back and forth between whatever shared library/shared memory segments the user process is accessing.

A performance problem arose when the shared libraries were introduced, causing increased process ID (pid) thrashing. To minimize this effect, a public protection ID was added to all shared-library mappings, thus effectively removing shared libraries from the pool of objects that were accessing the two protection ID registers.

Setting ``public_shlibs'' to ``1'' allows the system to assign public protection id's to shared libraries. Setting it to ``0'' disables public access and places a unique protection id on every shared library. The default value is ``1'', and any non-zero value is interpreted as ``1''.

Set the parameter to zero value !!only!! if there is some "security hole" or other reason why a public value should not be used.

rtsched_numpri

Specify the number of available, distinct real-time process scheduling priorities.

Acceptable Values:

Minimum: `` 32"
Maximum: ``512"
Default: `` 32"

Specify integer value.

Description

``rtsched_numpri" specifies the number of distinct priorities that can be set for real-time processes running under the real-time scheduler (POSIX Standard, P1003.4).

Appropriate Values

The default value of 32 satisfies the needs of most configurations. In cases where you need more distinct levels of priorities among processes, increase the value accordingly. However, be aware that increasing the value of ``rtsched_numpri" to specify a larger number of priorities can cause the system to spend more time evaluating eligible processes, thus resulting in possible reduced overall system performance.

remote_nfs_swap

``remote_nfs_swap" enables or disables the ability of the system to perform swap to NFS-mounted devices or file systems.

Acceptable Values:

Minimum: ``0"
Maximum: ``1"
Default: ``0"

Specify integer value.

Description

Use ``remote_nfs_swap" to enable or disable the ability of the system to perform swap to NFS-mounted devices or file systems. The default value of zero disables NFS swap. To enable, change the value to ``1".

This parameter was initially created to allow clients in an NFS cluster
to use disk space on the server for swap. NFS clusters are no longer
supported on HP-UX systems, and this parameter is set to zero by default
(remote NFS swap not allowed). Setting this parameter to allow remote
NFS swap is not very useful unless the system where it is allowed has
extremely fast NFS capabilities.

scsi_maxphys

Set the maximum record size for the SCSI I/O subsystem, in bytes.

Acceptable Values:

Minimum: `` 1048576 (1 MB)"
Maximum: ``16777215 (16MB - 1)"
Default: `` 1048576 (1 MB)"

Specify integer value.

Description

This parameter is used in conjunction with
``st_large_recs" to enable large tape record support without logical
record breakup and recombination.

scsi_max_qdepth

Set the maximum number of SCSI commands queued up for SCSI devices.

Acceptable Values:

Minimum: `` 1"
Maximum: ``255"
Default: `` 8"

Specify integer value.

Description

For devices that support a queue depth greater than the system
default, this parameter controls how many I/Os the driver will attempt to
queue to the device at any one time. Valid values are (1-255). Some
disk devices will not support the maximum queue depth settable by this
command. Setting the queue depth in software to a value larger than
the disk can handle will result in I/Os being held off once a QUEUE
FULL condition exists on the disk.

st_fail_overruns

If set, SCSI tape read resulting in data overrun causes failure.

Acceptable Values:

Disabled: ``0"
Enabled: ``1"
Default: ``0"

Specify ``0" or ``1".

Description

Certain technical applications depend on the fact that
reading a record smaller than the actual tape record size
should generate an error.

st_large_recs

If set, enables large record support for SCSI tape.

Acceptable Values:

Disabled: ``0"
Enabled: ``1"
Default: ``0"

Specify ``0" or ``1".

Description

This parameter is used in conjunction with
``scsi_maxphys"to enable large tape record support without logical
record breakup and recombination.

scroll_lines

Specify the number of display lines in ITE console screen buffer.

Acceptable Values:

Minimum: `` 60"
Maximum: ``999"

Default: ``100"

Specify integer value.

Description

``scroll_lines" defines the scrolling area (the number of lines of emulated terminal screen memory on each Internal Terminal Emulator (ITE) port configured into the system).

semmni

Specify maximum number of sets of IPC semaphores that can exist simultaneously on the system.

Acceptable Values:

Minimum: `` 2"
Maximum: Memory limited
Default: ``64"

Specify integer value or use integer formula expression.

Description

``semmni" defines the number of sets (identifiers) of semaphores available to system users.

When the system runs out of semaphore sets, the ``semget()" system call returns a ``ENOSPC" error message.

semmns

Define the system-wide maximum number of individual IPC semaphores that can be allocated for users.

Acceptable Values:

Minimum: `` 2"
Maximum: Memory limited
Default: ``128"

Specify integer value or use integer formula expression.

Description

``semmns'' defines the system-wide maximum total number of individual semaphores that can be made available to system users.

When the free-space map shows that there are not enough contiguous semaphore slots in the semaphore area of shared memory to satisfy a ``semget()'' request, ``semget()'' returns a ``ENOSPC'' error. This error can occur even though there may be enough free semaphores slots, but they are not contiguous.

semmnu

Define the maximum number of processes that can have undo operations pending on any given IPC semaphore on the system.

Acceptable Values:

Minimum: `` 1''
Maximum: ``nproc-4''
Default: ``30''

Specify integer value.

Description

An !!undo!! is a special, optional, flag in a semaphore operation which causes that operation to be undone if the process which invoked it terminates.

``semmnu'' specifies the maximum number of processes that can have undo operations pending on a given semaphore. It determines the size of the ``sem_undo'' structure.

A ``semop()'' system call using the ``SEM_UNDO'' flag returns an ``ENOSPC'' error if this limit is exceeded.

semmap

Specify size of the free-space resource map used for allocating new System V IPC semaphores in shared memory.

Acceptable Values:

Minimum: ``4''
Maximum: Memory limited
Default: ``SemMNI+2''

Specify integer value or use integer formula expression.

Description

Each set of semaphores allocated per identifier occupies 1 or more contiguous slots in the sem array. As semaphores are allocated and deallocated, the sem array might become fragmented.

``semmap'' dimensions the resource map which shows the free holes in the sem array. An entry in this map is used to point to each set of contiguous unallocated slots; the entry consists of a pointer to the set, plus the size of the set.

If semaphore usage is heavy and a request for a semaphore set cannot be accommodated, the following message appears:

danger: mfree map overflow

You should then configure a new kernel with a larger value for ``semmap''.

Fragmentation of the sem array is reduced if all semaphore identifiers have the same number of semaphores; ``semmap'' can then be somewhat smaller.

Four is the lower limit: 1 slot is overhead for the map and the second slot is always needed at system initialization to show that the sem array is free.

semume

Define the maximum number of IPC semaphores that a given process can have undo operations pending on.

Acceptable Values:

Minimum: `` 1''
Maximum: ``SemMNS''
Default: ``10''

Specify integer value.

Description

An !!undo!! is a special, optional, flag in a semaphore operation which causes that operation to be undone if the process which invoked it terminates.

``semume'' specifies the maximum number of semaphores that any given process can have undos pending on.

``semop'' is the value of the maximum number of semaphores you can change with one system call.  This value is specified in the file ``/usr/include/sys/sem.h''.

A ``semop()'' system call using the ``SEM_UNDO'' flag returns an ``EINVAL'' error if the ``semume'' limit is exceeded.

semvmx

Specify maximum possible semaphore value.

Acceptable Values:

Minimum: `` 1''
Maximum: ``65535''
Default: ``32767''

Specify integer value.

Description

``semvmx'' specifies the maximum value a semaphore can have. This limit must not exceed the largest number that can be stored in a 16-bit unsigned integer or undetectable semaphore overflows can occur.

Any ``semop()'' system call that tries to increment a semaphore value to greater than ``semvmx'' returns an ``ERANGE'' error.  If ``semvmx'' is greater than 65&sigspace;535, semaphore values can overflow without being detected.

``semop'' is the value of the maximum number of semaphores you can change with one system call.  This value is specified in the file ``/usr/include/sys/sem.h''.

sema

Enable or disable System V IPC semaphores support in kernel at system boot time (Series 700 only).

Acceptable Values:

Minimum: ``0'' (exclude System V IPC semaphore code from kernel)

Maximum: ``1'' (include System V IPC semaphore code in kernel)
Default: ``1''

Specify integer value of ``0'' or ``1''.

Description

``sema'' determines whether the code for System V IPC semaphore is
to be included in the kernel at system boot time (Series 700 systems
only).

``sema'' = 1 Code is included in the kernel (enable IPC shared
memory).

``sema'' = 0 Code is not included in the kernel (disable IPC shared
memory).

Series 800 systems: IPC shared memory is always enabled in the kernel.

Series 700 systems: If ``shmem'' is set to zero, all other IPC shared
memory parameters are ignored.

Starbase graphics library and some other HP-UX subsystems use
semaphores. Disable only if you are certain that no applications on
your system depend on System V IPC semaphores.

If ``sema'' is zero, any program that uses ``semget()'' or ``semop()''
system calls, will return a ``SIGSYS'' signal.

semaem

Define the maximum amount a semaphore value can be changed by a
semaphore "undo" operation.

Acceptable Values:

Minimum: ``0''
Maximum: ``SEMVMX'' or 32767, whichever is smaller''
Default: ``16384''

Specify integer value or use integer formula expression.

Description

An !!undo!! is an optional flag in a semaphore operation which
causes that operation to be undone if the process which invoked it
dies.

``semaem'' specifies the maximum amount the value of a semaphore can be
changed by an undo operation.

The undo value is cumulative per process, so if one process has more
than one undo operation on a semaphore, the values of each undo
operation are added together and the sum is stored in a variable named
``semadj''. ``semadj'' then contains the number by which the semaphore
will be incremented or decremented if the process dies.

sendfile_max

``sendfile_max'' defines the maximum number of pages of buffer cache
that can be in transit via the ``sendfile()'' system call at any given
time.

Acceptable Values:

Minimum: ``   0''
Maximum: ``0x40000''
Default: ``   0''

Specify integer value.

Description

``sendfile_max'' places a limit on the number of pages of buffer cache
that can be monopolized by the ``sendfile()'' system call at any given
time. ``sendfile()'' is a system call used by web servers so they
can avoid the overhead of copying data from user space to kernel space
using the ``send()'' system call. The networking software uses the
buffer-cache buffer directly while data is in-transit over the wire.
Normally this is a very short time period, but when sending data over a
slow link or when retransmitting due to errors, the in-transit period
can be much longer than usual.

``sendfile_max'' prevents ``sendfile()'' from locking up all of the
available buffer cache by limiting the amount of buffer cache memory
that sendfile can access at any given time.

``sendfile_max'' is the upper bound on the number of !!pages!! of
buffer cache that can be in transit via sendfile at any one time. The
minimum value of zero means there is no limit on the number of buffers.
Any other value limits buffer-cache access to the number of pages
indicated. The default value is 0.

Setting ``sendfile_max'' to ``1'' means, in effect, that no buffers are

available. Every buffer is at least one page, and that value prevents
any access because the first request for buffer space would exceed the
upper bound, forcing ``sendfile()'' to revert back to using ``malloc()''
and data-copy operations, which is what the ``send()'' system call does.

Setting ``sendfile_max'' to any other value up to 0x40000, allows the
adminstrator to protect the system against the possibility of
``sendfile()'' monopolizing too many buffers, if buffer availability
becomes a problem during normal system operation.

shmem

Enable or disable System V IPC shared memory support in kernel at system
boot time (Series 700 only).

Acceptable Values:

Minimum: ``0'' (exclude System V IPC shared memory code from kernel)
Maximum: ``1'' (include System V IPC shared memory code in kernel)
Default: ``1''

Specify integer value of ``0'' or ``1''.

Description

``shmem'' determines whether the code for System V IPC shared memory is
to be included in the kernel at system boot time (Series 700 systems
only).

``shmem'' = ``1''   Code is included in the kernel (enable IPC shared
                    memory).

``shmem'' = ``0''   Code is not included in the kernel (disable IPC
                    shared memory).

Series 800 systems: IPC shared memory is always enabled in the kernel.

Series 700 systems: If ``shmem'' is set to zero, all other IPC shared
memory parameters are ignored.

When to Disable Shared Memory

Some subsystems such as Starbase graphics require shared memory. Others
such as X Windows use shared memory (often in large amounts) for
server-client communication if it is available, or sockets if it is not.
If memory space is at a premium and such applications can operate,
albeit slower, without shared memory, you may prefer to run without

shared memory enabled.

shmmax

Specify system-wide maximum allowable shared memory segment size.

Acceptable Values:

Minimum: ``2048'' (2 Kbytes)
Maximum: ``1 Gbyte'' on 32-bit systems
Maximum: ``4 Tbyte'' on 64-bit systems
Default: ``0x04000000'' (64 Mbytes)

Specify integer value.

Description

``shmmax'' defines the system-wide maximum allowable shared memory
segment size in bytes. Any ``shmget()'' system call that requests a
segment larger than this limit returns an error.

The value used cannot exceed maximum available swap space. For minimum
and maximum allowable values, as well as the default value for any given
system, refer to values in ``/etc/conf/master.d/*'' files.

``shmmax'' can be set by rebuilding the kernel or be set in the running
kernel with ``settune()''. ``SAM'' and ``kmtune'' use ``settune()''.
``shmmax'' is only checked when a new shared memory segment is created.
Dynamically changing this parameter will only limit the size
of shared memory segments created after the call to ``settune()''.

shmmni

Specify system-wide maximum allowable number of shared memory segments
(by limiting the number of segment identifiers).

Acceptable Values:

Minimum: `` 3''
Maximum: (memory limited)
Default: `` 200'' identifiers

Specify integer value.

Description

``shmmni'' specifies the maximum number of shared memory segments allowed
to exist simultaneously, system-wide. Any ``shmget()'' system call
requesting a new segment when ``shmni'' segments already exist returns
an error. This parameter defines the number of entries in the shared memory segment
identifier list which is stored in non-swappable kernel space.

Setting ``shmmni'' to an arbitrarily large number wastes memory and can
degrade system performance. Setting the value too high on systems with
small memory configuration may consume enough memory space that the
system cannot boot. Select a value that is as close to actual system
requirements as possible for optimum memory usage. A value not
exceeding 1024 is recommended unless system requirements dictate
otherwise.

Starbase graphics requires that ``shmmni'' be set to not less than 4.

shmseg

Define maximum number of shared memory segments that can be simultaneously
attached to a single process.

Acceptable Values:

Minimum: ``1''
Maximum: ``shmmni''
Default: ``120''

Specify integer value.

Description

``shmseg'' specifies the maximum number of shared memory segments
that can be attached to a process at any given time. Any calls to
``shmat()'' that would exceed this limit return an error.

``shmseg'' can be set by rebuilding the kernel or be set in the running
kernel with ``settune()''. ``SAM'' and ``kmtune'' use ``settune()''.
``shmseg'' is only checked in ``shmat()'' whenever a segment is attached
to a process. Dynamically changing this parameter will only affect future
calls to ``shmat()''. Existing shared memory segments will be unaffected.

STRCTLSZ

Set the maximum number of control bytes allowed in the control portion
of any streams message on the system.

Acceptable Values:

Minimum: ``0''
Maximum: Memory limited
Default: ``1024'' bytes

Specify integer value.

Description

This parameter limits the number of bytes of control data that can be
inserted by ``putmsg()'' in the control portion of any streams message
on the system. If the parameter is set to zero, there is no limit on
how many bytes can be placed in the control segment of the message.

``putmsg()'' returns ``ERANGE'' if the buffer being sent is larger
than the current value of ``STRCTLSZ''.

STRMSGSZ

Set the maximum number of data bytes allowed in any streams message on
the system.

Acceptable Values:

Minimum: ``0''
Maximum: Memory limited
Default: ``8192'' bytes

Specify integer value.

Description

This parameter limits the number of bytes of control data that can be
inserted by ``putmsg()'' or ``write()'' in the data portion of any
streams message on the system. If the parameter is set to zero, there
is no limit on how many bytes can be placed in the data segment of the
message.

``putmsg()'' returns ``ERANGE'' if the buffer being sent is larger
than the current value of ``STRMSGSZ''; ``write()'' segments the
data into multiple messages.

``streampipes''

Force All Pipes to be Streams-Based.

Acceptable Values:

Minimum: ``0"
Maximum: ``1"
Default: ``0"

Specify integer value.

Description

This parameter determines the type of pipe that is created by the
``pipe()" system call. If set to the default value of zero, all pipes
created by ``pipe()" are normal HP-UX file-system pipes. If the value
is ``1", ``pipe()" creates streams-based pipes and modules can be pushed
onto the resulting stream.

If this parameter is set to a non-zero value, the ``pipemod" and
``pipedev" module and driver must be configured in file
``/stand/system".

swchunk

Specify chunk size to be used for swap.

Acceptable Values:

Minimum: `` 2048"
Maximum: ``65536"
Default: `` 2048"

Specify integer value.

Use the default value of ``2048" unless you need
to configure more than 32Gb of swap. See the help for
``maxswapchunks" before changing this parameter.

Description

``swchunk" defines the chunk size for swap. This value must be an
integer power of two.

Swap space is allocated in "chunks", each containing ``swchunk" blocks
of ``DEV_BSIZE" bytes each. When the system needs swap space, one swap
chunk is obtained from a device or file system. When that chunk has
been used and another is needed, a new chunk is obtained from a
different device or file system, thus distributing swap use over several

devices and/or file systems to improve system efficiency and minimize monopolization of a given device by the swap system.

swapmem_on

Enable pseudo-swap reservation.

Acceptable Values:

Minimum: ``0'' (disable pseudo-swap reservation)
Maximum: ``1'' (enable pseudo-swap reservation)
Default: ``1''

Specify integer value of ``0'' or ``1''.

Description

``swapmem_on'' enables or disables the reservation of pseudo-swap, which is space in system memory considered as available virtual memory space in addition to device swap space on disk. By default, pseudo-swap is enabled.

Virtual memory (swap) space is normally allocated from the device swap area on system disks. However, on systems that have massive amounts of installed RAM and large disks or disk arrays, there may be situations where it would be advantageous to not be restricted to the allocated device swap space.

For example, consider an administrator running a system in single-user mode that has 200 Mbytes of installed RAM, only 20 Mbytes of which is used by the kernel, and 1 Gbyte of swap area on the root disk array. Suppose a process is running that requires 1.1 Gbytes of swap space. Since no other users have processes running on the system, providing access to the unused RAM by the swap system would provide sufficient swap space. ``swapmem_on'' accomplishes this.

Administrators of workstations and smaller systems may prefer to disable this capability, depending on system and user needs.

``timeslice''

scheduling timeslice interval

Acceptable Values:

Minimum: ``   -1''

Maximum: ``2147483647'' (approximately 8 months)
Default: ``10'' (ten 10-msec ticks)

Specify integer value or use integer formula expression.

Description

The ``timeslice'' interval is the amount of time one process is allowed
to run before the CPU is given to the next process at the same priority.
The value of ``timeslice'' is specified in units of (10 millisecond) clock
ticks. There are two special values:

`` 0''   Use the system default value (currently ten
        10-msec ticks, or 100 milliseconds).

``-1''   Disable round-robin scheduling completely.

Impact on System

``timeslice'' imposes a time limit which, when it expires, forces a
process to check for pending signals. This guarantees that any
processes that do not make system calls can be terminated (such as a
runaway process in an infinite loop). Setting ``timeslice'' to a very
large value, or to −1, allows such processes to continue operating
without checking for signals, thus causing system performance
bottlenecks or system lock-up.

Use the default value for ``timeslice'' unless a different value is
required by system applications having specific real-time needs.

No memory allocation relates to this parameter. Some CPU time is spent
at each timeslice interval, but this time has not been precisely
measured.

timezone

Specify the time delay from Coordinated Universal Time west to the local
time zone.

Acceptable Values:

Minimum: ``-720''
Maximum: `` 720''
Default: `` 420''

Specify integer value.

Description

``timezone'' specifies the time delay in minutes from Coordinated
Universal Time in a westerly direction to the local time zone where the
system is located. A negative value is interpreted as minutes east from
Coordinated Unversal Time. The value is stored in a structure defined
in ``/usr/include/sys/time.h'' as follows:

struct timezone tz = { TimeZone, DST };
struct timezone {
int tz_minuteswest; /* minutes west of Greenwich */
int tz_dsttime;   /* type of dst correction */
};

```
#define DST_NONE    0   /* not on dst */
#define DST_USA     1   /* USA style dst */
#define DST_AUST    2   /* Australian style dst */
#define DST_WET     3   /* Western European dst */
#define DST_MET     4   /* Middle European dst */
#define DST_EET     5   /* Eastern European dst */
```

unlockable_mem

Specify minimum amount of memory that is to remain reserved for system
overhead and virtual memory management use.

Acceptable Values:

Minimum: ``0''
Maximum: Available memory indicated at power-up
Default: ``0'' (system sets to appropriate value)

Specify integer value.

Description

``unlockable_mem'' defines the minimum amount of memory that is to
always remain available for virtual memory management and system
overhead. Increasing the amount of unlockable memory decreases the
amount of lockable memory.

Specify ``unlockable_mem'' in 4-Kbyte pages. Note that current amounts
of available and lockable memory are listed along with the physical page
size in startup messages, which you can view later by running
``/etc/dmesg.''

If the value for ``unlockable_mem'' exceeds available system memory, it is set equal to available memory (reducing lockable memory to zero).

Any call that requires lockable memory may fail if the amount of lockable memory is insufficient. Note that lockable memory is available for virtual memory except when it is locked.

vas_hash_locks

vas_hash_locks is reserved for future use.

Acceptable Values:

Default: `` 128''

Customers should not attempt to change this parameter.

vmebpn_public_pages

``vmebpn_public_pages'' specifies the number of 4-Kbyte pages reserved for the VME slave I/O memory mapper.

Acceptable Values:

Minimum: `` 0''
Maximum: ``32''
Default: `` 1''

Specify integer value.

Description

``vmebpn_public_pages'' specifies the number of 4-Kbyte pages reserved for the VME slave I/O memory mapper.

Refer to VME documentation for further information about setting kernel parameters for the optional VME subsystem.

vmebpn_sockets

``vmebpn_sockets'' specifies whether the VME socket domain ``AF_VME_LINK'' is active or not.

Acceptable Values:

Minimum: ``0'' (``AF_VME_LINK'' inactive)
Maximum: ``1'' (``AF_VME_LINK'' active)
Default: ``1'' (``AF_VME_LINK'' active)

Specify integer value.

Description

``vmebpn_sockets'' enables or disables the VME socket domain
``AF_VME_LINK''.

Refer to VME documentation for further information about setting
kernel parameters for the optional VME subsystem.

vmebpn_tcp_ip

Maximum number of DLPI PPAs allowed.

Acceptable Values:

Minimum: ``0''
Maximum: ``1''
Default: ``1''

Specify integer value.

Description

``vmebpn_tcp_ip'' specifies the maximum number of DLPI PPAs
allowed on the system. If set to zero, TCP-IP is disabled.
Otherwise, the maximum value is ``1''.

Refer to VME documentation for further information about setting
kernel parameters for the optional VME subsystem.

vmebpn_tcp_ip_mtu

``vmebpn_tcp_ip_mtu'' specifies the maximum number of Kbytes allowed
in PPA transmission units.

Acceptable Values:

Minimum: `` 0''
Maximum: ``64''
Default: `` 8''

Specify integer value.

Description

``vmebpn_tcp_ip_mtu" specifies the maximum number of Kbytes allowed
in PPA transmission units.

Refer to VME documentation for further information about setting
kernel parameters for the optional VME subsystem.

vmebpn_total_jobs

``vmebpn_total_jobs" specifies the system-wide maximum number of VME
ports that can be open at any given time.

Acceptable Values:

Minimum: `` 0"
Maximum: ``8096"
Default: `` 16"

Specify integer value.

Description

``vmebpn_total_jobs" specifies the system-wide maximum number of VME
ports that can be open at any given time.

Refer to VME documentation for further information about setting
kernel parameters for the optional VME subsystem.

vme_io_estimate

``vme_io_estimate" specifies the number of 4-Kbyte pages in the kernel
I/O space that are needed by and are to be allocated to the VME
subsystem.

Acceptable Values:

Minimum: ``   0"
Maximum: ``0x800"
Default: ``0x800"

Specify integer value.

Description

``vme_io_estimate'' specifies how many 4-Kbyte pages in the kernel I/O space are to be allocated for use by the VME subsystem.

Refer to VME documentation for further information about setting kernel parameters for the optional VME subsystem.

vps_ceiling

Specify the maximum page size (in Kbytes) that the kernel can select when it chooses a page size based on system configuration and object size.

Acceptable Values:

Minimum: `` 4"
Maximum: ``65536"
Default: `` 16"

Specify integer value.

Description

This parameter is provided as a means to minimize lost cycle time caused by TLB (translation look-aside buffer) misses on systems using newer PA-RISC devices such as the PA-8000 that have smaller TLBs and no hardware TLB walker.

If a user application does not use the ``chatr'' command to specify a page size for program text and data segments, the kernel selects a page size that, based on system configuration and object size, appears to be suitable. This is called transparent selection. The selected size is then compared to the default maximum page-size value defined by ``vps_ceiling'' that is configured at system-boot time. If the the value is larger than ``vps_ceiling'', ``vps_ceiling'' is used.

The value is also compared with the default minimum page-size value defined by``vps_pagesize'' that is configured at system-boot time. If the the value is smaller than ``vps_pagesize'', ``vps_pagesize'' is used.

Note also that if the value specified by ``vps_ceiling'' is not a legitimate page size, the kernel uses the next !!lower!! valid value.

For more information about how these parameters are used, and how they affect system operation, refer to the whitepaper entitled !!Performance Optimized Page Sizing: Getting the Most out of your HP-UX Server!!.

This document is available on the World Wide Web at:
http://www.unixsolutions.hp.com/products/hpux/pop.html

vps_chatr_ceiling

Specify the maximum page size (in Kbytes) that can be specified when a
user process uses the ``chatr'' command to specify a page size.

Acceptable Values:

Minimum: `` 4'' Kbytes
Maximum: ``65536'' Kbytes
Default: ``65536'' Kbytes

Specify integer value.

Description

This parameter is provided as a means to minimize lost cycle time
caused by TLB (translation look-aside buffer) misses on systems
using newer PA-RISC devices such as the PA-8000 that have smaller
TLBs and no hardware TLB walker.

vps_pagesize

Specify the default user-page size (in Kbytes) that is used by the
kernel if the user application does not use the ``chatr'' command to
specify a page size.

Acceptable Values:

Minimum: `` 4''
Maximum: ``65536''
Default: `` 4''

Specify integer value.

Description

This parameter is provided as a means to minimize lost cycle time
caused by TLB (translation look-aside buffer) misses on systems
using newer PA-RISC devices such as the PA-8000 that have smaller
TLBs and no hardware TLB walker.

vxfs_max_ra_kbytes

Set the maximum amount of read-ahead data, in kilobytes,
that the kernel may have outstanding for a single VxFS filesystem.

Acceptable Values:

Minimum: `` 0"
Maximum: ``65536"
Default: `` 1024"

Specify integer value or use integer formula expression.

Description

When data is read from a disk drive, the system may read additional data
beyond that requested by the operation. This "read-ahead" speeds up sequential
disk accesses, by anticipating that additional data will be read, and
having it available in system buffers before it is requested.
This parameter limits the number of read-ahead blocks that the kernel
is allowed to have outstanding for any given VxFS filesystem. The
limit applies to each individual VxFS filesystem, !!not!! to the
system-wide total.

vxfs_ra_per_disk

Set the amount of VxFS filesystem

Acceptable Values:

Minimum: `` 0"
Maximum: ``8192"
Default: ``1024"

Specify an integer value or use an integer formula expression.

Description

When data is read from a disk drive, the system may read additional data
beyond that requested by the operation. This "read-ahead" speeds up sequential
disk accesses, by anticipating that additional data will be read, and
having it available in system buffers before it is requested.
This parameter specifies the amount of read-ahead permitted per disk drive.

The total amount of read-ahead is determined by multiplying
``vxfs_ra_per_disk" by the number of drives in the logical volume.
If the filesystem does not reside in a logical volume, then the number

of drives is effectively one

The total amount of read-ahead that the kernel may have
outstanding for a single VxFS filesystem is constrained by
``vxfs_max_ra_kbytes".

vx_ncsize

Specify the number of bytes to be reserved for the directory path-name
cache used by the VxFS file system.

Acceptable Values:

Minimum: ``0"
Maximum: None
Default: ``1024"

Specify integer value.

Description

The VxFS file system uses a name cache to store directory pathname
information related to recently accessed directories in the file system.
Retrieving this information from a name cache allows the system to
access directories and their contents without having to use direct disk
accesses to find its way down a directory tree every time it needs to
find a directory that is used frequently. Using a name cache in this
way can save considerable overhead, especially in large applications
such as databases where the system is repetitively accessing a
particular directory or directory path.

``vx_ncsize" specifies the how much space, in bytes, is set aside for
the VxFS file system manager to use for this purpose. The default value
is sufficient for most typical HP-UX systems, but for larger systems or
systems with applications that use VxFS disk I/O intensively, some
performance enhancement may result from expanding the cache size. The
efficiency gained, however, depends greatly on the variety of directory
paths used by the application or applications, and what percentage of
total process time is expended while interacting with the VxFS file
system.

Overview of Select Kernel Parameters

Asynchronous I/O Parameters

The following kernel parameters are used for managing asynchronous
I/O operations. The first four are related to POSIX asynchronous
I/O operations; the last pertains to open ports between processes
and the asynchronous disk-I/O driver:

"aio_listio_max"   Specifies how many POSIX asynchronous I/O
                     operations are allowed in a single "listio()"
                     call.

"aio_max_ops"   System-wide maximum number of POSIX asynchronous
                     I/O operations that are allowed at any given time.

"aio_physmem_pct"   Maximum total system memory that can be locked for
                     use in POSIX asynchronous I/O operations.

"aio_prio_delta_max" Maximum priority offset allowed in a POSIX
                     asynchronous I/O control block ("aiocb").

"max_async_ports"   Maximum number of ports to the asynchronous
                     disk-I/O driver that processes can have open at
                     any given time.

Configurable Parameters for Kernel-Panic Dumps

The following parameters affect dump operations when a kernel panic
occurs and parts of system memory are dumped to disk:

"alwaysdump"   Specifies which classes of system memory are to be
               dumped if a kernel panic occurs.

"dontdump"   Specifies which classes of system memory are !!not!!
               to be dumped if a kernel panic occurs.

"initmodmax"   Maximum number of kernel modules that "savecrash"
               will handle when processing system-crash dump data.

"modstrmax"   Maximum size, in bytes, of the "savecrash"
kernel-module table which contains module names and
their location in the file system.

Overview of Fiber Channel Kernel Parameters

Two kernel configuration parameters pertain to the Fiber Channel SCSI
subsystem and communication between the system processor and any
peripheral devices that interact with it using Fiber-Channel Protocol
(FCP). These parameters are used for adjusting the default amount and
type of memory allocated for supporting concurrent FCP read, write,
and/or control requests.

"num_tachyon_adapters"
Some of the memory that is allocated for FCP requests must meet
certain requirements. The "num_tachyon_adapters" parameter is
used on systems that do not provide I/O virtual addressing so that
memory meeting these requirements can be allocated. The value you
specify controls what type of memory is allocated, and specifies
the number of Tachyon-based Fiber-Channel adapters in the system.

"max_fcp_reqs"
This parameter sets a limit on the number of concurrent FCP requests
that are allowed on an FCP adapter. The default value of 512
requests can be changed by specifying a different value for this
parameter. The optimal limit on concurrent requests depends on a
number of factors such as configuration, device characteristics, I/O
load, host memory, and other values that FCP software cannot easily
determine.

Configurable File-System Parameters

The following parameters control various aspects of file-system
management:

Buffer Cache Group

"bufpages"
Number of 4-Kbyte pages in file-system buffer cache.

"dbc_min_pct"
Mimimum percentage of memory for dynamic buffer cache.

"dbc_max_pct"
Maximum percentage of memory for dynamic buffer cache.

"nbuf"
> System-wide number of file-system buffer and cache buffer headers.

Open/Locked Files Group

"maxfiles"
> Soft limit on how many files a single process can have opened or locked at any given time.

"maxfiles_lim"
> Hard limit on how many files a single process can have opened or locked at any given time.

"nfile"
> Maximum number of files that can be open simultaneously on the system at any given time.

"nflocks"
> Maximum combined total number of file locks that are available system-wide to all processes at any given time.

"ninode"
> Maximum number of open inodes that can be in memory.

Asynchronous Writes Group

"fs_async"
> Specify synchronous or asynchronous writes of file-system data structures to disk.

VxFS (Journaled) File-System Parameter

"vx_ncsize"
> Memory space reserved for VxFS directory path-name cache

Overview of Mass-Storage Kernel Parameters

Configurable parameters related to file system performance fall into the following categories:

File System Buffers   Allocating system physical memory resources for file system buffer cache space.

Open or Locked Files   Number of files that can be open or locked
              simultaneously.

Journal File Systems   Allocate space for the Directory-Name Lookup
              Cache (DNLC) associated with VxFS file-system
              inodes.

Asynchronous Writes   Asynchronous writes to file system allowed or
              not allowed.

Configurable Parameters for Logical Volume Manager (LVM)

Two configurable kernel parameters are provided that relate to kernel interaction
with the Logical Volume Manager:

maxvgs   Maximum number of volume groups configured by the
              Logical Volume Manager on the system.

no_lvm_disks   Flag that notifies the kernel when no logical
              volumes exist on the system. If set, all file
              systems coincide with physical disks on the system
              and physical disk boundaries. The only exception to
              this is when disks are configured for partitions or
              part of the disk is reserved for swap and other
              non-file-system uses.

Overview of LVM Operation

Logical Volume Manager (LVM) is a subsystem for managing file systems
and disk storage space that are structured into logical volumes rather
than being restricted to the beginning and end points of a physical
disk. Logical volumes can be smaller than the disk or disk array on
which they reside, or they can include all or part of several disks or
disk arrays. Logical volume boundaries are not required to coincide
with the boundaries of physical disks when multiple disks or arrays are
used.

Managing logical volumes is done by the Logical Volume Manager, not the
kernel. However, the kernel contains data structures for each volume
group on the system, and the space reserved for LVM data structures must
be sufficient to support the number of volume groups that exist on the
system. This is done by the "maxvgs" kernel configuration parameter.
A second parameter, "no_lvm_disks", is provided for notifying the
kernel at boot time that no logical volumes exist on the system. This
saves the system from having to identify and activate logical volumes at

boot time.
  Volume and Group Boundaries

Logical volume groups consist of one or more logical volumes. Logical volume boundaries within a volume group can be configured anywhere on a given disk. However, a single disk device cannot be shared between volume groups. Disk arrays configured as RAID (redundant array of independent disks) arrays for data protection are treated as a single disk device and cannot be shared between volume groups. Individual disks in any array that is not configured as a RAID array are treated as individual devices, and individual devices can be assigned to any volume group as desired by the administrator.

Configurable Parameters for Memory Paging

``allocate_fs_swapmap''   Enable or disable allocation of file-system swap space when ``swapon()'' is called as opposed to allocating swap space when ``malloc()'' is called. Enabling allocation reduces risk of insufficient swap space and is used primarily where high-availabilility is important.

``maxswapchunks''      This parameter, multiplied by ``swchunk'' times the system block size value (``DEV_BSIZE''), determines the combined maximum amount device swap and file-system swap space that can be configured, system-wide.

``nswapdev''   Maximum number of devices, system-wide, that can be used for device swap. Set to match actual system configuration.

``nswapfs''   Maximum number of mounted file systems, system-wide, that can be used for file-system swap. Set to match actual system configuration.

``page_text_to_local''   Enable or disable program text segment swapping to local swap device on cluster client. Increases load time for loading memory with new contents (text is written to local disk instead of discarding and reloading later from server), but reduces network traffic from server to client.

``remote_nfs_swap"   Enable or disable swap to mounted remote NFS
file system. Used on cluster clients for
swapping to NFS-mounted server file systems.

``swapmem_on"   Enable or disable pseudo-swap allocation.
This allows systems with large installed
memory to allocate memory space as well as
disk swap space for virtual memory use
instead of restricting availability to
defined disk swap area.

``swchunk"   Defines amount of space allocated for each
!!chunk!! of swap area. Chunks are
allocated from device to device by the
kernel. Changing this parameter requires extensive
knowledge of system internals. Without such knowledge,
Do not change this parameter from
the normal default value.

Variable-Page-Size Parameters

``vps_ceiling"   Defines the maximum system-selected page size
if the user does not specify a page size.

``vps_chatr_ceiling"   Defines the maximum page size a user can specify
by using the ``chatr" command in a program.

``page_size"   Defines the default minimum user page-size if
no page size is specified using ``chatr".

Overview of Memory Paging Parameters

Configurable kernel parameters for memory paging enforce operating
rules and limits related to virtual memory (swap space). They fall
into the following categories:

Total System Swap   Maximum swap space that can be allocated
system-wide.

Device Swap   Swap space allocated on hard disk devices.

File System Swap   Swap space allocated on mounted file
               systems.

Pseudo-Swap   Use of installed RAM as pseudo-swap,
               allowing virtual memory space allocation
               beyond the limit of swap space on disk
               devices.

Variable Page Sizes   The size of virtual memory pages can be
               altered to make swap operations more
               efficient in particular applications.

Undocumented Kernel Parameters

Some of the configurable parameters that appear in the kernel master
file are not documented, and some are not known to or are not supported
by SAM for any of several possible reasons:

* The parameter is obsolete. It is no longer used in current HP-UX
  releases, but might appear in an existing kernel configuration. If
  SAM encounters an obsolete parameter in the current kernel
  configuration, it does not display it in the list of configurable
  parameters that can be changed. It also removes that parameter when
  creating the new configuration file used to build the pending kernel.

* The parameter is not supported by SAM. As with obsolete parameters,
  it is not displayed in the list of configurable parameters, but it
  is retained in the new kernel configuration file to ensure that no
  malfunctions are introduced due to a missing parameter.

* The parameter is assigned a value by kernel configuration software,
  which is frequently based on external factors. The assigned value
  might be used when calculating values for one or more other
  parameters.

* The parameter is for HP factory or support use only. No change from
  the default value should be made unless specifically directed
  otherwise by official HP support personnel.

* The parameter supports obsolete or obsolescent sofware. For
  information about how to select a non-default value, consult the
  documentation furnished with the software that the parameter
  supports.

CHAPTER 5

Virtual Partitions and Devices

Background on Virtual Partitions and Devices

When working with Virtual Partitions you "carve up" your system in such a way that components are devoted to a Virtual Partition. This is done to accomplish the maximum isolation between Virtual Partitions in order to minimize the effect of one Virtual Partition on another Virtual Partition. At the time of this writing, components that are at or below the Local Bus Adapter (LBA) level are devoted to a partition. Since the layout of systems varies depending on the model, you need to become familiar with the layout of your system to the extent that you can determine the location of components in your system relative to the LBA level. We'll cover some examples of how to determine levels on your system in this chapter. Keep in mind, however, that new systems are introduced often, so there may not be an example covering your specific system in the upcoming examples.

Above the LBA level, system components may be shared to some extent. As we saw in Chapter 2, CPUs may be *bound* or *unbound* as they relate virtual partitions, memory is segmented into areas devoted to virtual partitions, and System Bus Adapters (SBAs) can be shared among virtual partitions.

In the next sections we'll take a look at system components and their paths. Although we specified components to add to virtual partitions in Chapter 2, we didn't take a close look at how you determine the components of which your system is comprised so that you can select which components you'll use in which partitions.

Table 5-1, which is taken from the tear out card supplied with this book, describes the way in which the components of your system are specified when working with vPars:

Table 5-1   Working with CPU, I/O, and Memory in vPars

Command	Description
Specify CPU Resources by:	Number of bound and unbound CPUs: *cpu::num* CPU hardware path(s): *cpu:path* Minimum and maximum number: *cpu:::[min][:[max]]*
Types of CPUs:	*Bound*: CPU is tied to a Virtual Partition when vPar is active. Allocation is done at the time vPar is created. Lowest number bound CPU is *monarch*. Interrupts handled by *bound* CPUs. *Unbound:* CPU that can be dynamically reassigned. Do not handle interrupts.
Specify Memory by:	Size *mem::size* Base and range: *mem:::base:range* combination of both above.
Specify I/O:	Use path: *io:path[:attr1[,attr2[...]]]* (see man page **vparresources** for details).
To add resources use: (This adds component relative to what already exists if running **vparmodify**.)	*-a cpu:path* *-a cpu::num* *[-a cpu::num] [-a cpu:::[min]:[max]] -[a cpu:path]* (**vparcreate** only) *-a io:path[:attr1[,attr2[...]]]* *-a mem::size* *-a mem:::base:range*
To delete resources use:	*-d cpu:path* *-d cpu::num* *-d io:path[:attr1[,attr2[...]]]* *-d mem::size* *-d mem:::base:range*

Command	Description
To modify resources use: (This modifies to absolute number rather than relative.)	*-m cpu:path* *-m cpu::num* *-m cpu:::min* *[-m cpu::num] [-m cpu:::min:[max]] -[m cpu:path]* *-m io:path[:attr1[,attr2[...]]]* *-m mem::size*

We'll use many commands related to these components in upcoming sections and specify the components in the manner shown in Table 5-1.

Virtual Partitions and Local Bus Adapters

First, let's run an **ioscan -f** to produce a full listing of the components in a system:

```
# ioscan -f
```
N-Class

```
Class       I   H/W Path    Driver    S/W State   H/W Type    Description
===========================================================================
root        0               root      CLAIMED     BUS_NEXUS
ioa         0   0           sba       CLAIMED     BUS_NEXUS   System Bus Adapter (803)
ba          0   0/0         lba       CLAIMED     BUS_NEXUS   Local PCI Bus Adapter (782)
lan         0   0/0/0/0     btlan3    CLAIMED     INTERFACE   PCI Ethernet (10110019)
ext_bus     0   0/0/1/0     c720      CLAIMED     INTERFACE   SCSI C895 Ultra
                                                              Wide Single-Ended
target      0   0/0/1/0.1   tgt       CLAIMED     DEVICE
disk        0   0/0/1/0.1.0 sdisk     CLAIMED     DEVICE      HP      DVD-ROM 305
target      1   0/0/1/0.7   tgt       CLAIMED     DEVICE
ctl         0   0/0/1/0.7.0 sctl      CLAIMED     DEVICE      Initiator
ext_bus     1   0/0/2/0     c720      CLAIMED     INTERFACE   SCSI C875 Ultra
                                                              Wide Single-Ended
target      2   0/0/2/0.6   tgt       CLAIMED     DEVICE
disk        1   0/0/2/0.6.0 sdisk     CLAIMED     DEVICE      SEAGATE ST336704LC
target      3   0/0/2/0.7   tgt       CLAIMED     DEVICE
ctl         1   0/0/2/0.7.0 sctl      CLAIMED     DEVICE      Initiator
ext_bus     2   0/0/2/1     c720      CLAIMED     INTERFACE   SCSI C875 Ultra
                                                              Wide Single-Ended
target      4   0/0/2/1.6   tgt       CLAIMED     DEVICE
disk        2   0/0/2/1.6.0 sdisk     CLAIMED     DEVICE      SEAGATE ST336704LC
target      5   0/0/2/1.7   tgt       CLAIMED     DEVICE
ctl         2   0/0/2/1.7.0 sctl      CLAIMED     DEVICE      Initiator
tty         0   0/0/4/0     asio0     CLAIMED     INTERFACE   PCI Serial (103c1048)
tty         1   0/0/5/0     asio0     CLAIMED     INTERFACE   PCI Serial (103c1048)
ba          1   0/1         lba       CLAIMED     BUS_NEXUS   Local PCI Bus Adapter (782)
ba          2   0/2         lba       CLAIMED     BUS_NEXUS   Local PCI Bus Adapter (782)
```

```
ba           3   0/4           lba        CLAIMED   BUS_NEXUS   Local PCI Bus Adapter (782)
lan          1   0/4/0/0       btlan5     CLAIMED   INTERFACE   HP A5230A/B5509BA
                                                                PCI 10/100Base-TX Addon
ba           4   0/5           lba        CLAIMED   BUS_NEXUS   Local PCI Bus Adapter (782)
ba           5   0/5/0/0       PCItoPCI   CLAIMED   BUS_NEXUS   PCItoPCI Bridge
lan          3   0/5/0/0/4/0   btlan      CLAIMED   INTERFACE   HP A5506B PCI
                                                                10/100Base-TX 4 port
lan          4   0/5/0/0/5/0   btlan      CLAIMED   INTERFACE   HP A5506B PCI
                                                                10/100Base-TX 4 port
lan          5   0/5/0/0/6/0   btlan      CLAIMED   INTERFACE   HP A5506B PCI
                                                                10/100Base-TX 4 port
lan          6   0/5/0/0/7/0   btlan      CLAIMED   INTERFACE   HP A5506B PCI
                                                                10/100Base-TX 4 port
ba           6   0/8           lba        CLAIMED   BUS_NEXUS   Local PCI Bus Adapter (782)
ba           7   0/10          lba        CLAIMED   BUS_NEXUS   Local PCI Bus Adapter (782)
ba           8   0/12          lba        CLAIMED   BUS_NEXUS   Local PCI Bus Adapter (782)
fc           0   0/12/0/0      td         CLAIMED   INTERFACE   HP Tachyon TL/TS Fibre
                                                                  Channel Mass Storage Adapter
fcp          0   0/12/0/0.1    fcp        CLAIMED   INTERFACE   FCP Domain
ioa          1   1             sba        CLAIMED   BUS_NEXUS   System Bus Adapter (803)
ba           9   1/0           lba        CLAIMED   BUS_NEXUS   Local PCI Bus Adapter (782)
ba          10   1/2           lba        CLAIMED   BUS_NEXUS   Local PCI Bus Adapter (782)
ba          11   1/4           lba        CLAIMED   BUS_NEXUS   Local PCI Bus Adapter (782)
ba          12   1/8           lba        CLAIMED   BUS_NEXUS   Local PCI Bus Adapter (782)
ba          13   1/10          lba        CLAIMED   BUS_NEXUS   Local PCI Bus Adapter (782)
fc           1   1/10/0/0      td         CLAIMED   INTERFACE   HP Tachyon TL/TS Fibre
                                                                  Channel Mass Storage Adapter
fcp          1   1/10/0/0.2    fcp        CLAIMED   INTERFACE   FCP Domain
ba          14   1/12          lba        CLAIMED   BUS_NEXUS   Local PCI Bus Adapter (782)
lan          2   1/12/0/0      btlan5     CLAIMED   INTERFACE   HP A5230A/B5509BA PCI
                                                                10/100Base-TX Addon
pbc          0   36            pbc        CLAIMED   BUS_NEXUS   Bus Converter
processor    0   37            processor  CLAIMED   PROCESSOR   Processor
pbc          1   44            pbc        CLAIMED   BUS_NEXUS   Bus Converter
processor    1   45            processor  CLAIMED   PROCESSOR   Processor
pbc          2   100           pbc        CLAIMED   BUS_NEXUS   Bus Converter
processor    2   101           processor  CLAIMED   PROCESSOR   Processor
pbc          3   108           pbc        CLAIMED   BUS_NEXUS   Bus Converter
processor    3   109           processor  CLAIMED   PROCESSOR   Processor
memory       0   192           memory     CLAIMED   MEMORY      Memory
#
```

With this full listing we can see the many components of which this N-Class system is comprised. All of the devices are *claimed*, meaning that software drivers exist for the devices and the software is bound. Going back to our earlier discussion regarding LBAs, we would like to know what components are on what LBAs so that we can plan the partition layout. Issuing the following command will produce a list of LBAs and SBAs:

```
# ioscan -f | grep ba
```

N-Class

```
ioa          0   0             sba        CLAIMED    BUS_NEXUS   System Bus Adapter (803)
ba           0   0/0           lba        CLAIMED    BUS_NEXUS   Local PCI Bus Adapter (782)
ba           1   0/1           lba        CLAIMED    BUS_NEXUS   Local PCI Bus Adapter (782)
ba           2   0/2           lba        CLAIMED    BUS_NEXUS   Local PCI Bus Adapter (782)
ba           3   0/4           lba        CLAIMED    BUS_NEXUS   Local PCI Bus Adapter (782)
ba           4   0/5           lba        CLAIMED    BUS_NEXUS   Local PCI Bus Adapter (782)
ba           5   0/5/0/0       PCItoPCI   CLAIMED    BUS_NEXUS   PCItoPCI Bridge
ba           6   0/8           lba        CLAIMED    BUS_NEXUS   Local PCI Bus Adapter (782)
ba           7   0/10          lba        CLAIMED    BUS_NEXUS   Local PCI Bus Adapter (782)
ba           8   0/12          lba        CLAIMED    BUS_NEXUS   Local PCI Bus Adapter (782)
ioa          1   1             sba        CLAIMED    BUS_NEXUS   System Bus Adapter (803)
ba           9   1/0           lba        CLAIMED    BUS_NEXUS   Local PCI Bus Adapter (782)
ba          10   1/2           lba        CLAIMED    BUS_NEXUS   Local PCI Bus Adapter (782)
```

```
ba          11  1/4        lba        CLAIMED     BUS_NEXUS  Local PCI Bus Adapter (782)
ba          12  1/8        lba        CLAIMED     BUS_NEXUS  Local PCI Bus Adapter (782)
ba          13  1/10       lba        CLAIMED     BUS_NEXUS  Local PCI Bus Adapter (782)
ba          14  1/12       lba        CLAIMED     BUS_NEXUS  Local PCI Bus Adapter (782)
#
```

On this N-Class system we have two SBAs, indicated by the leading *0* for one SBA and by the leading *1* indicating the second SBA. The SBAs exist one level above the LBAs at the system level. The first number of each item in the listing is the SBA, the next number is the LBA. Components on the same LBA can't be shared among multiple virtual partitions at the time of this writing. The two internal disks in the first **ioscan** (**ioscan -f**) listing, for instance, are both on *0/0/2*, which is SBA *0*, LBA *0*, and SCSI bus *2*.

Let's compare this to our L-Class system used in most of the examples of this book, which has only one SBA and two internal SCSI buses:

```
# ioscan -f | grep ba
```

L-Class

```
cvhdcon3:/ # ioscan -f | grep ba
ioa         0   0          sba        CLAIMED     BUS_NEXUS  System Bus Adapter (803)
ba          0   0/0        lba        CLAIMED     BUS_NEXUS  Local PCI Bus Adapter (782)
ba          1   0/1        lba        CLAIMED     BUS_NEXUS  Local PCI Bus Adapter (782)
ba          2   0/2        lba        CLAIMED     BUS_NEXUS  Local PCI Bus Adapter (782)
ba          3   0/3        lba        CLAIMED     BUS_NEXUS  Local PCI Bus Adapter (782)
ba          4   0/4        lba        CLAIMED     BUS_NEXUS  Local PCI Bus Adapter (782)
ba          5   0/5        lba        CLAIMED     BUS_NEXUS  Local PCI Bus Adapter (782)
ba          6   0/8        lba        CLAIMED     BUS_NEXUS  Local PCI Bus Adapter (782)
ba          7   0/9        lba        CLAIMED     BUS_NEXUS  Local PCI Bus Adapter (782)
ba          8   0/10       lba        CLAIMED     BUS_NEXUS  Local PCI Bus Adapter (782)
ba          9   0/12       lba        CLAIMED     BUS_NEXUS  Local PCI Bus Adapter (782)
cvhdcon3:/ #
```

Although this L-Class has only one SBA, as indicated by the leading *0* on all of the buses in the preceding listing, it has two SCSI buses on LBA *0/0*. The internal disks are normally mirrored across these two different SCSI buses. The following listing shows the internal disks on this L-Class mirrored across two different SCSI buses:

```
cvhdcon3:/ # ioscan -f | grep SEA
disk        1   0/0/1/1.0.0    sdisk    CLAIMED    DEVICE     SEAGATE ST173404LC
disk        2   0/0/1/1.2.0    sdisk    CLAIMED    DEVICE     SEAGATE ST173404LC
disk        3   0/0/2/0.0.0    sdisk    CLAIMED    DEVICE     SEAGATE ST173404LC
disk        4   0/0/2/0.2.0    sdisk    CLAIMED    DEVICE     SEAGATE ST173404LC
```

This listing shows that the four internal disks are at SBA *0*, LBA *0*, and SCSI buses *1* and *2*, respectively. At the time of this writing these disks have to be in the same vPar because they are on the same LBA.

To assign the LBA to which the L-Class disks are connected as well as the two disks to a vPar, we would use the full hardware paths of *-i 0/0* to assign the LBA to a Virtual Partition and *-i 0/0/1/1.2.0:boot* for the boot disk of that Virtual Partition.

The internal disks are not the only disks attached to our L-Class system. There is also an external disk enclosure on which we have created several Logical UNits (LUNs) that appear as separate disk drives. If we run **ioscan** and **grep** for disk we see that several of these exist:

```
cvhdcon3:/ # ioscan -f | grep disk
disk       0  0/0/1/0.1.0      sdisk    CLAIMED     DEVICE       HP      DVD-ROM 304
disk       1  0/0/1/1.0.0      sdisk    CLAIMED     DEVICE       SEAGATE ST173404LC
disk       2  0/0/1/1.2.0      sdisk    CLAIMED     DEVICE       SEAGATE ST173404LC
disk       3  0/0/2/0.0.0      sdisk    CLAIMED     DEVICE       SEAGATE ST173404LC
disk       4  0/0/2/0.2.0      sdisk    CLAIMED     DEVICE       SEAGATE ST173404LC
disk       7  0/8/0/0.8.0.5.0.0.0   sdisk    CLAIMED    DEVICE    HP    A5277A
disk      10  0/8/0/0.8.0.5.0.0.1   sdisk    CLAIMED    DEVICE    HP    A5277A
disk      11  0/8/0/0.8.0.5.0.0.2   sdisk    CLAIMED    DEVICE    HP    A5277A
disk      12  0/8/0/0.8.0.5.0.0.3   sdisk    CLAIMED    DEVICE    HP    A5277A
disk      15  0/8/0/0.8.0.5.0.1.0   sdisk    CLAIMED    DEVICE    HP    A5277A
disk      17  0/8/0/0.8.0.5.0.2.0   sdisk    CLAIMED    DEVICE    HP    A5277A
disk      18  0/8/0/0.8.0.5.0.3.0   sdisk    CLAIMED    DEVICE    HP    A5277A
disk       5  0/9/0/0.8.0.4.0.0.0   sdisk    CLAIMED    DEVICE    HP    A5277A
disk       6  0/9/0/0.8.0.4.0.0.1   sdisk    CLAIMED    DEVICE    HP    A5277A
disk       8  0/9/0/0.8.0.4.0.0.2   sdisk    CLAIMED    DEVICE    HP    A5277A
disk       9  0/9/0/0.8.0.4.0.0.3   sdisk    CLAIMED    DEVICE    HP    A5277A
disk      13  0/9/0/0.8.0.4.0.1.0   sdisk    CLAIMED    DEVICE    HP    A5277A
disk      14  0/9/0/0.8.0.4.0.2.0   sdisk    CLAIMED    DEVICE    HP    A5277A
disk      16  0/9/0/0.8.0.4.0.3.0   sdisk    CLAIMED    DEVICE    HP    A5277A
cvhdcon3:/ #
```

This listing shows first the DVD-ROM, then the four internal disks, and finally, the 14 LUNs configured on our external storage enclosure. We used one of these for the boot volume of *cable2*. The following **vparstatus -v** command shows the respective boot disks of *cable1* and *cable2*:

man page

vparstatus appendix a

```
# vparstatus -v


[Virtual Partition Details]
Name:          cable1
State:         Up
Attributes:    Dynamic,Manual
Kernel Path:   /stand/vmunix
Boot Opts:

[CPU Details]
```

```
Min/Max:   1/3
Bound by User [Path]:
Bound by Monitor [Path]:   33
Unbound [Path]:

[IO Details]
   0.0
      0.0.1.1.2.0   BOOT              <-- boot disk of cable1

[Memory Details]
Specified [Base   /Range]:
          (bytes) (MB)
Total Memory (MB):   1024

[Virtual Partition Details]
Name:          cable2
State:         Up
Attributes:    Dynamic,Manual
Kernel Path:   /stand/vmunix
Boot Opts:

[CPU Details]
Min/Max:   1/3
Bound by User [Path]:
Bound by Monitor [Path]:   37
Unbound [Path]:

[IO Details]
   0.8.0.0.8.0.5.0.0.0, BOOT          <-- boot disk of cable2
   0.10

[Memory Details]
Specified [Base   /Range]:
          (bytes) (MB)
Total Memory (MB):   1024
#
```

cable1 boots off of the internal disk at *0.0.1.1.2.0* and *cable2* boots off of the external disk at *0.8.0.0.8.0.5.0.0.0.*

You need a good working knowledge of the hardware of your system, including bus adapters and disks when working with Virtual Partitions. At the time of this writing, all vPar-related work takes place at the command line. Understanding the hardware of which your system is comprised and how to interrogate it at the command line is important.

You may want to review the backup material at the end of this chapter to familarize yourself with devices and related topics if you haven't worked with them before.

Virtual Partitions and Processors

When assigning processors in Chapter 2, we had a choice of making them *unbound* or *bound*. *Bound* CPUs are dedicated to a vPar and can't be dynamically removed or added to vPars. *Bound* CPUs handle I/O interrupts and should therefore be used with I/O-intensive applications. *Unbound* CPUs can be dynamically added and removed from vPars. *Unbound* CPUs do not handle I/O interrupts and should be used for CPU intensive applications. Working with processors is a little tricky because you have many options, some of which you can only execute when creating a vPar, others of which require the vPar to be down before executing, so let's take a look at one of the tables from the **vparstatus** man page (Table 5-2):

man page

vparstatus
appendix a

Table 5-2   Adding, Deleting, and Modifying Resources

Command	Description	Done with vPar Running?
To add resources use: (This adds component relative to what already exists if running **vparmodify**.)	*-a cpu:path* *-a cpu::num* *[-a cpu::num] [-a cpu:::[min]:[max]] -[a cpu:path]* (*:::***vparcreate** only) *-a io:path[:attr1[,attr2[...]]* *-a mem::size* *-a mem:::base:range*	No Yes - relative value **vparcreate** only No No No
To delete resources use:	*-d cpu:path* *-d cpu::num* *-d io:path[:attr1[,attr2[...]]* *-d mem::size* *-d mem:::base:range*	No Yes - relative value No No No
To modify resources use: (This modifies to absolute number rather than relative.)	*-m cpu::num* *-m cpu:::[min][:max]]* *-m io:path[:attr1[,attr2[...]]* *-m mem::size*	Yes-absolute value No No No

Table 5-2 shows that you have many options when adding, deleting, and modifying the resources related to your Virtual Partitions. The flexibility afforded you with Virtual Partitions is one of the most desirable aspects of working with this technology. At the same time, however; it is also one of the most confusing aspects.

There are many options embedded in this table. Let's talk about assigning CPUs when creating a vPar because most of the issues related to CPUs come into play when creating a vPar. At the time of this writing, *num* is used in some documentation and *total* in others, so for the purposes of this discussion, *num* and *total* are interchangeable.

path allows you to specify a specific processor to be used with a vPar. Using *path* will automatically assign *bound* processors. To add the processor at hardware path *45* to a vPar, you would use the following:

```
-a cpu:45
```

min refers to the minimum number of *bound* CPUs. Only if you create a vPar and specify *min* you get *min* number of CPU(s) with the system assigning the hardware paths of the *bound* CPU(s). The following will give you two *bound* CPUs, the hardware paths of which are defined by the system:

```
-a cpu:::2
```

max is the potential number of *bound* + *unbound* CPUs. You can, for instance, have two *min* and four *max* CPUs, which would give you two *bound*, as specified by the *min* of two, and as many as two *unbound,* as specified by the four *max*. If there are unused CPUs, they'll be allocated to your vPar, giving you a total of four. The following will give you this number:

```
-a cpu:::2:4
```

num is the current number of *bound* + *unbound* CPUs. This is different from the potential number described by *max*. To specify three CPUs total with *num*, three of which are *bound* with *min*, and one at hardware path *45* with *path*, you would use the following:

```
-a cpu::3 -a cpu:::3 -a cpu:45
```

An interesting nuance to this command is that to delete the hardware path we specified, we would issue the options in reverse order. The hardware path would come first, then the *min*, and finally, the *num*.

In my work with vPars the most common desire is to have a *min* number of *bound* CPUs in all vPars and then move around *unbound* CPUs as the

man page

vparcreate appendix a

applications in vPars need them. For instance, when **vparcreate** is run, we would specify the following:

> **vparcreate -p cable1 -a cpu:::1:3 -a cpu::1**

At the time of creation, *cable1* will have one *bound* CPU only because we specified a *min* of one and a *num* of one. *num* is the total *bound* + *unbound* CPUs, and since we specified one for *num,* we'll get one *bound* CPU. Since *max* is three, we have left the door open to add as many as two additional *unbound* CPUs. If we have two *unbound* CPUs on our system, we can move them among the vPars as required with **vparmodify**. To remove the two *unbound* CPUs from *cable2* and add them to *cable1,* we would issue the two following **vparmodify** commands:

man page

vparmodify appendix a

> **vparmodify -p cable2 -m cpu::1**   <-- reduces cable2 from 3 to 1
>
> vparmodify -p cable1 -m cpu::3   <-- increases cable1 from 1 to 3

We first removed the two *unbound* CPUs from *cable2* and then added them to *cable1*. If the two *unbound* CPUs were not assigned to a vPar, we would not have to remove them from *cable2* prior to adding them to *cable1*. *unbound* CPUs can be moved when a vPar is up or down but *bound* CPUs can be moved only when a vPar is down at the time of this writing.

Although you have a lot of options for specifying and modifying CPUs, you don't have to use all of them. vPars is like any other system adminstration endeavor, keep things simple.

Let's now take a look at some processors in a system.. The following listing shows the total CPUs on the L-Class system used in some of our earlier examples in the book before they were assigned to any vPars:

```
cvhdcon3:/ # ioscan -f | grep proc
processor     0   33              processor CLAIMED     PROCESSOR     Processor
processor     1   37              processor CLAIMED     PROCESSOR     Processor
processor     2   97              processor CLAIMED     PROCESSOR     Processor
processor     3   101             processor CLAIMED     PROCESSOR     Processor
```

The third field in this listing shows the hardware path of the processors that would be used when specifying the hardware path.

After assigning processors to vPars, you'll want to confirm that indeed each vPar has in it the number of processors you specified. If we had two vPars named *cable1* and *cable2*, each with two bound processors assigned to them, we could verify that we did indeed have two processors assigned to each vPar in a variety of ways. First we can check the processors portion only of **dmesg**, as shown below for *cable1*:

```
cvhdcon3:/ # dmesg  |  grep proc
33 processor
101 processor
cvhdcon3:/ #
```

This **dmesg** output confirms that our vPar *cable1*, which has a host-name of *cvhdcon3*, does indeed have only two processors assigned to it even though there are four processors in the system.

We can also verify the number of CPUs in a vPar by running Glance-Plus and selecting the *Process List* screen as we have done in Figure 5-1 for *cable1*:

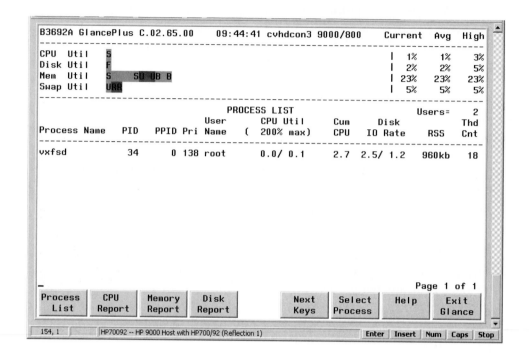

Figure 5-1 *CPU Report* in GlancePlus Showing Two Processors

The screen in Figure 5-1 confirms that we have two processors devoted to *cable1* (hostname *cvhdcon3*) by the *(200% max)* shown for *CPU Util* rather than the four (which would have read *400%*) that are in the systems. You can also run **top** to confirm the two processors in *cable1*, as shown in Figure 5-2:

```
System: cvhdcon3                                    Tue Jun 26 09:51:50 2001
Load averages: 0.53, 0.53, 0.53
127 processes: 111 sleeping, 16 running
Cpu states:
CPU   LOAD   USER   NICE    SYS    IDLE  BLOCK  SWAIT   INTR   SSYS
 0    0.17   0.0%   0.0%   1.0%   99.0%  0.0%   0.0%   0.0%   0.0%
 1    0.89   0.0%   0.0%   0.0%  100.0%  0.0%   0.0%   0.0%   0.0%
---   ----  -----  -----  -----  -----  -----  -----  -----  -----
avg   0.53   0.0%   0.0%   1.0%   99.0%  0.0%   0.0%   0.0%   0.0%

Memory: 93864K (61800K) real, 311236K (245020K) virtual, 1622548K free   Page# 1/
12

CPU TTY       PID USERNAME PRI NI    SIZE     RES STATE    TIME %WCPU   %CPU COMMAND
 1   ?         34 root     152 20      0K    960K run      0:03  0.31   0.31 vxfsd
 1   ?       1173 root     152 20   4644K   7244K run      0:11  0.30   0.30 prm3d
 0   ?       1473 root     158 10     76K    200K sleep    0:14  0.22   0.21 cclogd
 1   ?       1171 root     -16 20   5740K   5192K run      0:06  0.15   0.15 midaemon
 0   ?         13 root     152 20      0K    192K run      0:02  0.14   0.14 ioconfig
 1   ?        962 root     152 20   1416K   2212K run      0:00  0.10   0.10 dmisp
 1   ?       1292 root     152 20   1236K   2964K run      0:00  0.10   0.10 opcctla
 1   ?          3 root     128 20      0K     32K sleep    0:04  0.10   0.10 statdaem
 0  pts/ta  3775 root     158 20    496K    168K sleep    0:00  0.07   0.07 sh
 1   ?       1298 root     152 20    856K    960K run      0:00  0.05   0.05 opcmona_
```

```
 157, 80  |   HP70092 -- HP 9000 Host with HP700/92 (Reflection 1)        Enter  Insert  Num  Caps  Stop
```

Figure 5-2 **top** Screen Shot Showing Two Processors in *cable1*

top clearly shows two CPUs devoted to *cable1* (CPU 0 and 1 in Figure 5-2.)

Virtual Partitions and Memory

When assigning memory in Chapter 2, you use *size*. You can also specify *base* address and *range* as subset of *size* jusst as *hwpath* is a subset of *min* and *num* for CPUs. We chose to use the size. Table 5-1 shows the options related to assigning and changing memory. The first activity we have to perform is to find the amount of memory on a system so that we can assign portions of it to vPars. There are a variety of ways to determine the amount of memory on your system. The following shows only the memory-related output of the **dmesg** command when booting standard HP-UX in non-vPars mode:

```
# dmesg
    Memory Information:
    IWBD / > cal page size = 4096 bytes, logical page size = 4096 bytes
        Physical: 4194304 Kbytes, lockable: 3180924 Kbytes, available: 3655192 Kbytes

#
```

This listing shows a *Physical* memory of 4GBytes. You could also run GlancePlus and select the *Memory* screen.

Memory can easily be specified for a vPar with *m::size*, where size is in MBytes. To specify 2 GBytes in a virtual partition, you would use the option *m::2048.*

After assigning memory to vPars you'll want to confirm that indeed each vPar has in it the amount of memory you specified. You can verify this in a variety of ways. The first is by issuing **dmesg** when booting Virtual Partitions. The Virtual Partitions Monitor boots only the devices you have specified as part of a Virtual Partition. The following example shows only the memory-related output of **dmesg** for *cable1*:

```
Memory Information:
cvhdcon3:/ # page size = 4096 bytes, logical page size = 4096 bytes
    Physical: 2096128 Kbytes, lockable: 1576748 Kbytes, available: 1815620 Kbytes
```

Notice that this output shows 2 GBytes of RAM for *cable1*, as was specified when the vPar *cable1* was created. This is different from the example in Chapter 2, where *cable1* had one GByte of RAM. This is an indication of how low-level vPars work, in that resources were assigned to *cable1* at the time of boot, ensuring that only the specified resources were assigned to the vPar.

We can also view memory-related information by running GlancePlus and selecting the memory screen. The following screen shot shows the total memory of the system when booting standard HP-UX and not Virtual Partitions as we have done in Figure 5-3:

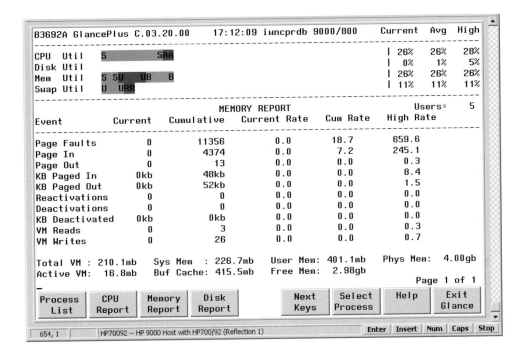

```
B3692A GlancePlus C.03.20.00      17:12:09 iuncprdb 9000/800    Current  Avg  High
--------------------------------------------------------------------------------
CPU  Util  S          SAA                                    | 26%   26%   28%
Disk Util                                                    |  0%    1%    5%
Mem  Util  S SU   UB   B                                     | 26%   26%   26%
Swap Util  U  URR                                            | 11%   11%   11%
--------------------------------------------------------------------------------
                             MEMORY REPORT                        Users=    5
Event            Current    Cumulative  Current Rate  Cum Rate  High Rate
--------------------------------------------------------------------------------
Page Faults          0        11356         0.0        18.7       659.6
Page In              0         4374         0.0         7.2       245.1
Page Out             0           13         0.0         0.0         0.3
KB Paged In        0kb         48kb         0.0         0.0         8.4
KB Paged Out       0kb         52kb         0.0         0.0         1.5
Reactivations        0            0         0.0         0.0         0.0
Deactivations        0            0         0.0         0.0         0.0
KB Deactivated     0kb          0kb         0.0         0.0         0.0
VM Reads             0            3         0.0         0.0         0.3
VM Writes            0           26         0.0         0.0         0.7

Total VM : 210.1mb   Sys Mem  : 226.7mb   User Mem: 401.1mb   Phys Mem:  4.00gb
Active VM:  16.8mb   Buf Cache: 415.5mb   Free Mem: 2.98gb
                                                           Page 1 of 1
--------------------------------------------------------------------------------
 Process   CPU     Memory    Disk          Next     Select    Help    Exit
  List    Report   Report   Report         Keys    Process           Glance
--------------------------------------------------------------------------------
 654, 1      HP70092 -- HP 9000 Host with HP700/92 (Reflection 1)   Enter  Insert  Num  Caps  Stop
```

Figure 5-3 *Phys Mem* in GlancePlus Showing 4 GBytes for System (non-vPars)

Now let's view the memory for *cable1* (hostname *cvhdcon3*) in GlancePlus. Figure 5-4 was obtained when the system loaded *cable1* at boot time:

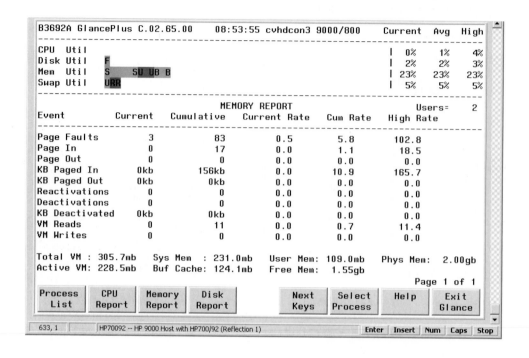

Figure 5-4 *Phys Mem* in GlancePlus Showing 2 GBytes for *cable1*

The *Phys Mem* in the bottom right-hand side of the screen is shown as 2 GBytes, as we had assigned for *cable1*. This confirms the 4 GBytes for the system and 2 GBytes for *cable1* shown with **dmesg**.

Because you have multiple Virtual Partitions running, you have to have multiple HP-UX kernels running. The kernel for a specific Virtual Partition has to be located within the memory range devoted to that Virtual Partition. The location of the kernel in memory is specified in the **/usr/conf/gen/map-file** file in HP-UX 11i. Among the entries in this file is the location in memory at which the kernel will be located. This line begins with *Text = LOAD*. This file exists on every file system for which you have a Virtual Partition and contains the kernel location for the respective Virtual Partition as well as other dynamic information. This file exists on HP-UX 11i for non-Virtual Partition systems as well and contains other information used by 11i. Working with the HP-UX 11i kernel and Virtual Partitions is covered in Chapter 4.

Virtual Partitions and LAN

The LAN cards on your system are also easy to identify with **ioscan**. To see only the listing of LAN cards on a system, we would issue the following command:

```
# ioscan -f | grep lan
lan       0  0/0/0/0     btlan3    CLAIMED   INTERFACE   PCI Ethernet (10110019)
lan       1  0/4/0/0     btlan5    CLAIMED   INTERFACE   HP A5230A/B5509BA
                                                         PCI 10/100Base-TX Addon
lan       3  0/5/0/0/4/0 btlan     CLAIMED   INTERFACE   HP A5506B
                                                         PCI 10/100Base-TX 4 port
lan       4  0/5/0/0/5/0 btlan     CLAIMED   INTERFACE   HP A5506B
                                                         PCI 10/100Base-TX 4 port
lan       5  0/5/0/0/6/0 btlan     CLAIMED   INTERFACE   HP A5506B
                                                         PCI 10/100Base-TX 4 port
lan       6  0/5/0/0/7/0 btlan     CLAIMED   INTERFACE   HP A5506B
                                                         PCI 10/100Base-TX 4 port
lan       2  1/12/0/0    btlan5    CLAIMED   INTERFACE   HP A5230A/B5509BA
                                                         PCI 10/100Base-TX Addon
#
```

This system has seven LAN interfaces. It has the built-in LAN interface, two add-on LAN cards, and a four-port card. Although this system was not used in our earlier example, I wanted to show a listing of a system with a variety of LAN interfaces present.

Going back to our earlier example, our system has three LAN interfaces as shown in the following **ioscan** listing:

```
cvhdcon3:/ # ioscan -f | grep lan
lan       0  0/0/0/0          btlan    CLAIMED   INTERFACE   HP PCI 10/100Ba
se-TX Core
lan       1  0/10/0/0         btlan    CLAIMED   INTERFACE   HP A5230A/B5509
BA PCI 10/100Base-TX Addon
lan       2  0/12/0/0         btlan    CLAIMED   INTERFACE   HP A5230A/B5509
BA PCI 10/100Base-TX Addon
cvhdcon3:/ #
```

The LAN card at *0/0* has been asssigned to *cable1*, and the card at *0/10* has been assigned to *cable2*, as shown in the following **vparstatus -v** listing:

man page

vparstatus
appendix a

```
# vparstatus -v

[Virtual Partition Details]
Name:        cable1
State:       Up
Attributes:  Dynamic,Manual
```

```
Kernel Path:   /stand/vmunix
Boot Opts:

[CPU Details]
Min/Max:  1/3
Bound by User [Path]:
Bound by Monitor [Path]:  33
Unbound [Path]:

[IO Details]
   0.0                           <-- cable1 LAN on 0/0 but not shown
   0.0.1.1.2.0   BOOT

[Memory Details]
Specified [Base  /Range]:
         (bytes) (MB)
Total Memory (MB):  1024

[Virtual Partition Details]
Name:          cable2
State:         Up
Attributes:    Dynamic,Manual
Kernel Path:   /stand/vmunix
Boot Opts:

[CPU Details]
Min/Max:  1/3
Bound by User [Path]:
Bound by Monitor [Path]:  37
Unbound [Path]:

[IO Details]
   0.8.0.0.8.0.5.0.0.0, BOOT
   0.10                          <-- cable2 LAN

[Memory Details]
Specified [Base  /Range]:
         (bytes) (MB)
Total Memory (MB):  1024
#
```

vparmodify
appendix a

vparcreate
appendix a

The LAN interface on the Core I/O card at *0/0/0/0* is not called out explicitly in the **vparstatus** output. The console at *0/0/4/0* is also an implied component of this vPar. Both of these components are part of the Core I/O card that we specified as part of *cable1* with the *-a io:0/0* argument to the **vparcreate** command.

The unassigned LAN interface can be added to *cable1* or *cable2* with the **vparmodify** command. At the time of this writing, however; I/O components can't be added dynamically, and the vPar would have to be *down* in order to add LAN or any other I/O component. You can, however; use Online Replacement and Addition (OLAR) of components in vPars. If you had, for instance, assigned an I/O path to a vPar and then you physically add a component to that I/O slot then it is part of the vPar.

Virtual Partitions and the Console

You can set up a dedicated physical console for each virtual partition. This would mean allocating a serial port for each of your virtual partitions. Alternatively, your virtual partitions can use virtual consoles. The Virtual CoNsole driver, *vcn*, handles I/O related to the virtual consoles. As shown in Figure 5-5, *vcn* communicates with the Virtual Partitions Monitor. The Virtual Partitions Monitor buffers I/O related to virtual consoles until it can be handled by the Virtual Console Slave (*vcs*). All vPars use Virtual Consoles and the physical console is assigned to one of the vPars as part of the I/O specification.

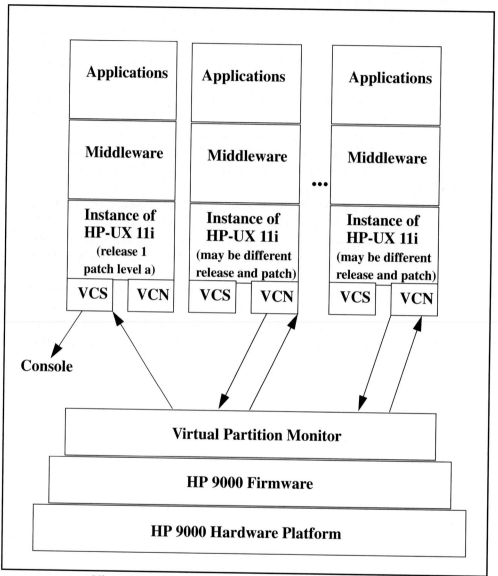

Figure 5-5 Virtual Partitions and Consoles

The leftmost virtual partition in Figure 5-5 has a physical port assigned to it for the console. The other partitions use the *vcn* driver. Console-related information on these Virtual Partitions goes through the *vcn* driver to the Virtual Partions Monitor. It, in turn, communicates with the *vcs* driver on the leftmost partition. You can then use the console on this partition to get access to the consoles of the other partitions.

If a hardware console port is not defined, the *vcn* driver is used automatically, so no configuration is required. The physical console, in our examples throughout this book were specified when the Core I/O card was included in one of the vPars.

You don't perform any console setup in order to use the virtual console. When you create a vPar and specify that the Core I/O card at *0/0* is to be added to the vPar the console is automatically created for you in that vPar. This is true also for the Core I/O built-in LAN card. The boot device, however, must be called out explicitly with its path and *:BOOT* following the path.

You would then toggle between any number of Virtual Partitions using *Ctrl-A*. The Virtual Partition Monitor buffers all data to be sent to the console. When you hit *Ctrl-A* to switch to the next vPar, the console information that has been buffered for the vPar to which you have switched is sent to the console.

Figure 5-6 shows using the console to view *cable1* with a hostname of *cvhdcon3*. Issuing *Ctrl-A* connects to vPar *cable2* with a hostname of *cvhdcon4*. When you issue *Ctrl-A* to switch to the next vPar in the console, you are supplied with the name of the vPar to which you have connected in brackets, such as *[cable1]*.

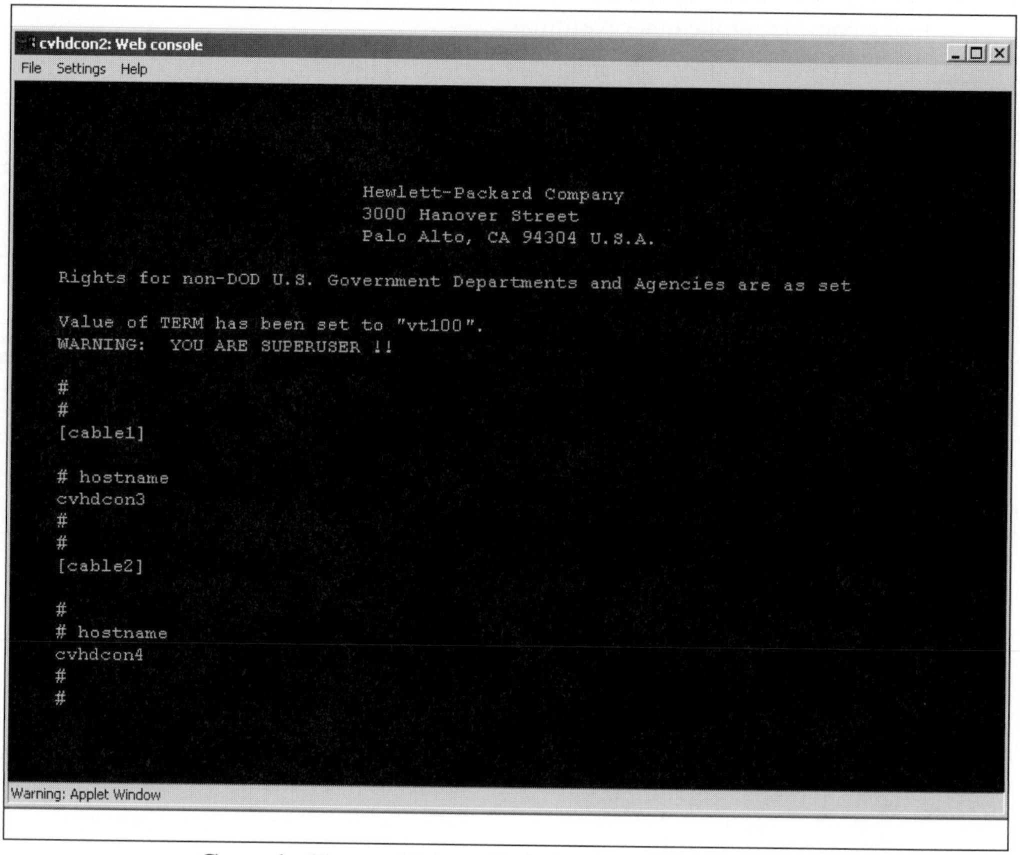

```
 cvhdcon2: Web console                                                    _ □ ×
File  Settings  Help




                        Hewlett-Packard Company
                        3000 Hanover Street
                        Palo Alto, CA 94304 U.S.A.

        Rights for non-DOD U.S. Government Departments and Agencies are as set

        Value of TERM has been set to "vt100".
        WARNING:   YOU ARE SUPERUSER !!

        #
        #
        [cable1]

        # hostname
        cvhdcon3
        #
        #
        [cable2]

        #
        # hostname
        cvhdcon4
        #
        #



Warning: Applet Window
```

Figure 5-6 Console Shown Using *Ctrl-A* to Toggle between vPars

In addition to using the console to switch between vPars, you can also
use the LAN cards configured into the respective vPars to open a *TELNET*
or other type of session to the vPars. This is the same technique you would
use to connect to any system over the network and is one of the primary reasons you always want to have a LAN card configured as part of every vPar.

Adding and Removing Devices in Virtual Partitions

Most of the work we've done related to Virtual Partitions has been static in nature; that is, we've configured a Virtual Partition with specific components and verified the configuration. We can add and remove devices from Virtual Partitions as well. In Chapter 2 we assigned an *unbound* CPU to vPar *cable1*. Let's review this process, which we can apply to tape drives as well as other devices.

In the upcoming example there is a four-processor system on which there are the two Virtual Partitions we just created: *cable1* and *cable2*. Each vPar has one *bound* CPU that was assigned by *min* when the vPars were created. Let's run **vparstatus** to see the components of which these two Virtual Partitions are comprised and confirm that each has one bound CPU:

man page

vparstatus
appendix a

```
# vparstatus -p cable1 -v

[Virtual Partition Details]
Name:        cable1
State:       Up
Attributes:  Dynamic,Manual
Kernel Path: /stand/vmunix
Boot Opts:

[CPU Details]
Min/Max:  1/3
Bound by User [Path]:
Bound by Monitor [Path]:  33      <-- one bound CPU @ 33
Unbound [Path]:

[IO Details]
   0.0
   0.0.1.1.2.0  BOOT

[Memory Details]
Specified [Base  /Range]:
          (bytes) (MB)
Total Memory (MB):  1024
#
```

```
# vparstatus -p cable2 -v


[Virtual Partition Details]
Name:          cable2
State:         Up
Attributes:    Dynamic,Manual
Kernel Path:   /stand/vmunix
Boot Opts:

[CPU Details]
Min/Max:  1/3
Bound by User [Path]:
Bound by Monitor [Path]:  37      <-- one CPU in use at 37
Unbound [Path]:

[IO Details]
    0.8.0.0.8.0.5.0.0.0   BOOT
    0.10

[Memory Details]
Specified [Base  /Range]:
          (bytes) (MB)
Total Memory (MB):  1024
#
```

man page

vparstatus
appendix a

The output of these two **vparstatus** commands shows that *cable1* has one *bound* CPU, and *cable2* has one *bound* CPU. On the L-Class system on which these vPars were created there are a total of four CPUs. This means that two CPUs should be available. Let's run **vparstatus -A** to view the available components on a system:

```
# vparstatus -A

[Unbound CPUs (path)]:  97
                        101
[Available CPUs]:  2

[Available I/O devices (path)]:   0.1
                                  0.2
                                  0.3
                                  0.4
                                  0.5
                                  0.9
                                  0.12
                                  32
                                  36
```

```
                                          96
                                          100

[Unbound memory (Base  /Range)]:   0x0/64
                (bytes) (MB)       0xc000000/1856
                                   0x180000000/128
[Available memory (MB)]:  2048
#
```

This output confirms that there are two CPUs available at hardware paths *97* and *101*. We can add these CPUs in a variety of ways. Let's use the **vparmodify** command to change the *num* of CPUs in *cable1* to two CPUs. We do this by *adding* one to the current number of CPUs with *-a*. This is a relative operation in that one CPU will be added to the current number of CPUs. You can use **vparmodify -m** if you want to specify the absolute number of CPUs for the vPar rather than the relative number. The following shows this **vparmodify** command:

man page

vparmodify
appendix a

```
# vparmodify -p cable1 -a cpu::1
#
```

We can now run **vparstatus -p cable1 -v** to confirm that the CPU has been added, shown in the following listing:

man page

vparstatus
appendix a

```
# vparstatus -p cable1 -v

[Virtual Partition Details]
Name:        cable1
State:       Up
Attributes:  Dynamic,Manual
Kernel Path: /stand/vmunix
Boot Opts:

[CPU Details]
Min/Max:  1/3
Bound by User [Path]:
Bound by Monitor [Path]:  33      <-- original CPU @ 33
Unbound [Path]:  97               <-- umbound CPU @ 97

[IO Details]
    0.0
    0.0.1.1.2.0  BOOT
```

```
[Memory Details]
Specified [Base  /Range]:
         (bytes) (MB)
Total Memory (MB):  1024
#
```

man page

vparstatus
appendix a

man page

vparmodify
appendix a

The **vparstatus** output shows that the CPU at hardware path *97* has indeed been added to *cable1* with the **vparmodify** command.

In addition, we can run GlancePlus or **top** to confirm that there are two CPUs in use on *cable2*. The following is a **top** output run on *cable2*:

```
# top

System: cvhdcon3                                    Thu Oct  4 15:30:42 2001
Load averages: 0.19, 0.51, 0.62
124 processes: 110 sleeping, 14 running
Cpu states:
CPU   LOAD   USER   NICE    SYS   IDLE   BLOCK   SWAIT   INTR   SSYS
 0    0.37   0.0%   0.2%   0.0%  99.8%   0.0%    0.0%    0.0%   0.0%
 1    0.02   0.0%   0.0%   0.8%  99.2%   0.0%    0.0%    0.0%   0.0%
---   ----   -----  -----  -----  -----  -----   -----   -----  -----
avg   0.19   0.0%   0.2%   0.4%  99.4%   0.0%    0.0%    0.0%   0.0%

Memory: 93636K (57816K) real, 322124K (239536K) virtual, 746284K free  Page# 1/4

CPU TTY          PID USERNAME PRI NI   SIZE    RES STATE    TIME %WCPU   %CPU COMMAND
 0   ?            36 root     152 20     0K   832K run      0:00  0.33   0.33 vxfsd
 1   ?          1342 root     158 10    80K   212K sleep    0:10  0.28   0.28 cclogd
 0   ?          1149 root     152 20  4644K  7260K run      0:06  0.21   0.21 prm3d
 1   ?           922 root     154 24   540K   808K sleep    0:00  0.15   0.15 hpterm
 0 pty/ttyp1    3114 root     186 24   596K   528K run      0:00  0.17   0.15 top
 1   ?          1146 root     -16 20  7788K  7240K run      0:03  0.14   0.13 midaemon
 1   ?             3 root     128 20     0K    32K sleep    0:04  0.11   0.11 statdaemon
 0   ?          2018 root     154 20  3908K  1908K sleep    0:00  0.05   0.04 alarmgen
 1   ?          1272 root     152 20   856K   960K run      0:00  0.04   0.04 opcmona
 1   ?          1372 root     152 20  1076K  2356K run      0:00  0.04   0.04 samd
 0   ?             0 root     128 20     0K     0K sleep    0:11  0.02   0.02 swapper
 1   ?             1 root     168 20   448K   204K sleep    0:00  0.02   0.02 init
 0   ?             2 root     128 20     0K    32K sleep    0:00  0.02   0.02 vhand
 0   ?             4 root     128 20     0K    32K sleep    0:00  0.02   0.02 unhashdaemo
 1   ?            20 root     147 20     0K    32K sleep    0:00  0.02   0.02 lvmkd
 0   ?            22 root     147 20     0K    32K sleep    0:00  0.02   0.02 lvmkd
 1   ?            24 root     147 20     0K    32K sleep    0:00  0.02   0.02 lvmkd
 0   ?           339 root     154 20   152K   204K sleep    0:00  0.02   0.02 syncer
 0   ?           342 root     168 20    76K   192K sleep    0:00  0.02   0.02 vphbd
 0   ?           345 root     168 20   156K   216K sleep    0:00  0.02   0.02 vpard
 0   ?           410 root     154 20    80K   224K sleep    0:00  0.02   0.02 syslogd
 0   ?           446 root     127 20   156K   424K sleep    0:00  0.02   0.02 netfmt
 0   ?           552 root     154 20   740K   816K sleep    0:00  0.02   0.02 rpc.statd
 0   ?           558 root     154 20  1004K  1032K sleep    0:00  0.02   0.02 rpc.lockd
 0   ?           586 root     154 20   180K   316K sleep    0:00  0.02   0.02 inetd
 0   ?           855 root     154 20  1064K   472K sleep    0:00  0.02   0.02 sendmail:
 0   ?           863 root     154 20   772K   712K sleep    0:00  0.02   0.02 snmpdm
 0   ?           896 root     154 20   620K   552K sleep    0:00  0.02   0.02 mib2agt
 0   ?           914 root     154 20  1332K   444K sleep    0:00  0.02   0.02 cmsnmpd
 1   ?           951 root     154 20  4044K  1840K sleep    0:00  0.02   0.02 rpcd
 1 pty/ttyp1     952 root     158 24   512K   180K sleep    0:00  0.02   0.02 sh
 0   ?           974 root     168 20   152K   304K sleep    0:04  0.02   0.02 scrdaemon
 0   ?           996 root     154 20   200K   336K sleep    0:00  0.02   0.02 pwgrd
 0   ?          1039 root     154 10   308K   428K sleep    0:00  0.02   0.02 diagmond
 0   ?          1093 root     154 20  1224K   816K sleep    0:00  0.02   0.02 ttd
 1   ?          1135 root     154 20  2588K  1624K sleep    0:00  0.02   0.02 perflbd
 0   ?          1156 root     154 20  2952K  1572K sleep    0:00  0.02   0.02 swagentd
 0   ?          1167 root     154 20   224K   252K sleep    0:00  0.02   0.02 emsagent
```

```
  0   ?      1168 root     127 20  2380K  2204K sleep    0:00  0.02  0.02 scopeux
```

This output show two CPUs labeled *0* and *1* in *cable1*. The *System* name of *cvhdcon3* is shown at the output because the hostname for *cable1* is *cvhdcon3*.

Although this is a simple example showing how a Virtual Partition can be modified, it also demonstrates the power of vPars. While both vPars on the system are running, a processor can be added to one or both without interruption of the programs running in the vPars.

Note that the *-a* option to **vparmodify** changed the number of CPUs *relative* to the current number. In our case the current number of CPUs was one and using *-a cpu::1* added one CPU to the current number of one resulting in two CPUs. This is true also when we use the *-d* option to **vparmodify** to remove processors. The following example shows running **vparstatus** to see the two CPUs, using **vparmodify** to change the number of CPUs back to one (this is also relative to the current number of CPUs which is two,) and a **vparstatus** to confirm that this change has taken place:

man page

vparmodify
appendix a

man page

vparstatus
appendix a

```
# vparstatus -p cable1 -v


[Virtual Partition Details]
Name:         cable1
State:        Up
Attributes:   Dynamic,Manual
Kernel Path:  /stand/vmunix
Boot Opts:

[CPU Details]
Min/Max:  1/3
Bound by User [Path]:
Bound by Monitor [Path]:   33        <-- bound CPU @ 33
Unbound [Path]:  97                  <-- unbound CPU @ 97

[IO Details]
   0.0
   0.0.0.0
   0.0.1.1.2.0  BOOT
   0.0.4.0  CONSOLE

[Memory Details]
Specified [Base  /Range]:
         (bytes) (MB)
Total Memory (MB):  1024
# vparmodify -p cable1 -d cpu::1
# vparstatus -p cable1 -v
```

```
[Virtual Partition Details]
Name:          cable1
State:         Up
Attributes:    Dynamic,Manual
Kernel Path:   /stand/vmunix
Boot Opts:

[CPU Details]
Min/Max:   1/3
Bound by User [Path]:
Bound by Monitor [Path]:   33      <-- original CPU @ 33
Unbound [Path]:                     <-- no unbound CPUs

[IO Details]
   0.0
   0.0.0.0
   0.0.1.1.2.0   BOOT
   0.0.4.0   CONSOLE

[Memory Details]
Specified [Base   /Range]:
          (bytes)  (MB)
Total Memory (MB):   1024
#
```

We could perform many other modifications to the vPars with the two *unbound* CPUs that are available, such as adding two CPUs to one of the vPars or one CPU to each vPar.

man page

vparmodify
appendix a

Please keep in mind the relative nature of components when using **vparmodify**, and that some changes, such as modifying memory or adding I/O components, require the vPar to be down at the time of this writing.

The following sections provide some background on device files in general for HP-UX 11i. You'll want to review the non-vPars-specific section of this chapter if you haven't worked much with device files on HP systems.

Non-vPar Specific Section of Chapter - Background on Device Files and Peripherals

HP-UX creates special files for most devices it finds attached at the time the system boots. You may, however, have to create your own device files or, at a minimum, have to understand some device files that exist on your system, so the information in this chapter is important for every system administrator to know. A typical installation will have terminals, printers, a tape drive, a DVD drive, and so on. Some devices are "standard," meaning that they are HP products or third-party products officially supported by HP. You have to be careful here, though, because what may seem as if it should work may not work after all and may not be supported. Almost always you can find a way to get things working eventually, but beware of devices you may be adding that aren't supported and may cause you trouble.

As you add additional peripherals to your system, you will have to either add device files manually or use SAM to create them for you. Most devices you add can be added through SAM. I find adding peripherals to be much like setting up networking; that is, I almost always use SAM, but I find it important to know what is going on in the background. As an example, you could add a printer to your system using SAM and never know what has been done to support the new printer. In the event that the printer does not work for some reason, you really can't begin troubleshooting the problem without an understanding of the device files.

The following section is a general overview of device files.

Device Files in HP-UX 11i

What could be more confusing in the UNIX world than device files? Fortunately, in HP-UX, device files for the Series 700 and Series 800 are nearly identical, so if you learn one, your knowledge applies to the other. In this section I cover:

- The structure of device files.

- Some commands associated with helping you work with device files.

• Some examples of creating device files.

A device file provides the HP-UX kernel with important information about a specific device. The HP-UX kernel needs to know a lot about a device before I/O operations can be performed. With HP-UX 11i, the device file naming convention is the same for workstations and server systems. Device files are in the **/dev** directory. There may also be a subdirectory under **/dev** used to further categorize the device files. An example of a sub-directory would be **/dev/dsk,** where disk device files are usually located, and **/dev/rmt**, where tape drive device files are located. Figure 5-7 shows the HP-UX 11i device file-naming convention.

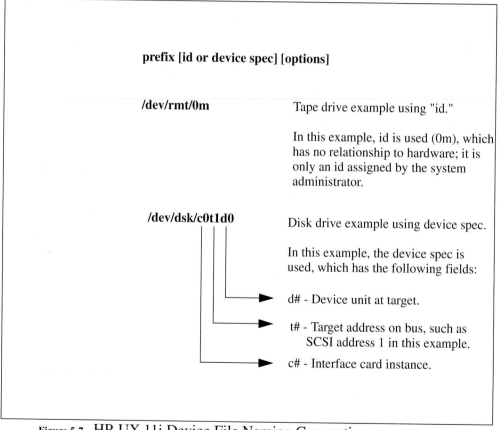

prefix [id or device spec] [options]

/dev/rmt/0m

Tape drive example using "id."

In this example, id is used (0m), which has no relationship to hardware; it is only an id assigned by the system administrator.

/dev/dsk/c0t1d0

Disk drive example using device spec.

In this example, the device spec is used, which has the following fields:

d# - Device unit at target.

t# - Target address on bus, such as SCSI address 1 in this example.

c# - Interface card instance.

Figure 5-7 HP-UX 11i Device File Naming Convention

There are a number of commands you can use as you go about creating device files. The **ioscan** command is the first of these. Some of the examples in this section were used in Chapter 3, when building a kernel was covered. The following is an **ioscan** output of the same Series 700 for which **sysdef** was run when describing how a kernel is created in Chapter 4. (Using *-f* with **ioscan** would have created a full listing; you should try it with and without *-f*.) I included four **ioscan** outputs so that you could see examples from a variety of different systems. The last listing is from a large V-Class system used in some of the examples in Chapter 9, where disks and filesystems are covered.

(on Series 700)

```
$ /usr/sbin/ioscan

H/W Path      Class              Description
==============================================================

              bc
1             graphics           Graphics
2             ba
2/0           unknown
2/0/1            ext_bus         Built-in SCSI
2/0/1.1             target
2/0/1.1.0              disk      HP        C2247
2/0/1.2             target
2/0/1.2.0             disk       TOSHIBA CD-ROM XM-3301TA
2/0/1.6             target
2/0/1.6.0             disk       HP        C2247
2/0/2            lan             Built-in LAN
2/0/4            tty             Built-in RS-232C
2/0/6            ext_bus         Built-in Parallel Interface
2/0/8            audio           Built-in Audio
2/0/10           pc              Built-in Floppy Drive
2/0/10.1            floppy       HP_PC_FDC_FLOPPY
2/0/11           ps2             Built-in Keyboard
8             processor          Processor
9             memory             Memory
```

The following is an **ioscan** output from a Series 800 system. Note the four processors shown in this output.

(on Series 800)

```
$ /usr/sbin/ioscan

H/W Path      Class           Description
====================================================================
              bc
8             bc              I/O Adapter
10            bc              I/O Adapter
10/0             ext_bus      GSC built-in Fast/Wide SCSI
10/0.3              target
10/0.3.0               disk   HP        C2490WD
10/0.4              target
10/0.4.0               disk   HP        C2490WD
10/0.5              target
10/0.5.0               disk   HP        C2490WD
10/0.6              target
10/0.6.0               disk   HP        C2490WD
10/4          bc              Bus Converter
10/4/0             tty        MUX
10/12         ba              Core I/O Adapter
10/12/0          ext_bus      Built-in Parallel Interface
10/12/5          ext_bus      Built-in SCSI
10/12/5.0           target
10/12/5.0.0            tape   HP        HP35480A
10/12/5.2           target
10/12/5.2.0            disk   TOSHIBA CD-ROM XM-4101TA
10/12/6           lan         Built-in LAN
10//12/7          ps2         Built-in Keyboard/Mouse
32            processor       Processor
34            processor       Processor
36            processor       Processor
38            processor       Processor
49            memory          Memory
```

And last is an **ioscan** output from a V-Class server. Note the eight processors shown in this output.

(on V-Class)

```
$ /usr/sbin/ioscan

H/W Path      Class               Description
============================================
              bc
0             ba                  PCI Bus Bridge - epic
0/0/0            lan              PCI(10110019)
0/1/0            unknown          PCI(107e0008)
```

```
2              ba                              PCI Bus Bridge - epic
2/0/0                       ext_bus           Ultra Wide SCSI
2/0/0.5                       target
2/0/0.5.0                       disk          SEAGATE ST34371W
2/0/0.6                       target
2/0/0.6.0                       disk          SEAGATE ST34371W
2/0/0.7                       target
2/0/0.7.0                         ctl         Initiator
2/1/0                       lan               PCI(10110019)
4              ba                              PCI Bus Bridge - epic
4/1/0                    fc                    HP Fibre Channel Mass
                                                  Storage Adapter
4/1/0.5                lan                     HP Fibre Channel Mass
                                                  Storage Cntl
4/1/0.8                      fcp               FCP Protocol Adapter
4/2/0                       ext_bus           Ultra Wide SCSI
4/2/0.0                       target
4/2/0.0.0                       disk          TOSHIBA CD-ROM XM-5701TA
4/2/0.1                       target
4/2/0.1.0                       tape          HP C1537A
4/2/0.7                       target
4/2/0.7.0                         ctl         Initiator
6              ba                              PCI Bus Bridge - epic
8              memory
15             ba                              Core I/O Adapter
15/1                    tty                    Built-in Serial Port DUART
15/2                    tty                    Built-in Serial Port DUART
15/3                    unknown                Unknown
17             processor                       Processor
19             processor                       Processor
20             processor                       Processor
22             processor                       Processor
25             processor                       Processor
27             processor                       Processor
28             processor                       Processor
30             processor                       Processor
```

The following is a full **ioscan** output from a V-Class server. This server has a large disk unit attached to it (XP 256), which resulted in a very long output that I had to abbreviate in the place where the three dots are shown.

(on V-Class)

```
# ioscan -f
Class      I  H/W Path        Driver      S/W State   H/W Type     Description
================================================================================
bc         0                  root        CLAIMED     BUS_NEXUS
ba         0  0               saga        CLAIMED     BUS_NEXUS    saga Bridge
lan        0  0/0/0           btlan6      CLAIMED     INTERFACE    PCI Ethernet (10110019)
```

```
ba         1    1                    saga        CLAIMED    BUS_NEXUS     saga Bridge
ext_bus    0    1/0/0                c720        CLAIMED    INTERFACE     Ultra2 Wide LVD SCSI
target     0    1/0/0.4              tgt         CLAIMED    DEVICE
disk       0    1/0/0.4.0            sdisk       CLAIMED    DEVICE        SEAGATE ST318275LW
target     1    1/0/0.5              tgt         CLAIMED    DEVICE
disk       1    1/0/0.5.0            sdisk       CLAIMED    DEVICE        SEAGATE ST318275LW
target     2    1/0/0.6              tgt         CLAIMED    DEVICE
disk       2    1/0/0.6.0            sdisk       CLAIMED    DEVICE        SEAGATE ST318275LW
target     3    1/0/0.7              tgt         CLAIMED    DEVICE
ctl        0    1/0/0.7.0            sctl        CLAIMED    DEVICE        Initiator
target     4    1/0/0.8              tgt         CLAIMED    DEVICE
disk       3    1/0/0.8.0            sdisk       CLAIMED    DEVICE        SEAGATE ST318275LW
ext_bus    1    1/1/0                c720        CLAIMED    INTERFACE     Ultra2 Wide LVD SCSI
target     5    1/1/0.7              tgt         CLAIMED    DEVICE
ctl        1    1/1/0.7.0            sctl        CLAIMED    DEVICE        Initiator
target     6    1/1/0.9              tgt         CLAIMED    DEVICE
disk       4    1/1/0.9.0            sdisk       CLAIMED    DEVICE        SEAGATE ST318275LW
target     7    1/1/0.10             tgt         CLAIMED    DEVICE
disk       5    1/1/0.10.0           sdisk       CLAIMED    DEVICE        SEAGATE ST318275LW
target     8    1/1/0.11             tgt         CLAIMED    DEVICE
disk       6    1/1/0.11.0           sdisk       CLAIMED    DEVICE        SEAGATE ST318275LW
target     9    1/1/0.12             tgt         CLAIMED    DEVICE
disk       7    1/1/0.12.0           sdisk       CLAIMED    DEVICE        SEAGATE ST318275LW
ba         2    2                    saga        CLAIMED    BUS_NEXUS     saga Bridge
fc         0    2/0/0                td          CLAIMED    INTERFACE     HP Tachyon TL/TS Fibre
Channel Mass Storage Adapter
fcp        0    2/0/0.8              fcp         CLAIMED    INTERFACE     FCP Protocol Adapter
ext_bus    7    2/0/0.8.0.0.0        fcparray    CLAIMED    INTERFACE     FCP Array Interface
target     12   2/0/0.8.0.0.0.0      tgt         CLAIMED    DEVICE
disk       9    2/0/0.8.0.0.0.0.0    sdisk       CLAIMED    DEVICE        HP        OPEN-8
disk       77   2/0/0.8.0.0.0.0.1    sdisk       CLAIMED    DEVICE        HP        OPEN-8
disk       78   2/0/0.8.0.0.0.0.2    sdisk       CLAIMED    DEVICE        HP        OPEN-8
disk       105  2/0/0.8.0.0.0.0.3    sdisk       CLAIMED    DEVICE        HP        OPEN-8
disk       106  2/0/0.8.0.0.0.0.4    sdisk       CLAIMED    DEVICE        HP        OPEN-8
disk       10   2/0/0.8.0.0.0.0.5    sdisk       CLAIMED    DEVICE        HP        OPEN-8
disk       107  2/0/0.8.0.0.0.0.6    sdisk       CLAIMED    DEVICE        HP        OPEN-8
disk       108  2/0/0.8.0.0.0.0.7    sdisk       CLAIMED    DEVICE        HP        OPEN-8
target     13   2/0/0.8.0.0.0.1      tgt         CLAIMED    DEVICE
disk       11   2/0/0.8.0.0.0.1.0    sdisk       CLAIMED    DEVICE        HP        OPEN-8
disk       109  2/0/0.8.0.0.0.1.1    sdisk       CLAIMED    DEVICE        HP        OPEN-8
disk       110  2/0/0.8.0.0.0.1.2    sdisk       CLAIMED    DEVICE        HP        OPEN-8
disk       111  2/0/0.8.0.0.0.1.3    sdisk       CLAIMED    DEVICE        HP        OPEN-8
disk       112  2/0/0.8.0.0.0.1.4    sdisk       CLAIMED    DEVICE        HP        OPEN-8
disk       113  2/0/0.8.0.0.0.1.5    sdisk       CLAIMED    DEVICE        HP        OPEN-8
disk       114  2/0/0.8.0.0.0.1.6    sdisk       CLAIMED    DEVICE        HP        OPEN-8
disk       176  2/0/0.8.0.0.0.1.7    sdisk       CLAIMED    DEVICE        HP        OPEN-8
target     14   2/0/0.8.0.0.0.2      tgt         CLAIMED    DEVICE
disk       12   2/0/0.8.0.0.0.2.0    sdisk       CLAIMED    DEVICE        HP        OPEN-8
disk       177  2/0/0.8.0.0.0.2.1    sdisk       CLAIMED    DEVICE        HP        OPEN-8
target     15   2/0/0.8.0.0.0.3      tgt         CLAIMED    DEVICE
disk       13   2/0/0.8.0.0.0.3.0    sdisk       CLAIMED    DEVICE        HP        DISK-SUBSYSTEM
target     16   2/0/0.8.0.0.0.4      tgt         CLAIMED    DEVICE
disk       14   2/0/0.8.0.0.0.4.0    sdisk       CLAIMED    DEVICE        HP        DISK-SUBSYSTEM
target     17   2/0/0.8.0.0.0.5      tgt         CLAIMED    DEVICE
disk       15   2/0/0.8.0.0.0.5.0    sdisk       CLAIMED    DEVICE        HP        DISK-SUBSYSTEM
target     18   2/0/0.8.0.0.0.6      tgt         CLAIMED    DEVICE
disk       16   2/0/0.8.0.0.0.6.0    sdisk       CLAIMED    DEVICE        HP        DISK-SUBSYSTEM
target     19   2/0/0.8.0.0.0.7      tgt         CLAIMED    DEVICE
disk       17   2/0/0.8.0.0.0.7.0    sdisk       CLAIMED    DEVICE        HP        DISK-SUBSYSTEM
target     20   2/0/0.8.0.0.0.8      tgt         CLAIMED    DEVICE
disk       18   2/0/0.8.0.0.0.8.0    sdisk       CLAIMED    DEVICE        HP        OPEN-8
disk       79   2/0/0.8.0.0.0.8.1    sdisk       CLAIMED    DEVICE        HP        OPEN-8
disk       80   2/0/0.8.0.0.0.8.2    sdisk       CLAIMED    DEVICE        HP        OPEN-8
disk       115  2/0/0.8.0.0.0.8.3    sdisk       CLAIMED    DEVICE        HP        OPEN-8
disk       116  2/0/0.8.0.0.0.8.4    sdisk       CLAIMED    DEVICE        HP        OPEN-8
disk       117  2/0/0.8.0.0.0.8.5    sdisk       CLAIMED    DEVICE        HP        OPEN-8
disk       118  2/0/0.8.0.0.0.8.6    sdisk       CLAIMED    DEVICE        HP        OPEN-8
disk       119  2/0/0.8.0.0.0.8.7    sdisk       CLAIMED    DEVICE        HP        OPEN-8
target     21   2/0/0.8.0.0.0.9      tgt         CLAIMED    DEVICE
disk       19   2/0/0.8.0.0.0.9.0    sdisk       CLAIMED    DEVICE        HP        OPEN-8
disk       120  2/0/0.8.0.0.0.9.1    sdisk       CLAIMED    DEVICE        HP        OPEN-8
disk       121  2/0/0.8.0.0.0.9.2    sdisk       CLAIMED    DEVICE        HP        OPEN-8
disk       122  2/0/0.8.0.0.0.9.3    sdisk       CLAIMED    DEVICE        HP        OPEN-8
disk       123  2/0/0.8.0.0.0.9.4    sdisk       CLAIMED    DEVICE        HP        OPEN-8
disk       124  2/0/0.8.0.0.0.9.5    sdisk       CLAIMED    DEVICE        HP        OPEN-8
```

```
disk     125  2/0/0.8.0.0.0.9.6    sdisk    CLAIMED  DEVICE           HP  OPEN-8
disk     178  2/0/0.8.0.0.0.9.7    sdisk    CLAIMED  DEVICE           HP  OPEN-8
target    22  2/0/0.8.0.0.0.10     tgt      CLAIMED  DEVICE
disk      20  2/0/0.8.0.0.0.10.0   sdisk    CLAIMED  DEVICE           HP  OPEN-8
disk     179  2/0/0.8.0.0.0.10.1   sdisk    CLAIMED  DEVICE           HP  OPEN-8
target    23  2/0/0.8.0.0.0.11     tgt      CLAIMED  DEVICE
disk      21  2/0/0.8.0.0.0.11.0   sdisk    CLAIMED  DEVICE           HP  DISK-SUBSYSTEM
target    24  2/0/0.8.0.0.0.12     tgt      CLAIMED  DEVICE
disk      22  2/0/0.8.0.0.0.12.0   sdisk    CLAIMED  DEVICE           HP  DISK-SUBSYSTEM
target    25  2/0/0.8.0.0.0.13     tgt      CLAIMED  DEVICE
disk      23  2/0/0.8.0.0.0.13.0   sdisk    CLAIMED  DEVICE           HP  DISK-SUBSYSTEM
target    26  2/0/0.8.0.0.0.14     tgt      CLAIMED  DEVICE
disk      24  2/0/0.8.0.0.0.14.0   sdisk    CLAIMED  DEVICE           HP  DISK-SUBSYSTEM

                        .
                        .
                        .

memory       0   8            memory      CLAIMED  MEMORY      Memory
ba           8  15            bus_adapter CLAIMED  BUS_NEXUS   Core I/O Adapter
tty          0  15/1    consp1          CLAIMED  INTERFACE  Built-in Serial Port DUART
tty          1  15/2    consp1          CLAIMED  INTERFACE  Built-in Serial Port DUART
unknown     -1  15/3            UNCLAIMED  UNKNOWN     Built-in Ethernet
processor    0  16            processor   CLAIMED  PROCESSOR   Processor
processor    1  18            processor   CLAIMED  PROCESSOR   Processor
processor    2  21            processor   CLAIMED  PROCESSOR   Processor
processor    3  23            processor   CLAIMED  PROCESSOR   Processor
processor    4  24            processor   CLAIMED  PROCESSOR   Processor
processor    5  26            processor   CLAIMED  PROCESSOR   Processor
processor    6  29            processor   CLAIMED  PROCESSOR   Processor
processor    7  32            processor   CLAIMED  PROCESSOR   Processor
processor    8  34            processor   CLAIMED  PROCESSOR   Processor
processor    9  37            processor   CLAIMED  PROCESSOR   Processor
processor   10  39            processor   CLAIMED  PROCESSOR   Processor
processor   11  40            processor   CLAIMED  PROCESSOR   Processor
processor   12  42            processor   CLAIMED  PROCESSOR   Processor
processor   13  45            processor   CLAIMED  PROCESSOR   Processor
```

The next command that helps you when creating device files is **lsdev**. **lsdev** lists the drivers configured into your system. When adding a device file, you need to have the driver for the device configured into the system. If it is not configured into the system, you can use SAM to configure it, or you can use the manual kernel configuration process covered earlier. There are columns for the major number for a character device and block device, the driver name, and the class of the driver. The major number, character device, and other parameters are defined later. The following is an example of running **lsdev** on the same Series 700 on which **ioscan** was run:

(on Series 700)

```
$ /usr/sbin/lsdev
```

```
Character      Block      Driver      Class
       0         -1       cn          pseudo
       1         -1       ansio0      tty
```

3	-1	mm	pseudo
16	-1	ptym	ptym
17	-1	ptys	ptys
24	-1	hil	hil
27	-1	dmem	pseudo
46	-1	netdiag1	unknown
52	-1	lan2	lan
64	64	lv	lvm
66	-1	audio	audio
69	-1	dev_config	pseudo
72	-1	clone	pseudo
73	-1	strlog	pseudo
74	-1	sad	pseudo
75	-1	telm	strtelm
76	-1	tels	strtels
77	-1	tlctls	pseudo
78	-1	tlcots	pseudo
79	-1	tlcotsod	pseudo
114	-1	ip	pseudo
115	-1	arp	pseudo
116	-1	echo	pseudo
119	-1	dlpi	pseudo
130	-1	rawip	pseudo
136	-1	tcp	pseudo
137	-1	udp	pseudo
138	-1	stcpmap	pseudo
139	-1	nuls	pseudo
140	-1	netqa	pseudo
141	-1	tun	pseudo
142	-1	btlan3	unknown
143	-1	fddi3	unknown
144	-1	fddi0	unknown
145	-1	fcT1_cntl	unknown
156	-1	ptm	strptym
157	-1	ptm	strptys
159	-1	ps2	ps2
164	-1	pipedev	unknown
168	-1	beep	graf_pseudo
169	-1	fcgsc_lan	lan
170	-1	lpr0	unknown
174	-1	framebuf	graf_pseudo
183	-1	diag1	diag
188	31	sdisk	disk
189	-1	klog	pseudo
196	-1	eeprom	da
203	-1	sctl	ctl
205	-1	stape	tape
207	-1	sy	pseudo
216	-1	CentIF	ext_bus
227	-1	kepd	pseudo
229	-1	ite	graf_pseudo
232	-1	diag2	diag

Next is an example of running **lsdev** on the same Series 800 on which
ioscan was run:

(on Series 800)

```
$ /usr/sbin/lsdev

Character       Block       Driver        Class
       0          -1        cn            pseudo
       1          -1        asio0         tty
       3          -1        mm            pseudo
      16          -1        ptym          ptym
      17          -1        ptys          ptys
      28          -1        diag0         diag
      46          -1        netdiag1      unknown
      52          -1        lan2          lan
      64          64        lv            lvm
      69          -1        dev_config    pseudo
      72          -1        clone         pseudo
      73          -1        strlog        pseudo
      74          -1        sad           pseudo
      75          -1        telm          strtelm
      76          -1        tels          strtels
      77          -1        tlctls        pseudo
      78          -1        tlcots        pseudo
      79          -1        tlcotsod      pseudo
     114          -1        ip            pseudo
     116          -1        echo          pseudo
     119          -1        dlpi          pseudo
     130          -1        rawip         pseudo
     136          -1        lpr0          unknown
     137          -1        udp           pseudo
     138          -1        stcpmap       pseudo
     139          -1        nuls          pseudo
     140          -1        netqa         pseudo
     141          -1        tun           pseuod
     142          -1        btlan3        unknown
     143          -1        fddi3         unknown
     144          -1        fddi0         unknown
     156          -1        ptm           strptym
     157          -1        ptm           strptys
     159          -1        ps2           ps2
     164          -1        pipedev       unknown
     168          -1        beep          graf_pseudo
     174          -1        framebuf      graf_pseudo
     188          31        sdisk         disk
```

```
189              -1         klog          pseudo
193              -1         mux2          tty
203              -1         sctl          ctl
205              -1         stape         tape
207              -1         sy            pseudo
216              -1         CentIF        ext_bus
227              -1         kepd          pseudo
229              -1         ite           graf_pseudo
```

And last, here is an example of running **lsdev** on the same V-class server on which the first **ioscan** was run:

(on V-Class)

```
$ /usr/sbin/lsdev
```

Character	Block	Driver	Class
0	-1	cn	pseudo
3	-1	mm	pseudo
16	-1	ptym	ptym
17	-1	ptys	ptys
27	-1	dmem	pseudo
28	-1	diag0	diag
46	-1	netdiag1	unknown
64	64	lv	lvm
69	-1	dev_config	pseudo
72	-1	clone	pseudo
73	-1	strlog	pseudo
74	-1	sad	pseudo
75	-1	telm	strtelm
76	-1	tels	strtels
77	-1	tlclts	pseudo
78	-1	tlcots	pseudo
79	-1	tlcotsod	pseudo
114	-1	ip	pseudo
115	-1	arp	pseudo
116	-1	echo	pseudo
119	-1	dlpi	pseudo
130	-1	rawip	pseudo
136	-1	tcp	pseudo
137	-1	udp	pseudo
138	-1	stcpmap	pseudo
139	-1	nuls	pseudo
140	-1	netqa	pseudo
141	-1	tun	pseudo
142	-1	fddi4	unknown
143	-1	fcT1_cntl	lan
144	-1	fcgsc_lan	lan

```
145        -1      lpr0        unknown
156        -1      ptm         strptym
157        -1      pts         strptys
164        -1      pipedev     unknown
169        -1      consp1      tty
170        -1      btlan6      lan
171        -1      fcp         fcp
188        31      sdisk       disk
189        -1      klog        pseudo
203        -1      sctl        ctl
205        -1      stape       tape
207        -1      sy          pseudo
227        -1      kepd        pseudo
232        -1      diag2       diag
```

From these three **lsdev** outputs, you can observe some minor differences in the devices. The Series 700, for instance, has such classes as audio and floppy, the Series 800 has a multiplexer, and the V-Class has a BaseTen network card.

You can use **ioscan** to show the device files for a particular peripheral. Going back to the Series 800 that had four disks and a CD-ROM attached to it, you could issue the following **ioscan** command to see the device files associated with *disk:*

(on Series 800)

```
$ /usr/sbin/ioscan -fn -C disk

Class  I  H/W Path    Driver  S/W State  H/W Type    Description
============================================================
disk   0 10/0.3.0     sdisk   CLAIMED    DEVICE      HP C2490WD
                      /dev/dsk/c0t3d0    /dev/rdsk/c0t3d0

disk   1 10/0.4.0     sdisk   CLAIMED    DEVICE      HP C2490WD
                      /dev/dsk/c0t4d0    /dev/rdsk/c0t4d0

disk   2 10/0.5.0     sdisk   CLAIMED    DEVICE      HP C2490WD
                      /dev/dsk/c0t5d0    /dev/rdsk/c0t5d0

disk   3 10/0.6.0     sdisk   CLAIMED    DEVICE      HP C2490WD
                      /dev/dsk/c0t6d0    /dev/rdsk/c0t6d0

disk   3 10/12/5/2/0 sdisk   CLAIMED    DEVICE      CD-ROM
                      /dev/dsk/c1t2d0    /dev/rdsk/c1t2d0
```

You can see from this **ioscan** all of the device files associated with *disk,* including the CD-ROM.

You could find out more information about one of these devices with the **diskinfo** command. Specify the character device you want to know more about, as shown below (using the *-v* option for verbose provides more detailed information).

```
$ diskinfo /dev/rdsk/c0t5d0

SCSI describe of /dev/rdsk/c0t5d0
             vendor: HP
         product id: C2490WD
               type: direct access
               size: 2082636 bytes
    bytes per sector: 512
```

An Example of Adding a Peripheral

In this section, we'll construct a device file for a tape drive. Chapter 9 covers the process of using device files and all Logical Volume Manager commands for adding disk devices that you may want to view as well. Before we construct a device file, let's view two existing device files on the Series 700 and see where some of this information appears. The first long listing is that of the tape drive, and the second is the disk, both of which are on the Series 700 in the earlier listings.

(on Series 700)

```
$ ll /dev/rmt/0m

crw-rw-rw- 2 bin bin 205 0x003000 Feb 12 03:00 /dev/rmt/0m
```

(on Series 700)

```
$ ll /dev/dsk/c0t1d0

brw-r----- 1 bin sys 31 0x001000 Feb 12 03:01 /dev/dsk/c0t1d0
```

The tape drive device file, **/dev/rmt/0m**, shows a major number of 205, corresponding to that shown for the *character* device driver *stape* from **lsdev**. The disk drive device file, **/dev/dsk/c0t6d0**, shows a major number of *31,* corresponding to the *block* device driver *sdisk* from **lsdev**. Since the tape drive requires only a character device file, and no major number exists for a block *stape* device, as indicated by the *-1* in the *block* column of **lsdev**, this file is the only device file that exists for the tape drive. The disk, on the other hand, may be used as either a block device or a character device (also referred to as the *raw device*). Therefore, we should see a character device file, **/dev/rdsk/c0t6d0**, with a major number of *188*, as shown in **lsdev** for *sdisk*.

(on Series 700)

```
$ ll /dev/rdsk/c0t0d0


crw-r-----   1   root   sys   188   0x001000   Feb   12   03:01
/dev/rdsk/c0t1d0
```

We can now create a device file for a second tape drive, this time at SCSI address 2, and a disk device file for a disk drive at SCSI address 5, using the mksf command. You can run mksf two different ways. The first form of mksf requires you to include less specific information, such as the minor number. The second form requires you to include more of this specific information. Some of these arguments relate only to the specific form of mksf you use.

-d	Use the device driver specified. A list of device drivers is obtained with the **lsdev** command.
-C	The device specified belongs to this class. The class is also obtained with the **lsdev** command.
-H	Use the hardware path specified. Hardware paths are obtained with the **ioscan** command.

-m   The minor number of the device is supplied.

-r   Create a character, also known as a raw device file. The default is to create a block file.

-v   Use verbose output, which prints the name of each special file as it is created.

We will now create the device files for a disk drive. Both a block and a character device file are required. The *0x005000* in the example corresponds to the address of 5 on the disk drive. This number, used in both the block and character device files, is unique for every disk drive created.

We can now create a *block* device file for a disk at SCSI address 5 using the following **mksf** command:

(on Series 700)

```
$ /sbin/mksf -v -C disk -m 0x005000 /dev/dsk/c0t5d0

    making /dev/dsk/c0t5d0 b 31 0x005000
```

Similarly, we can now create a *character* device file for a disk at SCSI address 5 using form two of **mksf**:

(on Series 700)

```
$ /sbin/mksf -v -r -C disk -m 0x005000 /dev/dsk/c0t5d0

    making /dev/rdsk/c0t5d0 c 188 0x005000
```

The *-v* option used in these examples prints out each device file as it is created. If you wanted to add a second tape drive at SCSI address 2 to your system in addition to the existing tape drive (**/dev/rmt/0m**), you might use the following **mksf** command:

(on Series 700)

```
$ /sbin/mksf  -v -C tape -m 0x002000 /dev/rmt/1m

      making /dev/rmt/1m c 205 0x002000
```

Character devices are automatically produced for tape drives, since no block device drivers are required. This fact was found in the output from the **lsdev** command, as indicated by a *-1* in the "Block" column.

With this level of device file background, you should have a good understanding of the device files that SAM will build for you when you add peripherals. By the way, printer device files look much different from the device files I covered here, but all the same principles apply.

Memory Management - Kind of Related to Device Files

Memory-related topics are almost never covered in system administration discussion. This is because memory is in too many different forms and there are too many factors affecting how much memory you need, what kind of memory you need, and so on. Let's cover some memory-related topics at a high level and look at some commands related to memory.

To begin with, most memory discussions begin with: what is swap, and how much do I need? HP-UX system administrators spend a lot of time worrying about swap. It must be very important. Swap is one part of the overall HP-UX memory management scheme, one of three parts to be exact. As any student of computer science will tell you, computers have three types of memory: cache memory, Random Access Memory (RAM), and disk memory. These are listed in order of their speed; that is, cache is much faster than RAM, which is much faster than disk.

Cache Memory

The HP Precision Architecture chip-set is configured with both data and instruction cache, which, I might add, are used very efficiently. You must rely on the operating system to use cache efficiently, since you have very little control over this. If you need information from memory and it is loaded in cache (probably because you recently accessed this information or accessed some information that is located close to what you now want), it will take very little time to get the information out of cache memory. This access, called a cache "hit," is instantaneous for all practical purposes. One of the reasons cache memory is so fast is that it typically is physically on the same chip as the processor. If putting large amounts of cache on-chip with the processor were possible, this would obviate the need for RAM and disk. This, however, is not currently possible, so efficient use of memory is a key to good overall system performance.

Checking Available RAM

Your system spells out to you what RAM is available. **/sbin/dmesg** gives you the amount of "physical" memory installed on the system, as shown below for a 64-MByte system:

```
Physical: 65536 Kbytes
```

Don't get too excited when you see this number, because it is not all "available" memory. Available memory is what is leftover after some memory is reserved for kernel code and data structures. You'll also see the available memory, in this case approximately 54 MBytes, with **/sbin/dmesg**:

```
available: 55336 Kbytes
```

Some of the available memory can also be "lockable." Lockable memory is that which can be devoted to frequently accessed programs and data. The programs and data that lock memory for execution will remain memory-resident and run more quickly. You will also see the amount of lockable memory, in this case approximately 44 MBytes, at the time of system startup:

```
lockable: 45228
```

/sbin/dmesg shows you these values and a summary of system-related messages. You should issue this command on your system to see what it supplies you. The following displays the output of both **bdf** and the **/sbin/dmesg** command issued on a large V-Class system with an XP 256 disk array unit attached to it.

```
# bdf
Filesystem           kbytes     used    avail %used Mounted on
/dev/vg00/lvol3      524288    40899   453231    8% /
/dev/vg00/lvol1       99669    29984    59718   33% /stand
/dev/vg00/lvol7     1048576   272706   728019   27% /var
/dev/vg00/lvol6     1048576   491445   522318   48% /usr
/dev/vgu10/lvol1   35860480    35632 35544976    0% /u10
/dev/vgu09/lvol1   35860480  4358224 31256152   12% /u09
/dev/vgu08/lvol1   35860480    21560 35576720    0% /u08
/dev/vgu07/lvol1   35860480   555544 35029128    2% /u07
/dev/vgu06/lvol1   35860480    13624 35566816    0% /u06
/dev/vgu05/lvol1   35860480   560432 35024280    2% /u05
/dev/vgu04/lvol1   35860480   575152 35009672    2% /u04
/dev/vgu03/lvol1   35860480    13624 35566816    0% /u03
/dev/vgu02/lvol1   35860480    13632 35566808    0% /u02
/dev/vgu01/lvol1   35860480  5611848 30012328   16% /u01
/dev/vg00/lvol5      204800     2273   189930    1% /tmp
/dev/vg00/lvol4     2097152   466824  1528479   23% /opt
/dev/vg00/lvol8      524288     2887   488858    1% /home
/dev/vgapp/lvol1   35860480  6485880 29146160   18% /app

# /sbin/dmesg

Jun 20 16:26
...
disk
5/0/0.8.0.0.0.9.2 sdisk
5/0/0.8.0.0.0.9.3 sdisk
5/0/0.8.0.0.0.9.4 sdisk
5/0/0.8.0.0.0.9.5 sdisk
5/0/0.8.0.0.0.9.6 sdisk
5/0/0.8.0.0.0.9.7 sdisk
5/0/0.8.0.0.0.10 tgt
5/0/0.8.0.0.0.10.0 sdisk
5/0/0.8.0.0.0.10.1 sdisk
5/0/0.8.0.0.0.10.2 sdisk
5/0/0.8.0.0.0.10.3 sdisk
5/0/0.8.0.0.0.10.4 sdisk
5/0/0.8.0.0.0.10.5 sdisk
5/0/0.8.0.0.0.11 tgt
5/0/0.8.0.0.0.11.0 sdisk
5/0/0.8.0.0.0.12 tgt
5/0/0.8.0.0.0.12.0 sdisk
5/0/0.8.0.0.0.13 tgt
5/0/0.8.0.0.0.13.0 sdisk
5/0/0.8.0.0.0.14 tgt
5/0/0.8.0.0.0.14.0 sdisk
5/0/0.8.0.255.0 fcpdev
5/0/0.8.0.255.0.0 tgt
5/0/0.8.0.255.0.0.0 sctl
Probing epic6
Probe of epic6 complete
6 saga
```

```
6/0/0 btlan6
Probing epic7
Probe of epic7 complete
7 saga
7/0/0 td
td: claimed Tachyon TL/TS Fibre Channel Mass Storage card at 7/0/0
7/0/0.8 fcp
7/0/0.8.0.0.0 fcparray
7/0/0.8.0.0.0.0 tgt
7/0/0.8.0.0.0.0.0 sdisk
7/0/0.8.0.0.0.0.1 sdisk
7/0/0.8.0.0.0.0.2 sdisk
7/0/0.8.0.0.0.0.3 sdisk
7/0/0.8.0.0.0.0.4 sdisk
7/0/0.8.0.0.0.0.5 sdisk
7/0/0.8.0.0.0.0.6 sdisk
7/0/0.8.0.0.0.0.7 sdisk
7/0/0.8.0.0.0.1 tgt
7/0/0.8.0.0.0.1.0 sdisk
7/0/0.8.0.0.0.1.1 sdisk
7/0/0.8.0.0.0.1.2 sdisk
7/0/0.8.0.0.0.1.3 sdisk
7/0/0.8.0.0.0.1.4 sdisk
7/0/0.8.0.0.0.1.5 sdisk
7/0/0.8.0.0.0.1.6 sdisk
7/0/0.8.0.0.0.1.7 sdisk
7/0/0.8.0.0.0.2 tgt
7/0/0.8.0.0.0.2.0 sdisk
7/0/0.8.0.0.0.2.1 sdisk
7/0/0.8.0.0.0.3 tgt
7/0/0.8.0.0.0.3.0 sdisk
7/0/0.8.0.0.0.4 tgt
7/0/0.8.0.0.0.4.0 sdisk
7/0/0.8.0.0.0.5 tgt
7/0/0.8.0.0.0.5.0 sdisk
7/0/0.8.0.0.0.6 tgt
7/0/0.8.0.0.0.6.0 sdisk
7/0/0.8.0.0.0.7 tgt
7/0/0.8.0.0.0.7.0 sdisk
7/0/0.8.0.0.0.8 tgt
7/0/0.8.0.0.0.8.0 sdisk
7/0/0.8.0.0.0.8.1 sdisk
7/0/0.8.0.0.0.8.2 sdisk
7/0/0.8.0.0.0.8.3 sdisk
7/0/0.8.0.0.0.8.4 sdisk
7/0/0.8.0.0.0.8.5 sdisk
7/0/0.8.0.0.0.8.6 sdisk
7/0/0.8.0.0.0.8.7 sdisk
7/0/0.8.0.0.0.9 tgt
7/0/0.8.0.0.0.9.0 sdisk
7/0/0.8.0.0.0.9.1 sdisk
7/0/0.8.0.0.0.9.2 sdisk
7/0/0.8.0.0.0.9.3 sdisk
7/0/0.8.0.0.0.9.4 sdisk
7/0/0.8.0.0.0.9.5 sdisk
7/0/0.8.0.0.0.9.6 sdisk
7/0/0.8.0.0.0.9.7 sdisk
7/0/0.8.0.0.0.10 tgt
7/0/0.8.0.0.0.10.0 sdisk
7/0/0.8.0.0.0.10.1 sdisk
7/0/0.8.0.0.0.11 tgt
7/0/0.8.0.0.0.11.0 sdisk
7/0/0.8.0.0.0.12 tgt
7/0/0.8.0.0.0.12.0 sdisk
7/0/0.8.0.0.0.13 tgt
7/0/0.8.0.0.0.13.0 sdisk
7/0/0.8.0.0.0.14 tgt
7/0/0.8.0.0.0.14.0 sdisk
7/0/0.8.0.255.0 fcpdev
7/0/0.8.0.255.0.0 tgt
7/0/0.8.0.255.0.0.0 sctl
8 memory
15 bus_adapter
15/1 consp1
15/2 consp1
```

```
16 processor
18 processor
21 processor
23 processor
24 processor
26 processor
29 processor
32 processor
34 processor
37 processor
39 processor
40 processor
42 processor
45 processor
btlan6: Initializing 10/100BASE-TX card at 0/0/0....
btlan6: Initializing 10/100BASE-TX card at 6/0/0....

System Console is on SPP DUART0 Interface
Entering cifs_init...
Initialization finished successfully... slot is 8
Logical volume 64, 0x3 configured as ROOT
Logical volume 64, 0x2 configured as SWAP
Logical volume 64, 0x2 configured as DUMP
    Swap device table:  (start & size given in 512-byte blocks)
        entry 0 - major is 64, minor is 0x2; start = 0, size = 2097152
    Dump device table:  (start & size given in 1-Kbyte blocks)
        entry 0 - major is 31, minor is 0x6000; start = 105312, size = 1048576
Starting the STREAMS daemons-phase 1
btlan6: NOTE: MII Link Status Not OK - Switch Connection to AUI at 0/0/0....
Create STCP device files
Starting the STREAMS daemons-phase 2
    B2352B/9245XB HP-UX (B.11.00) #1: Wed Nov  5 22:38:19 PST 1997

Memory Information:
    physical page size = 4096 bytes, logical page size = 4096 bytes
    Physical: 16773120 Kbytes, lockable: 13099368 Kbytes, available: 15031616 Ks

btlan6: timeout: DMA timeout occurred at 0/0/0
btlan6: reset state is 550 at 0/0/0....
btlan6: WARNING: AUI Loopback Failed at 0/0/0....
btlan6: timeout: DMA timeout occurred at 0/0/0
btlan6: reset state is 575 at 0/0/0....
btlan6: WARNING: BNC Loopback Failed at 0/0/0....
Unable to add all swap for device: /dev/vg00/lvol9. Increase the tunable parame.
#
```

As you can see, **dmesg** provides a lot of useful information in addition to the memory-related reporting we earlier covered. The memory information in this output is roughly 1.6 GBytes total and 1.3 GBytes lockable.

Managing Cache and RAM

If the information you need is not in cache memory but in RAM, then the access will take longer. The speed of all memory is increasing and RAM speed is increasing at a particularly rapid rate. You have a lot of control over the way in which RAM is used. First, you can decide how much RAM is configured into your system. The entire HP product line, both workstations and server systems, supports more RAM than you will need in the system.

RAM, at the time of this writing, is inexpensive and getting less expensive all the time. RAM is not a good area in which to cut corners in the configuration of your system. Moreover, you can use whatever RAM you have configured efficiently. One example is in configuring an HP-UX kernel that is efficient. The HP-UX kernel is always loaded in RAM. This means that if it is 2 or 3 MBytes too big for your needs, then this is 2 or 3 MBytes you don't have for other purposes. If you need to access some information in RAM, it will take roughly one order of magnitude longer to access than if it were in cache.

Virtual Memory

If your system had only cache and, say, 64 MBytes of RAM, then you would be able to have user processes that consumed only about 64 MBytes of physical memory. With memory management, you can have user processes that far exceed the size of physical memory by using virtual memory. Virtual memory allows you to load into RAM only parts of a process while keeping the balance on disk. You move blocks of data back and forth between memory and disk in pages.

Swap

Swap is used to extend the size of memory, that is, reserve an area on the disk to act as an extension to RAM. When the load on the system is high, swap space is used for part or all of the processes for which space is not available in physical memory. HP-UX handles all this swapping for you with the **vhand**, **statdaemon**, and **swapper** processes. You want to make sure that you have more than enough swap space reserved on your disk so that memory management can take place without running out of swap space.

Three types of swap space exist: primary swap, secondary swap, and filesystem swap. These are described next:

Primary swap   Swap that is available at boot. Primary swap is located on the same disk as the root file system.

If a problem occurs with this primary swap, you may have a hard time getting the system to boot.

Secondary swap   Swap that is located on a disk other than the root disk.

File system swap   This is a filesystem that supports both files and data structures as well as swapping.

Don't labor too much over the amount of swap to configure. At a minimum, swap should be twice the size of physical memory (this is the installation process default size). Also, our primary applications will define the amount of swap required. Most of the applications I've worked with make clear the maximum amount of swap required for the application. If you are running several applications, add together the swap required for each application if they are going to be running simultaneously.

CHAPTER 6

Users and Groups

Virtual Partitions and Users

Each Virutal Partition is like a separate server. This means that you have separate users in your respective Virtual Partitions. Any user-related information that needs to be shared between Virtual Partitions would be done in the same manner as sharing between physically separate servers. For instance, you may want to have users have the capability to remotely login from one Virtual Partition to another. You would accomplish this by setting up the appropriate network files in each Virtual Partition just as you would with separate servers (see Chapter 13 for Networking.) Figure 6-1 shows Virtual Partitions and the relationship to users:

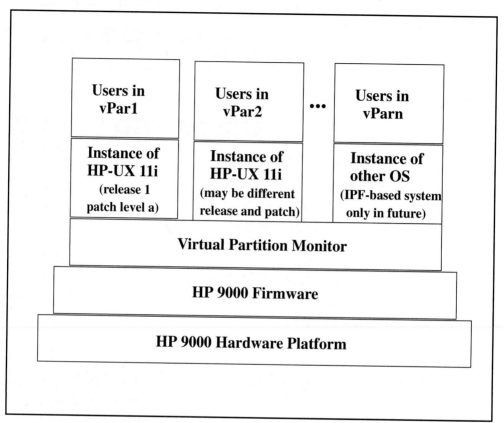

Figure 6-1 Virtual Partitions and Users

As Figure 6-1 shows, each Virtual Partition has its own instance of the operating system and its own set of users. The vPars are isolated from a software perspective, so it is just as if the users exist on different servers. In order to share information among users, such as a database of users, you would implement technology such as Network Information System (NIS). With NIS you could create a database of user information that would be shared among different systems, and in this case, different vPars because they are the same as different servers from a software standpoint.

Let's now create a new user on each of the two vPars. On *cable1* we'll create the user *cable1us* and verify that this user does not exist on *cable2*. On *cable2* we'll create the user *cable2us* and verify that this user does not exist on *cable1*. See the background portion of this chapter for detailed information on creating users.

Figure 6-2 shows a System Administration Manager (SAM) screen shot of creating a user *cable1us* in vPar *cable1*:

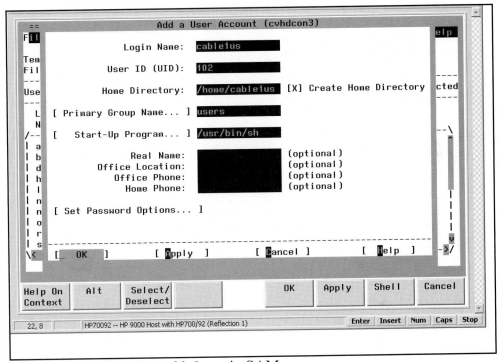

Figure 6-2 Creating *cable1user* in SAM

Figure 6-2 shows the hostname of *cvhdcon3*, which is the server name corresponding to vPar *cable1*.

The user *cable1us* was created in vPar *cable1* and exists only in *cable1*. We'll verify this shortly. We performed the same procedure creating user *cable2us* in vPar *cable2* using SAM.

There should now be one user in *cable1* that is not viewable in *cable2*, and vice versa. The following shows connecting to *cable1* and listing the contents of **/etc/passwd**.

```
cvhdcon3:/ # cat /etc/passwd                            cable1 listing
root:hiIXKsAzUIFy6:0:3::/:/sbin/sh
daemon:*:1:5::/:/sbin/sh
bin:*:2:2::/usr/bin:/sbin/sh
sys:*:3:3::/:
adm:*:4:4::/var/adm:/sbin/sh
uucp:*:5:3::/var/spool/uucppublic:/usr/lbin/uucp/uucico
lp:*:9:7::/var/spool/lp:/sbin/sh
nuucp:*:11:11::/var/spool/uucppublic:/usr/lbin/uucp/uucico
hpdb:*:27:1:ALLBASE:/:/sbin/sh
nobody:*:-2:-2::/:
www:*:30:1::/:
webadmin:*:40:1::/usr/obam/server/nologindir:/usr/bin/false
smbnull:*:101:101:DO NOT USE OR DELETE - needed by Samba:
                                         /home/smbnull:/sbin/sh
opc_op:*:777:77:OpC default operator:/home/opc_op:/usr/bin/ksh
cable1us::102:20:,,,:/home/cable1us:/usr/bin/sh      <-- cable1us
cvhdcon3:/ #
```

This listing for *cable1* shows that *cable1us* exists in the **/etc/passwd** file on *cable1*; however, there is no *cable2us* present in this file.

The following shows connecting to *cable2* and listing the contents of **/etc/passwd**.

```
# cat /etc/passwd                               cable2 listing
root:Jx66ARmhj.aBs:0:3::/:/sbin/sh
daemon:*:1:5::/:/sbin/sh
bin:*:2:2::/usr/bin:/sbin/sh
sys:*:3:3::/:
adm:*:4:4::/var/adm:/sbin/sh
uucp:*:5:3::/var/spool/uucppublic:/usr/lbin/uucp/uucico
lp:*:9:7::/var/spool/lp:/sbin/sh
nuucp:*:11:11::/var/spool/uucppublic:/usr/lbin/uucp/uucico
hpdb:*:27:1:ALLBASE:/:/sbin/sh
nobody:*:-2:-2::/:
www:*:30:1::/:
webadmin:*:40:1::/usr/obam/server/nologindir:/usr/bin/false
sam_exec:xxx:0:1::/home/sam_exec:/usr/bin/sh
cable2us::101:20:,,,:/home/cable2us:/usr/bin/sh     <-- cable2us
#
```

This listing for *cable2* shows that *cable2us* exists in the **/etc/passwd** file on *cable2*; however, there is no *cable1us* present in this file

This listing shows that the unique users for the respective vPars exist only on the vPar on which they were created. In addition, each vPar has its own *root* and other system-level users.

Next let's look at setup information of individual users in vPars.

Individual User Setup

As far as setup for users is concerned, you perform setup in a vPars environment just as you would in a non-vPars environment. The prompt, for instance, might include the hostname of your system. On a system where the hostname and vPar name are different, you still probably want your prompt to include the hostname. You can, however; also include the vPar name at the prompt if you wish. The following is the section of **/.profile** that includes some minor customization for the user *root*:

```
# Added for prompt, history etc.

        HISTFILE=~/.sh_history;                 export HISTFILE
        EDITOR=vi;                              export EDITOR
        PS1="`whoami`@`hostname`"'[${PWD}] > '; export PS1
```

This is the information I typically add for *root* to provide history file information and the prompt. I included the hostname here which would result in a prompt that includes the user's name, hostname, and present working directory, as shown below:

```
root@actappd1[/.root] >
```

If your users need to see the vPar name, this can be added to or substituted for the hostname in **.profile**. This is another example of the advantage to having your hostname and vPar name identical. It may be; however, that your hostname is very confusing, and substituting a simple vPar name in the prompt may be advantageous to users. In either case, your user setup does not change with vPars, since vPars are the same as separate systems from a user perspective.

Application Users

Users that are required for specific applications need to be set up on all vPars on which an application is going to run. Since vPars are like individual systems, you'll put the users, including application users, on the vPars where you need them and not on others. On a system running Broadvision and Oracle, for instance, you would set up the users required for those applications. The following shows an **/etc/passwd** output on a system running these two applications:

```
# cat /etc/passwd
root:9Obj3Cya98pFo:0:3::/.root:/sbin/sh
daemon:*:1:5::/:/sbin/sh
bin:*:2:2::/usr/bin:/sbin/sh
sys:*:3:3::/:
adm:*:4:4::/var/adm:/sbin/sh
uucp:*:5:3::/var/spool/uucppublic:/usr/lbin/uucp/uucico
lp:*:9:7::/var/spool/lp:/sbin/sh
nuucp:*:11:11::/var/spool/uucppublic:/usr/lbin/uucp/uucico
hpdb:*:27:1:ALLBASE:/:/sbin/sh
nobody:*:-2:-2::/:
www:*:30:1::/:
webadmin:*:40:1::/usr/obam/server/nologindir:/usr/bin/false
smbnull:*:101:101:DO NOT USE OR DELETE - needed by Samba:/home/smbnull:/sbin/sh
opc_op:*:777:77:OpC default operator:/home/opc_op:/usr/bin/ksh
stssmrp:HFQrTOZx920Fg:1108:20:Martin Paul:/home/stssmrp:/bin/ksh
stssmrpr:pugxhblYiahZI:0:3:Martin Paul:/home/stssmrp:/bin/ksh
stssjtf:VammVKnIwD/T.:1185:20:John Fontanilla:/home/stssjtf:/usr/bin/ksh
pbcombv:UzGN5gDTNfgQM:102:20:PB.COM User:/home/pbcombv:/usr/bin/ksh     <-- BV user
oracle:11Z/oQQfEHzOo:1012:111:Oracle User:/home/oracle:/bin/ksh    <-- Oracle user
#
```

Note the last two users in the file for Broadvision (*pvcombv*) and Oracle (*oracle*) with their respective home directories. With these two applications running on the Virtual Partition, the appropriate users had to be set up.

The remainder of this chapter covers background information related to users.

Non-vPar-Specific Section of Chapter - Set Up Users and Groups

As you may have guessed by now, performing system administration functions on your HP-UX system is easy; the planning is what takes time and effort. Setting up users and groups is no exception. Thanks to SAM, doing just about anything with users and groups is simple.

One exception exists to this easy setup: HP (Common Desktop Environment) CDE customization. SAM doesn't really help with HP CDE customization and it can be quite tricky to modify one's HP CDE setup manually. I have Chapter 13 to assist you with HP CDE customization.

You need to make a few basic decisions about users. Where should users' data be located? Who needs to access data from whom, thereby defining "groups" of users? What kind of particular startup is required by users and applications? Is there a shell that your users prefer?

You will want to put some thought into these important user-related questions. I spend a lot of time working with my customers, rearranging user data, for several reasons. It doesn't fit on a whole disk (for this reason, I strongly recommend using Logical Volume Manager or Veritas Volume Manager); users can't freely access one another's data, or even worse, users *can* access one another's data too freely.

We will consider these questions, but first, let's look at the basic steps to adding a user, whether you do this manually or rely on SAM. Here is a list of activities:

- Select a user name to add
- Select a user ID number
- Select a group for the user
- Create an **/etc/passwd** entry
- Assign a user password (including expiration options)
- Select and create a home directory for user
- Select the shell the user will run (I strongly recommend the default POSIX shell)
- Place startup files in the user's home directory
- Test the user account

This list may seem like a lot of work, but there is nothing to it if you run SAM and answer the questions. Most of what you do is entered in the **/etc/passwd** file, where information about all users is stored. You can make these entries to the **/etc/passwd** file with the **/usr/sbin/vipw** command. Figure 6-3 is a sample **/etc/passwd** entry.

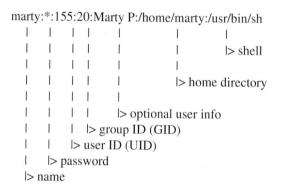

Figure 6-3   Sample **/etc/passwd** Entry

Here is a description of each of these fields:

name.   The user name you assign. This name should be easy for the user and other users on the system to remember. When sending electronic mail or copying files from one user to another, the easier it is to remember the user name the better. If a user has a user name on another system, you may want to assign the same user name on your HP-UX system. Some systems don't permit nice, easy user names, so you may want to break the tie with the old system and start using sensible, easy-to-remember user names on your HP-UX system. Remember, no security is tied to the user name; security is handled through the user's password and the file permissions.

password.   This is the user's password in encrypted form. If an asterisk appears in this field, the account can't be used. If it is empty, the user has no password assigned and can log in by typing only his or her user name. I strongly recommend that each user have a password that he or she changes periodically. Every system has different security needs, but at a minimum, every user on every system should have a password. When setting up a new user, you can force the user to create a password at first login by putting ,.. in the password field. Password aging can easily be set in SAM.

Some features of a good password are:

- A minimum of six characters that should include special characters such as a slash (/), a dot (.), or an asterisk (*).

- No words should be used for a password.

- Don't make the password personal such as name, address, favorite sports team, etc.

- Don't use something easy to type such as 123456, or qwerty.

- Some people say that misspelled words are acceptable, but I don't recommend using them. Spell-check programs that match misspelled words to correctly spelled words can be used to guess at words that might be misspelled for a password.

- A password generator that produces an intelligible passwords works the best.

user ID (UID). The identification number of the user. Every user on your system should have a unique UID. There are no conventions for UIDs. SAM will assign a UID for you when you add users, but you can always change this. I would recommend that you reserve UIDs less than 100 for system-level users.

group ID (GID). The identification number of the group. The members of the group and their GID are in the **/etc/group** file. You can change the GID assigned if you don't like it, but you may also have to change the GID of many files. As a user creates a file, his or her UID is assigned to the file as well as the GID. This means if you change the GID well after users of the same group have created many files and directories, you may have to change the GID of all these elements. I usually save GIDs less than 10 for system groups.

optional user info. In this space, you can make entries, such as the user's phone number or full name. SAM asks you for this information when you create a user. You can leave this blank, but if you manage a system or network with many users, you may want to add the user's full name and extension so that if you need to get in touch with him or her, you'll have the information at your fingertips. (This field is sometimes referred to as the GECOs field.)

home directory.   The home directory defines the default location for all the users' files and directories. This is the present working directory at the time of login.

shell.   This is the startup program the user will run at the time of login. The shell is really a command interpreter for the commands the user issues from the command line. I recommend using the default POSIX shell (/**usr/bin/sh**), but there are also three traditional, popular shells in the HP-UX environment: the C shell (**/usr/bin/csh**); Bourne shell (**/usr/old/bin/sh**); and Korn shell (**/usr/bin/ksh**). Shell programming for the system administrator is covered in Chapter 6.

The location of the user's home directory is another important entry in the **/etc/passwd** file. You have to select a location for the user's "home" directory in the file system where the user's files will be stored. With some of the advanced networking technology that exists, such as NFS, the user's home directory does not even have to be on a disk that is physically connected to the computer he or she is using! The traditional place to locate a user's home directory on an HP-UX system is the **/home** directory in HP-UX 11.x.

The **/home** directory is typically the most dynamic area in terms of growth. Users create and delete files in their home directory on a regular basis. This means you have to do more planning related to your user area than in more static areas, such as the root file system and application areas. You would typically load HP-UX and your applications and then perform relatively few accesses to these in terms of adding and deleting files and directories. The user area is continuously updated, making it more difficult to maintain.

Assigning Users to Groups

After defining all user-related information, you need to consider groups. Groups are often overlooked in the HP-UX environment until the system administrator finds that all his or her users are in the very same group, even though from an organizational standpoint, they are in different groups. Before I cover the groups in general, let's look at a file belonging to a user and the way access is defined for a file:

```
$ ll
-rwxr-x--x   1 marty      users     120 Jul 26 10:20 sort
```

For every file on the system, HP-UX supports three classes of access:

- User access (u). Access is granted to the owner of the file

- Group access (g). Access granted to members of the same group as the owner of the file

- Other access (o). Access granted to everyone else

These access rights are defined by the position of r (read), write (w), and execute (x) when the long listing command is issued. For the long listing (**ll**) above, you see the permissions in Table 6-1.

TABLE 6-1 Long Listing Permissions

Access	User Access	Group Access	Other
Read	r	r	-
Write	w	-	-
Execute	x	x	x

You can see that access rights are arranged in groups of three. Three groups of permissions exist with three access levels each. The owner, in this case, marty, is allowed read, write, and execute permissions on the file. Anyone in the group users is permitted read and execute access to the file. Others are permitted only execute access of the file.

These permissions are important to consider as you arrange your users into groups. If several users require access to the same files, then you will want to put those users in the same group. The trade-off here is that you can give all users within a group rwx access to files, but then you run the risk of several users editing a file without other users knowing it, thereby causing confusion. On the other hand, you can make several copies of a file so that each user has his or her personal copy, but then you have multiple versions of a file. If possible, assign users to groups based on their work.

When you run SAM and specify the groups to which each user belongs, the file **/etc/group** is updated. The **/etc/group** file contains the group name, an encrypted password (which is rarely used), a group ID, and a list of users in the group. Here is an example of an **/etc/group** file:

```
root::0:root
other::1:root, hpdb
bin::2:root,bin
sys::3:root,uucp
adm::4:root,adm
daemon::5:root,daemon
mail::6:root
lp::7:root,lp
tty::10:
nuucp::11:nuucp
military::25:jhunt,tdolan,vdallesandro
commercial::30:ccascone,jperwinc,devers
nogroup:*:-2:
```

This **/etc/group** file shows two different groups of users. Although all users run the same application, a desktop publishing tool, some work on documents of "commercial" products while others work on only "military" documents. It made sense for the system administrator to create two groups, one for commercial document preparation and the other for military document preparation. All members of a group know what documents are current and respect one another's work and its importance. You will have few problems among group members who know what the other members are doing and you will find that these members don't delete files that shouldn't be deleted. If you put all users into one group, however, you may find that you spend more time restoring files, because users in this broader group don't find files that are owned by other members of their group to be important. Users can change group with the **newgrp** command.

NIS for Managing Users

One of the most popular ways to manage user-related information in a distributed environment is the Network Information System (NIS). NIS provides a method for multiple systems to share a centralized database of password, group, and other optional databases such as services and/or hosts. By doing so, the administration of user accounts is simplified for both end-users and system administrators. You will also often hear NIS referred to as "Yellow Pages" or "YP"; in fact, most of the NIS commands begin with the letters "yp".

NIS and other such technologies are required only in a distributed environment where users have to be managed on many systems. This is because changes in information, such as adding and removing users, must be disseminated to many systems. This is normally not required in a centralized environment, where only a small number of copies of such information must be maintained.

NIS on HP-UX is interoperable with Solaris and Sun-licensed NIS implementations, including Linux. Like most of these implementations, HP's NIS is not implemented in C2 or Trusted System mode. Additionally, Microsoft-based operating systems such as Windows do not use or interoperate with NIS.

What Does NIS Manage?

NIS can manage many different databases. We'll focus on the user password and group information. Table 6-2 is a list of some of the databases NIS can manage:

TABLE 6-2   Some NIS Databases That NIS Can Manage

Filename	Information Contained in File
/etc/passwd	Usernames, user IDs primary groups, and encrypted passwords.
/etc/group	User group memberships.
/etc/hosts	Hostnames and IP addresses.
/etc/services	Network port numbers and service names.
/etc/aliases	Aliases and mailing lists for the mail system.
/etc/netgroup	Netgroup definitions.
/etc/rpc	Remote procedure call program numbers.
/etc/protocols	Network protocol names and numbers.
	The following are optional for HP, but not used by HP-UX NIS clients.
/etc/bootparms	Information about diskless nodes.
/etc/ethers	Ethernet numbers (MAC addresses).
/etc/netmasks	Network masks.

NIS also calls each of these databases a *map*. These are called maps because NIS allows you to map a key, such as a username, to a value field, such as the user's **passwd** entry from the **passwd** map on the NIS Master Server.

How Do I Plan For NIS?

NIS requires one NIS Master Server and typically at least one NIS Slave Server per IP subnet. A NIS Master or Slave Server answers requests from NIS clients typically seeking user password information when a user login occurs. NIS is designed in a "top-down" or hierarchical manner, with all changes being made through the NIS Master Server. When a change is made to the NIS Master, the changes can be made visible to the NIS Slaves by "pushing" the updated database to the Slaves. Generally, an NIS server should satisfy the demands of 25 to 50 NIS clients. NIS Masters and Slaves are typically also NIS clients.

On the NIS Master server, you need to decide where you want to keep the NIS database "source" files. Most typically, the **/etc** files are used on the NIS Master for all databases except passwords, which are generally put into an "alternate" or "private" password file such as **/etc/passwd.nis**. Put only the user password database there and not the "system" users, such as root, sys, bin and so on. The "system" users should always be put in **/etc/passwd** on any NIS server or client.

NIS will provide a small additional network and system load on an NIS Slave and Master server. Most typically, this extra load is encountered when updating a map or database and pushing the changes to the Slave servers.

The design of NIS requires that you first configure the NIS Master Server, then the NIS Slave Servers, and finally, the NIS clients.

How Do I Configure an NIS Master Or Slave Server?

You can configure an NIS Master and Slave Server either by using SAM or by performing the process manually. If you use SAM to perform this process most of the work will take place for you in the background. You enter the pertinent information and SAM performs the configuration. You perform the steps in the manual procedure. There are many good documents that can help you in this configuration, including HP's *Installing and Administering NFS Services* manual. This manual covers configuring Master and Slave Servers and can be obtained from *www.docs.hp.com*. HP support likes when you follow these step-by-step procedures so that should you encounter a problem, your execution of the steps can be reviewed.

To configure with SAM, select *Networking/Communications*, then *NIS*. You will first be prompted to specify the NIS domain name. After that, you can proceed to the *Enable NIS Master Server* or *Enable NIS Slave Server* menus.

How Do I Configure an NIS Client?

You can also configure an NIS client by either using SAM or by performing the process manually. Once again, the *Installing and Administering NFS Services* manual provides an excellent step-by-step procedure for configuring the client.

To configure with SAM, select *Networking/Communications*, then *NIS*. You will first be prompted to specify the NIS domain name. After that you can proceed to the *Enable NIS Client* menu.

In either case, I have two additional tips. First, HP supplies the following **/etc/nsswitch.compat** file as a template to copy into **/etc/nsswitch.conf**. This allows you to use the "+" and "-" syntax in **/etc/passwd** and **/etc/group**:

```
# /etc/nsswitch.compat:
#
# An example file that could be copied over to
# /etc/nsswitch.conf; it
# uses NIS (YP) in conjunction with files. #

passwd:         compat
group:          compat
hosts:          nis [NOTFOUND=return] files
networks:       nis [NOTFOUND=return] files
protocols:      nis [NOTFOUND=return] files
rpc:            nis [NOTFOUND=return] files
publickey:      nis [NOTFOUND=return] files
netgroup:       nis [NOTFOUND=return] files
automount:      files nis
aliases:        files nis
services:       files nis
```

Second, you may prefer DNS over NIS to manage the hosts database and use the following "hosts" entry in **/etc/nsswitch.conf**:

```
hosts:          files [NOTFOUND=continue] dns ...
```

or

```
hosts:          dns    [NOTFOUND=continue,UNAVAILABLE=continue]
files [NOTFOUND=continue,UNAVAILABLE=continue] nis
```

How Do I Maintain My NIS Environment?

The most common user activity is changing a user password. A user can use either the **passwd -r nis** or **yppasswd** command to do this. This will prompt for the old NIS passwd, the new password, make the change on the NIS server, and by default, re-make the NIS map and push it out to all the Slave Servers.

A system administrator can change user passwords either with SAM or with shell scripts or commands such as **passwd -r nis** *<username>* or **yppasswd** *<username>*. You can also use SAM to add new users, or you can do this with shell scripts or commands.

Often, when a user changes a database file by editing with **vi**, the changes need to be compiled into the NIS maps (called "making" a map) and pushing the maps out to the Slave Servers if the "make" does not do this. For example, after modifying some users' home directories in **/etc/passwd.nis**, the system administrator needs to:

```
1. cd /var/yp   # Change to directory of NIS Makefile
2. make passwd  # "make" or compile the passwd map
3. yppush passwd (if step #2 did not push to the NIS
slaves)
```

Here is a tip that applies to HP-UX and to any NIS vendor's implementation with group files: There are times when users are members of multiple groups, producing lines in **/etc/group** that are longer than the NIS limitation of 1024 characters per line. To work around this, use different group names for the same GID, for example:

```
102 support:brian,sam,charlie
102 support1:bill,julie,maria
```

Note that you don't need to specify a user's primary group membership in **/etc/group** since that is already specified by their GID in **/etc/passwd**. If users are members of multiple groups, you only need to put their username in **/etc/group** entries for their secondary groups.

NIS provides a centralized database scheme for managing user password and group information. Administration techniques used for NIS setup and administration are well documented, integrated into SAM, and are generally interoperable with other NIS implementations.

CHAPTER 7

Backup

Backup of Virtual Partitions

Backup of Virtual Partitions takes place in almost the same manner as in non-vPars systems. The primary difference is that rather than run one backup on a physical system, you'll have to run a backup of every Virtual Partition that exists on your physical system. You'll also want to run a **make_net_recovery** on every Virtual Partition as well. This will create a bootable recovery archive for the Virtual Partition. This is covered in the Ignite/UX Chapter 10.

man page

make_net
_ recovery
10

We'll perform a backup of the first vPar on a system that has the tape drive configured as one of its components (this is a backup to a local tape drive.) We'll then perform a backup of a second vPar on the same computer to the tape drive that is configured on the first vPar (this is a backup to a remote tape drive.) The tape drive is remote to the second vPar because it does not have the tape drive configured as one of its I/O components. Since the two vPars are distinct and independent systems, the tape drive on the first vPar is remote to the second vPar.

Backup to a Tape Drive on the Local Virtual Partition

Let's now backup a vPar called *cable1* to the local DDS drive at path *0.0.1.0.3.0*. This is a backup of a vPar to a local tape drive, meaning that the tape drive resource is tied to the vPar for which the backup will be performed. The following **vparstatus** shows that the Local Bus Adapter (LBA) at *0.0* is dedicated to *cable1*:

```
# vparstatus -p cable1 -v

[Virtual Partition Details]
Name:         cable1
State:        Up
Attributes:   Dynamic,Manual
Kernel Path:  /stand/vmunix
Boot Opts:

[CPU Details]
Min/Max:  1/3
Bound by User [Path]:
Bound by Monitor [Path]:   33
Unbound [Path]:  97

[IO Details]
   0.0                              <-- path of Core I/O card
   0.0.0.0
   0.0.1.1.2.0  BOOT
   0.0.4.0  CONSOLE

[Memory Details]
Specified [Base  /Range]:
        (bytes) (MB)
Total Memory (MB):  1024

#
```

Although the tape drive at *0.0.1.0.3.0* does not appear in this **vparstatus -v** output, the tape drive is connected to the Core I/O card at *0.0* and is therefore accessible to *cable1* to use as a backup device.

As a side note, if the tape interface were not on the Core I/O card, which is devoted to *cable1*, we could move the interface from *cable1* to a second vPar on the same computer called *cable2*, confirm that the driver is in **/stand/system**, and then backup *cable2*

Since there are many devices that you may want to move among the vPars running on your system you want to make sure that you have all of the device drivers required to support these devices in your kernel.

Let's now run **fbackup** with *u* to update the backup database, *0* for a full backup, *f* to specify the file to which we want to write the backup, *g* to specify our graph file, *I* to specify the name of the index file, and finally, we'll redirect messages to a file that will contain the backup log. We'll add the date and time to the end of the index and backup log files.

The following example shows the **fbackup** command issued:

```
fbackup -0u -f /dev/rmt/0m -g /tmp/backupgraph -I
        /tmp/backupindex.`date '+%y%m%d.%H:M'` 2>
        /tmp/backuplog.`date '+%y%m%d.%H:%M'`
```

Graph files are used to specify the files to be included in the backup. Index files contain a list of files produced as part of the backup. The graph file contains the files we wish to include (*i*) or exclude (*e*) as part of the backup. In our case the file contains only the following line:

```
i /var/tmp
```

Let's now see what files were produced as a result of having issued this command. First let's look at the backup index and backup logfiles:

```
# ls -l /tmp/backup*
-rw-rw-rw-   1 root     sys        11 Aug 29 14:45 backupgraph
-rw-------   1 root     sys       778 Aug 29 15:08 backupindex.010829.15:08
-rw-rw-rw-   1 root     sys       521 Aug 29 15:08 backuplog.010829.15:08
#
```

```
# cat /tmp/backupindex.010829.15:08
1024                   1 /
1024                   1 /var
1024                   1 /var/tmp
108                    1 /var/tmp/aaaa04686
1241                   1 /var/tmp/ems_inittab.old
28                     1 /var/tmp/envd.action2
28                     1 /var/tmp/envd.action5
4106                   1 /var/tmp/inetd.conf.old
96                     1 /var/tmp/ntp
0                      1 /var/tmp/rdskUBAa02185
0                      1 /var/tmp/rdskWAAa01840
```

```
310                        1 /var/tmp/sh1649.1
343                        1 /var/tmp/sh1649.2
166                        1 /var/tmp/sh1649.3
440                        1 /var/tmp/sh1649.4
611                        1 /var/tmp/swagent.log
0                          1 /var/tmp/sysstat_em.fmt
22734848                   1 /var/tmp/vmunix.noreloc
#


# cat /tmp/backupgraph
i/var/tmp
#


# cat /tmp/backuplog.010829.15:08
fbackup(1417): cannot open the dates file /var/adm/fbackupfiles/dates
for reading
fbackup(1004): session begins on Wed Aug 29 15:08:10 2001
fbackup(3203): volume 1 has been used 1 time(s)
fbackup(3024): writing volume 1 to the output file /dev/rmt/0m
fbackup(1423): WARNING: could not open the dates file /var/adm/fbackup-
files/dates for writing
fbackup(1030): warnings encountered during backup
fbackup(3055): total file blocks read for backup: 44432
#
```

The two files with the date appended (*8/29/01 time 15:08*) to the end of the filename were produced by the **fbackup** command issued earlier. The date appended to the end of the file can help in the organization of backup files. We could restore any or all of these files with **frestore**.

The backup of vPar *cable1* to the local tape drive is a backup of the system with a hostname of *cvhdcon3*. The other vPar running on this system, *cable2*, was not included in the backup because its host, *cvhdcon4,* is viewed as a separate system. In the next section we'll see how we would backup *cable2* to the tape drive dedicated to *cable1*.

Backup to a Tape Drive on a Different Local Virtual Partition

The tape drive in the preceding section was connected to *cable1* and used to backup *cable1*. Let's now backup *cable2* with the tape drive as part of the *cable1* Virtual Partition. Keep in mind that vPar *cable2* with its hostname *cvhdcon4* is a separate system from *cable1* and its hostname *cvhdcon3*. We will, therefore, have to backup vPar *cable2* to a remote tape drive on *cable1*.

We will backup to a remote tape, connected to *cable1*, with **fbackup** by specifying the system name and tape drive, or file, to which we want to store the files. The following example uses **fbackup** options covered later in this chapter in the non-vPar-specific part of the chapter. We are connected to *cable2* and specify that it is to be backed up to the tape drive on *cable1* (hostname *cvhdcon3*.) The **fbackup** command below will perform the backup to the remote tape drive:

```
# fbackup -f cvhdcon3:/dev/rmt/0m -i /var/tmp -v


fbackup(1004): session begins on Wed Aug 29 16:09:28 2001
fbackup(3307): volume 1 has been used 6 time(s)  (maximum: 100)
fbackup(3024): writing volume 1 to the output file cvhdcon3:/dev/rmt/0m
    1: /
    2: /tmp
    3: /tmp/.AgentSockets
    4: /tmp/.AgentSockets/A
    5: /tmp/X11_newfonts.log
    6: /tmp/install.vars
    7: /tmp/llbdbase.dat
    8: /tmp/lost+found
    9: /tmp/portmap.file
   10: /tmp/rpcbind.file
   11: /tmp/sd_ipd_acl.1417
   12: /tmp/services
   13: /tmp/swlist
   14: /tmp/typescript
fbackup(1005): run time: 17 seconds
fbackup(3055): total file blocks read for backup: 141
fbackup(3056): total blocks written to output file
cvhdcon3:/dev/rmt/0m: 0
#
```

It takes a little getting used to running **fbackup** to a remote device even when the device is physically connected to the computer on which you're working. Since the two vPars are different hosts, however, it makes sense that a tape drive used by a different vPar would indeed be remote.

The **fbackup** runs over the network from *cable2* to *cable1*. This is one of the many reasons that you want to have a network card for every vPar on your system.

We would issue other remote backup commands as well. The following example shows running **cpio** on *cable2* to the tape drive on *cable1* (hostname *cvhdcon3*:)

```
# find . -print | cpio -oBv | (remsh cvhdcon3 dd of=/dev/rmt/0m)
.
lost+found
.AgentSockets
Socket <.AgentSockets/A> not backed up
typescript
install.vars
swlist
X11_newfonts.log
sd_ipd_acl.1417
services
rpcbind.file
portmap.file
llbdbase.dat
140 blocks

140+0 records in
140+0 records out
#
```

This command performs the backup of **/tmp** on vPar *cable2* by sending the files to the tape drive on system *cvhdcon3* (vPar *cable1.*)

Backup of Virtual Partitions Using SAM

All of the work we've done backing *cable1* and *cable2* can be done through SAM. This includes the backup of *cable2* to the remote tape drive on *cable1*.

Let's first perform a backup of *cable1* using *Backup and Recovery - Interactive Backup and Recovery* in SAM. Figure 7-1 is a CDE screen shot showing some of the SAM windows related to *Interactive Backup and Recovery* for *cable1*:

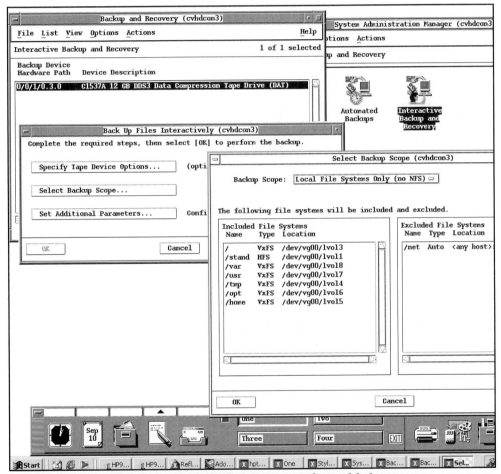

Figure 7-1 *Interactive Backup and Recovery* for *cable1*

All of the SAM windows in Figure 7-1 have in the top of them the hostname *cvhdcon3,* which corresponds to vPar *cable1.* The top left window shows that the DDS drive that was configured as part of the *cable1* vPar is selected as the backup device. The bottom-right window is the one in which we can specify the backup scope.

Performing this interactive backup of *cable1* could not be simpler with SAM. Let's now see if we can backup *cable2* to the remote tape drive on *cable1.* Keep in mind that as far as SAM is concerned these are two completely different systems, even though vPars *cable1* and *cable2* are running on the same computer. This means that the backup of *cable2* to the tape drive on *cable1* is remote.

We can initiate the backup of *cable2* in two different ways. The first would be to invoke SAM on *cable2* and specify all of the appropriate information. The second is to run SAM remotely from vPar *cable1.* We'll chose the latter approach. We first specify from *cable1* the name of the remote system on which we want to run SAM, as shown in Figure 7-2:

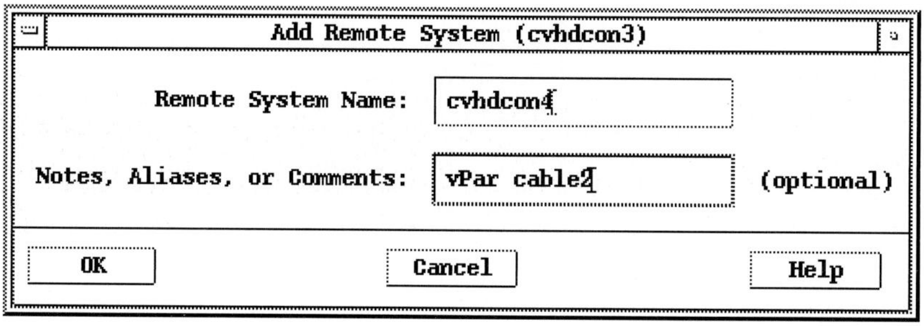

Figure 7-2   Add vPar *cable2* as Remote System on Which to Run SAM

After we specify the hostname *cvhdcon4* and make a note that this is vPar *cable2* we press *OK* and SAM configures this as a remote host.

We can now select the remote host and run SAM on it as shown in Figure 7-3:

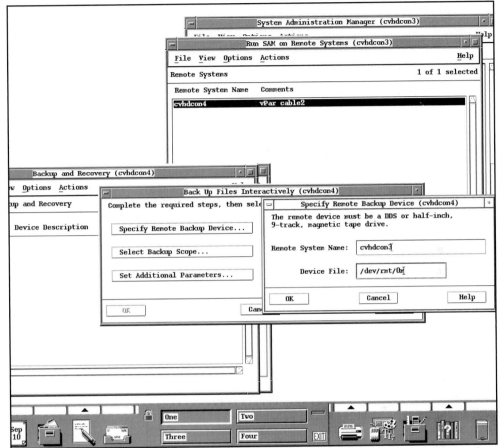

Figure 7-3 Configure Remote Tape Device on *cable1* for Backup of *cable2*

All of the SAM windows in Figure 7-3 now show a hostname of *cvhdcon4*, which is the remote hostname for *cable2*. The top right window shows that we have selected vPar *cable2* (hostname *cvhdcon4*) as the remote system on which to run SAM. The bottom-right window shows that we have selected */dev/rmt/0m* on *cvhdcon3* (the hostname for vPar *cable1*) as the device on which the backup will take place.

We have now performed all of the setup required to proceed with the backup to the remote tape drive. After selecting **/var/tmp** as the directory to backup SAM opened the window shown in Figure 7-4 which indicated that the backup of **/var/tmp** is taking place:

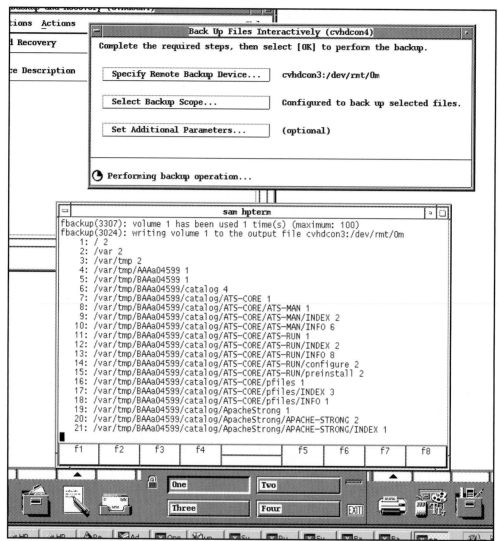

Figure 7-4 *Interactive Backup and Recovery* for *cable1*

This backup was completed with no problems.

This backup work of two different vPars on the same computer demonstrates the kind of isolation that vPars provide. The work we perform in one vPar does not affect the other vPar. To use a tape drive on the same computer but in a different vPar requires us to specify the tape drive as a remote device. If you're accustomed to using SAM to perform your local and remote backups, you can continue to use SAM in your vPars environments as long as you treat different vPars as separate systems from the perspective of SAM.

The remainder of this chapter provides background information on backup programs.

Non-vPar-Specific Section of Chapter - Built-in Backup Programs

Most HP-UX system administrators employ a dual backup strategy. The first is to use the **make_recovery** command of Ignite-UX to create a bootable backup tape of their root volume (**make_recovery** is covered in Chapter 10). Secondly, a backup program is used to back up the balance of data on the system. In this chapter I'll give an overview of several backup commands. I won't cover any advanced backup programs such as HP's OmniBack. Advanced backup tools, however, can make tasks such as centralized backup and overall management of backup much easier.

Here is a brief overview of backup programs I'll cover in upcoming sections:

tar   **tar** is widely considered the most *portable* of the backup and restore programs. **tar** is the most popular generic backup utility. You will find that many applications are shipped on **tar** tapes. This is the most widely used format for exchanging data with other UNIX systems. **tar** is the oldest UNIX backup method and therefore runs on all UNIX systems. You can append files to the end of a **tar** tape, which you can't do with **fbackup**. When sending files to another UNIX user, I would strongly recommend **tar**. **tar** is as slow as molasses, so you won't want to use it for your full or incremental backups. One highly desirable aspect of **tar** is that when you load files onto a tape with **tar** and then restore them onto another system, the original users and groups are retained.

cpio   **cpio** is also portable and easy to use, like **tar**. In addition, **cpio** is much faster than **tar** - not as fast as **fbackup**, but much faster than **tar**. **cpio** is good for replicating directory trees.

fbackup   **fbackup** is the utility used by SAM. It has a lot of functionality associated with it, such as specifying whether the backup is full or incremental, different *levels* of backup, files and directories to be included or excluded, support for a *graph* file which specifies files to be included and excluded, and other advanced features. **fbackup** is an HP-UX-only utility, and tapes can be read using **frecover** on HP-UX systems only.

dd   This is a bit-for-bit copy. It is not smart in the sense that it does not copy files and ownerships; it just copies bits. You could not, therefore, select an individual file from a **dd** tape as you could with **frecover**, **tar**, **restore** or **cpio**. **dd** is mainly used for converting data such as EBCDIC to ASCII.

dump   **dump** is similar to **fbackup**. If you use **fbackup** on HP-UX, you will see much similarity when you use **dump**. **dump** provides the same-level backup scheme as **fbackup** and creates **/var/adm/dumpdates,** which lists the last time a file system was backed up. **restore** is used to read information backed up with **dump**. **dump**, however, works only with HFS file systems and not VxFS, and it assumes that you are using a reel tape.

tar

tar is widely considered the most *portable* of the backup and restore programs. You will find that many applications are shipped on tar tapes and many UNIX files downloaded from the Internet are in tar format. This is the most widely used format for exchanging data with other UNIX systems. tar is the oldest UNIX backup method and therefore runs on all UNIX systems. You can append files to the end of a tar tape, which you can't do with many other programs. When sending files to another UNIX user, I would strongly recommend tar. tar is as slow as molasses, so you won't want to use it for your full or incremental backups if you have a lot of data to back up. One highly desirable aspect of tar is that when you load files onto a tape with tar and then restore them onto another system, the original users and groups are retained.

We'll use several tar commands in the upcoming examples, including the following:

```
# tar cf /dev/rmt/0m /var        ;use tar to create (c) an archive of
                                  the directory /var and put it on
                                  tape /dev/rmt/0m.


# tar tvf /dev/rmt/0m            ;obtain table of contents (t) from
                                   tape /dev/rmt/0m and produce
                                   produce verbose (v) output.


# tar xvf /dev/rmt/0m            ;extract (x) the entire contents
                                   of the archive on tape /dev/rmt/0m
                                 to default destination.


# tar xvf /dev/rmt/0m file1      ;extract (x) only file1
                                   from the archive on tape /dev/rmt/0m
                                   to default destination.
```

You'll notice when you view the man pages for tar that options are preceded by a hyphen. The command works without the hyphen, so most tar examples, including those in this chapter, omit the hyphen.

Let's take a look at some examples using tar. Let's begin by performing a tar backup (usually called *creating an archive*) of the directory /var to tape device /dev/rmt/0m. We use the c option to create a backup and the f option to specify the file of the tape drive /dev/rmt/0m:

```
# tar cf /dev/rmt/0m /var
tar: /var/opt/dce/rpc/local/01060/reaper is not a file. Not dumped
tar: /var/opt/dce/rpc/local/00997/reaper is not a file. Not dumped
tar: /var/opt/dce/rpc/local/00997/c-3/7000 is not a file. Not dumped
tar: /var/opt/dce/rpc/local/00997/c-3/shared is not a file. Not dumped
tar: /var/opt/dce/rpc/local/00997/c-3/7002 is not a file. Not dumped
tar: /var/opt/dce/rpc/local/s-0/135 is not a file. Not dumped
tar: /var/opt/dce/rpc/local/s-0/2121 is not a file. Not dumped
tar: /var/opt/dce/rpc/local/s-3/135 is not a file. Not dumped
tar: /var/opt/dce/rpc/local/s-3/2121 is not a file. Not dumped
tar: /var/spool/sockets/pwgr/client933 is not a file. Not dumped
tar: /var/spool/sockets/pwgr/client1028 is not a file. Not dumped
tar: /var/spool/sockets/pwgr/client1152 is not a file. Not dumped
tar: /var/spool/sockets/pwgr/client1172 is not a file. Not dumped
tar: /var/spool/sockets/pwgr/client1173 is not a file. Not dumped
tar: /var/spool/sockets/pwgr/client1139 is not a file. Not dumped
tar: /var/spool/sockets/pwgr/client2500 is not a file. Not dumped
tar: /var/spool/sockets/pwgr/client2592 is not a file. Not dumped
tar: /var/spool/sockets/pwgr/client2490 is not a file. Not dumped
tar: /var/spool/sockets/pwgr/client2593 is not a file. Not dumped
tar: /var/spool/pwgr/daemon is not a file. Not dumped
#
```

The result of this command printed only problem-related messages to *standard output*. You will often see the *v* option used with **tar** to produce verbose output, which would have listed both the messages above and those related to files that were successfully written to the tape archive.

Next let's take a look at only the files on the tape with the string *eaaa* in them. To produce a table of contents, we will use the *t* option. The following example also uses *v* for verbose output:

```
# tar tvf /dev/rmt/0m | grep eaaa
rw-rw-rw-    0/3        28 Jul 11 15:37 2000 /var/tmp/eaaa01299
rw-rw-rw-    0/3        28 Jul 11 15:37 2000 /var/tmp/eaaa01333
rw-rw-rw-    0/3        28 Jul 11 15:38 2000 /var/tmp/eaaa01354
rw-rw-rw-    0/3        28 Jul 11 15:40 2000 /var/tmp/eaaa01380
rw-rw-rw-    0/3        28 Jul 11 15:40 2000 /var/tmp/eaaa01405
rw-rw-rw-    0/3        28 Jul 11 15:45 2000 /var/tmp/eaaa01487

#
```

This output shows several files that begin with *eaaa* on the tape. We'll delete the last of these files from the computer and restore it from tape using the *x* option to extract the file from the **tar** archive. We'll then list the directory on the system to confirm that the file we deleted has been restored to the directory from tape.

```
# rm /var/tmp/eaaa01487
#
# tar xvf /dev/rmt/0m /var/tmp/eaaa01487

x /var/tmp/eaaa01487, 28 bytes, 1 tape blocks

#
# ls -l /var/tmp/eaaa*
-rw-rw-rw-   1 root       sys            28 Jul 11 15:37 /var/tmp/eaaa01299
-rw-rw-rw-   1 root       sys            28 Jul 11 15:37 /var/tmp/eaaa01333
-rw-rw-rw-   1 root       sys            28 Jul 11 15:38 /var/tmp/eaaa01354
-rw-rw-rw-   1 root       sys            28 Jul 11 15:40 /var/tmp/eaaa01380
-rw-rw-rw-   1 root       sys            28 Jul 11 15:40 /var/tmp/eaaa01405
-rw-rw-rw-   1 root       sys            28 Jul 11 15:45 /var/tmp/eaaa01487

#
```

This backup and restore using **tar** is simple and gets the job done.

A common use for **tar** is to back up files from one directory and restore them to another directory. We'll backup the contents of **/var/tmp** and restore them to the directory **/tmp/puttarfileshere**. In the following example, we will create a **tar** backup archive to a file rather than to tape. The file is called **tartest**. We will then move this file to the destination directory and extract it there. We don't use a tape at all in this example.

```
# cd /var/tmp
# ls -l
total 72
-rw-------   1 root       sys             0 Jul 11 15:57 OBAMFEAa01630
-rw-------   1 root       sys             0 Jul 11 15:20 OBAMHBAa01020
-rw-------   1 root       sys             0 Jul 11 15:50 OBAMHBAa01540
-rw-rw-rw-   1 root       sys           102 Jul 11 15:20 aaaa01112
-rw-rw-rw-   1 root       sys           102 Jul 11 15:37 aaaa01299
-rw-rw-rw-   1 root       sys           102 Jul 11 15:37 aaaa01333
-rw-rw-rw-   1 root       sys           102 Jul 11 15:38 aaaa01354
-rw-rw-rw-   1 root       sys           102 Jul 11 15:40 aaaa01380
-rw-rw-rw-   1 root       sys            99 Jul 11 15:40 aaaa01405
```

```
        •
        •
        •
 1 root        sys              28 Jul 11 15:37 eaaa01333
-rw-rw-rw-  1 root        sys          28 Jul 11 15:38 eaaa01354
-rw-rw-rw-  1 root        sys          28 Jul 11 15:40 eaaa01380
-rw-rw-rw-  1 root        sys          28 Jul 11 15:40 eaaa01405
-rw-rw-rw-  1 root        sys          28 Jul 11 15:45 eaaa01487
-rwxr--r--  1 root        root         28 Jul 11 16:04 envd.action2
-rwxr--r--  1 root        root         28 Jul 11 16:04 envd.action5
dr-xr-xr-x  2 bin         bin          96 Jul 11 13:50 ntp
-rw-r--r--  1 root        sys         600 Jul 11 15:27 swagent.log
#
# tar cvf /tmp/tartest `ls`
a OBAMFEAa01630 0 blocks
a OBAMHBAa01020 0 blocks
a OBAMHBAa01540 0 blocks
a aaaa01112 1 blocks
a aaaa01299 1 blocks
a aaaa01333 1 blocks
a aaaa01354 1 blocks
a aaaa01380 1 blocks
a aaaa01405 1 blocks


        •
        •
        •
a eaaa01354 1 blocks
a eaaa01380 1 blocks
a eaaa01405 1 blocks
a eaaa01487 1 blocks
a envd.action2 1 blocks
a envd.action5 1 blocks
a swagent.log 2 blocks
#
# cd /tmp
# mkdir puttarfileshere
# cp tartest puttarfileshere
# cd puttarfileshere
# ls -l
total 80
-rw-rw-rw-  1 root        sys       40960 Jul 11 17:09 tartest
#
# tar xvf tartest
x OBAMFEAa01630, 0 bytes, 0 tape blocks
x OBAMHBAa01020, 0 bytes, 0 tape blocks
x OBAMHBAa01540, 0 bytes, 0 tape blocks
x aaaa01112, 102 bytes, 1 tape blocks
x aaaa01299, 102 bytes, 1 tape blocks
x aaaa01333, 102 bytes, 1 tape blocks
x aaaa01354, 102 bytes, 1 tape blocks
x aaaa01380, 102 bytes, 1 tape blocks
x aaaa01405, 99 bytes, 1 tape blocks

        •
        •
```

•

```
x daaa01405,  28 bytes,  1 tape blocks
x daaa01487,  28 bytes,  1 tape blocks
x eaaa01299,  28 bytes,  1 tape blocks
x eaaa01333,  28 bytes,  1 tape blocks
x eaaa01354,  28 bytes,  1 tape blocks
x eaaa01380,  28 bytes,  1 tape blocks
x eaaa01405,  28 bytes,  1 tape blocks
x eaaa01487,  28 bytes,  1 tape blocks
x envd.action2,  28 bytes,  1 tape blocks
x envd.action5,  28 bytes,  1 tape blocks
x swagent.log,  600 bytes,  2 tape blocks
#
```

When creating the **tar** backup, I first changed to the **/var/tmp** directory and then used the **ls** command (a *grav* or *accent*, which is near the upper left of most keyboards on the same key as a *tilde*, appears before and after the **ls**). This produced relative pathnames that I could easily restore to the **/tmp/ puttarfileshere** directory. Alternatively, I could also have just changed directory to **/var** and issued the command **tar cf /dev/rmt/0m tmp** to back up the entire contents of the **/var/tmp** directory.

This entire process could have been done on a single command line. The following line is from the **tar** file man page and shows the procedure for producing an archive in the *fromdir* and restoring it to the *todir*:

cd *fromdir* ; **tar cf - .** | (**cd** *todir* ; **tar xf -i**)

The "-" in the **tar cf** command tells **tar** to send its data to *standard output*. The "-" in the **tar xf** command tells **tar** to look to *standard input* for data, which is the data produced by **tar cf**, issued earlier on the command line.

cpio

cpio is a powerful utility that is used in conjunction with **find** in order to perform full and incremental backups. **cpio** is an established UNIX utility that
works similarly on most UNIX variants.

We'll use several commands in the upcoming examples, including the
following:

```
# find . -print | cpio -oBv > /dev/rmt/0m   ;find the contents of
                                              the current dir and
                                              write them to tape.


# cpio -it < /dev/rmt/0m        ;read table of contents (t) of tape.


# cpio -icvBdum < /dev/rmt/0m ;restore (i) the contents of tape,
                               this is the most widely used
                               cpio command.



# find . -print | cpio -oBv | (remsh tapesys dd of=/dev/rmt/0m)
              ;find the contents of the current dir and
               write (o) them to tape on remote machine tapesys.


# remsh tapesys "dd if=/dev/rmt/0m bs=8k" | cpio -icvBdum
                 ;restore the contents (i) of a tape on remote system
                  tapesys to the local system.
```

The first command we'll issue is to **find** the contents in **/var/tmp** and
write them to our tape device **/dev/rmt/0m**. The options to **cpio** used in the
following example are *o* for output mode, *B* for block output, and *v* for verbose reporting:

```
# cd /var/tmp
# find . -print | cpio -oBv > /dev/rmt/0m
(Using tape drive with immediate report mode enabled (reel #1).)
.
envd.action2
```

```
envd.action5
swagent.log
ntp
OBAMHBAa01020
aaaa01558
aaaa01426
aaaa01112
OBAMHBAa01540
aaaa01299



                              .

                              .

                              .


eaaa01487
OBAMFEAa01630
cmd_res8215
tmp_cfg_file
cmd_res8708
exclude.temp
arch.include.1
3570 blocks
#
```

In the example, we first changed the directory to **/var/tmp**, then issue the **find** command and pipe its output to **cpio**. **cpio** is almost always used in conjunction with **find** in the manner shown in the example. This produced a backup with relative pathnames because we changed to the directory **/var/tmp** before issuing the backup commands.

Next we'll view the contents of the tape to see the files we wrote to it with **cpio**. The *i* option is used for input, and the *t* option is used to get a table of contents in the following listing:

```
# cpio -it < /dev/rmt/0m
       .
envd.action2
envd.action5
swagent.log
ntp
OBAMHBAa01020
aaaa01558
aaaa01426
aaaa01112
OBAMHBAa01540
aaaa01299



                            .

                            .

                            .
```

```
eaaa01487
OBAMFEAa01630
cmd_res8215
tmp_cfg_file
cmd_res8708
exclude.temp
arch.include.1
3570 blocks
#
```

Now that we have written to the tape and viewed its table of contents, we'll restore the contents of **/var/tmp**. In the following example we use several options to **cpio**, including *i* for input mode, *c* for ASCII header format, *v* for verbose, *B* for block output, *d* for directories, *u* for unconditional write over existing files, and *m* to restore the original modification times:

```
# cpio -icvBdum < /dev/rmt/0m
.
envd.action2
envd.action5
swagent.log
ntp
OBAMHBAa01020
aaaa01558
aaaa01426
aaaa01112
OBAMHBAa01540
aaaa01299

                    .

                    .

                    .

eaaa01487
OBAMFEAa01630
cmd_res8215
tmp_cfg_file
cmd_res8708
exclude.temp
arch.include.1
3570 blocks
#
```

The **cpio** command produces a list of files that will be read from the tape and restored to the system. Since we included the verbose option, we'll see all the information related to the restore.

Now that we've seen how to write a tape, produce a table of contents, and read the contents of a tape on a local system, let's work with a tape drive on a remote system. We'll perform a backup to a remote tape drive, view the table of contents on the tape, and then restore using the remote tape drive.

First let's perform a backup to a remote tape drive. The local system, which does not have a tape drive attached to it, is *orl*. The remote system, which has a tape drive attached to it, is *tapesys*. We'll run **cpio** (using the same three options earlier described) on *orl* and run a remote shell and **dd** on *tapesys,* which will store the contents of the backup. We'll run these commands from **/var/tmp** on *orl* in the following example:

```
# find . -print | cpio -oBv | (remsh tapesys dd of=/dev/rmt/0m)
.
envd.action2
envd.action5
swagent.log
ntp
OBAMHBAa01020
aaaa01558
aaaa01426
aaaa01112
OBAMHBAa01540
aaaa01299
              .
              .
              .
eaaa01487
OBAMFEAa01630
cmd_res8215
tmp_cfg_file
cmd_res8708
exclude.temp
arch.include.1
3570 blocks
#
```

Now let's come back to our local system without the tape drive and restore the contents of the **cpio** tape we just produced, but let's restore them to a different directory. The directory to which we'll restore the contents of the tape (originally in **/var/tmp**) is **/tmp/remotecpiofiles**. This is similar to the process we performed in the **tar** section earlier in this chapter, in which we restored **tar** files to a different location.

In the following example, we issue a series of commands while on *or1*. The last of these commands is to issue a **remsh** to system *tapesys*, which has on it a tape drive with the **cpio** tape we just created. We **dd** the information and pipe it through **cpio** to restore the contents of the tape. In this example, we use the same restore options to **cpio**, including *i* for input mode, *c* for ASCII header format, *v* for verbose, *B* for block output, *d* for directories, *u* for unconditional write over existing files, and *m* to restore original modification times:

```
# hostname
or1
# cd /tmp
# mkdir remotecpiofiles
# cd remotecpiofiles
# pwd
/tmp/remotecpiofiles
# remsh tapesys "dd if=/dev/rmt/0m bs=8k" | cpio -icvBdum
.
envd.action2
envd.action5
swagent.log
ntp
OBAMHBAa01020
aaaa01558
aaaa01426
aaaa01112
OBAMHBAa01540
aaaa01299
                        .
                        .
                        .
eaaa01487
OBAMFEAa01630
cmd_res8215
tmp_cfg_file
cmd_res8708
exclude.temp
arch.include.1
3570 blocks
#
# pwd
/tmp/remotecpiofiles
# ls
envd.action2
```

```
envd.action5
swagent.log
ntp
OBAMHBAa01020
aaaa01558
aaaa01426
aaaa01112
OBAMHBAa01540
aaaa01299

                    .

                    .

                    .

eaaa01487
OBAMFEAa01630
cmd_res8215
tmp_cfg_file
cmd_res8708
exclude.temp
arch.include.1
#
```

The **ls** we issued at the end of this example confirmed that we did indeed write the contents of the tape on the remote system to the new directory **/tmp/remotecpiofiles**. You may want to add the *-a* command to the **ls** option to ensure that the files have contents.

You can build from the simple examples in this **cpio** section to develop backup and restore commands to meet your needs in a modest environment.

fbackup and frecover

fbackup and **frecover** are the preferred backup and restore programs on HP-UX. Backups produced with **fbackup** are not portable to other UNIX variants. If you're working in a heterogeneous environment, you won't be able to take **fbackup** tapes produced on an HP-UX system and recover them to a system running a different UNIX variant.

In this section I'll cover issuing **fbackup** and **frecover** at the command line. You can also manage backups using these commands with SAM (covered in Chapter 3). SAM helps you manage both *Automated Backups* and *Interactive Backup and Recovery.* Although **fbackup** and **frecover** are the most advanced programs bundled with your HP-UX system for backup and restore, your needs may go beyond these programs. There are also advanced backup programs that you can procure from both HP and third parties. In general, I find that the capabilities of **fbackup** and **frecover** are sufficient for new HP-UX installations. If, however, you have a highly distributed environment, or need to back up large amounts of data, perform backups on systems with a variety of operating systems, or need to use several backup devices simultaneously, you may want to consider a more advanced product.

fbackup has the capability of performing backups at different *levels.* The levels define the amount of information to be included in the backup. A full backup, which is covered in this section, is backup level 0. The other levels define various degrees of incremental backups. I am a strong advocate of performing a full backup, and then performing incremental backups of every file that has changed since the *last full backup.* This means that to recover from a completely "hosed" (a technical term meaning *destroyed*) system, you would need your full backup tape and only one incremental tape (you would restore your root volume with a bootable Ignite-UX tape produced with **make_recovery**, which is covered in Chapter 10). If, for instance, you performed a full backup on Sunday and incremental backups on Monday through Friday, you would need to load only Sunday's full backup tape and Friday's incremental backup tape to completely restore your system. **fbackup** supports this scheme.

Keep in mind that although we'll be issuing **fbackup** and **frecovery** commands at the command line in this chapter, these can be managed more easily through SAM. The following is an explanation of the **fbackup** command and *some* of its options:

```
/usr/sbin/fbackup -f device [-0-9] [-u] [-i path] [-e path] [-g graph]
```

-f device	The tape drive for the backup, such as **/dev/rmt/0m** for your local tape drive.
[-0-9]	This is the level of the backup. If you run a full backup on Sunday at level 0, then you would run an incremental backup at level 1 the other days of the week. An incremental backup will back up all information changed since a backup was made at a lower level. You could back up at 0 on Sunday, 1 on Monday, 2 on Tuesday, and so on. However, to recover your system, you would need to load Sunday's tape, then Monday's tape, then Tuesday's tape, and so on, to fully recover.
[-u]	This updates the database of past backups so that it contains such information as the backup level, time of the beginning and end of the backup session, and the graph file (described below) used for the backup session. This is valid only with the *-g* (graph) option.
[-i path]	The specified path is to be included in the backup. This can be issued any number of times.
[-e path]	The specified path is to be excluded from the backup. This can also be specified any number of times.
[-g graph]	The graph file contains the list of files and directories to be included or excluded from the backup.

Although **fbackup** is quite thorough and easy to use, it does not have embedded in it the day and time at which full and incremental backups will be run. You have to make a **cron** entry to run **fbackup** automatically. SAM will make a **cron** entry for you, thereby running **fbackup** whenever you like. (**cron** is covered in Chapter 11.)

In its simplest form, we could run **fbackup** and specify only the tape drive with the *f* option and the directory to back up with the *i* option as shown in the following example:

```
# fbackup -f /dev/rmt/0m -i /var/tmp
fbackup(1004): session begins on Wed Jul 12 14:26:30 2000
fbackup(3205): WARNING: unable to read a volume header
fbackup(3024): writing volume 1 to the output file /dev/rmt/0m
fbackup(3055): total file blocks read for backup: 3606
fbackup(3056): total blocks written to output file /dev/rmt/0m: 3857
fbackup(1030): warnings encountered during backup
#
```

fbackup did not produce a list of files included in the backup since we did not include the *v* option for verbose.

To view the contents of the tape, we run **frecover** with the options *r* for read, *N* to prevent the contents of the tape from being restored to the system, and *v* for verbose, as shown in the following command:

```
# frecover -rNv -f /dev/rmt/0m
drwxr-xr-x        root    root     /
dr-xr-xr-x        bin     bin      /var
drwxrwxrwx        bin     bin      /var/tmp
-rw-------        root    sys      /var/tmp/OBAMFEAa01630
-rw-------        root    sys      /var/tmp/OBAMHBAa01020
-rw-------        root    sys      /var/tmp/OBAMHBAa01540
-rw-------        root    sys      /var/tmp/OBAMHBAa07762
-rw-rw-rw-        root    sys      /var/tmp/aaaa01112
                         .
                         .
                         .
-rw-rw-rw-        root    sys      /var/tmp/eaaa01487
-rwxr--r--        root    root     /var/tmp/envd.action2
-rwxr--r--        root    root     /var/tmp/envd.action5
-rw-rw-rw-        root    sys      /var/tmp/exclude.temp
dr-xr-xr-x        bin     bin      /var/tmp/ntp
-rw-r--r--        root    sys      /var/tmp/swagent.log
-rw-rw-rw-        root    sys      /var/tmp/tmp_cfg_file
#
```

Let's now delete a file from the system that was included as part of the **fbackup**. We'll then restore only the file we deleted. We'll use the *x* option for extract and the *i* option to specify the file to include with **frecover** as shown in the following example:

```
# cd /var/tmp
# ls -l aa*
-rw-rw-rw-    1 root         sys              102 Jul 11 15:20 aaaa01112
-rw-rw-rw-    1 root         sys              102 Jul 11 15:37 aaaa01299
-rw-rw-rw-    1 root         sys              102 Jul 11 15:37 aaaa01333
-rw-rw-rw-    1 root         sys              102 Jul 11 15:38 aaaa01354
-rw-rw-rw-    1 root         sys              102 Jul 11 15:40 aaaa01380
-rw-rw-rw-    1 root         sys               99 Jul 11 15:40 aaaa01405
-rw-rw-rw-    1 root         sys              102 Jul 11 14:57 aaaa01426
-rw-rw-rw-    1 root         sys               99 Jul 11 15:45 aaaa01487
-rw-rw-rw-    1 root         sys              102 Jul 11 14:24 aaaa01558
# rm aaaa01487
# cd /
# frecover -x -i /var/tmp/aaaa01487 -f /dev/rmt/0m
# cd /var/tmp
# ls -l aaa*
-rw-rw-rw-    1 root         sys              102 Jul 11 15:20 aaaa01112
-rw-rw-rw-    1 root         sys              102 Jul 11 15:37 aaaa01299
-rw-rw-rw-    1 root         sys              102 Jul 11 15:37 aaaa01333
-rw-rw-rw-    1 root         sys              102 Jul 11 15:38 aaaa01354
-rw-rw-rw-    1 root         sys              102 Jul 11 15:40 aaaa01380
-rw-rw-rw-    1 root         sys               99 Jul 11 15:40 aaaa01405
-rw-rw-rw-    1 root         sys              102 Jul 11 14:57 aaaa01426
-rw-rw-rw-    1 root         sys               99 Jul 11 15:45 aaaa01487
-rw-rw-rw-    1 root         sys              102 Jul 11 14:24 aaaa01558
#
```

In the previous example, we successfully restored the file **/var/tmp/ aaa01487** from the tape using **frestore**.

There are some powerful aspects to **fbackup** that we did not employ in our example. These include *backup levels, graph files*, and *index files*.

fbackup supports backup levels 0-9. 0 is used for full backups and the other digits indicate various incremental backup levels.

Graph files are used to specify the files to be included in the backup.

Index files contain a list of files produced as part of the backup.

Let's take a look at an example that employs all of these functions. First, we create a graph file that contains the files we wish to include (*i*) or exclude (*e*) as part of the backup. In our case the file will contain only the following line:

```
i /var/tmp
```

Let's now run **fbackup** with *u* to update the backup database, *0* for a full backup, *f* to specify the file to which we want to write the backup (we'll use a file rather than tape in this example), *g* to specify our graph file, *I* to specify the name of the index file, and finally, we'll redirect messages to a

file that will contain the backup log. We'll add the date and time to the end
of the index and backup log files.

```
# fbackup -0u -f /tmp/testbackup -g /tmp/backupgraph
           -I /tmp/backupindex.`date '+%y%m%d.%H:%M'` 2>
           /tmp/backuplog.`date '+%y%m%d.%H:%M'`
#
```

Let's now see what files were produced as a result of having issued this
command. First let's look at the backup index and backup logfiles:

```
# ls /tmp/backup*
backupgraph
backupgraph000712.15.04
backupindex.000712.15:04
backuplog.000712.15:04
#
# cat /tmp/backupindex000712.15:04
1024                  1 /
1024                  1 /var
2048                  1 /var/tmp
0                     1 /var/tmp/OBAMFEAa01630
0                     1 /var/tmp/OBAMHBAa01020
0                     1 /var/tmp/OBAMHBAa01540
336                   1 /var/tmp/OBAMHBAa07762
102                   1 /var/tmp/aaaa01112
                  .
                  .
                  .
28                    1 /var/tmp/eaaa01487
28                    1 /var/tmp/envd.action2
28                    1 /var/tmp/envd.action5
4608                  1 /var/tmp/exclude.temp
96                    1 /var/tmp/ntp
1595                  1 /var/tmp/swagent.log
205                   1 /var/tmp/tmp_cfg_file
#
# cat /tmp/backupgraph000712.15:04
i/var/tmp
#
# cat /tmp/backuplog000712.15:04

fbackup(1004): session begins on Wed Jul 12 14:56:19 2000
fbackup(3024): writing volume 1 to the output file /tmp/testbackup
fbackup(1030): warnings encountered during backup
fbackup(3055): total file blocks read for backup: 3614
fbackup(3056): total blocks written to output file /tmp/testbackup:3876
#
```

The three files with the date appended (*7/12/00 time 15:04*) to the end
of the filename were produced by the **fbackup** command issued earlier. The
date appended to the end of the file can help in the organization of backup
files. We could restore any or all of these files with **frestore** from the file that
contains the backup information (**/tmp/testbackup**), as demonstrated earlier.

We are not restricted to performing backups to a tape drive attached to
the local system. We can backup to a remote tape with **fbackup** by specifying the system name and tape drive, or file, to which we want to store the
files. The following example uses **fbackup** options covered earlier and also
includes the name of the system with the tape drive:

```
# fbackup -f tapesys:/dev/rmt/0m -i /var/tmp -v
fbackup(1004): session begins on Wed Jul 12 15:56:22 2000
fbackup(3307): volume 1 has been used -1 time(s) (maximum: 100)
fbackup(3024): writing vol 1 to output file tapesys:/dev/rmt/0m
    1: / 2
    2: /var 2
    3: /var/tmp 4
    4: /var/tmp/AAAa11812 0
    5: /var/tmp/AAAa11992 0
    6: /var/tmp/BEQ19522 19
    7: /var/tmp/DCE19522 0
    8: /var/tmp/DEC19522 0
    9: /var/tmp/ISPX19522 0
                        .
                        .
                        .
   73: /var/tmp/eaaa13306 1
   74: /var/tmp/ems_inittab.old 2
   75: /var/tmp/envd.action2 1
   76: /var/tmp/envd.action5 1
   77: /var/tmp/inetd.conf.old 9
   78: /var/tmp/net19522 1799
   79: /var/tmp/swagent.log 16
fbackup(1005): run time: 43 seconds
fbackup(3055): total file blocks read for backup: 1974
fbackup(3056): total blocks written to output file or1:/dev/rmt/0m: 0
#
```

This command performs the backup of **/var/tmp** on system *or1* by
sending the files to the tape drive on system *tapesys*. We could have used
many additional options to **fbackup** as demonstrated in earlier examples, but
I wanted to keep the example simple so that it would be easy to see the
remote tape drive specification.

dd

dd is a utility for writing the contents of a device, such as a disk, to tape. You can also use **dd** to copy an image of a tape to a file on your system, and then you can look at the file.

First, let's write the contents of a directory to tape using **tar**, then we'll use **dd** to copy the tape contents as a file. The only option to **dd** required in this example is *if,* which specifies the input file as the tape drive.

```
# cd /var/tmp
# tar cf /dev/rmt/0m `ls`
# cd /tmp
# dd if=/dev/rmt/0m > /tmp/tapecontents
183+0 records in
183+0 records out
# tar tv /tmp/tapecontents
rw-------    0/3        0 Jul 11 15:57 2000 OBAMFEAa01630
rw-------    0/3        0 Jul 11 15:20 2000 OBAMHBAa01020
rw-------    0/3        0 Jul 11 15:50 2000 OBAMHBAa01540
rw-------    0/3      336 Jul 12 13:18 2000 OBAMHBAa07762
rw-------    0/3        0 Jul 12 13:44 2000 OBAMHBAa08333
rw-rw-rw-    0/3      102 Jul 11 15:20 2000 aaaa01112
                           .
                           .
                           .
rw-rw-rw-    0/3       28 Jul 11 15:45 2000 eaaa01487
rwxr--r--    0/0       28 Jul 11 21:53 2000 envd.action2
rwxr--r--    0/0       28 Jul 11 21:53 2000 envd.action5
rw-rw-rw-    0/3     2304 Jul 12 12:42 2000 exclude.temp
r-xr-xr-x    2/2        0 Jul 11 13:50 2000 ntp/
rw-r--r--    0/3     1595 Jul 12 12:23 2000 swagent.log
rw-rw-rw-    0/3      205 Jul 12 12:39 2000 tmp_cfg_file
#
```

Now we can look at the contents of the file with **tar**, as shown in an earlier section, with the following command:

```
# tar tv /tmp/tapecontents
```

Another common use of **dd** is to extract a **cpio** archive from a tape drive on a remote system to a local system. In the following example the local system without a tape drive is *or1* and the remote system with a tape drive is *tapesys*. We'll read the tape to a directory on *or1* using **dd** and **cpio** (see the earlier **cpio** section for an explanation of the options) in the following example:

```
# hostname
or1
# pwd
/tmp/remotecpiofiles
# remsh tapesys "dd if=/dev/rmt/0m bs=8k" | cpio -icvBdum
.
envd.action2
envd.action5
swagent.log
ntp
OBAMHBAa01020
aaaa01558
              .
              .
              .
eaaa01487
OBAMFEAa01630
cmd_res8215
tmp_cfg_file
cmd_res8708
OBAMHBAa07762
exclude.temp
arch.include.1
3580 blocks
0+358 records in
0+358 records out
#
```

This command runs a remote shell (**remsh**) to run the **dd** command on *tapesys*. The output of this command is piped to **cpio** on our local system to extract the archive. In this example, only the *if* option was used to specify the input file. The *of* option, which specifies the output file was not needed. If you were to perform a **dd** of a disk device to a tape drive, the *of* would be the tape drive on your system, such as **/dev/rmt/0m**.

dump and restore

dump is similar to **fbackup**. If you use **fbackup** on HP-UX, you will see much similarity when you use **dump**. **dump** provides levels as part of the backup scheme and creates **/var/adm/dumpdates,** which lists the last time a filesystem was backed up. **restore** is used to read information backed up with **dump**. **dump**, however, works only with HFS filesystems, and not with VxFS, and it assumes that you are using a reel tape. **vxdump** and **vxrestore** are used for VxFS. Generally speaking, you will not find **dump** (and **vxdump**) and **restore** (and **vxrestore**) recommended as backup and restore programs on HP-UX. **fbackup** and **cpio** are the preferred backup programs on HP-UX. There is, however, no reason why you can't use **dump** and **restore** as long as you keep in mind the filesystem type limitation.

Let's take a look at some examples using **dump** and **restore**. Our examples will actually use **vxdump** and **vxrestore**; however. Nearly the same usage applies to both the HFS and VxFS programs. We'll use several commands in the upcoming examples, including the following:

```
# vxdump 0fu /dev/rmt/0m /var        ;dump vxfs file system /var to tape
                                      /dev/rmt/0m using level 0 and
                                      update /var/adm/dumpdates.


# vxrestore tf /dev/rmt/0m | grep eaaa   ;obtain table of contents from
                                          tape /dev/rmt/0m and look for
                                          file name containing "eaaa"

# vxrestore -x -f /dev/rmt/0m ./tmp/eaaa01487   ;restore file to
                                                 current directory
```

Let's take a look at some of these commands in more detail and I'll provide more explanation for what is taking place.

Our first example runs **vxdump** to back up the directory **/var** with a backup level of *0* for full backup, the *f* option to specify the output file **/dev/rmt/0m**, and *u* for a write to **/var/adm/dumpdates**:

```
# vxdump 0fu /dev/rmt/0m /var
  vxdump: Date of this level 0 dump: Tue Jul 11 16:41:27 2000
  vxdump: Date of last level 0 dump: the epoch
  vxdump: Dumping /dev/vg00/rlvol10 to /dev/rmt/0m
  vxdump: mapping (Pass I) [regular files]
  vxdump: mapping (Pass II) [directories]
  vxdump: estimated 428058 blocks (209.01MB).
  vxdump: dumping (Pass III) [directories]
  vxdump: dumping (Pass IV) [regular files]
  vxdump: vxdump: 214146 tape blocks on 1 volumes(s)
  vxdump: level 0 dump on Tue Jul 11 16:41:27 2000
  vxdump: Closing /dev/rmt/0m
  vxdump: vxdump is done
#
```

vxdump provides information related to the backup to *standard output*.

Next, let's view the table of contents on the tape using **vxrestore**, looking for files that begin with *eaaa*. We'll then delete one of these files from the system and use **vxrestore** to restore it from tape. To produce the table of contents, we use the *t* option, and to extract the file from tape, we use the *x* option to **vxrestore** as shown in the following listing:

```
#
# vxrestore tf /dev/rmt/0m | grep eaaa
       404        ./tmp/eaaa01299
       678        ./tmp/eaaa01333
       700        ./tmp/eaaa01354
       736        ./tmp/eaaa01380
       741        ./tmp/eaaa01405
       717        ./tmp/eaaa01487
#
#
# rm /var/tmp/eaaa01487
#
# vxrestore -x -f /dev/rmt/0m ./tmp/eaaa01487
You have not read any tapes yet.
Unless you know which volume your file(s) are on you should start
with the last volume and work towards the first.
Specify next volume #: 1
set owner/mode for '.'? [yn] y

# cd /var/tmp
# ls -l eaaa01487
total 2
-rw-rw-rw-   1 root        sys              28 Jul 11 15:45 eaaa01487
#
```

Notice that as part of restoring the file, we had to specify a volume number of *1* and whether or not we wanted to set the mode for the file.

The examples in this section showed creating a backup tape with **vxdump**, producing a table of contents, and restoring with **vxrestore**. Although **fbackup** and **cpio** are the recommended backup solutions on HP-UX, you can use **dump** and **restore** if you are familiar with these programs and would like to use them. Due to the portability of **tar**, it is often used for backup and restore as well.

CHAPTER 8

System Startup and Shutdown Scripts

System Startup and Shutdown Scripts in Virtual Partitions

Every Virtual Partition has separate startup and shutdown scripts just as you would have separate scripts on individual systems. There isn't any unique activity that takes place from a startup and shutdown standpoint due to Virtual Partitions; however, since each vPar is running its own HP-UX, you can customize the startup and shutdown to meet the needs of the applications you're running in each vPar. In addition, there is a *heartbeat* deamon that is used to synchronize the Virtual Partition database every few seconds.

Let's take a look at an application running in a vPar and the startup and shutdown procedures employed to support this application. In addition we'll view the the means by which the *heartbeat* deamon is started and stopped to synchronize the Virtual Partition database.

Application Startup in Virtual Partitions

Each Virtual Partition is like a separate server. The applications running in a vPar run independently of applications and activity running in other vPars.

415

All applications in a vPar require startup scripts to be run as they would on any system (please see the non-vPar-specific section of this chapter if you need information on how HP-UX startup and shutdown operates.)

In the vPar used in this example we have a variety of applications running, including Broadvision. Let's take a look at **/etc/rc.config.d**, where the configuration variable scripts are located, to see what *bv* files (those that relate to Broadvision) exist:

```
# ll | grep bv
-rwxr-xr-x   1 root        sys            9 Sep 26 09:31 bv
# cat bv
BV_CTL=1
#
```

This listing shows the **bv** file and its contents. The *BV_CTL=1* variable indicates that Broadvision is to be started when the system boots.

Starting the *bv* application processes results in several Broadvision-related daemons being started, including those shown in the following listing:

```
# ps -ef | grep bv1
pbcombv  3111  3096  0  Sep 26  ?  0:04 bvconf_srv p_1221_3 -f -install_name bv1to1/bvconf_srv_a
pbcombv  3404  3096  0  Sep 26  ?  1:19 cntdb p_1221_5 -install_name bv1to1/cntdb_1
pbcombv  3707  3096  0  Sep 26  ?  0:20 genericdb p_1221_8 -install_name bv1to1/genericdb_1
pbcombv  3479 3096  0 Sep 26 ? 0:05 cntdb p_1221_7 -install_name bv1to1/
                              DiscussionForum_cntdb_1
root  7572  7232  0 13:17:33 pts/0     0:00 grep bv1
#
```

You can see that there are many processes related to the *bv1to1* application running on this system. These are started automatically as part of the startup structure of HP-UX. The following listing shows the link in **/sbin/rc1.d**, for run level one, and **/sbin/rc2.d**, for run level two, for *bv*.

```
# ll /sbin/rc1.d | grep bv
lrwxr-xr-x   1 root        sys           15 Sep 26 10:42 K105bv -> /sbin/init.d/bv
# ll /sbin/rc2.d | grep bv
lrwxr-xr-x   1 root        sys           15 Sep 26 10:41 S930bv -> /sbin/init.d/bv
#
```

The *bv kill* script, as indicated by the "K" preceding the link, is shown in **/sbin/rc1.d**, and the *start* script, as indicated by the "S" preceding the link, is shown in **/sbin/rc2.d**.

The script **/sbin/init.d/bv,** which is shown in the links, runs a variety of commands at both startup and shutdown of the Virtual Partition. The following listing shows the **/sbin/init.d/bv** script:

```
#
# <Insert comment about your script here>
#

# Allowed exit values:
#        0 = success; causes "OK" to show up in checklist.
#        1 = failure; causes "FAIL" to show up in checklist.
#        2 = skip; causes "N/A" to show up in the checklist.
#            Use this value if execution of this script is overridden
#            by the use of a control variable, or if this script is not
#            appropriate to execute for some other reason.
#        3 = reboot; causes the system to be rebooted after execution.
#        4 = background; causes "BG" to show up in the checklist.
#            Use this value if this script starts a process in background mode.

# Input and output:
#        stdin is redirected from /dev/null
#
#        stdout and stderr are redirected to the /etc/rc.log file
#        during checklist mode, or to the console in raw mode.

PATH=/usr/sbin:/usr/bin:/sbin
export PATH

# NOTE: If your script executes in run state 0 or state 1, then /usr might
#       not be available.  Do not attempt to access commands or files in
#       /usr unless your script executes in run state 2 or greater.  Other
#       file systems typically not mounted until run state 2 include /var
#       and /opt.

rval=0

# Check the exit value of a command run by this script.  If non-zero, the
# exit code is echoed to the log file and the return value of this script
# is set to indicate failure.

set_return() {
        x=$?
        if [ $x -ne 0 ]; then
                echo "EXIT CODE: $x"
                rval=1  # script FAILed
        fi
}

# Kill the named process(es).
# $1=<search pattern for your process>

killproc() {
        pid=`ps -el | awk '( ($NF ~ /'"$1"'/) && ($4 != mypid) && ($5 != mypid)  ){
print $4 }' mypid=$$ `
        if [ "X$pid" != "X" ]; then
                if kill "$pid"; then
                        echo "$1 stopped"
                else
                        rval=1
                        echo "Unable to stop $1"
                fi
        fi
}
```

```
case $1 in
'start_msg')
        # Emit a _short_ message relating to running this script with
        # the "start" argument; this message appears as part of the checklist.
        echo "Starting the BroadVision subsystem"
        ;;

'stop_msg')
        # Emit a _short_ message relating to running this script with
        # the "stop" argument; this message appears as part of the checklist.
        echo "Stopping the BroadVision subsystem"
        ;;

'start')

        # source the system configuration variables
        if [ -f /etc/rc.config.d/bv ] ; then
                . /etc/rc.config.d/bv
        else
                echo "ERROR: /etc/rc.config.d/bv defaults file MISSING"
        fi

        # Check to see if this script is allowed to run...
        if [ "$BV_CTL" != 1 ]; then
                rval=2
        else

        # Execute the commands to start your subsystem
        su - pbcombv -c "/opt/bv1to1/bin/bvconf execute"
        :
        fi
        ;;

'stop')
        # source the system configuration variables
        if [ -f /etc/rc.config.d/bv ] ; then
                . /etc/rc.config.d/bv
        else
                echo "ERROR: /etc/rc.config.d/bv defaults file MISSING"
        fi

        # Check to see if this script is allowed to run...
        if [ "$BV_CTL" != 1 ]; then
                rval=2
        else
        :
        # Execute the commands to stop your subsystem
        su - pbcombv -c "/opt/bv1to1/bin/bvconf shutdown"
        fi
        ;;

*)
        echo "usage: $0 {start|stop|start_msg|stop_msg}"
        rval=1
        ;;
esac

exit $rval
```

Note that all of the *start* and *stop* information related to the Broadvision is present in this file because this script is run for both *kill* (*K*) and *start* (*S*.) Note also the line

```
if [ "$BV_CTL" != 1 ]; then
```

which checks to see if the variable we viewed earlier in **/etc/rc.con-fig.d/bv** is equal to one as it was when we checked the file.

The installation and startup of Broadvision is required in all Virtual Partitions in which you want to run this application. What is taking place in vPar used in this example is what you would see in every vPar running Broadvision.

Virtual Partition Startup

Let's take a look at **/etc/rc.config.d**, where the configuration variable scripts are located to see what vPar-related scripts exist (please see the non-vPar-specific section of this chapter if need information on how HP-UX startup and shutdown operates.) We'll perform a long listing of this directory and search for *vpar*:

```
# ll /etc/rc.config.d | grep vpar
-r--r--r--   1 bin        bin           291 Aug 21 14:38 vpard
-r--r--r--   1 bin        bin           399 Aug 13 14:31 vparhb
-r--r--r--   1 bin        bin           702 Aug 13 14:30 vparinit
#
```

This listing shows three vPar-related configuration variable scripts. We'll focus on **vparhb** the *heartbeat* daemon.

The *heartbeat* deamon is used to synchronize the Virtual Partition database every few seconds among the vPars running on a server. Modifications you make related to Virtual Partitions update the Virtual Partition database **/stand/vpdb**. The following listing shows the contents of **/stand** in a Virtual Partition:

```
# ll /stand
total 143232
-rw-r--r--   1 root       sys            19 Jul 13 15:04 bootconf
drwxr-xr-x   4 root       sys          2048 Sep 17 15:47 build
drwxrwxrwx   5 root       root         1024 Sep 17 15:52 dlkm
drwxrwxrwx   5 root       sys          1024 Sep 17 14:10 dlkm.vmunix.prev
-rw-r--r--   1 root       sys          3388 Sep 26 13:01 ioconfig
-r--r--r--   1 root       sys            82 Jul 13 15:34 kernrel
drwxr-xr-x   2 root       sys          1024 Sep 26 13:04 krs
drwxr-xr-x   2 root       root         1024 Sep 26 13:01 krs_lkg
drwxr-xr-x   2 root       root         1024 Sep 26 13:04 krs_tmp
```

```
drwxr-xr-x   2 root        root        8192 Jul 13 15:04 lost+found
-rw-------   1 root        root          12 Sep 26 13:01 rootconf
-r--r--r--   1 root        sys         2035 Sep 17 14:09 system
-r--r--r--   1 root        sys          994 Jul 13 15:28 system.01
-r--r--r--   1 root        sys          999 Jul 13 15:56 system.02
-r--r--r--   1 root        sys          994 Jul 13 15:28 system.base
drwxr-xr-x   2 root        sys         1024 Jul 13 15:37 system.d
-r--r--r--   1 root        sys         2030 Sep 17 14:07 system.prev
-rwxr-xr-x   1 root        root    22682568 Sep 17 15:52 vmunix
-rwxr-xr-x   1 root        sys     21916712 Sep 17 14:10 vmunix.prev
-rw-------   1 root        root        8232 Sep 26 13:01 vpdb
-rw-------   1 root        root        8232 Jul 17 14:11 vpdb.OLD
-r-xr-xr-x   1 bin         bin       837616 Aug 31 18:59 vpmon
-rw-------   1 root        root     5078504 Jul 18 11:36 vpmon.dmp
#
#
```

Among the files shown in this listing is **vpdb**. If this **vpdb** were to be modified, or another **vpdb** on this server were to be modified, the *heartbeat* daemon **vphb** would ensure that all of the databases on the server in all of the running vPars would be synchronized. The non-running vPars cannot be synchronized until they are started.

The *heartbeat* daemon **vphb** is shown in the following **ps -ef** listing:

```
# ps -ef | grep vphb
    root   352      1  0 13:01:53 ?        0:00 vphbd -d 10 -p /var/run/vphbd.pid
    root  7289   7232  1 12:18:28 pts/0    0:00 grep vphb
#
```

vphb is started automatically as part of the startup structure of HP-UX. The following lisitng shows all of the links in **/sbin/rc0.d**, for run level zero, including the two vPar-related links at the very beginning of this listing:

```
# ll /sbin/rc0.d
total 0
lrwxr-xr-x   1 bin     bin     18 Sep 17 14:11 K425vpard -> /sbin/init.d/vpard
lrwxr-xr-x   1 bin     bin     19 Sep 17 14:11 K431vparhb -> /sbin/init.d/vparhb
lrwxr-xr-x   1 root    root    19 Jul 13 15:08 K480syncer -> /sbin/init.d/syncer
lrwxr-xr-x   1 root    root    15 Jul 13 15:08 K650kl -> /sbin/init.d/kl
lrwxr-xr-x   1 root    root    20 Jul 13 15:08 K800killall -> /sbin/init.d/killall
lrwxr-xr-x   1 root    root    19 Jul 13 15:08 K888kminit -> /sbin/init.d/kminit
lrwxr-xr-x   1 root    root    20 Jul 13 15:08 K890kmbuild -> /sbin/init.d/kmbuild
lrwxr-xr-x   1 root    root    23 Jul 13 15:08 K900localmount -> /sbin/init.d/localmount
#
```

These are *kill* scripts, as indicated by the "K" preceding each link. The links to the *start* scripts are found in **/sbin/rc1.d**.

We'll take a look at the file **/sbin/init.d/vparhb** that is shown in the *heartbeat* link and that is run at startup in the following listing:

```
# cat /sbin/init.d/vparhb
#!/sbin/sh

#
# NOTE: This script is not configurable!  Any changes made to this
#        script will be overwritten when you upgrade to the next
#        release of HP-UX.
#

#
# vphbd startup: Startup and kill script for the virtual partition
#                heartbeat daemon
#

PATH=/sbin:/usr/sbin:/usr/bin
export PATH

if [ -r /etc/rc.config.d/vparhb ]
then . /etc/rc.config.d/vparhb
fi

case "$1" in

    'start_msg') echo "Starting Virtual Partition Heartbeat Daemon" ;;

    'start')
            vphbd -d "${VPHBD_DELAY-10}" -p "${VPHBD_PID_FILE-/var/run/vphbd.pid}"
            exit $?
            ;;

    'stop_msg') echo "Stopping Virtual Partition Heartbeat Daemon" ;;

    'stop')
            [ ! -r "${VPHBD_PID_FILE=/var/run/vphbd.pid}" ] && exit 2
            pid=`cat "$VPHBD_PID_FILE"`
            [ "$pid" -le "0" ] && exit 1
            kill "$pid"
            rm -f "$VPHBD_PID_FILE"
            exit 0
            ;;

    *)
            echo "Usage: $0 { start | start_msg | stop | stop_msg }"
            ;;

esac

exit 0
#
```

Note that all of the *start* and *stop* information related to the *heartbeat* daemon is present in this file because this script is run for both *kill* (*K*) and *start* (*S*.)

The vPar-specific startup and shutdown setup, such as the *heartbeat* daemon we just covered, are automatically performed for you when vPars software is installed. Your application-related startup configuration must be performed on each vPar just as it would on separate servers.

The remainder of this chapter covers background information related to startup and shutdown of vPars.

Non-vPar Specific-Section of Chapter - Introduction

A variety of topics related to startup and shutdown scripts are covered in this chapter, including:

- The overall organization of the startup and shutdown mechanism in HP-UX
- Example of a startup file
- **/etc/inittab** file
- **shutdown** command

System Startup and Shutdown Scripts

Startup and shutdown scripts for HP-UX 11.x are based on a mechanism that separates the actual startup and shutdown scripts from configuration information. In order to modify the way your system starts or stops, you don't have to modify scripts, which in general is considered somewhat risky; you can, instead, modify configuration variables. The startup and shutdown sequence is based on an industry standard that is similar to many other UNIX-based systems, so your knowledge of HP-UX applies to many other systems.

Startup and shutdown are going to become increasingly more important to you as your system administration work becomes more sophisticated. As you load and customize more applications, you will need more startup and shutdown knowledge. What I do in this section is give you an overview of startup and shutdown and the commands you can use to control your system.

The following components are in the startup and shutdown model:

Execution Scripts

Execution scripts read variables from configuration variable files and run through the startup or shutdown sequence. These scripts are located in **/sbin/init.d**.

Configuration Variable Scripts

These are the files you would modify to set variables that are used to enable or disable a subsystem or perform some other function at the time of system startup or shutdown. These are located in **/etc/rc.config.d**.

Link Files

These files are used to control the order in which scripts execute. These are actually links to execution scripts to be executed when moving from one run level to another. These files are located in the directory for the appropriate run level, such as **/sbin/rc0.d** for run level 0, **/sbin/rc1.d** for run level 1, and so on.

Sequencer Script

This script invokes execution scripts based on run-level transition. This script is located in /**sbin/rc**.

Figure 8-1 shows the directory structure for startup and shutdown scripts.

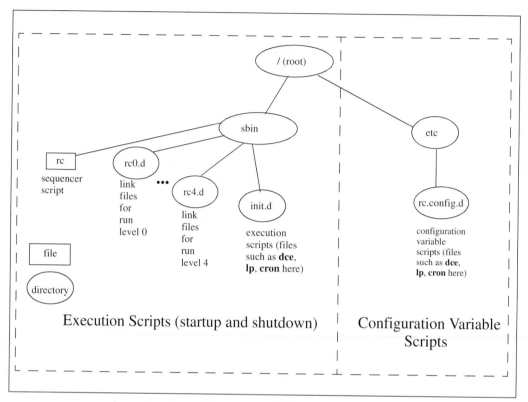

Figure 8-1 Organization of Startup and Shutdown Files

Execution scripts perform startup and shutdown tasks. **/sbin/rc** invokes the execution script with the appropriate start or stop arguments, and you can view the appropriate start or stop messages on the console. The messages you see will have one of the three following values:

OK   This indicates that the execution script started or shut down properly.

FAIL   A problem occurred at startup or shutdown.

N/A   The script was not configured to start.

In order to start up a subsystem, you would simply edit the appropriate configuration file in **/etc/rc.config.d**.

Let's take a look at an example startup and shutdown file for an application loaded onto an HP-UX system that is widely used for Internet applications called Cold Fusion. Like many applications loaded on HP-UX systems, Cold Fusion installs startup and shutdown scripts as a standard part of the installation of the product.

As mentioned earlier, the script used as part of the startup and shutdown process is in **/etc/init.d**. In our case, the name of the program is **/etc/init.d/coldfusion** and is shown in the following listing:

```
# cat /sbin/init.d/coldfusion
#!/bin/sh
#
# Start the Cold Fusion servers
#

# set at install
CFHOME=/apps/coldfusion
CFBIN=$CFHOME/bin

export CFHOME

#
# Start/stop processes for Cold Fusion
#

rval=0

case "$1" in

    start_msg)
        print "Starting ColdFusion Application Server"
        ;;

    stop_msg)
        print "Stopping ColdFusion Application Server"
        ;;

    'start')
        #First, check "on/off switch", to set CF_AUTOSTART, in config.d file.
        RCFILE=/etc/rc.config.d/coldfusion
        if [ -f $RCFILE ] ; then
                . $RCFILE
        else
                print "Warning: $RCFILE defaults file missing."
                print "         Starting ColdFusion by default."
                CF_AUTOSTART=1
        fi

        # Start CF if switch is on.
        if [ "$CF_AUTOSTART" -eq 1 ]; then
            if [ -x $CFBIN/start ]; then
                $CFBIN/start
                rval=$?
            else
                print "Error: ColdFusion startup script $CFBIN/start missing."
                print "         ColdFusion not started."
                rval=1
            fi
        else
            print "Notice: ColdFusion startup disabled in $RCFILE"
            rval=2
        fi
        ;;
```

```
        'stop')
            if [ -x $CFBIN/stop ]; then
                    $CFBIN/stop -force
            fi
            ;;

    *)
            echo "Usage: $0 { start | stop }"
            rval=1
            ;;
esac

exit $rval

#
```

The startup and shutdown scripts in **/etc/init.d** generally perform both startup and shutdown functions. The startup and shutdown scripts, including the one in our example, recognize the following four arguments:

- *start_msg* - This is an argument passed to scripts so that the script can report a message indicating what the "start" action will do.
- *stop_msg* - This is an argument passed to scripts so that the script can report a message indicating what the "stop" action will do.
- *start* - The script will start the application.
- *stop* - The script will shut down the application.

All startup and shutdown scripts, including the one in the preceding listing, obtain configuration data from variables in **/etc/rc.config.d**. Our example script checks the value of the "on/off" switch in **/etc/rc.confi.d/ coldfusion**, which is shown in the following listing to determine if Cold Fusion should be started:

```
# cat /etc/rc.config.d/coldfusion
# ColdFusion Application Server configuration file
#
CF_AUTOSTART=1  #Set to 1 to restart at boot time

#
```

The variable in this file is set to *one,* so the application will start at the time of system boot.

Startup and shutdown scripts are run based on the directory in which a link to the script appears. Our example script should be started at run level *three*. Therefore, a link to the script appears in the directory **/sbin/rc3.d**, shown as the third link in the following listing:

```
# ls -l /sbin/rc3.d
total 0
lrwxr-xr-x  1 root      sys     23 Apr 26 14:32 S100nfs.server -> /sbin/init.d/nfs.server
lrwxr-xr-x  1 root      sys     19 Apr 26 14:52 S200tps.rc -> /sbin/init.d/tps.rc
lrwxrwxrwx  1 root      sys     20 May 16 20:57 S790coldfusion -> ../init.d/coldfusion
lrwxr-xr-x  1 root      sys     23 Apr 26 14:44 S990dtlogin.rc -> /sbin/init.d/dtlogin.rc
#
```

We'll get to the significance of the naming of the link shortly. For the time being, it is sufficient to know that a link called **/sbin/rc3.d/ S790coldfusion** points to our script **/init.d/coldfusion**.

Applications are shut down in the opposite order from which they were started. This means that a link to the startup and shutdown script will appear in a lower-level directory for shutdown. In our example, the startup link appears in **/sbin/rc3.d** but the shutdown link appears in **/etc/rc1.d**, as shown in the following listing:

```
# ls -l /sbin/rc1.d

lrwxr-xr-x  1 root      sys     17 Apr 26 14:52 K220slsd -> /sbin/init.d/slsd
lrwxr-xr-x  1 root      sys     18 Apr 26 14:45 K230audio -> /sbin/init.d/audio
lrwxr-xr-x  1 root      sys     21 Apr 26 14:46 K240auditing -> /sbin/init.d/auditing
lrwxr-xr-x  1 root      sys     17 Apr 26 14:43 K250envd -> /sbin/init.d/envd
lrwxr-xr-x  1 root      sys     17 Apr 26 14:43 K270cron -> /sbin/init.d/cron
lrwxr-xr-x  1 root      sys     15 Apr 26 14:45 K278pd -> /sbin/init.d/pd
lrwxr-xr-x  1 root      sys     15 Apr 26 14:45 K280lp -> /sbin/init.d/lp
lrwxr-xr-x  1 root      sys     21 Apr 26 14:49 K290hparamgr -> /sbin/init.d/hparamgr
lrwxr-xr-x  1 root      sys     20 Apr 26 14:43 K290hparray -> /sbin/init.d/hparray
lrwxrwxrwx  1 root      sys     20 May 16 20:57 K300coldfusion -> ../init.d/coldfusion
                 .
                 .
                 .
```

The link called **/sbin/rc3.d/K300coldfusion** points to our script **/init.d/ coldfusion**. Startup for this application takes place at run level 3, and shutdown takes place at run level 1.

There is significance associated with the names of the links shown in the preceding two listings. Let's take a look at the startup link in our example:

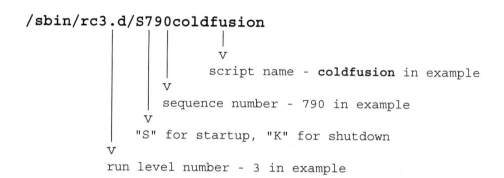

```
/sbin/rc3.d/S790coldfusion
        |  |||        |
        |  |||        V
        |  |||           script name - coldfusion in example
        |  ||V
        |  || sequence number - 790 in example
        |  |V
        |  | "S" for startup, "K" for shutdown
        |  V
        V  run level number - 3 in example
```

This example is for our Cold Fusion startup script. Startup links begin with an "S" for startup. The shutdown script has a similar entry in **/sbin/ rc1.d**, but it has a "K" as the first character of the link name to indicate kill.

Scripts are executed in lexicographical order. Gaps are left between startup scripts at a given run level and between shutdown scripts at a given run level, so when additional scripts are added, you don't have to renumber any existing scripts within a run level.

Because applications are shut down in the opposite order in which they are started, shutdown scripts do not usually have the same numbers as their startup counterparts. Two applications that start in a given order due to dependencies will usually be shut down in the opposite order in which they were started. In our example, the startup number is *S790coldfusion* and the shutdown number is *K300coldfusion*.

Scripts are run when there is a change in run level. **/sbin/rc** is a program that is run whenever there is a change in run level. The following listing shows **/etc/inittab**, which invokes **/sbin/rc** on the system used in our example:

```
init:3:initdefault:
ioin::sysinit:/sbin/ioinitrc >/dev/console 2>&1
tape::sysinit:/sbin/mtinit > /dev/console 2>&1
muxi::sysinit:/sbin/dasetup    </dev/console >/dev/console 2>&1 # mux init
stty::sysinit:/sbin/stty 9600 clocal icanon echo opost onlcr ixon icrnl ignpar </dev/
systty
brc1::bootwait:/sbin/bcheckrc </dev/console >/dev/console 2>&1 # fsck, etc.
link::wait:/sbin/sh -c "/sbin/rm -f /dev/syscon; \
```

```
                        /sbin/ln /dev/systty /dev/syscon" >/dev/console 2>&1
cprt::bootwait:/sbin/cat /etc/copyright >/dev/syscon           # legal req
sqnc::wait:/sbin/rc </dev/console >/dev/console 2>&1           # system init
#powf::powerwait:/sbin/powerfail >/dev/console 2>&1            # powerfail
cons:123456:respawn:/usr/sbin/getty console console           # system console
#ttp1:234:respawn:/usr/sbin/getty -h tty0p1 9600
#ttp2:234:respawn:/usr/sbin/getty -h tty0p2 9600
#ttp3:234:respawn:/usr/sbin/getty -h tty0p3 9600
#ttp4:234:respawn:/usr/sbin/getty -h tty0p4 9600
#ttp5:234:respawn:/usr/sbin/getty -h tty0p5 9600
#ups::respawn:rtprio 0 /usr/lbin/ups_mond -f /etc/ups_conf
```

The **/sbin/rc** line is always present in the **/etc/inittab** file. There is more information about **/etc/inittab** coming shortly.

If you are booting your system to run level 3, then **/sbin/rc** will run the startup scripts present in **/sbin/rc1.d**, **/sbin/rc2.d**, and **/sbin/rc3.d**.

I have mentioned run levels several times in this discussion. Both the startup and shutdown scripts described here, as well as the **/etc/inittab** file, depend on run levels. In HP-UX 11.x, the following run levels exist:

0	Halted run level.
s	Run level s, also known as single-user mode, is used to ensure that no one else is on the system so you can proceed with system administration tasks.
1	Run level 1 starts various basic processes.
2	Run level 2 allows users to access the system. This is also known as multi-user mode.
3	Run level 3 is for exporting NFS file systems.
4	Run level 4 starts the graphical manager, including HP Common Desktop Environment (HP CDE).
5 and 6	Not currently used.

/etc/inittab is also used to define a variety of processes that will be run, and it is used by **/sbin/init**. The **/sbin/init** process ID is 1. It is the first process started on your system and it has no parent. The **init** process looks at /etc/inittab to determine the run level of the system.

Entries in the **/etc/inittab** file have the following format:

id:run state:action:process

id	The name of the entry. The id is up to four characters long and must be unique in the file. If the line in **/etc/inittab** is preceded by a "#", the entry is treated as a comment.
run state	Specifies the run level at which the command is executed. More than one run level can be specified. The command is executed for every run level specified.
action	Defines which of 11 actions will be taken with this process. The 11 choices for action are: *initdefault, sysinit, boot, bootwait, wait, respawn, once, powerfail, powerwait, ondemand,* and *off.*
process	The shell command to be executed *if* the run level and/or action field so indicates.

Here is an example of an **/etc/inittab** entry:

```
cons:123456:respawn:/usr/sbin/getty   console console
  |    |            |                   |
  |    |            |               |> process
  |    |            |> action
  |    |> run state
  |> id
```

This is in the **/etc/inittab** file, as opposed to being defined as a startup script, because the console may be killed and have to be restarted whenever it dies, even if no change has occurred in run level. **respawn** starts a process if it does not exist and restarts the process after it dies. This entry shows all run states, since you want the console to be activated at all times.

Another example is the first line from **/etc/inittab**:

init:3:initdefault:

The default run level of the system is defined as *3*.

The basics of system startup and shutdown described here are important to understand. You will be starting up and shutting down your system and possibly even modifying some of the files described here. Please take a close look at the startup and shutdown files before you begin to modify them.

Now let's take a look at the commands you can issue to shut down your system.

System Shutdown

What does it mean to shut down the system? Well, in its simplest form, a shutdown of the system simply means issuing the **/sbin/shutdown** command. The **shutdown** command is used to terminate all processing. It has many options, including the following:

-r	Automatically reboots the system; that is, brings it down and brings it up.
-h	Halts the system completely.
-y	Completes the shutdown without asking you any questions that it would normally ask.
grace	Specifies the number of seconds you wish to wait before the system is shut down, in order to give your users time to save files, quit applications, and log out.

Here are some of the things your system does when you issue the **shutdown** command:

- Checks to see whether the user who executed **shutdown** does indeed have permission to execute the command.

- Changes the working directory to root (/).

- Sets *PATH* to **/usr/bin/:/usr/sbin:/sbin**.

- Updates all superblocks.

- Informs users that a **shutdown** has been issued and asks them to log out.

- Executes **/sbin/rc,** which does such things as shut down subsystems via shutdown scripts such as the spooler and CDE, unmount file systems and other such tasks.

- Runs **/sbin/reboot** if the *-r* option is used.

To shut down and automatically reboot the system, you would type:

```
$ shutdown -r
```

To halt the system, you would type:

```
$ shutdown -h
```

You will be asked whether you want to type a message to users, informing them of the impending system shutdown. After you type the message, it is immediately sent to all users. After the specified time elapses (60 seconds is the default), the system begins the shutdown process. Once you receive a message that the system is halted, you can power off all your system components.

To shut down the system in two minutes without being asked any questions or sending any message, type:

```
$ shutdown -h -y 120
```

At times, you will need to go into single-user mode with **shutdown** to perform some task such as a backup or to expand a logical volume, and then reboot the system to return it to its original state.

To shut down the system into single-user mode, you would type:

```
$ shutdown
```

The **shutdown** command with no options puts you into single-user mode. On older versions of the operating system, you could go to single-user mode by using the **init** command with the *s* option (**init s**). However, this is highly discouraged because this command does not terminate other system activity nor does it log users off; therefore, it does not result in a true single-user state.

If the system is already in single-user mode or you like to live dangerously, you can execute **/usr/sbin/reboot**. I strongly suggest that you issue **shutdown,** which will call **reboot**. The **reboot** command abruptly terminates all processes and then halts or reboots the system. Also, with dynamically loadable kernel modules, **reboot** will not load these modules; only **shutdown** will.

Again, I recommend using the **shutdown** command, not **reboot**.

CHAPTER 9

File Systems

Virtual Partition File Systems

Every Virtual Partition has its own full HP-UX file system, just as you would have separate file systems on individual servers. The file systems work completely independently of one another. If you wanted to share file system information between two vPars, you would use the same method you use to share file system information between servers, such as Network File System (NFS). This complete independence of file systems of different vPars ensures the full software isolation of vPars.

In the upcoming section we'll cover some vPars file-system-related topics and then file-system background in the non-vPars specific part of this chapter.

Separate vPars File Systems

The file systems for vPars will differ on two different vPars just as they would differ on two different servers. This means that the disk space consumed by two vPars running on one server may very well be twice the disk space consumed by one standard HP-UX running on the same server. Each of the two vPars require their own operating system, applications, user home directories, and so on. This may double your storage requirements since none of the files ystems are shared beyond the NFS file systems that would normally be shared in a networked environment. Let's take a look at the file systems running on two different vPars.

The following is a **bdf** run on the first vPar running on a server (hostname *actappd1:*)

```
# hostname
actappd1
# bdf
Filesystem          kbytes     used    avail %used Mounted on
/dev/vg00/lvol3     245760    40769   192184   18% /
/dev/vg00/lvol1     111637    74350    26123   74% /stand
/dev/vg00/lvol8    1732608   598033  1063751   36% /var
/dev/vg00/lvol7    1732608   755560   915987   45% /usr
/dev/vg00/u001     1228800   466878   714321   40% /u001
/dev/vg00/lvol4     258048    69857   176476   28% /tmp
/dev/vg00/lvol6    1531904  1381306   141226   91% /opt
/dev/vg00/lvol5     819200   176005   603031   23% /home
#
```

This listing shows *vg00*, the only volume group configured on the system, and the capacity setup in each logical volume.

Next is a **bdf** run on the second vPar running on a server (hostname *ecvpard2:*)

```
# hostname
actappd1
# bdf
Filesystem          kbytes     used    avail %used Mounted on
/dev/vg00/lvol3     143360    43174    93951   31% /
/dev/vg00/lvol1     111637    73632    26841   73% /stand
/dev/vg00/lvol8    1536000   965183   535326   64% /var
/dev/vg00/lvol7    1593344   740643   799434   48% /usr
/dev/vg00/lvol4     258048    68619   177641   28% /tmp
/dev/vg00/lvol6    2084864   563709  1426107   28% /opt
/dev/vg00/lvol5     819200     1314   766771    0% /home
#
```

You can see from these two listings that the space consumed by the two *vg00* volume groups is roughly twice the space that would be consumed without vPars running. You may very well get twice the work done on this

server by running two vPars, so this is probably disk space well spent; however; you need to think about the space being consumed as part of your planning.

The first vPar we listed earlier also has several applications running on
it. One is Broadvision, which requires its own directory under **/opt/bv1to1**
as shown in the following listing:

```
# hostname
actappd1
# ll /opt
total 32
dr-xr-xr-x    7 bin     bin         96 Jul 13 15:27 Migration
dr-xr-xr-x    9 bin     bin       1024 Jul 13 15:26 OV
drwxrwxr-x   18 bin     bin       1024 Jul 13 15:23 apache
dr-xr-xr-x    6 bin     bin         96 Jul 13 15:12 asx
dr-xr-xr-x    6 bin     bin         96 Jul 13 15:24 audio
drwxr-xr-x   22 root    bin       1024 Sep 21 13:34 bv1to1
drwxr-xr-x    8 root    users     1024 Jul 13 15:26 cifsclient
dr-xr-xr-x    4 bin     bin         96 Jul 13 15:26 cmcluster
dr-xr-xr-x    4 bin     bin         96 Jul 13 15:25 cmom
dr-xr-xr-x   10 bin     bin       1024 Jul 13 15:10 dce
dr-xr-xr-x    4 bin     bin       1024 Jul 13 15:35 dcelocal
dr-xr-xr-x    4 bin     bin         96 Jul 13 15:13 dmi
dr-xr-xr-x    4 bin     bin         96 Jul 13 15:11 fcms
dr-xr-xr-x    3 bin     bin         96 Jul 13 15:17 graphics
dr-xr-xr-x    4 bin     bin         96 Jul 13 15:08 hparray
dr-xr-xr-x    3 bin     bin         96 Jul 13 15:14 ifor
dr-xr-xr-x   16 bin     bin       1024 Jul 19 15:03 ignite
dr-xr-xr-x    3 bin     bin         96 Jul 13 15:14 image
drwxr-xr-x    4 bin     bin         96 Jul 13 15:25 java1.2
drwxrwxrwx    7 bin     bin       1024 Aug 24 16:34 java1.3
drwxr-xr-x    2 root    root        96 Jul 13 15:04 lost+found
drwxr-xr-x    7 root    sys         96 Aug 24 17:26 make
drwxr-xr-x    8 root    sys       1024 Jul 13 15:27 mx
dr-xr-xr-x    9 bin     bin       1024 Jul 13 15:26 netscape
dr-xr-xr-x    7 bin     bin         96 Jul 13 15:09 nettladm
dr-xr-xr-x    2 bin     bin         96 Jul 13 15:11 networkdocs
dr-xr-xr-x    4 bin     bin         96 Jul 13 15:16 parmgr
dr-xr-xr-x    7 bin     bin         96 Jul 13 15:13 pd
dr-xr-xr-x   12 root    bin       1024 Jul 13 15:25 perf
dr-xr-xr-x    9 bin     bin       1024 Jul 13 15:26 prm
dr-xr-xr-x    4 bin     bin         96 Jul 13 15:11 raid4si
dr-xr-xr-x    6 bin     bin         96 Jul 13 15:12 resmon
drwxr-xr-x   10 root    users     1024 Jul 13 15:25 samba
drwxr-xr-x    3 root    users       96 Jul 13 15:24 samba_src
dr-xr-xr-x    8 bin     bin       1024 Jul 13 15:16 scr
drwxr-xr-x    3 root    bin         96 Aug 24 13:42 tivoli
drwxrwxr-x   11 bin     bin       1024 Jul 13 15:24 tomcat
dr-xr-xr-x    5 bin     bin         96 Jul 13 15:10 upgrade
dr-xr-xr-x    4 bin     bin         96 Jul 13 15:25 video
dr-xr-xr-x    6 bin     bin         96 Jul 13 15:26 webadmin
drwxr-xr-x   10 bin     bin       1024 Jul 13 15:27 wlm
#
```

The **bv1to1** directory is the directory in which the Broadvision application is loaded. This directory will appear on every vPar on which Broadvision is to be run. The following listing shows the capacity consumed by each directory under **/opt** with the **du** command:

```
# hostname
actappd1
# cd /opt
# hostname
actappd1
# pwd
/opt
# du -s *
13842    Migration
80456    OV
57604    apache
250      asx
1912     audio
1402052  bv1to1              <-- Broadvision directory
5072     cifsclient
2304     cmcluster
4720     cmom
22214    dce
2        dcelocal
446      dmi
296      fcms
620      graphics
44848    hparray
28708    ifor
146206   ignite
2064     image
136598   java1.2
136910   java1.3
0        lost+found
2386     make
53634    mx
54444    netscape
1292     nettladm
512      networkdocs
1076     parmgr
35770    pd
216234   perf
112774   prm
2182     raid4si
850      resmon
26874    samba
10514    samba_src
8648     scr
87810    tivoli
8628     tomcat
1998     upgrade
1272     video
28684    webadmin
5908     wlm
#
```

This application will be loaded in every vPar in which it is to be run and consume the disk space associated with it. This is true for all applications.

Issuing **swlist** on this vPar shows all applications that have been loaded on it, including vPars software and the Broadvision application:

```
# swlist
# Initializing...
# Contacting target "actappd1"...
#
# Target:  actappd1:/
#

#
# Bundle(s):
#

  B9788AA                          1.3.0.01        Java 2 SDK 1.3 for HP-UX (700/800),
                                                   PA1.1 + PA2.0 Add On
  BUNDLE11i                        B.11.11.0102.2 Required Patch Bundle for HP-UX 11i
  CDE-English                      B.11.11         English CDE Environment
  FDDI-00               B.11.11.01     PCI FDDI;Supptd HW=A3739A/A3739B;SW=J3626AA
  FibrChanl-00                     B.11.11.06      PCI/HSC FibreChannel;
                                                   Supptd HW=A6684A,A6685A,A5158A
  GOLDAPPS11i                      B.11.11.0106.9 Gold Applications Patches
                                                   for HP-UX 11i, June 2001
  GOLDBASE11i           B.11.11.0106.9 Gold Base Patches for HP-UX 11i, June 2001
  GigEther-00                      B.11.11.14      PCI/HSC GigEther;Supptd
                                       HW=A4926A/A4929A/A4924A/A4925A;SW=J1642AA
  HPUX11i-OE-MC                    B.11.11.0106    HP-UX Mission Critical
                                                   Operating Environment Component
  HPUXBase64                       B.11.11         HP-UX 64-bit Base OS
  HPUXBaseAux                      B.11.11.0106    HP-UX Base OS Auxiliary
  HWEnable11i                      B.11.11.0106.8 Hardware Enablement Patches for
                                                   HP-UX 11i, June 2001
  IUX-Recovery                     B.3.3.116       Ignite-UX network recovery tool subset
  J4258BA                          B.04.13         Netscape Directory Server v4 for HP-UX
  OnlineDiag                       B.11.11.04     HPUX 11.11 Support Tools Bundle, Jun 2001
  RAID-00                          B.11.11.01      PCI RAID; Supptd HW=A5856A
#
# Product(s) not contained in a Bundle:
#

  BVSN1to1                         6.0             BroadVision One-To-One Enterprise
  BVSN6-0AA             6.0             BroadVision One-To-One Enterprise 6.0 Patch AA
  BVSNCommerceB2BMKT               6.0.0           BroadVision 1:1 Business-To-
                                                   Business Contract Utility Installation
  BVSNTradingConnector             6.0.0          BroadVision 1:1 Adapter TradingConnector
                                                   Application Installation
  BVSNb2b                          6.0.0           BroadVision 1:1 Commerce Business-To-
                                                   Business Installation
  BVSNb2bAA                        6.0.0-AA        BroadVision 1:1 Commerce Business
                                                   Commerce Patch AA Installation
  BVSNcwa              6.0.0           BroadVision 1:1 Core Commerce Base Installation
  BVSNcwaAA                        6.0.0-AA        BroadVision 1:1 Core Commerce Patch AA
                                                   Installation
  BVSNcwaAB                        6.0.0-AB        BroadVision 1:1 Core Commerce Patch
                                                   AB Installation
  BVSNverity261                    2.6.1           Verity v2.6.1 Developer Kit
  PHCO_23578                       1.0             Software Distributor Cumulative Patch
  PHCO_24625                       1.0             Virtual Partitions manpages cumul patch
  PHKL_24546                       1.0             vPar enablement patch
  PHKL_24547                       1.0             vPar enablement patch
  PHKL_24548                       1.0             vPar enablement patch
  PHKL_24549                       1.0             vPar enablement patch
  PHKL_24550              1.0             early boot panic, Psets & vPar enablement
  PHKL_24551              1.0             thread nostop, vPar, Psets, load averages
  PHKL_24552                       1.0             vPar enablement patch
```

```
PHKL_24553              1.0              console, chassis code, crash/dump, vPar
PHKL_24554              1.0                 vPar enablement patch
PHKL_24555              1.0                 PREFETCH_LOCK I/O, PA 8700 2.2, vPar
PHKL_24556              1.0                 vPar enablement patch
PHKL_24557              1.0                 vPar enablement patch
PHKL_24558              1.0                 vPar enablement patch
PHKL_24559              1.0              Syslog overflow, high temp alerts, vPar
PHKL_24560              1.0                 vPar enablement patch
PHKL_24561              1.0                 Psets & vPar Enablement
PHKL_24562              1.0                 vPar enablement patch
PHKL_24563              1.0                 vPar enablement patch
PHKL_24564              1.0                 vPar enablement patch
PHKL_24565              1.0                 vPar Enablement patch
PHKL_24566              1.0              Kernel Memory allocation, Psets Enablement
PHKL_24570              1.0                 Boot hang, Psets & vPar enablement
PHKL_24582              1.0                 iCOD Support, Psets Enablement Patch
PHKL_24585              1.0                 Psets & vPar enablement patch
PHKL_24960              1.0                 vPar enablement patch
PHKL_25080              1.0                 vPar enablement patch
PHNE_23715             1.0                 Cumulative STREAMS Patch
PHSS_22535              1.0              ld(1) and linker tools cumulative patch
TIVsm                   4.1.2               Tivoli Storage Manager
VirtualPartition        A.01.00.08      HP-UX Virtual Partitions Functionality
make                    3.79.1              make
#
```

The revision of *VirtualPartition* software you see on your system will be later than that shown in the example.

Maintaining additional HP-UX file systems, which is probably going to be the case when you run vPars, requires you to think about the additional disk space required as well as techniques to ensure that your systems run smoothly such as recovery and operating system and application updates. Be sure to have a current inventory of your systems and perform backups and create bootable recovery tapes often.

Non-vPar-Specific Section of Chapter: Introduction

In this section of the chapter we'll focus on the following:

- Veritas Volume Manager overview

- Logical Volume Manager (LVM) - You will probably be using LVM to manange the data on your system. I provide LVM background in this section.

- Example of adding XP 256 disks to your system using LVM.

- Example of Using LVM to Reconfigure Disks - I include an example of a complex disk reconfiguration performed on a real system to show how many LVM commands are used. Although this disk reconfiguration may not be required on your system(s), it is a good example of using LVM commands.

- Some additional file-system commands.

Veritas Volume Manager

New to HP-UX 11i is the Veritas Volume Manager, which is bundled with the operating system.

Unlike Logical Volume Manager, most of the work you perform with Vertias Volume Manager is performed through the Java-based graphical interface. The examples in this section all use the graphical interface to introduce you to Veritas Volume Manager.

Logical Volume Manager Background

Logical Volume Manager is a disk management subsystem that allows you to manage physical disks as logical volumes. This means that a file system can span multiple physical disks. You can view Logical Volume Manager as a flexible way of defining boundaries of disk space that are independent of one another. Not only can you specify the size of a logical volume, but you can also change its size if the need arises. This possibility is a great advancement over dedicating a disk to a files ystem or having fixed-size partitions on a disk. Logical volumes can hold file systems, raw data, or swap space. You can now specify a logical volume to be any size you wish, have logical volumes that span multiple physical disks, and then change the size of the logical volume if you need to do so!

So what do you need to know in order to set up Logical Volume Manager and realize all these great benefits? First, you need to know the terminology, and second, you need to know Logical Volume Manager commands. As with many other system administration tasks, you can use SAM to set up Logical Volume Manager for you. In fact, I recommend that you use SAM to set up Logical Volume Manager on your system(s). But, as usual, I recommend that you read this overview and at least understand the basics of Logical Volume Manager before you use SAM to set up Logical Volume Manager on your system. The SAM chapter (Chapter 11) has an example of using SAM to create logical volumes. After reading this section, you may want to take a quick look at that example.

For use with the Journaled Filesystem (JFS), Hewlett-Packard has an add-on product called HP OnLineJFS. This handy product allows you to perform many of the LVM functions without going into single-user mode. For example, when a filesystem needs to be expanded, the logical volume on which it resides needs to be unmounted before the expansion takes place. Normally, that unmounting would mean shutting the system down into single-user mode so that no user or process could access the volume and it could then be unmounted. With OnLineJFS, the logical volumes and file systems are simply expanded with the system up and running and no interruption to users or processes.

Logical Volume Manager Terms

The following terms are used when working with Logical Volume Manager. They are only some of the terms associated with Logical Volume Manager, but they are enough for you to get started with Logical Volume Manager. You can work with Logical Volume Manager without knowing all these terms if you use SAM. It is a good idea, however, to read the following brief overview of these terms if you plan to use Logical Volume Manager, so you have some idea of what SAM is doing for you.

Volume   A volume is a device used for a file system, swap, or raw data. Without Logical Volume Manager, a volume would be either a disk partition or an entire disk drive.

Physical Volume

A disk that has been not been initialized for use by Logical Volume Manager. An entire disk must be initialized if it is to be used by Logical Volume Manager; that is, you can't initialize only part of a disk for Logical Volume Manager use and the rest for fixed partitioning.

Volume Group   A volume group is a collection of logical volumes that are managed by Logical Volume Manager. You would typically define which disks on your system are going to be used by Logical Volume Manager and then define how you wish to group these into volume groups. Each individual disk may be a volume group, or more than one disk may form a volume group. At this point, you have created a pool of disk space called a *volume group*. A disk can belong to only one volume group. A volume group may span multiple physical disks.

Logical Volume This is space that is defined within a volume group. A volume group is divided up into logical volumes. This is like a disk partition, which is of a fixed size, but you have the flexibility to change its size. A logical volume is contained within a volume group, but the volume group may span multiple physical disks. You can have a logical volume that is bigger than a single disk.

Physical Extent A set of contiguous disk blocks on a physical volume. If you define a disk to be a physical volume, then the contiguous blocks within that disk form a physical extent. Logical Volume Manager uses the physical extent as the unit for allocating disk space to logical volumes. If you use a small physical extent size, such as 1 MByte, then you have a fine granularity for defining logical volumes. If you use a large physical extent size such as 256 MBytes, then you have a coarse granularity for defining logical volumes. The default size is 4 MBytes.

Logical Extent   A logical volume is a set of logical extents. Logical extents and physical extents are the same size within a volume group. Although logical and physical extents are the same size, this doesn't mean that two logical extents will map to two contiguous physical extents. It may be that you have two logical extents that end up being mapped to physical extents on different disks!

Figure 9-1 graphically depicts some of the logical volume terms we just covered. In this diagram, you can see clearly that logical extents are not mapped to contiguous physical extents, because some of the physical extents are not used.

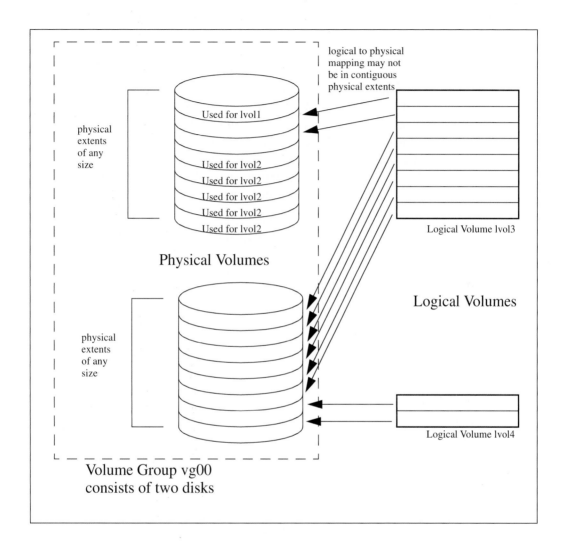

Figure 9-1 Logical Volume Manager Partial Logical to Physical Mapping

Disk Mirroring

Logical volumes can be mirrored one or more times, creating an identical image of the logical volume. This means that a logical extent can map to more than one physical extent if mirrored.

You may have an environment where you wish to mirror some or all of the logical volumes. SAM can be used to set up disk mirroring for you. You must first, however, decide the characteristics of your mirroring. There is a mirroring policy called "strict." You define one of the following three strict policies when you create the logical volume using the following options:

n	<u>N</u>o, this is not a strict allocation policy, meaning that mirrored copies of a logical extent can share the same physical volume. This means that your original data and mirrored data may indeed be on the same physical disk. If you encounter a disk mechanism problem of some type, you may lose both your original and mirrored data.
y	<u>Y</u>es, this is a strict allocation policy, meaning that mirrored copies of a logical extent may not share the same physical volume. This is safer than allowing mirrored copies of data to share the same physical volume. If you have a problem with a disk in this scenario, you are guaranteed that your original data is on a different physical disk from your mirrored data. Original data and mirrored data are always part of the same volume group even if you want them on different physical volumes.
g	Mirrored data will not be on the same Physical Volume Group (PVG) as the original data. This policy is called a PVG-strict allocation policy.

The strict allocation policy depends on your environment. Most installations that employ mirroring buy sufficient disk drives to mirror all data. In an environment such as this, I would create two volume groups, one for the original data and one for the mirrored data, and use the "strict -g" option when creating logical volumes so that the original data is on one volume group and the mirrored data on the other.

Logical Volume Manager Commands

The following are definitions of some of the more common Logical Volume Manager Commands. Many of these commands are found in the log file that SAM creates when setting up logical volumes for you. I am giving a description of these commands here so that when you see them, you'll have an idea of each command's use. Although these are not all of the Logical Volume Manager commands, these are the ones I use most often and are the commands you should have knowledge of when using Logical Volume Manager. The commands are grouped by physical volume (pv) commands, volume group (vg) commands, and logical volume (lv) commands. These commands are found in the manual pages. Some of the commands such as **vgdisplay**, **pvdisplay**, and **lvdisplay**, were issued so that you could see examples of these. The following output of **bdf** will be helpful to you when you view the output of Logical Volume Manager commands that are issued. The output of **bdf** shows several logical volumes mounted (**lvol1, lvol3, lvol4, lvol5, lvol6, lvol7, lvol8**), all of which are in volume group **vg00** (see the **bdf** command overview later in this chapter).

$ **bdf**

Files system	Kbytes	used	avail	%used	Mounted on
/dev/vg00/lvol3	47829	18428	24618	43%	/
/dev/vg00/lvol1	67733	24736	36223	41	/stand
/dev/vg00/lvol8	34541	8673	22413	28%	/var
/dev/vg00/lvol7	299157	149449	119792	56%	/usr
/dev/vg00/lvol4	23013	48	20663	0%	/tmp
/dev/vg00/lvol6	99669	32514	57188	36%	/opt

Files system	Kbytes	used	avail	%used	Mounted on
/dev/vg00/lvol5	19861	9	17865	0%	/home
/dev/dsk/c0t6d0	802212	552120	169870	76%	/mnt/9.x

Physical Volume Commands

pvchange   This command is used to change a physical volume in some way. For example, you may wish to allow additional physical extents to be added to a physical volume if they are not permitted, or prohibit additional physical extents from being added to a physical volume if, indeed, they are allowed.

pvcreate   This command is used to create a physical volume that will be part of a volume group. Remember that a volume group may consist of several physical volumes. The physical volumes are the disks on your system.

pvdisplay   This command shows information about the physical volumes you specify. You can get a lot of information about the logical to physical mapping with this command if you use the verbose (*-v*) option. With *-v* **pvdisplay** will show you the mapping of logical to physical extents for the physical volumes specified.

You get a lot of other useful data from this command, such as the name of the physical volume; the name of the volume group to which the physical volume belongs; the status of the physical volume; the size of physical extents on the physical volume; the total number of physical extents; and the number of free physical extents.

The following is a partial example of running **pvdisplay**:

```
$  pvdisplay -v /dev/dsk/c0t6d0

--- Physical volumes ---
PV Name                  /dev/dsk/c0t1d0
VG Name                  /dev/vg00
PV Status                available
Allocatable              yes
VGDA                     2
Cur LV                   7
PE Size (Mbytes)         4
Total PE                 157
Free PE                  8
Allocated PE             149
Stale PE                 0

    --- Distribution of physical volume ---
    LV Name              LE of LV      PE for LV
    /dev/vg00/lvol1      12            12
    /dev/vg00/lvol2      17            17
    /dev/vg00/lvol6      75            75
    /dev/vg00/lvol7      9             9
    /dev/vg00/lvol4      25            25
    /dev/vg00/lvol5      6             6
    /dev/vg00/lvol3      5             5

    --- Physical extents ---
    PE    Status   LV                    LE
    0000  current  /dev/vg00/lvol1       0000
    0001  current  /dev/vg00/lvol1       0001
    0002  current  /dev/vg00/lvol1       0002
    0003  current  /dev/vg00/lvol1       0003
    0004  current  /dev/vg00/lvol1       0004
    0005  current  /dev/vg00/lvol1       0005
    0006  current  /dev/vg00/lvol1       0006
    0007  current  /dev/vg00/lvol1       0007
    0008  current  /dev/vg00/lvol1       0008
    0009  current  /dev/vg00/lvol1       0009
    0010  current  /dev/vg00/lvol1       0010
    0011  current  /dev/vg00/lvol1       0011
    0012  current  /dev/vg00/lvol2       0000
    0013  current  /dev/vg00/lvol2       0001
    0014  current  /dev/vg00/lvol2       0002
    0015  current  /dev/vg00/lvol2       0003
    0016  current  /dev/vg00/lvol2       0004
```

```
0017 current   /dev/vg00/lvol2        0005
0018 current   /dev/vg00/lvol2        0006
0019 current   /dev/vg00/lvol2        0007
0020 current   /dev/vg00/lvol2        0008
0021 current   /dev/vg00/lvol2        0009
0022 current   /dev/vg00/lvol2        0010
0023 current   /dev/vg00/lvol2        0011
0024 current   /dev/vg00/lvol3        0000
0025 current   /dev/vg00/lvol3        0001
0026 current   /dev/vg00/lvol3        0002
0027 current   /dev/vg00/lvol3        0003
0028 current   /dev/vg00/lvol3        0004
0029 current   /dev/vg00/lvol4        0000
0030 current   /dev/vg00/lvol4        0001
0031 current   /dev/vg00/lvol4        0002
0032 current   /dev/vg00/lvol4        0003
0033 current   /dev/vg00/lvol4        0004
0034 current   /dev/vg00/lvol4        0005
0035 current   /dev/vg00/lvol4        0006


             .
             .
             .

0156 free                             0000
```

From this listing, you can see that *lvol1*, which is roughly 48 MBytes, has many more physical extents assigned to it than *lvol3*, which is roughly 20 MBytes.

pvmove

You can move physical extents from one physical volume to other physical volumes with this command. By specifying the source physical volume and one or more destination physical volumes, you can spread data around to the various physical volumes you wish with this command.

Volume Group Commands

vgcfgbackup   This command is used to save the configuration information for a volume group. Remember that a volume group is made up of one or more physical volumes. SAM automatically runs this command after you make an LVM change.

vgcfgrestore   This command is used to restore the configuration information for a volume group.

vgchange   This command makes a volume group active or inactive. With the -*a* option, you can deactivate (-*a n*) a volume group or activate (-*a y*) a volume group.

vgcreate   You can create a volume group and specify all of its parameters with this command. You specify a volume group name and all of the associated parameters for the volume group when creating it.

vgdisplay   This displays all information related to the volume group if you use the verbose (-*v*) option, including the volume group name; the status of the volume group; the maximum, current, and open logical volumes in the volume group; the maximum, current, and active physical volumes in the volume group; and physical extent-related information.

The following is an example of using **vgdisplay** for the volume group *vg00*:

```
$ vgdisplay /dev/vg00

--- Volume groups ---
VG Name                 /dev/vg00
VG Write Access         read/write
VG Status               available
Max LV                  255
Cur LV                  7
Open LV                 7
Max PV                  16
Cur PV                  1
Act PV                  1
Max PE per PV           2000
VGDA                    2
PE Size (Mbytes)        4
Total PE                157
Alloc PE                149
Free PE                 8
Total PVG               0
```

vgexport   This command removes a logical volume group from the system, but does not modify the logical volume information on the physical volumes. These physical volumes can then be imported to another system using **vgimport.**

vgextend   Physical volumes can be added to a volume group with this command by specifying the physical volume to be added to the volume group.

vgimport   This command can be used to import a physical volume to another system.

vgreduce   The size of a volume group can be reduced with this command, by specifying which physical volume(s) to remove from a volume group. Make sure that the physical volume to be removed has no data on it before doing this.

vgremove	A volume group definition can be completely removed from the system with this command.
vgscan	In the event of a catastrophe of some type, you can use this command to scan your system in an effort to rebuild the **/etc/lvmtab** file.
vgsync	There are times when mirrored data in a volume group becomes "stale" or out-of-date. **vgsync** is used to synchronize the physical extents in each mirrored logical volume in a volume group.

Logical Volume Commands

lvcreate	This command is used to create a new logical volume. A logical volume is created within a volume group. A logical volume may span multiple disks, but must exist within a volume group. SAM will execute this command for you when you create a logical volume using SAM. Many options exist for this command, and two that you would often use are *-L* to define the size of the logical volume and *-n* to define the name of the logical volume.
lvchange	This command is used to change the logical volume in some way. For example, you may wish to change the permission on a logical volume to read-write (w) or read (r) with the *-p* option. Or, you may want to change the strict policy (described under Disk Mirroring) to strict (y), not strict (n), or PVG strict (g).
lvdisplay	This command shows the status and characteristics of every logical volume that you specify. If you use the verbose (*-v*) option of this command,

you get a lot of useful data in many categories, including:

1) Information about the way in which the logical volumes are set up, such as the physical volume on which the logical extents appear; the number of local extents on a physical volume; and the number of physical extents on the physical volume.

2) Detailed information for logical extents, including the logical extent number and some information about the physical volume and physical extent for the logical extent.

The following is an example of **lvdisplay** for the first of the logical volumes (*lvol1*) shown in the earlier **bdf** example:

```
$  lvdisplay -v /dev/vg00/lvol1

--- Logical volumes ---
LV Name                   /dev/vg00/lvol1
VG Name                   /dev/vg00
LV Permission             read/write
LV Status                 available/syncd
Mirror copies             0
Consistency Recovery      MWC
Schedule                  parallel
LV Size (Mbytes)          48
Current LE                12
Allocated PE              12
Stripes                   0
Stripe Size (Kbytes)      0
Bad block                 off
Allocation                strict/contiguous

    --- Distribution of logical volume ---
    PV Name               LE on PV   PE on PV
    /dev/dsk/c0t1d0       12            12

    --- Logical extents ---
    LE    PV1               PE1      Status 1
    0000  /dev/dsk/c0t1d0   0000     current
```

```
0001 /dev/dsk/c0t1d0    0001   current
0002 /dev/dsk/c0t1d0    0002   current
0003 /dev/dsk/c0t1d0    0003   current
0004 /dev/dsk/c0t1d0    0004   current
0005 /dev/dsk/c0t1d0    0005   current
0006 /dev/dsk/c0t1d0    0006   current
0007 /dev/dsk/c0t1d0    0007   current
0008 /dev/dsk/c0t1d0    0008   current
0009 /dev/dsk/c0t1d0    0009   current
0010 /dev/dsk/c0t1d0    0010   current
0011 /dev/dsk/c0t1d0    0011   current
```

Although most of what is shown in this example is self-explanatory, some entries require explanation. The size of the logical volume is 48 MBytes, which consists of 12 Logical Extents (LEs,) and 12 Physical Extents (PE). This means that each physical extent is 4 MBytes in size (4 MBytes x 12 extents = 48 MBytes). We can verify this by running the command to display the characteristics of the physical volume. At the bottom of this listing, you can see the mapping of logical extents onto physical extents. In this case a direct mapping takes place between logical extents *0000 - 0011* and physical extents *0000 - 0011*.

lvextend   This command is used to increase the number of physical extents allocated to a logical volume. We sometimes underestimate the size required for a logical volume, and with this command, you can easily correct this problem. You may want to extend a logical volume to increase the number of mirrored copies (using the *-m* option), to increase the size of the logical volume (using the *-L* option), or to increase the number of logical extents (using the *-l* option).

extendfs   Use this command after **lvextend**. Whereas the **lvextend** command expands the logical volume, **extendfs** expands the filesystem within the logical volume. If you forget to issue the **extendfs** command, the logical volume inside SAM will look expanded, but issuing the **bdf** command will not show the expansion.

lvlnboot   Use this to set up a logical volume to be a root, boot, primary swap, or dump volume (this can be undone with **lvrmboot**). Issuing the **lvlnboot** command with the -*v* option gives the current settings.

lvsplit and **lvmerge**

These commands are used to split and merge mirrored logical volumes, respectively. If you have a mirrored logical volume, **lvsplit** will split this into two logical volumes. **lvmerge** merges two logical volumes of the same size, increasing the number of mirrored copies.

lvmmigrate   This command prepares a root file system in a disk partition for migration to a logical volume. You would use this if you had a partition to convert into a logical volume.

lvreduce   Use this to decrease the number of physical extents allocated to a logical volume. When creating logical volumes, we sometimes overestimate the size of the logical volume. This command can be used to set the number of mirrored copies (with the -*m* option), decrease the number of logical extents (with the -*l* option), or decrease the size of the logical volume (with the -*L* option). Be careful when decreasing the size of a logical volume. You may make it smaller than the data in it. If you choose to do this, make sure that you have a good backup of your data.

lvremove

After emptying a logical volume, you can use this command to remove logical volumes from a volume group.

lvrmboot

Use this if you don't want a logical volume to be root, boot, primary swap, or a dump device (this is the converse of the **lvlnboot** command). However, unless you have a disk partition to boot from, don't leave the system without a root or boot device designated with the **lvlnboot** command or the system won't know where to boot from.

lvsync

There are times when mirrored data in a logical volume becomes "stale" or out-of-date. **lvsync** is used to synchronize the physical extents in a logical volume.

Adding Disks

In this section, we're going to do some work with XP 256 disks. We want to create ten volume groups with five primary disks and five alternate disks per volume group.

Let's take a look at the file that contains the physical disks to be used for the primary and alternate paths on the XP 256. The XP 256 is an advanced storage device that has in it the capability to fail over to an alternate controller, should the primary controller fail. The same set of disks are connected to the primary and alternate controllers, but the disks are given two different sets of device files. One set is for the disks when connected to the primary controller and the second set is for the same disks when connected to the alternate controller. This is the same concept that you may have come across if you are a ServiceGuard user. There are a set of disks connected through two different paths, so you must define the disks with different names depending on whether they are connected through the primary or alternate path. The following is a listing of the file **pri**, containing the primary disks in groups of five:

```
c9t0d0  c9t0d1  c9t0d2  c8t0d0   c8t0d1
c7t0d0  c7t0d1  c7t0d2  c10t0d0  c10t0d1
c9t0d3  c9t0d4  c9t0d5  c8t0d3   c8t0d4
c7t0d3  c7t0d4  c7t0d5  c10t0d3  c10t0d4
c9t0d6  c9t0d7  c9t1d0  c8t0d6   c8t0d7
c7t0d6  c7t0d7  c7t1d0  c10t0d6  c10t0d7
c9t1d1  c9t1d2  c9t1d3  c8t1d1   c8t1d2
c7t1d1  c7t1d2  c7t1d3  c10t1d1  c10t1d2
c9t1d4  c9t1d5  c9t1d6  c8t1d4   c8t1d5
c7t1d4  c7t1d5  c7t1d6  c10t1d4  c10t1d5
```

Notice that in this listing, the disks have been grouped in fives. Each group of five disks will constitute a volume group. There are a total of *10* groups of five disks that will be placed in volume groups *vgu01* through *vgu10*.

There will also be an alternate group of five disks. The alternate disks will be used in the event of a disk controller failover as described earlier. The following is a listing of the file **alt**, which contains a list of alternate disks in groups of five:

```
c8t8d0   c8t8d1   c8t8d2   c9t8d0  c9t8d1
c10t8d0  c10t8d1  c10t8d2  c7t8d0  c7t8d1
c8t8d3   c8t8d4   c8t8d5   c9t8d3  c9t8d4
c10t8d3  c10t8d4  c10t8d5  c7t8d3  c7t8d4
c8t8d6   c8t8d7   c8t9d0   c9t8d6  c9t8d7
c10t8d6  c10t8d7  c10t9d0  c7t8d6  c7t8d7
c8t9d1   c8t9d2   c8t9d3   c9t9d1  c9t9d2
c10t9d1  c10t9d2  c10t9d3  c7t9d1  c7t9d2
c8t9d4   c8t9d5   c8t9d6   c9t9d4  c9t9d5
c10t9d4  c10t9d5  c10t9d6  c7t9d4  c7t9d5
```

There are a total of *10* groups of alternate disks shown in this listing that will also be part of volume groups *vgu01* through *vgu10*. Using these primary and alternate disks that have been set up on the XP 256, we'll set up the appropriate volumes on the host system. In this example, the host system is a V-Class system.

Let's now cover the steps to create one of these volume groups. First, we'll create a physical volume for each of the disks in the volume group with the **pvcreate** command. Next, we'll create a directory for the volume group with **mkdir**, then we'll create a device special file for the volume group within the directory with **mknod**. This will set up the directory and special file required for the first of the *10* volume groups. Then we'll create the volume group in which the five primary disks will be contained using **vgcreate**. We'll specify the first disk when we create the volume group and then include the other disks in the volume group with **vgextend**. Then we extend the volume group with **vgextend** to include the five alternate disks. The final step is to create a single logical volume for the entire volume group. You might want to create several logical volumes within a volume group, but in our example, we need only one logical volume that consumes the entire capacity of the volume group, which is 8755 physical extents. The following procedure is the list of manual steps to create the first volume group:

```
# pvcreate /dev/rdsk/c9t0d0      # run for each of the 5 pri disks


# mkdir /dev/vgu01               # make dir for first vol group


# mknod /dev/vgu01/group -c 64 0x01000
                                 # create special file with major
                                   and minor numbers shown
# vgcreate /dev/vgu01 /dev/dsk/c9t0d0
                                 # Place first disk in volume group


# vgextend /dev/vgu01 /dev/dsk/c9t0d1
                                     # extend volume with remaining four
                                       primary disks disks


# vgextend /dev/vgu01 /dev/dsk/c8t8d0
                                     # extend volume group to include five
                                       alternte disks

# lvcreate -l 8755 /dev/vgu01    # creates lvol1 (lvol1 by default)
                                   that consumes all 8755 extents
```

We completed the procedure for only one disk, and there are nine additional disks in this volume group. In addition, there are another nine volume groups for which this procedure must be completed. That is a total of an additional 99 disks for which various commands must be run. There is a lot of room for error with that much typing involved so this is an ideal process to automate.

-- Read this only if you wish to see how to automate the procedure --

Since there are a primary set of disks and an alternate set of disks we'll write a short program to automate each procedure. The following program performs all of the steps required to create a physical volume for each disk, create a volume group, and include the primary disks in it:

```
#!/bin/ksh
set -x              ;set tracing on

  vgnum=$1          ;first item on each line is the volume group no.
  shift             ;shift to get to first disk

  for i in $*       ;run pvcreate for every disk name in first line
  do
     pvcreate /dev/rdsk/$i
  done

  reada             ;pause program to view what has been run

mkdir /dev/vgu$vgnum                        ;mkdir for volume group
mknod /dev/vgu$vgnum/group c 0x$(vgnum)0000  ;mknod for volume group
vgcreate /dev/vgu$vgnum /dev/dsk/$1          ;vgcreate 1st disk in vg

  shift             ;shift over to second disk

  for i in $*       ;extend volume group to include remaining four disks
  do
     vgextend /dev/vgu$vgnum /dev/dsk/$i
  done

  lvcreate -l 8755 /dev/vgu$vgnum   ;create single log vol for entire vg
```

I use **set -x** in this file to turn on execution tracing. I always do this when first debugging a shell program so I can see that the lines in the shell program as they are executed. The line being executed will appear with a "+" in front of it, followed by what you would normally see when the program is run. The **read a** is a way of pausing the program to wait for input so I can review what has been run to that point of the program.

In order for this program to run, we must slightly modify the file containing the primary disk devices and add the volume group number to the beginning of each line. In addition, I decided to call the program from the file that has the primary disks in it and operate on one line of disks at a time. The following listing shows the updated file containing the name of the shell program in the previous listing (**vg.sh**), followed by the volume group number and then the list of five primary disks names for each volume group:

```
#vg.sh 01 c9t0d0 c9t0d1 c9t0d2 c8t0d0 c8t0d1
#read a
#vg.sh 02 c7t0d0 c7t0d1 c7t0d2 c10t0d0 c10t0d1
#read a
#vg.sh 03 c9t0d3 c9t0d4 c9t0d5 c8t0d3 c8t0d4
#read a
#vg.sh 04 c7t0d3 c7t0d4 c7t0d5 c10t0d3 c10t0d4
#read a
#vg.sh 05 c9t0d6 c9t0d7 c9t1d0 c8t0d6 c8t0d7
#read a
#vg.sh 06 c7t0d6 c7t0d7 c7t1d0 c10t0d6 c10t0d7
#read a
#vg.sh 07 c9t1d1 c9t1d2 c9t1d3 c8t1d1 c8t1d2
#read a
#vg.sh 08 c7t1d1 c7t1d2 c7t1d3 c10t1d1 c10t1d2
#read a
#vg.sh 09 c9t1d4 c9t1d5 c9t1d6 c8t1d4 c8t1d5
#read a
#vg.sh 10 c7t1d4 c7t1d5 c7t1d6 c10t1d4 c10t1d5
```

The **read a** between lines of this file will pause and wait for you to enter a *Return* before the next line will be executed. I did this in case I decided to run several lines and I wanted to check the results between the execution of lines.

We can now uncomment the first line of the file and type the file name **pri**, which will call **vg.sh** and run the program (you must give appropriate permissions to the files and make sure both **vg.sh** and **pri** are executable.) I like to run such files one line at a time and check the volume groups as they are created. The script is written to run one line at a time but is easily modifiable to run all ten lines.

We need to do much less work with the alternate disk names. The physical volumes have already been created, and the volume group and single logical volume have already been set up in **vg.sh**. We'll create another script called **vga.sh**, "a" for alternate), in which we'll extend the volume group to include the alternate name for each disk. This script is shown in the listing below:

```
#!/bin/ksh
set -x                  ;set tracing on

  vgnum=$1              ;first item on each line is the volume group number
  shift                ;shift to get to first disk

  for i in $*          ;extend vol group to include all five disks on line

    vgextend /dev/vgu$vgnum /dev/dsk/$i

  done
```

This script performs only the task of extending the volume group *vgnum* to include all five disks that appear on the line. Much like the file **pri**, the file **alt** will call the script **vga.alt**, as shown in the following listing:

```
#vga.sh 01 c8t8d0   c8t8d1   c8t8d2   c9t8d0 c9t8d1
#vga.sh 02 c10t8d0  c10t8d1  c10t8d2  c7t8d0 c7t8d1
#vga.sh 03 c8t8d3   c8t8d4   c8t8d5   c9t8d3 c9t8d4
#vga.sh 04 c10t8d3  c10t8d4  c10t8d5  c7t8d3 c7t8d4
#vga.sh 05 c8t8d6   c8t8d7   c8t9d0   c9t8d6 c9t8d7
#vga.sh 06 c10t8d6  c10t8d7  c10t9d0  c7t8d6 c7t8d7
#vga.sh 07 c8t9d1   c8t9d2   c8t9d3   c9t9d1 c9t9d2
#vga.sh 08 c10t9d1  c10t9d2  c10t9d3  c7t9d1 c7t9d2
#vga.sh 09 c8t9d4   c8t9d5   c8t9d6   c9t9d4 c9t9d5
#vga.sh 10 c10t9d4  c10t9d5  c10t9d6  c7t9d4 c7t9d5
```

You would uncomment the line for which you wanted to run the script. Again, you could run all ten lines, but I like to check what has taken place after each line has been run. You could add **read a** between the lines of this file if you wanted to run several lines and have a pause between them to check the results.

These two scripts automate a lot of typing. There are 100 disks for which commands must be run as well as other Logical Volume Manager commands. This is the type of HP-UX system administration task that is ideally suited to shell programming.

----------- End of Automated Procedure -----------

I completed the steps that had to be run for the additional disks to complete the work, such as the **vgcreate** for the additional four disks and the **vgextend** for the additional nine disk devices. I included only the first disk in the examples so you could see the initial step that had to be run.

We don't have to set up any RAID levels within the primary or alternate volume because this is being done internally to the XP 256.

The following **vgdisplay** listing shows the disks we set up for volume group *vgu01* with both the group of five primary and alternate disks:

```
# vgdisplay /dev/vgu01 -v
```

```
VG Name                    /dev/vgu01
VG Write Access            read/write
VG Status                  available
Max LV                     255
Cur LV                     1
Open LV                    1
Max PV                     16
Cur PV                     5
Act PV                     5
Max PE per PV              1751
VGDA                       10
PE Size (Mbytes)           4
Total PE                   8755
Alloc PE                   8755
Free PE                    0
Total PVG                  0
Total Spare PVs            0
Total Spare PVs in use     0

   --- Logical volumes ---
   LV Name                 /dev/vgu01/lvol1
   LV Status               available/syncd
   LV Size (Mbytes)        35020
   Current LE              8755
   Allocated PE            8755
```

```
       Used PV                        5


       --- Physical volumes ---
       PV Name                        /dev/dsk/c9t0d0
       PV Name                        /dev/dsk/c8t8d0Alternate Link
       PV Status                      available
       Total PE                       1751
       Free PE                        0

       PV Name                        /dev/dsk/c9t0d1
       PV Name                        /dev/dsk/c8t8d1Alternate Link
       PV Status                      available
       Total PE                       1751
       Free PE                        0

       PV Name                        /dev/dsk/c9t0d2
       PV Name                        /dev/dsk/c8t8d2Alternate Link
       PV Status                      available
       Total PE                       1751
       Free PE                        0

       PV Name                        /dev/dsk/c8t0d0
       PV Name                        /dev/dsk/c9t8d0Alternate Link
       PV Status                      available
       Total PE                       1751
       Free PE                        0

       PV Name                        /dev/dsk/c8t0d1
       PV Name                        /dev/dsk/c9t8d1Alternate Link
       PV Status                      available
       Total PE                       1751
       Free PE                        0
```

There are some points of interest to cover in this **vgdisplay**. The first is that there is a primary and an alternate path to the same disk because we defined them earlier. For instance, the first disk in the volume group has a primary pathname of *c9t0d0* and an alternate pathname of *c8t8d0*. Next, both the volume group *vgu01* and the only logical volume in it, *lvol1*, consist of a total of 8755 PE or physical extents (the size of the volume group is PE x PE size, or 8755 x 4MB in our case).

We should also check one logical volume on *vgu01*, called *lvol1*. We can check the parameters of this logical volume with the **lvdisplay** command as shown in the following example:

```
# lvdisplay -v /dev/vgu01/1*

--- Logical volumes ---
```

```
LV Name                       /dev/vgu01/lvol1
VG Name                       /dev/vgu01
LV Permission                 read/write
LV Status                     available/syncd
Mirror copies                 0
Consistency Recovery          MWC
Schedule                      parallel
LV Size (Mbytes)              35020
Current LE                    8755
Allocated PE                  8755
Stripes                       0
Stripe Size (Kbytes)          0
Bad block                     on
Allocation                    strict
IO Timeout (Seconds)          default

   --- Distribution of logical volume ---
   PV Name              LE on PV   PE on PV
   /dev/dsk/c9t0d0        1751       1751
   /dev/dsk/c9t0d1        1751       1751
   /dev/dsk/c9t0d2        1751       1751
   /dev/dsk/c8t0d0        1751       1751
   /dev/dsk/c8t0d1        1751       1751

   --- Logical extents ---
   LE     PV1                PE1      Status 1
   00000  /dev/dsk/c9t0d0    00000    current
   00001  /dev/dsk/c9t0d0    00001    current
   00002  /dev/dsk/c9t0d0    00002    current
   00003  /dev/dsk/c9t0d0    00003    current
   00004  /dev/dsk/c9t0d0    00004    current
   00005  /dev/dsk/c9t0d0    00005    current
   00006  /dev/dsk/c9t0d0    00006    current
   00007  /dev/dsk/c9t0d0    00007    current
   00008  /dev/dsk/c9t0d0    00008    current
   00009  /dev/dsk/c9t0d0    00009    current
   00010  /dev/dsk/c9t0d0    00010    current
   00011  /dev/dsk/c9t0d0    00011    current
   00012  /dev/dsk/c9t0d0    00012    current
   00013  /dev/dsk/c9t0d0    00013    current
   00014  /dev/dsk/c9t0d0    00014    current
   00015  /dev/dsk/c9t0d0    00015    current
   00016  /dev/dsk/c9t0d0    00016    current
   00017  /dev/dsk/c9t0d0    00017    current
   00018  /dev/dsk/c9t0d0    00018    current
   00019  /dev/dsk/c9t0d0    00019    current
   00020  /dev/dsk/c9t0d0    00020    current
   00021  /dev/dsk/c9t0d0    00021    current
   00022  /dev/dsk/c9t0d0    00022    current
   00023  /dev/dsk/c9t0d0    00023    current
   00024  /dev/dsk/c9t0d0    00024    current
   00025  /dev/dsk/c9t0d0    00025    current
   00026  /dev/dsk/c9t0d0    00026    current
   00027  /dev/dsk/c9t0d0    00027    current
   00028  /dev/dsk/c9t0d0    00028    current
   00029  /dev/dsk/c9t0d0    00029    current
   00030  /dev/dsk/c9t0d0    00030    current
   00031  /dev/dsk/c9t0d0    00031    current
```

```
00032 /dev/dsk/c9t0d0        00032 current
                    .
                    .
                    .
08733 /dev/dsk/c8t0d1        01729 current
08734 /dev/dsk/c8t0d1        01730 current
08735 /dev/dsk/c8t0d1        01731 current
08736 /dev/dsk/c8t0d1        01732 current
08737 /dev/dsk/c8t0d1        01733 current
08738 /dev/dsk/c8t0d1        01734 current
08739 /dev/dsk/c8t0d1        01735 current
08740 /dev/dsk/c8t0d1        01736 current
08741 /dev/dsk/c8t0d1        01737 current
08742 /dev/dsk/c8t0d1        01738 current
08743 /dev/dsk/c8t0d1        01739 current
08744 /dev/dsk/c8t0d1        01740 current
08745 /dev/dsk/c8t0d1        01741 current
08746 /dev/dsk/c8t0d1        01742 current
08747 /dev/dsk/c8t0d1        01743 current
08748 /dev/dsk/c8t0d1        01744 current
08749 /dev/dsk/c8t0d1        01745 current
08750 /dev/dsk/c8t0d1        01746 current
08751 /dev/dsk/c8t0d1        01747 current
08752 /dev/dsk/c8t0d1        01748 current
08753 /dev/dsk/c8t0d1        01749 current
08754 /dev/dsk/c8t0d1        01750 current
```

This listing has been abbreviated where the three dots are shown. Only the beginning of the first disk and end of the last disk are shown. The **lvdisplay** does indeed show the five primary disks of which the logical volume is comprised.

The final step is to place a file system on the logical volume we set up in *vgu00*. This is a task for which SAM is ideally suited. Figure 9-2 shows the SAM screen shot of the logical volumes we created. There is one logical volume created for each of the ten volume groups.

```
═══                Disks and File Systems (o2) (1)
File List View Options Actions                                     Help
                   Press CTRL-K for keyboard help.


Logical Volumes                                      0 of 19 selected


                                        Total    Mirror   Mount
    Logical Volume   Volume Group   Use   Mbytes   Copies   Directory

    ▌lvol1           vgu01        Unused   35020    0
    lvol1            vgu02        Unused   35020    0
    lvol1            vgu03        Unused   35020    0
    lvol1            vgu04        Unused   35020    0
    lvol1            vgu05        Unused   35020    0
    lvol1            vgu06        Unused   35020    0
    lvol1            vgu07        Unused   35020    0
    lvol1            vgu08        Unused   35020    0
    lvol1            vgu09        Unused   35020    0
    lvol1            vgu10        Unused   35020    0
```

Figure 9-2 *lvol1* on *vgu01* through *vgu10*

lvol1 appears for volume groups *vgu01* through *vgu10*. We want a file system on each of the logical volumes for the application we are running. Although we could issue the appropriate commands at the command line, we'll use SAM for this task.

Figure 9-3 shows the SAM screen used to add a file system to one of the logical volumes:

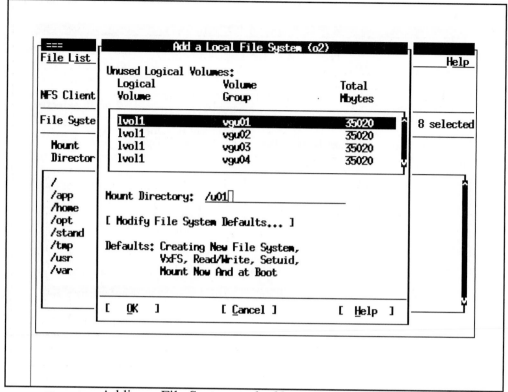

Figure 9-3 Adding a File System to *lvol1* on *vgu01*

We have selected *lvol1* on *vgu01* to add a file system as shown in this figure.

Next, we want to modify the defaults for the logical volume as shown in Figure 9-4:

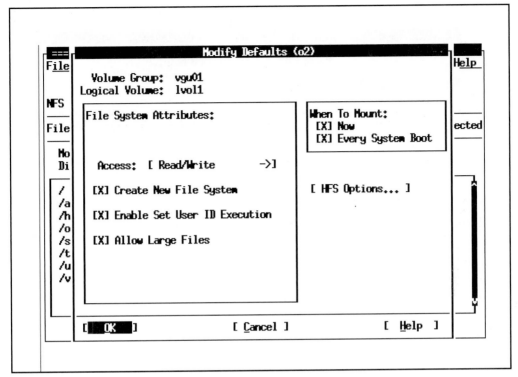

Figure 9-4 Modify Filesystem Defaults

We want to be sure to *Allow Large Files* in this screen because we'll be running a database application that creates many large files. If we were to create a filesystem without large files, we could use the **fsadm** command to convert to large files if we're running Online JFS. We want to mount this file system now and at the time of system boot so an entry gets made in **/etc/ fstab** for us.

Figure 9-5 shows the result of having created the ten filesystems on the ten logical volumes:

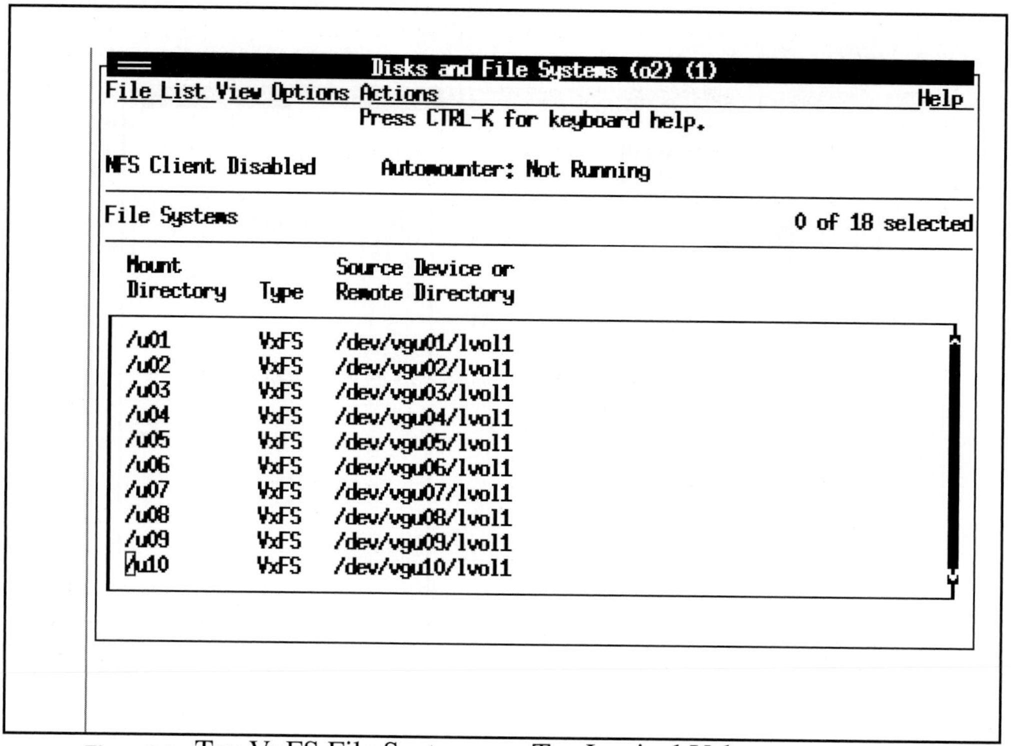

Figure 9-5 Ten VxFS File Systems on Ten Logical Volumes

Using SAM, we created ten VxFS filesystems on all ten *lvol1*s. We had to create all ten individually in SAM, so this may have been a good candidate for automating with a shell program.

SAM automatically adds these entries to **/etc/fstab** because we specified them to be mounted both now and at the time of system boot, as shown in the following listing:

```
# System /etc/fstab file.  Static information about the file systems
# See fstab(4) and sam(1M) for further details on configuring devices.
/dev/vg00/lvol3 / vxfs delaylog 0 1
/dev/vg00/lvol1 /stand hfs defaults 0 1
/dev/vg00/lvol4 /opt vxfs delaylog 0 2
/dev/vg00/lvol5 /tmp vxfs delaylog 0 2
/dev/vg00/lvol6 /usr vxfs delaylog 0 2
/dev/vg00/lvol7 /var vxfs delaylog 0 2
/dev/vg00/lvol8 /home vxfs delaylog 0 2
/dev/vg00/lvol9 ... swap pri=0 0 0
/dev/vgapp/lvol1 /app vxfs rw,suid,largefiles,delaylog,datainlog 0 2
/dev/vgu01/lvol1 /u01 vxfs rw,suid,largefiles,delaylog,datainlog 0 2
```

```
/dev/vgu02/lvol1 /u02 vxfs rw,suid,largefiles,delaylog,datainlog 0 2
/dev/vgu03/lvol1 /u03 vxfs rw,suid,largefiles,delaylog,datainlog 0 2
/dev/vgu04/lvol1 /u04 vxfs rw,suid,largefiles,delaylog,datainlog 0 2
/dev/vgu05/lvol1 /u05 vxfs rw,suid,largefiles,delaylog,datainlog 0 2
/dev/vgu06/lvol1 /u06 vxfs rw,suid,largefiles,delaylog,datainlog 0 2
/dev/vgu07/lvol1 /u07 vxfs rw,suid,largefiles,delaylog,datainlog 0 2
/dev/vgu08/lvol1 /u08 vxfs rw,suid,largefiles,delaylog,datainlog 0 2
/dev/vgu09/lvol1 /u09 vxfs rw,suid,largefiles,delaylog,datainlog 0 2
/dev/vgu10/lvol1 /u10 vxfs rw,suid,largefiles,delaylog,datainlog 0 2
```

This listing shows our ten logical volumes with the parameters we set up such as VxFS and support for large files as the last ten entries.

There is no reason why we could not have run the filesystem-related commands such as **newfs** and **fsadm** at the command line as we did with the volume-related commands earlier. Since most people use SAM for these procedures, I thought it would be best illustrated using SAM.

The next section provides tips on various procedures you may want to perform using logical volume manager. These are procedures I have used many times, and they may help you when you need to perform similar tasks.

Commonly Used LVM Procedures

System administrators tend to be careful before running any intrusive (there is a chance something LVM-related will be changed) LVM commands. Always back up your system and create a bootable recovery tape with Ignite-UX before you run any intrusive LVM commands. The following are some procedures for tasks I have encountered on a regular basis. Please modify them to suit your needs. Don't run the commands as shown. You will need to prepare your system, substitute the names of your volumes, and perform additional steps. These commands, however, serve as good examples for ways in which the tasks shown can be performed.

The first task we'll perform is to replace a bad disk in a system that is not mirrored (Figure 9-6).

vgcfgrestore - /dev/vgXX /dev/rdsk/cxtxdx   ; volume group configuration restore

vgchange -a y /dev/vgXX   ; change volume group to available (*-a y*)

newfs -F fstype /dev/vgXX/rlvolx   ; create filesystem for every *lvol* on physical volume

mount */mountpointname*   ; mount every new filesystem

Notes:

Confirm you have **/etc/lvmconf/vgXX.conf**

vgcfgbackup is run automatically

Defective disk was not mirrored before it failed

Additional steps may be required on your system

Figure 9-6 Replace a Non-Mirrored Disk

In this example we had a nonmirrored and nonroot disk that was defective and had to be replaced. After replacing the disk, the volume group information was restored for the specific disk with **vgcfgrestore**. We then changed the volume group to available, ran a **newfs** on the disk, and mounted the file systems that used the disk.

In Figure 9-7 we will again replace a defective nonroot disk, but this time, the disk will be mirrored.

vgcfgrestore - /dev/vgXX /dev/rdsk/cxtxdx   ; volume group configuration restore

vgchange -a y /dev/vgXX   ; change volume group to available (*-a y*)

vgsync /dev/vgXX   ; resync logical volumes in volume group

Notes:

Defective disk was mirrored before it failed

Additional steps may be required on your system

Figure 9-7   Replace a Mirrored Disk

In this example, we performed the same first two steps of restoring the volume group configuration and changing the volume group to available. Because the disk was mirrored, we only have to synchronize the data on the new disk with that on its mirror with **vgsync**.

In Figure 9-8 we will again replace a mirrored disk, but this time, the disk will have a boot area on it.

```
# vgcfgrestore - /dev/vgXX /dev/rdsk/cxtxdx      ; volume group configuration restore

# vgchange -a y /dev/vgXX                        ; change volume group to available (-a y)

# vgsync /dev/vgXX                               ; resync logical volumes in volume group

# mkboot /dev/rdsk/cxtxdx                         ; create boot area on disk

# mkboot -a "hpux lq" /dev/rdsk/cxtxdx            ; specify low quorum in boot area

# shutdown <desired options>                      ; reboot system to take effect

vgcfgbackup is run automatically

Notes:

Confirm you have /etc/lvmconf/vgXX.conf

Defective disk was mirrored before it failed

Addtional steps may be required on your system
```

Figure 9-8   Replace a Mirrored Disk Boot Disk

In this example, we performed the same first three steps as in the previous example, but we also have to create a boot area on the disk. The system has to be rebooted in order for this to take effect.

In Figure 9-9, we want to move a volume group onto a different system.

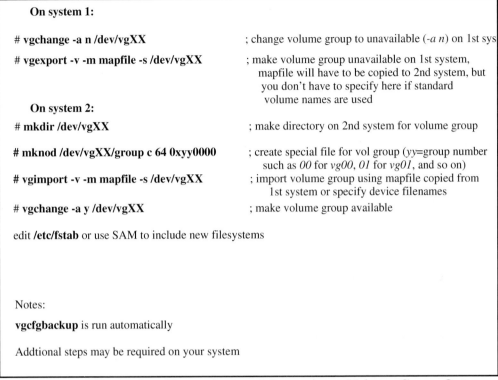

On system 1:

vgchange -a n /dev/vgXX   ; change volume group to unavailable (*-a n*) on 1st sys

vgexport -v -m mapfile -s /dev/vgXX   ; make volume group unavailable on 1st system,
                                           mapfile will have to be copied to 2nd system, but
                                           you don't have to specify here if standard
                                           volume names are used

On system 2:

mkdir /dev/vgXX   ; make directory on 2nd system for volume group

mknod /dev/vgXX/group c 64 0xyy0000 ; create special file for vol group (*yy*=group number
                                           such as *00* for *vg00*, *01* for *vg01*, and so on)

vgimport -v -m mapfile -s /dev/vgXX ; import volume group using mapfile copied from
                                           1st system or specify device filenames

vgchange -a y /dev/vgXX   ; make volume group available

edit **/etc/fstab** or use SAM to include new filesystems

Notes:

vgcfgbackup is run automatically

Addtional steps may be required on your system

Figure 9-9 Exporting (Removing) and Importing a Volume Group Onto Another System

In this example we performed the first two steps on the system from which we're moving the volume group. We make the volume group unavailable and then export the volume group. The mapfile from the first system needs to be copied to the second system. You don't have to specify the mapfile name if standard names such as **/dev/vg01** are used. In any event, the mapfile has to be copied to the system to which the volume group is being migrated.

On the second system we create a directory and device special file for the new volume group. We then import the mapfile for the volume group and make the volume group active. The last step involved making additions to **fstab** for the filesystems to be mounted.

Figure 9-10 shows extending a VxFS file system by 800 MBytes.

---

lvextend -L 800 /dev/vgXX/rlvolY   ; extend logical volume *rlvolY* by 800 MBytes

fsadm -F vxfs -b 800M */mountpointname*   ; use **fsadm** to extend or **extendfs** on non-JFS

Notes:

This is a VxFS file system and Online JFS is installed on system

Additional steps may be required on your system

Figure 9-10 Extend VxFS File System Using Online JFS

First, we use **lvextend** to specify the size and raw logical volume to be extended. Next we use **fsadm** to make the change.

The Figure 9-11 shows changing a VxFS file system to support large files.

 # fsadm -F vxfs -o largefiles /dev/vgXX/rlvolY   ; use *fsadm* and specify *largefile* option

Notes:

This is VxFS file system, you can substitute *hfs* for *vxfs* in above example for an *hfs* filesystem and use
        lvolY in place of *rlvolY*
Unmount file system before running

Additional steps may be required on your system

Figure 9-11   Change a Logical Volume to Support Large Files

Using **fsadm**, we specify the raw logical volume on which we want large files supported.

This change would be unnecessary had the logical volume been created to support large files.

Reconfiguring Some Disks: An Example of Using Some Logical Volume Commands

I have always advised in my books and articles to take great care when you first set up disks on your HP-UX systems to make sure that the disk layout you select is one you can live with for a long time. No matter how careful you are, however, you often need to perform some logical volume reconfiguration. It is much more difficult to make changes to an existing logical volume layout than it is to set up your system correctly when it is first installed. This section describes the steps performed to make some changes to the dump and mirror on an existing system.

This is not a procedure you should follow. It is an example of some advanced Logical Volume Manager (LVM) commands used to reconfigure some disks on a specific system. It is a good procedure for illustrating how several LVM commands can be used.

Why Change?

Figure 9-12 shows the original configuration of disks on a system and the updated configuration we wish to implement.

The overall objective here is to move the 4 GByte disk used as the mirror of the root disk to a different SCSI channel and to install a 2 GByte dump device on the same SCSI channel as the root disk.

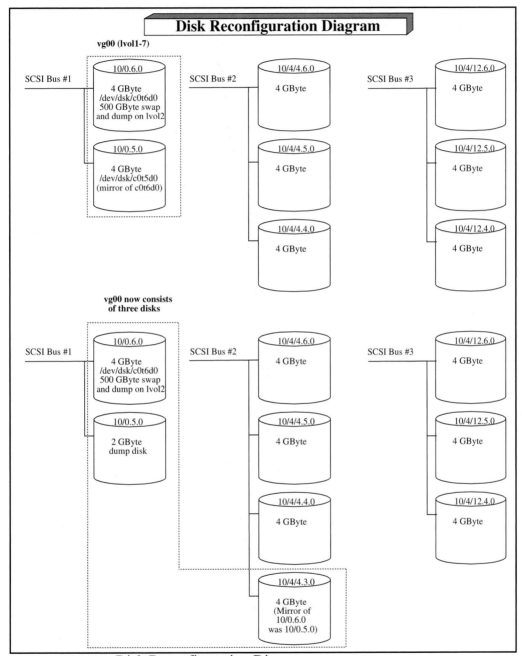

Figure 9-12 Disk Reconfiguration Diagram

The procedure consists of several parts. The first is to obtain a snapshot of the system before any reconfigurations. This serves two purposes. The first is to have documentation of the original system configuration that can be included in the system administration notebook. Should any questions arise in the future as to the original configuration and changes made to it, the original configuration will be in the system administration notebook. The second purpose of having this information is to have all of the relevant information about the configuration available as you proceed with the reconfiguration process.

The second part of the procedure is to shut down the system, install the new 2 GByte disk, and move the 4 GByte disk.

The last part of the procedure is to perform the system administration reconfiguration of the dump and mirror.

Figures 9-13, 9-14, and 9-15 show a flowchart depicting the procedure we'll follow throughout this section. The step numbers in the upcoming procedure correspond to the step numbers shown in these figures. Let's now proceed beginning with the snapshot of the system.

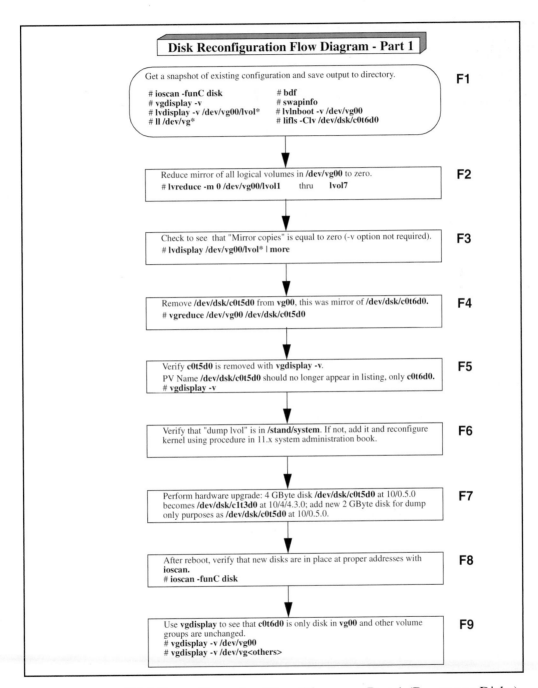

Disk Reconfiguration Flow Diagram - Part 1

F1 Get a snapshot of existing configuration and save output to directory.

```
# ioscan -funC disk          # bdf
# vgdisplay -v               # swapinfo
# lvdisplay -v /dev/vg00/lvol*    # lvlnboot -v /dev/vg00
# ll /dev/vg*                # lifls -Clv /dev/dsk/c0t6d0
```

F2 Reduce mirror of all logical volumes in **/dev/vg00** to zero.

```
# lvreduce -m 0 /dev/vg00/lvol1     thru     lvol7
```

F3 Check to see that "Mirror copies" is equal to zero (-v option not required).

```
# lvdisplay /dev/vg00/lvol* | more
```

F4 Remove **/dev/dsk/c0t5d0** from **vg00**, this was mirror of **/dev/dsk/c0t6d0**.

```
# vgreduce /dev/vg00 /dev/dsk/c0t5d0
```

F5 Verify **c0t5d0** is removed with **vgdisplay -v**.
PV Name **/dev/dsk/c0t5d0** should no longer appear in listing, only **c0t6d0**.

```
# vgdisplay -v
```

F6 Verify that "dump lvol" is in **/stand/system**. If not, add it and reconfigure kernel using procedure in 11.x system administration book.

F7 Perform hardware upgrade: 4 GByte disk **/dev/dsk/c0t5d0** at 10/0.5.0 becomes **/dev/dsk/c1t3d0** at 10/4/4.3.0; add new 2 GByte disk for dump only purposes as **/dev/dsk/c0t5d0** at 10/0.5.0.

F8 After reboot, verify that new disks are in place at proper addresses with **ioscan.**

```
# ioscan -funC disk
```

F9 Use **vgdisplay** to see that **c0t6d0** is only disk in **vg00** and other volume groups are unchanged.

```
# vgdisplay -v /dev/vg00
# vgdisplay -v /dev/vg<others>
```

Figure 9-13 Disk Reconfiguration Flow Diagram - Part 1 (Rearrange Disks)

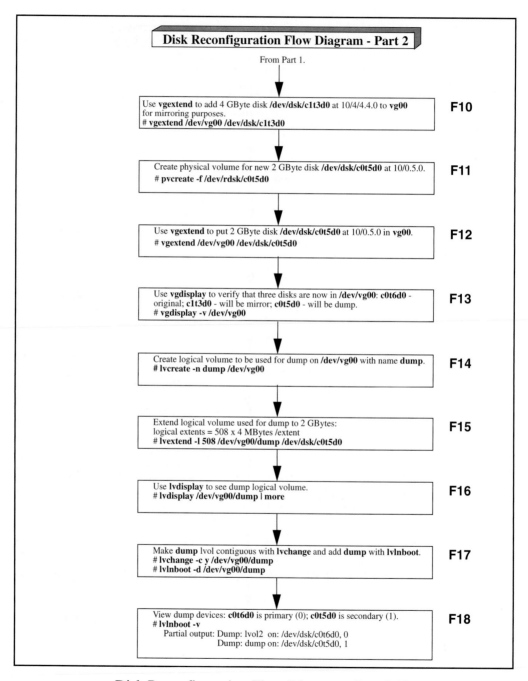

Disk Reconfiguration Flow Diagram - Part 2

From Part 1.

Use **vgextend** to add 4 GByte disk **/dev/dsk/c1t3d0** at 10/4/4.4.0 to **vg00** for mirroring purposes.
vgextend /dev/vg00 /dev/dsk/c1t3d0   **F10**

Create physical volume for new 2 GByte disk **/dev/dsk/c0t5d0** at 10/0.5.0.
pvcreate -f /dev/rdsk/c0t5d0   **F11**

Use **vgextend** to put 2 GByte disk **/dev/dsk/c0t5d0** at 10/0.5.0 in **vg00**.
vgextend /dev/vg00 /dev/dsk/c0t5d0   **F12**

Use **vgdisplay** to verify that three disks are now in **/dev/vg00**: **c0t6d0** - original; **c1t3d0** - will be mirror; **c0t5d0** - will be dump.
vgdisplay -v /dev/vg00   **F13**

Create logical volume to be used for dump on **/dev/vg00** with name **dump**.
lvcreate -n dump /dev/vg00   **F14**

Extend logical volume used for dump to 2 GBytes:
logical extents = 508 x 4 MBytes /extent
lvextend -l 508 /dev/vg00/dump /dev/dsk/c0t5d0   **F15**

Use **lvdisplay** to see dump logical volume.
lvdisplay /dev/vg00/dump | more   **F16**

Make **dump** lvol contiguous with **lvchange** and add **dump** with **lvlnboot**.
lvchange -c y /dev/vg00/dump
lvlnboot -d /dev/vg00/dump   **F17**

View dump devices: **c0t6d0** is primary (0); **c0t5d0** is secondary (1).
lvlnboot -v
    Partial output: Dump: lvol2 on: /dev/dsk/c0t6d0, 0
                          Dump: dump on: /dev/dsk/c0t5d0, 1   **F18**

Figure 9-14   Disk Reconfiguration Flow Diagram - Part 2 (Set Up Dump)

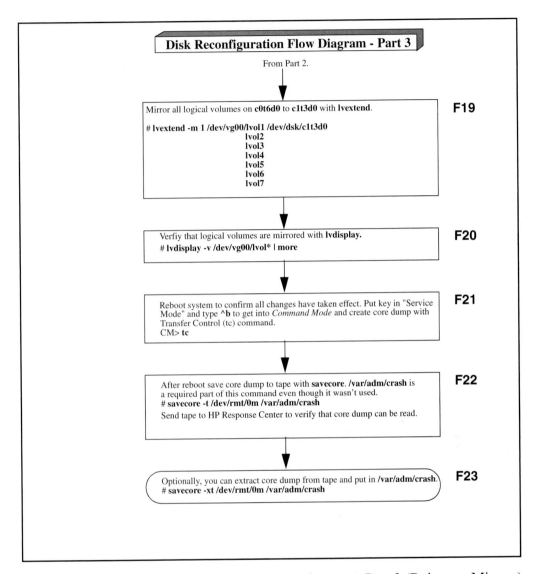

Figure 9-15   Disk Reconfiguration Flow Diagram - Part 3 (Reinstate Mirrors)

F1 - to scan

First let's run **ioscan** to see the disks on the system.

```
$ /usr/sbin/ioscan -funC disk
```

```
Class    I  H/W Path      Driver      S/W State H/W Type  Description
=====================================================================
disk     2  10/0.5.0      sdisk       CLAIMED   DEVICE     SEAGATE ST15150W
                          /dev/dsk/c0t5d0    /dev/rdsk/c0t5d0
disk     3  10/0.6.0      sdisk       CLAIMED   DEVICE     SEAGATE ST15150W
                          /dev/dsk/c0t6d0    /dev/rdsk/c0t6d0
disk     6  10/4/4.4.0    sdisk       CLAIMED   DEVICE     SEAGATE ST15150W
                          /dev/dsk/c1t4d0    /dev/rdsk/c1t4d0
disk     7  10/4/4.5.0    sdisk       CLAIMED   DEVICE     SEAGATE ST15150W
                          /dev/dsk/c1t5d0    /dev/rdsk/c1t5d0
disk     8  10/4/4.6.0    sdisk       CLAIMED   DEVICE     SEAGATE ST15150W
                          /dev/dsk/c1t6d0    /dev/rdsk/c1t6d0
disk     9  10/4/12.4.0   sdisk       CLAIMED   DEVICE     SEAGATE ST15150W
                          /dev/dsk/c2t4d0    /dev/rdsk/c2t4d0
disk    10  10/4/12.5.0   sdisk       CLAIMED   DEVICE     SEAGATE ST15150W
                          /dev/dsk/c2t5d0    /dev/rdsk/c2t5d0
disk    11  10/4/12.6.0   sdisk       CLAIMED   DEVICE     SEAGATE ST15150W
                          /dev/dsk/c2t6d0    /dev/rdsk/c2t6d0
disk     5  10/12/5.2.0   sdisk       CLAIMED   DEVICE     TOSHIBA CD-ROM XM-5401TA
                          /dev/dsk/c3t2d0    /dev/rdsk/c3t2d0
```

Note that the disks in this configuration correspond to those on the top of Figure 9-4. We haven't yet looked at the logical volume information related to these disks, only their physical addresses.

F1 - vgdisplay

Next run **vgdisplay** to see the volume groups. **lvol2** on **vg00** is the dump logical volume we are going to move to a separate 2 GByte disk. We don't yet know if **lvol1-7** on **vg00** are all mirrored.

```
# vgdisplay -v
 --- Volume groups ---
VG Name                 /dev/vg00
VG Write Access         read/write
VG Status               available
Max LV                  255
Cur LV                  7
Open LV                 7
Max PV                  16
Cur PV                  2
Act PV                  2
```

```
Max PE per PV          1023
VGDA                   4
PE Size (Mbytes)       4
Total PE               2046
Alloc PE               688
Free PE                1358
Total PVG              0

     --- Logical volumes ---
LV Name                /dev/vg00/lvol1
LV Status              available/syncd
LV Size (Mbytes)       92
Current LE             23
Allocated PE           46
Used PV                2

LV Name                /dev/vg00/lvol2
LV Status              available/syncd
LV Size (Mbytes)       500
Current LE             125
Allocated PE           250
Used PV                2

LV Name                /dev/vg00/lvol3
LV Status              available/syncd
LV Size (Mbytes)       20
Current LE             5
Allocated PE           10
Used PV                2

LV Name                /dev/vg00/lvol4
LV Status              available/syncd
LV Size (Mbytes)       252
Current LE             63
Allocated PE           126
Used PV                2

LV Name                /dev/vg00/lvol5
LV Status              available/syncd
LV Size (Mbytes)       32
Current LE             8
Allocated PE           16
Used PV                2

LV Name                /dev/vg00/lvol6
LV Status              available/syncd
LV Size (Mbytes)       320
Current LE             80
Allocated PE           160
Used PV                2
LV Name                /dev/vg00/lvol7
LV Status              available/syncd
LV Size (Mbytes)       160
Current LE             40
Allocated PE           80
Used PV                2

     --- Physical volumes ---
PV Name                /dev/dsk/c0t6d0
PV Status              available
Total PE               1023
Free PE                679

PV Name                /dev/dsk/c0t5d0
PV Status              available
Total PE               1023
Free PE                679
```

F1 - lvdisplay

View detailed logical volume information with **lvdisplay**. Note that all
of these logical volumes are mirrored and that each has "current" status.
Only **lvol1** and **lvol2** are shown in the listing. **lvol3** through **lvol7** are not
shown.

```
# lvdisplay -v /dev/vg00/lvol*
   --- Logical volumes ---
LV Name                    /dev/vg00/lvol1
VG Name                    /dev/vg00
LV Permission              read/write
LV Status                  available/syncd
Mirror copies              1
Consistency Recovery       MWC
Schedule                   parallel
LV Size (Mbytes)           92
Current LE                 23
Allocated PE               46
Stripes                    0
Stripe Size (Kbytes)       0
Bad block                  off
Allocation                 strict/contiguous

   --- Distribution of logical volume ---
PV Name              LE on PV  PE on PV
/dev/dsk/c0t6d0      23          23
/dev/dsk/c0t5d0      23          23


   --- Logical extents ---
LE    PV1                  PE1   Status 1 PV2           PE2   Status 2
0000 /dev/dsk/c0t6d0      0000  current  /dev/dsk/c0t5d0 0000  current
0001 /dev/dsk/c0t6d0      0001  current  /dev/dsk/c0t5d0 0001  current
0002 /dev/dsk/c0t6d0      0002  current  /dev/dsk/c0t5d0 0002  current
0003 /dev/dsk/c0t6d0      0003  current  /dev/dsk/c0t5d0 0003  current
0004 /dev/dsk/c0t6d0      0004  current  /dev/dsk/c0t5d0 0004  current
0005 /dev/dsk/c0t6d0      0005  current  /dev/dsk/c0t5d0 0005  current
0006 /dev/dsk/c0t6d0      0006  current  /dev/dsk/c0t5d0 0006  current
0007 /dev/dsk/c0t6d0      0007  current  /dev/dsk/c0t5d0 0007  current
0008 /dev/dsk/c0t6d0      0008  current  /dev/dsk/c0t5d0 0008  current
0009 /dev/dsk/c0t6d0      0009  current  /dev/dsk/c0t5d0 0009  current
0010 /dev/dsk/c0t6d0      0010  current  /dev/dsk/c0t5d0 0010  current
0011 /dev/dsk/c0t6d0      0011  current  /dev/dsk/c0t5d0 0011  current
0012 /dev/dsk/c0t6d0      0012  current  /dev/dsk/c0t5d0 0012  current
0013 /dev/dsk/c0t6d0      0013  current  /dev/dsk/c0t5d0 0013  current
0014 /dev/dsk/c0t6d0      0014  current  /dev/dsk/c0t5d0 0014  current
0015 /dev/dsk/c0t6d0      0015  current  /dev/dsk/c0t5d0 0015  current
0016 /dev/dsk/c0t6d0      0016  current  /dev/dsk/c0t5d0 0016  current
0017 /dev/dsk/c0t6d0      0017  current  /dev/dsk/c0t5d0 0017  current
0018 /dev/dsk/c0t6d0      0018  current  /dev/dsk/c0t5d0 0018  current
0019 /dev/dsk/c0t6d0      0019  current  /dev/dsk/c0t5d0 0019  current
0020 /dev/dsk/c0t6d0      0020  current  /dev/dsk/c0t5d0 0020  current
0021 /dev/dsk/c0t6d0      0021  current  /dev/dsk/c0t5d0 0021  current
0022 /dev/dsk/c0t6d0      0022  current  /dev/dsk/c0t5d0 0022  current

LV Name                    /dev/vg00/lvol2
VG Name                    /dev/vg00
LV Permission              read/write
LV Status                  available/syncd
Mirror copies              1
Consistency Recovery       MWC
Schedule                   parallel
LV Size (Mbytes)           500
Current LE                 125
Allocated PE               250
Stripes                    0
```

```
Stripe Size (Kbytes)     0
Bad block                off
Allocation               strict/contiguous

--- Distribution of logical volume ---

PV Name                LE on PV   PE on PV
/dev/dsk/c0t6d0        125        125
/dev/dsk/c0t5d0        125        125

--- Logical extents ---

LE    PV1                  PE1    Status 1  PV2                  PE2    Status 2

0000  /dev/dsk/c0t6d0      0023   current   /dev/dsk/c0t5d0      0023   current
0001  /dev/dsk/c0t6d0      0024   current   /dev/dsk/c0t5d0      0024   current
0002  /dev/dsk/c0t6d0      0025   current   /dev/dsk/c0t5d0      0025   current
0003  /dev/dsk/c0t6d0      0026   current   /dev/dsk/c0t5d0      0026   current
0004  /dev/dsk/c0t6d0      0027   current   /dev/dsk/c0t5d0      0027   current
0005  /dev/dsk/c0t6d0      0028   current   /dev/dsk/c0t5d0      0028   current
0006  /dev/dsk/c0t6d0      0029   current   /dev/dsk/c0t5d0      0029   current
0007  /dev/dsk/c0t6d0      0030   current   /dev/dsk/c0t5d0      0030   current
0008  /dev/dsk/c0t6d0      0031   current   /dev/dsk/c0t5d0      0031   current
0009  /dev/dsk/c0t6d0      0032   current   /dev/dsk/c0t5d0      0032   current
0010  /dev/dsk/c0t6d0      0033   current   /dev/dsk/c0t5d0      0033   current
0011  /dev/dsk/c0t6d0      0034   current   /dev/dsk/c0t5d0      0034   current
0012  /dev/dsk/c0t6d0      0035   current   /dev/dsk/c0t5d0      0035   current
0013  /dev/dsk/c0t6d0      0036   current   /dev/dsk/c0t5d0      0036   current
                             .
                             .
                             .
0111  /dev/dsk/c0t6d0      0134   current   /dev/dsk/c0t5d0      0134   current
0112  /dev/dsk/c0t6d0      0135   current   /dev/dsk/c0t5d0      0135   current
0113  /dev/dsk/c0t6d0      0136   current   /dev/dsk/c0t5d0      0136   current
0114  /dev/dsk/c0t6d0      0137   current   /dev/dsk/c0t5d0      0137   current
0115  /dev/dsk/c0t6d0      0138   current   /dev/dsk/c0t5d0      0138   current
0116  /dev/dsk/c0t6d0      0139   current   /dev/dsk/c0t5d0      0139   current
0117  /dev/dsk/c0t6d0      0140   current   /dev/dsk/c0t5d0      0140   current
0118  /dev/dsk/c0t6d0      0141   current   /dev/dsk/c0t5d0      0141   current
0119  /dev/dsk/c0t6d0      0142   current   /dev/dsk/c0t5d0      0142   current
0120  /dev/dsk/c0t6d0      0143   current   /dev/dsk/c0t5d0      0143   current
0121  /dev/dsk/c0t6d0      0144   current   /dev/dsk/c0t5d0      0144   current
0122  /dev/dsk/c0t6d0      0145   current   /dev/dsk/c0t5d0      0145   current
0123  /dev/dsk/c0t6d0      0146   current   /dev/dsk/c0t5d0      0146   current
0124  /dev/dsk/c0t6d0      0147   current   /dev/dsk/c0t5d0      0147   current
```

F1 - ll /dev/vg00

Next, view **/dev/vg00** to have a record of the logical volumes.

```
# ll /dev/vg00

/dev/vg00:
total 0
crw-r--r--   1 root     sys       64 0x000000 May 29 04:44 group
brw-r-----   1 root     sys       64 0x000001 May 29 04:44 lvol1
brw-r-----   1 root     sys       64 0x000002 Jul  9 17:10 lvol2
brw-r-----   1 root     sys       64 0x000003 May 29 04:44 lvol3
brw-r-----   1 root     sys       64 0x000004 May 29 04:44 lvol4
brw-r-----   1 root     sys       64 0x000005 May 29 04:44 lvol5
brw-r-----   1 root     sys       64 0x000006 May 29 04:44 lvol6
brw-r-----   1 root     sys       64 0x000007 May 29 04:44 lvol7
crw-r-----   1 root     sys       64 0x000001 May 29 04:44 rlvol1
crw-r-----   1 root     sys       64 0x000002 Jul  9 17:10 rlvol2
crw-r-----   1 root     sys       64 0x000003 May 29 04:44 rlvol3
crw-r-----   1 root     sys       64 0x000004 May 29 04:44 rlvol4
crw-r-----   1 root     sys       64 0x000005 May 29 04:44 rlvol5
```

```
crw-r-----  1 root     sys       64 0x000006 May 29 04:44 rlvol6
crw-r-----  1 root     sys       64 0x000007 May 29 04:44 rlvol7
```

F1 - ll /dev/vg_nw

Next, view **/dev/vg_nw** and any other volume groups.

```
# ll /dev/vg_nw

/dev/vg_nw:
total 0
crw-rw-rw-  1 root     sys       64 0x010000 Jul  9 12:03 group
brw-r-----  1 root     sys       64 0x010003 Jul  9 13:01 lv_nwbackup
brw-r-----  1 root     sys       64 0x010004 Jul  9 13:01 lv_nwlog
brw-r-----  1 root     sys       64 0x010002 Jul  9 12:54 lv_nwsys
brw-r-----  1 root     sys       64 0x010001 Jul  9 12:53 lv_nwtext
crw-r-----  1 root     sys       64 0x010003 Jul  9 13:01 rlv_nwbackup
crw-r-----  1 root     sys       64 0x010004 Jul  9 13:01 rlv_nwlog
crw-r-----  1 root     sys       64 0x010002 Jul  9 12:55 rlv_nwsys
crw-r-----  1 root     sys       64 0x010001 Jul  9 12:54 rlv_nwtext
```

F1 - bdf

Next, view the file systems with **bdf**. Notice that **lvol2** is not shown because this is a swap and dump device.

```
# bdf
Filesystem              kbytes     used    avail %used Mounted on
/dev/vg00/lvol1          91669    31889    50613   39% /
/dev/vg00/lvol7         159509    83630    59928   58% /var
/dev/vg00/lvol6         319125   197912    89300   69%
/usr /dev/vg00/lvol5     31829    11323    17323   40% /tmp
/dev/vg00/lvol4         251285    67854   158302   30% /opt
/dev/vg_nw/lv_nwtext   4099465  2070905  1618613   56% /nwtext
/dev/vg_nw/lv_nwsys    4099465  1063909  2625609   29% /nwsys
/dev/vg_nw/lv_nwlog      99669    17313    72389   19% /nwlog
/dev/vg_nw/lv_nwbackup 2552537   377388  1919895   16% /nwbackup
/dev/vg00/lvol3          19861     2191    15683   12% /home
```

F1 - swapinfo

Next, run **swapinfo** to see that **lvol2** is the only swap device.

```
# swapinfo
              Kb       Kb       Kb  PCT  START/      Kb
TYPE       AVAIL     USED     FREE USED  LIMIT RESERVE  PRI  NAME
dev       512000        0   512000   0%      0       -    1  /dev/vg00/lvol2
reserve        -   512000  -512000
memory   1670828  1474704   196124  88%
```

F1 - lvlnboot

Next, look at the boot information with **lvlnboot**. **lvol2** on **vg00** is the dump device.

```
# lvlnboot -v /dev/vg00
Boot Definitions for Volume Group /dev/vg00:
Physical Volumes belonging in Root Volume Group:
        /dev/dsk/c0t6d0 (10/0.6.0) -- Boot Disk
        /dev/dsk/c0t5d0 (10/0.5.0) -- Boot Disk
Root: lvol1        on: /dev/dsk/c0t6d0
                       /dev/dsk/c0t5d0
Swap: lvol2        on: /dev/dsk/c0t6d0
                       /dev/dsk/c0t5d0
Dump: lvol2        on: /dev/dsk/c0t6d0, 0
```

F1 - lifls

Look at the boot area with **lifls**.

```
#lifls -Clv /dev/dsk/c0t6d0

volume ISL10 data size 7984 directory size 8 94/11/04 15:46:53
filename   type   start  size    implement  created
=====================================================================
ODE        -12960 584    496     0          95/05/19 13:36:50
MAPFILE    -12277 1080   32      0          95/05/19 13:36:50
SYSLIB     -12280 1112   224     0          95/05/19 13:36:50
CONFIGDATA -12278 1336   62      0          95/05/19 13:36:50
SLMOD      -12276 1400   70      0          95/05/19 13:36:50
SLDEV      -12276 1472   68      0          95/05/19 13:36:50
SLDRIVERS  -12276 1544   244     0          95/05/19 13:36:50
MAPPER     -12279 1792   93      0          95/05/19 13:36:51
IOTEST     -12279 1888   150     0          95/05/19 13:36:51
PERFVER    -12279 2040   80      0          95/05/19 13:36:51
PVCU       -12801 2120   64      0          96/09/16 09:04:01
SSINFO     -12286 2184   1       0          94/11/04 15:46:53
ISL        -12800 2192   240     0          94/11/04 15:46:53
AUTO       -12289 2432   1       0          94/11/04 15:46:54
HPUX       -12928 2440   800     0          96/05/29 01:49:55
LABEL      BIN    3240   8       0          
```

F2

After all the appropriate information has been saved for the existing configuration, we can begin the reconfiguration. First, we break the mirror with **lvreduce** and the **-m** option.

```
# lvreduce -m 0 /dev/vg00/lvol1
Logical volume "/dev/vg00/lvol1" has been successfully reduced.
Volume Group configuration for /dev/vg00 has been saved in /etc/lvmconf/vg00.conf
# lvreduce -m 0 /dev/vg00/lvol2
Logical volume "/dev/vg00/lvol2" has been successfully reduced.
Volume Group configuration for /dev/vg00 has been saved in /etc/lvmconf/vg00.conf
# lvreduce -m 0 /dev/vg00/lvol3
Logical volume "/dev/vg00/lvol3" has been successfully reduced.
Volume Group configuration for /dev/vg00 has been saved in /etc/lvmconf/vg00.conf
# lvreduce -m 0 /dev/vg00/lvol4
Logical volume "/dev/vg00/lvol4" has been successfully reduced.
Volume Group configuration for /dev/vg00 has been saved in /etc/lvmconf/vg00.conf
# lvreduce -m 0 /dev/vg00/lvol5
Logical volume "/dev/vg00/lvol5" has been successfully reduced.
Volume Group configuration for /dev/vg00 has been saved in /etc/lvmconf/vg00.conf
# lvreduce -m 0 /dev/vg00/lvol6
Logical volume "/dev/vg00/lvol6" has been successfully reduced.
Volume Group configuration for /dev/vg00 has been saved in /etc/lvmconf/vg00.conf
# lvreduce -m 0 /dev/vg00/lvol7
Logical volume "/dev/vg00/lvol7" has been successfully reduced.
Volume Group configuration for /dev/vg00 has been saved in /etc/lvmconf/vg00.conf
```

You can type each command or make a file with the **lvreduce** commands in it and run the file. You can call the file **/tmp/reduce** with the following entries:

```
lvreduce -m 0 /dev/vg00/lvol1
lvreduce -m 0 /dev/vg00/lvol2
lvreduce -m 0 /dev/vg00/lvol3
lvreduce -m 0 /dev/vg00/lvol4
lvreduce -m 0 /dev/vg00/lvol5
lvreduce -m 0 /dev/vg00/lvol6
lvreduce -m 0 /dev/vg00/lvol7
```

After you create this file, change it to executable and then run with the following two commands.

```
# chmod 555 /tmp/reduce
# /tmp/reduce
```

You will then see all the output of having run the **lvreduce** commands.

F3

Check to see that mirroring of **lvol1-7** has been reduced with **lvdisplay**. Look to see that mirrored copies are equal to 0. Only **lvol1** through **lvol3** are shown in this listing.

```
# lvdisplay -v /dev/vg00/lvol* | more

--- Logical volumes ---
LV Name                  /dev/vg00/lvol1
VG Name                  /dev/vg00
LV Permission            read/write
LV Status                available/syncd
Mirror copies            0
Consistency Recovery     MWC
Schedule                 parallel
LV Size (Mbytes)         92
Current LE               23
Allocated PE             23
Stripes                  0
Stripe Size (Kbytes)     0
Bad block                off
Allocation               strict/contiguous

LV Name                  /dev/vg00/lvol2
VG Name                  /dev/vg00
LV Permission            read/write
LV Status                available/syncd
Mirror copies            0
Consistency Recovery     MWC
Schedule                 parallel
LV Size (Mbytes)         500
Current LE               125
Allocated PE             125
Stripes                  0
Stripe Size (Kbytes)     0
Bad block                off
Allocation               strict/contiguous

LV Name                  /dev/vg00/lvol3
VG Name                  /dev/vg00
LV Permission            read/write
LV Status                available/syncd
Mirror copies            0
Consistency Recovery     MWC
Schedule                 parallel
LV Size (Mbytes)         20
Current LE               5
Allocated PE             5
Stripes                  0
Stripe Size (Kbytes)     0
Bad block                on
Allocation               strict
```

F4

Now remove **c0t5d0** from **vg00** with **vgreduce**. Since there is no mirroring in place, this approach will work. This disk will be put on a different SCSI controller and again used for mirroring later in the procedure.

```
# vgreduce /dev/vg00 /dev/dsk/c0t5d0
Volume group "/dev/vg00" has been successfully reduced.
Volume Group configuration for /dev/vg00 has been saved in /etc/lvmconf/vg00.conf
```

F5

At this point **c0t5d0** is no longer in **vg00**. Verify that "PV Name" **c0t5d0** is no longer in **vg00** with **vgdisplay**.

```
# vgdisplay -v
```

There should be no **c0t5d0** in **vg00**.

F6

Verify that "dump lvol" is in **/stand/system**. If not, add "dump vol" and reconfigure the kernel. See the kernel rebuild procedure in Chapter 1.

F7

Now the hardware upgrade takes place. The system is shut down, disk drives are added and moved, and the system is rebooted. The 4 GByte disk **/dev/dsk/c0t5d0** becomes **/dev/dsk/c1t3d0** at address 10/4/4.3.0, and a new 2 GByte disk is introduced as 10/0.5.0 with the device name **/dev/dsk/c0t5d0**. The second half of Figure 9-4 depicts this change.

F8

The first activity to perform after the hardware upgrade is to view the new disks with **ioscan**. There is now a 2 GByte disk at 10/0.5.0 and a 4 GByte disk at 10/4/4.3.0.

```
# ioscan -funC disk
Class      I  H/W Path    Driver     S/W State H/W Type  Description
===================================================================
disk       2  10/0.5.0    sdisk      CLAIMED   DEVICE SEAGATE   ST32550W
                          /dev/dsk/c0t5d0    /dev/rdsk/c0t5d0
disk       3  10/0.6.0    sdisk      CLAIMED   DEVICE    SEAGATE ST15150W
```

```
                               /dev/dsk/c0t6d0    /dev/rdsk/c0t6d0
disk   12  10/4/4.3.0    disc3      CLAIMED    DEVICE      SEAGATE ST15150W
                               /dev/dsk/c1t3d0    /dev/rdsk/c1t3d0
                               /dev/floppy/c1t3d0 /dev/rfloppy/c1t3d0
disk    6  10/4/4.4.0    disc3      CLAIMED    DEVICE      SEAGATE ST15150W
                               /dev/dsk/c1t4d0    /dev/rdsk/c1t4d0
                               /dev/floppy/c1t4d0 /dev/rfloppy/c1t4d0
disk    7  10/4/4.5.0    disc3      CLAIMED    DEVICE      SEAGATE ST15150W
                               /dev/dsk/c1t5d0    /dev/rdsk/c1t5d0
                               /dev/floppy/c1t5d0 /dev/rfloppy/c1t5d0
disk    8  10/4/4.6.0    disc3      CLAIMED    DEVICE      SEAGATE ST15150W
                               /dev/dsk/c1t6d0    /dev/rdsk/c1t6d0
                               /dev/floppy/c1t6d0 /dev/rfloppy/c1t6d0
disk    9  10/4/12.4.0   disc3      CLAIMED    DEVICE      SEAGATE ST15150W
                               /dev/dsk/c2t4d0    /dev/rdsk/c2t4d0
                               /dev/floppy/c2t4d0 /dev/rfloppy/c2t4d0
disk   10  10/4/12.5.0   disc3      CLAIMED    DEVICE      SEAGATE ST15150W
                               /dev/dsk/c2t5d0    /dev/rdsk/c2t5d0
                               /dev/floppy/c2t5d0 /dev/rfloppy/c2t5d0
disk   11  10/4/12.6.0   disc3      CLAIMED    DEVICE      SEAGATE ST15150W
                               /dev/dsk/c2t6d0    /dev/rdsk/c2t6d0
                               /dev/floppy/c2t6d0 /dev/rfloppy/c2t6d0
disk    5  10/12/5.2.0   sdisk      CLAIMED    DEVICE      TOSHIBA CD-ROM XM-5401TA
                               /dev/dsk/c3t2d0    /dev/rdsk/c3t2d0
```

F9

Now we run **vgdisplay** to see new volume group information. Only
c0t6d0 is in **vg00** and no mirroring is yet configured. The other volume
groups have remained the same. Only **lvol1** through **lvol3** are shown in our
example.

```
# vgdisplay -v /dev/vg00

--- Volume groups ---
VG Name                  /dev/vg00
VG Write Access          read/write
VG Status                available
Max LV                   255
Cur LV                   7
Open LV                  7
Max PV                   16
Cur PV                   1
Act PV                   1
Max PE per PV            1023
VGDA                     2
PE Size (Mbytes)         4
Total PE                 1023
Alloc PE                 344
Free PE                  679
Total PVG                0

--- Logical volumes ---
LV Name                  /dev/vg00/lvol1
LV Status                available/syncd
LV Size (Mbytes)         92
Current LE               23
Allocated PE             23
Used PV                  1
```

```
LV Name              /dev/vg00/lvol2
LV Status            available/syncd
LV Size (Mbytes)     500
Current LE           125
Allocated PE         125
Used PV              1

LV Name              /dev/vg00/lvol3
LV Status            available/syncd
LV Size (Mbytes)     20
Current LE           5
Allocated PE         5
Used PV              1
```

(F9 continued)

Only the first three logical volumes in **/dev/vg_nw** are shown.

```
# vgdisplay -v /dev/vg_nw
VG Name              /dev/vg_nw
VG Write Access      read/write
VG Status            available
Max LV               255
Cur LV               4
Open LV              4
Max PV               16
Cur PV               6
Act PV               6
Max PE per PV        1023
VGDA                 12
PE Size (Mbytes)     4
Total PE             6138
Alloc PE             5416
Free PE              722
Total PVG            2
   --- Logical volumes ---
LV Name              /dev/vg_nw/lv_nwtext
LV Status            available/syncd
LV Size (Mbytes)     4092
Current LE           1023
Allocated PE         2046
Used PV              2

LV Name              /dev/vg_nw/lv_nwsys
LV Status            available/syncd
LV Size (Mbytes)     4092
Current LE           1023
Allocated PE         2046
Used PV              2

LV Name              /dev/vg_nw/lv_nwbackup
LV Status            available/syncd
LV Size (Mbytes)     2548
Current LE           637
Allocated PE         1274
Used PV              2
```

F10

Use **vgextend** to add the 4 GByte disk to **vg00** for mirroring (you may also have to run **pvcreate** here, too).

```
# vgextend /dev/vg00 /dev/dsk/c1t3d0
Volume group "/dev/vg00" has been successfully extended. Volume Group configuration for
/dev/vg00 has been saved in /etc/lvmconf/vg00.conf
```

F11

Now we can create the new 2 GByte disk and add it to **vg00** using the two following commands: **pvcreate** (F11) to create the physical volume and **vgextend** (F12) to extend the volume group.

```
# pvcreate -f /dev/rdsk/c0t5d0
Physical volume "/dev/rdsk/c0t5d0" has been successfully created.
```

F12

```
# vgextend /dev/vg00 /dev/dsk/c0t5d0
Volume group "/dev/vg00" has been successfully extended.
Volume Group configuration for /dev/vg00 has been saved in /etc/lvmconf/vg00.conf
```

F13

We can check to see that these two disks have indeed been added to **vg00** with **vgdisplay**. Only **lvol1** through **lvol3** are shown in our example.

The end of the display is the significant part of the listing showing three physical volumes.

```
# vgdisplay -v /dev/vg00

   --- Volume groups ---
VG Name                  /dev/vg00
VG Write Access          read/write
VG Status                available
Max LV                   255
Cur LV                   7
Open LV                  7
Max PV                   16
Cur PV                   3
Act PV                   3
Max PE per PV            1023
VGDA                     6
PE Size (Mbytes)         4
Total PE                 2554
Alloc PE                 344
Free PE                  2210
Total PVG                0

   --- Logical volumes ---

LV Name                  /dev/vg00/lvol1
LV Status                available/syncd
LV Size (Mbytes)         92
Current LE               23
Allocated PE             23
Used PV                  1

LV Name                  /dev/vg00/lvol2
LV Status                available/syncd
LV Size (Mbytes)         500
Current LE               125
Allocated PE             125
Used PV                  1

LV Name                  /dev/vg00/lvol3
LV Status                available/syncd
LV Size (Mbytes)         20
Current LE               5
Allocated PE             5
Used PV                  1

                    .
                    .
                    .


   --- Physical volumes ---

PV Name                  /dev/dsk/c0t6d0
PV Status                available
Total PE                 1023
Free PE                  679

PV Name                  /dev/dsk/c1t3d0
PV Status                available
Total PE                 1023
Free PE                  1023

PV Name                  /dev/dsk/c0t5d0
PV Status                available
Total PE                 508
Free PE                  508
```

F14

We can now create the dump logical volume in **vg00** with **lvcreate** (F14), extend it to 2 GBytes with **lvextend** (F15), and view it with **lvdisplay** (F16).

```
# lvcreate -n dump  /dev/vg00
Logical volume "/dev/vg00/dump" has been successfully created with character de-
vice
"/dev/vg00/rdump".
Volume Group configuration for /dev/vg00 has been saved in /etc/lvmconf/vg00.conf
```

F15

```
# lvextend -l 508 /dev/vg00/dump /dev/dsk/c0t5d0
Logical volume "/dev/vg00/dump" has been successfully extended.
Volume Group configuration for /dev/vg00 has been saved in /etc/lvmconf/vg00.conf
```

F16

```
# lvdisplay /dev/vg00/dump | more

--- Logical volumes ---
LV Name                 /dev/vg00/dump
VG Name                 /dev/vg00
LV Permission           read/write
LV Status               available/syncd
Mirror copies           0
Consistency Recovery    MWC
Schedule                parallel
LV Size (Mbytes)        2032
Current LE              508
Allocated PE            508
Stripes                 0
Stripe Size (Kbytes)    0
Bad block               on
Allocation              strict

--- Distribution of logical volume ---
PV Name           LE on PV  PE on PV
/dev/dsk/c0t5d0   508       508
                  .
                  .
                  .
```

F17

In order to make **/dev/vg00/dump** the dump device, we must first make it contiguous with **lvchange** and then make it a dump device with **lvln-boot**.

```
# lvchange -C y /dev/vg00/dump
```

```
# lvlnboot -d /dev/vg00/dump
```

F18

View dump devices.

```
# lvlnboot -v | more
Boot Definitions for Volume Group /dev/vg00:
Physical Volumes belonging in Root Volume Group:
            /dev/dsk/c0t6d0 (10/0.6.0) -- Boot Disk
            /dev/dsk/c1t3d0 (10/4/4.3.0) -- Boot Disk
            /dev/dsk/c0t5d0 (10/0.5.0)
Root: lvol1      on:      /dev/dsk/c0t6d0
Swap: lvol2      on:      /dev/dsk/c0t6d0
Dump: lvol2      on:      /dev/dsk/c0t6d0, 0
Dump: dump       on:      /dev/dsk/c0t5d0, 1
```

This may not be what we want. The primary dump device, as indicated by the "0" is **/dev/dsk/c0t6d0** and the secondary dump device, indicated by the "1," is **/dev/dsk/c0t5d0**. We can optionally redo this. Let's proceed with mirroring the lvols on **/dev/vg00** and come back to dump devices.

F19

Let's now extend all the volumes in **vg00** for one mirror using **lvextend**.

```
# lvextend -m 1 /dev/vg00/lvol1 /dev/dsk/c1t3d0
The newly allocated mirrors are now being synchronized.
This operation will take some time. Please wait ....
Logical volume "/dev/vg00/lvol1" has been successfully extended.
Volume Group configuration for /dev/vg00 has been saved in /etc/lvmconf/vg00.conf
```

Put the following in **/tmp/mirror** and run. **lvol1** was extended earlier; **lvol2** is swap and doesn't need to be extended:

```
lvextend -m 1 /dev/vg00/lvol3 /dev/dsk/c1t3d0
lvextend -m 1 /dev/vg00/lvol4 /dev/dsk/c1t3d0
lvextend -m 1 /dev/vg00/lvol5 /dev/dsk/c1t3d0
lvextend -m 1 /dev/vg00/lvol6 /dev/dsk/c1t3d0
lvextend -m 1 /dev/vg00/lvol7 /dev/dsk/c1t3d0
```

```
The newly allocated mirrors are now being synchronized.
This operation will take some time.
Please wait .... Logical volume "/dev/vg00/lvol2" has been successfully extended.
Volume Group configuration for /dev/vg00 has been saved in /etc/lvmconf/vg00.conf
                    .
                    .
                    .
```

F20

Let's now verify that the mirroring is in place with **lvdisplay** (only **lvol1** and **lvol2** are shown).

```
# lvdsisplay -v /dev/vg00/lvol* | more

--- Logical volumes ---
LV Name                 /dev/vg00/lvol1
VG Name                 /dev/vg00
LV Permission           read/write
LV Status               available/syncd
Mirror copies           1
Consistency Recovery    MWC
Schedule                parallel
LV Size (Mbytes)        92
Current LE              23
Allocated PE            46
Stripes                 0
Stripe Size (Kbytes)    0
Bad block               off
Allocation              strict/contiguous

--- Distribution of logical volume ---
PV Name           LE on PV     PE on PV
/dev/dsk/c0t6d0     23           23
/dev/dsk/c1t3d0     23           23

--- Logical extents ---
LE    PV1                PE1   Status 1 PV2              PE2   Status 2
0000  /dev/dsk/c0t6d0    0000  current  /dev/dsk/c1t3d0  0000  current
0001  /dev/dsk/c0t6d0    0001  current  /dev/dsk/c1t3d0  0001  current
0002  /dev/dsk/c0t6d0    0002  current  /dev/dsk/c1t3d0  0002  current
0003  /dev/dsk/c0t6d0    0003  current  /dev/dsk/c1t3d0  0003  current
                     .
                     .
```

You can see from this listing that **c0t6d0** is mirrored on **c1t3d0**.

F21

Reboot the system to confirm that all changes have taken effect.

After reboot, do the following to create a dump. The key must be in the "Service" position for **^b** to work (you must be on a server and at the system console for this to work).

Use **^b** to get the **CM>** prompt.

Use the **tc** command at the **CM>** prompt to create core dump

F22

The system will automatically reboot after a core dump. Use the following command to save the core dump to tape. The **/var/adm/crash** file name is required even though the core dump is in the dump logical volume and not in the **/var/adm/crash** directory.

```
# savecore -t /dev/rmt/0m /var/adm/crash
```

F23

Then use **savecore -xt** and the directory name to the extract core dump. If you do not have room for the core dump, or you want a more thorough check, you can place a call and ask the HP Response Center to verify that the **savecore** to tape has worked.

```
# savecore -xt /dev/rmt/0m /var/adm/crash
```

The core dump space requirement is calculated from the end of dump back toward the front. For this reason, about roughly 1.5 GBytes is written to the **dump** logical volume and then roughly 600 MBytes are written to **lvol2**.

Optional Procedure to Exchange Dump Priorities

This procedure removes all boot definitions, including swap and dump, from **/dev/vg00** with **lvrmboot** and recreates them with **lvlnboot**. This needs to be done because **lvol2** is the primary dump logical volume (0) and dump is the secondary dump logical volume (1).

You must reboot in order for these changes to take effect. Figure 9-16 shows the steps required to complete this optional procedure.

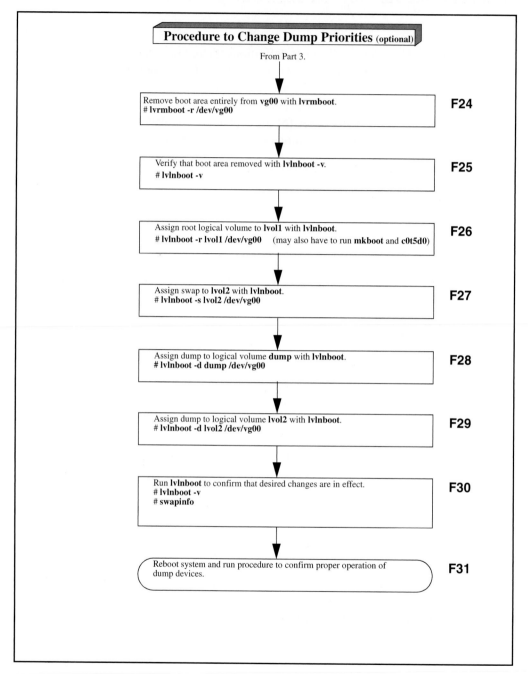

Figure 9-16 Procedure to Change Dump Priorities (Optional)

F24

Remove the boot area entirely from **vg00** with **lvrmboot**.

```
# lvrmboot -r /dev/vg00
```

F25

Verify that the boot area was removed with lvlnboot.

```
# lvlnboot -v
Boot Definitions for Volume Group /dev/vg00: The Boot Data Area is empty.
```

F26

Assign the root logical volume to **lvol1** on **/dev/vg00** with **lvlnboot**.

```
# lvlnboot -r lvol1 /dev/vg00
```

F27

Assign the swap to **lvol2** on **/dev/vg00**.

```
# lvlnboot -s lvol2 /dev/vg00

# swapinfo
          Kb        Kb       Kb   PCT  START/       Kb
TYPE      AVAIL     USED     FREE USED LIMIT RESERVE PRI NAME
dev       512000      0   512000   0%     0       -   1 /dev/vg00/lvol2
reserve        -  23144   -23144
memory   1671008  27324  1643684   2%
```

F28

Assign the dump to the logical volume **dump** on **/dev/vg00**.

```
# lvlnboot -d dump /dev/vg00
```

F29

     Assign the secondary dump device as **lvol2** (primary swap) on **lvol2**.

```
# lvlnboot -d lvol2 /dev/vg00
```

F30

     Run **lvlnboot** to confirm that the dump and swap are properly configured with priority "0" on 2 GByte disk **c0t5d0** and "1" on **c0t6d0**.

```
# lvlnboot -v      # after adding lvol2 as secondary dump

Boot Definitions for Volume Group /dev/vg00:
Physical Volumes belonging in Root Volume Group:
                /dev/dsk/c0t6d0 (10/0.6.0) -- Boot Disk
                /dev/dsk/c1t3d0 (10/4/4.3.0) -- Boot Disk
                /dev/dsk/c0t5d0 (10/0.5.0)
Root: lvol1        on:      /dev/dsk/c0t6d0
                            /dev/dsk/c1t3d0
Swap: lvol2        on:      /dev/dsk/c0t6d0
                            /dev/dsk/c1t3d0
Dump: dump         on:      /dev/dsk/c0t5d0, 0
Dump: dump         on:      /dev/dsk/c0t6d0, 1
```

F31

     Reboot the system and run steps F21-F23 to confirm proper operation of dump devices.

     Although this procedure to reconfigure disks is for a specific system, it is useful for illustrating the many LVM commands required to perform such tasks. LVM, and disk management in general, are the areas that I find consumes the most system administration time in mature HP-UX installations. There are many commands used in this procedure for which there is no way to "back out," so use caution whenever using LVM commands.

HP VERITAS Volume Manager

At the time of this writing HP Veritas Volume Manager (which I'll call VxVM throughout much of this chapter) is a software product loaded from the HP-UX 11i Application CD-ROM. There is a version of VxVM bundled with 11i called Base HP VERITAS Volume Manager and a full version called HP VERITAS Volume Manager. The Base product is a subset of the full version. With both versions of VxVM there is a Java-based administration interface, striping (RAID 0), concatenation, path failover support, online resizing of volumes, and a task monitor. The full version performs all of the functions in the Base product and also supports load balancing, hot relocation and unrelocation, mirroring of up to 32 copies (RAID 1), mirrored stripes, striped mirrors, RAID 5, online migration, and online relayout. The features of each are described in the *HP VERITAS Volume Manager Release Notes.*

On the system used for the examples compiled for the VxVM part of this chapter the root disk setup at the time 11i was originally loaded on the system was under control of Logical Volume Manager (LVM.) After loading HP Veritas Volume Manager as an application we can then perform storage administration on other disks on the system. The root disk will remain under LVM control and not be placed under VxVM control.

In the upcoming sections, we'll load HP Veritas Volume Manager and perform some basic storage management tasks so you can get a feel for this product. This is a product that has a lot of functionality and manuals devoted to using it, so in this part of the chapter we'll cover some of the basics. Please see *docs.hp.com* for a complete list of manuals on VxVm. Two that contain much more detailed information on configuring and using VxVM are *HP VERITAS Volume Manager Release Notes* and *HP VERITAS Volume Manager Administrator's Guide.*

HP VERITAS Volume Manager Setup

After loading HP Veritas from the Applications CD-ROM we have to decide what disk(s) we want to control with VxVM. Let's run **ioscan** to view the disks in our L-Class system:

```
# ioscan -funC disk
```

```
Class    I  H/W Path     Driver S/W State   H/W Type     Description

=======================================================================

disk     0  0/0/1/1.2.0  sdisk CLAIMED      DEVICE       SEAGATE ST318203LC

                         /dev/dsk/c1t2d0    /dev/rdsk/c1t2d0

disk     1  0/0/2/0.2.0  sdisk CLAIMED      DEVICE       SEAGATE ST318203LC

                         /dev/dsk/c2t2d0    /dev/rdsk/c2t2d0

disk     2  0/0/2/1.4.0  sdisk CLAIMED      DEVICE       TOSHIBA CD-ROM XM-6201TA

                         /dev/dsk/c3t4d0    /dev/rdsk/c3t4d0
```

This output shows two internal disks and a CD-ROM drive (we'll later add two more disks to demonstrate a setup of mirroring and striping). The root disk under LVM control is *c1t2d0*. We want to use VxVM to perform various storage management functions on disk *c2t2d0*. If there is any LVM header information on this disk, it must be removed prior to proceeding with any VxVM functions on the disk. The following two LVM-related commands were issued to create and remove this disk from LVM:

pvcreate -f /dev/rdsk/c2t2d0

```
Physical volume "/dev/rdsk/c2t2d0" has been successfully created.
```

pvremove /dev/rdsk/c2t2d0

```
The physical volume associated with "/dev/rdsk/c2t2d0" has been
removed.

#
```

You may not have to issue the **pvcreate** command; however, I have found that issuing both commands works every time. This procedure is outlined in the *Release Notes* I mentioned earlier.

Next, we run **vxinstall** to perform the initial setup of VxVM. In the following procedure, we run **vxinstall** and select a *Quick Installation,* which walks us through evaluating the disks on the system and allows us to select those that we want to put under VxVM control:

vxinstall

Populating VxVM DMP device directories ....
Generating list of attached controllers....
Volume Manager Installation

Menu: VolumeManager/Install

The Volume Manager names disks on your system using the controller
and disk number of the disk, substituting them into the following

   pattern:
                    c<controller>t<disk>d<disk>

   NOTE: With the Dynamic Multipathing (DMP) facility of VxVM, the
   controller number represents a multipath pseudo controller number
   for those disk devices with multiple access paths. For example,
   if a disk has 2 paths from controllers c0 and c1, then the Volume
   Manager displays only one of them, such as c0, to represent both
   of the controllers.

   Some examples would be:

                    c0t0d0- first controller, first target, first disk
                    c1t0d0- second controller, first target, first disk
                    c1t1d0- second controller, second target, first disk

   The Volume Manager has detected the following controllers on your
system:

                    c1:
                    c2:

Hit RETURN to continue.

_____

Volume Manager Installation
Menu: VolumeManager/Install
   You will now be asked if you wish to use Quick Installation or
   Custom Installation. Custom Installation allows you to select how
   the Volume Manager will handle the installation of each disk
   attached to your system.

   Quick Installation examines each disk attached to your system and
   attempts to create volumes to cover all disk partitions that might
   be used for file systems or for other similar purposes.

   If you do not wish to use some disks with the Volume Manager, or if
   you wish to reinitialize some disks, use the Custom Installation

```
option Otherwise, we suggest that you use the Quick Installation
option.


Hit RETURN to continue.
```

```
Volume Manager Installation Options
Menu: VolumeManager/Install


1                Quick Installation
2                Custom Installation
?                Display help about menu
??               Display help about the menuing system
q                Exit from menus


Select an operation to perform: 1
```

```
Volume Manager Quick Installation
Menu: VolumeManager/Install/QuickInstall/c1

Generating list of attached disks on c1....
<excluding c1t2d0>
No disks were found attached to controller c1 !


Hit RETURN to continue.
```

```
Volume Manager Quick Installation
Menu: VolumeManager/Install/QuickInstall/c2

Generating list of attached disks on c2....
  The Volume Manager has detected the following disks on controller
c2:
  c2t2d0

Hit RETURN to continue.
```

```
Volume Manager Quick Installation For Controller c2

Menu: VolumeManager/Install/QuickInstall/c2

Initialize all disks on this controller ? (destroys data on these
disks)
[y,n,q,?] (default: n) y


Are you sure ? (destroys data on these disks)
[y,n,q,?] (default: n) y

 Volume Manager will now initialize all the disks on this controller

Hit RETURN to continue.

_____


Volume Manager Quick Installation
Menu: VolumeManager/Install/QuickInstall/c2/Init

Use default disk names for these disks? [y,n,q,?] (default: y) y

   The c2t2d0 disk will be given disk name disk01

Hit RETURN to continue.

_____



Volume Manager Quick Installation
Menu: VolumeManager/Install/QuickInstall


   The following is a summary of your choices.
                 c2t2d0New Disk
Is this correct [y,n,q,?] (default: y)
   The Volume Manager is now reconfiguring (partition phase)...
   Volume Manager: Initializing c2t2d0 as a new disk.
   The Volume Manager is now reconfiguring (initialization phase)...
   Volume Manager: Adding disk01 (c2t2d0) as a new disk.

   The Volume Daemon has been enabled for transactions
   Starting the relocation daemon, vxrelocd.
#
```

Notice that **vxinstall** found the one disk on our system not under LVM control and asked us if we wanted to initialize this disk. Since we have only one potential disk to place under VxVM control, it is the only disk found by

vxinstall. The *Quick Installation* we chose, as opposed to *Custom Installation*, makes some of the decisions for us, and in this case, helped us configure the disk quickly.

After running **vxinstall**, we can view the processes that have been started to support VxVM:

```
# ps -ef | grep vx
  root     34      0  0 12:52:28 ?           0:01 vxfsd
  root   2978      0  0 12:58:59 ?           0:00 vxiod
  root   4170   4156  0 13:07:35 ttyp4       0:00 vxnotify
  root   4079      1  0 13:05:51 ?           0:00 vxconfigd -k -m enable
  root   4165      1  0 13:07:35 ttyp4       0:00 /sbin/sh -
                                     /usr/lib/vxvm/bin/vxrelocd root
  root   4173   4165  0 13:07:35 ttyp4       0:00 vxnotify -f -w 15
  root   4628   2900  1 13:16:12 ttyp4       0:00 grep vx
#
```

The initial load and setup of VxVM is quick and easy. I suggest that you obtain documents from *docs.hp.com* if you don't have them in hardcopy in case you need to refer to them as part of the setup. Without the *Release Notes* I would have not known the procedure to free the second disk from LVM control so that I could place it under VxVM control.

Volume Manager Storage Administrator

After the setup of HP Veritas Volume Manager is complete, its graphical interface is invoked with **/opt/HPvmsa/bin/vmsa** for the Volume Manager Storage Administrator (I'll call this vmsa occasionally in this section). Figure 9-17 shows the interface for our L-Class system:

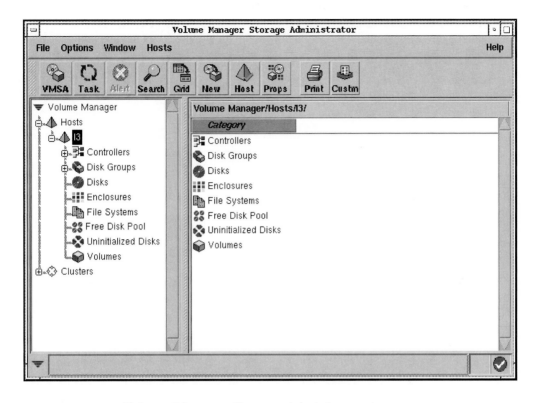

Figure 9-17 *Volume Manager Storage Administrator*

Figure 9-17 shows the many areas of administration that can be performed in this interface under our system name *l3*. We could also perform
storage administration on additional systems, *Hosts*, and *Clusters*, which
would be shown in the left-hand window along with system *l3* which is now
shown.

Let's now select some of the administration icons and see what is
reported for our L-Class system. Figure 9-18 shows the *Controllers* on our
system:

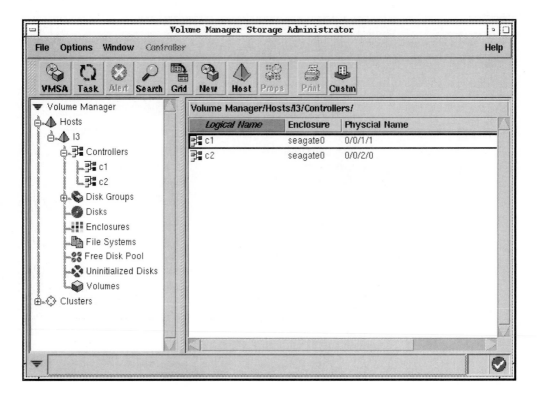

Figure 9-18 *Controllers*

Figure 9-18 shows two internal controllers on our system, *c1* and *c2*. All L-Class systems have two internal controllers, and in our case, there are no additional controllers. We could also select these controllers individually to see what disks are connected to them if we so desired.

Let's now view the *Disk Groups* on our system as shown in Figure 9-19:

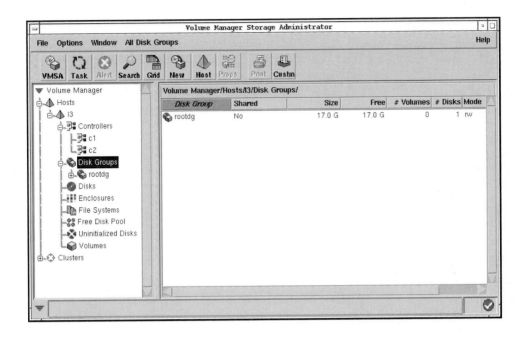

Figure 9-19 *Disk Groups*

Figure 9-19 shows one disk group, called *rootdg* which consists of one 17 GByte disk drive. This is the VxVM disk group we set up earlier. Notice that the LVM disk is not shown because it is not under VxVM control.

Next, we'll view *Disks* in Figure 9-20:

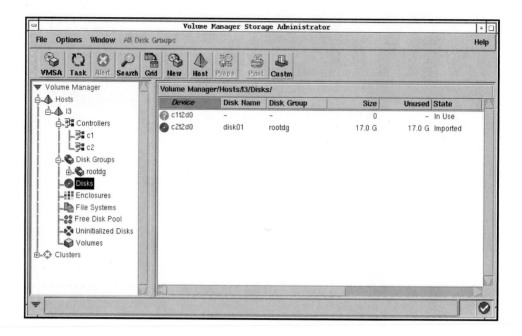

Figure 9-20 *Disks*

Figure 9-20 shows the two internal disks of our L-Class system. The first is in use by the Logical Volume Manager (root disk) and is not under the control of Veritas Volume Manager. It therefore has very little information associated with it because the VxVM interface does not recognize any of the LVM information. The second is our unused disk in *rootdg* that is called *disk01*.

Figure 9-21 shows the *File Systems* in use on our system:

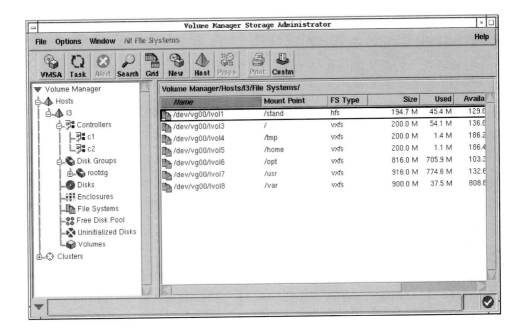

Figure 9-21 *File Systems*

Figure 9-21 shows many filesystems in use. Notice that all but one of these filesystems is a Veritas filesystem as indicated by the *vxfs*. This is sometimes a point of confusion. There is a Veritas file system (*vxfs*) that defines the type of file system and there is the Veritas Volume Manager, which we're covering in this section and is used to manage filesystems. You can also manage Veritas file systems on HP-UX using LVM.

We know that we have one disk in *rootdg* that is unused at this time. Let's issue a couple of **vx** commands and compare these to what we see in the graphical interface. Table 9-1 at the end of this section that describes the use of some **vx** commands.

First, let's get a list of disks on the system with **vxdisk**:

```
# vxdisk list
DEVICE      TYPE      DISK      GROUP      STATUS
c1t2d0      simple    -         -          LVM
```

```
c2t2d0        simple    disk01      rootdg        online
#
```

The output of **vxdisk** shows two disks in our system. The first is the root disk, which is under LVM control, and the second is *disk01,* which is under VxVM control.

Next, let's get some detailed information with **vxprint -ht**:

```
# vxprint -ht
Disk group: rootdg
DG NAME           NCONFIG      NLOG     MINORS    GROUP-ID
DM NAME           DEVICE       TYPE     PRIVLEN   PUBLEN    STATE
RV NAME           RLINK_CNT    KSTATE   STATE     PRIMARY   DATAVOLS   SRL
RL NAME           RVG          KSTATE   STATE     REM_HOST  REM_DG     REM_RLNK
V  NAME           RVG          KSTATE   STATE     LENGTH    USETYPE    PREFPLEX RDPOL
PL NAME           VOLUME       KSTATE   STATE     LENGTH    LAYOUT     NCOL/WID MODE
SD NAME           PLEX         DISK     DISKOFFS  LENGTH    [COL/]OFF  DEVICE   MODE
SV NAME           PLEX         VOLNAME  NVOLLAYR  LENGTH    [COL/]OFF  AM/NM    MODE
dg rootdg         default      default  0         969390349.1025.13
dm disk01         c2t2d0       simple   1024      17782088  -
#
```

Notice that only the information related to *rootdg,* which is under the control of the Veritas Volume Manager, has been produced. The *dg* is information related to the *disk group* and *dm* is information about the *disk mechanism.* In an upcoming **vxprint,** we'll add the *-q* option to eliminate the extensive header information produced with this output.

Next let's see what we have free on *rootdg* with the **vxdg** command:

```
# vxdg free
GROUP         DISK        DEVICE      TAG        OFFSET    LENGTH    FLAGS
rootdg        disk01      c2t2d0      c2t2d0     0         17782088  -
```

This output shows that we have nearly the full 18 GBytes of the disk free at this time.

We can now go back to the graphical interface and create a usable volume by selecting *rootdg* and entering information related to the new volume as shown in Figure 9-22:

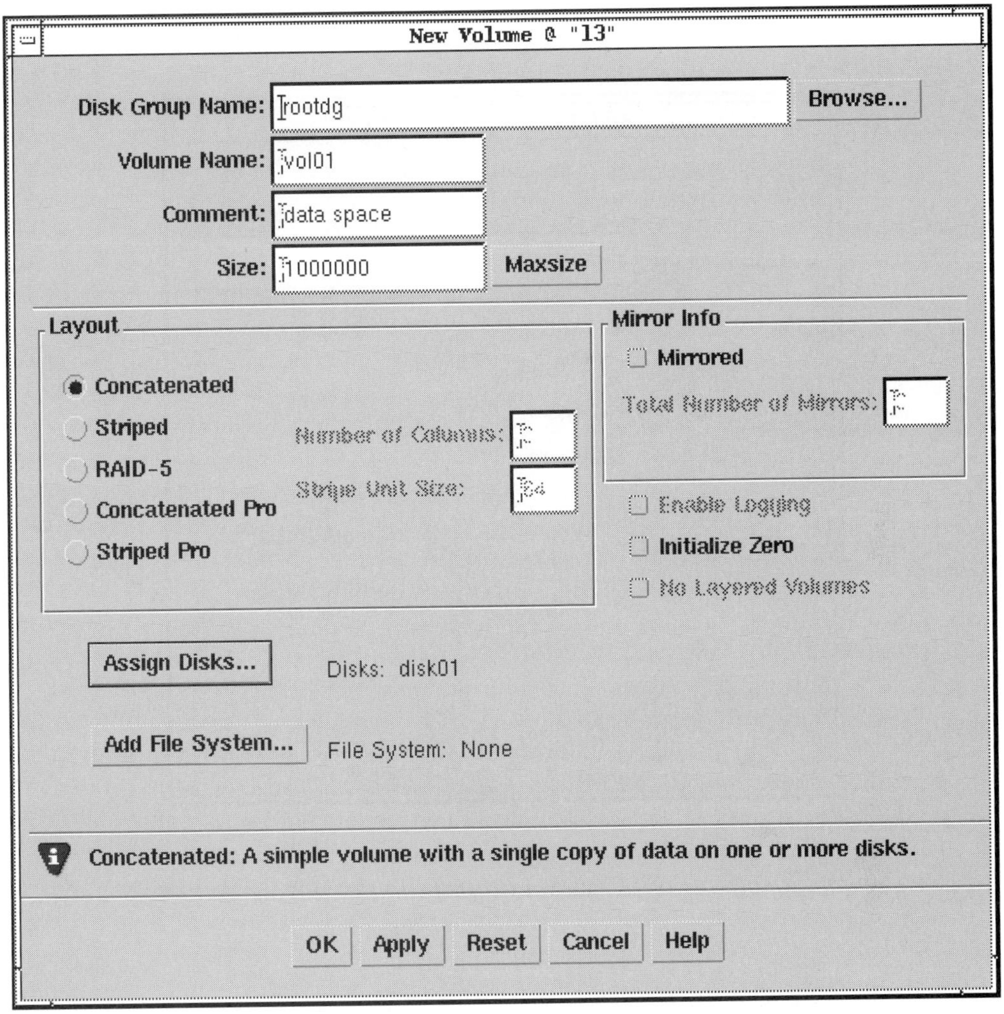

Figure 9-22   *Creating a New Volume*

The maximum size that we could have made this volume is the total size of the unused disk of which *rootdg* is comprised, which is 17781760 bytes. We have selected about 1 GByte without RAID 5 because another disk would have been required. The default name of *vol01* is used. In addition, selecting *Add File System...* from the bottom of Figure 9-22 brought up the window in Figure 9-23:

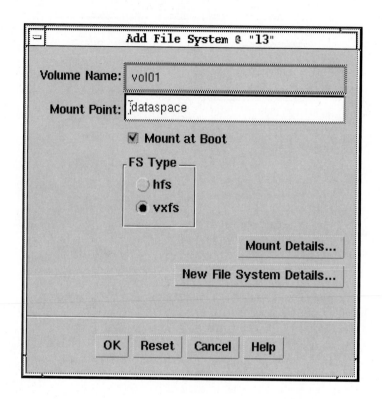

Figure 9-23 *Specifying File System Information of a New Volume*

In Figure 9-23 we selected a name of *dataspace* as the mount point and have selected *vxfs* as the file-system type. After clicking *OK*, a new volume is created, as shown in Figure 9-24:

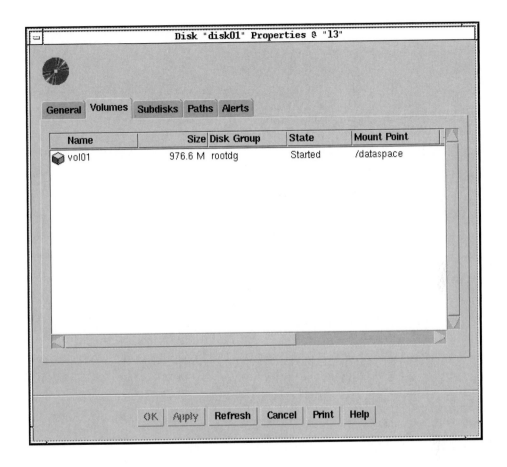

Figure 9-24 *vol01*

Figure 9-24 shows *vol01* with a mount point of */dataspace*. We can use the **vxprint** command with some useful options to see volume information. This includes information on the volume we just created. The following **vxprint** shows some useful options in the following listing:

```
# vxprint -AGtsq
Disk group: rootdg

dg rootdg     default     default   0       969390349.1025.13
sd disk01-01  vol01-01    disk01    0       1000000   0         c2t2d0    ENA
#
```

This output shows that our roughly 1 GByte area on *c2t2d0* is in place. We issued this **vxprint** with the *-q* option to eliminate the header information shown in the earlier example.

This simple example demonstrates the ease with which volumes can be added using VxVM. In the next section, we'll add two disks to the system and perform some additional setup.

HP VERITAS Volume Manager Mirroring and Striping

Now that we've covered the basics of VxVM, let's take the next step and add two additional disks to our system and use mirroring and striping.

To begin with, let's again use the **vxdisk** command to see the two new disks we've added to the system:

```
# vxdisk list
DEVICE      TYPE       DISK       GROUP       STATUS
c1t0d0      simple     -          -           online invalid
c1t2d0      simple     -          -           LVM
c2t0d0      simple     -          -           online invalid
c2t2d0      simple     disk01     rootdg      online
#
```

At this point, the disks are listed, but they have not been configured in any way. These disks were physically added to the system, and no additional commands were issued prior to the **vxdisk**.

Let's now go to the graphical interface and configure these disks. Figure 9-25 shows a total of four disks, including our two new unconfigured disks:

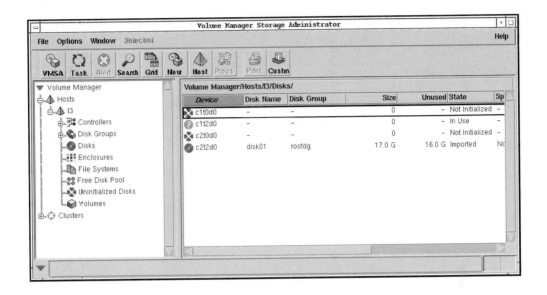

Figure 9-25 *Two New Disks in* ***vmsa***

Figure 9-25 shows that disks *c1t0d0* and *c2t0d0* are installed and *Not Initialized*. Let's now add these disks to a new disk group, called *test,* using the graphical interface as shown in Figure 9-26 for the first of the two disks:

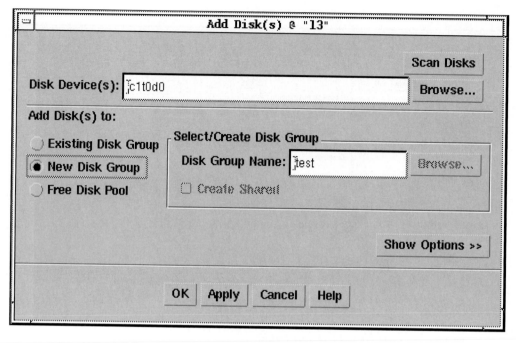

Figure 9-26   Adding New Disk to Group *test*

We add both disks to *test* graphically using the *Add Disk(s)* window. This results in the screen shown in Figure 9-27, in which both new disks, *test01* and *test02*, are part of *test*:

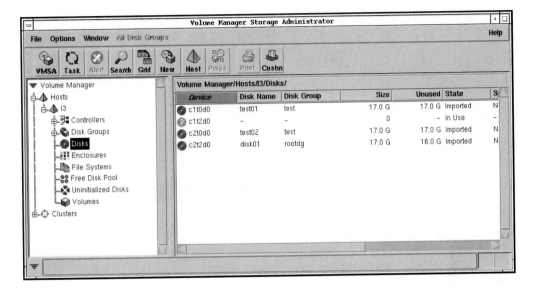

Figure 9-27 Two New Disks Added to Group *test*

We can confirm the disks in *test* with the **vxdisk** command as shown in the following listing:

```
# vxdisk list
DEVICE       TYPE       DISK        GROUP        STATUS
c1t0d0       simple     test01      test         online
c1t2d0       simple     -           -            LVM
c2t0d0       simple     test02      test         online
c2t2d0       simple     disk01      rootdg       online
#
```

The disks are now shown as configured with names of *test01* and *test02* and both are *online*. Both of these disks are part of *Group test*.

Next, let's create a striped and mirrored volume in our new *disk group test*. Selecting *New* from the items on the *vmsa* window brings up the dialog box shown in Figure 9-28.

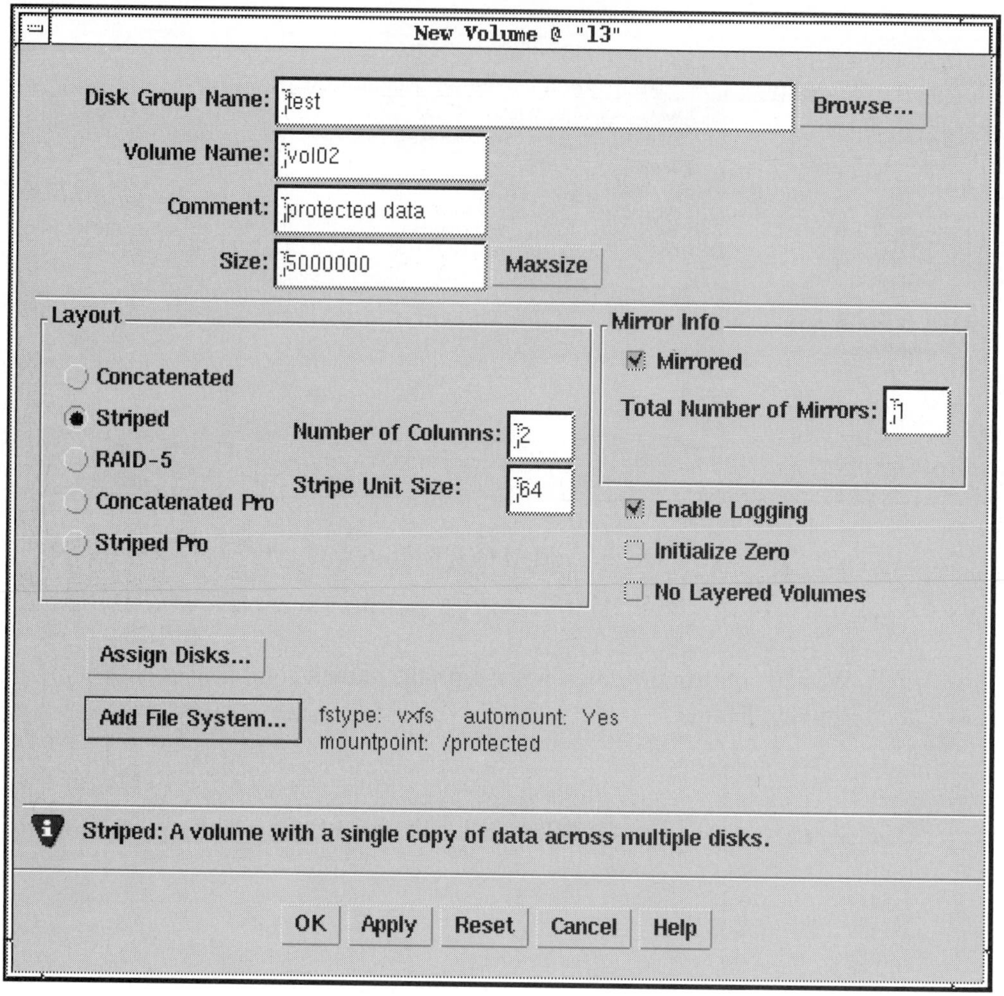

Figure 9-28 *Creating a New Volume That is Striped and Mirrored*

From Figure 9-28, you can see all of the characteristics specified for *vol02*. It is roughly 5 GBytes in size, it is striped, and it has one mirror copy. It is a file system type of *vxfs* and has a mount point of **/protected**.

After adding this volume, it appears in the *vmsa* window as shown in Figure 9-29:

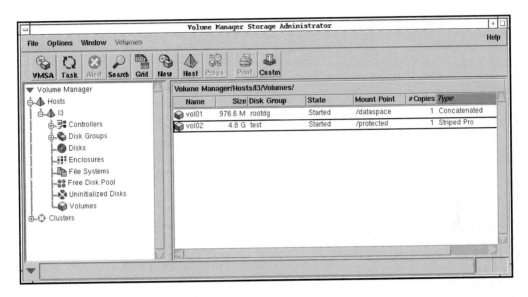

Figure 9-29   Volume *vol02*

We could go to the command line to confirm the presence of *vol02* with **vxprint** and no options, as shown in the following listing:

```
# vxprint
Disk group: rootdg

TY NAME         ASSOC        KSTATE     LENGTH     PLOFFS    STATE     TUTIL0    PUTIL0
dg rootdg       rootdg       -          -          -         -         -         -

dm disk01       c2t2d0       -          17782088   -         -         -         -

v  vol01        fsgen        ENABLED    1000000    -         ACTIVE    -         -
pl vol01-01     vol01        ENABLED    1000000    -         ACTIVE    -         -
sd disk01-01    vol01-01     ENABLED    1000000    0         -         -         -

Disk group: test

TY NAME         ASSOC        KSTATE     LENGTH     PLOFFS    STATE     TUTIL0    PUTIL0
dg test         test         -          -          -         -         -         -

dm test01       c1t0d0       -          17782088   -         -         -         -
dm test02       c2t0d0       -          17782088   -         -         -         -

v  vol02        fsgen        ENABLED    5000000    -         ACTIVE    -         -
pl vol02-03     vol02        ENABLED    5000064    -         ACTIVE    -         -
sv vol02-S01    vol02-03     ENABLED    2500032    0         -         -         -
```

```
sv vol02-S02      vol02-03     ENABLED  2500032  0      -       -      -

v  vol02-L01      fsgen        ENABLED  2500032  -      ACTIVE  -      -
pl vol02-P01      vol02-L01    ENABLED  LOGONLY  -      ACTIVE  -      -
sd test01-03      vol02-P01    ENABLED  33       LOG    -       -      -
pl vol02-P02      vol02-L01    ENABLED  2500032  -      ACTIVE  -      -
sd test01-04      vol02-P02    ENABLED  2500032  0      -       -      -

v  vol02-L02      fsgen        ENABLED  2500032  -      ACTIVE  -      -
pl vol02-P03      vol02-L02    ENABLED  LOGONLY  -      ACTIVE  -      -
sd test01-05      vol02-P03    ENABLED  33       LOG    -       -      -
pl vol02-P04      vol02-L02    ENABLED  2500032  -      ACTIVE  -      -
sd test02-02      vol02-P04    ENABLED  2500032  0      -       -      -
#
```

This output shows our 5 GByte volume as mirrored.

In addition, we want to see **/protected** as a mounted file system with **bdf**:

```
# bdf

Filesystem             kbytes    used    avail %used Mounted on
/dev/vg00/lvol3        204800   55509   140002  28% /
/dev/vg00/lvol1        199381   46526   132916  26% /stand
/dev/vg00/lvol8        921600   38739   827833   4% /var
/dev/vg00/lvol7        937984  793162   135806  85% /usr
/dev/vg00/lvol4        204800    1529   190628   1% /tmp
/dev/vg00/lvol6        835584  722803   105775  87% /opt
/dev/vg00/lvol5        204800    1162   190917   1% /home
/dev/vx/dsk/rootdg/vol01
                      1000000    1349   936243   0% /dataspace
/dev/vx/dsk/test/vol02
                      5000000    2693  4685038   0% /protected
#
```

Our new volume, *vol02,* has been created with a size of 5 GBytes and a mount point of **/protected**.

Several of the basics of using VxVM were covered in the previous examples. This by no means is an exhaustive coverage of VxVM, but hopefully, it serves as a good introduction. Please refer to the detailed information in the manuals related to VxVM.

Although we focused mostly on *vmsa* in this section there are a number of **vx** commands that you can issue that perform the same functions as the graphical interface. I sometimes like to issue commands to view volume-related work that I have performed in the graphical interface just to confirm the results. Table 9-1 lists some of the most commonly used **vx** commands and their functions.

TABLE 9-1   VxVM Commands

Command	Description
vxassist	Create and change volumes.
vxdctl	Manage the vxconfigd daemon.
vxdg	Perform tasks related to disk groups.
vxdisk	Perform tasks related to disks.
vxdiskadd	Used to add disks.
vxedit	Change VxVM objects.
vxmake	Create VxVM objects.
vxmend	Correct configuration problems.
vxplex	Perform plex-related tasks.
vxprint	Print configuration information.
vxsd	Perform tasks on subdisks.
vxstat	Print volume statistics.
vxtrace	Trace volume tasks.
vxunrelocate	Move relocated subdisks.
vxvol	Perform volume tasks.

These commands are covered in the HP documentation set, and there are also man pages available which provide detailed usage information on the commands.

Some Additional File-System-Related Commands

Viewing File Systems with bdf

You can manually view the file systems you have mounted with the **bdf** command. **bdf** provides the following output:

File system	Block device file system name. In the following example, several logical volumes are shown.
KBytes	Number of KBytes of total disk space on the file system.
used	The number of used KBytes on the file system.
avail	The number of available KBytes on the file system.
%used	The percentage of total available disk space that is used on the file system.
Mounted on	The directory name on which the file system is mounted.
iused	Number of inodes in use (only if you use the -*i* option with **bdf**).
ifree	Number of free inodes (only if you use the -*i* option with **bdf**).
%iuse	Percentage of inodes in use (only if you use the **-*i*** option with **bdf**).

Here is an example of **bdf** that is also in "Logical Volume Manager Background," covered earlier in this chapter:

$ **/usr/bin/bdf**

File system	kbytes	used	avail	%used	Mounted on
/dev/vg00/lvol3	47829	18428	24618	43%	/
/dev/vg00/lvol1	67733	24736	36223	41%	/stand
/dev/vg00/lvol8	34541	8673	22413	28%	/var
/dev/vg00/lvol7	299157	149449	119792	56%	/usr
/dev/vg00/lvol4	23013	48	20663	0%	/tmp
/dev/vg00/lvol6	99669	32514	57188	36%	/opt
/dev/vg00/lvol5	19861	9	17865	0%	/home
/dev/dsk/c0t6d0	802212	552120	169870	76%	/mnt/9.x

File System Maintenance with fsck

fsck is a program used for file system maintenance on HP-UX systems. **fsck** checks file system consistency and can make many "life-saving" repairs to a corrupt file system. **fsck** can be run with several options, including the following:

-F   This option allows you to specify the file system type. Be sure to specify a file system type. On some UNIX variants **/etc/fstab** will be used to determine the file system type on others it will not be used. See the **fstab** description later in this section.

-m   This is a sanity check of the file system. If you run this, you'll be told whether your file system is okay or not. I did the following to check lvol5, which is mounted as **/home**:

```
$ umount /home
$ fsck -m /dev/vg00/lvol5

vxfs fsck: sanity check: /dev/vg00/lvol5 OK
```

-y   **fsck** will ask questions if run in interactive mode, which is the default. Using the -y option causes a "yes" response to all questions asked by **fsck**. Don't use this! If you have a serious problem with your file system, data will probably have to be removed, and the -y indicates that the response to every question, including removing data, will be "yes".

-n   The response to all questions asked by **fsck** will be "no." Don't use this, either. If your file system is in bad shape, you may have to respond "yes" to some questions in order to repair the file system. All "no" responses will not do the job.

Since your system runs **fsck** on any file systems that were not marked as clean at the time you shut down the system, you can rest assured that when your system boots, any disks that were not properly shut down will be checked. It is a good idea to run **fsck** interactively on a periodic basis just so you can see firsthand that all of your file systems are in good working order.

Should **fsck** find a problem with a directory or file, it would place these in the **lost+found** directory, which is at the top level of each file system. If a file or directory appears in **lost+found,** you may be able to identify the file or directory by examining it and move it back to its original location. You can use the **file, what**, and **strings** commands on a file to obtain more information about it to help identify its origin.

How are file system problems created? The most common cause of a file system problem is improper shutdown of the system. The information written to file systems is first written to a buffer cache in memory. It is later written to the disk with the **sync** command by unmounting the disk, or through the normal use of filling the buffer and writing it to the disk. If you walk up to a system and shut off the power, you will surely end up with a file system problem. Data in the buffer that was not synchronized to the disk will be lost, the file system will not be marked as properly shut down, and **fsck** will be run when the system boots. A sudden loss of power can also cause an improper system shutdown.

Proper shutdown of the system is described with the **shutdown** command. Although **fsck** is a useful utility that has been known to work miracles on occasion, you don't want to take any unnecessary risks with your file systems. So be sure to properly shut down your system.

The **/etc/fstab** file mentioned earlier is used by **fsck** to determine the sequence of the file system check if it is required at the time of boot. The sequence of entries in **/etc/fstab** is important if a "pass number" for any of the entries does not exist. Here is an example of the **/etc/fstab** file:

```
# System /etc/fstab file. Static information about the file
# systems. See fstab(4) and sam(1m) for further details.

/dev/vg00/lvol3    /            vxfs   delaylog    0    1
/dev/vg00/lvol1    /stand       hfs    defaults    0    1
/dev/vg00/lvol4    /tmp         vxfs   delaylog    0    2
/dev/vg00/lvol6    /opt         vxfs   delaylog    0    2
/dev/vg00/lvol5    /home        vxfs   delaylog    0    2
/dev/vg00/lvol7    /usr         vxfs   delaylog    0    2
/dev/vg00/lvol8    /var         vxfs   delaylog    0    2
/dev/dsk/c0tt6d0   /tmp/mnt9.x  hfs    rw, suid    0    2
         |              |          |         |          |     |
         v              v          v         v          v     v
```

device special file	directory	type	options	backup frequency	pass #

device special file

> This is the device block file, such as **/dev/ vg00/lvol1** in the example.

directory

> The name of the directory under which the device special file is mounted.

type

> Can be one of several types including:
> *cdfs* (local CD-ROM file system)

hfs (high performance local file system)
nfs (network file system)
vxfs (journaled file system)
swap or
swapfs

options
: Several options are available, including those shown in the example. *rw* is read and write; *ro* is read only.

backup frequency
: To be used by backup utilities in the future.

pass #
: Used by **fsck** to determine the order in which file system checks (**fsck**) will take place.

comment
: Anything you want, as long as it's preceded by a #.

Initializing with mediainit

A command you probably won't use, but should be aware of, is **mediainit**. When you use SAM to set up disks for you, the **mediainit** command may be run to initialize new media.

Here are some of the options of **mediainit**:

-*v*
: This is the verbose option. **mediainit** normally just prints error messages to the screen. You can get continuous feedback on what **mediainit** is doing with the -*v* option.

-i interleave   This allows you to specify the interleave factor, which is the relationship between
sequential logical and physical records.
mediainit will provide this if one is not
specified.

-f format   The format option allows you to specify format options for devices, such as floppy
disks, that support different format options.
This is not required for hard disks.

pathname   This is the character device file to be used
for **mediainit**.

newfs, which was used in some of the earlier examples, is used to create a new file system. **newfs** calls the **mksf** command earlier covered. **newfs**
builds a file system of the type you specify (this is one of the commands that
uses the *-F* option, so you can specify the file system type).

CHAPTER 10

Ignite-UX

Ignite-UX Bootable Recovery Achive for Virtual Partitions

Using Ignite-UX it's easy to create bootable recovery archives for all of your Virtual Partitions. From either the Ignite-UX server or client you can initiate the process of creating an image of your Virtual Partition that is stored on the server. In the event of a failure on your Virtual Partition, you can boot your cleint from the image stored on the server and restore your vPar. With vPars you'll have many more images of HP-UX to manage than without vPars. For instance, on an N-Class system running without vPars, you would have only one instance of HP-UX, but with vPars you might have four instances of HP-UX, with two CPUs each to manage. You may have many additional system management-related challenges as a result of the additional images of HP-UX to manage; however, Ignite-UX will make creating the bootable recovery archives easy for you.

In the Virtual Partition-specific part of this chapter we'll focus on creating the bootable recovery archive using the Graphical User Interface (GUI) of Ignite-UX on the server. We'll walk through the process of creating the bootable recovery archives as well as take a look at some of the activities taking place in the background. Then a step-by-step procedure to use Ignite-UX and vPars, developed by an HP lab engineer, will be included. In the

535

non-vPars-specific section of this chapter, a lot of background and examples of Ignite-UX will be covered.

Keep in mind that Ignite-UX to create a bootable recovery archive is used in conjunction with regular backups to protect all of your data. Please see Chapter 7 for backup-related information.

Creating Bootable Recovery Archives for vPars

In this section we'll create a bootable recovery archive for a Virtual Partition using the Ignite-UX GUI. In addition, we'll take a look at some of what is taking place in the background such as:

- Disk space consumed by a bootable recovery archive on the server.

- Server files created and modified to support creating the client archives (**/etc/exports**, others.)

- Command issued by server on client to produce the archive.

- In the next section we'll restore a client by booting from the archive created on the server (note that the relocatable kernel is different from a standard kernel.)

Using Ignite-UX GUI to Create a vPar Archive

After the Ignite-UX tool is loaded on the server there is some initial client setup that is required and managed through the Ignite-UX Graphical User Interface (GUI). There are also some modifications made to the server. One of these changes is to make entries for the cleints to be managed in **/etc/exports**. Ignite-UX automatically included entries in **/etc/exports** for the cleints that were set up. The following **/etc/exports** listing shows an entry for two clients on the server *chess2*:

```
root@chess2 > cat /etc/exports

/var/opt/ignite/clients -anon=2
/var/opt/ignite/recovery/archives/actappd1 -anon=2,access=actappd1
/var/opt/ignite/recovery/archives/ecvpard2 -anon=2,access=ecvpard2

root@chess2 >
```

The three entries include the general *clients* directory used by the Ignite-UX server, and *archives* directories for the two clients that were setup on the Ignite-UX server, called *actappd1* and *ecvpard2*. These two hosts are Virtual Partitions running on the same server. *chess2*, the Ignite-UX server, is a different server than that on which the two vPars are running.

In addition to **/etc/exports** updates that were automatically made when specifying clients, you may want to manually create entries in **/.rhosts** on both the server and client so that you won't have to respond with the client password on the server when you initiate creating the bootable recovery archive. The server is running a program remotely on the client, and in order to do so without issuing a password, the **/.rhosts** file must have the appropriate entries. Keep in mind, though, that including entries in **/.rhosts** reduces the overall security level of your system.

Once this has been completed you can initiate the process of creating the bootable recovery archive as shown in Figure 10-1 on our server *chess2*:

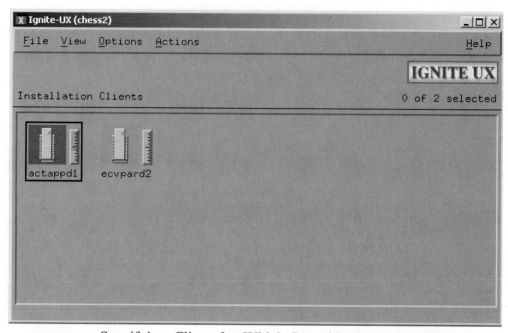

Figure 10-1 Specifying Client for Which Bootable Recovery Archive Will Be Produced

The two clients shown in the Ignite-UX GUI were those for which we saw entries in **/etc/exports**. Keep in mind that the two systems shown in the Ignite-UX GUI are two Virtual Partitions running on the same server.

There are several *Actions* from which we can choose once a client has been selected, as shown in Figure 10-2:

Figure 10-2 *Actions* Menu after Client Has Been Selected

With *actappd1* selected we'll choose *Create Network Recovery Archive* from the *Actions* menu.

Making this menu selection brings up a window that contains a series of defaults for creating the archive, as shown in Figure 10-3:

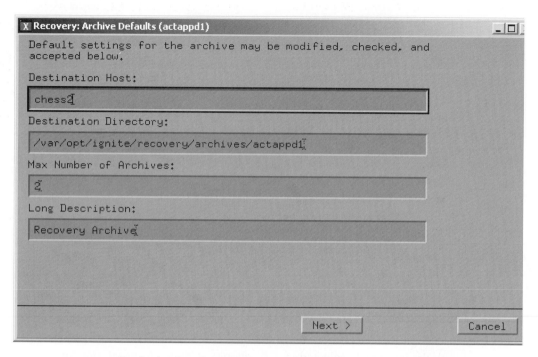

Figure 10-3 Defaults for Creating a Bootable Recovery Archive

man page

make_net
_recovery
10

After we progress through these basic screens, Ignite-UX begins the process of creating the archive.

The server issued the **make_net_recovery** command on the client in order to create the archive. The following is the output of **ps -ef** for only this command on the client (*actappd1*) for which the archive is being produced:

```
root@actappd1 > ps -ef | grep make

/opt/ignite/bin/make_net_recovery -i -b -P s -l 0x00306E0981D4

root@actappd1 >
```

This command is now running in the background on our client, which is a Virtual Partition, and writing an archive across the network to the server. This process takes about three hours on our client and produces a file over 600 MBytes in size.

If you're interested in the many options to **make_net_recovery**, you can view the online man page for the command. In this example the *i* is for *interactive*, *b* for *background*, *-P* for *partial*, *s* for *server*, and *-l* for *lanic id* of the client. You could issue this command from the client as well as from the server. Some system administrators prefer to manage the creation of the archives centrally from the server and others prefer to create **cron** entries on the clients and initiate this process from the client. Both the setup and syntax of the **make_net_recovery** command appear in its man page (at the time of this writing, **make_net_recovery** is the latest command.)

man page

make_net
_recovery
10

There are many files created as a result of initiating the creation of the recovery archive for the client. The following listing shows some of the more interesting directories and files. The man page for **make_net_recovery** provides an explanation for all of the important directories and files created for clients. Let's take a look at some of the more interesting ones on the Ignite-UX server used in our example in this chapter.

The following is a long listing of the **/var/opt/ignite/clients** directory on the server:

```
root@chess2[/var/opt/ignite/clients] > ll
total 4
drwxrwxrwx   3 bin        bin         1024 Jul 20 12:23 0x001083F7C4FC
drwxr-xr-x   3 bin        bin         1024 Jul 19 17:54 0x00306E0981D4
drwxr-xr-x   2 root       sys           96 Jul 19 14:13 161.228.212.121
lrwxr-xr-x   1 bin        bin           14 Jul 27 14:01 actappd1 -> 0x00306E0981D4
lrwxr-xr-x   1 bin        bin           14 Jul 20 09:53 ecvpard2 -> 0x001083F7C4FC
lrwxrwxrwx   1 root       sys           14 May 25 15:53 sample -> 0x999999999999
```

Notice that there are entries for both of our clients in this directory. There is a link that allows you to specify the client name rather than the ID of the LAN card because the client name is much easier to remember and type.

Next, let's change to the directory of the client for which we are creating our archive and perform a long listing:

```
root@chess2[/var/opt/ignite/clients] > cd actappd1
root@chess2[/var/opt/ignite/clients/actappd1] > ll
total 18
-rw-r--r--   1 bin        bin          987 Jul 24 18:33 CINDEX
```

```
-rw-r--r--   1 bin        bin                9 Jul 19 15:15 client_name
-rw-r--r--   1 bin        bin               28 Jul 19 15:15 client_status
-rw-r--r--   1 bin        bin              300 Jul 19 15:15 config.sys
-rw-r--r--   1 bin        bin              336 Jul 19 15:15 host.info
-rw-r--r--   1 bin        bin              940 Jul 19 15:15 hw.info
-rw-r--r--   1 bin        bin              231 Jul 19 15:15 install.log
-rw-r--r--   1 bin        bin                0 Jul 19 15:20 lockfile
drwxr-xr-x   3 bin        bin             1024 Jul 27 14:01 recovery
-rw-r--r--   1 bin        bin              585 Jul 27 13:39 server.state
```

There is a lot of client-related information in this directory. The **recovery** directory has the most interesting files related to our client, so let's change to that directory and perform a long listing:

```
root@chess2[/var/opt/ignite/clients/actappd1] > cd recovery
root@chess2[/var/opt/ignite/clients/actappd1/recovery] > ll
total 8
drwxr-xr-x   2 bin        bin             1024 Jul 27 14:05 2001-07-27,13:55
-rw-r--r--   1 bin        bin              252 Jul 27 14:03 archive_content
-rw-r--r--   1 bin        bin              247 Jul 27 14:05 client_status
-rw-r--r--   1 bin        bin              411 Jul 27 14:03 defaults
lrwxr-xr-x   1 bin        bin               16 Jul 27 14:01 latest -> 2001-07-27,13:55
```

man page

**make_net
_recovery
10**

The **archive_content** file has in it the files and directories to be included or excluded. **client_status** is used to communicate with the client to provide the status of the **make_net_recovery** command. A status window is shown in the GUI after the creation of the archive is initiated. **latest** is a link to the directory that has in it the newest recovery files. If we change to this directory and perform a long listing, we see the files in the following listing:

```
root@chess2[/var/opt/ignite/clients/actappd1/recovery] > cd 2001-07-27,13:55
@chess2[/var/opt/ignite/clients/actappd1/recovery/2001-07-27,13:55] > ll
total 3704
-rw-r--r--   1 bin        bin             3089 Jul 27 14:05 archive_cfg
-rw-r--r--   1 bin        bin              252 Jul 27 14:03 archive_content
-rw-r--r--   1 bin        bin              269 Jul 27 14:03 control_cfg
-rw-r--r--   1 bin        bin          1880616 Jul 27 14:05 flist
-rw-r--r--   1 bin        bin             2510 Jul 27 14:05 recovery.log
-rw-r--r--   1 root       sys             5588 Jul 27 13:58 system_cfg
```

The **recovery.log** file contains information about the archive we are currently creating. The following output contains the contents of the file:

```
======= 07/27/01 13:55:54 EDT  Started /opt/ignite/bin/make_net_recovery. (Fri
        Jul 27 13:55:54 EDT 2001)
        @(#) Ignite-UX Revision B.3.4.115
        @(#) net_recovery (opt) $Revision: 10.543 $


        * User interface starting.
NOTE:     Detected entries in the defaults file at
          /var/opt/ignite/recovery/client_mnt/0x00306E0981D4/recovery/defaults.

        * User interface completed successfully.
NOTE:     Detected entries in the defaults file at
          /var/opt/ignite/recovery/client_mnt/0x00306E0981D4/recovery/defaults.

        * Checking Versions of Recovery Tools
        * Creating System Configuration.
        * /opt/ignite/bin/save_config -f /var/opt/ignite/recovery/client_mnt/0x0
          0306E0981D4/recovery/2001-07-27,13:55/system_cfg vg00
        * Backing Up Volume Group /dev/vg00
        * /usr/sbin/vgcfgbackup /dev/vg00
Volume Group configuration for /dev/vg00 has been saved in /etc/lvmconf/vg00.conf
        * Creating Map Files for Volume Group /dev/vg00
        * /usr/sbin/vgexport -p -m /etc/lvmconf/vg00.mapfile /dev/vg00
vgexport: Volume group "/dev/vg00" is still active.

        * Creating Control Configuration.
        * Creating Archive File List
        * Creating Archive Configuration

        * /opt/ignite/bin/make_arch_config -c /var/opt/ignite/recovery/client_mn
          t/0x00306E0981D4/recovery/2001-07-27,13:55/archive_cfg -g /var/opt/ign
          ite/recovery/client_mnt/0x00306E0981D4/recovery/2001-07-27,13:55/flist
          -n 2001-07-27,13:55 -r 64 -d Recovery\ Archive -L
          /var/opt/ignite/recovery/arch_mnt -l
          chess2:/var/opt/ignite/recovery/archives/actappd1 -i 1
        * Saving the information about archive to
          /var/opt/ignite/recovery/previews
        * Creating The Networking Archive

        * /opt/ignite/data/scripts/make_sys_image -d
          /var/opt/ignite/recovery/arch_mnt -t n -s local -n 2001-07-27,13:55 -m
          t -w /var/opt/ignite/recovery/client_mnt/0x00306E0981D4/recovery/2001-
          07-27,13:55/recovery.log -u -R -g /var/opt/ignite/recovery/client_mnt/
          0x00306E0981D4/recovery/2001-07-27,13:55/flist -a 905500

        * Preparing to create a system archive
        * The archive is estimated to reach 452750 kbytes.
        * Free space on /var/opt/ignite/recovery/arch_mnt
          after archive should be about 4066 kbytes.

        * Archiving contents of actappd1 via tar to
          /var/opt/ignite/recovery/arch_mnt/2001-07-27,13:55.
@chess2[/var/opt/ignite/clients/actappd1/recovery/2001-07-27,13:55] > ll
total 3704
-rw-r--r--   1 bin      bin          3089 Jul 27 14:05 archive_cfg
-rw-r--r--   1 bin      bin           252 Jul 27 14:03 archive_content
-rw-r--r--   1 bin      bin           269 Jul 27 14:03 control_cfg
-rw-r--r--   1 bin      bin       1880616 Jul 27 14:05 flist
-rw-r--r--   1 bin      bin          2510 Jul 27 14:05 recovery.log
-rw-r--r--   1 root     sys          5588 Jul 27 13:58 system_cfg
```

There are many useful files produced for each client; however, the one in which we are most interested is the recovery archive. The following listing shows three archives that have been produced for our client.

```
root@chess2[/var/opt/ignite/recovery/archives/actappd1] > ls -l
total 1432116
-rw-------   1 bin        bin          623288688 Jul 24 18:33 2001-07-24,13:08
-rw-------   1 bin        bin           36152098 Jul 25 16:08 2001-07-25,15:42
-rw-------   1 bin        bin           73728000 Jul 27 14:42 2001-07-27,13:55
root@chess2[/var/opt/ignite/recovery/archives/actappd1] >
```

The first is a complete archive created at an earlier date, the second is a partial archive that was not complete because it was aborted, and the third is the archive we were creating at the time this listing was produced.

This shows that our Virtual Partition consumed over 600 MBytes of disk space for the complete archive. You'll want to consider the number of clients for which you wish to store bootable recovery archives on your server and plan your volume space accordingly. For the archive we are currently producing, there have been about 73 MBytes of what will be an over 600 MByte recovery archive present, and we have been running **make_net_recovery** on the client for about 20 minutes.

man page

make_net _recovery 10

After our archive has been fully created we can progress to booting it as a test. I usually create an archive as soon as a Virtual Partition has been produced and test it before I perform a lot of customization on the vPar. This will give you peace of mind that you know the process of booting from the recovery archive.

Virtual Partition Recovery

man page

vparboot appendix a

Now that we've created the bootable recovery archive for our Virtual Partition, we can restore our vPar using it. You can restore one vPar from another using the **vparboot** command. This means that while one vPar is running, you can restore another vPar on the same system using the following **vparboot** command:

```
vparboot -p vp_name -I ignite_kernel
```

This is different from the **vparboot** form used in Chapter 2 when we booted a vPar using a kernel that was located on the same system as opposed to an Ignite-UX server. That form of the **vparboot** is as follows:

```
vparboot -p vp_name [-b kernel_path] [-o boot_opts] [-B boot_addr]
```

In examples in early chapters we simply specified the name of the Virtual Partition we wanted to boot, such as **vparboot -p cable1**. With this form of **vparboot** we specify a boot kernel on the local system with the *-b* option. The man page for **vparboot** and the other vPar commands are found in Appendix A.

You would normally boot a recovery archive from the PDC prompt, that is, your system is down and you are recovering it. Since we have multiple vPars on our system, we can recover one vPar on a system from a running vPar on the same system using **vparboot**.

We'll issue the following **vparboot** command from our running vPar in order to restore vPar *actappd1* from an Ignite-UX server at the command line:

```
# vparboot -p actappd1 -I 161.228.212.110,/opt/ignite/boot/WINSTALL
```

The IP address of our Ignite-UX server is specified. The **WINSTALL** file used in this **vparboot** command is different from that used for normal HP-UX recovery (without vPars.) A relocatable kernel is required for vPars, so the **WINSTALL** used in the **vparboot** command is one that is required for vPars. This **WINSTALL** is supplied with vPars.

man page

vparboot
appendix a

The ability to recover a Virtual Partition from a running vPar using **vparboot** means that fewer users are affected. The users in the running vPar are unaffected by the recovery taking place, on another vPar. After the recovery of the root volume group (*vg00*) takes place you can restore the balance of information on your vPar from the latest backup. Be sure to create the bootable recovery archive often so that your entire root volume group can be recovered with the latest data.

Virtual Partition Installation with Ignite-UX

This section contains a step-by-step procedure to set up an Ignite-UX server to install vPars. This procedure was supplied by HP lab engineer Geff Blaha. Since you'll be installing many instances of HP-UX 11i and vPars software in a vPars environment, this procedure may save you a lot of time.

In examples in early chapters, we simply specified the name of the Virtual Partition we wanted to boot, such as **vparboot -p cable1**. With this form of **vparboot** we specify a boot kernel on the local system with the *-b* option. The man pages for **vparboot** and the other vPar commands are found in Appendix A.

Ignite-UX and vPars Cookbook

man page

vparboot
appendix a

Use the **vparboot** command from a Virtual Partition to install HP-UX and vPar software to a target vPar. An Ignite-UX server is used as the source depot for this installation process.

The following is an overall vPars installation process (assuming that a new server is being installed)

- Install the server and peripherals
- Install any required patches for vPars (i.e., Gold Quality Pack, etc.)
- Install HP-UX 11i (stand-alone.)
- Install vPars software.
- Plan for desired vPars.

man page

vparcreate
appendix a

- Create vPars using the **vparcreate** command: this creates the vPars database **/stand/vpdb**.
- Shut down HP-UX and place the server into BCH (Boot Console Handler) mode.
- Boot from the HP-UX/vPars disk and stop (interact) at the ISL prompt.
- Load and run the vPars monitor.
- Boot the first vPar (previously installed) with the **vparload** command.
- Use the **vparboot** command to install HP-UX and vPars software to all remaining vPars. Use the *Ctrl A* command to switch the virtual console

between vPars and the monitor.

An Ignite-UX server is used as the source depot for the **vparboot** installation process. If an Ignite-UX server does not already exist for use with this process, install and configure one, preferably on another system, starting with steps 1 through 3 below. If an Ignite-UX server does exist, or is older than revision B.3.4.115, it will need to be updated. If your Ignite-UX server is already at revision B.3.4.115, continue with step 4 below.

1) Obtain Ignite-UX software.

Sources include CDROM, *software.hp.com,* and SD-UX depot files.

Note: the revision of Ignite-UX supported for the first release of vPars is **B.3.4.115:**

```
# what /opt/ignite/bin/ignite
    /opt/ignite/bin/ignite:
                ignite user interface $Revision: 10.643 $
                Ignite-UX Revision B.3.4.115
                install/h $Revision: 10.102 $
```

This revision can be found on the September 2001 application distribution. Although previous versions of Ignite-UX may work, they are not supported for use with vPars, and may have problems with the relocatable **WINSTALL** file, which was built using libraries based on the B.3.4.115 revision of Ignite-UX.

2) Install or update Ignite-UX software.

Use **swinstall** to install Ignite-UX.

3) Update *PATH*.

Add the following search path to your login script(s):

```
export PATH=${PATH}:/opt/ignite/bin
```

If an Ignite-UX server already exists (revision B.3.4.115), add HP-UX 11i server OEs and vPars software to the Ignite-UX server (Note, there are various methods to install and configure software on the Ignite-UX server; described below is one method):

4) Set up software within Ignite-UX to be installed on target vPars:

- Create HP-UX 11i OE depots from September 2001 media (example using CDROM device *c0t3d0*):

```
# make_depots -r B.11.11 -s /dev/dsk/c0t3d0
```

- Create a vPars application depot so that it will appear within the *Software* tab of *itool* during installation (using a tar-format depot file, and another example using an Ignite-UX server):

```
# make_depots -r B.11.11 -a 800 -s /tmp/vpar_IC9.tar
```

or

```
# make_depots -r B.11.11 -a 800 -s flatcat.cup.hp.com:/opt/VPAR/ic9/depot
```

Note: the above assumes that vPars source was available as a tar (depot) file or another Ignite-UX depot on the *flatcat* computer. A CDROM source will also work. The above example commands will create and copy vPars within the **"apps_800" depot.**

- Create an Ignite-UX config file for the above depots (11i OEs and vPars):

```
# make_config -r B.11.11
```

The above command creates the **/var/opt/ignite/data/Rel_B.11.11/ apps_800_cfg** configuration file.

- Manage the Ignite-UX index file for applications:

```
# manage_index -a -f /var/opt/ignite/data/Rel_B.11.11/
  apps_800_cfg
```

- Create HP-UX 11i OE depots from September 2001 media:

Once the above steps are completed, copy the relocatable **WINSTALL** file for use with vPars to the Ignite-UX boot directory:

```
# cd /opt/ignite/boot
# cp WINSTALL WINSTALL_NoReloc
# cp <source_path>/WINSTALL .    (may also need to perform
a chmod and chown.)
```

Note that the *<source_path>* above means any source where **WINSTALL** exists.

Using the **WINSTALL** bundled within Ignite-UX will not work (presently) for vPars, as it is not relocatable. The following is to verify that the correct **WINSTALL** is being used:

```
# /usr/ccs/bin/elfdump -r /opt/ignite/boot/WINSTALL|fgrep -i relocation
```

If no output is supplied from the above command then **WINSTALL** is not relocatable.

5) Start the Ignite-UX server manager:

```
# /opt/ignite/bin/ignite
```

6) Complete the Ignite-UX server configuration

Select: *Options -> Server Configuration...*
    - Select the *Server Options tab*
    - Default Configuration: *HP-UX B.11.11 Default.*
    - Client timeouts: *40*

- Run client installation UI on: *server*

Select: *Options -> Server Configurations... -> Session Options*
  - Verify that only these options are set:
    - *Confirm new clients*
    - *Show the welcome screen for the install server*
  - Ensure that the option *Halt the client after installation* is not selected.

man page

**vparboot
appendix a**

Once the Ignite-UX server is installed and configured to install HP-UX OEs and vPars, proceed to use **vparboot** to install all remaining vPars as needed.

More information on Ignite-UX is available in the *Ignite-UX Administration Guide*.

As I mentioned at the beginning of this chapter, you'll probably have more instances of HP-UX 11i to manage when you use vPars. Intalling these vPars from an Ignite-UX server will save you a lot of time and ensure that you have a consistent base of software for your installation.

Non-vPar-Specific Section of Chapter: Ignite-UX Overview

Ignite-UX is quite a versatile product. It has a great deal of functionality associated with it that would take an entire book to cover. This background section was written with an older versin of Ignite-UX and did not include any vPar-related information. It is, however; a good overview of Ignite-UX for those who have never used it. I'll cover what I believe to be the two major functional areas of Ignite-UX that I see used. These are:

- Network installation of client, or target, systems from a server that has on it software depots. These depots are usually created by copying software from media into depots on the Ignite-UX server. This is somewhat the same as the software installation covered in Chapter 2, except that the software is on a server rather than media. There is also a graphical user interface that allows you to control this process from the server. This technique would allow you to select the specific software that you want to load on each individual client. You can either "push" software from the server to the client or "pull" software to the client from the server. In addition to creating software depots from media, you can create an operating system archive from a "golden image." The "golden image" is a perfectly running system that you wish to replicate to many systems. The **make_sys_image** command produces a compressed image of a "golden system." In this chapter we'll focus on the software depots created from copying media into depots on the server.

- Creating a bootable system recovery tape. This feature allows you to create an image of your root volume on tape. You could later boot off of this tape and restore the root volume group directly from tape.

Let's take a look at these two aspects of Ignite-UX in the upcoming sections. Be sure to check *www.docs.hp.com* to obtain some good documents available on Ignite-UX and *www.software.hp.com* to obtain the latest Ignite-UX software. Some of these documents have much more detail than I provide in the upcoming "how to" sections.

I'll assume that you already have the Ignite-UX product loaded on your server system. This software comes bundled with HP-UX 11i and 11.0, so it is just a matter of loading it on your server system from media. You can be sure that you're getting the latest version of Ignite-UX if you download it from the *software.hp.com* Web site. The process of working with Ignite-UX in this chapter is nearly identical for HP-UX 10.20, 11.0, and 11i. You'll find this chapter applicable regardless of which version of HP-UX you're running.

After installing Ignite-UX, you may want to update your path so that you don't have to type the full path for every Ignite-UX command. For the default POSIX shell, you would issue the following:

```
# export PATH=${PATH}:/opt/ignite/bin
```

This command updates your path to include the directory for most Ignite-UX executables, **/opt/ignite/bin**.

Set up Server with Depots and Install Clients

You can use most any system as your Ignite-UX server. You can have depots on your server for HP-UX 11i, 11.0, and 10.20. I would recommend using an 11.00 or 11i system as an Ignite-UX server because I have seen problems with a 10.20 system acting as a server for loading clients with 11.00 and 11i. I have never seen a problem with an 11.0 or 11i system acting as a server for loading clients with any version of HP-UX. In general, though, the server acts as a host for depots, and its operating system is not an integral part of loading software onto clients. We'll use a workstation (model J2240) running 11.00 in our examples. From the 11.00 depot we create on this system, we can load a variety of clients. The fact that we're using a workstation rather than a server doesn't matter as far as loading clients is concerned. I find that many system administrators use a workstation as an Ignite-UX server even though they're loading primarily servers, such as N-Class systems.

The software depots you create on your Ignite-UX server consume a lot of disk space. A core operating system with many applications could take up several GBytes of disk space. I like to devote several GBytes of disk space to Ignite servers so I don't have to increase the size of **/var** (the default location for software depots) when additional depots are loaded on a system. My rule of thumb is **/var** at 6 GBytes to support several depots.

Just to give you an idea of the disk space consumed by depots, I have issued the following **bdf** commands upon initial system installation without any software depots and then again after creating a core operating system and application depot. The location of the software depots is **/var** by default; however, you can load the depots in any directory. I would recommend creating a file system such as **/var/depots** as a depot area. In the following example, we'll focus on the capacity of **/var** since it is used as the destination for depots in upcoming examples.

```
# bdf
Filesystem          kbytes      used    avail %used Mounted on
/dev/vg00/lvol3     204800     19830   173464   10% /
/dev/vg00/lvol1      83733     13654    61705   18% /stand
/dev/vg00/lvol8    6553600    156292  5998347    3% /var
/dev/vg00/lvol7     512000    341251   160127   68% /usr
/dev/vg00/lvol4     102400      1522    94578    2% /tmp
/dev/vg00/lvol6     602112    186976   389238   32% /opt
/dev/vg00/lvol5     204800      1157   190923    1% /home
/dev/dsk/c1t2d0    2457600   2457600        0  100%
                                       /var/tmp/cddirAAAa02574
```

The following **bdf**, which was taken immediately after the core operating system depot for 11.0 was created, shows that **/var** availability has been reduced to about 5.667 GBytes from 5.998 GBytes. This represents roughly 330 MBytes of data that were loaded as part of the core operating system.

```
# bdf
Filesystem          kbytes      used    avail %used Mounted on
/dev/vg00/lvol3     204800     19943   173357   10% /
/dev/vg00/lvol1      83733     13654    61705   18% /stand
/dev/vg00/lvol8    6553600    507003  5668779    8% /var
/dev/vg00/lvol7     512000    341255   160123   68% /usr
/dev/vg00/lvol4     102400      3350    92862    3% /tmp
/dev/vg00/lvol6     602112    186976   389238   32% /opt
/dev/vg00/lvol5     204800      1157   190923    1% /home
/dev/dsk/c1t2d0    2457600   2457600        0  100% /iuxcdrom0
#
```

The disk space consumed by the core operating system depot can be confirmed by viewing the location of the depot as shown in the following listing:

```
# cd /var/opt/ignite/depots
# du -s *
688842  Rel_B.11.00
#
```

This listing of the **du** command shows that roughly 330 MBytes (688K blocks divided by 2048 bytes/block) are in the core operating system directory. This 330 MBytes of disk space consumed by the core operating system depot is nothing compared with all of the application software we're going to load into the **depots** directory. We're going to put both the core operating system and applications in this directory, so substantially more space will be consumed.

To further drive home the point of the amount of disk space consumed, the following **du** command shows the amount of disk space consumed by both the core operating system depot (still about 330 MBytes) and the total applications contained on the three CD-ROMs that came with the release of the operating system for which we're creating our depots. The **/var/opt/ignite/depots/app** directory, which is the depot for the contents of the three application CD-ROMs, is roughly 3.7 GBytes!

```
# cd /var/opt/ignite/depots
# du -s *
688874  Rel_B.11.00
3722622 app
#
```

The space consumed by the applications is over 10 times the space consumed by the core operating system. This 3.7 GBytes consists of every application available for the 11.0 release of the operating system; however, this gives you an idea of the space required when using Ignite-UX to create depots.

Run Ignite-UX GUI

After loading the Ignite-UX tool, you can type **ignite** if you have set up your path for **/opt/ignite/bin**, or you can type the full path **/opt/ignite/bin/ignite** to bring up the graphical interface for Ingite-UX as shown in Figure 10-4:

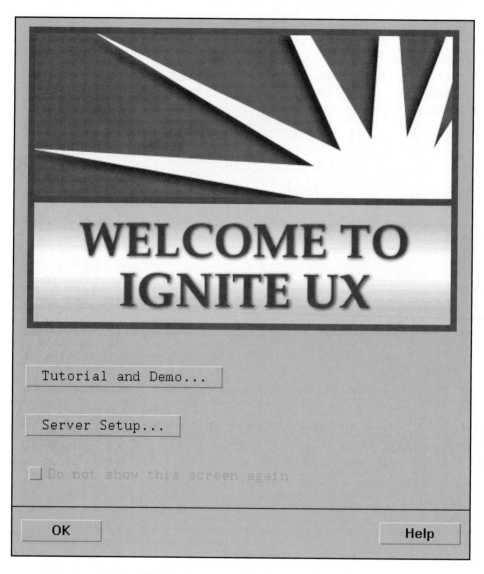

Figure 10-4 Ignite-UX Welcome Screen

    From this window we can make various selections to configure Ignite-UX for our environment. The first configuration we'll perform is *Server Setup*. When we select *Server Setup,* we're shown the screen in Figure 10-5,

Which allows use to set up IP addresses for the clients we wish to manage from Ignite-UX under option 1.

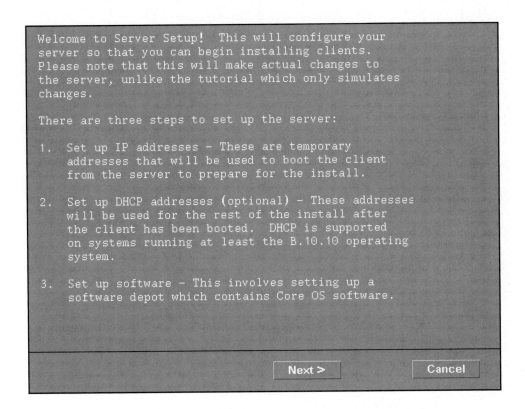

Figure 10-5 Set Up Client IP Address

We'll set up a bank of addresses for several clients we anticipate loading through the Ignite-UX interface as shown in Figure 10-6. Be sure to put entries for these clients in your host database, such as the file **/etc/hosts** as well.

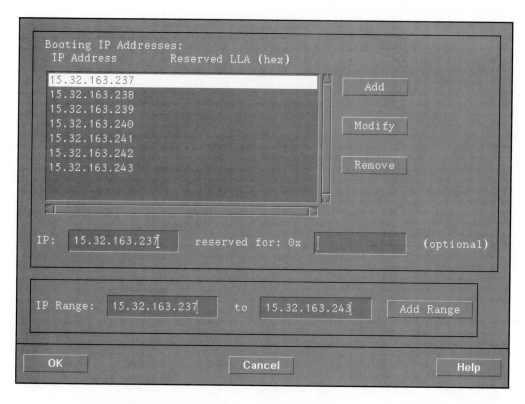

Figure 10-6 A Bank of Client IP Addresses

We have set up a bank of seven clients that we wish to manage from Ignite-UX.

Next, let's create a core operating system depot for HP-UX 11.0 through the graphical interface. We'll copy the core operating system from the orginal CD-ROM, which is the selection we make in Figure 10-7:

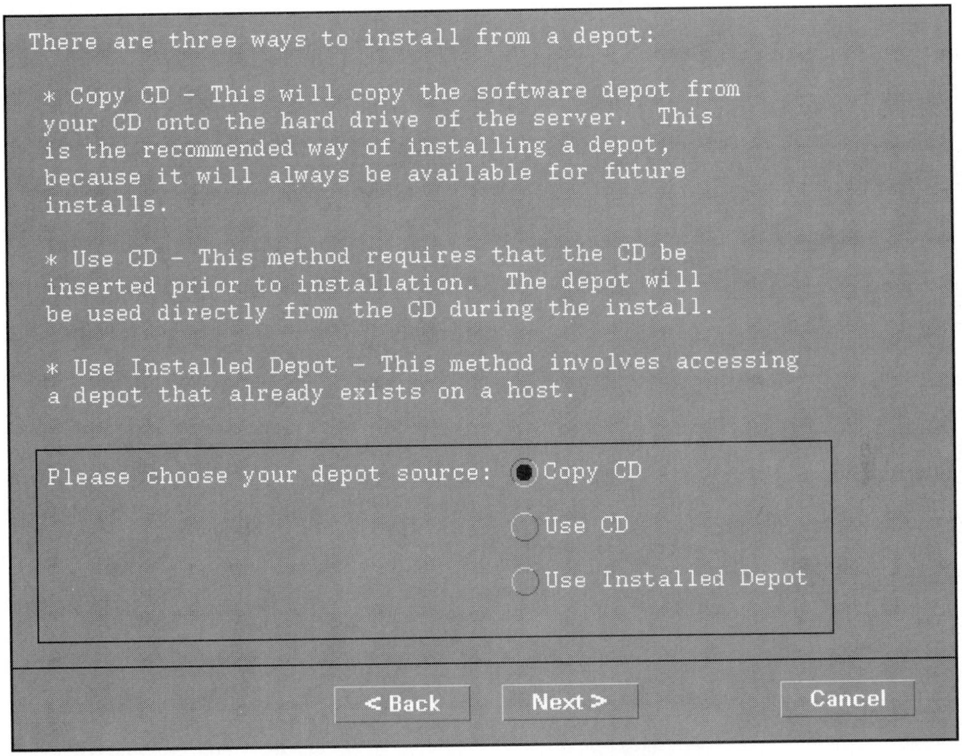

```
There are three ways to install from a depot:

* Copy CD - This will copy the software depot from
your CD onto the hard drive of the server.  This
is the recommended way of installing a depot,
because it will always be available for future
installs.

* Use CD - This method requires that the CD be
inserted prior to installation.  The depot will
be used directly from the CD during the install.

* Use Installed Depot - This method involves accessing
a depot that already exists on a host.
```

Please choose your depot source: ● Copy CD

                               ○ Use CD

                               ○ Use Installed Depot

[< Back]   [Next >]   [Cancel]

Figure 10-7 Install a Software Depot

After making the selection to load from the CD-ROM, another window appears, which is not shown in our example. Here, we specify the location in which the depot will be loaded. By default the directory is **/var/opt/ignite/depots** (full path **/var/opt/ignite/depots/Rel_B.11.11/core** as an example for the 11.11 release of HP-UX); however, we can specify any directory location for the depots. If you have a lot of unused disk space in **/localapps**, for instance, you could make the full path **/localapps/depots/Rel_B.11.11/core**. Next, we receive a status window showing the progression of the software copy and depot creation shown in Figure 10-8:

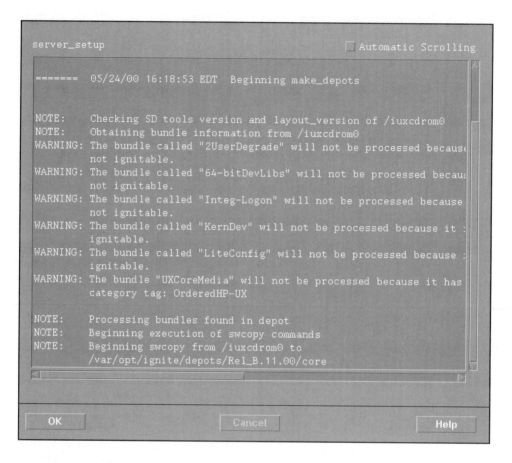

Figure 10-8 Status of Software Depot Creation

Upon completion of software copy and depot setup, we are given the window shown in Figure 10-9:

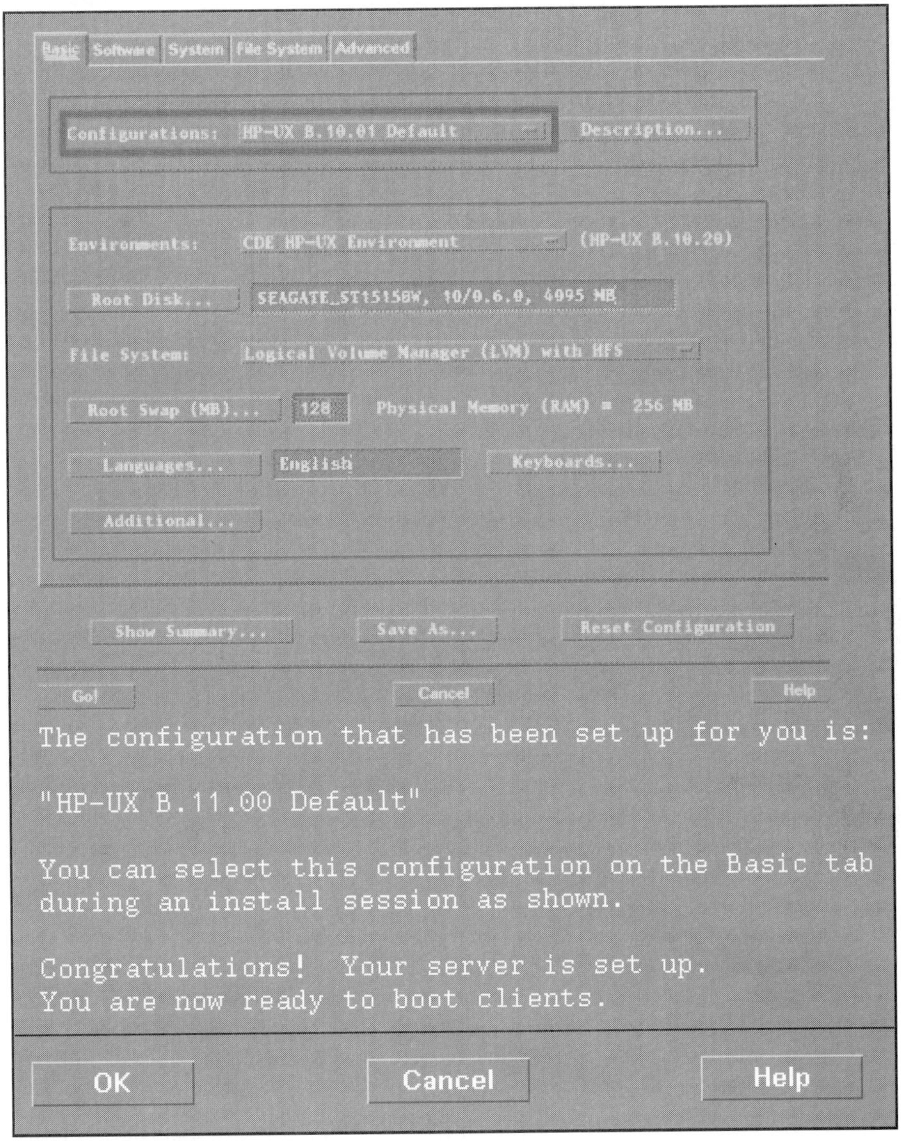

Figure 10-9 The Software Depot Is Complete

The depot for the core operating system was automatically created under **/var/opt/ignite/depots/Rel_B.11.00**. As described earlier in the chapter, this depot consumes about 330 MBytes of disk space.

At this point, we have created only the core operating system depot and configured the clients all through the graphical interface on the Ignite-UX server. At the time of this writing, there is no way to use the graphical interface to create the applications software depot. We'll use three Ignite-UX commands to create the applications depot. First we'll run the **make_depots** command for all three applications CD-ROMs we wish to load into the depot. Then we'll run the **make_config** command one time for the applications depot we have created. Finally, we'll run the **manage_index** one time for the applications depot we created. Let's take a look at each of these commands in the upcoming listings.

```
# /opt/ignite/bin/make_depots -d /var/opt/ignite/depots/app -s /dev/dsk/c1t2d0
# /opt/ignite/bin/make_depots -d /var/opt/ignite/depots/app -s /dev/dsk/c1t2d0
# /opt/ignite/bin/make_depots -d /var/opt/ignite/depots/app -s /dev/dsk/c1t2d0
```

We add the *-d* option to specify a destination directory called **app** for the contents of the application media. We could also specify an alternate destination directory. Using the earlier example, we could specify the destination with **-d /localapps/depots/app**, for instance. We'll load the entire application media, in this case, three CD-ROMs. Next, we run **make_config**:

```
# /opt/ignite/bin/make_config -s /var/opt/ignite/depots/app
              -c /var/opt/ignite/data/Rel_B.11.00/app_cfg
```

NOTE: make_config can sometimes take a long time to complete. Please be
         patient!

We placed the **app_cfg** file in the directory for our specific release of the operating system. This is a method of organizing the configuration files in such a way that those pertaining to a specific release of the operating system are grouped together. If we had used a different location for the application directory, we would have specified it with **-s /localapps/depots/app** but have left the **app_cfg** file in the same location. You will want to take a look at the configuration files in **/var/opt/ignite/data/<*yourHP-UXrelease*>** to see their contents. These files contain the information about all of the software you have loaded as part of your Ignite-UX depot.

The **manage_index** command is required to manage the index file used by Ignite-UX, as shown in the following example:

```
# /opt/ignite/bin/manage_index -a -f /var/opt/ignite/data/Rel_B.11.00/app_cfg
```

We have now set up the core operating system depot using the Ignite-UX graphical interface and the application depot using the three Ignite-UX commands at the command line. You now also have an entry for your release of the operating system in **/var/opt/ignite/INDEX**. This is a file you will want to view so that you can see the entry made for your release of the operating system.

Let's now get back to using the Ignite-UX graphical interface on the server. We can get information about a specific client through the Ignite-UX interface on the server. The window that appears on the server is shown in Figure 10-10 for the client we'll be booting through Ignite-UX:

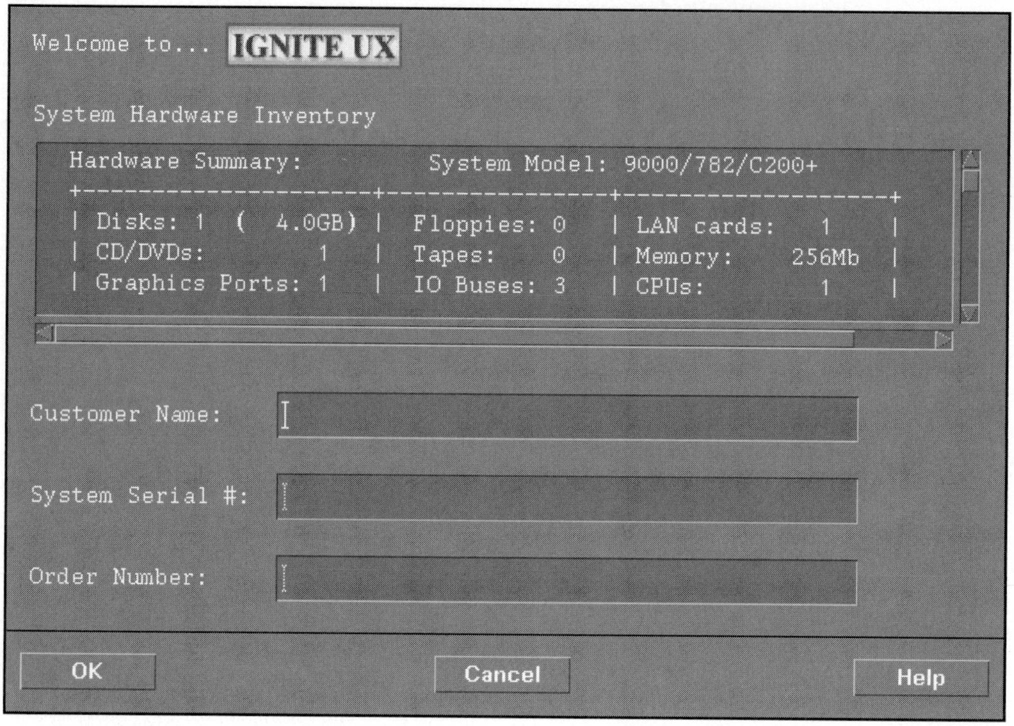

```
Welcome to...  IGNITE UX

System Hardware Inventory

   Hardware Summary:        System Model: 9000/782/C200+
   +--------------------+----------------+--------------------+
   | Disks: 1  ( 4.0GB) |  Floppies: 0   | LAN cards:   1     |
   | CD/DVDs:         1  |  Tapes:    0   | Memory:    256Mb   |
   | Graphics Ports: 1   |  IO Buses: 3   | CPUs:        1     |


Customer Name:     [

System Serial #:   [

Order Number:      [


     OK                      Cancel                    Help
```

Figure 10-10   Information about Client

Now that we've created both a core operating system and applications depot, we can boot and load one of our clients through Ignite-UX on the server.

In addition to controlling the client as we have done using the Ignite-UX graphical interface in "push" fashion from the server, you can also work from the client in "pull" fashion. In order to boot the client from the server while sitting at the server, you would issue the following command from PDC (Processor Dependent Code; see Chapter 1) after interrupting the boot process:

BOOT ADMIN> `boot lan 15.32.163.26 install`

man page

boot - 3

The IP address specified is that of the server, where we set up the software depot. While sitting at the client, you would see the Ignite-UX interface in character mode and proceed with the installation while sitting at the client using the software depot we set up on the server.

Getting back to the GUI, we select the software we wish to load through the familiar Ignite-UX interface that is part of any initial operating system load as shown in Figure 10-11:

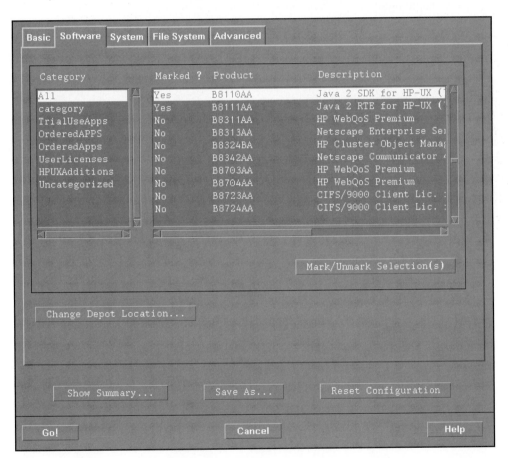

Figure 10-11 Selecting Software to Load on Client

Notice in Figure 10-11 that we are in the *Software* tab at the top of the screen. We'll progress through the *System* and *File System* tabs in two upcoming figures. Remember, all of this work is being done on the Ignite-UX server we set up.

We have selected a Java product that was part of the applications depot we created in Figure 10-11. The core operating system and other software selections were also made in the *Software* window.

In addition to the software load, we can also perform additional configuration on the server for the client we are loading, such as providing the system name under the *System* tab as shown in Figure 10-12:

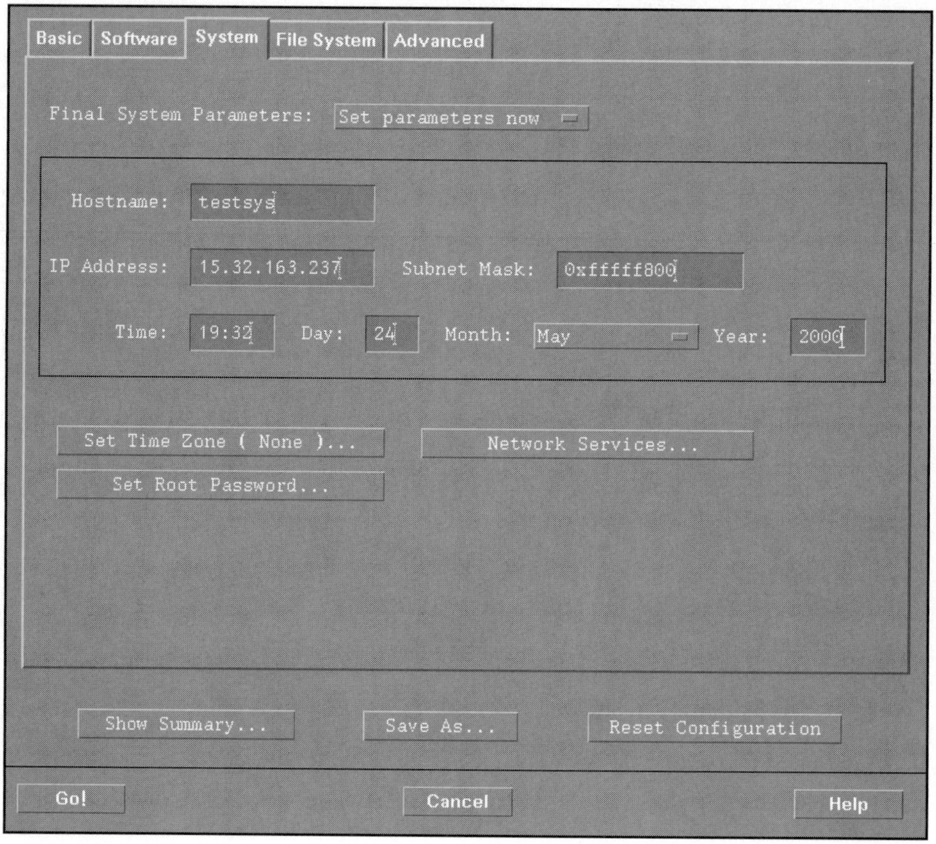

Figure 10-12 Set Up the Client System

Next we can perform file-system-related configuration under the *File System* tab as shown in Figure 10-13:

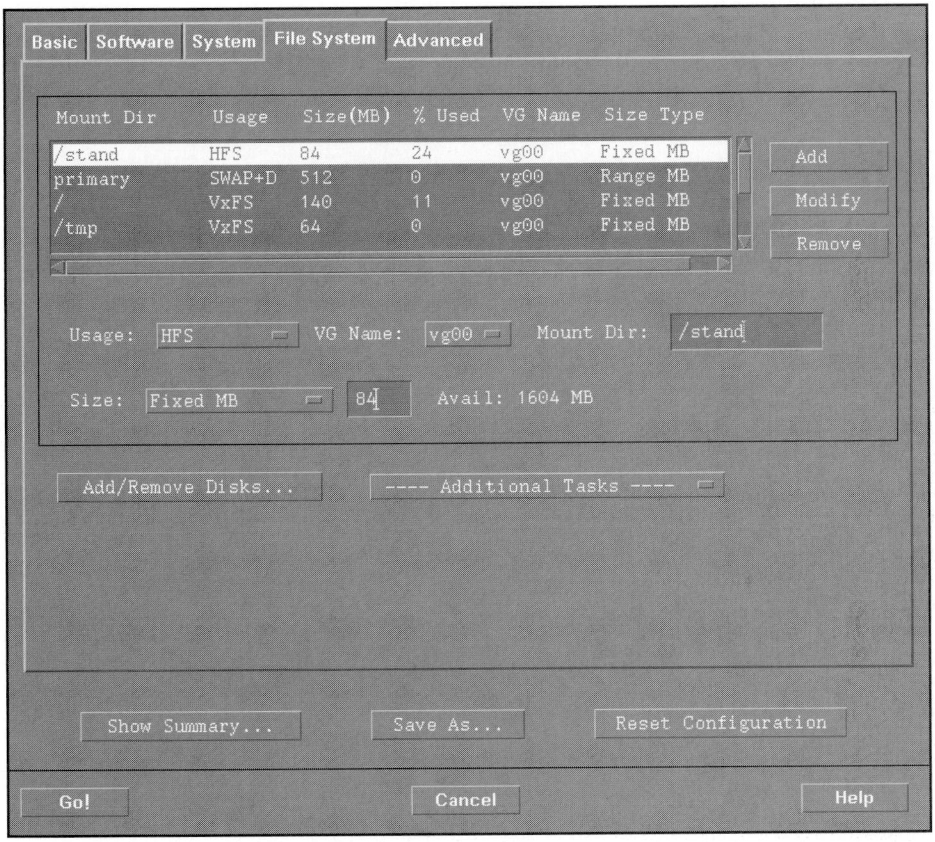

```
 Basic  Software  System | File System | Advanced

    Mount Dir      Usage    Size(MB)   % Used   VG Name   Size Type
   /stand          HFS       84          24       vg00     Fixed MB
   primary         SWAP+D    512          0       vg00     Range MB
   /               VxFS      140         11       vg00     Fixed MB      Add
   /tmp            VxFS      64           0       vg00     Fixed MB      Modify
                                                                        Remove


    Usage:  HFS          ▭  VG Name:  vg00 ▭   Mount Dir:  /stand

    Size:  Fixed MB      ▭    84     Avail: 1604 MB


     Add/Remove Disks...        ---- Additional Tasks ----  ▭




       Show Summary...        Save As...       Reset Configuration

  Go!                           Cancel                           Help
```

Figure 10-13 Set Up the Client File Systems

After we have completed all of our initial work in the Ignite-UX for the client while working on the server, we can proceed with the client load. Figure 10-14 shows two Ignite-UX windows that appear on the server when we begin configuring and loading the client:

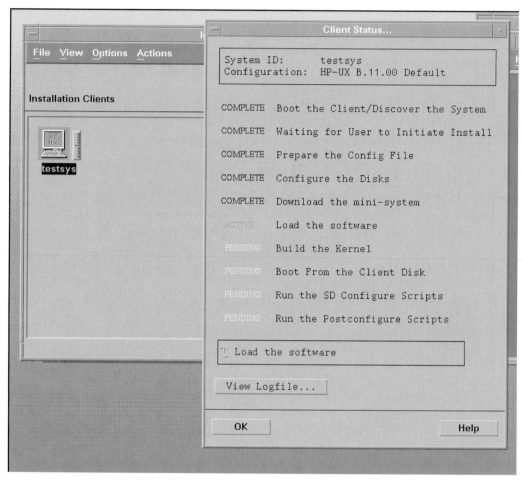

Figure 10-14 Status of Client Load

The leftmost window in Figure 10-14 shows the icon for the system we are working on and the rightmost window provides the status of the client load. Since we are working on only one system, only one icon appears in the leftmost window. The status of the software load in the rightmost window indicates that *Load the software* is an *ACTIVE* process. Several process have been *COMPLETE,* and several others are *PENDING.*

Although you can't see the colors in the original screen shot, the status messages are color-coded.

There is substantially more that you can accomplish with Ignite-UX, such as grouping the configuration files into sets that you can select when loading clients, installing patch depots, and many other useful tasks. The *Ignite-UX Administrator Guide* at *www.docs.hp.com* covers many additional topics.

From the procedure we performed in this section, however, you can see how easy it is to create software depots and manage clients.

System Recovery with Ignite-UX

Ignite-UX is a product bundled with HP-UX 11i that provides a process to create a bootable system recovery tape. The tape contains a boot area and an operating system archive. Should your root disk fail or corruption of the root disk take place, you can recover using the bootable system recovery tape.

make_recovery is the Ignite-UX tool that is used to create the bootable system recovery tape. **make_recovery** is being replaced by **make_net_recovery** at the time of this writing but **make_recovery** will be used throughout this section because the **check_recovery** function covered in this section was not yet implemented with **make_net_recovery**. You could boot and restore from the system recovery tape and then use your system backup to fully restore the system. If your root disk were to fail, in a non-mirrored environment, you would perform the following steps to recover from the failure:

- Replace the defective root disk.
- Boot from the recovery tape by selecting the tape device.
- Monitor the restoration of the operating system archive from the recovery tape.
- Restore the balance of data on the system with backup information.

The bootable system recovery tape consists of both a Logical Interchange Format (LIF) volume as well as the operating system archive. The LIF volume contains all the components necessary to boot from the tape. The operating system archive contains only the core operating system by default.

You can include additional files in the operating system archive, if you wish, using two different techniques. The first is to edit the file **/var/opt/ignite/recovery/makrec.append** and add to it the file name, directory name, or software distributor product name you wish to include in the operating system archive. The second technique is to run **make_recovery** in preview mode with the -*p* option, manually add files to include and/or exclude from the archive, and resume **make_recovery** with the -*r* option. The manual pages for **/opt/ignite/bin/make_recovery** and **/opt/ignite/bin/ignite** are online on your HP-UX system.

You can also determine whether your recovery tape is up-to-date by using the **check_recovery** command. Running **make_recovery** with the -*C* option produces a system recovery status file. **check_recovery** compares the system recovery status file to the current state of the system and produces a list of discrepancies. From this list you can determine whether or not you should produce another system recovery tape. The manual page for **/opt/ignite/bin/check_recovery** is online on your HP-UX system.

The recovery feature is only one component of the Ignite-UX product. Ignite-UX provides a means to install systems over the network by either pushing the installation to a client from an Ignite server or pulling the installation from the Ignite server to the client. With Ignite-UX, "golden images" of your standard installation setup can be created and systems can be set up in a matter of minutes by "igniting" them from this image over the network. More information about Ignite-UX can be viewed on the Internet at *http://www.software.hp.com/products/IUX* and read about in the "Configuring an Ignite-UX Server" and "Installing from the Ignite-UX Server" chapters as well as Appendix C: "Ignite-UX System Administration" of the *Installing HP-UX 11.0 and Upgrading 10.x to 11.0* manual from Hewlett-Packard. The "HP-UX System Recovery" chapter of the same manual gives additional information about the **make_recovery** feature of Ignite-UX.

An Example of Creating a Bootable System Recovery Tape

Now that we have covered the basic components and capabilities of the Ignite-UX recovery process, let's look at an example of creating a bootable system recovery tape.

Let's first run **make_recovery** with the *-p* option so that we cansee the way Ignite-UX reports the information it is including on the tape. I'll also use the *-A* option, which specifies that the entire root volume group is to be included. I sometimes use **make_recovery** to clone identical systems by producing a recovery tape with the *-A* option and then loading the tape on systems that I want to be identical to the original system. You would not use the *-A* option if you have a large root volume group or if you perform normal backups and don't need to include all root volume group information on the recovery tape. In addition to *-p* for preview and *-A* for all, I'll also use the *-v* for the verbose option and *-C* to create the system status file in the following preview command example:

```
# make_recovery -p -v -A -C


        *** Previewing only ***
    Option -A specified. Entire Core Volume Group/disk will be backed up.



    *****************************************
    HP-UX System Recovery
    Validating append file
            Done

    File Systems on Core OS Disks/Volume Groups:

            vg name = vg00
            pv_name =  /dev/dsk/c0t5d0

            vg00        /dev/vg00/lvol3        /
            vg00        /dev/vg00/lvol4        /home
            vg00        /dev/vg00/lvol5        /opt
            vg00        /dev/vg00/lvol1        /stand
            vg00        /dev/vg00/lvol6        /tmp
            vg00        /dev/vg00/lvol7        /usr
            vg00        /dev/vg00/lvol8        /var

      Create mount points
       /apps
       /work
       /spill
       /spill2
       /rbdisk01
       /rbdisk02
       /rbdisk03
       /rbdisk04
       /rbdisk05
       /rbdisk06
       /rbdisk07
       /rbdisk09
       /rbdisk10
       /rbdisk11
       /rbdisk12
       /rbdisk13
       /rbdisk14
       /rbdisk15
       /rbdisk16
       /rbdisk17
       /rbdisk18
       /nfs

            /opt is a mounted directory
              It is in the Core Volume Group
              Mounted at /dev/vg00/lvol5


            /var is a mounted directory
              It is in the Core Volume Group
              Mounted at /dev/vg00/lvol8

    Destination = /dev/rmt/0m
    Boot LIF location = /var/tmp/uxinstlf.recovery



    *****************************************
```

```
    Preview only. Tape not created

The /var/opt/ignite/recovery/arch.include file has been created.
This can be modified to exclude known files.
Only delete files or directories that are strictly user created.
The creation of the System Recovery tape can then be
resumed using the -r option.

No further checks will be performed by the commands.
        Cleanup
```

The **arch.include** file has been produced at this point. This file lists the files that will be part of the archive that you can modify. The following is an abbreviated listing of **arch.include**, showing just the very beginning and very end of the file:

```
/
/lost+found
/etc
/etc/vue
/etc/vue/config
/etc/vue/config/types
/etc/vue/config/types/tools
/etc/vue/config/types/tools/System_Admin
/etc/vue/config/types/tools/System_Admin/FontClientSrvr
/etc/vue/config/types/tools/System_Admin/SetNetworking
/etc/vue/config/types/tools/System_Admin/ShutdownSystem
/etc/vue/config/types/tools/System_Admin/VerifyPEX
/etc/vue/config/types/tools/System_Admin/VerifyPEX
/etc/vue/config/types/tools/Media

.
.
.

/spp/scripts/tc_standalone
/spp/scripts/sppconsole.old
/spp/unsupported
/spp/unsupported/cbus
/spp/unsupported/clear_pid
/spp/unsupported/ex_shm
/spp/unsupported/rdr_dumper.fw
/spp/unsupported/rdr_formatter
/spp/unsupported/reset_jtag
/spp/unsupported/scan_sram
/users
/users/sppuser
/users/sppuser/.Xdefaults
/users/sppuser/.cshrc
/users/sppuser/.kshrc
/users/sppuser/.login
```

```
/users/sppuser/.mwmrc
/users/sppuser/.profile
/users/sppuser/.x11start
/users/sppuser/.x11startlog
/users/sppuser/.sh_history
/users/sppuser/.sw
/users/sppuser/.sw/sessions
/users/sppuser/.sw/sessions/swlist.last
/users/sppuser/.history
/.sh_history
/.profile
/lib
/lib
/bin
/bin
/core
/ignite_10.20.tar
/var/tmp/makrec.lasttmp
/var/opt/ignite/recovery/chkrec.include
/var/opt/ignite/recovery/config.recover
```

On the system on which this **make_recovery** was performed, the **arch.include** file had over 44,000 lines in it, as shown below:

```
# cat /var/opt/ignite/recovery/arch.include | wc
44142 44146 1730818
```

Now let's resume **make_recovery**, which was running in preview mode with the *-r* option for resume, the *-v* option for verbose, and the *-C* option to create the system status file. The *-d* option will not be specified because the default tape device will be used. The *-A* option, which was specified earlier in preview mode, specifies that the entire root volume group is to be included.

```
# make_recovery -r -C -v
make_recovery(306): In Resume mode. Do you wish to continue?y


        *****************************************
        HP-UX System Recovery

        File Systems on Core OS Disks/Volume Groups:

                vg name = vg00
                pv_name =  /dev/dsk/c0t5d0
```

```
                          vg00        /dev/vg00/lvol3      /
                          vg00        /dev/vg00/lvol4      /home
                          vg00        /dev/vg00/lvol5      /opt
                          vg00        /dev/vg00/lvol1      /stand
                          vg00        /dev/vg00/lvol6      /tmp
                          vg00        /dev/vg00/lvol7      /usr
                          vg00        /dev/vg00/lvol8      /var

          Create mount points
           /apps
           /work
           /spill
           /spill2
           /rbdisk01
           /rbdisk02
           /rbdisk03
           /rbdisk04
           /rbdisk05
           /rbdisk06
           /rbdisk07
           /rbdisk09
           /rbdisk10
           /rbdisk11
           /rbdisk12
           /rbdisk13
           /rbdisk14
           /rbdisk15
           /rbdisk16
           /rbdisk17
           /rbdisk18
           /nfs

                  /opt is a mounted directory
                     It is in the Core Volume Group
                     Mounted at /dev/vg00/lvol5


                  /var is a mounted directory
                     It is in the Core Volume Group
                     Mounted at /dev/vg00/lvol8

  Destination = /dev/rmt/0m
  Boot LIF location = /var/tmp/uxinstlf.recovery


  ****************************************
  Creating the configuration file.
          Done
  Modifying the configuration file.
          Done
  Backing up vg configurations
          Volume Group vg00
          Volume Group vg01
          Volume Group vg03
          Volume Group vg02
          Done
  Creating the /var/opt/ignite/recovery/makrec.last file
          Done
  Going to create the tape.
  Processing tape
          Invoking instl_adm -T
          Creating boot LIF
          Done
          Writing boot LIF to tape /dev/rmt/0mn
```

```
            Done
            Creating archive - this may take about 30 minutes.
            Done
        System Recovery Tape successfully created.
#
```

A system recovery tape has now been produced. You could now boot from the system recovery tape and restore the entire volume group **vg00** on this system.

Running the check_recovery Command

You can run the **check_recovery** command any time to view the changes that have been made to the system since the last time the system recovery status file was created with the *-C* option. The following example shows running the **check_recovery** command:


```
# check_recovery

Since the last System Recovery Image was created, the following software
product changes have been detected.

(Added)      Auxiliary-OptB.11.01.01    Auxiliary Optimizer for HP Languages.
(Added)      OBJCOBOLB.12.50               Object COBOL Developer

Since the last System Recovery Image was created, the following system
files (or links) have been added to the current system.

  /apps/informix7.3/lib/iosm07a.sl
  /apps/informix7.3/lib/ipldd07a.sl
  /apps/informix7.3/lib/liborb_r.sl
  /dev/vg13/lvol01
  /dev/vg13/rlvol01
  /etc/sam/custom/scjjs.cf
  /etc/sam/custom/scrar.cf
  /sbin/init.d/flex
  /sbin/rc2.d/S989flex
  /usr/lib/iosm07a.sl
  /usr/lib/iosm07a.sl.980709
  /usr/lib/ipldd07a.sl.980709
  /usr/lib/liborb_r.sl
  /usr/local/adm/bin/user_watch.pl
  /usr/local/adm/etc/rept
  /usr/local/flexlm/bin/lmcksum
  /usr/local/flexlm/bin/lmdiag
  /usr/local/flexlm/bin/lmdown
  /usr/local/flexlm/bin/lmgrd
  /usr/local/flexlm/bin/lmhostid
  /usr/local/flexlm/bin/lmremove
  /usr/local/flexlm/bin/lmreread
  /usr/local/flexlm/bin/lmstat
  /usr/local/flexlm/bin/lmswitchr
```

```
/usr/local/flexlm/bin/lmutil
/usr/local/flexlm/bin/lmver
/usr/local/flexlm/daemons/HPCUPLANGS
/usr/local/flexlm/licenses/license.dat
/usr/local/flexlm/licenses/license.log
/usr/share/man/cat1.Z/X.1
/usr/share/man/cat1.Z/Xserver.1
/usr/share/man/cat1.Z/grep.1
/usr/share/man/cat1.Z/mwm.1
/usr/share/man/cat1.Z/xhost.1
/usr/share/man/cat1.Z/xset.1
/usr/share/man/cat2.Z/exec.2
```

Since the last System Recovery Image was created, the following system files (or links) have been deleted from the current system.

```
/dev/vg13/lvol1
/dev/vg13/rlvol1
/stand/build/conf.o
```

Since the last System Recovery Image was created, the following system files (or links) have been modified on the current system.

```
                              Current              makrec.last
                              -------              -----------
/dev/pty/ttyp2
        permissions           crw-rw-rw-           crw--w----
        uid                   0                    102
        gid                   0                    10
/dev/pty/ttyp3
        permissions           crw--w----           crw-rw-rw-
        uid                   102                  0
        gid                   10                   0
/dev/pty/ttyp4
        permissions           crw--w----           crw-rw-rw-
        gid                   10                   0
/dev/pty/ttyp5
        permissions           crw-rw-rw-           crw--w----
        uid                   0                    102
        gid                   0                    10
/dev/pty/ttyp6
        permissions           crw-rw-rw-           crw--w----
        uid                   0                    102
        gid                   0                    10
/dev/pty/ttyp8
        uid                   0                    2
        gid                   0                    10
/dev/ttyp2
        permissions           crw-rw-rw-           crw--w----
        uid                   0                    102
        gid                   0                    10
/dev/ttyp3
        permissions           crw--w----           crw-rw-rw-
        uid                   102                  0
        gid                   10                   0
/dev/ttyp4
        permissions           crw--w----           crw-rw-rw-
        gid                   10                   0
/dev/ttyp5
        permissions           crw-rw-rw-           crw--w----
        uid                   0                    102
        gid                   0                    10
/dev/ttyp6
        permissions           crw-rw-rw-           crw--w----
        uid                   0                    102
```

```
        gid                 0               10
/dev/ttyp8
        uid                 0               2
        gid                 0               10
/etc/MANPATH
        checksum            1982379524      497249200
/etc/PATH
        checksum            562953260       2784298760
/etc/SHLIB_PATH
        checksum            2664385509      241316845
/etc/fstab
        checksum            3014086519      200239819
/etc/fstab.old
        checksum            682979636       2528618126
/etc/group
        checksum            368341889       127908837
/etc/lvmconf/vg13.conf
        checksum            1522028984      929609311
/etc/lvmconf/vg13.conf.old
        checksum            1830986219      3891043243
/etc/lvmtab
        checksum            4141778997      3277790772
/etc/passwd
        checksum            1661378396      2350540120
/etc/profile
        checksum            510591831       2645970599
/stand/build/conf.SAM.c
        checksum            3973853979      4022316306
/stand/build/conf.SAM.o
        checksum            4142700410      118504989
/stand/build/conf.o.old
        checksum            2526740160      1129366190
/stand/build/config.SAM.mk
        checksum            2849240259      1706527948
/stand/build/function_names.c
        checksum            2434797998      1240646943
        permissions         rw-rw-rw-       rw-r--r--
/stand/build/function_names.o
        checksum            3857693076      1165263911
        permissions         rw-rw-rw-       rw-r--r--
/stand/build/space.h
        permissions         rw-rw-rw-       rw-r--r--
/stand/build/tune.h
        checksum            2763942582      2084822502
/stand/dlkm.vmunix.prev/symtab
        checksum            2086890351      1785861028
        permissions         rw-r--r--       rw-rw-rw-
/stand/dlkm.vmunix.prev/system
        checksum            3376707916      2873910478
/stand/dlkm/symtab
        checksum            2368412414      2086890351
        permissions         rw-rw-rw-       rw-r--r--
/stand/dlkm/system
        checksum            2855591959      3376707916
/stand/system
        checksum            4141126356      1910321628
        permissions         rw-rw-rw-       r--r--r--
/stand/system.prev
        checksum            1910321628      253499711
        permissions         r--r--r--       rw-rw-rw-
/stand/vmunix
        checksum            2977157561      2742478025
/stand/vmunix.prev
        checksum            2742478025      3594881120
/usr/lib/ipldd07a.sl
        linkname            /apps/informix7.3/lib/ipldd07a.sl
```

```
            /apps/informix/lib/ipldd07a.sl
    /usr/local/samba.1.9.18p3/var/locks/browse.dat
        checksum       2594069517              2221092461
    /usr/local/samba.1.9.18p3/var/log.nmb
        checksum       4219117043              2190854115
    /usr/local/samba.1.9.18p3/var/log.smb
        checksum       2251415300              1791314631
    /var/spool/cron/crontabs/root
        checksum       2015828837              1660287231
#
```

This output indicates that many changes have been made to the system, including software additions and system file additions, deletions, and modifications. If **check_recovery** produces any significant changes to the system, you should rerun the **make_recovery** command so that the system recovery tape reflects the current state of your system. As a result of completing the procedure covered in this section, many files were produced. Some that you may want to take a look at are in the **/var/opt/ignite/recovery** directory shown in the following listing:

```
# cd /var/opt/ignite/recovery
# 11
total 5412
-rw-rw-rw-  1 root     sys        1737051 Jul 13 16:17 arch.include
-rw-rw-rw-  1 root     sys            250 Jul 13 16:12 chkrec.include
-rw-rw-rw-  1 root     sys           4872 Jul 13 16:17 config.recover
-rw-rw-rw-  1 root     sys           4872 Jul 13 16:17 config.recover.prev
-rw-rw-rw-  1 root     sys           1682 Jul 13 16:12 fstab
-rw-rw-rw-  1 root     sys            390 Jul 13 16:29 group.makrec
-r--r--r--  1 root     sys           1971 Jun 25 12:27 makrec.append
-r--r--r--  1 bin      bin           1971 Apr 24 00:32 makrec.append.org
-rw-rw-rw-  1 root     sys        1010844 Jul 13 16:28 makrec.last
-rw-rw-rw-  1 root     sys           2573 Jul 13 16:29 passwd.makrec
```

Manual Pages for Commands Used in Chapter 10

The following section contains the **make_net_recovery** manual page.

make_net_recovery

make_net_recovery - Create an Ignite-UX system recovery archive.

```
make_net_recovery(1M)
```

NAME
     make_net_recovery - network based system recovery archive creation

SYNOPSIS
     /opt/ignite/bin/make_net_recovery -s Ignite-UX_server [-v] [-P
          partial_inclusion_indicator] [-i|-ib] [-a
          archive_server:archive_dir] [-d description] [-f
content_file] [-l
          lanic_id] [-n num_archives] [-x content-options] [XToolkit-
          Options]

DESCRIPTION
     The make_net_recovery tool creates a system recovery archive and
     stores the archive on the network. The archive created by
     make_net_recovery is specific to the system it was created for and its
     identity includes hostname, ip_address, networking information, etc.
     In the event of a root disk failure, the recovery archive can be
     installed via Ignite-UX to restore the system.

     The contents of the system recovery archive will always include all
     files and directories which are considered essential to bringing up a
     functional system. This "essential" list is pre-defined by
     make_net_recovery. By running make_net_recovery in interactive mode,
     the directories and files which make up the "essential list" can be
     displayed. In addition to the essential list, data can be included in
     the archive on a disk/volume group, file, or directory basis. Non-
     essential files and directories can also be excluded.

  Options
    make_net_recovery recognizes the following options:

          -a archive_server:archive_dir
                 Specifies the NFS server and location to store the archive.
                 The archive directory must be NFS exported (See section
                 "Exporting Archive Directory") and sufficient disk space is
                 required. The default is the hostname of the Ignite-UX
                 server followed by the directory which holds the archive.
                 e.g.,

      Serverhost:/var/opt/ignite/recovery/archives/<hostname>.

The hostname is the name of the system being archived. Each make_net_recovery client will create a subdirectory named after the client hostname under the specified directory to store the archives.

-b   When used in combination with the -i option, it causes make_net_recovery to run in the background after the interactive user interface completes.

-d description
         One line description of the system recovery archive. Quotation marks must be enclosed around the description if spaces are included in the description. This description will be displayed when choosing the archive as a configuration from the Ignite-UX Graphical User Interface. The default description is Recovery Archive.

-f content_file
         Location of the file which identifies keywords to specify inclusions and exclusions for the archive. Default is

         /var/opt/ignite/clients/0x{LLA}/recovery/archive_content

         This file is located on the Ignite-UX server and accessed by the client through an NFS mount. The absolute path name to the archive_content file must be supplied as an argument to the -f option. This option may be useful when there is a desire to manage multiple files which specify the content of the archive. The -f option is not allowed when using the -x options to specify the contents of the archive.

-i   Causes make_net_recovery to run interactively to allow you to select which files and directories are to be included in the recovery archive. It is preferable to use the ignite GUI command on the Ignite-UX server when running an interactive make_net_recovery session. Running it from ignite causes any additional server configuration of NFS mounts to be performed. It also gives you a better progress report.

-l lanic id
         The lanic id of the system being archived. Used to create the per-client directory on the Ignite-UX server.

-n num_archives
         Specifies the number of archives that should remain on the server at any given time. The default is 2. If num_archives=2 and there are already 2 archives present when a 3rd is being created, make_net_recovery will remove the oldest archive after successfully creating the 3rd archive.

-P s|w|e
         When a disk or volume group is partially included in the system recovery archive, generate an ERROR(e), WARNING(w), or SUPPRESS(s) any warning messages that would normally be generated when partial inclusions occur. The default is w, thus causing Warning messages to be produced when partial inclusions of disks and/or volume groups are detected.

When e is specified, an Error message will be displayed to stdout and to the logfile, and execution of make_net_recovery will stop once the Error message is displayed.

-s Ignite-UX_server
Specifies the hostname of the Ignite-UX server. The configuration files, defaults and contents files for the client system will be read from the Ignite-UX server in /var/opt/ignite/clients/0x{LLA}/recovery. The make_net_recovery tool will NFS mount the per-client directory to access this information.

-v   Display verbose progress messages while creating the system recovery archive. Includes information such as which volume groups/disks will be included in the system recovery archive.

-x include=file|dir
Includes the file or directory in the recovery archive but does not cross any mount points.

-x inc_cross=file|dir
Includes the file or directory in the recovery archive and crosses mount points to access any directories that are mounted or files contained in directories that are mounted.

-x inc_entire=/dev/dsk/<name>|vg_name
Includes all file systems contained on the specified disk or volume group. Use a block device file of the format /dev/dsk/<name> when specifying a whole-disk (non-LVM) file system. Use the volume group name (such as vg00) when you want all file systems that are part of that LVM volume group to be included in the archive.

-x exclude=file|dir
Excludes the file or directory from the archive. When a directory is specified, no files beneath that directory will be stored in the archive.

XToolkit-Options
The make_net_recovery command supports a subset of the standard X Toolkit options to control the appearance of the GUI when the -i option is specified. The supported options are: -bg, -background, -fg, -foreground, -display, -name, -xrm, and -synchronous. See the X(1) manual page for a definition of these options.

Including and Excluding From Archive
The contents of the archive can be controlled from the contents file. The full path for the contents file is /var/opt/ignite/clients/0x{LLA}/recovery/archive_content on the Ignite-UX Server. This file consists of keyword identifiers which specify the inclusion of files, directories, or entire disks and volume groups. The keyword identifiers also instruct make_net_recovery whether to follow mount points when creating the system recovery archive. The contents file has the following keywords identifiers:

```
include <filename | directory>
        Includes the specified filename or directory and all
        subdirectories and associated files. Mount points are not
        crossed and symbolic links are not followed.

inc_cross <filename | directory >
        Include the specified filename or directory and all
        subdirectories and files contained underneath
        subdirectories. Local mount points are crossed but symbolic
        links are not followed.

inc_entire <volume group | disk >
        Include the entire specified volume group (e.g. "vg00") or
        disk (block device - e.g. "/dev/dsk/c0t5d0").  Do not
        specify a disk if it is part of a volume group.

exclude <filename | directory >
        Exclude the specified filename or directory and all
        subdirectories and files contained under the subdirectories.
```

make_net_recovery reads the contents file to generate the list of
files that will be used to create the system recovery archive. The
contents file can be modified by hand or by running make_net_recovery
in interactive mode. When modifying the contents file, keep the
following points in mind:

+   No essential file or directory can be excluded. Exclusions of
    essential files or directories will be ignored.

+   Exclusions take precedence over inclusions. Anything that is
    both included and excluded will be excluded from the archive.

+   The ordering of inclusions and exclusions within the defaults
    file is not significant.

Using Settings From Previous Archive Creation
    The defaults file stores input specified by interacting with the
    make_net_recovery GUI. Options are preserved until the next archive is
    generated by interacting with the GUI. Command line options will
    override settings in the defaults file. The full path for the defaults
    file is /var/opt/ignite/clients/0x{LLA}/recovery/defaults on the
    Ignite-UX server. This directory is accessed via NFS from the client.

    ###### defaults file ######

RECOVERY_LOCATION=15.1.2.3:/var/opt/ignite/recovery/archives/{client_name}
    RECOVERY_DESCRIPTION="Recovery Archive"
    SAVE_NUM_ARCHIVES=2

Using the Recovery Archive
    To recover a failed system using the network recovery archive:

+ If the client system is being replaced, or the LAN card has
  changed since make_net_recovery was last used, you should
  manually rename the old client directory prior to starting the
  recovery. Not doing so will cause a new directory to be
  created and you will not see the recovery archives created
  under the old client directory. To rename the client
  directory, obtain the new LLA address (you may use the
  LanAddress boot-ROM command in the information menu), then use
  the mv command. For example:
      cd /var/opt/ignite/clients
      mv 0x00108305463A 0x0060B0C43AB7
  If you have already booted the new system, you will need to
  remove the new client before renaming the old directory. Be
  careful not to remove the old directory containing the
  recovery information.

+ Boot the system using either a network boot, a tape created
  using make_boot_tape, or using the bootsys command if the
  system is still running.

+ Do not interact with ISL

+ Select: [Install HP-UX]

+ From the Ignite-UX GUI: select the icon for the client

+ Choose "Install/New Install"

+ Select the recovery configuration to use

Exporting Archive Directory
  The directory used to store the archives must be exported from the
  archive server to each client. Exporting the archive directory from
  the system where the archive will be stored enables make_net_recovery
  to create and access the archive via NFS. The archive server by
  default is the Ignite-UX server but can be changed using the -a option
  to be a different remote server, or even the local client if you want
  to capture the archives as part of the client's regular backup. Note
  however, that if the archives are stored on the client itself, they
  must be put onto a remote server if the client ever needs to be
  recovered using them.

  For security reasons, it is best to export each client-specific
  archive directory to just the individual client. If the recovery
  archive creation is initiated from the ignite graphical user interface
  on the Ignite-UX server, and the archive server is the same as the
  Ignite-UX server, the /etc/exports file will be edited automatically
  so the archive can be stored in the desired location. Otherwise, if
  make_net_recovery is run directly on the client the following steps
  are required to be done on the archive server.

    + On the archive server, create a directory for each client to hold
      the archive of the client's files. It is important that the
      directory be owned by the user "bin". Replace <client> in the
      commands below with the hostname of the client. If you use the -a
      option to make_net_recovery to specify an alternate location or
      the archives, you will need to use that path instead of the
      default which is shown below.

```
mkdir -p /var/opt/ignite/recovery/archives/<client>
chown bin:bin /var/opt/ignite/recovery/archives/<client>
```

+ Edit /etc/exports to add an entry for each client. Replace
  <client> with the client's hostname in the example shown:

```
/var/opt/ignite/recovery/archives/<client> -anon=2,access =<client>
```

+ Run the exportfs command to have the edits to the exports file
  take effect:

```
/usr/sbin/exportfs -av
```

Networking Features
    Two NFS mount points are established on the client by
    make_net_recovery. The /var/opt/ignite/clients directory on the
    Ignite-UX server is mounted to the client system to store
    configuration files which describe the client configuration and
    location of the recovery archive. The second mount point is made to
    the archive_server:archive_dir (see the -a option) and is used to
    store the recovery archive of the client system. After successful or
    unsuccessful completion of the system recovery archive, the NFS mount
    points are un-mounted.

    The NFS mount for the archive directory may be exported on a per-
    client bases. A separate archive directory is used for each client.
    This allows you to NFS export each directory only to the individual
    client owning the archive, which provides security.

    If the client system does not have the most recent versions of
    Ignite-UX tools, The Ignite-UX GUI uses swinstall(1M) to install the
    "recovery package" which includes all necessary files to perform the
    recovery.

RETURN VALUE
    make_net_recovery will return 0 upon successful completion. When
    warnings occur, 2 will be returned. Otherwise, when a failure occurs 1
    will be returned.

EXAMPLES
    Create a system recovery archive by interacting with the Ignite-UX
GUI
    from the Ignite-UX server:

```
export DISPLAY=<hostname>:0
ignite
```

    Create a system recovery archive from the client, using settings from
    the last invocation of the Ignite-UX GUI. Use the options file on the
    Ignite-UX server (myserver) in the default location:
    /var/opt/ignite/clients/0x{LLA}/recovery.

```
make_net_recovery -s myserver
```

    Create a system recovery archive that includes files from all file
    systems in the vg00 volume group:

```
make_net_recovery -s myserver -x inc_entire=vg00
```

Create a system recovery archive that includes all of the vg00 and
vg01 volume groups, but that excludes the /depots directory.

```
make_net_recovery -s myserver -x inc_entire=vg00 -x inc_entire=vg01
        -x exclude=/depots
```

Below is an example shell script that can be run on each client.It
can help you to keep from ever having to update Ignite-UX on each
client when a new release is loaded on the server. It will
automatically update the network recovery software if the server has a
newer version. It may be suitable for use in a crontab entry. This
example assumes that the /var/opt/ignite/depots/recovery_cmds software
depot has been created. This depot is created by running ignite GUI
at least once to make a recovery archive of a system (See also
pkg_rec_depot(1M)). Once created, this depot will automatically be
updated each time Ignite-UX is updated on the server.

```
        myserver=iuxserver
        /opt/ignite/lbin/check_version -s $myserver
        if [ $? != 0 ]
        then
            swinstall -s
$myserver:/var/opt/ignite/depots/recovery_cmds '*'
        fi
        /opt/ignite/bin/make_net_recovery -s $myserver
```

WARNINGS
    Disks Will be Reformatted
        If any file from a disk or volume group is included in the recovery
        archive, that disk (or all disks in the volume group) will be
        reformatted during the recovery, and only the files included will be
        recovered. Any files that were not included in the archive, will have
        to be restored from your normal backups.

        Disks and volume groups that did not have any files included in the
        archive are not reformatted during a recovery and are re-imported and
        re-mounted at the end of the recovery.

    Logical Volume Physical Extent Allocation Not Preserved:
        The make_net_recovery tool captures enough information from the system
        so that during a recovery it can reconstruct most all visible aspects
        of the prior LVM configuration. This includes logical volume and
        volume group names, attributes, and even minor number values. The
        tool also ensures that the new logical volumes reside on the same
        disks within the volume group as they did before.

        make_net_recovery does not, however, ensure that logical volumes are
        extended in the same exact order as they were originally. This means
        the LVM physical extents allocated to a logical volume may be in a
        different location on the disk than before. The recovery tools use a
        very specific and complex algorithm for extending logical volumes to
        ensure success (such as extending contiguous volumes before non-
        contiguous). An example effect of this is that swap/dump volumes will
        reside on the root disk ahead of some other volumes even though that
        may not have been the original layout.

VxVM disk groups not included in The disk groups managed by VERITAS
Volume Manager (VxVM) cannot be included in the Ignite-UX archive. If they are
included, make_net_recovery will error out. Those disk groups will be left
undisturbed and re-integrated to the system after the recovery is complete.

LVM Disk Mirrors not Restored
The make_net_recovery tool will create a recovery backup for a system
with mirrored disks but it will not restore the mirrored disk
configuration. If the system is later recovered, previously mirrored
volumes will no longer be mirrored. They can be manually re-mirrored
after the system is up. Using the config.local file in the clients
directory, you can specify the LVM commands to restore mirrored disks
to be executed automatically after the system has been restored. For
more details, see the white paper /opt/ignite/share/doc/diskmirror.pdf.

DEPENDENCIES
The Ignite-UX GUI must be run from the Ignite-UX Server, see
ignite(5). make_net_recovery depends on several other Ignite-UX
tools. When running the Ignite-UX server GUI, Ignite-UX checks
whether the client system, that make_net_recovery runs on, has the
same versions of Ignite-UX tools.

If running make_net_recovery from the command line without ever
interacting with the Ignite-UX GUI, commands will need to be
installed
using swinstall(1M) from the Ignite-UX server to the client system
that make_net_recovery will run on.

AUTHOR
Ignite-UX and make_net_recovery were developed by the Hewlett-Packard
company.

DIAGNOSTICS
All major steps within network recovery are logged on the server and
displayed via the Ignite-UX Server GUI.

FILES
/opt/ignite/recovery/mnr_essentials Lists the files and directories that
are considered essential and are always included in the archive if they
exist on the system.

/var/opt/ignite/recovery/mnr_essentials
Lists the files and directories that are essentials, but actsas
the user modifiable version, so that the original mnr_essentials
file can be maintained. When this file exists, its content is
checked before the file /opt/ignite/recovery/mnr_essentials.

/var/opt/ignite/clients/0x{LLA}/CINDEX
This file contains a list of Ignite-UX configurations that are
specific to the particular client with a network LAN link address
(LLA) as shown in the path. This file supplies Ignite-UX with
the config files created by make_net_recovery and provides a list
of client-specific selections a user can pick from during a
system recovery.

/var/opt/ignite/clients/0x{LLA}/recovery
The per-clients recovery directory. It holds the client's
recovery configuration files as described below.

/var/opt/ignite/clients/0x{LLA}/recovery/defaults
>Supplies the default options to make_net_recovery. Created by
>the ignite GUI.

/var/opt/ignite/clients/0x{LLA}/recovery/archive_content
>Supplies files and directories to be included or excluded. Using
>the -x command line arguments will cause this file to be ignored.

/var/opt/ignite/clients/0x{LLA}/recovery/client_status
>File used to communicate the status of the make_net_recovery
>command back to the ignite GUI running on the Ignite-UX

server.

/var/opt/ignite/clients/0x{LLA}/recovery/latest
>A symlink to the <date,time> directory containing the newest set
>of recovery files as described below.

/var/opt/ignite/clients/0x{LLA}/recovery/<date,time>
>Directory containing files pertaining to the make_net_recovery
>command that was run at the date and time indicated in the
>directory name. An example path looks like:
>/var/opt/ignite/clients/0x080009123456/1999-12-20,13:50

/var/opt/ignite/clients/0x{LLA}/recovery/<date,time>/system_cfg
>Configuration file which describes the file system and networking
>configuration of the system (generated by the save_config(1M)
>command).

/var/opt/ignite/clients/0x{LLA}/recovery/<date,time>/archive_cfg
>Configuration file which supplies the location and access method
>to the archive containing the files to be restored.

/var/opt/ignite/clients/0x{LLA}/recovery/<date,time>/control_cfg
>Configuration file which supplies control parameters and the
>command scripts to import volume groups that will be preserved
>and not created during the recovery.

/var/opt/ignite/clients/0x{LLA}/recovery/config.local
>An optional config file that the user may create to add
>configuration information to be used during the recovery of the
>client. For example, you may want to add to this file a
>post_config_cmd to re-mirror disks that the recovery process un-
>mirrored. (See the document:
>/opt/ignite/share/doc/diskmirror.pdf for an example). Once this
>file is created, make_net_recovery will automatically add it to
>any new configurations that it adds to the CINDEX file.

/var/opt/ignite/clients/0x{LLA}/recovery/<date,time>/recovery.log
>Default logfile location for make_net_recovery.

/var/opt/ignite/clients/0x{LLA}/recovery/<date,time>/manifest
>Software and Hardware manifest information installed and
>configured for the system at the time the archive was created
>(See print_manifest(1M)).

/var/opt/ignite/recovery/archives/<hostname>
>The default location on the Ignite-UX server for the client to
>store the recovery archive. The <hostname> directory must be NFS
>exported to the individual client with the matching hostname.

SEE ALSO
        ignite(5), instl_adm(4), make_medialif(1M), make_boot_tape(1M),
        manage_index(1M), pkg_rec_depot(1M), save_config(1M), swinstall(1M).

CHAPTER 11

System Administration Manager (SAM)

SAM and Virtual Partitions

Virtual Partitions are viewed as separate systems even though you may have several instances of HP-UX running on the same computer. When you invoke SAM in a Virtual Partition you can manage the resources of that Virtual Partition. Other Virtual Partitions, even those running on the same server, are viewed as remote systems.

In the upcoming sections we'll run some tasks in SAM in Virtual Partitions to show that this is identical to running these tasks on separate systems. We'll also show an example of setting up and running System Configuration Repository (SCR) on a vPar. SCR records a lot of useful information about your system. With multiple instances of HP-UX running on one computer you have more configuration information to keep track of and SCR helps with this data management.

There is substantial background information on SAM and ServiceControl Manager (SCM) in the overview at the end of this chapter. SCM allows you to perform tasks on multiple systems rather than one at a time. With mulitple instances of HP-UX running on one computer, this may save you time in performing your management tasks.

Virtual Partitions

Each Virtual Partition is an independent host. As such, vPars have unique hostnames and are viewed by SAM as independent systems. Figure 11-1 shows SAM running on two different vPars with the respective hostnames in the top of the SAM windows.

The hostnames used are *actappd1*(this is also the name of the first vPar) and *ecvpard2* (this is also the name of the second vPar.) Using the same name for both the host and vPar is recommended when configuring Virtual Partitions to reduce confusion. I'll use the name vPar *1* for the first vPar and vPar *2* for the second vPar throughout this section.

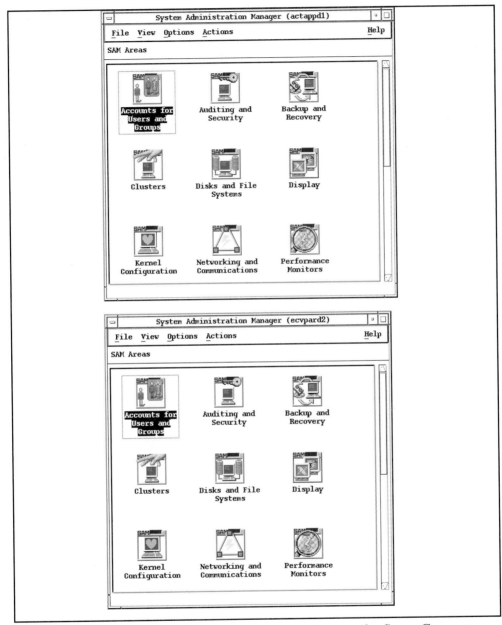

Figure 11-1   Partial SAM Windows of Two vPars on the Same Computer

Since the concept of isolation is very important in the world of Virtual Partitions we would expect to see only the information related to vPar *1* when working in SAM on this vPar. The same is true of vPar *2*, that is, we'd expect to see only information related to vPar *2* when working in SAM on this vPar.

man page

vparstatus
appendix a

Let's start by running **vparstatus** to see which components are associated with vPar *1* and which components are associated with vPar *2*, as shown in the following listing:

```
root@actappd1[/.root] > vparstatus -v

[Virtual Partition Details]
Name:           actappd1        <-- begininng of vPar 1 information
State:          Up
Attributes:     Dynamic,Manual
Kernel Path:    /stand/vmunix
Boot Opts:

[CPU Details]
Min/Max:  2/2
Bound [Path]:   33
                37
Unbound [Path]:

[IO Details]
    0.0.1.1.2.0   BOOT
    0.0.4.0   CONSOLE
    0.0
    0.0.2.0.2.0   ALTBOOT

[Memory Details]
Specified [Base  /Range]:
        (bytes) (MB)
Total Memory (MB):  2048

[Virtual Partition Details]
Name:           ecvpard2        <-- beginning of vPar 2 information
State:          Up
Attributes:     Dynamic,Autoboot
Kernel Path:    /stand/vmunix
Boot Opts:

[CPU Details]
Min/Max:  2/2
Bound [Path]:   97
                101
Unbound [Path]:

[IO Details]
    0.12.0.0.1.0, BOOT
    0.8
```

```
[Memory Details]
Specified [Base  /Range]:
          (bytes) (MB)
Total Memory (MB):  1920
root@actappd1[/.root] >
```

I took the information for vPars *1* and *2* from the **vparstatus** output and summarize it below:

man page

vparstatus
appendix a

vPar *1*

name	ecvpard1	<-- **we'll call this vPar 1**
processors	two bound added by path (I/O intensive app)	
	33 and 37	
memory	2048 MB	
LAN	0/0/0/0	
boot disk	0/0/1/1.2.0	
kernel	/stand/vmunix	
console	0/0/4/0	

vPar *2*

name	ecvpard2	<-- **we'll call this vPar 2)**
processors	two bound added by path (I/O intensive app)	
	97 and 101	
memory	2048 MB	
LAN	0/0/8/0	
boot disk	0.12.0.0.1.0	
kernel	/stand/vmunix	

We'll refer to some of these components in upcoming SAM screen shots.

Let's now look at *Peripheral Devices - Cards* functional area of SAM in Figure 11-2 and see if indeed only the components related to vPar *1* are shown when working with this vPar and that the components of vPar *2* are shown when working with this vPar in SAM.

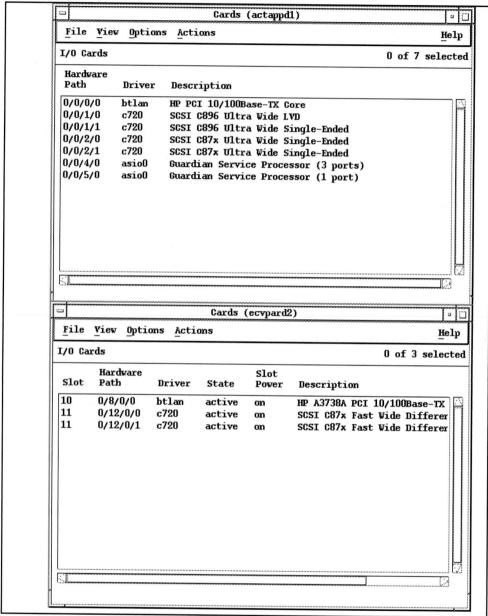

Figure 11-2 *Peripheral Devices - Cards* for vPar *1* and vPar *2*

All of the components associated with the Core I/O card are part of vPar *1*. All of the components of the Core I/O card must be part of the same vPar since they are on the same Local Bus Adapter (LBA) and are shown in the top window of Figure 11-2.

The second vPar has in it the cards specified when the vPar was created, including boot disk (*0/12*) and LAN (*0/8.*) The cards shown for the respective vPars can be manipulated only in the SAM window to which the cards are dedicated.

These cards have many devices associated with them as well. Figure 11-3 shows the *Peripheral Devices - Device List* functional area of SAM for vPar *1* and vPar *2*.

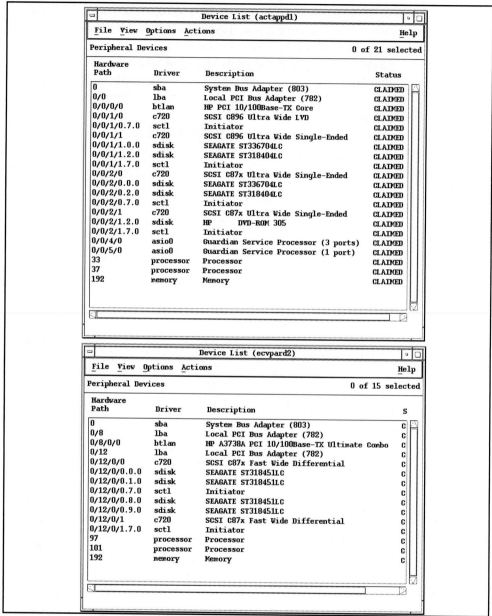

Figure 11-3 *Peripheral Devices - Device List* for vPar *1* and vPar *2*

There are many devices associated with the Core I/O card that are part of vPar *1*. Also shown for vPar *1* are the two processors and memory. Note that there are four internal disk drives associated with vPar *1*. We specified only a boot disk at *0/0/1/1.2.0*; however, the three additional internal disks are shown. These are associated with the Core I/O LBA and can therefore be used by vPar *1*. If we run an **ioscan** on vPar *1* and look for its disks only, we'll see all four internal disks as well as the DVD-ROM:

```
root@actappd1[/.root] > ioscan -f | grep disk
disk        0  0/0/1/1.0.0  sdisk    CLAIMED    DEVICE      SEAGATE
ST336704LC
disk        1  0/0/1/1.2.0  sdisk    CLAIMED    DEVICE      SEAGATE
ST318404LC
disk        2  0/0/2/0.0.0  sdisk    CLAIMED    DEVICE      SEAGATE
ST336704LC
disk        3  0/0/2/0.2.0  sdisk    CLAIMED    DEVICE      SEAGATE
ST318404LC
disk        4  0/0/2/1.2.0  sdisk    CLAIMED    DEVICE      HP
                          DVD-ROM 305
```

The second vPar has in it all of the devices on *0/12* and *0/8* as well as its two processors and memory. All of the disks on LBA *0/12* are shown as vPar *2* devices, just as all of the internal disk devices were associated with vPar *1*.

As with the cards, the devices are isolated between the two Virtual Partitions even though they are on the same computer. Some devices on the system, such as the Memory Controller (*192*) and System Bus Adapter (*0*), are under the control of the Virtual Partition Monitor and appear under both vPars.

We could perform the same checks for many additional areas of SAM, however; we've seen that the isolation we'd expect by vPars when using SAM is indeed in place. This means that the work you perform on one vPar in SAM will not affect the other vPars running on your system.

We can also use SAM to view all aspects of the kernel and make changes to the kernel for vPars. Keep in mind that running SAM in different vPars is like running SAM on different systems. Figure 11-4 shows a screen shot of SAM displaying drivers for vPar *cable1* (hostname of *cvhdcon4* shown in the top of all of the SAM windows):

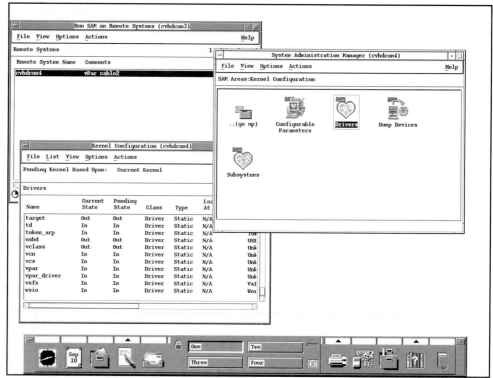

Figure 11-4   SAM Showing Virtual Console-Related Drivers

Chapter 4 covers many aspects of performing vPar kernel-related work at the command line. All of this kernel-related work can also be performed in SAM. The background portion of this chapter covers many aspects of kernel-related work in SAM.

Backup Using SAM

Chapter 7 covered backup and Virtual Partitions. Much of the work done in Chapter 7 was at the command line. Backup can also be managed through SAM. This backup section is from Chapter 7, but I've included it here to save you the trouble of flipping to Chapter 7. Let's take a look at the SAM backup functional area for two vPars - *cable1* and *cable2*. A substantial amount of work was done at the command line to perform a backup of these two vPars in Chapter 7. This same backup can be achieved using SAM. This includes the backup of *cable2* to the remote tape drive on *cable1*. Although *cable1* and *cable2* are on the same computer system the tape drive connected to *cable1* is considered remote to *cable2* since these are two different vPars.

Let's first perform a backup of *cable1* using *Backup and Recovery - Interactive Backup and Recovery* in SAM. Figure 11-5 is a full CDE screen shot showing some of the SAM windows related to *Interactive Backup and Recovery* for *cable1*:

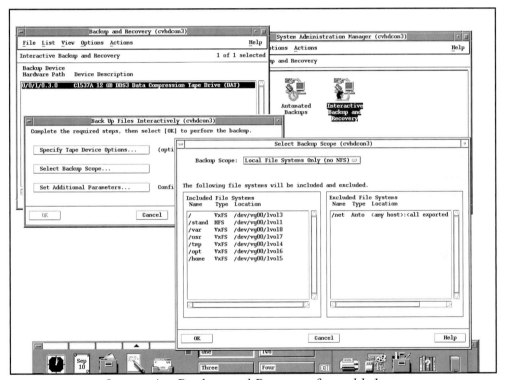

Figure 11-5 *Interactive Backup and Recovery* for *cable1*

All of the SAM windows in Figure 11-5 have in the top of them the hostname of *cvhdcon3*, which is the hostname for *cable1*. The top-left window shows that the DDS drive that was configured as part of the *cable1* vPar is selected as the backup devices. The bottom-right windows is the one in which we can specify the backup scope.

Performing this interactive backup of *cable1* could not be simpler with SAM. Let's now see if we can back up *cable2* to the remote tape drive on *cable1*. Keep in mind that as far as SAM is concerned, these are two completely different systems, even though vPars *cable1* and *cable2* are running on the same computer. This means that the backup of *cable2* to the tape drive on *cable1* is remote.

We can initiate the backup of *cable2* in two different ways. The first would be to invoke SAM on *cable2* and specify all of the appropriate information. The second is to run SAM remotely. We'll chose the latter approach. We first specify from *cable1* the name of the remote system on which we want to run SAM, as shown in Figure 11-6:

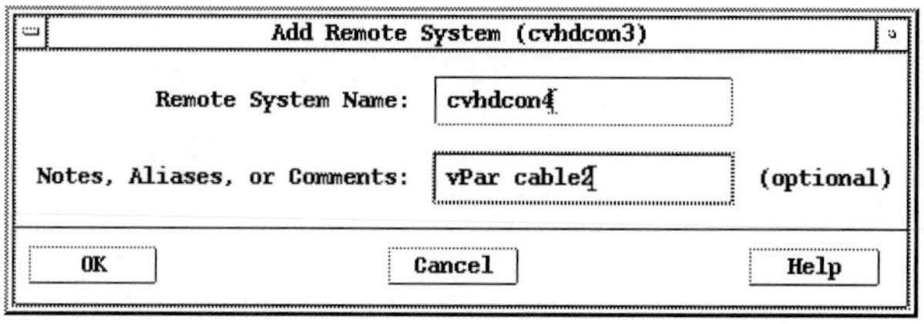

Figure 11-6 Add vPar *cable2* as a Remote System on Which to Run SAM

After we specify the hostname of *cvhdcon4* and make a note that this is vPar *cable2,* we press *OK* and SAM configures this as a remote host.

We can now run select the remote host and run SAM on it as shown in Figure 11-7:

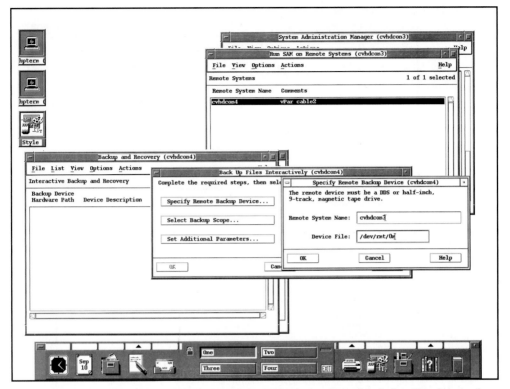

Figure 11-7 Configure Remote Tape Device on *cable1* for Backup of *cable2*

All of the SAM windows in Figure 11-7 now show a hostname of *cvhdcon4*, which is the remote hostname for *cable2*. The top-right window shows that we have selected vPar *cable2* (hostname *cvhdcon4*) as the remote system on which to run SAM. The bottom-right window shows that we have selected */dev/rmt/0m* on *cvhdcon3* (the hostname for vPar *cable1*) as the device on which the backup will take place.

We have now performed all of the setup required to proceed with the backup to the remote tape drive. After selecting **/var/tmp** as the directory to backup SAM opened, the window shown in Figure 11-8 indicated that the backup of **/var/tmp** is taking place:

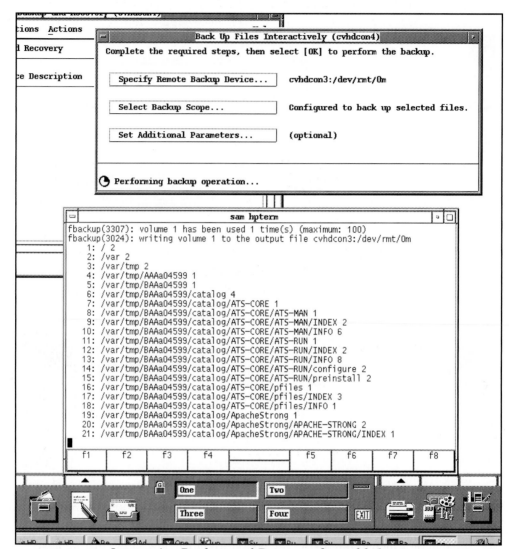

Figure 11-8 *Interactive Backup and Recovery* for *cable1*

This backup completed with no problems.

This backup work of two different vPars on the same computers demonstrates the kind of isolation that vPars provide. The work we perform in one vPar does not affect the other vPar. To use a tape drive on the same computer but in a different vPar requires us to specify the tape drive as a remote device. If you're accustomed to using SAM to perform your local and remote backups, you can continue to use SAM in your vPars environments as long as you treat different vPars as separate systems from the perspective of SAM.

Users and SAM

Chapter 6 covered users and Virtual Partitions. This is the part of Chapter 6 that covers users and SAM. I've included it here to save you the trouble of flipping to Chapter 6. Let's now create a new user on each of the two vPars called *cable1* and *cable2*. On *cable1* we'll create the user *cable1us* and verify that this user does not exist on *cable2*. On *cable2* we'll create the user *cable2us* and verify that this user does not exist on *cable1*. See the background portion of this chapter for detailed information on creating users.

Figure 11-9 shows a System Administration Manager (SAM) screen shot of creating a user *cable1us* in vPar *cable1*:

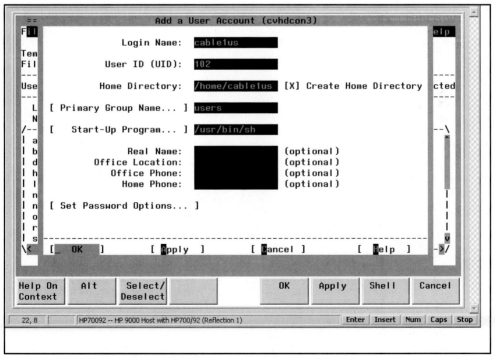

Figure 11-9 Creating *cable1user* in SAM

The user *cable1us* was created in vPar *cable1* and exists only in *cable1*. We'll verify this shortly. We performed the same procedure creating user *cable2us* in vPar *cable2* using SAM.

There should now be one user in *cable1* that is not viewable in *cable2*, and vice versa. The following shows connecting to *cable1* and listing the contents of **/etc/passwd**.

```
cvhdcon3:/ # cat /etc/passwd
root:hiIXKsAzUIFy6:0:3::/:/sbin/sh
daemon:*:1:5::/:/sbin/sh
bin:*:2:2::/usr/bin:/sbin/sh
sys:*:3:3::/:
adm:*:4:4::/var/adm:/sbin/sh
uucp:*:5:3::/var/spool/uucppublic:/usr/lbin/uucp/uucico
lp:*:9:7::/var/spool/lp:/sbin/sh
nuucp:*:11:11::/var/spool/uucppublic:/usr/lbin/uucp/uucico
hpdb:*:27:1:ALLBASE:/:/sbin/sh
nobody:*:-2:-2::/:
www:*:30:1::/:
webadmin:*:40:1::/usr/obam/server/nologindir:/usr/bin/false
smbnull:*:101:101:DO NOT USE OR DELETE - needed by Samba:
                                        /home/smbnull:/sbin/sh
opc_op:*:777:77:OpC default operator:/home/opc_op:/usr/bin/ksh
cable1us::102:20:,,,:/home/cable1us:/usr/bin/sh
cvhdcon3:/ #
```

This listing for *cable1* shows that *cable1us* exists in the **/etc/passwd** file on *cable1*, however, there is no *cable2us* present in this file.

The following shows connecting to *cable2* and listing the contents of **/etc/passwd**.

```
# cat /etc/passwd
root:Jx66ARmhj.aBs:0:3::/:/sbin/sh
daemon:*:1:5::/:/sbin/sh
bin:*:2:2::/usr/bin:/sbin/sh
sys:*:3:3::/:
adm:*:4:4::/var/adm:/sbin/sh
uucp:*:5:3::/var/spool/uucppublic:/usr/lbin/uucp/uucico
lp:*:9:7::/var/spool/lp:/sbin/sh
nuucp:*:11:11::/var/spool/uucppublic:/usr/lbin/uucp/uucico
hpdb:*:27:1:ALLBASE:/:/sbin/sh
nobody:*:-2:-2::/:
www:*:30:1::/:
```

```
webadmin:*:40:1::/usr/obam/server/nologindir:/usr/bin/false
sam_exec:xxx:0:1::/home/sam_exec:/usr/bin/sh
cable2us::101:20:,,,:/home/cable2us:/usr/bin/sh
#
```

This listing for *cable2* shows that *cable2us* exists in the **/etc/passwd** file on *cable2*, however, there is no *cable1us* present in this file

This listing shows that unique users for the respective vPars exist only on the vPar on which they were created. In addition, each vPar has its own *root* and other system-level users.

ServiceControl Manager (SCM) and Virtual Partitions

SCM allows you to replicate tasks over multiple systems. Tasks that have traditionally been performed individually on many systems can now be performed across multiple systems in a cluster managed by SCM. This is particularly relevent to Virtual Partitions since you have one computer system with more than one Virtual Partition running on it. In most cases you'll want to have SCM control of these Virtual Partitions since they're running on the same computer system even though you have multiple instances of HP-UX.

You can take a command or tool that runs on an individual system, such as the **find** or **df** command, dispatch it to run on multiple systems or Virtual Partitions, and collect the results for review in SCM.

More advanced tools that were designed to run on multiple systems, such as Ignite-UX, can also be run in the same manner using SCM.

Specific tasks can be assigned to specific individuals with SCM, thus creating a role-based environment. This obviates the need for root access to systems because specific management activities are assigned to specific users on specific nodes. These user roles provide great flexibility in defining the tasks that individual users can perform.

You can define the systems and/or Virtual Partitions of which an SCM cluster is composed. The Central Management Server (CMS) in an SCM environment is the focal point in which management takes place. Agents on the managed nodes communicate with CMS to perform management functions. The CMS could be one of your Virtual Partitions.

SCM is available on the applications media of 11i and loaded with Software Distributor like any other application. You'll want to load SCM on onel of the HP-UX 11i vPar instances for your CMS.

The overview section at the end of this chapter describes the details of setting up and running SCM.

System Configuration Repository (SCR) and Virtual Partitions

System Configuration Repository, which I'll call SCR in this section, gathers a lot of system information that can be used for viewing and can be compared to previously gathered data to produce a list of differences. SCR will view each Virtual Partition as a separate system and should be run separately in each Virtual Partition. SCR is easy to use, so the best way to learn about it is to run some SCR commands. It is particularly important in an environment with Virtual Partitions to use SCR. The more instances of HP-UX you have, the more important it is to maintain information about your system. You can only keep so much information about your vPars in your system log book and SCR may help you maintain more useful information about your vPars and systems.

You can obtain documents related to SCR from *www.docs.hp.com*. When writing this chapter I obtained two documents that were helpful for installing and using SCR. The first is *Troubleshooting Guide for SCR+DMI* and the second is *System Configuration Repository User's Reference*.

Using SCR

 SCR is easy to use. The first command to issue is **scrconfig** with the option *-n* to register nodes to be managed by SCR. Since you can have a central system act as the SCR server on which information for all managed nodes will be kept, you can issue the **scrconfig** command on the central system for all systems to be managed. We'll issue it only for the first Virtual Partition used for our earlier vPar example called *actappd1* (vPar *1*):

```
root@actappd1[/] > scrconfig -n +actappd1
"actappd1" is registered as a managed node. Default parameters are applied:
    Schedule time:         Off
    Interval:              1 week
    Expiration period:     3 months
    Collection timeout:    15 minutes
```

To register additional nodes, you would list the node names preceded by the plus sign on the same line in the format:

```
# scrconfig -n +node1 +node2 +node3 ...
```

Since the L-Class system in our earlier example had two vPars running on it, we'll register the second vPar called *ecvpard2* (vPar *2*) as well:

```
root@actappd1[/] > scrconfig -n +ecvpard2
"ecvpard2" is registered as a managed node. Default parameters are applied
    Schedule time:         Off
    Interval:              1 week
    Expiration period:     3 months
    Collection timeout:    15 minutes
```

We now have both vPars registered with SCR and we can collect on one or both.

You can schedule data collection for a node to take place at any time. The **scrconfig** command is also used to schedule data collection. We'll specify the node name with the *-n* option and use *-s* to specify the date and time at which we want collection to take place. The following example collects data on *09/06/2001* at *13:05* on vPar *1*:

```
root@actappd1[/] > date
Thu Sep  6 12:59:03 EDT 2001
root@actappd1[/] > scrconfig -n actappd1 -s 200109061305
Parameter for "actappd1" is set to:
    Schedule time:         09/06/2001 13:05 EDT
```

This command has scheduled collection on vPar *1* on the specified date and time. Note that the time is in 24-hour format. We could initiate data collection on-demand on node 11 by omitting the *-s* option and date and time with **scrconfig -n actappd1**. Each time data is collected from a node, it is callled a *snapshot*. A *snapshot* will not be saved if there are no changes since the last snapshot that was obtained from the system. If you try to obtain snapshots in very close succession with one another, the second snapshot will probably not be obtained because no changes have occurred to the system.

Let's now issue **scrconfig** for vPar *1* with the *-l* option to list the details for vPar *1*:

```
root@actappd1[/] > scrconfig -n actappd1 -l
NODE                    SCHEDULE TIME           INTERVAL    EXPIRATION   TIMEOUT
actappd1                09/06/2001 13:05 EDT    1 week      3 months     15 minutes
```

The output shows our scheduled collection for node vPar *1*. If we had other scheduled collections, they would show up in this output as well.

Next, we'll check the data collection status of all nodes that have been registered to see what collections have taken place and what collections are scheduled with **scrstatus**:

```
root@actappd1[/] > scrstatus
TIME        (START - STOP)          NODE            STATUS      DETAIL

09/06/2001 13:05 -          EDT     actappd1        Scheduled
```

This output shows our scheduled collection. Let's run the command again after the scheduled collection has taken place:

```
root@actappd1[/] > scrstatus
TIME        (START - STOP)          NODE            STATUS      DETAIL
09/06/2001 13:05 - 13:06 EDT        actappd1        Completed

09/13/2001 13:05 -          EDT     actappd1        Scheduled
root@actappd1[/] >
```

This shows that our collection is complete and that a collection has automatically been scheduled for same time one week later. The status of the collection already run is *Completed* and the status of the upcoming collection is *Scheduled*.

Next, we'll use the command **scrviewer** to see data that has been collected for system *11*. We specify the system for which we want the file produced as well as collection we want to view. Because the output is long (very long) I have also redirected the output to a file:

```
root@actappd1[/] > scrviewer actappd1:latest > /tmp/actappd1_scr.txt &
[1]     10871
```

You'll be amazed at the amount of data that has been collected for your system. The following is a very small subset of the data collected by SCR for vPar *1*:

Example of software information produced by SCR:

```
COMPONENT NAME                                    VALUE
     GROUP NAME
          ATTRIBUTE NAME
"HP-UX Installed Software Definition"
     "Bundle Contents"
          "scr dmi class"                         HPUX_BundleContents_
          "scr dmi version"                       001
          "scr dmi key"                           "Bundle Software Specification,Index"
          [Bundle Software Specification]         B9788AA,r=1.3.0.01,a=HP-UX_B.11.00_32/
64,v=HP
          [Index]                                 1
          [Content]                                    Java2-JDK13_base,r=1.3.0.01,a=HP-
UX_B.11.00_32/64,v=HP

          [Bundle Software Specification]         B9788AA,r=1.3.0.01,a=HP-UX_B.11.00_32/
64,v=HP
          [Index]                                 2
          [Content]                                    Java2-JDK13_perf,r=1.3.0.01,a=HP-
UX_B.11.00_32/64,v=HP

          [Bundle Software Specification]         B9788AA,r=1.3.0.01,a=HP-UX_B.11.00_32/
64,v=HP
```

Example of device information produced by SCR:

```
     "Host Processor"
          "scr dmi class"                         "HPUX_Host Processor_"
          "scr dmi version"                       001
          "scr dmi key"                           "Host Processor Index"
          [Host Processor Index]                  1
          [Processor Firmware ID]                 "HP PA_RISC2.0"
          [Processor Allocated]                   1:True

          [Host Processor Index]                  2
          [Processor Firmware ID]                 "HP PA_RISC2.0"
          [Processor Allocated]                   1:True
     "Host Storage"
          "scr dmi class"                         "HPUX_Host Storage_"
          "scr dmi version"                       001
          "scr dmi key"                           "Host Storage Index"
          [Host Storage Index]                    1
          [Storage Type]                          4:FixedDisk
          [Description]                           " SEAGATE    ST336704LC      "
          [Allocation Unit Size]                  1024
          [Total Allocation Units]                34732
          [Allocation Units Used]                 0
          [Storage Allocation Failures]           0

          [Host Storage Index]                    2
          [Storage Type]                          4:FixedDisk
          [Description]                           " SEAGATE    ST318404LC      "
          [Allocation Unit Size]                  1024
```

```
[Total Allocation Units]                          17366
[Allocation Units Used]                           11580
[Storage Allocation Failures]                     0

[Host Storage Index]                              3
[Storage Type]                                    4:FixedDisk
[Description]                                      "  SEAGATE     ST336704LC       "
[Allocation Unit Size]                            1024
[Total Allocation Units]                          34732
[Allocation Units Used]                           0
[Storage Allocation Failures]                     0

[Host Storage Index]                              4
[Storage Type]                                    4:FixedDisk
[Description]                                      "  SEAGATE     ST318404LC       "
[Allocation Unit Size]                            1024
[Total Allocation Units]                          17366
[Allocation Units Used]                           11580
[Storage Allocation Failures]                     0
```

Example of kernel information produced by SCR:

```
"Kernel Configure Group"
    "scr dmi class"                               "HPUX_Kernel Configure Group_"
    "scr dmi version"                             001
    "scr dmi key"                                 "Kernel Configure Group Index"
    [Kernel Configure Group Index]                1
    [Parameter Name]                              STRMSGSZ
    [Parameter Value]                             65535

    [Kernel Configure Group Index]                2
    [Parameter Name]                              nstrpty
    [Parameter Value]                             60

    [Kernel Configure Group Index]                3
    [Parameter Name]                              maxswapchunks
    [Parameter Value]                             4096

    [Kernel Configure Group Index]                4
    [Parameter Name]                              bufpages
    [Parameter Value]                             0

    [Kernel Configure Group Index]                5
    [Parameter Name]                              dbc_max_pct
    [Parameter Value]                             15

    [Kernel Configure Group Index]                6
    [Parameter Name]                              dbc_min_pct
    [Parameter Value]                             2

    [Kernel Configure Group Index]                7
    [Parameter Name]                              max_thread_proc
    [Parameter Value]                             256

    [Kernel Configure Group Index]                8
    [Parameter Name]                              maxdsiz
    [Parameter Value]                             0x20000000
```

Among the data produced for vPar *1* is extensive software-related information early in the listing, logical volume-related information, and hardware-related information at the end of the listing. There is information produced for many categories. The **scrfilter** command is used to control what is collected or to manipulate the view of information already collected. Issuing **scrfilter -l** shows that the following information can be filtered as part of the SCR output:

> # **scrfilter -l**
> Disk
> FileSystem
> LVM
> Network
> Patch
> Probe
> Software
> SystemProperty

This is the type of information system administrators want to know about their system.

There are several other SCR-related commands and options to commands we've covered that you can issue. Among the most useful commands is **scrdiff**, which produces a report of differences between collections. The following command would produce a report of differences between the *latest* and *oldest* collections for vPar *1*:

```
root@actappd1[/] > scrdiff actappd1:oldest actappd1:latest
[1]     2728
```

Table 11-1 summarizes SCR-related commands. There are manual pages loaded for these commands along with SCR.

TABLE 11-1   System Configuration Repository Commands

Command	Description
scrconfig	Configure and query configuration information.
scrdelete	Delete configuration information.
scrdiff	Report differences between two configuration reports.
scrfilter	Generate, modify, or delete view filter.
scrhist	Produce configuration history.
scrstatus	Produce data collection status report.
scrtag	Manage tag names for snapshots.
scrviewer	Display configuration information.
scrlog_viewer	SCR log file viewer.
scr (not command)	System Configuration Repository.

SCR uses the Desktop Management Interface (DMI) to obtain collection data from nodes. DMI provides the Application Programming Interfaces (APIs) that are called by SCR to obtain data. The central management system, which is vPar *1* in our examples, requires both DMI and SCR.

There is no additional background material at the end of this chapter on SCR since we covered this product thoroughly in this section.

Non-vPar-Specific Section of Chapter: SAM Overview

SAM is a program you can use to automate and perform various system administration tasks. SAM has been refined over many releases of HP-UX and is now a highly functional and reliable tool for performing routine system administration tasks. As you'll see in the upcoming sections, SAM has many *functional areas* in which you can perform system administration tasks. Since there is a lot of "coverage" with SAM, meaning that most system administration tasks can be performed with SAM, combined with its reliability in performing these tasks, I have found more and more system administrators using SAM for performing system administration tasks.

Four features of SAM that make it particularly useful are:

1. It provides a central point from which system administration tasks can be performed. This includes both the built-in tasks that come with SAM as well as those you can add into the SAM menu hierarchy. You can run SAM on a remote system and display it locally so that you truly have a central point of control.

2. It provides an easy way to perform tasks that are difficult, in that you would have to perform many steps. SAM performs these steps for you.

3. It provides a summary of what your system currently looks like for any of the categories of administration tasks that you wish to perform. If you want to do something with the disks on your system, SAM first lists the disks that you currently have connected. If you want to play with a printer, SAM first lists all your printers and plotters for you. This capability cuts down on mistakes by putting your current configuration right in front of you.

4. You can assign non-root users to perform some of the system administration functions in SAM. If, for instance, you feel comfortable assigning one of your associates to manage users, you can give them permission to perform user-related tasks and give another user permission to perform backups, and so on.

There are some tasks SAM can't perform for you. SAM does most routine tasks for you, but troubleshooting a problem is not considered routine. Troubleshooting a problem gives you a chance to show off and hone your system administration skills.

When SAM is performing routine tasks for you, it isn't doing anything you couldn't do yourself by issuing a series of HP-UX commands. SAM provides a simple user interface that allows you to perform tasks by selecting menu items and entering pertinent information essential to performing the task.

Running and Using SAM as Superuser

To run SAM, log in as root and type:

sam   (or **sam &**)

This will invoke SAM. If you have a graphics display, SAM will run with the Motif interface. If you have a character-based display, SAM will run in character mode. You have nearly all the same functionality in both modes, but the Motif environment is much more pleasant to use.

If you have a graphics display and SAM does not come up in a Motif window, you probably don't have your *DISPLAY* variable set for root.

Type the following to set the *DISPLAY* variable for default POSIX, Korn, and Bourne shells:

DISPLAY=system_name:0.0
export DISPLAY

Just substitute the name of your computer for *system_name*. This can be set in your local **.profile** file. If you're running HP CDE, you may want to put these lines in your **.dtprofile** file.

Type the following to set the *DISPLAY* variable for C shell:

setenv DISPLAY system_name:0.0

Again, you would substitute the name of your computer for *system_name*. This would typically be done in your **.login** file, but if you're running HP CDE, you may want to put this in your **.dtprofile** file. Most CDE users, however, have **.dtprofile** as the source for **.profile** or **.login**.

Figure 11-10 shows the System Administration Manager running in graphics mode. This is the top-level window of the hierarchical SAM environment called the *Functional Area Launcher* (*FAL*). The many categories, or areas, of management shown are the default functional areas managed by SAM. You can select one of these functional areas to be placed in a subarea. Because SAM is hierarchical, you may find yourself working your way down through several levels of the hierarchy before you reach the desired level. I'll cover each of these categories, or areas, in this chapter.

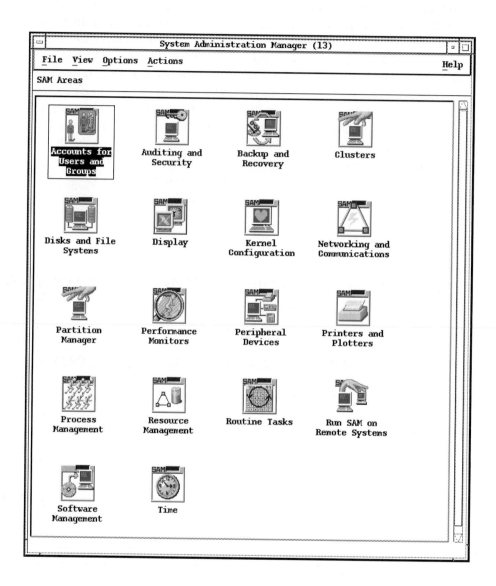

Figure 11-10   HP-UX 11i SAM Startup Window in Graphics Mode

In addition to selecting a functional area, you can select from the pull-down menu bar across the top of the SAM window. I will indicate selections made in SAM and keyboard keys in this chapter with italics. The five selections are *File, View, Options, Actions,* and *Help.* The title line shown in Figure 11-10 reads *SAM Areas.* If you're running Restricted SAM Builder, you will also see a status line with the message *"Privileges for user: <username>."* As you progress down the hierarchy, the title line will change to reflect your level in the SAM hierarchy. You can move into one of the areas shown, such as *Backup and Recovery,* by double-clicking the left mouse button on this functional area. You move back up the hierarchy by double-clicking the *..(go up)* icon, if available, or by selecting the *Actions-Close Level* menu commands.

You don't need a graphics display to run SAM. You have access to nearly all the same functionality on a text terminal as you do on a graphics terminal. Figure 11-11 is SAM running in character mode with the same functional areas you have in graphics mode, although the bottom selections are not shown in the figure:

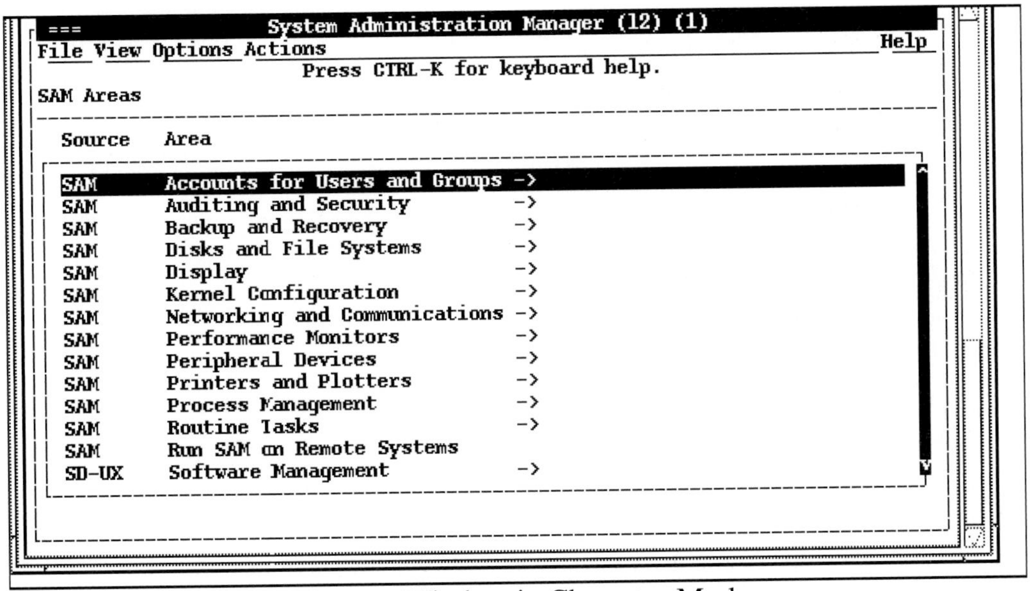

```
===              System Administration Manager (12) (1)
File View Options Actions                                          Help
                      Press CTRL-K for keyboard help.

SAM Areas
_____

  Source    Area
_____

   SAM      Accounts for Users and Groups ->
   SAM      Auditing and Security         ->
   SAM      Backup and Recovery           ->
   SAM      Disks and File Systems        ->
   SAM      Display                       ->
   SAM      Kernel Configuration          ->
   SAM      Networking and Communications ->
   SAM      Performance Monitors          ->
   SAM      Peripheral Devices            ->
   SAM      Printers and Plotters         ->
   SAM      Process Management            ->
   SAM      Routine Tasks                 ->
   SAM      Run SAM on Remote Systems
   SD-UX    Software Management           ->
```

Figure 11-11   SAM Startup Window in Character Mode

The *View* menu can be used in character mode to tailor the information desired, filter out some entries, or search for particular entries.

Because you don't have a mouse on a text terminal, you use the keyboard to make selections. The point-and-click method of using SAM when in graphics mode is highly preferable to using the keyboard; however, the same structure to the functional areas exists in both environments. When you see an item in reverse video on the text terminal (such as *Accounts for Users and Groups* in Figure 11-11), you know that you have that item selected. After having selected *Accounts for Users and Groups* as shown in Figure 11-11, you would then use the *tab* key (or *F4*) to get to the menu bar, use the <--> *(arrow)* keys to select the desired menu, and use the *space bar* to display the menu. This situation is where having a mouse to make your selections is highly desirable. Figure 11-12 shows a menu bar selection for both text and graphic displays. In both cases, the *Actions* menu has been selected.

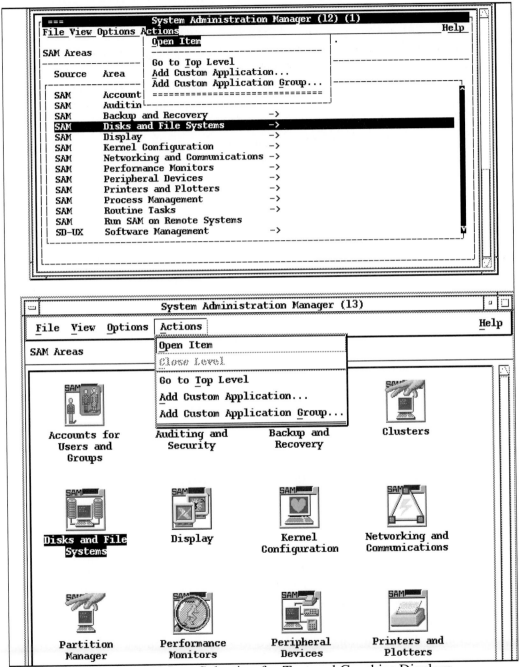

Figure 11-12   SAM Menu Selection for Text and Graphics Displays

Of particular interest on the pull-down menu are *Add Custom Application* and *Add Custom Application Group*. When you use *Add Custom Application Group*, you are prompted for a *Label* and optional *Help File* for the group. After you enter this information, a new icon appears, if you have a graphics display, with the name of your application group. You can then go into this application group and *Add Custom Applications*. This means that you can customize SAM to meet your specific administration needs by adding functionality to SAM. After you familiarize yourself with the aspects of system administration SAM can help you with, you'll want to test adding your own application to SAM. Adding a simple application like opening a log file or issuing the **/usr/bin/find** command will take you only seconds to create.

You can also create users who have restricted access to SAM. You can specify areas within SAM to which specific users can have access. You may have users to whom you would like to give access to backup and restore, or managing users, or handling the print spooler. Invoking SAM with the *-r* option will allow you to select a user to whom you want to give access to a SAM area and then select the specific area(s) to which you want to enable that user to have access. You can also give a user partial access to some areas, such as providing access to backup and recovery, but not providing access to handling automated backups. As you progress through the detailed descriptions of SAM areas in this chapter, you'll want to think about which of these areas may be appropriate for some of your users to access.

Author's Disclaimer: SAM is a Moving Target

SAM is improving all the time. The SAM you are using on your HP-UX 11i system may have been enhanced and may therefore differ in some ways from what I cover in this chapter. The HP 9000 product line also improves requiring SAM to be enhanced. In the functional area *Partitions,* for instance, will be enhanced to support many of the functions we've been performing throughout this book related to vPars and hard partitions (nPartitions) as well.

Running Restricted SAM Builder

SAM can be configured to provide a subset of its overall functionality to specified users such as operators. You may, for instance, wish to give a user the ability to start a backup but not the ability to manage disks and file systems. With the Restricted SAM Builder, you have control of the functional areas to which specified users have access.

When specifying the functionality you wish to give a user, you invoke SAM with the *-r* option, initiating a Restricted SAM Builder session. After you have set up a user with specific functionality, you can then invoke SAM with both the *-r* and *-f* options with the login name of a user you wish to test. The functionality of the user can be tested using these two options along with the login name.

Initially Setting User Privileges

When you invoke SAM with the *-r* option, you are first asked to select the user to whom you want to assign privileges. You will then be shown a list of default privileges for a new restricted SAM user. Figure 11-13 shows the default privileges SAM recommends for a new restricted user; note that custom SAM functional areas are disabled by default.

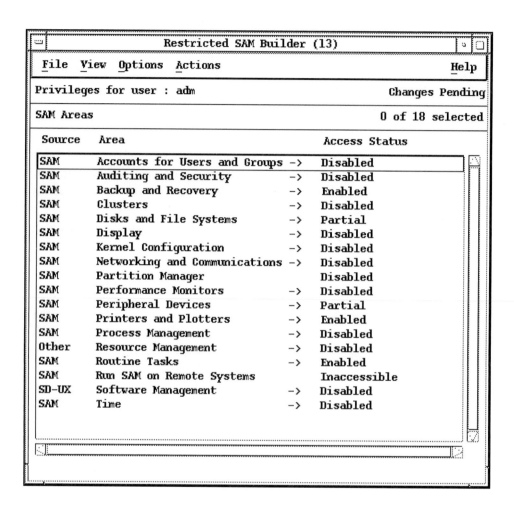

Figure 11-13   Restricted SAM Builder Screen

You can select from the *Actions* shown in Figure 11-13 to control access to functional areas. Of particular interest is the ability to save the privileges, which you may later use as a template for other users with *Load User Privileges* from the *Actions* menu.

The user will now have only access to the functional areas specified and therefore be able to execute tasks in only the areas to which they have access.

Accounts for Users and Groups

In Chapter 5, I explained the information that is associated with each user and group. There is an entry in the **/etc/passwd** file for each user and an entry in **/etc/group** for each group. To save you the trouble of flipping back to Chapter 5, Figure 11-14 is an example of a user entry from **/etc/passwd** and an example of a group entry from **/etc/group**:

User Example:

```
vinny:*:204:20:Vinny Emmaddebra,,,:/home/vinny:/usr/bin/sh
 |   |   |   |                  |               |        |
 |   |   |   |                  |               |        |> shell
 |   |   |   |                  |               |
 |   |   |   |                  |               |> home directory
 |   |   |   |                  |
 |   |   |   |                  |> optional user info
 |   |   |   |> group ID (GID)
 |   |   |> user ID (UID)
 |   |> password
 |> name
```

Group Example:

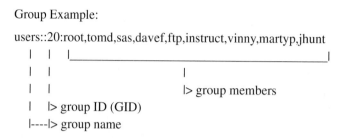

Figure 11-14   Sample **/etc/passwd** and **/etc/group** Entry

The *Accounts for Users and Groups* top-level SAM category, or area, has beneath it only two picks: *Groups* and *Users*. The menu hierarchy for "Users and Groups" is shown in Figure 11-15.

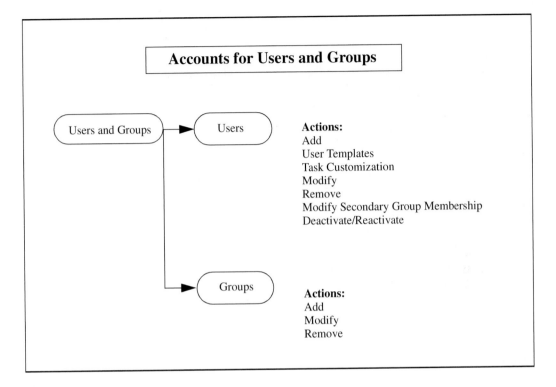

Figure 11-15 Accounts for Users and Groups

When you select *Accounts for Users and Groups* and then *Users* from the SAM menu, you are provided a list of all the users on your system. Figure 11-16 is a list of users provided by SAM for a system including Oracle users:

```
┌─────────────────────────────────────────────────────────────────────┐
│ ⊡        Accounts for Users and Groups (o2)                    ▫ □    │
├─────────────────────────────────────────────────────────────────────┤
│  File   List   View   Options   Actions                        Help  │
├─────────────────────────────────────────────────────────────────────┤
│ Template In Use: None                                                │
│ Filtering:  Displaying all users                                     │
├─────────────────────────────────────────────────────────────────────┤
│ Users                                            0 of 18 selected     │
├─────────────────────────────────────────────────────────────────────┤
```

Login Name	User ID (UID)	Real Name	Primary Group	Office Phone	Office Location
Oracle2	105		oinstall		
adm	4		adm		
akhan	103		users		
bin	2		bin		
daemon	1		daemon		
dm	104		users		
hpdb	27		other		
lp	9		lp		
ms	102		users		
nobody	-2		nogroup		
nuucp	11		nuucp		
opc_op	777	OpC default operator	opcgrp		
oracle	101	Oracle8i	oinstall		Data Center
root	0		sys		
sam_exec	0		other		
sys	3		sys		
uucp	5		sys		
www	30		other		

Figure 11-16 List of Users

Adding a User

SAM is ideal for performing administration tasks related to users and groups. These are routine tasks that are not complex but require you to edit the **/etc/passwd** and **/etc/group** files, make directories, and copy default files, all of which SAM performs for you. Finally, take a minute to check what SAM has done for you, especially if you modify an existing user or group.

To add an additional user, you would select *Add* from the *Actions* menu under *Users* and then fill in the information as shown in Figure 11-17:

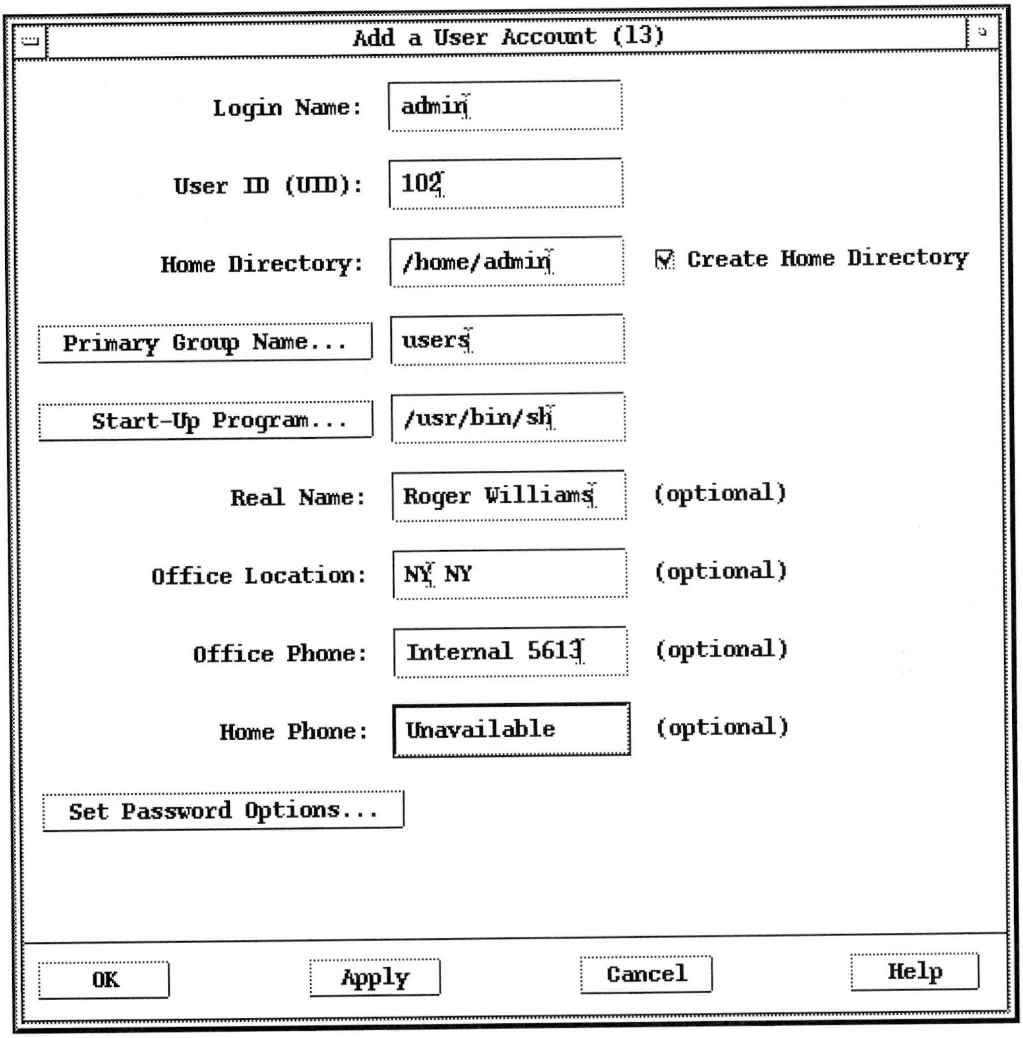

```
 ┌─────────────────────────────────────────────────────────────────────────┐
 │ ─              Add  a  User  Account  (13)                             ᴗ │
 │ ┌───────────────────────────────────────────────────────────────────────┤
 │ │                                                                         │
 │ │          Login  Name:  │ admin͏                        │                 │
 │ │                                                                         │
 │ │       User  ID  (UID):  │ 102                          │                 │
 │ │                                                                         │
 │ │      Home  Directory:  │ /home/admin                  │  ☑ Create Home Directory │
 │ │                                                                         │
 │ │ │ Primary  Group  Name...  │  │ users                 │                 │
 │ │                                                                         │
 │ │ │ Start–Up  Program...  │  │ /usr/bin/sh              │                 │
 │ │                                                                         │
 │ │          Real  Name:  │ Roger Williams               │  (optional)     │
 │ │                                                                         │
 │ │      Office  Location:  │ NY NY                        │  (optional)     │
 │ │                                                                         │
 │ │        Office  Phone:  │ Internal 5613                │  (optional)     │
 │ │                                                                         │
 │ │          Home  Phone:  │ Unavailable                  │  (optional)     │
 │ │                                                                         │
 │ │ │ Set  Password  Options...  │                                          │
 │ │                                                                         │
 │ ├───────────────────────────────────────────────────────────────────────┤
 │ │   │ OK │        │ Apply │        │ Cancel │           │ Help │          │
 │ └───────────────────────────────────────────────────────────────────────┘
 └─────────────────────────────────────────────────────────────────────────┘
```

Figure 11-17 Example of Adding a New User

There are some restrictions when entering this information. For instance, a comma and colon are not permitted in the *Office Location* field. When I tried to enter a comma, SAM informed me that this was not permitted.

To see the **/etc/passwd** entry that was made I issued the following **cat** and **grep** commands, which showed two users who had *admin* in their names:

```
# cat /etc/passwd | grep admin
webadmin:*:40:1::/usr/obam/server/nologindir:/usr/bin/false
admin::102:20:Roger  Williams,NY  NY,Internal  5613,Unavailable:/home/admin:/usr/
bin/sh
#
```

This user admin has no password entry, as indicated by the **::**, which is a poor practice. You want to make sure that there are passwords for all users.

You can view the log file that SAM produces with the menu selection *Options - View SAM Log.* Figure 11-18 shows the end of the log file, indicating that our user was successfully added:

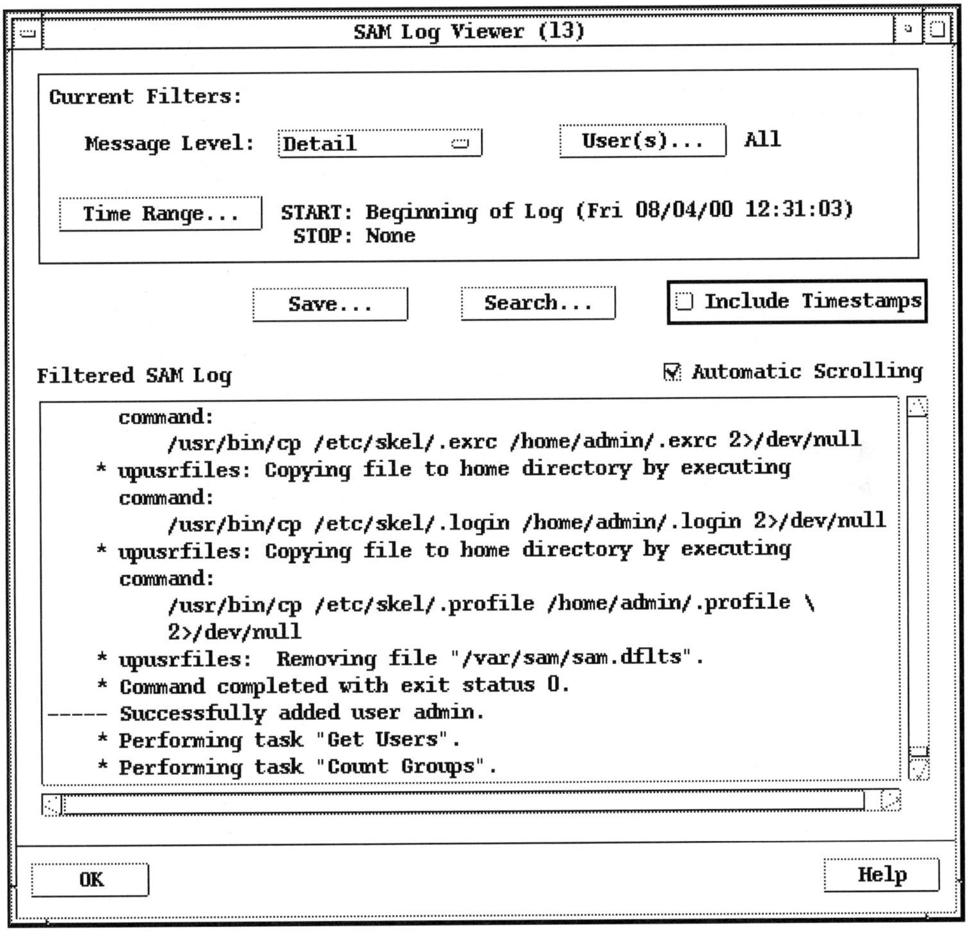

```
┌─────────────────────────────────────────────────────────────────────────┐
│ □                        SAM Log Viewer (13)                       ▫  □   │
├───────────────────────────────────────────────────────────────────────────┤
│  ┌──────────────────────────────────────────────────────────────────────┐ │
│  │ Current Filters:                                                     │ │
│  │                                                                      │ │
│  │    Message Level:  │Detail          ⌐│      │ User(s)... │  All      │ │
│  │                                                                      │ │
│  │    │ Time Range... │  START: Beginning of Log (Fri 08/04/00 12:31:03)│ │
│  │                       STOP: None                                     │ │
│  └──────────────────────────────────────────────────────────────────────┘ │
│                                                                            │
│              │   Save...   │    │  Search...  │   │ □ Include Timestamps │  │
│                                                                            │
│  Filtered SAM Log                          ☑ Automatic Scrolling           │
│  ┌──────────────────────────────────────────────────────────────────────┐ │
│  │      command:                                                      ▲ │ │
│  │           /usr/bin/cp /etc/skel/.exrc /home/admin/.exrc 2>/dev/null│ │ │
│  │    * upusrfiles: Copying file to home directory by executing       │ │ │
│  │      command:                                                      │ │ │
│  │           /usr/bin/cp /etc/skel/.login /home/admin/.login 2>/dev/null│ │
│  │    * upusrfiles: Copying file to home directory by executing       │ │ │
│  │      command:                                                      │ │ │
│  │           /usr/bin/cp /etc/skel/.profile /home/admin/.profile \    │ │ │
│  │           2>/dev/null                                              │ │ │
│  │    * upusrfiles:  Removing file "/var/sam/sam.dflts".              │ │ │
│  │    * Command completed with exit status 0.                        │ │ │
│  │ ----- Successfully added user admin.                              │ │ │
│  │    * Performing task "Get Users".                                 ▼ │ │
│  │    * Performing task "Count Groups".                                 │ │
│  └──────────────────────────────────────────────────────────────────────┘ │
│  ◄                                                                     ►   │
│  ┌─────────┐                                              ┌──────────┐     │
│  │   OK    │                                              │  Help    │     │
│  └─────────┘                                              └──────────┘     │
└─────────────────────────────────────────────────────────────────────────┘
```

Figure 11-18   SAM Log Viewer for Adding a User

The scroll bar on the right-hand side of the SAM Log Viewer allows you to scroll to any point in the log file. We are viewing only the part of the log file that pertains to adding the user *Roger Williams.* You can select the level of detail you wish to view with the log file. The four levels are *Summary, Detail, Verbose,* and *Commands Only.* The level shown in Figure 11-18 is *Detail.* I like this level because you can see what has taken place without getting mired down in too much detail. When you view the log file you typically see the calls to SAM scripts that SAM has made as well as other commands that SAM is issuing.

Adding a Group

Adding an additional group is similar to adding a new user. To add an additional group, you would select *Add* from the *Actions* menu under *Groups*. Figure 11-19 shows the Add a New Group window:

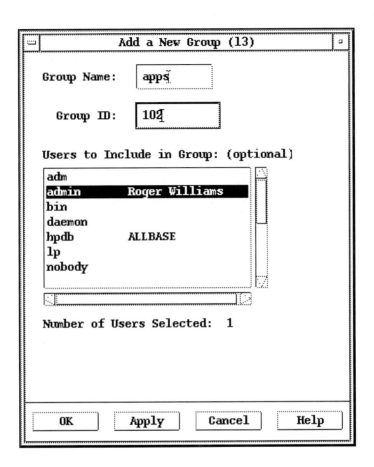

Figure 11-19 Example of Adding a New Group

In Figure 11-19, I added a new group called *apps* with a group ID of *102*, and into that group I added the user *admin* that we had earlier created.

Auditing and Security

Under *Auditing and Security,* you manage the security of your system. This is becoming an increasingly important aspect of system management. Some installations care very little about security because of well-known, limited groups of users who will access a system. Other installations, such as those connected to the Internet, may go to great pains to make their systems into fortresses, with firewalls checking each and every user who attempts to access a system. I suggest that you take a close look at all the ramifications of security, and specifically a trusted system, before you enable security. You'll want to review the "Managing System Security" section of the "Administering A System" chapter of the *Managing Systems and Workgroups* manual, which replaces the 10.x manual *HP-UX System Administration Tasks Manual.* Although SAM makes creating and maintaining a trusted system easy, a lot of files are created for security management, which takes place under the umbrella of Auditing and Security. Among the modifications that will be made to your system, should you choose to convert to a trusted system, is the **/etc/rc.config.d/auditing** file, which will be updated by SAM. In addition, passwords in the **/etc/passwd** file will be replaced with "*," and the encrypted passwords are moved to a password database. All users are also given audit ID numbers. Figure 11-20 shows the menu hierarchy of Auditing and Security.

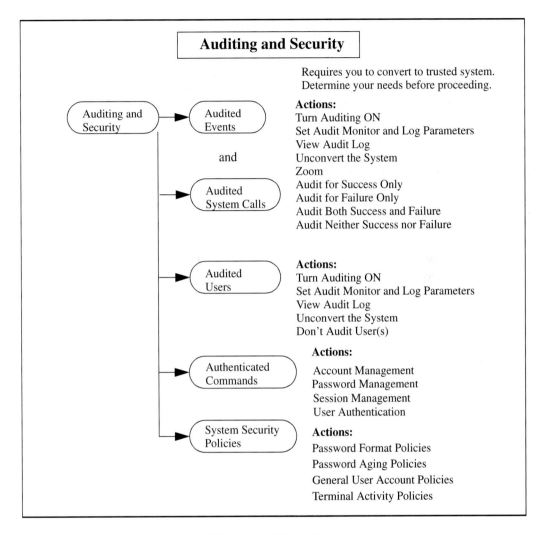

Auditing and Security

Requires you to convert to trusted system.
Determine your needs before proceeding.

Auditing and Security → Audited Events

Actions:
Turn Auditing ON
Set Audit Monitor and Log Parameters
View Audit Log
Unconvert the System
Zoom
Audit for Success Only
Audit for Failure Only
Audit Both Success and Failure
Audit Neither Success nor Failure

and

Audited System Calls

Audited Users

Actions:
Turn Auditing ON
Set Audit Monitor and Log Parameters
View Audit Log
Unconvert the System
Don't Audit User(s)

Authenticated Commands

Actions:
Account Management
Password Management
Session Management
User Authentication

System Security Policies

Actions:
Password Format Policies
Password Aging Policies
General User Account Policies
Terminal Activity Policies

Figure 11-20 Auditing and Security Menu Structure

One choice to observe in Figure 11-20 is an *Actions* menu choice to *Unconvert the System*. This means to reverse the trusted system environment. I have tried this on various systems and it seems to work fine, but you should have a good idea of what a trusted system can do for and to you before you make the conversion.

I hope that I have given you a reasonably good overview of Auditing and Security, because in order to investigate it yourself, you must first convert to a trusted system. Before you do, please read this section to get an idea of the functionality this will provide and then convert to a trusted system if you think there is adequate benefit.

Audited Events and Audited System Calls

Under *Audited Events,* you can select the particular events you wish to analyze and detect, which may cause security breaches. Under *Audited System Calls,* you can monitor system calls. This option is a function of the trusted system to which you must convert in order to perform auditing. You may have in mind particular events and system calls that are most vital to your system's security that you wish to audit, and not bother with the balance. There are a number of events and system calls that you may wish to keep track of for security reasons.

Auditing these events gives you a detailed report of each event. The same is true of system calls. SAM uses the auditing commands of HP-UX, such as **audsys**, **audusr**, **audevent**, **audomon**, and **audisp**, to perform auditing.

Audited Users

Under *Audited Users,* you can use the *Actions* menu to turn auditing on and off for specific users. Since the audit log files, which you can also control and view through the *Actions* menu, grow large very quickly, you may want to select specific users to monitor to better understand the type of user audit information that is created.

Authenticated Commands

This security feature is the ability to perform authentication based on user, password, session, or account. This industry-standard authentication framework is known as the Pluggable Authentication Module, or PAM. The PAM framework allows for authentication modules to be implemented without modifying any applications. Authentication is currently provided for CDE components, HP-UX standard commands, trusted systems, and DCE (the Distributed Computing Environment), as well as third-party modules.

System Security Policies

The most important part of HP-UX security is the policies you put in place. If, for instance, you choose to audit each and every system call, but don't impose any restrictions on user passwords, you are potentially opening up your system to any user. You would be much better off restricting users and not worrying so much about what they're doing. Being proactive is more important in security than being reactive.

Password Aging Policies, when enabled, allows you to set:

• Time between Password Changes

• Password Expiration Time

• Password Expiration Warning Time

• Password Life Time

• Expire All User Passwords Immediately

General User Account Policies, when enabled, allows you to specify the time at which an account will become inactive and lock it. In addition, you can specify the number of unsuccessful login tries that are permitted.

Terminal Security Policies allows you to set:

• Number of unsuccessful Login Tries Allowed

• Delay between Login Tries

• Login Timeout Value in Seconds

• Required Login upon Boot to Single-User State

Backup and Recovery

The most important activities that you'll perform as a system administrator are system backup and recovery. The SAM team put a lot of thought into giving you all the options you need to ensure the integrity of your system through backup and recovery. You may also want to see Chapter 7, which covers various backup commands available on HP-UX. Figure 11-21 shows the hierarchy of the *Backup and Recovery* SAM menu:

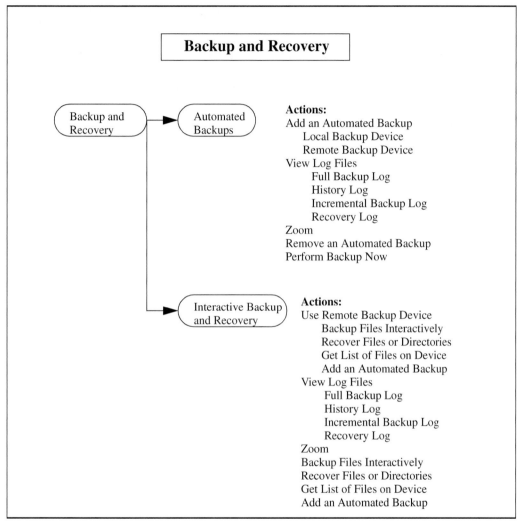

Figure 11-21   Backup and Recovery Menu Structure

Scheduling a Backup

The first step is to enter the *Automated Backups* subarea. You won't see that any automated backups appear in the list until you have specified one. Using the *Actions* menu and selecting *Add an Automated Backup,* you can specify all the information about your automated backup. When you select *Add an Automated Backup,* you have to specify whether your backup will be to a local or a remote backup device. You will have to enter information pertaining to the backup scope, backup device, backup time, and additional parameters.

Select Backup Scope

You can view the backup scope as the files that will be included and excluded from the backup. This can include Network File System (NFS)-mounted file systems as well. Figure 11-22 shows the window used to specify files to be included and excluded from a backup:

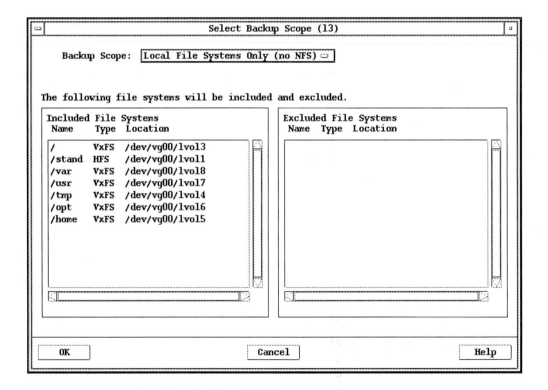

Figure 11-22   Selecting the Backup Scope

In the selections shown in Figure 11-22 are several directories speci-fied under *Included Files*. These were selected with the *Local File Systems Only (no NFS)* option. We could easily have excluded files and directories from the backup scope as well.

Select Backup Device

If you plan to back up to a local backup device, then those attached to your system will be listed and you select the desired device from the list.

If you plan to use a remote backup device, then you will be asked to specify the remote system name and device file.

Select Backup Time

As with the backup scope, you are provided with a window in which you can enter all the information about backup time for both full and incremental backups, as shown in Figure 11-23. If *Incremental Backup* is *Enabled,* then you must provide all pertinent information about both the full and incremen-tal backup, as shown in the figure.

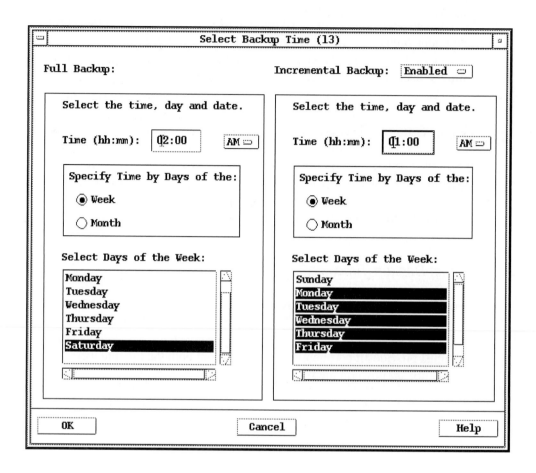

Figure 11-23 Selecting the Backup Time

A key point to keep in mind here is that the incremental backup that SAM creates for you includes files that have been changed *since the last full backup.* This means that you need only the full backup and last incremental backup to recover your system; that is, you do not need to restore the full backup and each incremental backup.

Set Additional Parameters

You can also specify additional parameters such as whether or not to create an index log, which I strongly suggest that you do, and to whom to mail the results of a backup. After specifying backup information, you can view the **crontab** entry that SAM has made for root for your backups. The **crontab** file is used to schedule jobs that are automatically executed by **cron**. **crontab** files are in the **/var/spool/cron/crontabs** directory. **cron** is a program that runs other programs at the specified time. **cron** reads files that specify the operation to be performed and the date and time it is to be performed. Since we want to perform backups on a regular basis, SAM will activate **cron**.

The format of entries in the **crontab** file is as follows:

minutehourmonthday   month   weekday   user name   command

minute - the minute of the hour, from 0-59
hour - the hour of the day, from 0-23
monthday - the day of the month, from 1-31
month - the month of the year, from 1-12
weekday - the day of the week, from 0 (Sunday) - 6 (Saturday)
user name - the user who will run the command if necessary
              (not used in the example)
command - specifies the command line or script file to run

You have many options in the **crontab** for specifying the *minute, hour, monthday, month,* and *weekday* to perform a task. You could list one entry in a field and then a space, several entries in any field separated by a comma, two entries separated by a dash indicating a range, or an asterisk, which corresponds to all possible entries for the field.

To list the contents of the **crontab** file, you would issue the command **crontab -l**. SAM will create a **crontab** entry for any backups you specify.

You will see various *crontab* **commands** when you use the *SAM Log Viewer* to see what SAM has done for you to create the **crontab** files. For instance, if you change your backup plan, SAM will remove the old **crontab** file with the command:

```
$ crontab -r
```

This will remove the **crontab** file for the user from the **/var/spool/cron/crontabs** directory.

To place a file in the **crontab** directory, you would simply issue the **crontab** command and the name of the **crontab** file:

```
$ crontab crontabfile
```

You can schedule cron jobs using SAM. The section in this chapter covering *Process Management* has a section called *Scheduling Cron Jobs*.

Interactive Backup and Recovery

The *Interactive Backup and Recovery* subarea is used to perform a backup interactively or restore information that was part of an earlier backup. When you enter this area, you are asked to select a backup device from a list that is produced, in the same way that you are asked to select a backup device when you first enter the *Automated Backups* subarea.

After selecting a device from the list, you may select an item from the *Actions* menu shown earlier. If you decide to use *Backup Files Interactively,* you are again provided a window from which you can specify files to be included and excluded from the backup. You are asked to *Select Backup Scope, Specify Tape Device Options*, and *Set Additional Parameters.* You are not, however, asked to *Select Backup Time,* since the backup is taking place interactively.

The steps in this area will vary, depending on the tape devices you have selected.

The index files can be reviewed from the *Actions* menu. These are stored in the **/var/sam/log** directory. The following shows the very top and bottom of an index file for an interactive backup:

```
#  1 /
#  1 /.profile
#  1 /.rhosts
#  1 /.sh_history
#  1 /.sw
#  1 /.sw/sessions
#  1 /.sw/sessions/swinstall.last
```

```
#  1 /.sw/sessions/swlist.last
#  1 /.sw/sessions/swmodify.last
#  1 /.sw/sessions/swreg.last
#  1 /.dt
#  1 /.dt/Desktop
#  1 /.dt/Desktop/Two                    TOP
#  1 /.dt/Desktop/Four
#  1 /.dt/Desktop/One
#  1 /.dt/Desktop/Three

                         .
                         .
                         .


#  1 /var/uucp/.Log/uucico
#  1 /var/uucp/.Log/uucp
#  1 /var/uucp/.Log/uux
#  1 /var/uucp/.Log/uuxqt
#  1 /var/uucp/.Old
#  1 /var/uucp/.Status
#  1 /var/varspool/sw
#  1 /var/varspool/sw/catalog/dfiles
#  1 /var/varspool/sw/catalog/swlock
#  1 /var/varspool/sw/swagent.log
#  1 /var/yp
#  1 /var/yp/Makefile                    BOTTOM
#  1 /var/yp/binding
#  1 /var/yp/securenets
#  1 /var/yp/secureservers
#  1 /var/yp/updaters
#  1 /var/yp/ypmake
#  1 /var/yp/ypxfr_1perday
#  1 /var/yp/ypxfr_1perhour
#  1 /var/yp/ypxfr_2perday
```

Performing a Restore

A full or incremental backup, however, is only as good as the files it restores. To retrieve a file from the backup tape, you specify a backup device and then many options related to the backup. Figure 11-24 shows one device selected from among four DLT units connected to a system:

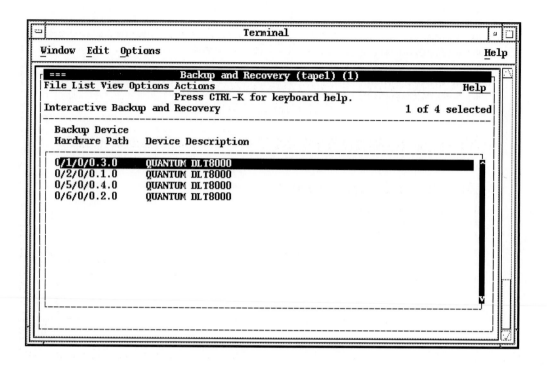

Figure 11-24   Selecting from among Four DLT Units

After selecting a device, there are a number of options from which you can select, including those shown in Figure 11-25:

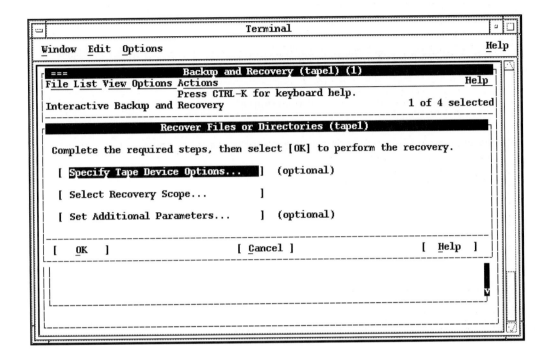

Figure 11-25 *Recover Files Interactively*

In this window you supply information in three areas: *Select Recovery Scope; Specify Tape Device Options;* and *Set Additional Parameters.* The device options you specify will depend on the tape device you are using.

Select Recovery Scope allows you to either enter a file name that contains the files to be recovered or manually list the files to be included in the recovery. You can optionally list files to be excluded from the recovery as well.

A list of tape device files is provided in *Specify Tape Device Options,* from which you can select the tape device. In this step, you may select the tape device file; in other cases, you might make selections such as a magneto-optical surface, or you may have nothing to select at all.

Under *Set Additional Parameters,* you can select any of the following options:

Overwrite Newer Files

Preserve Original File Ownership

Recover Files Using Full Path Name

Place Files in Non-Root Directory

After you make all the desired selections, the recovery operation begins. If a file has been inadvertently deleted and you wish to restore it from the recovery tape, you would select the Preserve Original File Owner-ship and Recover Files Using Full Path Name options. You will receive status of the recovery as it takes place and may also View Recovery Log from the Actions menu after the recovery has completed. If you choose View Recovery Log, you will receive a window that provides the name of the index log and the names of the files recovered.

Clusters

High availability clusters can be managed through SAM. Such tasks as add-ing applications and adding application groups can be performed using SAM. Since high availability is a highly customized aspect of a computing environment, I won't cover this area of SAM. If, however, you have to man-age clusters of systems, you will want to review this SAM area to see if it would help in your cluster-related work.

Disks and File Systems

Disks and File Systems helps you manage disk devices, file systems, logical volumes, swap, and volume groups (you may also manage other HP disk devices such as XP and disk arrays through SAM if you have these installed on your system.) There is no reason to manually work with these, since SAM does such a good job of managing these for you. Figures 11-26 and 11-27 show the hierarchy of *Disks and File Systems*:

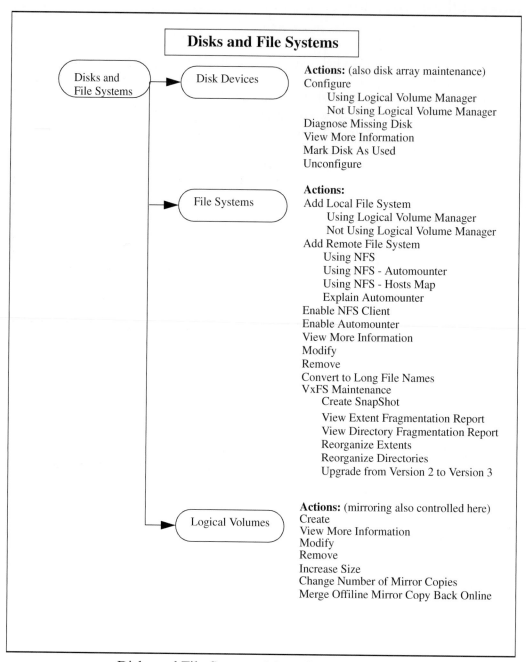

Figure 11-26 Disks and File Systems Menu Structure

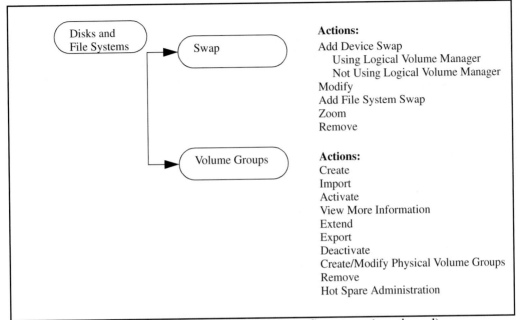

Figure 11-27 Disks and File Systems Menu Structure (continued)

Disk Devices

When you enter this subarea, SAM shows you the disk devices connected to your system. Figure 11-28 shows a listing of the disks for a Series 800 unit:

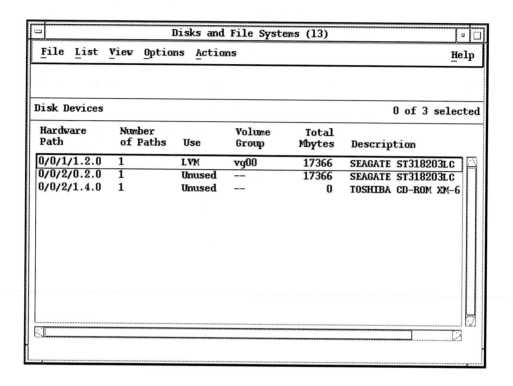

Figure 11-28 *Disk Devices* Window

The first two entries refer to internal disks in an L-Class system. The third entry is a CD-ROM drive. Let's compare this output to what we would see when we run **ioscan**:

```
$ /usr/sbin/ioscan -funC disk

Class    I  H/W Path     Driver S/W State  H/W Type     Description
======================================================================
disk     1  0/0/1/1.2.0  sdisk CLAIMED     DEVICE       SEAGATE ST318203LC
                         /dev/dsk/c1t2d0   /dev/rdsk/c1t2d0
disk     2  0/0/2/0.2.0  sdisk CLAIMED     DEVICE       SEAGATE ST318203LC
                         /dev/dsk/c2t2d0   /dev/rdsk/c2t2d0
disk     3  0/0/2/1.4.0  sdisk CLAIMED     DEVICE       TOSHIBA CD-ROM XM-6201TA
                         /dev/dsk/c3t4d0   /dev/rdsk/c3t4d0
```

The **ioscan** output jives with the disk information produced by SAM. The SAM output also indicates that the first disk is used and the second unused, which **ioscan** does not show.

We can now add one of the unused disks in SAM by selecting *Add* from the *Actions* menu. Using Logical Volume Manager, we can create a new volume group or select the volume group to which we wish to add the new disk. We would then select the new logical volumes we wanted on the volume group or extend the size of existing logical volumes. Other information such as the mount directory and size of the logical volume, would be entered as well.

Most disks connected to your system can be managed through SAM. Figure 11-29 shows a SAM screen shot of a V-Class system with an XP-256 attached to it:

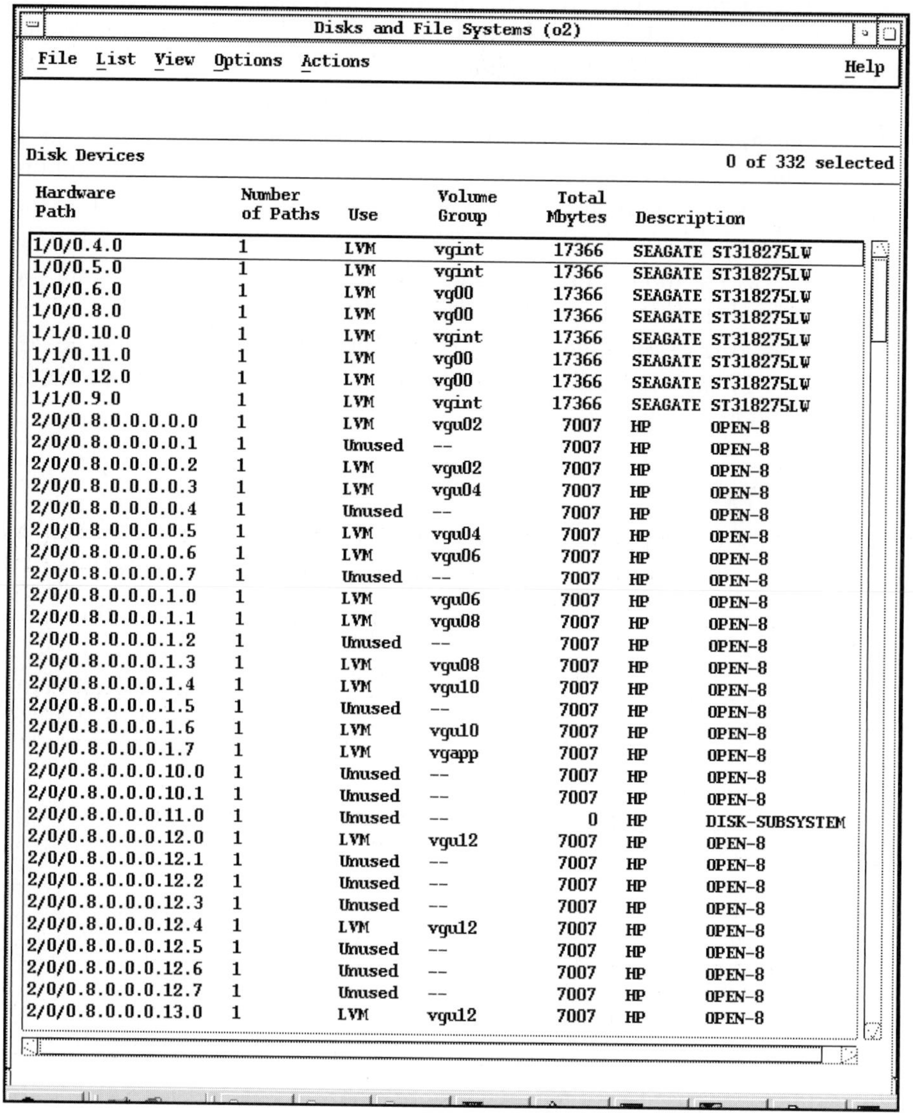

```
┌──────────────────────────────────────────────────────────────────────┐
│ ▭              Disks and File Systems (o2)                       □ □   │
│ File  List  View  Options  Actions                            Help    │
│                                                                        │
│                                                                        │
│ Disk Devices                                  0 of 332 selected        │
├──────────────────────────────────────────────────────────────────────┤
│ Hardware           Number              Volume    Total                 │
│ Path               of Paths   Use      Group     Mbytes   Description   │
│ ┌────────────────────────────────────────────────────────────────────┐│
│ │1/0/0.4.0           1         LVM      vgint      17366   SEAGATE ST318275LW││
│ │1/0/0.5.0           1         LVM      vgint      17366   SEAGATE ST318275LW││
│ │1/0/0.6.0           1         LVM      vg00       17366   SEAGATE ST318275LW││
│ │1/0/0.8.0           1         LVM      vg00       17366   SEAGATE ST318275LW││
│ │1/1/0.10.0          1         LVM      vgint      17366   SEAGATE ST318275LW││
│ │1/1/0.11.0          1         LVM      vg00       17366   SEAGATE ST318275LW││
│ │1/1/0.12.0          1         LVM      vg00       17366   SEAGATE ST318275LW││
│ │1/1/0.9.0           1         LVM      vgint      17366   SEAGATE ST318275LW││
│ │2/0/0.8.0.0.0.0.0   1         LVM      vgu02      7007    HP    OPEN-8 ││
│ │2/0/0.8.0.0.0.0.1   1         Unused   --         7007    HP    OPEN-8 ││
│ │2/0/0.8.0.0.0.0.2   1         LVM      vgu02      7007    HP    OPEN-8 ││
│ │2/0/0.8.0.0.0.0.3   1         LVM      vgu04      7007    HP    OPEN-8 ││
│ │2/0/0.8.0.0.0.0.4   1         Unused   --         7007    HP    OPEN-8 ││
│ │2/0/0.8.0.0.0.0.5   1         LVM      vgu04      7007    HP    OPEN-8 ││
│ │2/0/0.8.0.0.0.0.6   1         LVM      vgu06      7007    HP    OPEN-8 ││
│ │2/0/0.8.0.0.0.0.7   1         Unused   --         7007    HP    OPEN-8 ││
│ │2/0/0.8.0.0.0.1.0   1         LVM      vgu06      7007    HP    OPEN-8 ││
│ │2/0/0.8.0.0.0.1.1   1         LVM      vgu08      7007    HP    OPEN-8 ││
│ │2/0/0.8.0.0.0.1.2   1         Unused   --         7007    HP    OPEN-8 ││
│ │2/0/0.8.0.0.0.1.3   1         LVM      vgu08      7007    HP    OPEN-8 ││
│ │2/0/0.8.0.0.0.1.4   1         LVM      vgu10      7007    HP    OPEN-8 ││
│ │2/0/0.8.0.0.0.1.5   1         Unused   --         7007    HP    OPEN-8 ││
│ │2/0/0.8.0.0.0.1.6   1         LVM      vgu10      7007    HP    OPEN-8 ││
│ │2/0/0.8.0.0.0.1.7   1         LVM      vgapp      7007    HP    OPEN-8 ││
│ │2/0/0.8.0.0.0.10.0  1         Unused   --         7007    HP    OPEN-8 ││
│ │2/0/0.8.0.0.0.10.1  1         Unused   --         7007    HP    OPEN-8 ││
│ │2/0/0.8.0.0.0.11.0  1         Unused   --         0       HP    DISK-SUBSYSTEM││
│ │2/0/0.8.0.0.0.12.0  1         LVM      vgu12      7007    HP    OPEN-8 ││
│ │2/0/0.8.0.0.0.12.1  1         Unused   --         7007    HP    OPEN-8 ││
│ │2/0/0.8.0.0.0.12.2  1         Unused   --         7007    HP    OPEN-8 ││
│ │2/0/0.8.0.0.0.12.3  1         Unused   --         7007    HP    OPEN-8 ││
│ │2/0/0.8.0.0.0.12.4  1         LVM      vgu12      7007    HP    OPEN-8 ││
│ │2/0/0.8.0.0.0.12.5  1         Unused   --         7007    HP    OPEN-8 ││
│ │2/0/0.8.0.0.0.12.6  1         Unused   --         7007    HP    OPEN-8 ││
│ │2/0/0.8.0.0.0.12.7  1         Unused   --         7007    HP    OPEN-8 ││
│ │2/0/0.8.0.0.0.13.0  1         LVM      vgu12      7007    HP    OPEN-8 ││
│ └────────────────────────────────────────────────────────────────────┘│
└──────────────────────────────────────────────────────────────────────┘
```

Figure 11-29 *Disk Devices* Window with XP-256 Disks Shown

A small subset of the total disks attached is shown in the screen shot. The first eight disks are internal to the V-Class and the remainder are XP disks. All of the devices shown in this figure can be managed through SAM.

File Systems

File Systems shows the *Mount Directory, Type* of file system, and *Source Device or Remote Directory.* Figure 11-30 shows the information you see when you enter *File Systems* for the L-Class system used in earlier examples:

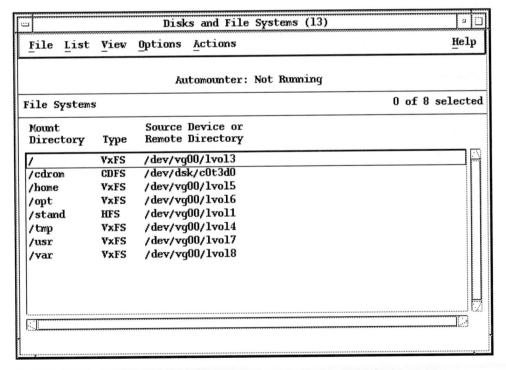

Figure 11-30 *File Systems* Window

At this level, you can perform such tasks as *Add Local File System* and *Add Remote File System,* and you can perform *VxFS Maintenance* from the *Actions* menu.

Several types of file systems may be listed under the *Type* column. The most common are:

Auto-Indirect	Directory containing auto-mountable remote NFS file systems. You may see the **/net** directory here if you have auto-mounter running.
Auto-Mount	Auto-mountable remote NFS file system.
CDFS	CD-ROM file system if it is currently mounted. If, for instance, you have a CD-ROM mounted as /SD_CDROM, you will see this as type CDFS in the list.
HFS	Local HFS file system. These are local HFS file systems that are part of your system. HP's version of the UNIX File System. This was the most common file system under earlier versions of HP-UX.
NFS	Remote NFS file system that is currently mounted.
LOFS	Loopback file system that allows you to have the same file system in multiple places.
VxFS	Local Journaled File System (JFS). This is the HP-UX implementation of the Veritas

journaled file system (VxFS), which supports fast file system recovery. JFS is the default HP-UX file system.

Add Local File System allows you to mount an unmounted, local file system. *Add Remote File System* gives you the ability to mount a file system from another host. The *VxFS Maintenance* subarea is where you can perform some file system maintenance tasks on your JFS file system. Here, you can create reports on extent and directory fragmentation. Once these are reviewed and you find that you do indeed need to perform maintenance, you can choose the option to reorganize either the extents or the directory.

Logical Volumes

You can perform several functions related to logical volume manipulation in SAM. Such tasks as *Create, Modify, Remove,* and *Increase Size* can be performed in SAM. Figure 11-31 shows increasing the size of lvol5 (**/home**) from 52 MBytes to 6 MBytes:

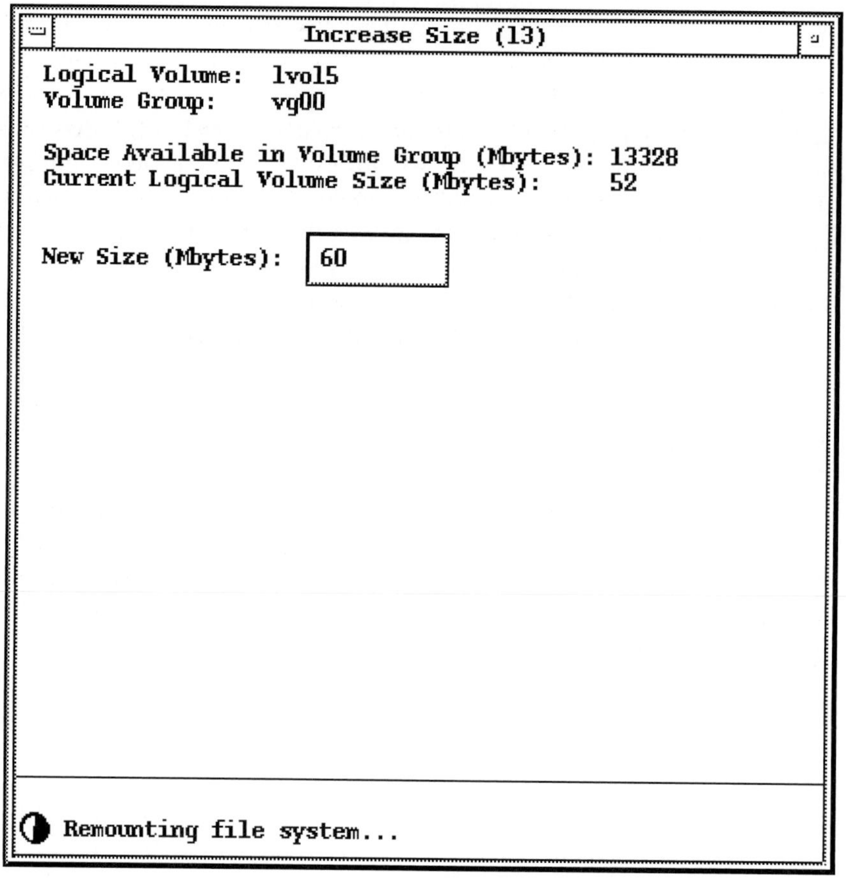

```
┌──────────────────────────────────────────────────────────────┐
│ ▢│              Increase Size (13)                        │▫│ │
│  Logical Volume:   lvol5                                        │
│  Volume Group:     vg00                                         │
│                                                                 │
│  Space Available in Volume Group (Mbytes): 13328                │
│  Current Logical Volume Size (Mbytes):     52                   │
│                                                                 │
│                                                                 │
│  New Size (Mbytes):    ┌──────────────────┐                     │
│                        │ 60               │                     │
│                        └──────────────────┘                     │
│                                                                 │
│                                                                 │
│                                                                 │
│                                                                 │
│                                                                 │
│                                                                 │
│                                                                 │
│                                                                 │
│                                                                 │
│                                                                 │
│                                                                 │
│ ◗ Remounting file system...                                     │
└──────────────────────────────────────────────────────────────┘
```

Figure 11-31 *Increase Size* Window

SAM will increase the size of the logical volume only if it can be unmounted. Viewing the log file after this task has been completed shows that SAM ran such commands as **/sbin/lvextend** and **/sbin/extendfs** to extend the size of the logical volume and file system, and **/usr/sbin/umount** and **/usr/sbin/mount** to unmount and mount the file system.

See the Logical Volume Manager detail in Chapter 9 for definitions of Logical Volume Manager terms. There is also a description of some Logical Volume Manager commands.

Increasing the Size of a Logical Volume in SAM

SAM may create a unique set of problems when you attempt to increase the size of a logical volume. Problems may be encountered when increasing the size of a logical volume if it can't be unmounted. If, for instance, you wanted to increase the size of the **/opt** logical volume, it would first have to be unmounted by SAM. If SAM can't **umount /opt**, you will receive a message from SAM indicating that the device is busy. You can go into single-user state, but you will have to have some logical volumes mounted, such as **/usr** and **/var**, in order to get SAM to run. You would then need to reboot your system with **shutdown -r** after you have completed your work. This works for directories such as **/opt**, which SAM does not need in order to run.

Alternatively, you could exit SAM and kill any processes accessing the logical volume you wish to extend the size of, and then manually unmount that logical volume. You could then use SAM to increase the size of the logical volume.

The HP OnLineJFS add-on product allows you to perform many of these LVM functions without going into single-user mode. For example, with OnLineJFS, logical volumes and file systems are simply expanded with the system up and running and no interruption to users or processes.

Swap

Both device swap and file system swap are listed when you enter *Swap*. Listed for you are the *Device File/Mount Directory, Type, Mbytes Available*, and *Enabled.* You can get more information about an item by highlighting it and selecting *Zoom* from the *Actions* menu.

Volume Groups

Listed for you when you enter volume groups are *Name, Mbytes Available, Physical Volumes*, and *Logical Volumes*. If you have an unused disk on your system, you can extend an existing volume group or create a new volume group. This window is useful to see how much disk space within a volume group has not been allocated yet. Another function here is the ability to import volume groups from other systems or ready a volume group for export to a remote system. You would use this when moving a volume group contained on an entire disk drive or set of disk drives from one system to another.

Display

In this SAM area, you can perform work related to the graphics display(s) on your system. This work is self-explanatory in SAM, so I won't cover this functional area of SAM.

Kernel Configuration

Your HP-UX kernel is a vitally important part of your HP-UX system that is often overlooked by HP-UX administrators. Perhaps this is because administrators are reluctant to tinker with such a critical and sensitive part of their system. Your HP-UX kernel, however, can have a big impact on system performance, so you want to be sure that you know how it is configured. This doesn't mean that you have to make a lot of experimental changes, but you should know how your kernel is currently configured so that you can assess the possible impact that changes to the kernel may have on your system.

SAM allows you to view and modify the four basic elements of your HP-UX kernel. There is a great deal of confusion among new HP-UX system administrators regarding these four elements. Before I get into the details of each of these four areas, I'll first give you a brief description of each.

- *Configurable Parameters* - These are parameters that have a *value* associated with them. When you change the value, there is a strong possibility that you will affect the performance of your system. An example of a *Configurable Parameter* is **nfile**, which is the maximum number of open files on the system. Many configurable parameters in HP-UX 11i can be modified and included in the kernel without a reboot required. We'll cover this in one of the upcoming examples.

- *Drivers* - Drivers are used to control the hardware on your system. You have a driver called **CentIF** for the parallel interface on your system, one called **sdisk** for your SCSI disks, and so on.

- *Dump Devices* - A dump device is used to store the contents of main memory in the event that a serious kernel problem is encountered. If no dump device is configured, then the contents of main memory are saved on the primary swap device, and this information is copied into one of the directories (usually **/var/adm/crash**) when the system is booted. It is not essential that you have a dump device, but the system will boot faster after a crash if you have a dump device because the contents of main memory don't need to be copied to a file after a crash. A dump device is different from a swap device.

- *Subsystems* - A subsystem is different from a driver. A subsystem is an area of functionality or support on your system such as **CD-ROM/9000**, which is CD-ROM file system support; **LVM,** which is Logical Volume Manager support; and so on.

When you go into one of the four subareas described above, the configuration of your system for the respective subarea is listed for you. The first thing you should do when entering *Kernel Configuration* is to go into each of the subareas and review the list of information about your system in each.

In *Kernel Configuration* is a *current* kernel and *pending* kernel. The *current* kernel is the one you are now running, and the *pending* kernel is the one for which you are making changes.

Figure 11-32 shows the SAM menu hierarchy for *Kernel Configuration*.

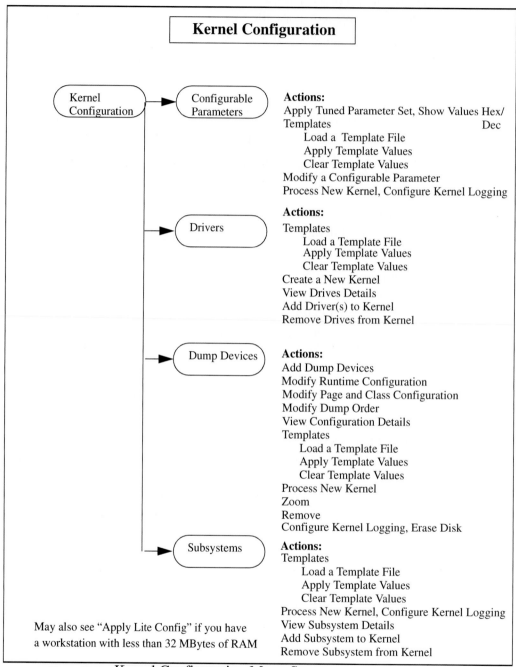

Kernel Configuration

Kernel Configuration → Configurable Parameters

Actions:
Apply Tuned Parameter Set, Show Values Hex/
Templates   Dec
    Load a Template File
    Apply Template Values
    Clear Template Values
Modify a Configurable Parameter
Process New Kernel, Configure Kernel Logging

Drivers

Actions:
Templates
    Load a Template File
    Apply Template Values
    Clear Template Values
Create a New Kernel
View Drives Details
Add Driver(s) to Kernel
Remove Drives from Kernel

Dump Devices

Actions:
Add Dump Devices
Modify Runtime Configuration
Modify Page and Class Configuration
Modify Dump Order
View Configuration Details
Templates
    Load a Template File
    Apply Template Values
    Clear Template Values
Process New Kernel
Zoom
Remove
Configure Kernel Logging, Erase Disk

Subsystems

Actions:
Templates
    Load a Template File
    Apply Template Values
    Clear Template Values
Process New Kernel, Configure Kernel Logging
View Subsystem Details
Add Subsystem to Kernel
Remove Subsystem from Kernel

May also see "Apply Lite Config" if you have
a workstation with less than 32 MBytes of RAM

Figure 11-32 Kernel Configuration Menu Structure

Configurable Parameters

Selecting *Configurable Parameters* lists all your configurable kernel parameters. For each configurable parameter, the following information is listed:

- Name - Name of the parameter.

- Current Value - Value of the parameter in **/stand/vmunix**.

- Pending Value - Value of the parameter in the kernel to be built.

- Type - Shows whether parameters are part of the static kernel or a loadable module.

- Associated Module - Lists module parameter is part of if type is loadable.

- Description - A few words describing the parameter.

You can then take a number of *Actions,* including the following:

Apply Tuned Parameter Set

Several sets of configurable parameters have been tuned for various environments. When you select this from the *Actions* menu, the tuned parameter sets on your system, such as a database server system, are listed for you and you can select from among them.

Templates

You can select a kernel template to load that is basically a different kernel configuration from the one you are currently running.

Process New Kernel

> After making whatever changes you like to
> the *Pending Value* of a configurable parame-
> ter, you can have SAM create a new kernel
> for you.

Modify Configurable Parameter

> You can change the value of a parameter in
> the *pending* kernel. You simply highlight a
> parameter and select this from the *Actions*
> menu.

Modifying a configurable parameter is made much easier by SAM. But although the logistics of changing the parameter are easier, determining the value of the parameter is still the most important part of this process.

Many applications recommend modifying one or more of these parameters for optimal performance of the application. Keep in mind, though, that many of these parameters are related; modifying one may adversely affect another parameter. Many applications will request that you change the *maxuprc* to support more processes. Keep in mind that if you have more processes running, you may end up with more open files and also you may have to change the *maxfiles* per process. If you have a system primarily used for a single application, you can feel more comfortable in modifying these. But if you run many applications, make sure that you don't improve the performance of one application at the expense of another.

When you do decide to modify the value of a configurable parameter, be careful. The range on some of these values is broad. The *maxuprc* (maximum number of user processes) can be reduced as low as three processes. I can't imagine what a system could be used for with this low a value, but SAM ensures that the parameter is set within supported HP-UX ranges for the parameter. "Let the administrator beware" when changing these values. You may find that you'll want to undo some of your changes. Here are some tips: Keep careful notes of the values you change, in case you have to undo a change. In addition, change as few values at a time as possible. That way, if you're not happy with the results, you know which configurable parameter caused the problem.

In Chapter 4, when covering the kernel, we manually modified the *maxuprc* kernel parameter. Since this parameter is dynamic, there was not a reboot required in order for it to take effect. Let's now use SAM to modify this parameter and again demonstrate that since it is dynamic, no reboot is required if it is modified with SAM.

Figure 11-33 shows *maxuprc* selected in a SAM screen shot:

```
 _____
|_|||                     Kernel Configuration (13)                    |o|□||
|  ||====================================================================|  |
|  ||   File  List  View  Options  Actions                         Help  |  |
|  ||--------------------------------------------------------------------|  |
|  ||  Pending Kernel Based Upon:    Current Kernel                       |  |
|  ||                                                                     |  |
|  ||--------------------------------------------------------------------|  |
|  ||  Configurable Parameters                        1 of 128 selected   |  |
|  ||                                                                     |  |
|  ||                  Current      Pending            Associated         |  |
|  ||  Name             Value        Value     Type    Module        D    |  |
|  ||  ----------------------------------------------------------------   |  |
|  ||  max_thread_proc      64           64    Static   N/A          M ^  |  |
|  ||  maxdsiz        268435456    268435456   Static   N/A          M    |  |
|  ||  maxdsiz_64bit 1073741824   1073741824   Static   N/A          M    |  |
|  ||  maxfiles             60           60    Static   N/A          S    |  |
|  ||  maxfiles_lim       1024         1024     Dynamic  N/A          H    |  |
|  ||  maxssiz         8388608      8388608    Static   N/A          M    |  |
|  ||  maxssiz_64bit   8388608      8388608    Static   N/A          M    |  |
|  ||  maxswapchunks       512          512    Static   N/A          M    |  |
|  ||  maxtsiz        67108864     67108864    Dynamic  N/A          M    |  |
|  ||  maxtsiz_64bit 1073741824   1073741824   Dynamic  N/A          M    |  |
|  ||  maxuprc              80           80    Dynamic  N/A          M    |  |
|  ||  maxusers             32           32    Static   N/A          V    |  |
|  ||  maxvgs              10           10    Static   N/A          M    |  |
|  ||  mesg                 1            1    Static   N/A          E    |  |
|  ||  modstrmax          500          500    Static   N/A          M    |  |
|  ||  msgmap              42           42    Static   N/A          M    |  |
|  ||  msgmax            8192         8192     Dynamic  N/A          M    |  |
|  ||  msgmnb           16384        16384     Dynamic  N/A          M    |  |
|  ||  msgmni              50           50    Static   N/A          N    |  |
|  ||  msgseg            2048         2048    Static   N/A          N    |  |
|  ||  msgssz               8            8    Static   N/A          M    |  |
|  ||  msgtql              40           40    Static   N/A          N    |  |
|  ||  nbuf                 0            0    Static   N/A          N v  |  |
|  ||                                                                     |  |
 ---------------------------------------------------------------------------
```

Figure 11-33   *maxuprc* Selected in a SAM Window

Let's now increase the value of *maxuprc* from *80* to *100* as shown in Figure 11-34:

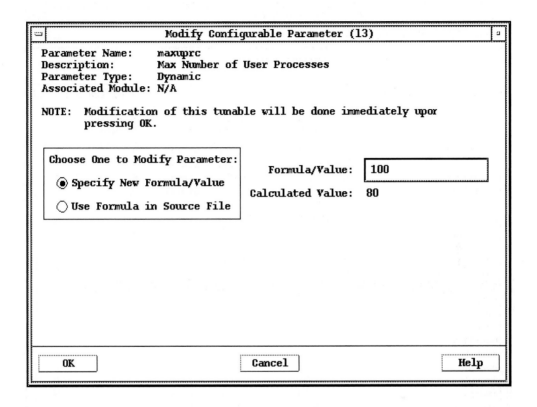

Figure 11-34 *maxuprc* from *80* to *100*

Clicking *OK* results in changing *maxuprc* from *80* to *100* on the system immediately, without a reboot required, as shown in Figure 11-35:

```
┌─────────────────────────────────────────────────────────────────┐
│ ─                    Kernel Configuration (13)              ⌐  ☐ │
├─────────────────────────────────────────────────────────────────┤
│  File  List  View  Options  Actions                        Help  │
│                                                                   │
│ Pending Kernel Based Upon:    Current Kernel                      │
│                                                                   │
│ Configurable Parameters                        1 of 128 selected  │
│                                                                   │
│                    Current     Pending          Associated        │
│  Name               Value       Value    Type    Module      D    │
│ ───────────────────────────────────────────────────────────────  │
│  max_thread_proc        64          64   Static   N/A        M     │
│  maxdsiz          268435456   268435456  Static   N/A        M     │
│  maxdsiz_64bit   1073741824  1073741824  Static   N/A        M     │
│  maxfiles               60          60   Static   N/A        S     │
│  maxfiles_lim         1024        1024   Dynamic  N/A        H     │
│  maxssiz           8388608     8388608   Static   N/A        M     │
│  maxssiz_64bit     8388608     8388608   Static   N/A        M     │
│  maxswapchunks         512         512   Static   N/A        M     │
│  maxtsiz          67108864    67108864   Dynamic  N/A        M     │
│  maxtsiz_64bit   1073741824  1073741824  Dynamic  N/A        M     │
│ ▐maxuprc               100         100   Dynamic  N/A        M▌    │
│  maxusers               32          32   Static   N/A        V     │
│  maxvgs                 10          10   Static   N/A        M     │
│  mesg                    1           1   Static   N/A        E     │
│  modstrmax             500         500   Static   N/A        M     │
│  msgmap                 42          42   Static   N/A        M     │
│  msgmax               8192        8192   Dynamic  N/A        M     │
│  msgmnb             16384       16384   Dynamic  N/A        M     │
│  msgmni                 50          50   Static   N/A        N     │
│  msgseg               2048        2048   Static   N/A        N     │
│  msgssz                  8           8   Static   N/A        M     │
│  msgtql                 40          40   Static   N/A        N     │
│  nbuf                    0           0   Static   N/A        N     │
└─────────────────────────────────────────────────────────────────┘
```

Figure 11-35   *maxuprc* Increase Takes Effect Immediately

Figure 11-35 shows that both the *Current Value* and *Pending Value* of *maxuprc* are *100,* without a reboot required. Dynamic configurable parameters and dynamically loadable kernel modules can be updated in this fashion without a reboot required.

Drivers

When you select *Drivers*, the drivers for your current kernel, the template file on which your current kernel is based, and the pending kernel are listed. You'll know that the drivers displayed are for more than your current kernel because you'll see that some of the drivers listed are *Out* of both your current and pending kernels. The following information is listed for you when you enter the *Drivers* subarea:

- Name - Name of the driver.

- Current State - Lists whether the driver is *In* or *Out* of **/stand/vmunix**.

- Pending State - Lists whether the driver is *In* or *Out* of the pending kernel to be built.

- Class - Identifies element as a driver or module.

- Type - Identifies driver as part of the static kernel or a loadable module.

- Load Module at Boot? - Lists whether driver is automatically loaded at boot time if it is a loadable module.

- Description - A few words describing the driver.

The *Current State* indicates whether or not the driver selected is in **/stand/vmunix.**

The *Pending State* indicates whether or not you have selected this driver to be added to or removed from the kernel. *In* means that the driver is part of the kernel or is pending to be part of the kernel. *Out* means that the driver is not part of the kernel or is pending to be removed from the kernel.

Typically, drivers are added statically. In other words, they are added to the kernel and left there. However, if the driver is a specially created module for a particular purpose, then it may be configured as loadable. This means that it can be loaded and unloaded from the kernel without rebooting the system. This advanced feature is discussed in detail in the "Managing Dynamically Loadable Kernel Modules" chapter of the *Managing Systems and Workgroups* book from Hewlett-Packard.

Using the *Actions* menu, you can select one of the drivers and add or remove it. You can also pick *View Driver Details* from the *Actions* menu after you select one of the drivers. You can select *Process New Kernel* from the *Actions* menu. If you have indeed modified this screen by adding or removing drivers, you want to recreate the kernel. SAM asks whether you're sure that you want to rebuild the kernel before it does this for you. The only recommendation I can make here is to be sure that you have made your selections carefully before you rebuild the kernel.

Dump Devices

When you enter this subarea, both the *Current Dump Devices* and *Pending Dump Devices* are listed for you. A dump device is used when a serious kernel problem occurs with your system, and main memory is written to disk. This information is a core dump that can later be read from disk and used to help diagnose the kernel problem.

Prior to HP-UX 11.x, memory dumps contained the entire image of physical memory. As a result, in order to get a full memory dump, you needed to create a dump area at least as large as main memory. With systems with memory size into the gigabits, a large amount of disk space was wasted just waiting around for a system panic to occur. With HP-UX 11.x comes a new, fast dump feature. This allows you to pick and choose what to dump. The fast dump feature not only prevents such things as unused memory pages and user text pages from being dumped, but it also allows you to configure what memory page classes to dump.

The sizes of the dump areas can be configured somewhat smaller than main memory in your system. You can specify a disk or logical volume as a dump device (you can also specify a disk section, but I don't recommend that you use disk sections at all). The entire disk or logical volume is then reserved as a dump device.

If no dump device is specified or if the size of the dump area is less than what is configured to be dumped, then the core dump is written to primary swap. At the time of system boot, the core dump is written out to a core file, usually in **/var/adm/crash**. This is the way that most systems I have worked on operate; that is, there is no specific dump device specified and core dumps are written to primary swap and then to **/var/adm/crash**. This approach has sometimes been a point of confusion; that is, primary swap may indeed be used as a dump device, but a dump device is used specifically for core dump purposes, whereas primary swap fills this role in the event there is no dump device specified. As long as you don't mind the additional time it takes at boot to write the core dump in primary swap to a file, you may want to forgo adding a specific dump device to your system.

Since you probably won't be allocating an entire disk as a dump device, you may be using a logical volume. You must select a logical volume in the root volume group that is unused or is used for non-file-system swap. This is done by selecting *Add* from the *Actions* menu to add a disk or logical volume to the list of dump devices.

You will want to get acquainted with the *View Dump Configuration Details* subarea of *Dump Devices*. It is here where you can see what the current dump configuration is, what the current and pending kernel dump configurations are, and what the current runtime dump configuration is.

Subsystems

Selecting *Subsystems* lists all of your subsystems. For each subsystem, the following information is listed:

- *Name* - Name of the subsystem.

- *Current Value* - Lists whether the subsystem is *In* or *Out* of **/stand/vmunix**.

- *Pending Value* - Lists whether the subsystem is *In* or *Out* of the pending kernel.

- *Description* - A few words describing the parameter.

You can then take a number of *Actions,* including the following:

Templates	You can select a kernel template to load that is basically a different kernel configuration from the one you are currently running.
Process New Kernel	After making whatever changes you like to the *Pending State* of a subsystem, you can have SAM create a new kernel for you.
View Subsystem Details	

You get a little more information about the subsystem when you select this.

Add Subsystem to Kernel

When you highlight one of the subsystems and select this from the menu, the *Pending State* is changed to *In* and the subsystem will be added to the kernel when you rebuild the kernel.

Remove Subsystem from Kernel

When you highlight one of the subsystems and select this from the menu, the *Pending State* is changed to *Out* and the subsystem will be removed from the kernel when you rebuild the kernel.

After making selections, you can rebuild the kernel to include your pending changes or back out of them without making the changes.

Networking and Communications

The menu hierarchy for *Networking and Communications* is shown in Figures 11-36 through 11-38. This area contains many advanced networking features. Because there are so many networking areas to cover in SAM, I'll go over just a few so you can get a feel for working in this area. The bubble diagram shows the many areas related to networking configuration for which you can use SAM, so you can refer back to it if you have a question about whether or not some specific networking can be configured using SAM.

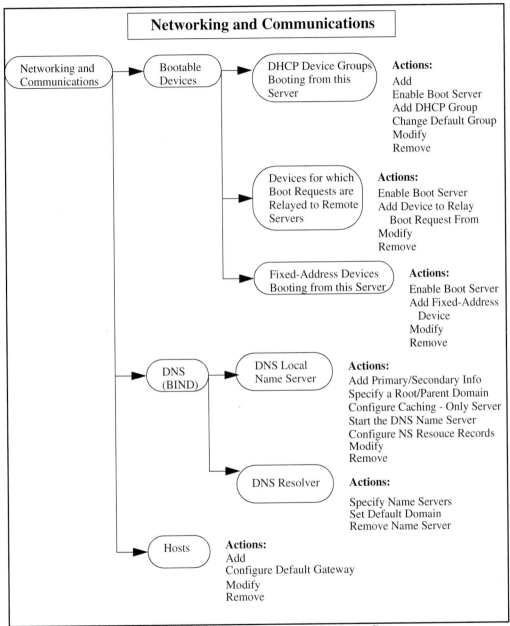

Figure 11-36 Networking and Communications Menu Structure

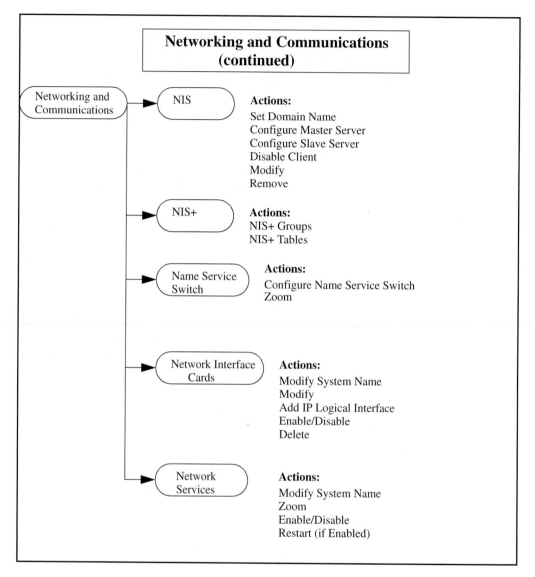

Figure 11-37 Networking and Communications Menu Structure (cont)

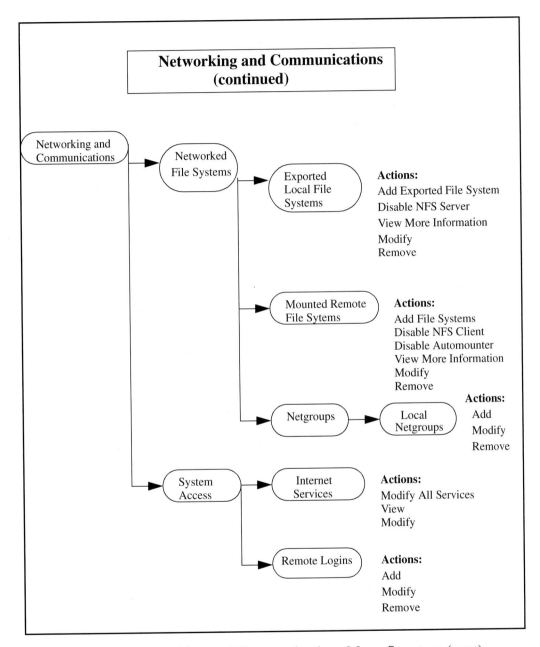

Figure 11-38 Networking and Communications Menu Structure (cont)

Bootable Devices

The *Bootable Devices* area is further subdivided into three subareas: *DHCP Device Groups Booting from this Server, Devices for which Boot Requests are Relayed to Remote Servers,* and *Fixed-Address Devices Booting from this Server.* I will briefly describe each subarea and its use. DHCP (Dynamic Host Configuration Protocol) is now available on HP-UX and is used by many services.

The *DHCP Device Groups Booting from this Server* subarea is where the device groups can be configured. Each group would contain a set of IP addresses for use by that device group. Devices could be such things as specific types of printers or specific types of terminals.

In the *Devices for which Boot Requests are Relayed to Remote Servers* subarea, you can view information about Bootstrap Protocol (Bootp) client devices that get their booting information from remote Bootp or DHCP servers. Information is displayed on the client or client groups, including the IP addresses of the remove servers and the maximum number of hops a boot request from a client or client group can be relayed.

In the *Fixed-Address Devices Booting from this Server* subarea, you can specify systems that will boot from your system using Bootstrap Protocol (Bootp) or DHCP. Bootp is a means by which a system can discover network information and boot automatically. The Bootp software must be loaded on your system in order for other devices to use it as a boot source (see the **swlist** command in Chapter 2 regarding how to list software installed on your system). In this subarea, you can add, modify, or remove a Bootp device. In addition, you can enable or disable the Bootp Server. Similarly, DHCP allows the client to use one of a pool of IP addresses in order to boot automatically. Applications such as Ignite-UX can be configured to use this protocol.

When you enter the *Fixed-Address Devices Booting from this Server* subarea, you immediately receive a list of devices that can boot off your system. You can choose *Add* from the *Actions* menu and you'll be asked to enter the following information about the device you are adding:

- Host Name

- Internet Address

- Subnet Mask (this is optional)

- Station Address in hex or client ID (this is optional)

- Boot File Name

- Whether you'll be using Ethernet or IEEE 802.3 for booting

- Whether to send the hostname to the client or device

You can select *Enable Protocol Server* or *Disable Protocol Server* from the *Actions* menu, depending on whether your system is currently disabled or enabled to support this functionality. When you *Enable Protocol Server,* you also enable Trivial File Transfer Protocol (TFTP), which boot devices use to get boot files. When you enable or disable this, the **/etc/inetd.conf** is edited. This file contains configuration information about the networking services running on your system. If a line in **/etc/inetd.conf** is preceded by a "#", then it is viewed as a comment. The daemon that reads the entries in this file is **/usr/sbin/inetd**. Before enabling or disabling Bootp, you may want to view the **/etc/inetd.conf** file and see what services are enabled. After you make your change through SAM, you can again view **/etc/inetd.conf** to see what has been modified. See *System Access* for security related to **/etc/inetd.conf.** The following is the *beginning* of the **/etc/inetd.conf** file from a system showing Bootp and TFTP enabled. Also, a brief explanation of the fields in this file appears at the beginning of the file:

```
## Configured using SAM by root
##
#
# Inetd  reads its configuration information from this file upon ex-
# ecution and at some later time if it is reconfigured.
#
# A line in the configuration file has the following fields separated
# by tabs and/or spaces:
#
#    service name         as in /etc/services
#    socket type          either "stream" or "dgram"
#    protocol             as in /etc/protocols
#    wait/nowait           only applies to datagram sockets, stream
#                         sockets should specify nowait
#    user                 name of user as whom the server should run
#    server program       absolute pathname for the server inetd
#                         will execute
#    server program args.  arguments server program uses as they
```

```
#                               normally are starting with argv[0] which
#                               is the name of the server.
#
# See the inetd.conf(4) manual page for more information.
##


##
#
#              ARPA/Berkeley services
#
##
ftp            stream tcp nowait root /usr/lbin/ftpd       ftpd -l
telnet         stream tcp nowait root /usr/lbin/telnetd    telnetd

# Before uncommenting the "tftp" entry below, please make sure
# that you have a "tftp" user in /etc/passwd. If you don't
# have one, please consult the tftpd(1M) manual entry for
# information about setting up this service.

tftp           dgram  udp wait    root  /usr/lbin/tftpd       tftpd
bootps         dgram  udp wait    root  /usr/lbin/bootpd      bootpd
#finger        stream tcp nowait  bin   /usr/lbing/fingerd    fingerd
login          stream tcp nowait  bin   /usr/lbin/rlogind     rlogind
shell          stream tcp nowait  bin   /usr/lbin/remshd      remshd
exec           stream tcp nowait  root  /usr/lbin/rexecd      rexecd
#uucp          stream tcp nowait  bin   /usr/sbin/uucpd       uucpd
```

                                            .
                                            .
                                            .

If you select *Fixed-Address Device Client Names*, you can then select *Modify* or *Remove* from the *Actions* menu and either change one of the parameters related to the client, such as its address or subnet mask, or completely remove the client.

DNS (BIND)

Domain Name Service (DNS) is a name server used to resolve hostname-to-IP addressing. HP-UX uses BIND, Berkeley InterNetworking Domain, one of the name services that can be used to implement DNS. A DNS server is responsible for the resolution of all hostnames on a network or subnet. Each DNS client would rely on the server to resolve all IP address-to-hostname issues on the client's behalf. A boot file is used by the server to locate database files. The database files map hostnames to IP addresses and IP addresses to hostnames. Through SAM, a DNS server can be easily set up.

Information about DNS and its setup and administration is described in the HP-UX manual *Installing and Administering Internet Services*.

Hosts

The *Hosts* subarea is for maintaining the default gateway and remote hosts on your system. When you enter this subarea, you receive a list of hosts specified on your system. This information is retrieved from the **/etc/ hosts** file on your system.

You can then *Add* a new host, *Specify Default Gateway*, *Modify* one of the hosts, or *Remove* one of the hosts, all from the *Actions* menu. When adding a host, you'll be asked for information pertaining to the host, including its Internet Address, system name, aliases for the system, and comments.

NIS

Network Information Service (NIS) is a database system used to propagate common configuration files across a network of systems. Managed on a master server are such files as **/etc/passwd**, **/etc/hosts**, and **/etc/auto***, files used by automounter. Formerly called "yellow pages," NIS converts these files to its own database files, called maps, for use by clients in the NIS domain. When a client requests information, such as when a user logs in and enters their password, the information is retrieved from the server rather than from the client's system. Thus, this information only needs to be maintained only on the server.

Through SAM, the NIS master server, slave servers, and clients can be configured, enabled, disabled, and removed. Once the master, slaves, and clients are established, you can easily build, modify, and push the various maps to the slaves.

NIS is not available on trusted systems.

NIS+

HP-UX 11i supports NIS+. This is not an enhancement of NIS, but rather, a new service that includes standard and trusted systems and non-HP-UX systems. If you already use NIS, a compatibility mode version of NIS+ allows servers to answer requests from both NIS and NIS+ clients. When NIS+ is configured on a trusted system, in the *Auditing and Security* area of SAM, a new subarea, *Audited NIS+ Users*, is displayed.

Name Service Switch

The Name Service Switch file, **/etc/nsswitch.conf**, can now be configured through SAM. This service allows you to prioritize which name service (FILES, NIS, NIS+, DNS, or COMPAT) to use to look up information. Unless you specifically use one of these services, the default of FILES should be used. The FILES designation supports the use of the local **/etc** directory for such administrative files as **/etc/passwd**, **/etc/hosts**, and **/etc/services**. (COMPAT is used with the compatibility mode of NIS+.)

More information about the Name Service Switch file and its setup is described in the HP-UX manual *Installing and Administering NFS Services*.

Network Interface Cards

This subarea is used for configuring any networking cards in your system. You can *Enable, Disable*, and *Modify* networking cards as well as *Modify System Name,* all from the *Actions* menu. Under *Add IP Logical Interface,* you can add additional logical IP addresses to an existing network card.

The *Network Interface Cards* screen lists the network cards installed on your system, including the information listed below. You may have to expand the window or scroll over to see all this information.

- Card Type, such as Ethernet, IEEE 802.3, Token Ring, FDDI, etc.

- Card Name

- Hardware Path

- Status, such as whether or not the card is enabled

- Internet Address

- Subnet Mask

- Station Address in hex

Included under *Configure* for Ethernet cards is *Advanced Options,* which will modify the Maximum Transfer Unit (MTU) for this card. Other cards included in your system can also be configured here, such as ISDN, X.25, ATM, and so on.

Network Services

This subarea is used to enable or disable *some* of the network services on your system. You will recognize some of the network services in Figure 11-39 from the **/etc/inetd.conf** file shown earlier. This screen has three columns, which are the Name, Status, and Description of the network services. Figure 11-39 from the *Network Services* subarea shows some of the network services that can be managed:

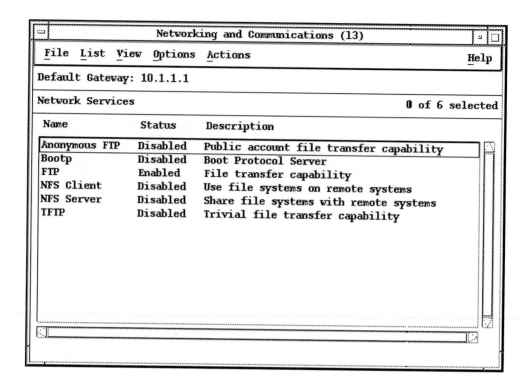

Figure 11-39 Network Services Window

After selecting one of the network services shown, you can *Enable* or *Disable* the service, depending on its current status, *Restart* the service if it is currently enabled, get more information about the service with *Zoom,* or *Modify System Name,* all from the *Actions* menu.

Network File Systems

This subarea is broken down into *Exported Local File Systems, Mounted Remote File Systems,* and *Netgroups.* NFS is broken down into these first two areas because you can export a local file system without mounting a remote file system, and vice versa. This means that you can manage these independently of one another. You may have an NFS server in your environment that won't mount remote file systems, and you may have an NFS client that will mount only remote file systems and never export its local file system. *Entropies,* a part of NIS, allows you to group a set of systems or users to be used together. Among other things, netgroup designations can be used to export file systems to.

Under *Exported Local File Systems,* you can select the file systems you want to export. The first time you enter this screen you have no exported file systems listed. When you select *Add Exported File System* from the *Actions* menu, you enter such information as:

- Local directory name

- User ID

- Whether or not to allow asynchronous writes

- Permissions

After this exported file system has been added, you can select it and choose from a number of *Actions,* including *Modify* and *Remove.*

Under *Mounted Remote File Systems,* you have listed for you all of the directories and files that are mounted using NFS. These can be either mounted or unmounted on demand with automounter. After selecting one of the mounted file systems, you can perform various *Actions.* For every remote file system mounted, you have the following columns:

- *Mount Directory,* which displays the name of the local directory name used to mount the remote directory.

- *Type,* which is either *NFS* for standard NFS or *Auto* for automounter (see the paragraph below).

- *Remote Server,* which displays the name of the remote system where the file or directory is mounted.

- *Remote Directory,* which is the name of the directory under which the directory is remotely mounted.

You should think about whether or not you want to use the NFS automounter. With automounter, you mount a remote file or directory on demand, that is, when you need it. Using a master map, you can specify which files and directories will be mounted when needed. The files and directories are not continuously mounted with automounter, resulting in more efficiency as far as how system resources are being used. There is, however, some overhead time associated with mounting a file or directory on-demand, as opposed to having it continuously mounted. From a user standpoint, this may be slightly more undesirable, but from an administration standpoint, using the automounter offers advantages. Since the automounter is managed through SAM, there is very little additional work you need to perform to enable it.

System Access

This subarea is broken down into *Internet Services* and *Remote Logins.*

When you select *Internet Services,* the screen lists the networking services that are started by the Internet daemon **/usr/sbin/inetd**. I earlier covered **/etc/inetd.conf**, which is a configuration file that lists all of the network services supported by a system that is read by **inetd**. There is also a security file, **/var/adm/inetd.sec**, that serves as a security check for **inetd**. Although many other components are involved, you can view **inetd**, **/etc/inetd.conf**, and **/var/adm/inetd.sec** as working together to determine what network services are supported and the security level of each.

Listed for you in the *System Access* subarea are *Service Name, Description, Type,* and *System Permission*. Figure 11-40 shows the defaults for my system:

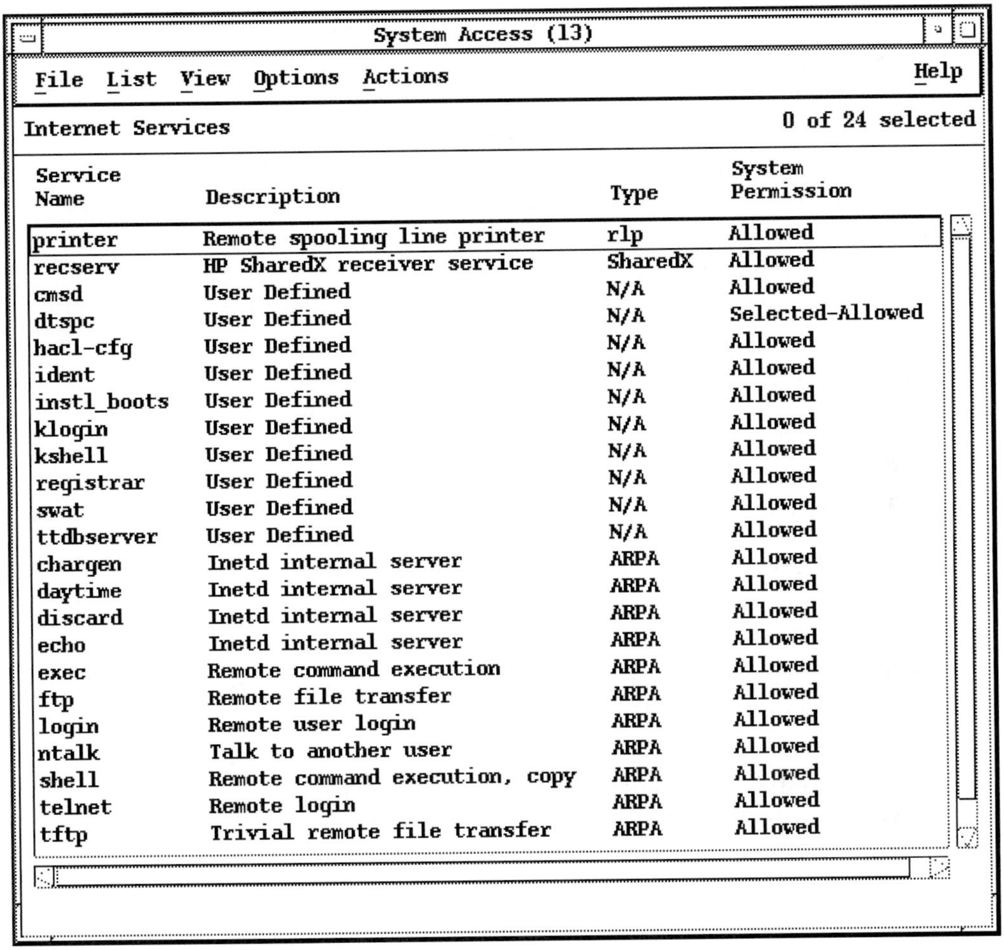

```
┌──────────────────────────────────────────────────────────────────────┐
│ ▄           ▄▄▄▄▄▄▄▄▄▄  System Access (13) ▄▄▄▄▄▄▄▄▄▄▄▄▄▄▄▄▄     □ □   │
├──────────────────────────────────────────────────────────────────────┤
│  File  List  View  Options  Actions                           Help    │
│                                                                        │
│  Internet Services                              0 of 24 selected       │
├──────────────────────────────────────────────────────────────────────┤
│  Service                                          System               │
│  Name           Description               Type    Permission           │
│ ┌──────────────────────────────────────────────────────────────────┐  │
│ │printer         Remote spooling line printer  rlp    Allowed       │  │
│ │recserv         HP SharedX receiver service   SharedX Allowed       │  │
│ │cmsd            User Defined                   N/A    Allowed       │  │
│ │dtspc           User Defined                   N/A    Selected-Allowed│ │
│ │hacl-cfg        User Defined                   N/A    Allowed       │  │
│ │ident           User Defined                   N/A    Allowed       │  │
│ │instl_boots     User Defined                   N/A    Allowed       │  │
│ │klogin          User Defined                   N/A    Allowed       │  │
│ │kshell          User Defined                   N/A    Allowed       │  │
│ │registrar       User Defined                   N/A    Allowed       │  │
│ │swat            User Defined                   N/A    Allowed       │  │
│ │ttdbserver      User Defined                   N/A    Allowed       │  │
│ │chargen         Inetd internal server          ARPA   Allowed       │  │
│ │daytime         Inetd internal server          ARPA   Allowed       │  │
│ │discard         Inetd internal server          ARPA   Allowed       │  │
│ │echo            Inetd internal server          ARPA   Allowed       │  │
│ │exec            Remote command execution       ARPA   Allowed       │  │
│ │ftp             Remote file transfer           ARPA   Allowed       │  │
│ │login           Remote user login              ARPA   Allowed       │  │
│ │ntalk           Talk to another user           ARPA   Allowed       │  │
│ │shell           Remote command execution, copy ARPA   Allowed       │  │
│ │telnet          Remote login                   ARPA   Allowed       │  │
│ │tftp            Trivial remote file transfer   ARPA   Allowed       │  │
│ └──────────────────────────────────────────────────────────────────┘  │
└──────────────────────────────────────────────────────────────────────┘
```

Figure 11-40   System Access - Internet Services Window

You could change the permission for any of these entries by selecting them, using the *Modify* command from the *Actions* menu, and selecting the desired permissions.

Remote Logins is used to manage security restrictions for remote users who will access the local system. Two HP-UX files are used to manage users. The file **/etc/hosts.equiv** handles users, and **/.rhosts** handles superusers (root). When you enter this subarea, you get a list of users and the restrictions on each. You can then *Add, Remove*, or *Modify* login security.

Partition Manager

Many HP 9000 systems running HP-UX 11i support partitions. At the time of this writing, however, partitions were just emerging as an advanced technology and I did not have access to any systems supporting partitions. The two partition types supported on HP 9000 systems running HP-UX 11i are hard (*nPartition*) and Virtual Partitions (*vPars*), covered throughout this book. At the time of this writing, hard partitions are available on Superdome and the rp8400 systems and consist primarily of hardware components that are combined to form the hard partition. The vPars we've been working with throughout this book at the command line are, or will soon be, available on all HP 9000 systems.

Performance Monitors

Under *Performance Monitors,* you can view the performance of your system in several different areas such as disk and virtual memory. Figure 11-41 shows the menu hierarchy of *Performance Monitors*:

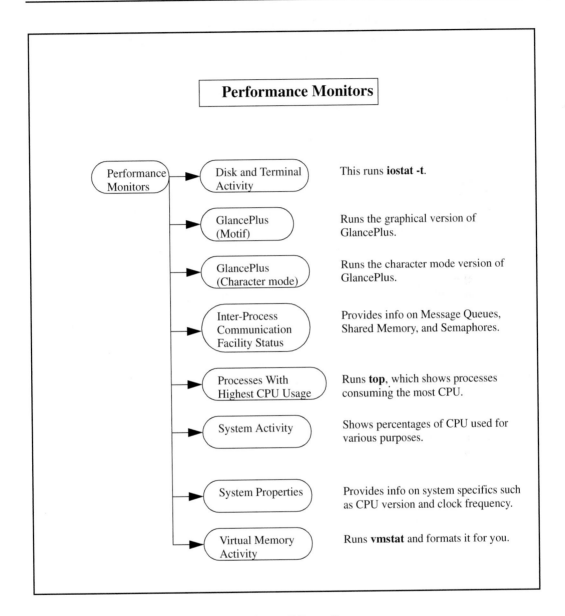

Figure 11-41 *Performance Monitors* Menu Structure

Performance Monitors provides you with a window into several areas of your system. If you are serious about becoming familiar with the tools available on your system to help you understand how your system resources are being used, you should take a close look at Chapter 12. Chapter 12 is devoted to getting a handle on how your system resources are being used, including many built-in HP-UX commands. Some of the performance monitors you can select in this subarea are HP-UX commands, which you'll need some background in before you can use them. I'll cover these areas only briefly because this material will be covered in more detail in Chapter 12.

Disk and Terminal Activity

Selecting *Disk and Terminal Activity* opens a window that shows the output of **iostat -t**. I have included the description of **iostat** from Chapter 12 to save you the trouble of flipping ahead. When the *Disks and Terminal Activity* window with the output of **iostat** is opened for you, it shows a single **iostat** output. When you press *Return,* the window is automatically closed for you.

The **iostat** command gives you an indication of the level of effort the CPU is putting into I/O and the amount of I/O taking place among your disks and terminals. The following example shows the **iostat -t** command, which will be executed every three seconds, and associated output from an HP-UX 11.x system:

```
# iostat -t 3
                        tty                    cpu
               tin    tout          us      ni     sy    id
               78      42            2       0     28    70
/dev/dsk/c0t1d0              /dev/dsk/c0t4d0               /dev/dsk/c0t6d0
bps  sps  msps              bps   sps  msps               bps  sps  msps
 0    0     0                33   8.3  25.2                 7    1   19.5
                        tty                    cpu
               tin    tout          us      ni     sy    id
               66      24            0       0     30    70
/dev/dsk/c0t1d0              /dev/dsk/c0t4d0               /dev/dsk/c0t6d0
bps  sps  msps              bps   sps  msps               bps  sps  msps
 5   12    15.9             36    9.7   21                 7   1.2   13.8
                        tty                    cpu
               tin    tout          us      ni     sy    id
               90      29            1       0     25    73
```

/dev/dsk/c0t1d0			/dev/dsk/c0t4d0			/dev/dsk/c0t6d0		
bps	sps	msps	bps	sps	msps	bps	sps	msps
12	1.7	15.5	24	3	19.1	14	2.1	14.6

tty		cpu			
tin	tout	us	ni	sy	id
48	16	1	0	16	83

/dev/dsk/c0t1d0			/dev/dsk/c0t4d0			/dev/dsk/c0t6d0		
bps	sps	msps	bps	sps	msps	bps	sps	msps
0	0	0	62	9.3	18	12	2	17.2

tty		cpu			
tin	tout	us	ni	sy	id
32	48	7	0	14	79

/dev/dsk/c0t1d0			/dev/dsk/c0t4d0			/dev/dsk/c0t6d0		
bps	sps	msps	bps	sps	msps	bps	sps	msps
1	0.3	14.4	5	.9	16.2	171	29.4	18.2

tty		cpu			
tin	tout	us	ni	sy	id
2	40	20	1	42	27

/dev/dsk/c0t1d0			/dev/dsk/c0t4d0			/dev/dsk/c0t6d0		
bps	sps	msps	bps	sps	msps	bps	sps	msps
248	30.9	20.8	203	29.2	18.8	165	30.6	22.1

Descriptions of the reports you receive with **iostat** for terminals, the CPU, and mounted file systems follow.

For every terminal you have connected (tty), you see a "tin" and "tout," which represent the number of characters read from your terminal and the number of characters written to your terminal, respectively. The *-t* option produces this terminal report.

For your CPU, you see the percentage of time spent in user mode ("us"), the percentage of time spent running user processes at a low priority called nice ("ni"), the percentage of time spent in system mode ("sy"), and the percentage of time the CPU is idle ("id").

For every locally mounted file system, you receive information on the kilobytes transferred per second ("bps"), number of seeks per second ("sps"), and number of milliseconds per average seek ("msps"). For disks that are NFS-mounted or disks on client nodes of your server, you will not receive a report; **iostat** reports only on locally mounted file systems.

GlancePlus

GlancePlus is available here if it is installed on your system. You are given the choice of using either the Motif (graphical) version or the character mode version of GlancePlus. GlancePlus and other HP VantagePoint products are covered in Chapter 12.

Inter-Process Communication Facility Status

Inter-Process Communication Facility Status shows categories of information related to communication between processes. You receive status on Message Queues, Shared Memory, and Semaphores. This is a status window only, so again, when you press *Return,* and the window closes.

Processes with Highest CPU Usage

Processes with Highest CPU Usage is a useful window that lists the processes consuming the most CPU on your system. Such useful information as the *Process ID*, its *Resident Set Size*, and the *Percentage of CPU* it is consuming are listed.

System Activity

System Activity provides a report of CPU utilization. You receive the following list:

%usr   Percent of CPU spent in user mode.

%sys   Percent of CPU spent in system mode.

%wio	Percent of CPU idle with some processes waiting for I/O, such as virtual memory pages moving in or moving out.
%idle	Percent of CPU completely idle.

System Properties

System Properties gives you a great overview of system specifics. Included here are those hard-to-find items such as processor information, CPU version, clock frequency, kernel support (32-bit or 64-bit), memory information, operating system version, and network IP and MAC addresses.

Virtual Memory Activity

Virtual Memory Activity runs the **vmstat** command. This too is covered in Chapter 12, but I have included the **vmstat** description here so that you don't have to flip ahead. Some of the columns of **vmstat** are moved around a little when the *Virtual Memory Activity* window is opened for you.

vmstat provides virtual memory statistics. It provides information on the status of processes, virtual memory, paging activity, faults, and a breakdown of the percentage of CPU time. In the following example, the output was produced ten times at five-second intervals. The first argument to the **vmstat** command is the interval; the second is the number of times you would like output produced.

 # vmstat 5 10:

procs			memory				page					faults			cpu		
r	b	w	avm	free	re	at	pi	po	fr	de	sr	in	sy	cs	us	sy	id
4	0	0	1161	2282	6	22	48	0	0	0	0	429	289	65	44	18	38
9	0	0	1161	1422	4	30	59	0	0	0	0	654	264	181	18	20	62
6	0	0	1409	1247	2	19	37	0	0	0	0	505	316	130	47	10	43

vmstat 5 10:

procs			memory		page						faults			cpu		
r	b	w	avm	free	re	at	pi	po	fr	de	sr	in	sy	cs	us	sy	id
1	0	0	1409	1119	1	10	19	0	0	0	0	508	254	180	69	15	16
2	0	0	1878	786	0	1	6	0	0	0	0	729	294	217	75	17	8
2	0	0	1878	725	0	0	3	0	0	0	0	561	688	435	67	32	1
2	0	0	2166	98	0	0	20	0	0	0	66	728	952	145	8	14	78
1	0	0	2310	90	0	0	20	0	0	0	171	809	571	159	16	21	63
1	0	0	2310	190	0	0	8	1	3	0	335	704	499	176	66	14	20
1	0	0	2316	311	0	0	3	1	5	0	376	607	945	222	4	11	85

You will get more out of the **vmstat** command than you want. Next is a brief description of the categories of information produced by **vmstat**:

Processes are classified into one of three categories: runnable ("r"), blocked on I/O or short-term resources ("b"), or swapped ("w").

Next you will see information about memory. "avm" is the number of virtual memory pages owned by processes that have run within the last 20 seconds. If this number is roughly the size of physical memory minus your kernel, then you are near paging. The "free" column indicates the number of pages on the system's free list. It doesn't mean that the process has finished running and these pages won't be accessed again; it just means that they have not been accessed recently.

Next is paging activity. The first field (*re*) shows the pages that were reclaimed. These pages made it to the free list but were later referenced and had to be salvaged. Check to see that "re" is a low number. If you are reclaiming pages that were thought to be free by the system, then you are wasting valuable time salvaging these. Reclaiming pages is also a symptom that you are short on memory.

Next you see the number of faults in three categories: interrupts per second, which usually come from hardware ("in"); system calls per second ("sy"); and context switches per second ("cs").

The final output is CPU usage percentage for user ("us"), system ("sy"), and idle ("id"). This is not as complete as the **iostat** output, which also shows **nice** entries.

Peripheral Devices

With *Peripheral Devices,* you can view any I/O cards installed in your system and peripherals connected to your system. These include both used and unused devices. You can also quickly configure any peripheral, including printers, plotters, tape drives, terminals, modems, and disks. This is a particularly useful area in SAM, because configuring peripherals in HP-UX is tricky. You perform one procedure to connect a printer, a different procedure to connect a disk, and so on, when you use the command line. In SAM, these procedures are menu-driven and therefore much easier.

Two of the six subareas, *Disks and File Systems* and *Printers and Plotters,* have their own dedicated hierarchy within SAM and are covered in this chapter. I don't cover these again in this section. The other four subareas, *Cards, Device List, Tape Drives*, and *Terminals and Modems,* are covered in this section.

It's impossible for me to cover every possible device that can be viewed and configured in SAM. What I'll do is give you examples of what you would see reported as devices on a server so that you can get a feel for what you can do under *Peripheral Devices* with SAM. From what I show here, you should be comfortable that SAM can help you configure peripherals.

Figure 11-42 shows the hierarchy of *Peripheral Devices*:

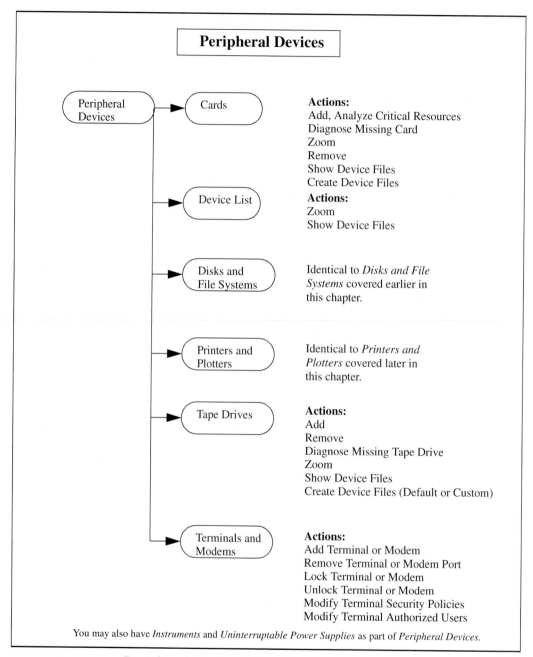

Figure 11-42 *Peripheral Devices* Menu Structure

Cards

When you select *Cards,* you are provided with a list of I/O cards in your system. You can also perform such tasks as adding and removing cards. Having this list of I/O cards is useful. Figure 11-43 shows a listing of I/O cards for an L-Class system:

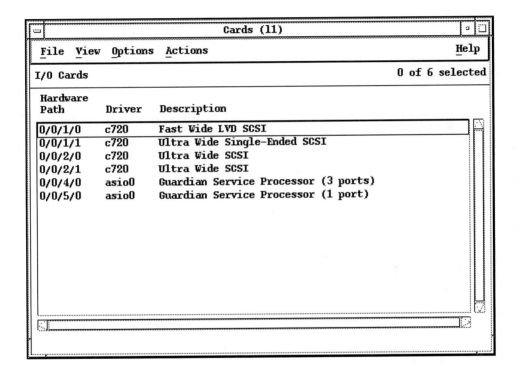

Figure 11-43 *I/O Cards* Window for L-Class System

In *Cards,* you can perform the following *Actions*:

Add   You can add a new I/O card in the window
                            that is opened for you.

Diagnose Missing Card

                          If a card you have installed is not included in
                          the list, you can select this to determine the
                          reason.

Zoom   If you highlight a card and select *Zoom,* you
                          will be provided such information as the
                          hardware path, driver, and description of the
                          card.

Remove   If you highlight a card and select *Remove,* a
                          window will appear that walks you through
                          removing the card from the system.

Show Device Files

                          If you select this, a window will be opened in
                          which the device files associated with the
                          card will be listed.

Create Device Files

                          Creates device files for the selected card.
                          This takes place without any user interaction.

Device List

Device List shows all the peripherals configured into the system. Figure 11-44 shows a device list for an L-Class system:

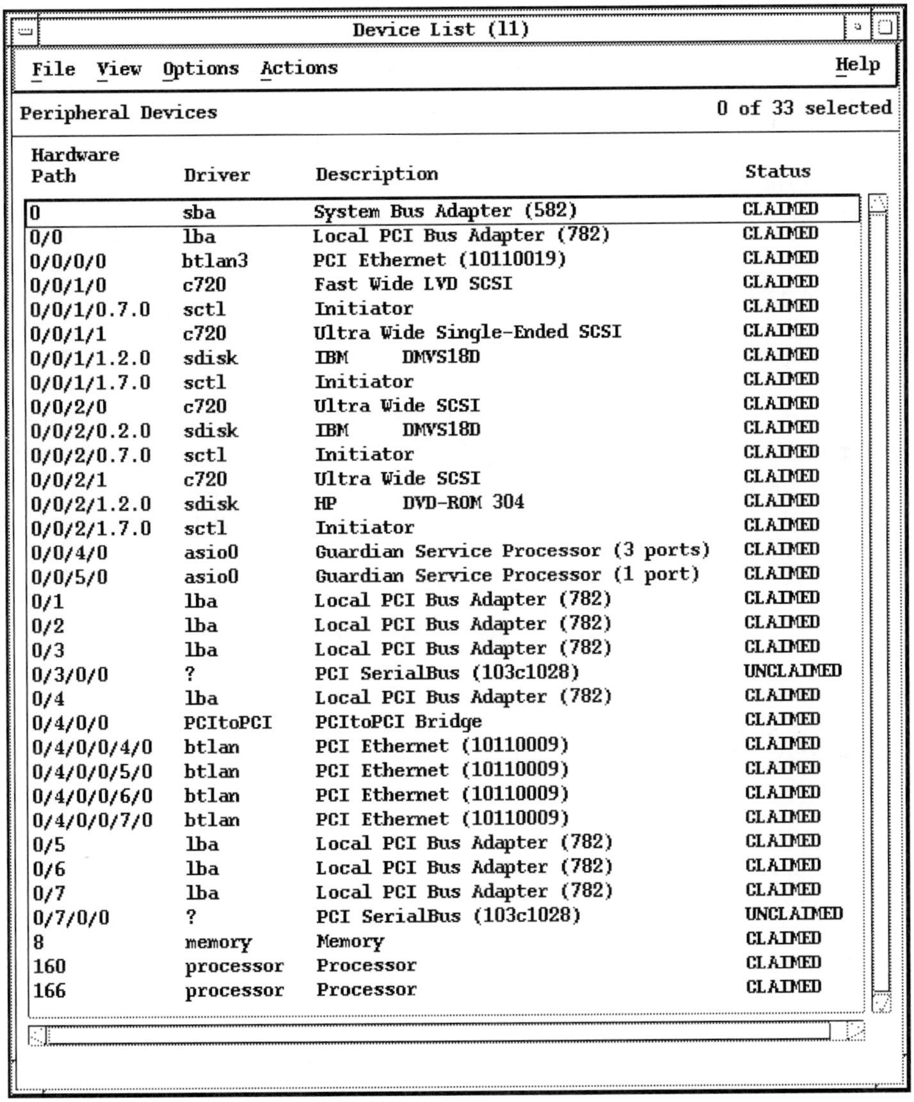

```
┌────────────────────────────────────────────────────────────────────┐
│  ⊟ ║                       Device List (11)                    │ ॰│▢ │
├────────────────────────────────────────────────────────────────────┤
│    File   View   Options   Actions                          Help    │
├────────────────────────────────────────────────────────────────────┤
│  Peripheral Devices                           0 of 33 selected      │
│                                                                      │
│   Hardware                                                           │
│   Path          Driver     Description                  Status       │
│  ┌────────────────────────────────────────────────────────────┬──┐ │
│  │0             sba        System Bus Adapter (582)     CLAIMED │▲ │ │
│  │0/0           lba        Local PCI Bus Adapter (782)  CLAIMED │  │ │
│  │0/0/0/0       btlan3     PCI Ethernet (10110019)      CLAIMED │  │ │
│  │0/0/1/0       c720       Fast Wide LVD SCSI           CLAIMED │  │ │
│  │0/0/1/0.7.0   sctl       Initiator                    CLAIMED │  │ │
│  │0/0/1/1       c720       Ultra Wide Single-Ended SCSI CLAIMED │  │ │
│  │0/0/1/1.2.0   sdisk      IBM      DMVS18D             CLAIMED │  │ │
│  │0/0/1/1.7.0   sctl       Initiator                    CLAIMED │  │ │
│  │0/0/2/0       c720       Ultra Wide SCSI              CLAIMED │  │ │
│  │0/0/2/0.2.0   sdisk      IBM      DMVS18D             CLAIMED │  │ │
│  │0/0/2/0.7.0   sctl       Initiator                    CLAIMED │  │ │
│  │0/0/2/1       c720       Ultra Wide SCSI              CLAIMED │  │ │
│  │0/0/2/1.2.0   sdisk      HP       DVD-ROM 304         CLAIMED │  │ │
│  │0/0/2/1.7.0   sctl       Initiator                    CLAIMED │  │ │
│  │0/0/4/0       asio0      Guardian Service Processor (3 ports) CLAIMED │  │ │
│  │0/0/5/0       asio0      Guardian Service Processor (1 port)  CLAIMED │  │ │
│  │0/1           lba        Local PCI Bus Adapter (782)  CLAIMED │  │ │
│  │0/2           lba        Local PCI Bus Adapter (782)  CLAIMED │  │ │
│  │0/3           lba        Local PCI Bus Adapter (782)  CLAIMED │  │ │
│  │0/3/0/0       ?          PCI SerialBus (103c1028)     UNCLAIMED│  │ │
│  │0/4           lba        Local PCI Bus Adapter (782)  CLAIMED │  │ │
│  │0/4/0/0       PCItoPCI   PCItoPCI Bridge              CLAIMED │  │ │
│  │0/4/0/0/4/0   btlan      PCI Ethernet (10110009)      CLAIMED │  │ │
│  │0/4/0/0/5/0   btlan      PCI Ethernet (10110009)      CLAIMED │  │ │
│  │0/4/0/0/6/0   btlan      PCI Ethernet (10110009)      CLAIMED │  │ │
│  │0/4/0/0/7/0   btlan      PCI Ethernet (10110009)      CLAIMED │  │ │
│  │0/5           lba        Local PCI Bus Adapter (782)  CLAIMED │  │ │
│  │0/6           lba        Local PCI Bus Adapter (782)  CLAIMED │  │ │
│  │0/7           lba        Local PCI Bus Adapter (782)  CLAIMED │  │ │
│  │0/7/0/0       ?          PCI SerialBus (103c1028)     UNCLAIMED│  │ │
│  │8             memory     Memory                       CLAIMED │  │ │
│  │160           processor  Processor                    CLAIMED │  │ │
│  │166           processor  Processor                    CLAIMED │▼ │ │
│  └────────────────────────────────────────────────────────────┴──┘ │
│   ◁ ║════════════════════════════════════════════════════════════▷ │
└────────────────────────────────────────────────────────────────────┘
```

Figure 11-44 *Peripheral Devices* Window

The two *Action* menu picks here are *Zoom* and *Show Device Files.* Selecting *Zoom* produces a window with such information as hardware path, driver, description, and status. The devices files associated with the item you have highlighted will be shown if you select *Show Device Files*.

Disks and File Systems was covered earlier in this chapter.

Instruments may appear if your system supports HP-IB cards.

Printers and Plotters is covered later in this chapter.

Tape Drives

Tape Drives lists the tape drives connected to your system. You are shown the *Hardware Path*, *Driver*, and *Description* for each tape drive. You can add, remove, diagnose tape drives, list tape drive device files, and add new tape drive device files. Figure 11-45 shows a four-drive DLT unit attached to the system:

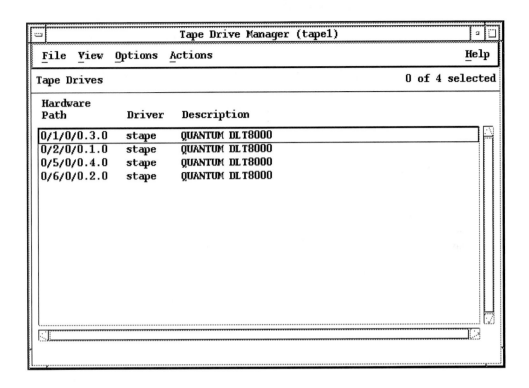

Figure 11-45 *Tape Drives* Window

Terminals and Modems

Your system's terminals and modems are listed for you when you enter this subarea. You can perform a variety of tasks from the *Actions* menu, including the following:

- *Add Terminal or Modem*

- *Remove Terminal or Modem Port*

- *Lock Terminal or Modem Port*

- *Unlock Terminal or Modem Port*

- *Modify Terminal Security Policies*

- *Modify Terminal Security Policies*

- *Modify Terminal Authorized Users*

- *Additional Information*

Uninterruptable Power Supplies

Your system's uninterruptable power supplies are listed for you when you enter this area, including the UPS type, device file of the UPS, hardware path, port number, and whether or not shutdown is enabled. The *Actions* you can select are: *Modify Global Configuration, Add, Zoom, Remove,* and *Modify.*

Printers and Plotters

Printers and Plotters is divided into two subareas: *HP Distributed Print Service* and *LP Spooler. HP Distributed Print Service* (HPDPS) is part of the Distributed Computing Environment (DCE). It is not covered in this book. *LP Spooler* is covered in this section; Figure 11-46 shows the hierarchy of *Printers and Plotters*:

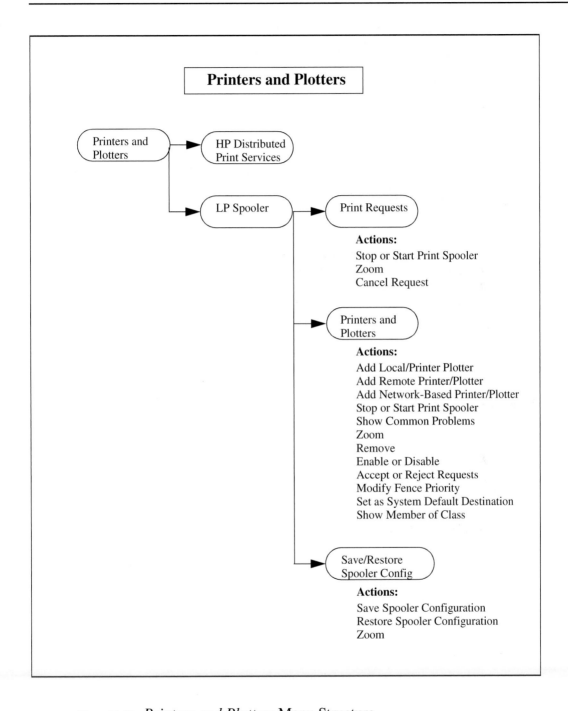

Figure 11-46 *Printers and Plotters* Menu Structure

Print Requests

Under *Print Requests,* you can manage the print spooler and specific print jobs. You can start or stop the print spooler and cancel print jobs. The following information on print requests is listed for you:

Request ID   An ID is associated with each print job. This is the Printer Name followed by a number.

Owner   The name of the user who requested the print job.

Priority   The priority of a print job is assigned when the job is submitted. The *-p* option of **lp** can be used to assign a priority to a job. Each print destination has a default priority that is assigned to jobs when *-p* is not used on the **lp** command.

File   The name of the file sent to the print queue.

Size   The size of the print job in bytes.

The *Actions* menu allows you to act on print jobs by cancelling them. In addition, the print spooler can be stopped and started.

Printers and Plotters

You can configure both local and remote printers in *Printers and Plotters*. When you select *Add Local Printer/Plotter* from the *Actions* menu and then the appropriate type of printer, a window is opened for you in which you can supply the specifics about the printer. Before this window is opened, however, you must specify whether the *type* of printer to be added is: parallel serial; HP-IB; non-standard device file; or a printer connected to a TSM terminal, as well as to which I/O card to add the printer. One huge advantage to adding the printer using SAM is that this process is entirely menu-driven, so you only have to select from among the information that is supplied.

The window appears to ask you for the following information:

Printer Name   You can pick any name for the printer. I usually like to use a name that is somewhat descriptive, such as *ljet5* for a LaserJet 5. The name is limited to 14 alphanumeric characters and underscores.

Printer Model/Interface

SAM supplies a list of all interface models for you when this window is opened. These models are located in the **/usr/lib/lp/model** directory. Each printer has an interface program that is used by the spooler to send a print job to the printer. When an interface model is selected, the model is copied to **/etc/lp/interface/**<*printername*>, where it becomes the printer's interface program. Models can be used without modification, or you can create customized interface programs.

Printer Class   You can define a group of printers to be in a
                       class, which means that print requests won't
                       go to a specific printer but will go to the first
                       available printer within the class. This is
                       optional.

Default Request Priority

                       This defines the default priority level of all
                       requests sent to this printer.

Default Destination

                       Users who do not specify a printer when
                       requesting a print job will have the print
                       request sent to the default printer.

You could use SAM to view printers or you could use the **lpstat** command showing printers configured on a system as shown in the following
example:

```
$ /usr/bin/lpstat -t
scheduler is running
system default destination: ljet5
members of class laser:
        ljet5
device for ljet5: /dev/c1t0d0_lp
ljet5 accepting requests since Nov 21 22:45
printer ljet5 is idle. enabled since Nov 21 22:45
        fence priority : 0
no entries
```

As with all the other tasks SAM helps you with, you can manage printers and plotters manually or you can use SAM. Not only does SAM make
this easier for you, but I have also had nothing but good results having SAM
do this for me. As you go through the SAM Log file, you will see a variety
of **lp** commands that were issued. Some of the more common commands,
including the **lpstat** command issued earlier, are listed in Table 11-2:

TABLE 11-2 lp Commands

Command	Description
/usr/sbin/accept	Start accepting jobs to be queued.
/usr/bin/cancel	Cancel a print job that is queued.
/usr/bin/disable	Disable a device for printing.
/usr/bin/enable	Enable a device for printing.
/usr/sbin/lpfence	Set minimum priority for spooled file to be printed.
/usr/bin/lp	Queue a job or jobs for printing.
/usr/sbin/lpadmin	Configure the printing system with the options provided.
/usr/sbin/lpmove	Move printing jobs from one device to another.
/usr/sbin/lpsched	Start the **lp** scheduling daemon.
/usr/sbin/lpshut	Stop the **lp** scheduling daemon.
/usr/bin/lpstat	Show the status of printing based on the options provided.
/usr/sbin/reject	Stop accepting jobs to be queued.

Save/Restore Spooler Configuration

Occasionally, the spooler can get into an inconsistent state (usually, something else has to go wrong with your system that ends up somehow changing or renaming some of the spooler configuration files). SAM keeps a saved version of the spooler's configuration each time it is used to make a change (only the most recent one is saved). This saved configuration can be restored by SAM to recover from the spooler having gotten into an inconsistent state. Your latest configuration is automatically saved by SAM, provided that you used SAM to create the configuration, as opposed to issuing **lp** commands at the command line, and it can be restored with *Restore Spooler Configuration* from *Save/Restore Spooler Config*. This screen allows you to save your current spooler configuration or restore a previously saved spooler configuration information.

Process Management

Process Management is broken down into two areas that allow you to control and schedule processes. *Process Control* allows you to control an individual process by performing such tasks as viewing it, changing its *nice* priority, killing it, stopping it, or continuing it. You can also view and schedule **cron** jobs under *Scheduled Cron Jobs*. Figure 11-47 shows the menu hierarchy of *Process Management*:

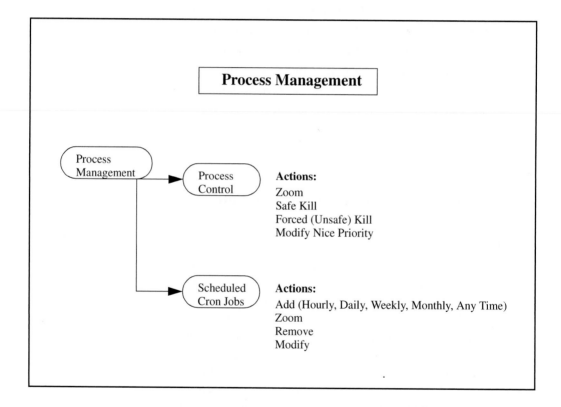

Figure 11-47 *Process Management* Menu Structure

Process Control

When you pick *Process Control,* SAM lists the processes on your system and allows you to perform various actions. Using *Process Control* is a much easier way of controlling the processes on your system than executing commands such as **ps**, **nice**, and so on. Figure 11-48 shows a partial listing of processes:

```
┌─────────────────────────────────────────────────────────────────────────────┐
│ ▭                        Process Management (13)                      ◦ │ ▯ │
├─────────────────────────────────────────────────────────────────────────────┤
│  File  List  View  Options  Actions                                    Help  │
├─────────────────────────────────────────────────────────────────────────────┤
│ Process Control                                          0 of 91 selected    │
├─────────────────────────────────────────────────────────────────────────────┤
│                        Nice                                                   │
│  User     Priority    Priority   Command                                      │
│ ┌───────────────────────────────────────────────────────────────────────┐   │
│ │root        128         20     swapper                                   │▒▒│
│ │root        168         20       init                                    │  │
│ │root        152         20        /usr/sbin/syncer                       │  │
│ │root        154         20        /usr/sbin/syslogd -D                   │  │
│ │root        155         20        /usr/sbin/ptydaemon                    │  │
│ │root        127         20        /usr/lbin/nktl_daemon 0 0 0 0 0 1 -2    │  │
│ │root        127         20        /usr/lbin/ntl_reader 0 1 1 1 1000 2 /var/adm/ne │
│ │root        127         20          /usr/sbin/netfmt -C -F -f /var/adm/nettl.LOGO │
│ │root        154         20        /usr/sbin/rpcbind                      │  │
│ │root        154         20        /usr/sbin/inetd                        │  │
│ │root        154         20        /usr/sbin/snmpdm                       │  │
│ │root        154         20        /usr/sbin/hp_unixagt                   │  │
│ │root        154         20        /usr/sbin/mib2agt                      │  │
│ │root        154         20        /usr/sbin/trapdestagt                  │  │
│ │root        154         20        /usr/lbin/cmsnmpd                      │  │
│ │root        154         20        /opt/dce/sbin/rpcd                     │  │
│ │root        152         20        /usr/dmi/bin/dmisp                     │  │
│ │root        152         20        /var/dmi/bin/hpuxci                    │  │
│ │root        152         20        /var/dmi/bin/sdci                      │  │
│ │root        152         20        /var/dmi/bin/swci                      │  │
│ │root        168         20        /opt/scr/lbin/scrdaemon                │  │
│ │root         64         20        /usr/sbin/rbootd                       │  │
│ │root        154         20        /usr/sbin/pwgrd                        │  │
│ │root        154         20        /usr/sbin/cron                         │  │
│ │root        154         20        /usr/sbin/envd                         │  │
│ │root        154         20        /opt/perf/bin/ttd                      │  │
│ │root        154         20        /opt/perf/bin/perflbd                  │  │
│ │root        154         20         /opt/perf/bin/rep_server -t SCOPE /var/opt/pe │
│ │root        154         20         /opt/perf/bin/agdbserver -t alarmgen /var/opt │
│ │root        154         20          /opt/perf/bin/alarmgen -svr 1811 -t alarmge │
│ │root        -16         20        /opt/perf/bin/midaemon                 │  │
│ │root        152         20        /opt/prm/bin/prm3d                     │  │
│ │root        127         20        /opt/perf/bin/scopeux                  │  │
│ │root        154         20        /usr/sbin/swagentd -r                  │  │
│ │root        154         20        /etc/opt/resmon/lbin/emsagent          │  │
│ │root        152         20      opcctla -start                           │  │
│ │root        152         20        opcmsga                                │  │
│ │root        152         20        opcacta                                │▒▒│
│ └───────────────────────────────────────────────────────────────────────┘   │
└─────────────────────────────────────────────────────────────────────────────┘
```

Figure 11-48   Partial *Process Control* Listing.

There are the four columns of information listed:

- *User* - The name of the user who owns the process.

- *Priority* - The priority of the process determines its scheduling by the CPU. The lower the number, the higher the priority. Unless you have modified these priorities, they will be default priorities. Changing the priority is done with the **nice** command, which will be covered shortly.

- *Nice Priority* - If you have a process that you wish to run at a lower or higher priority, you could change this value. The lower the value, the higher the CPU scheduling priority.

- *Command* - Lists the names of all the commands currently being run or executed on the system.

In addition to these four columns, there are several others you can specify to be included in the list by selecting *Columns* from the *View* menu. You can include such information as the *Process ID, Parent Process ID, Processor Utilization, Core Image Size*, and so on. Adding *Processor Utilization* as a column, for instance, shows me how much of the processor all processes are consuming, including SAM.

You can now select one of the processes and an *Actions* to perform.

When you select a process to kill and pick *Safe Kill* from the *Actions* menu, you will see a message that indicates the process number killed and that it may take a few minutes to kill it in order to terminate cleanly. If you select a process to kill and pick *Forced Kill* from the *Actions* menu, you don't get any feedback; SAM just kills the process and you move on.

Chapter 5 covered the **kill** command. To save you the trouble of flipping ahead, I have included some of the information related to **kill** here. The **kill** command can be either **/usr/bin/kill** or **kill**, which is part of the POSIX shell. The POSIX shell is the default shell for HP-UX 11i. The other shells provide their own **kill** commands as well. We use the phrase "kill a process" in the UNIX world all the time, I think, because it has a powerful connotation associated with it. What we are really saying is that we want to terminate a process. This termination is done with a signal. The most common signal to send is "SIGKILL," which terminates the process. There are other signals you can send to the process, but SIGKILL is the most common. As an alternative to sending the signal, you could send the corresponding signal number. A list of signal numbers and corresponding signals is shown below:

Signal Number	Signal
0	SIGNULL
1	SIGHUP
2	SIGINT
3	SIGQUIT
9	SIGKILL
15	SIGTERM
24	SIGSTOP
25	SIGTSTP
26	SIGCONT

I obtained this list of processes from the **kill** manual page.

To **kill** a process with a process ID of *234*, you would issue the following command:

```
$ kill -9 234
      |   |   |
      |   |   |> process id (PID)
      |   |> signal number
      |> kill command to terminate the process
```

The final selection from the *Actions* menu is to *Modify Nice Priority* of the process you have selected. If you were to read the manual page on **nice,** you would be very happy to see that you can modify this with SAM. Modifying the **nice** value in SAM simply requires you to select a process and specify its new **nice** value within the acceptable range.

Scheduling Cron Jobs

The *Scheduled Cron Jobs* menu selection lists all the **cron** jobs you have scheduled and allows you to *Add, Zoom, Remove*, and *Modify* **cron** jobs through the *Actions* menu. **cron** was described earlier in this chapter in "Backup and Recovery." I have included some of the **cron** background covered earlier to save you the trouble of flipping back.

The **crontab** file is used to schedule jobs that are automatically executed by **cron**. **crontab** files are in the **/var/spool/cron/crontabs** directory.

cron is a program that runs other programs at the specified time. **cron** reads files that specify the operation to be performed and the date and time it is to be performed.

The format of entries in the **crontab** file is as follows:

minute   hour monthday   month   weekday   user name   command

minute - the minute of the hour, from 0-59
hour - the hour of the day, from 0-23
monthday - the day of the month, from 1-31
month - the month of the year, from 1-12
weekday - the day of the week, from 0 (Sunday) - 6 (Saturday)
user name - the user who will run the command if necessary
command - specifies the command line or script file to run

You have many options in the **crontab** file for specifying the *minute, hour, monthday, month,* and *weekday* to perform a task. You could list one entry in a field and then a space, several entries in any field separated by a comma, two entries separated by a dash indicating a range, or an asterisk, which corresponds to all possible entries for the field.

To list the contents of a **crontab** file, you would issue the **crontab -l** command.

Routine Tasks

The following subareas exist under *Routine Tasks* in SAM:

- Backup and Recovery

- Selective File Removal

- System Log Files

- System Shutdown

The hierarchy of *Routine Tasks* is shown in Figure 11-49. Please note that *Backup and Recovery* is identical to the SAM top-level *Backup and Recovery* area discussed earlier in this chapter.

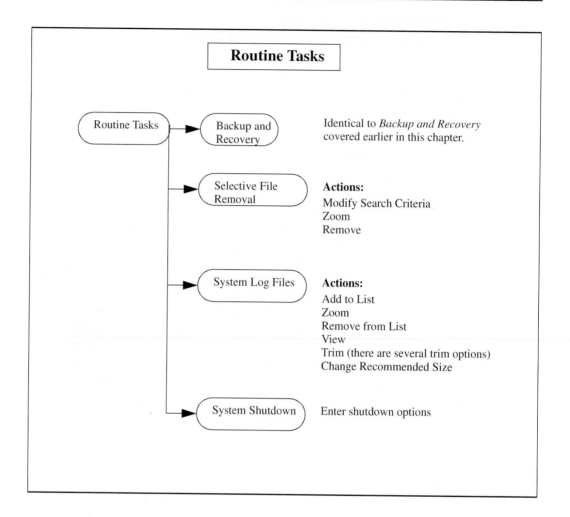

Figure 11-49 Routine Tasks Menu Structure

Backup and Recovery

This is identical to the *Backup and Recovery* area covered earlier in this chapter.

Selective File Removal

Selective File Removal allows you to search for files to remove. You can specify a variety of criteria for selecting files to remove including the following:

Type of file   There are three different file types you can search for: *Large Files, Unowned Files*, and *Core Files*. A pop-up menu allows you to select which of these to search for. With *Large Files,* you are searching for files of a minimum size that haven't been modified in the specified time. *Unowned Files* are files owned by someone other than a valid system user. *Core Files* contain a core image of a terminated process when the process was terminated under certain conditions. Core files are usually related to a problem with a process and contain such information as data, stack, etc.

Mount Points   Specify whether or not you want to search across non-NFS mount points. If you select *Yes,* this means that the search will include mount points on your system, but not extend to NFS mount points. I chose not to include other mount points in the example.

Beginning Path   Your search can begin at any point in the system hierarchy. You can specify the start point of the search in this field. If you want to search only the **/home** directory for files, then change this entry to **/home** and you will search only that directory, as I did in the example.

Minimum Size   Specify the smallest size file in bytes that you want to search for. Files smaller than this size will not be reported as part of the search. The minimum size in the example is 500,000 bytes.

Last Modification

If you select *Large Files*, you can make an entry in this field. You enter the minimum number of days since the file was last modified, and files that have been modified within that time period will be excluded from the search. This is *30* days in the example.

Figure 11-50 shows an example of specifying which files to search for:

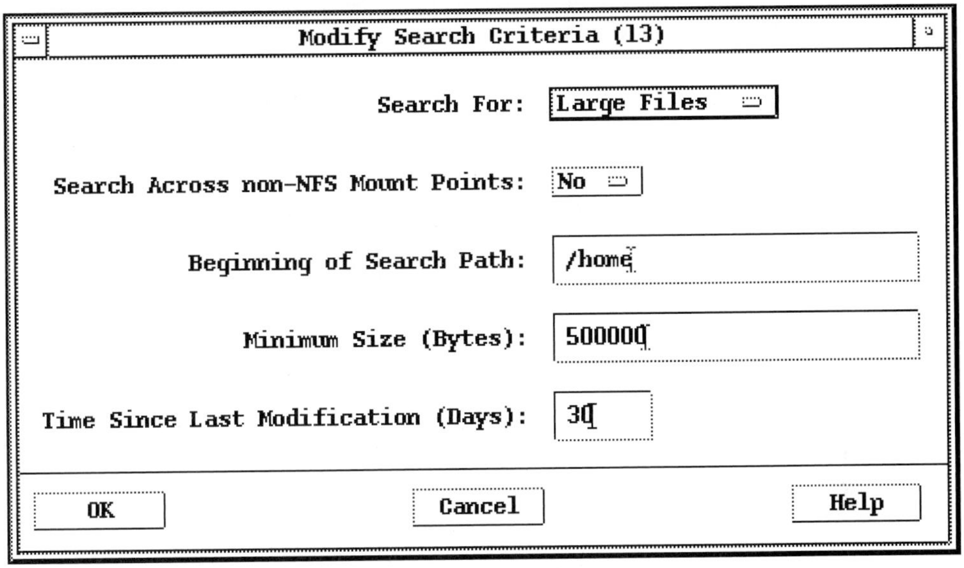

Figure 11-50 Searching for Files to Remove

The way to approach removing files is to start with an exceptionally large file size and work your way down in size. It may be that you have a few "unexpected" large files on your system that you can remove and ignore the smaller files.

System Log Files

System Log Files is used to manage the size of your system log files. Log files are generated by HP-UX for a variety of reasons, including backup, shutdown, **cron**, and so on. Your applications may very well be generating log files as well. Some of these log files can grow in size indefinitely, creating a potential catastrophe on your system by growing and crashing your system. You can be proactive and manage these log files in this subarea.

SAM is aware of many of the log files generated by HP-UX. When you enter the *System Log Files* subarea, information related to these log files is listed. You can add to the list of log files SAM knows about and have a complete list of log files presented to you each time you enter this subarea. SAM lists the following information related to log files each time you enter this subarea. (You may have to increase the size of the window to see all this information:)

File Name   The full path name of the log file.

Percent Full   SAM has what it thinks should be the maximum size of a log file. You can change this size by selecting *Change Recommended Size* from the *Actions* menu. The *Percent Full* is the percentage of the recommended size the log file consumes.

Current Size   The size of the file in bytes is listed for you. You may want to take a look at this. The current size of a log file may be much bigger than you would like. You could then change the recommended size and quickly see which files are greater than 100 percent. The converse may also be true. You may think the recommended size for a log file is far too small and change the recommended size to a larger value. In either case, you would like to quickly see which files are much bigger than recommended.

Recommended Size

                     This is what you define as the recommended size of the file. Check to make sure that you agree with this value.

Present on System

> *Yes* if this file is indeed present on your system; *No* if it is not present on your system. If a file is not present on your system and it simply does not apply to you, then you can select *Remove from List* from the *Actions* menu. For example, you may not be running UUCP and therefore want to remove all the UUCP related log files.

File Type

> The only file types listed are *ASCII* and *Non-ASCII*. I found it interesting that **/var/sam/log/samlog** was not one of the log files listed. This is not an ASCII file and must be viewed through *View SAM Log* from the *Actions* menu, but it is indeed a log file that I thought would appear in the list.

You can trim a log file using the *Trim* command from the *Actions* menu. You then have several options for trimming the file having to do with the size of the file when the trim is complete, and so on.

System Shutdown

SAM offers you the following three ways to shut down your system:

- *Halt the System*

- *Reboot (Restart) the System*

- *Go to Single-User State*

In addition, you can specify the number of minutes before shutdown occurs.

Run SAM on Remote Systems

I think SAM is great. If it works well on one system, then you, as the system administrator, may as well use it on other systems from a central point of control. *Run SAM on Remote Systems* allows you to set up the system on which you will run SAM remotely from a central point of control.

You can specify any number of remote systems to be controlled by a central system. With the *Actions* menu, you can elect among the following:

Add System   A window opens up in which you can specify the name of the remote system you wish to administer locally.

Run SAM   You can select the remote system on which you want to run SAM.

Remove System(s)

Remote systems can be removed from the list of systems on which you will run SAM remotely.

Software Management

Software Management under SAM uses Software Distributor-HP-UX (I'll call this Software Distributor), which was covered in detail in Chapter 1. SAM is giving you an interface to Software Distributor that allows you to perform software management by selecting the task you want to perform. In the end, all of the same Software Distributor commands are run, so I won't cover those again in this section. The following subareas exist under *Software Management* in SAM:

• Copy Software to Depot

- Install Software to Local Host

- List Software

- Remove Software

The hierarchy of *Software Management* is shown in Figure 11-51:

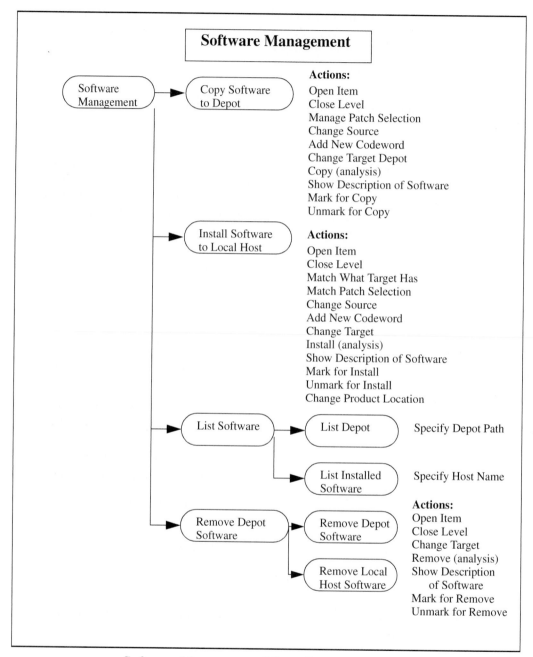

Figure 11-51 *Software Management* Menu Structure

As you can see from this diagram, when you select a task you want to perform, SAM is selecting the Software Distributor command to run. Chapter 1 covers many of these commands.

Time

The *Time* area of SAM allows you to configure Network Time Protocol, or NTP, and set the system clock. NTP is a service that allows you to synchronize the time on all your systems utilizing a Universal Coordinated Time server. I won't cover this area of SAM other than to say that NTP can be a little tricky to configure, so using SAM for this greatly simplifies NTP.

NFS Diskless Concepts

Rather than cover NFS Diskless as an area to manage, I'm going to deviate from the format found throughout this chapter and instead provide a brief description of NFS Diskless.

This topic was introduced with HP-UX 10.x. Diskless nodes were implemented with Distributed HP-UX (DUX) in HP-UX 9.x and earlier releases. Distributed HP-UX was first introduced in HP-UX 6.0 in 1986 and was successfully used in many HP installations. The new implementation of diskless nodes as of HP-UX 10.x is NFS Diskless. It has many desirable features, including the following:

- NFS Diskless is the current de facto standard.

- It is not a proprietary solution.

- High-end diskless servers and clients can be symmetric multi-processing systems.

- Many file system types and features are available, such as UNIX File System, Journaled File System, Logical Volume Manager, disk mirroring, and so on.

- The System V Release 4 file system layout described throughout this book is implemented. This file system layout is conducive to extensive file sharing, which is used in NFS Diskless.

- Read-only NFS mounts, such as **/usr** and **/opt/**<*application*> are supported.

- Distributed HP-UX functionality, such as context-dependent files, has been removed.

- Servers can be both Series 700 and Series 800 units.

- The physical link doesn't matter, so servers can use many interfaces such as IEEE 802.3 and FDDI. A server can also assign some diskless systems to one network card, and other systems to other network cards.

- Diskless systems can boot across a gateway, thereby allowing subnets to be used.

- Booting is implemented with standard Boot Protocol (BOOTP) and Trivial File Transfer Protocol (TFTP) protocols.

- Clients can swap to a local disk or swap using NFS to a remote disk.

Many additional features of NFS Diskless exist; however, since our focus is on management, let's take a closer look at this. Using SAM, all tasks related to NFS Diskless administration can be performed. This means that you have a single point of administration for the cluster. You have cluster-wide resources, such as printers and file systems, that can be managed from any node in the cluster. You can defer some operations until a later point in time if a node is unreachable. And, of course, you can add and delete clients in SAM.

Using SAM, you get a single point of administration for several NFS Diskless systems. This means that performing an operation in SAM affects all systems in the cluster. The single point of administration areas in SAM include:

- Printers/Plotters

- File Systems

- Users/Groups

- Home Directories

- Electronic Mail

- Backups

Although a great deal could be covered on NFS Diskless and the many improvements in this area over Distributed HP-UX, the key point from an administrative perspective is that SAM provides a central point of administration for NFS Diskless administration. All tasks related to NFS Diskless administration can be performed through SAM.

ServiceControl Manager (SCM) Overview

SCM allows you to replicate tasks over multiple systems. Tasks that have traditionally been performed individually on many systems can now be performed across multiple systems in a cluster managed by SCM.

You can take a command or tool that runs on an individual system, such as the **find** or **df** command, dispatch it to run on multiple systems, and collect the results for review in SCM.

More advanced tools that were designed to run on multiple systems, such as Ignite-UX, can also be run in the same manner using SCM.

Specific tasks can be assigned to specific individuals with SCM, thus creating a role-based environment. This obviates the need for root access to systems because specific management activities are assigned to specific users on specific nodes. These user roles provide great flexibility in defining the tasks that individual users can perform.

You can define the systems of which an SCM cluster is composed. The Central Management Server (CMS) in an SCM environment is the focal point in which management takes place. Agents on the managed nodes communicate with CMS to perform management functions.

SCM is available on the applications media of 11i and loaded with Software Distributor like any other application.

After having loaded SCM from the Applications CD-ROM for HP-UX 11i, we'll run the program to set up SCM called **mxsetup**. Most of the programs related to SCM begin with *"mx"* and the application itself is loaded in **/opt/mx**, and the repository of SCM data is kept in **/var/opt/mx**.

```
# mxsetup

Please enter the ServiceControl repository password

Please re-enter the ServiceControl repository password

Please enter a name for your Managed Cluster
(default name: 'HP Managed Cluster'): servicecluster

Please enter the login name of the initial ServiceControl trusted user
martyp

Would you like mxsetup to backup the ServiceControl repository after
it has initially configured it?(Y/N) [Y]:

Please enter the file path where mxsetup will store the backup data
(default path: /var/opt/mx/data/scm.backup) :
```

```
   ----------------------------------------------------------------
   You have entered,

   ServiceControl Managed Cluster Name  : servicecluster
   Initial ServiceControl trusted user  : martyp
   Backup the ServiceControl repository : y
   Backup file path                     : /var/opt/mx/data/scm.backup
   ----------------------------------------------------------------
   Would you like to continue? (Y/N) [Y] :

Please enter the file path where mxsetup will store the backup data
(default path: /var/opt/mx/data/scm.backup) :

   ----------------------------------------------------------------
   You have entered,

   ServiceControl Managed Cluster Name  : servicecluster
   Initial ServiceControl trusted user  : martyp
   Backup the ServiceControl repository : y
   Backup file path                     : /var/opt/mx/data/scm.backup
   ----------------------------------------------------------------
   Would you like to continue? (Y/N) [Y] :

   ================================================================
   ServiceControl Manager configuration has '8' Tasks and
   it may take a while to do the configuration.

   Please wait while mxsetup configures the ServiceControl Manager...
   ================================================================

1: Creating Agent Depots..

2: Naming the ServiceControl Managed Cluster
   as  'servicecluster'....................... OK

3: Configuring the ServiceControl daemons......... OK

4: Starting the ServiceControl daemons............ OK

5: Installing the AgentConfig.................... OK

6: Initializing ServiceControl................... OK

7: Adding Tools ................................. OK

8: Backing up the Repository.................... OK

The ServiceControl Manager was successfully configured
Please see /var/opt/mx/logs/scmgr-setup.log for details.

To start the ServiceControl Manager:
    - set DISPLAY environment variable
    - and enter '/opt/mx/bin/scmgr'

#
```

After the setup is complete, you can issue a **ps** to view processes that begin with an *mx* to see the daemons started in order to run SCM.

With SCM having been set up, we can now run the graphical interface to it with **/opt/mx/bin/scmgr**, as shown in Figure 11-52:

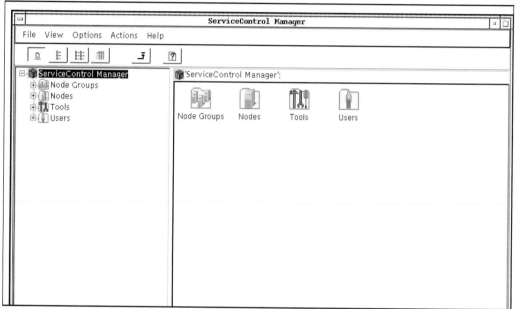

Figure 11-52   ServiceControl Manager *scmgr* Screen

The four icons shown are launch points for the tasks you'll perform in SCM as described below:

1. *Node Groups* provides a view of the managed nodes as groups. Once the node groups are displayed, a user can perform a task on a selected group of nodes.

2. *Nodes View* provides a view of all nodes that are managed. This is the point from which you can perform a variety of node-related tasks such as adding and removing nodes.

3. *Tools View* provides a view of SCM tools.

4. Users View provides a view of HP-UX users who are part of SCM. A trusted user can perform a variety of user-related tasks from this view, such as adding or removing users.

If all of your systems are 11i, you won't have to load any software on clients in order to manage them from the central SCM system. If you have 11.0 or 10.20 systems, additional software is required on client systems. You can obtain the *Planning, Installing, Configuring and Updating ServiceControl Manager* document from *docs.hp.com* which provides procedures for installing all SCM-related software.

In order to add managed nodes, you would go to the *Actions - New - Node...* menu pick and then select the nodes you wish to add.

Also under this menu pick is a tab area for *Users and Roles*. In Figure 11-53, we've added a user *martyp* with an *operator* role:

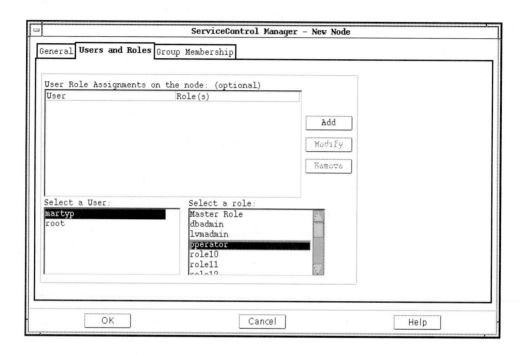

Figure 11-53 Selecting an *operator* Role for a User on a New Node

After adding nodes and grouping them, and adding users and defining their roles, you have set up the SCM management environment. You can use the pre-defined tools for users and add your own custom tools as well.

Figure 11-54 shows some of the software management tools that are predefined in SCM:

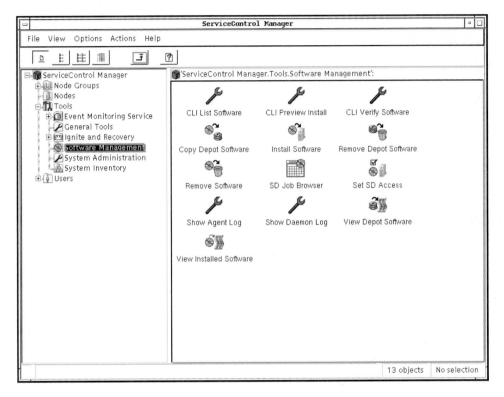

Figure 11-54 SCM *Software Management* Tools

The tools shown in Figure 11-54 are the default tools for software management. You can define and add your own tools as well. Note the categories of tools shown at the left-hand side of the figure.

From the graphical environment shown in Figure 11-54 you can launch into SCM-related work. You can also work with SCM from the command line. Table 11-3 lists some of the more commonly used SCM commands you can issue at the command line:

TABLE 11-3 Commonly Used SCM Commands

COMMAND	DESCRIPTION
mxauth	Add, remove, or list authorizations in SCM.
mxexec	Run an SCM tool.
mxngroup	Add, modify, remove, or list node groups in SCM.
mxnode	Add, remove, or list nodes in SCM.
mxrepositoryrestore	Restore the SCM repository.
mxrepositorysave	Back up the SCM repository.
mxrole	List or modify SCM roles.
mxsetup	Set up or uninstall the Central Management Server of an SCM-managed cluster.
mxtool	Add, modify, remove, or list tools in SCM.
mxuser	Add, modify, remove, or list users in SCM.

To view SCM roles, you would issue the following command:

```
# mxrole -lt

NAME            ENABLED?    DESCRIPTION
role16          true        For use by ServiceControl administrators
role15          true        For use by ServiceControl administrators
role14          true        For use by ServiceControl administrators
role13          true        For use by ServiceControl administrators
role12          true        For use by ServiceControl administrators
role11          true        For use by ServiceControl administrators
role10          true        For use by ServiceControl administrators
role9           true        For use by ServiceControl administrators
role8           true        For use by ServiceControl administrators
role7           true        For use by ServiceControl administrators
role6           true        For use by ServiceControl administrators
lvmadmin        true        A role for LVM Administrators
operator        true        A read-only role for operators
webadmin        true        A role for WEB Server Administrators
dbadmin         true        A role for Database Administrators
Master Role     true        The ServiceControl Master Role
#
```

This output shows the default roles that have been set up for SCM and a brief description of each. Since you can perform most any function you want in the graphical version of SCM, I don't expect you'll be running many functions at the command line; however, it's good to know these commands exist.

CHAPTER 12

Performance Topics

Performance and Virtual Partitions

In the upcoming sections we'll run some commands associated with performance analysis to see how the output of these differ from the output you would see on a non-vPars system. Since the commands we're going to cover are the basis for much performance analysis-related work, it is important to know what differences you'll see in the output of these commands. The non-vPars-specific part of this chapter covers performance analysis in general. Performance analysis on a vPar is performed in the same manner as performance analysis on a non-vPar system except that the output of some commands will not display all of the components on your system. Instead, only the components devoted to the vPar on which you're performing analysis will be displayed and analyzed. This is the area we'll focus on in the first part of this chapter, the output you'll see for some commonly used commands.

On a purely performance-related note, you do indeed have additional software running on your system with vPars, the Virtual Partition Monitor. Some of the resources on a vPars system are shared, in the sense that they're owned by the Virtual Partition Monitor rather than an individual vPar such as System Bus Adapters and the Memory Controller. The Virtual Partition software consumes a minimal amount of overall system resources. The components in a vPar are devoted exclusively to the operation of the vPar to which they are assigned. This means that when we run a performance analysis on a vPar, we are analyzing only the components devoted to the vPar.

Let's take a look at some commonly used performance analysis commands in the upcoming sections and see what the vPars outputs look like. This is by no means an exhaustive list of commands, but it will give you an idea of what you'll see with vPars.

sar and ioscan with Disks

Running **ioscan** on your vPars system will show you only the components that are contained in the vPar. The following **ioscan** searches for disks on a vPar named *cable1* and shows only the disks connected to the LBA *0/0. 0/0* was the lone I/O component of *cable1* when it was created with *-a io:0/0*:

```
# ioscan -funC disk
Class     I  H/W Path      Driver S/W State  H/W Type      Description
=======================================================================
disk      0  0/0/1/0.1.0   sdisk CLAIMED     DEVICE        HP      DVD-ROM 304
                           /dev/dsk/c0t1d0   /dev/rdsk/c0t1d0
disk      1  0/0/1/1.0.0   sdisk CLAIMED     DEVICE        SEAGATE ST173404LC
                           /dev/dsk/c1t0d0   /dev/rdsk/c1t0d0
disk      2  0/0/1/1.2.0   sdisk CLAIMED     DEVICE        SEAGATE ST173404LC
                           /dev/dsk/c1t2d0   /dev/rdsk/c1t2d0
disk      3  0/0/2/0.0.0   sdisk CLAIMED     DEVICE        SEAGATE ST173404LC
                           /dev/dsk/c2t0d0   /dev/rdsk/c2t0d0
disk      4  0/0/2/0.2.0   sdisk CLAIMED     DEVICE        SEAGATE ST173404LC
                           /dev/dsk/c2t2d0   /dev/rdsk/c2t2d0
#
```

This listing shows that the four internal disks are at SBA *0*, LBA *0*, and SCSI busses *1* and *2,* respectively. At the time of this writing these disks have to be in the same vPar because they are on the same LBA.

There are many more disks connected to this server beyond those shown in the previous listing, however; those disks are connected to LBAs that are not part of *cable1* and therefore don't appear in the listing.

The following output of **sar -d** shows only performance data for the one disk configured into *cable1*. The disk off which the other vPar on this system (*cable2*) is running at the time this output was produced is not shown in this output:

```
# sar -d 4 3

HP-UX cvhdcon3 B.11.11 U 9000/800     10/15/01

14:28:42   device   %busy   avque   r+w/s   blks/s   avwait   avserv
14:28:46   c1t2d0    0.25    0.50      1        3      0.49     8.29
14:28:50   c1t2d0    0.50    0.50      1        2      1.49     8.77
14:28:54

Average    c1t2d0    0.25    0.50      1        2      0.92     8.50
```

You would have to connect to the other vPar, in this case *cable2*, and run **ioscan** and **sar -d** to get a list of devices and performance data for the disk off which *cable2* is running. This is a clear example of the way in which vPars running on the same server are like separate servers. All of the vPars are running their own instance of HP-UX 11i and applications and must be analyzed as though they are separate servers.

uptime

uptime produces information about the time at which the system booted and some load data. Let's run this command for two different vPars running on the same server as shown below:

```
# hostname
cvhdcon3
# uptime
  2:32pm  up  3:02,  2 users,  load average: 2.26, 1.96, 1.60
#

# hostname
cvhdcon4
# uptime
  2:31pm  up  2:41,  2 users,  load average: 0.25, 0.22, 0.23
#
```

The information produced by **uptime** is vPar-specific. The first output we see in this output is the time at which the first vPar booted, and the second output is the time at which the second vPar booted. The other information in this output is also for the specific vPar on which **uptime** was run. Like most of the commands you'll execute when vPars are running, you'll see vPar-specific information, not system-specific information.

Next, we'll take a look at some networking commands in vPars.

Networking

Networking information produced by commands is also peculiar to the vPar on which you've issued the command. Networking configuration of vPars is covered in Chapter 13. Let's take a look at the network interface on two different vPars configured on the same server. First let's look at the output of vPar *cable1* with a hostname of *cvhdcon3*:

```
# hostname
cvhdcon3
# netstat -I lan0
Name     Mtu  Network          Address        Ipkts    Ierrs Opkts   Oerrs Coll
lan0     1500 172.16.15.0      cvhdcon3       12785    0     11855   0     3
#
# netstat -in
Name     Mtu  Network          Address        Ipkts    Ierrs Opkts   Oerrs Coll
lan0     1500 172.16.15.0      172.16.15.36   12990    0     12052   0     3
lo0      4136 127.0.0.0        127.0.0.1      7616     0     7616    0     0
#
# lanscan
Hardware Station           Crd Hdw   Net-Interface   NM   MAC        HP-DLPI DLPI
Path     Address           In# State NamePPA         ID   Type       Support Mjr#
0/0/0/0  0x00306E06F6BA    0   UP    lan0 snap0      1    ETHER      Yes     119
#
```

This output shows that *lan0* is the network interface devoted to vPar *cable1* on this server. The **lanscan** output shows that this interface has a hardware path of *0/0/0/0*. This is on the Core I/O card that was configured as a component of the vPar when it was created with *-a io:0/0*. The LAN interface on the Core I/O card was not explicitly called out when *cable1* was created because *0/0/0/0* is an implied component of the Core I/O card at *0/0*.

Let's now take a look at the second vPar running on this server, called *cable2* with a hostname of *cvhdcon4*:

```
# hostname
cvhdcon4
# netstat -I lan1
Name     Mtu  Network          Address        Ipkts    Ierrs Opkts   Oerrs Coll
lan1     1500 172.16.14.0      cvhdcon4       3463     0     1603    0     2
#
# netstat -in
```

```
Name      Mtu  Network        Address       Ipkts Ierrs Opkts Oerrs Coll
lan1      1500 172.16.14.0    172.16.14.44  3819  0     1948  0     2
lo0       4136 127.0.0.0      127.0.0.1     916   0     916   0     0
#
# lanscan
Hardware Station        Crd Hdw  Net-Interface NM  MAC    HP-DLPI DLPI
Path     Address        In# State NamePPA       ID  Type   Support Mjr#
0/10/0/0 0x00306E0653E8 1   UP   lan1 snap1    1   ETHER  Yes     119
#
```

This output shows that *lan1* is the network interface devoted to vPar *cable2* on this server. The **lanscan** output shows that this interface has a hardware path of *0/10/0/0*. The LBA of *0/10* was configured as a component of the vPar when it was created with *-a io:0/10/*. Unlike the LAN interface on the Core I/O card that was an implied component, this LAN interface is in a separate PCI slot and LBA and therefore had to be specified explicitly when the vPar was created.

Running **lanadmin** on *cable1* produces more detailed output related to *lan0*, as shown in the following listing:

```
# lanadmin

          LOCAL AREA NETWORK ONLINE ADMINISTRATION, Version 1.0
                    Mon, Oct 15,2001  14:41:23

              Copyright 1994 Hewlett Packard Company.
                    All rights are reserved.

Test Selection mode.

        lan     = LAN Interface Administration
        menu    = Display this menu
        quit    = Terminate the Administration
        terse   = Do not display command menu
        verbose = Display command menu

Enter command: lan

LAN Interface test mode. LAN Interface PPA Number = 0

        clear   = Clear statistics registers
        display = Display LAN Interface status and statistics registers
        end     = End LAN Interface Administration, return to Test Selection
        menu    = Display this menu
        ppa     = PPA Number of the LAN Interface
        quit    = Terminate the Administration, return to shell
        reset   = Reset LAN Interface to execute its selftest
        specific = Go to Driver specific menu

Enter command: d
                    LAN INTERFACE STATUS DISPLAY
                    Mon, Oct 15,2001  14:42:33

PPA Number                 = 0
Description                = lan0 HP PCI 10/100Base-TX Core [100BASE-TX,HD,AUTO,TT=1500
Type (value)               = ethernet-csmacd(6)
MTU Size                   = 1500
Speed                      = 100000000
Station Address            = 0x306e06f6ba
```

```
Administration Status (value)     = up(1)
Operation Status (value)          = up(1)
Last Change                       = 755
Inbound Octets                    = 2101014
Inbound Unicast Packets           = 9830
Inbound Non-Unicast Packets       = 1692
Inbound Discards                  = 0
Inbound Errors                    = 0
Inbound Unknown Protocols         = 772
Outbound Octets                   = 1184028
Outbound Unicast Packets          = 9613
Outbound Non-Unicast Packets      = 8
Outbound Discards                 = 0
Outbound Errors                   = 0
Outbound Queue Length             = 0
Specific                          = 655367

Press <Return> to continue
```

This **lanadmin** output shows *lan0* as the configured LAN interface on *cable1*. Let's now run **lanadmin** on *cable2* and see for what LAN interface it produces an output:

```
# lanadmin


            LOCAL AREA NETWORK ONLINE ADMINISTRATION, Version 1.0
                    Mon, Oct 15,2001  14:41:23

              Copyright 1994 Hewlett Packard Company.
                    All rights are reserved.

Test Selection mode.

        lan       = LAN Interface Administration
        menu      = Display this menu
        quit      = Terminate the Administration
        terse     = Do not display command menu
        verbose   = Display command menu

Enter command: lan

LAN Interface test mode. LAN Interface PPA Number = 1

        clear     = Clear statistics registers
        display   = Display LAN Interface status and statistics registers
        end       = End LAN Interface Administration, return to Test Selection
        menu      = Display this menu
        ppa       = PPA Number of the LAN Interface
        quit      = Terminate the Administration, return to shell
        reset     = Reset LAN Interface to execute its selftest
        specific  = Go to Driver specific menu

Enter command: d

                    LAN INTERFACE STATUS DISPLAY
                    Mon, Oct 15,2001  14:40:48

PPA Number                        = 1
Description                       = lan1 HP A5230A/B5509BA PCI 10/100Base-TX Addon 100BASE-TX
Type (value)                      = ethernet-csmacd(6)
MTU Size                          = 1500
Speed                             = 100000000
Station Address                   = 0x306e0653e8
Administration Status (value)     = up(1)
Operation Status (value)          = up(1)
Last Change                       = 726
Inbound Octets                    = 4329654
Inbound Unicast Packets           = 3157
```

```
Inbound Non-Unicast Packets    = 23708

Inbound Discards               = 0

Inbound Errors                 = 0

Inbound Unknown Protocols      = 20720

Outbound Octets                = 401517

Outbound Unicast Packets       = 3189

Outbound Non-Unicast Packets   = 7

Outbound Discards              = 0

Outbound Errors                = 0

Outbound Queue Length          = 0

Specific                       = 655367


Press <Return> to continue
```

This **lanadmin** output shows *lan1* as the configured LAN interface on *cable2*.

Producing information specific to the vPar in which you issue a command is what you can expect when working at the command line with vPars.

Next, let's take a look at a couple of GlancePlus/UX outputs.

HP GlancePlus/UX

Working with Glance in vPars is identical to working with Glance on a non-vPars system, except with vPars you will see in Glance only the components that are assigned to the vPar you are analyzing. This means that if you're running two vPars on a system, you would run Glance in whatever vPar in which you want to perform analysis.

Figure 12-1 shows a Glance screen shot of vPar *cable1*, which has a hostname of *cvhdcon3*:

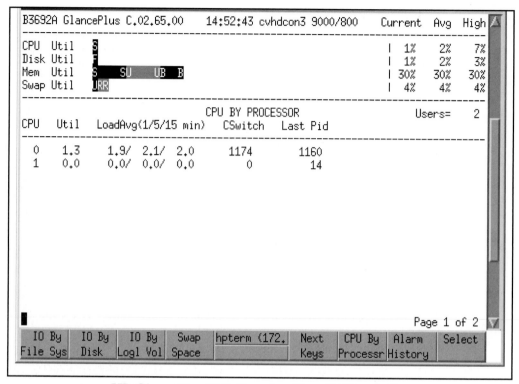

Figure 12-1 HP GlancePlus/UX Showing Two CPUs of vPar

Figure 12-1 shows that there are two CPUs present in this vPar. The system on which this vPar is running is a four-processor L-Class system. The vPar was configured with only two CPUs, so even though this is a four-processor system only two are shown in the Glance screen shot of this vPar. Where are the other processors you ask? It may be that the vPar(s) in which the other processors are configured are not even running, so the CPUs my be unused at this time. It may be that the other vPar(s) are up-and-running and one or two additional CPUs, depending on how the additional vPar(s) are configured, are in use. If the other vPar(s) are running, invoking Glance in those vPars would show the additional CPU(s) in use.

The other components of which your vPar is comprised will also be shown in Glance. Figure 12-2 shows the disks of vPar *cable1*:

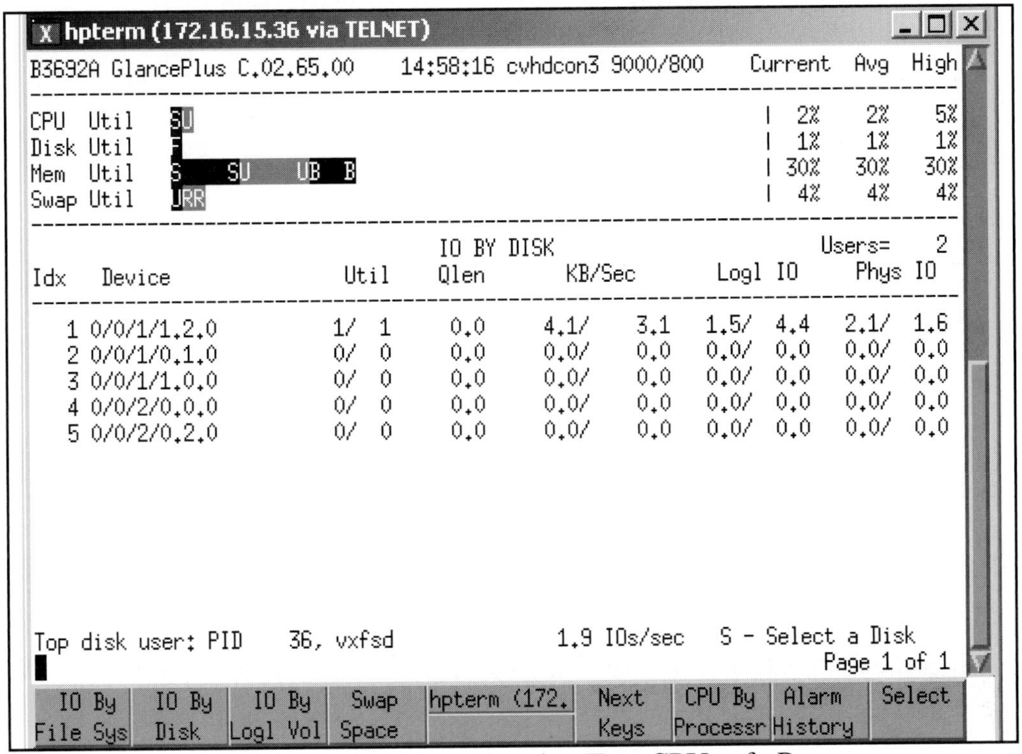

```
 X  hpterm (172.16.15.36 via TELNET)                          _ □ X
B3692A GlancePlus C.02.65.00    14:58:16 cvhdcon3 9000/800    Current  Avg  High

CPU  Util  SU                                            |   2%    2%    5%
Disk Util  F                                             |   1%    1%    1%
Mem  Util  S     SU     UB   B                           |  30%   30%   30%
Swap Util  URR                                           |   4%    4%    4%
-----------------------------------------------------------------------------
                             IO BY DISK                          Users=   2
Idx   Device          Util   Qlen    KB/Sec      Logl IO      Phys IO

  1 0/0/1/1.2.0       1/ 1    0.0   4.1/  3.1   1.5/ 4.4    2.1/ 1.6
  2 0/0/1/0.1.0       0/ 0    0.0   0.0/  0.0   0.0/ 0.0    0.0/ 0.0
  3 0/0/1/1.0.0       0/ 0    0.0   0.0/  0.0   0.0/ 0.0    0.0/ 0.0
  4 0/0/2/0.0.0       0/ 0    0.0   0.0/  0.0   0.0/ 0.0    0.0/ 0.0
  5 0/0/2/0.2.0       0/ 0    0.0   0.0/  0.0   0.0/ 0.0    0.0/ 0.0




Top disk user: PID   36, vxfsd              1.9 IOs/sec   S - Select a Disk
█                                                           Page 1 of 1
 IO By   IO By   IO By   Swap  hpterm (172.  Next   CPU By  Alarm   Select
File Sys  Disk  Logl Vol Space              Keys  Processr History
```

Figure 12-2 HP GlancePlus/UX Showing Two CPUs of vPar

This is the same list of disks as we saw for *cable1* in the **ioscan -funC disk** output. Only the first disk shown in Figure 12-2 has been included in the vPar for which the Glance screen shot was produced. The other devices shown are also connected to the SCSI channels that are part of the Core I/O card that was included when the vPar was created with *-a io:0/0*. The boot disk was explicitly included when the vPar was created with *-a io:0.0.1.1.2.0:BOOT,* so you would expect it to be shown in Glance. The other devices are part of the vPar also because they are part LBA at *0/0*. There are other implied components of this vPar as well, including the LAN interface at *0/0/0/0* and the console at *0/0/4/0*. For more information on how vPars were created please see Chapter 2 as well as the tear-out card included in this book.

The remainder of this chapter includes background information on commands and tools used for performance analysis.

Non-vPar-Specific Section of Chapter: Introduction

You can take a variety of approaches to performance analysis on your system. These choices range from quick snapshots that take but a few seconds to create, to long-range capacity planning programs that you may want to run for weeks or months before you even begin to analyze the data they produce. This chapter contains examples from a variety of systems, including HP-UX 11i systems. I left in the examples from non-HP-UX systems because some readers of my books are coming from UNIX variants other than HP-UX. Most of the HP-UX examples in this chapter have been updated to reflect 11i systems, however, I'm not aware of any differences between these performance examples on 11i vs. 11.0.

In this chapter, we'll focus on some commonly used UNIX commands and a couple of advanced tools that run on several UNIX variants. These are by no means an exhaustive list of UNIX commands and tools related to performance management; however, I provide enough good information to give you an overview. Your UNIX system may support additional commands and have advanced performance analysis tools. This chapter will give a good overview of performance analysis, including examples of the most commonly used UNIX performance-related commands.

Standard UNIX Commands

To begin, let's look at some commands you can issue from the UNIX prompt to give you some information about your system. The commands I'll cover are:

- **iostat**
- **vmstat**
- **netstat**
- **ps**
- **kill**
- **showmount**
- **swapinfo and swap**
- **sar**

We'll first look at each of these commands so that you get an understanding of the output produced by them and how this output may be used. There are online manual pages for many of the commands covered on your HP-UX system.

Please keep in mind that, like all topics we have covered, the output of these commands may differ somewhat among UNIX variants. The basic information produced on most UNIX variants is the same; however, the format of the outputs may differ somewhat. This usually is not significant if you're viewing the outputs; however, if you're writing programs that accept these outputs and manipulate them in some way, then the format of the outputs is important.

I/O and CPU Statistics with iostat

The **iostat** command gives you an indication of the level of effort the CPU is putting into I/O and the amount of I/O taking place among your disks and terminals. **iostat** provides a lot of useful information; however, it acts somewhat differently among UNIX variants. The following examples show issuing **iostat** on a Solaris system, an HP-UX system, and an AIX system. **iostat** was not supported on the Linux system I was using for this chapter. Note that on some systems, using the *-t* option for terminal information produces just terminal information, and on some systems it produces a full output. You will, of course, have to determine the best options for your needs on your UNIX variant. The following examples show the **iostat** command:

Here is a Solaris example executed ten times at five-second intervals:

```
# iostat 5 10
        tty          fd0           sd1           sd3           sd6            cpu
 tin tout kps tps serv kps tps serv kps tps serv kps tps serv us sy wt id
   0    0   0   0    0   0   0    0   3   0   57   0  79    0   0  7 49 43
   0   47   0   0    0   0   0    0  14   2   75   0   0    0   0  2  0 98
   0   16   0   0    0   0   0    0   0   0    0   0   0    0   0  1  0 98
   0   16   0   0    0   0   0    0   0   0    0   0   0    0   0  2  0 98
   0   16   0   0    0   0   0    0   0   0    0   0   0    0   0  0  0 100
   0   16   0   0    0   0   0    0   0   0    0   0   0    0   0  0  0 100
   0   16   0   0    0   0   0    0   0   0    0   0   0    0   0  1  0 99
   0   16   0   0    0   0   0    0   0   0    0   0   0    0   0  0  0 100
   0   16   0   0    0   0   0    0   6   1   35   0   0    0   0  4  0 96
   0   16   0   0    0   0   0    0   0   0    0   0   0    0   0  0  0 100
```

An HP-UX example includes the *-t* option executed five times at five-second intervals:

```
# iostat -t 5 5
                     tty                cpu
               tin tout          us  ni  sy  id
                1    58           5   1  10  84

   device    bps      sps     msps

   c1t2d0      0      0.0      1.0


                     tty                cpu
               tin tout          us  ni  sy  id
                0    30           0   2  26  72

   device    bps      sps     msps

   c1t2d0    484    249.6      1.0


                     tty                cpu
               tin tout          us  ni  sy  id
                0    31           1   3  23  73

   device    bps      sps     msps

   c1t2d0    517    256.1      1.0


                     tty                cpu
               tin tout          us  ni  sy  id
                0    35           0   2  23  75

   device    bps      sps     msps

   c1t2d0    456    254.4      1.0


                     tty                cpu
               tin tout          us  ni  sy  id
                0   744           1   6  38  55

   device    bps      sps     msps

   c1t2d0    155     83.1      1.0


#
```

Here is an AIX example executed ten times at five-second intervals:

```
# iostat 5 10

tty:      tin           tout     avg-cpu:  % user   % sys    % idle   % iowait
          0.0            0.0                  0.3     1.0      98.4      0.3

Disks:        % tm_act      Kbps       tps    Kb_read   Kb_wrtn
hdisk0          0.4          2.7       0.4    2366635    959304
hdisk1          0.0          0.0       0.0      18843     37928
hdisk2          0.1          0.6       0.1     269803    423284
```

```
hdisk3          0.0       0.0       0.0      20875        172
cd0             0.0       0.0       0.0         14          0

tty:    tin         tout   avg-cpu:  % user   % sys    % idle    % iowait
        0.0        108.2               0.0     0.2      99.8       0.0

Disks:       % tm_act      Kbps      tps   Kb_read   Kb_wrtn
hdisk0          0.0       0.0       0.0         0          0
hdisk1          0.0       0.0       0.0         0          0
hdisk2          0.0       0.0       0.0         0          0
hdisk3          0.0       0.0       0.0         0          0
cd0             0.0       0.0       0.0         0          0

tty:    tin         tout   avg-cpu:  % user   % sys    % idle    % iowait
        0.0        108.4               0.2     0.8      99.0       0.0

Disks:       % tm_act      Kbps      tps   Kb_read   Kb_wrtn
hdisk0          0.0       0.0       0.0         0          0
hdisk1          0.0       0.0       0.0         0          0
hdisk2          0.0       0.0       0.0         0          0
hdisk3          0.0       0.0       0.0         0          0
cd0             0.0       0.0       0.0         0          0

tty:    tin         tout   avg-cpu:  % user   % sys    % idle    % iowait
        0.0        108.4               0.4     0.2      99.4       0.0

Disks:       % tm_act      Kbps      tps   Kb_read   Kb_wrtn
hdisk0          0.0       0.0       0.0         0          0
hdisk1          0.0       0.0       0.0         0          0
hdisk2          0.0       0.0       0.0         0          0
hdisk3          0.0       0.0       0.0         0          0
cd0             0.0       0.0       0.0         0          0

tty:    tin         tout   avg-cpu:  % user   % sys    % idle    % iowait
        0.0        108.2               0.4     0.6      99.0       0.0

Disks:       % tm_act      Kbps      tps   Kb_read   Kb_wrtn
hdisk0          0.0       0.0       0.0         0          0
hdisk1          0.0       0.0       0.0         0          0
hdisk2          0.0       0.0       0.0         0          0
hdisk3          0.0       0.0       0.0         0          0
cd0             0.0       0.0       0.0         0          0

tty:    tin         tout   avg-cpu:  % user   % sys    % idle    % iowait
        0.0        108.4               0.0     0.4      99.6       0.0

Disks:       % tm_act      Kbps      tps   Kb_read   Kb_wrtn
hdisk0          0.0       0.0       0.0         0          0
hdisk1          0.0       0.0       0.0         0          0
hdisk2          0.0       0.0       0.0         0          0
hdisk3          0.0       0.0       0.0         0          0
cd0             0.0       0.0       0.0         0          0

tty:    tin         tout   avg-cpu:  % user   % sys    % idle    % iowait
        0.0        108.4               0.6     0.0      99.4       0.0

Disks:       % tm_act      Kbps      tps   Kb_read   Kb_wrtn
hdisk0          0.0       0.0       0.0         0          0
hdisk1          0.0       0.0       0.0         0          0
hdisk2          0.0       0.0       0.0         0          0
hdisk3          0.0       0.0       0.0         0          0
cd0             0.0       0.0       0.0         0          0

tty:    tin         tout   avg-cpu:  % user   % sys    % idle    % iowait
        0.0        108.2               0.2     0.8      99.0       0.0

Disks:       % tm_act      Kbps      tps   Kb_read   Kb_wrtn
hdisk0          0.0       0.0       0.0         0          0
hdisk1          0.0       0.0       0.0         0          0
hdisk2          0.0       0.0       0.0         0          0
hdisk3          0.0       0.0       0.0         0          0
cd0             0.0       0.0       0.0         0          0

tty:    tin         tout   avg-cpu:  % user   % sys    % idle    % iowait
        0.0        108.4               0.4     0.0      99.6       0.0
```

```
Disks:          % tm_act     Kbps      tps    Kb_read    Kb_wrtn
hdisk0            0.0         0.0       0.0        0          0
hdisk1            0.0         0.0       0.0        0          0
hdisk2            0.0         0.0       0.0        0          0
hdisk3            0.0         0.0       0.0        0          0
cd0               0.0         0.0       0.0        0          0

tty:        tin          tout    avg-cpu:  % user    % sys    % idle    % iowait
            0.0         108.4                0.4       0.4      99.2        0.0

Disks:          % tm_act     Kbps      tps    Kb_read    Kb_wrtn
hdisk0            0.0         0.0       0.0        0          0
hdisk1            0.0         0.0       0.0        0          0
hdisk2            0.0         0.0       0.0        0          0
hdisk3            0.0         0.0       0.0        0          0
cd0               0.0         0.0       0.0        0          0
```

Here are descriptions of the reports you receive with **iostat** for terminals, the CPU, and mounted file systems. Because the reports are somewhat different, I have included detailed information from the HP-UX output. A more detailed description of these fields is included in the **iostat** online manual page available on your HP-UX system. Most of the fields appear in the outputs; however, the outputs of the commands differ somewhat among UNIX variants.

For every terminal you have connected (*tty*), you see a "tin" and "tout," which represent the number of characters read from your terminal and the number of characters written to your terminal, respectively.

For your CPU, you see the percentage of time spent in user mode ("us"), the percentage of time spent running user processes at a low priority called nice ("ni"), the percentage of time spent in system mode ("sy"), and the percentage of time the CPU is idle ("id").

For every locally mounted file system, you receive information on the kilobytes transferred per second ("bps"), number of seeks per second ("sps"), and number of milliseconds per average seek ("msps"). For disks that are NFS-mounted or disks on client nodes of your server, you will not receive a report; **iostat** reports only on locally mounted file systems.

When viewing the output of **iostat**, there are some parameters to take note of.

First, note that the time that your CPU is spending in the four categories shown. The CPU report is produced with the *-t* option. I have worked on systems with poor performance that the administrator assumed to be a result of a slow CPU because the "id" number was very high, indicating that the CPU was actually idle most of the time. If the CPU is mostly idle, the chances are that the bottleneck is not the CPU, but may be I/O, memory, or networking. If the CPU is indeed busy most of the time ("id" is very low), see whether any processes are running "nice" (check the "ni" number). It may be that there are some background processes consuming a lot of CPU time that can be changed to run "nice."

Second, compare the number of transfers taking place. These are usually indicated by something like blocks per second (bps), transfers per second (*tps*), or seeks per second (*sps*). These numbers give an indication of the amount of activity taking place on a disk. If one volume is consistently much higher than other volumes, then it may be performing an inordinate amount of the workload. Notice on HP-UX that the milliseconds per average seek (*msps*) for all disks is always equal to one.

Virtual Memory Statistics with vmstat

vmstat provides virtual memory statistics. It provides information on the status of processes, virtual memory, paging activity, faults, and a breakdown of the percentage of CPU time. **vmstat** acts somewhat differently among UNIX variants. The following examples show issuing **vmstat** on a Solaris system, an HP-UX system, an AIX system, and a Linux system. You will, of course, have to determine the best options for your needs on your UNIX variant. In the following examples, the output was produced nine times at five-second intervals. The first argument to the **vmstat** command is the interval; the second is the number of times you would like the output produced.

Solaris example:

```
# vmstat 5 9
 procs     memory            page            disk          faults      cpu
 r b w   swap  free  re  mf pi po fr de sr f0 s1 s3 s6   in   sy   cs us sy id
 0 0 0    4480  4696   0   0  1  0  0  0  0  0  0  0 79  864  130  297  0  7 92
 0 0 0 133020  5916   0   3  0  0  0  0  0  0  0  3  0  102   42   24  0  2 98
 0 0 0 133020  5916   0   0  0  0  0  0  0  0  0  0  0   70   48   24  0  0 100
 0 0 0 133020  5916   0   0  0  0  0  0  0  0  0  0  0   74   42   24  0  0 100
 0 0 0 133020  5916   0   0  0  0  0  0  0  0  0  0  0   35   45   23  0  0 99
 0 0 0 133020  5916   0   0  0  0  0  0  0  0  0  0  0   65   66   26  0  0 100
 0 0 0 133020  5916   0   0  0  0  0  0  0  0  0  0  0   52   44   23  0  1 99
 0 0 0 133020  5916   0   0  0  0  0  0  0  0  0  0  0   53   54   24  0  1 99
 0 0 0 133020  5916   0   0  0  0  0  0  0  0  0  1  0   60   53   25  0  2 98
```

HP-UX example:

```
# vmstat 5 9

 procs       memory              page                   faults       cpu
 r  b  w    avm    free   re  at  pi   po   fr   de   sr   in     sy    cs  us sy id
 5 240 0 17646   3979    2   0   0    0    0    0    0    0    778   193  17  3 80
 4 242 0 16722   4106    0   0   0    0    0    0    0  814  20649   258  89 10  2
 4 240 0 16649   4106    0   0   0    0    0    0    0   83  18384   218  91  9  0
 4 240 0 16468   4106    0   0   0    0    0    0    0  792  19552   273  89 11  1
```

```
5 239 0 15630    4012    9   0   0   0   0   0   0   804  18295   270  93   8  -1
5 241 0 16087    3934    6   0   0   0   0   0   0   920  21044   392  89  10   0
5 241 0 15313    3952   11   0   0   0   0   0   0   968  20239   431  90  10   0
4 242 0 16577    4043    3   0   0   0   0   0   0   926  19230   409  89  10   0
6 238 0 17453    4122    0   0   0   0   0   0   0   837  19269   299  89   9   2
```

AIX example:

```
martyp $ vmstat 5 9
kthr      memory                    page                  faults           cpu
-----  -----------  ------------------------  ------------  -----------
 r  b    avm   fre  re  pi  po  fr   sr  cy   in   sy   cs  us sy id wa
 0  0  16604   246   0   0   0   0    2   0  149   79   36   0  1 98  0
 0  0  16604   246   0   0   0   0    0   0  153  125   41   0  0 99  0
 0  0  16604   246   0   0   0   0    0   0  143   83   33   0  0 99  0
 0  0  16604   246   0   0   0   0    0   0  140   94   35   0  1 99  0
 0  0  16604   246   0   0   0   0    0   0  166   62   32   0  0 99  0
 0  0  16604   246   0   0   0   0    0   0  150  102   38   1  0 99  0
 0  0  16604   246   0   0   0   0    0   0  183   78   34   0  0 99  0
 0  0  16604   246   0   0   0   0    0   0  132   87   33   0  1 99  0
 0  0  16604   246   0   0   0   0    0   0  147   84   38   0  0 99  0
```

Linux example:

```
# vmstat 5 5
   procs                  memory      swap        io      system        cpu
 r  b  w   swpd   free   buff  cache  si   so    bi   bo   in    cs   us  sy  id
 1  0  0   9432   1160   656   12024   1    2    14    1  138   274    3   1  96
 1  0  0   9684    828   652   12148   0   50     0   14  205  8499   82  18   0
 1  0  0   9684    784   652   11508   0    0     0    1  103  8682   81  19   0
 1  0  0   9684    800   652   10996   0    0     0    0  101  8683   80  20   0
 0  0  0   9772    796   652    9824  12   18     3    4  160  6577   66  17  18
```

You certainly get a lot for your money out of the **vmstat** command. Here is a brief description of the categories of information produced by **vmstat**. I have included a description of the fields in the HP-UX example because of the manual page that appears at the end of this chapter for HP-UX. You can see, however, that the outputs are very similar.

Processes are classified into one of three categories: runnable ("r"), blocked on I/O or short-term resources ("b"), or swapped ("w").

Next you will see information about memory. "avm" is the number of virtual memory pages owned by processes that have run within the last 20 seconds. If this number is roughly the size of physical memory minus your kernel, then you are near forced paging. The "free" column indicates the number of pages on the system's free list. It doesn't mean that the process is finished running and these pages won't be accessed again; it just means that they have not been accessed recently. I suggest that you ignore this column.

Next is paging activity. The first field ("re") shows the pages that were reclaimed. These pages made it to the free list but were later referenced and had to be salvaged.

Next you see the number of faults in three categories: interrupts per second, which usually come from hardware ("in"), system calls per second ("sy"), and context switches per second ("cs").

The final output is CPU usage percentage for user ("us"), system ("sy"), and idle ("id"). This is not as complete as the **iostat** output, which also shows **nice** entries.

If you are running an I/O-intensive workload, you may indeed see a lot of activity in runnable processes ("r"), blocked processes("b"), and the runnable but swapped ("w") processes. If you have many runnable but swapped processes, then you probably have an I/O bottleneck.

Network Statistics with netstat

netstat provides information related to network statistics. Because network bandwidth has as much to do with performance as the CPU and memory in some networks, you want to get an idea of the level of network traffic you have.

I use two forms of **netstat** to obtain network statistics. The first is **netstat -i**, which shows the state of interfaces that are autoconfigured. Although **netstat -i** gives a good rundown of the primary LAN interface, such as the network it is on, its name, and so on, it does not show useful statistical information.

The following shows the output of **netstat -i**:

```
# netstat -i
```

Name	Mtu	Network	Address	Ipkts	Ierrs	Opkts	Oerrs	Col
lan0	1497	151.150	a4410.e.h.c	242194	120	107665	23	19884

netstat provides a concise output. Put another way, most of what you get from **netstat** is useful. Here is a description of the nine fields in the **netstat** example:

Name	The name of your network interface (Name), in this case, "lan0."
Mtu	The "maximum transmission unit," which is the maximum packet size sent by the interface card.
Network	The network address of the LAN to which the interface card is connected (151.150).
Address	The host name of your system. This is the symbolic name of your system as it appears in the **/etc/hosts** file if your networking is configured to use **/etc/hosts**.

Below is the statistical information. Depending on the system you are using, or revision of OS, you may not see some of these commands:

Ipkts	The number of packets received by the interface card, in this case, "lan0."
Ierrs	The number of errors detected on incoming packets by the interface card.
Opkts	The number of packets transmitted by the interface card.
Oerrs	The number of errors detected during the transmission of packets by the interface card.
Col	The number of collisions that resulted from packet traffic.

netstat provides cumulative data since the node was last powered up; therefore, you might have a long elapsed time over which data was accumulated. If you are interested in seeing useful statistical information, you can use **netstat** with different options. You can also specify an interval to report statistics. I usually ignore the first entry, because it shows all data since the system was last powered up. This means that the data includes non-prime hours when the system was idle. I prefer to view data at the time the system is working its hardest. The following examples show running **netstat -I** and specifying the *lan* interface for Solaris, HP-UX, and AIX. These outputs are nearly identical, although the name of the network interface does vary among UNIX variants. The **netstat** command is run at an interval of five seconds. The Linux version of this command, which is not shown, does not allow me to specify an interval.

Solaris example:

```
# netstat -I le0 5
     input   le0          output             input   (Total)      output
packets errs  packets errs  colls  packets errs  packets errs  colls
116817990 0     3299582 11899 1653100 116993185 0     3474777 11899 1653100
185       0   3       0     0      185       0   3       0     0
273       0   8       0     0      273       0   8       0     0
153       0   3       0     0      153       0   3       0     0
154       0   3       0     0      154       0   3       0     0
126       0   3       0     0      126       0   3       0     0
378       0   2       0     0      378       0   2       0     0
399       0   4       0     0      399       0   4       0     0
286       0   2       0     0      286       0   2       0     0
```

HP-UX example (10.x):

netstat -I lan0 5

(lan0)-> input		output			(Total)-> input		output		
packets	errs	packets	errs	colls	packets	errs	packets	errs	colls
269841735	27	256627585	1	5092223	281472199	27	268258048	1	5092223
1602	0	1238	0	49	1673	0	1309	0	49
1223	0	1048	0	25	1235	0	1060	0	25
1516	0	1151	0	42	1560	0	1195	0	42
1553	0	1188	0	17	1565	0	1200	0	17
2539	0	2180	0	44	2628	0	2269	0	44
3000	0	2193	0	228	3000	0	2193	0	228
2959	0	2213	0	118	3003	0	2257	0	118
2423	0	1981	0	75	2435	0	1993	0	75

AIX example:

```
# netstat -I en0 5
     input   (en0)        output             input   (Total)      output
packets  errs  packets errs colls  packets errs  packets errs colls
46333531 0    1785025 0    0      47426087 0    2913405 0    0
203      0    1       0    0      204      0    2       0    0
298      0    1       0    0      298      0    1       0    0
293      0    1       0    0      304      0    12      0    0
191      0    1       0    0      191      0    1       0    0
150      0    2       0    0      151      0    3       0    0
207      0    3       0    0      218      0    15      0    0
162      0    3       0    0      162      0    4       0    0
120      0    2       0    0      120      0    2       0    0
```

With this example, you get multiple outputs of what is taking place on the LAN interface, including the totals on the right side of the output. As I mentioned earlier, you may want to ignore the first output, because it includes information over a long time period. This may include a time when your network was idle, and therefore the data may not be important to you.

You can specify the network interface on which you want statistics reported by using **-I interface**; in the case of the example, it was   **-I** and either *le0*, *lan0*, or *en0*. An interval of five seconds was also used in this example.

Analyzing **netstat** statistical information is intuitive. You want to verify that the collisions (Colls) are much lower than the packets transmitted (Opkts). Collisions occur on output from your LAN interface. Every collision your LAN interface encounters slows down the network. You will get varying opinions about what is too many collisions. If your collisions are less than 5 percent of "Opkts," you're probably in good shape and better off spending your time analyzing some other system resource. If this number is high, you may want to consider segmenting your network in some way such as installing networking equipment between portions of the network that don't share a lot of data.

As a rule of thumb, if you reduce the number of packets you are receiving and transmitting ("Ipkts" and "Opkts"), then you will have less overall network traffic and fewer collisions. Keep this in mind as you plan your network or upgrades to your systems. You may want to have two LAN cards in systems that are in constant communication. That way, these systems have a "private" LAN over which to communicate and do not adversely affect the performance of other systems on the network. One LAN interface on each system is devoted to intrasystem communication. This provides a "tight" communication path among systems that usually act as servers. The second LAN interface is used to communicate with any systems that are usually clients on a larger network.

You can also obtain information related to routing with **netstat** (see Chapter 13). The *-r* option to **netstat** shows the routing tables, which you usually want to know about, and the *-n* option can be used to print network addresses as numbers rather than as names. In the following examples, **netstat** is issued with the *-r* option (this will be used when describing the **netstat** output) and the *-rn* options, so that you can compare the two outputs:

$ netstat -r

Routing tables Destination	Gateway	Flags	Refs	Use	Interface	Pmtu
hp700	localhost	UH	0	28	lo0	4608
default	router1	UG	0	0	lan0	4608
128.185.61	system1	U	347	28668	lan0	1500

$ netstat -rn

Routing tables Destination	Gateway	Flags	Refs	Use	Interface	Pmtu
127.0.0.1	127.0.0.1	UH	0	28	lo0	4608
default	128.185.61.1	UG	0	0	lan0	4608
128.185.61	128.185.61.2	U	347	28668	lan0	1500

With **netstat**, some information is provided about the router, which is the middle entry. The *-r* option shows information about routing, but there are many other useful options to this command are available. Of particular interest in this output is "Flags," which defines the type of routing that takes place. Here are descriptions of the most common flags, which may be different among UNIX variants, from the online manual page on my HP-UX system.

1=*U*   Route to a *network* via a gateway that is the local host itself.

3=*UG*   Route to a *network* via a gateway that is the remote host.

5=*UH*   Route to a *host* via a gateway that is the local host itself.

7=*UGH*   Route to a *host* via a remote gateway that is a host.

The first line is for the local host, or loopback interface called, *lo0* at address 127.0.0.1 (you can see this address in the **netstat -rn** example). The *UH* flags indicate that the destination address is the local host itself. This

Class A address allows a client and server on the same host to communicate with one another via TCP/IP. A datagram sent to the loopback interface won't go out onto the network; it will simply go through the loopback.

The second line is for the default route. This entry says to send packets to Router 1 if a more specific route can't be found. In this case, the router has a *UG* under *Flags*. Some routers are configured with a *U*; others, such as the one in this example, with a *UG.* I've found that I usually end up determining through trial and error whether a *U* or *UG* is required. If there is a *U* in *Flags* and I am unable to ping a system on the other side of a router, a *UG* entry usually fixes the problem.

The third line is for the system's network interface, *lan0*. This means to use this network interface for packets to be sent to 128.185.61.

Checking Processes with ps

Knowing about the processes running on your system, and knowing how to stop them, are important to both system administration and performance.

To find the answer to "What is my system doing?," use **ps -ef**. This command provides information about every running process on your system. If, for instance, you want to know whether NFS is running, you simply type **ps -ef** and look for NFS daemons. Although **ps** tells you every process that is running on your system, it doesn't provide a good summary of the level of system resources being consumed. I would guess that **ps** is the most often issued system administration command. There are a number of options you can use with **ps**. I normally use *e* and *f*, which provide information about every ("*e*") running process and lists this information in full ("*f*"). **ps** outputs are almost identical from system to system. The following three examples are from a Solaris, AIX, and HP-UX system, respectively:

Solaris example:

```
martyp $ ps -ef
    UID   PID  PPID  C    STIME TTY       TIME CMD
   root     0     0  0   Feb 18 ?         0:01 sched
   root     1     0  0   Feb 18 ?         1:30 /etc/init -
   root     2     0  0   Feb 18 ?         0:02 pageout
   root     3     0  1   Feb 18 ?       613:44 fsflush
   root  3065  3059  0   Feb 22 ?         5:10 /usr/dt/bin/sdtperfmeter -f -H -r
   root    88     1  0   Feb 18 ?         0:01 /usr/sbin/in.routed -q
   root   478     1  0   Feb 18 ?         0:00 /usr/lib/saf/sac -t 300
   root    94     1  0   Feb 18 ?         2:50 /usr/sbin/rpcbind
   root   150     1  0   Feb 18 ?         6:03 /usr/sbin/syslogd
   root    96     1  0   Feb 18 ?         0:00 /usr/sbin/keyserv
```

```
    root    144     1   0   Feb 18 ?          50:37 /usr/lib/autofs/automountd
    root   1010     1   0   Apr 12 ?           0:00 /opt/perf/bin/midaemon
    root    106     1   0   Feb 18 ?           0:02 /usr/lib/netsvc/yp/ypbind -broadt
    root    156     1   0   Feb 18 ?           0:03 /usr/sbin/cron
    root    176     1   0   Feb 18 ?           0:00 /usr/lib/lpsched
    root    129     1   0   Feb 18 ?           0:00 /usr/lib/nfs/lockd
  daemon    130     1   0   Feb 18 ?           0:01 /usr/lib/nfs/statd
    root  14798     1   0   Mar 09 ?          31:10 /usr/sbin/nscd
    root    133     1   0   Feb 18 ?           0:10 /usr/sbin/inetd -s
    root    197     1   0   Feb 18 ?           0:00 /usr/lib/power/powerd
    root    196     1   0   Feb 18 ?           0:35 /etc/opt/licenses/lmgrd.ste -c /d
    root    213     1   0   Feb 18 ?        4903:09 /usr/sbin/vold
    root    199   196   0   Feb 18 ?           0:03 suntechd -T  4 -c /etc/optd
    root    219     1   0   Feb 18 ?           0:08 /usr/lib/sendmail -bd -q15m
    root    209     1   0   Feb 18 ?           0:05 /usr/lib/utmpd
    root   2935   266   0   Feb 22 ?          48:08 /usr/openwin/bin/Xsun :0 -nobanna
    root  16795 16763   1   07:51:34 pts/4     0:00 ps -ef
    root   2963  2954   0   Feb 22 ?           0:17 /usr/openwin/bin/fbconsole
    root    479     1   0   Feb 18 console     0:00 /usr/lib/saf/ttymon -g -h -p sunc
    root  10976     1   0   Jun 01 ?           0:00 /opt/perf/bin/ttd
    root   7468     1   0   Feb 24 ?           0:13 /opt/perf/bin/pvalarmd
    root    266     1   0   Feb 18 ?           0:01 /usr/dt/bin/dtlogin -daemon
  martyp  16763 16761   0   07:46:46 pts/4     0:01 -ksh
    root  10995     1   0   Jun 01 ?           0:01 /opt/perf/bin/perflbd
    root    484   478   0   Feb 18 ?           0:00 /usr/lib/saf/ttymon
    root    458     1   0   Feb 18 ?          20:06 /usr/lib/snmp/snmpdx -y -c /etc/f
    root  16792  3059   0   07:50:37 ?         0:00 /usr/dt/bin/dtscreen -mode blank
    root    471     1   0   Feb 18 ?           0:07 /usr/lib/dmi/dmispd
    root    474     1   0   Feb 18 ?           0:00 /usr/lib/dmi/snmpXdmid -s
    root    485   458   0   Feb 18 ?         739:44 mibiisa -r -p 32874
    root   2954  2936   0   Feb 22 ?           0:01 /bin/ksh /usr/dt/bin/Xsession
    root   2936   266   0   Feb 22 ?           0:00 /usr/dt/bin/dtlogin -daemon
    root   3061  3059   0   Feb 22 ?           1:32 dtwm
    root   3058     1   0   Feb 22 pts/2       0:01 /usr/dt/bin/ttsession
    root    712   133   0   Feb 18 ?           0:01 rpc.ttdbserverd
    root  11001 11000   0                      0:01 <defunct>
    root   2938     1   0   Feb 22 ?           0:00 /usr/openwin/bin/fbconsole -d :0
    root   2999  2954   0   Feb 22 pts/2       0:16 /usr/dt/bin/sdt_shell -c      unt
    root   3059  3002   0   Feb 22 pts/2     283:35 /usr/dt/bin/dtsession
    root   3063  3059   0   Feb 22 ?           0:03 /usr/dt/bin/dthelpview -helpVolur
    root   3099  3062   0   Feb 22 ?           0:13 /usr/dt/bin/dtfile -geometry +700
    root  11000 10995   0   Jun 01 ?           0:02 /opt/perf/bin/agdbserver -t alar/
    root   3002  2999   0   Feb 22 pts/2       0:01 -ksh -c        unset DT;    DISPLg
    root    730   133   0   Feb 18 ?           1:37 rpc.rstatd
    root   3062  3059   0   Feb 22 ?           2:17 /usr/dt/bin/dtfile -geometry +700
    root   3067     1   0   Feb 22 ?           0:00 /bin/ksh /usr/dt/bin/sdtvolcheckm
    root   3000     1   0   Feb 22 ?           0:00 /usr/dt/bin/dsdm
    root   3078  3067   0   Feb 22 ?           0:00 /bin/cat /tmp/.removable/notify0
    root  10984     1   0   Jun 01 ?          12:42 /opt/perf/dce/bin/dced -b
    root  16761   133   0   07:46:45 ?         0:00 in.telnetd
  martyp $
```

AIX example:

```
martyp $ ps -ef
    UID    PID  PPID   C    STIME  TTY  TIME CMD
    root     1     0   0   Feb 24   -   5:07 /etc/init
    root  2208 15520   0   Feb 24   -   8:21 dtwm
    root  2664     1   0   Feb 24   -   0:00 /usr/dt/bin/dtlogin -daemon
    root  2882     1   0   Feb 24   - 158:41 /usr/sbin/syncd 60
    root  3376  2664   5   Feb 24   - 3598:41 /usr/lpp/X11/bin/X -D /usr/lib/
    root  3624  2664   0   Feb 24   -   0:00 dtlogin <:0>          -daemon
    root  3950     1   6   Feb 24   - 5550:30 /usr/lpp/perf/bin/llbd
    root  4144     1   0   Feb 24   -   0:00 /usr/lpp/perf/bin/midaemon
    root  4490     1   0   Feb 24   -   0:48 /usr/lpp/perf/bin/perflbd
    root  4906     1   0   Feb 24   -   0:00 /usr/lib/errdemon
    root  5172     1   0   Feb 24   -   0:00 /usr/sbin/srcmstr
    root  5724  5172   0   Feb 24   -   9:54 /usr/sbin/syslogd
    root  6242  5172   0   Feb 24   -   0:00 /usr/sbin/biod 6
    root  6450  5172   0   Feb 24   -   0:02 sendmail: accepting connections
```

```
root   6710   5172   0   Feb 24      -   7:34  /usr/sbin/portmap
root   6966   5172   0   Feb 24      -   0:23  /usr/sbin/inetd
root   7224   5172   0   Feb 24      -   1:09  /usr/sbin/timed -S
root   7482   5172   0   Feb 24      -  11:55  /usr/sbin/snmpd
root   8000      1   0   Feb 24      -   9:17  ovspmd
root   8516   8782   0   Feb 24      -   0:00  netfmt -CF
root   8782      1   0   Feb 24      -   0:00  /usr/OV/bin/ntl_reader 0 1 1 1
root   9036   8000   0   Feb 24      -  10:09  ovwdb -O -n5000
root   9288   8000   0   Feb 24      -   0:44  pmd -Au -At -Mu -Mt -m
root   9546   8000   0   Feb 24      -  20:05  trapgend -f
root   9804   8000   0   Feb 24      -   0:28  trapd
root  10062   8000   0   Feb 24      -   0:47  orsd
root  10320   8000   0   Feb 24      -   0:33  ovesmd
root  10578   8000   0   Feb 24      -   0:30  ovelmd
root  10836   8000   0   Feb 24      -  13:12  ovtopmd -O
root  11094   8000   0   Feb 24      -  17:50  netmon -P
root  11352   8000   0   Feb 24      -   0:02  snmpCollect
root  11954      1   0   Feb 24      -   1:22  /usr/sbin/cron
root  12140   5172   0   Feb 24      -   0:01  /usr/lib/netsvc/yp/ypbind
root  12394   5172   0   Feb 24      -   1:39  /usr/sbin/rpc.mountd
root  12652   5172   0   Feb 24      -   0:29  /usr/sbin/nfsd 8
root  12908   5172   0   Feb 24      -   0:00  /usr/sbin/rpc.statd
root  13166   5172   0   Feb 24      -   0:29  /usr/sbin/rpc.lockd
root  13428      1   0   Feb 24      -   0:00  /usr/sbin/uprintfd
root  14190   5172   0   Feb 24      -  72:59  /usr/sbin/automountd
root  14452   5172   0   Feb 24      -   0:17  /usr/sbin/qdaemon
root  14714   5172   0   Feb 24      -   0:00  /usr/sbin/writesrv
root  14992      1   0   Feb 24      - 252:26  /usr/lpp/perf/bin/scopeux
root  15520   3624   1   Feb 24      -  15:29  /usr/dt/bin/dtsession
root  15742      1   0   Feb 24      -   0:00  /usr/lpp/diagnostics/bin/diagd
root  15998      1   0   Feb 24   lft0  0:00  /usr/sbin/getty /dev/console
root  16304  18892   0   Feb 24  pts/0  0:00  /bin/ksh
root  16774      1   0   Feb 24      -   0:00  /usr/lpp/perf/bin/ttd
root  17092   4490   0   Feb 24      -  68:54  /usr/lpp/perf/bin/rep_server -t
root  17370  19186   3                 0:00  <defunct>
root  17630  15520   0   Mar 25      -   0:00  /usr/dt/bin/dtexec -open 0 -ttp
root  17898  15520   0   Mar 20      -   0:00  /usr/dt/bin/dtexec -open 0 -ttp
root  18118  19888   0   Feb 24  pts/1  0:00  /bin/ksh
root  18366   6966   0   Feb 24      -   0:00  rpc.ttdbserver 100083 1
root  18446  15520   0   Mar 15      -   0:00  /usr/dt/bin/dtexec -open 0 -ttp
root  18892  15520   0   Feb 24      -   3:46  /usr/dt/bin/dtterm
root  19186  16304   0   Feb 24  pts/0  0:01  /usr/lpp/X11/bin/msmit
root  19450      1   0   Feb 24      -  26:53  /usr/dt/bin/ttsession -s
root  19684   2208   0   Feb 24      -   0:00  /usr/dt/bin/dtexec -open 0 -ttp
root  19888  19684   0   Feb 24      -   0:00  /usr/dt/bin/dtterm
root  20104  15520   0   Feb 27      -   0:00  /usr/dt/bin/dtexec -open 0 -ttp
root  20248  20104   0   Feb 27      -   0:03  /usr/dt/bin/dtscreen
root  20542  29708   0   May 14      -   0:03  /usr/dt/bin/dtscreen
root  20912  26306   0   Apr 05      -   0:03  /usr/dt/bin/dtscreen
root  33558      1   0   May 18      -   3:28  /usr/atria/etc/lockmgr -a /var/
root  33834   6966   3  07:55:49      -   0:00  telnetd
root  34072      1   0   May 18      -   0:00  /usr/atria/etc/albd_server
martyp 36296  36608  13  07:56:07  pts/2  0:00  ps -ef
martyp 36608  33834   1  07:55:50  pts/2  0:00  -ksh
root  37220  15520   0   May 28      -   0:00  /usr/dt/bin/dtexec -open 0 -ttp
martyp $
```

HP-UX example (partial listing):

```
martyp $ ps -ef

    UID    PID   PPID C   STIME   TTY    TIME    COMMAND
   root      0      0  0   Mar  9   ?   107:28 swapper
   root      1      0  0   Mar  9   ?     2:27 init
   root      2      0  0   Mar  9   ?    14:13 vhand
   root      3      0  0   Mar  9   ?   114:55 statdaemon
   root      4      0  0   Mar  9   ?     5:57 unhashdaemon
   root      7      0  0   Mar  9   ?   154:33 ttisr
```

```
   root     70      0  0  Mar   9  ?        0:01 lvmkd
   root     71      0  0  Mar   9  ?        0:01 lvmkd
   root     72      0  0  Mar   9  ?        0:01 lvmkd
   root     13      0  0  Mar   9  ?        9:54 vx_sched_thread
   root     14      0  0  Mar   9  ?        1:54 vx_iflush_thread
   root     15      0  0  Mar   9  ?        2:06 vx_ifree_thread
   root     16      0  0  Mar   9  ?        2:27 vx_inactive_cache_thread
   root     17      0  0  Mar   9  ?        0:40 vx_delxwri_thread
   root     18      0  0  Mar   9  ?        0:33 vx_logflush_thread
   root     19      0  0  Mar   9  ?        0:07 vx_attrsync_thread
                           .
                           .
                           .
   root     69      0  0  Mar   9  ?        0:09 vx_inactive_thread
   root     73      0  0  Mar   9  ?        0:01 lvmkd
   root     74      0 19  Mar   9  ?     3605:29 netisr
   root     75      0  0  Mar   9  ?        0:18 netisr
   root     76      0  0  Mar   9  ?        0:17 netisr
   root     77      0  0  Mar   9  ?        0:14 netisr
   root     78      0  0  Mar   9  ?        0:48 nvsisr
   root     79      0  0  Mar   9  ?        0:00 supsched
   root     80      0  0  Mar   9  ?        0:00 smpsched
   root     81      0  0  Mar   9  ?        0:00 smpsched
   root     82      0  0  Mar   9  ?        0:00 sblksched
   root     83      0  0  Mar   9  ?        0:00 sblksched
   root     84      0  0  Mar   9  ?        0:00 strmem
   root     85      0  0  Mar   9  ?        0:00 strweld
   root   3730      1  0  16:39:22 console  0:00 /usr/sbin/getty console console
   root    404      1  0  Mar   9  ?        3:57 /usr/sbin/swagentd
 oracle    919      1  0  15:23:23 ?        0:00 oraclegprd (LOCAL=NO)
   root    289      1  2  Mar   9  ?       78:34 /usr/sbin/syncer
   root    426      1  0  Mar   9  ?        0:10 /usr/sbin/syslogd -D
   root    576      1  0  Mar   9  ?        0:00 /usr/sbin/portmap
   root    429      1  0  Mar   9  ?        0:00 /usr/sbin/ptydaemon
   root    590      1  0  Mar   9  ?        0:00 /usr/sbin/biod 4
   root    442      1  0  Mar   9  ?        0:00 /usr/lbin/nktl_daemon 0 0 0 0 0 1 -2
 oracle   8145      1  0  12:02:48 ?        0:00 oraclegprd (LOCAL=NO)
   root    591      1  0  Mar   9  ?        0:00 /usr/sbin/biod 4
   root    589      1  0  Mar   9  ?        0:00 /usr/sbin/biod 4
   root    592      1  0  Mar   9  ?        0:00 /usr/sbin/biod 4
   root    604      1  0  Mar   9  ?        0:00 /usr/sbin/rpc.lockd
   root    598      1  0  Mar   9  ?        0:00 /usr/sbin/rpc.statd
   root    610      1  0  Mar   9  ?        0:16 /usr/sbin/automount -f /etc/auto_master
   root    638      1  0  Mar   9  ?        0:06 sendmail: accepting connections
   root    618      1  0  Mar   9  ?        0:02 /usr/sbin/inetd
   root    645      1  0  Mar   9  ?        5:01 /usr/sbin/snmpdm
   root    661      1  0  Mar   9  ?       11:28 /usr/sbin/fddisubagtd
   root    711      1  0  Mar   9  ?       30:59 /opt/dce/sbin/rpcd
   root    720      1  0  Mar   9  ?        0:00 /usr/sbin/vtdaemon
   root    867    777  1  Mar   9  ?        0:00 <defunct>
     lp    733      1  0  Mar   9  ?        0:00 /usr/sbin/lpsched
   root    777      1  0  Mar   9  ?        8:55 DIAGMON
   root    742      1  0  Mar   9  ?        0:15 /usr/sbin/cron
 oracle   7880      1  0  11:43:47 ?        0:00 oraclegprd (LOCAL=NO)
   root    842      1  0  Mar   9  ?        0:00 /usr/vue/bin/vuelogin
 oracle   5625      1  0  07:00:14 ?        0:01 ora_smon_gprd
   root    781      1  0  Mar   9  ?        0:00 /usr/sbin/envd
   root    833    777  0  Mar   9  ?        0:00 DEMLOG   DEMLOG;DEMLOG;0;0;
   root    813      1  0  Mar   9  ?        0:00 /usr/sbin/nfsd 4
   root    807      1  0  Mar   9  ?        0:00 /usr/sbin/rpc.mountd
   root    815    813  0  Mar   9  ?        0:00 /usr/sbin/nfsd 4
   root    817    813  0  Mar   9  ?        0:00 /usr/sbin/nfsd 4
   root    835    777  0  Mar   9  ?        0:13 PSMON   PSMON;PSMON;0;0;
```

Here is a brief description of the headings:

UID	The user ID of the process owner.
PID	The process ID (you can use this number to kill the process).
PPID	The process ID of the parent process.
C	Processor utilization. On a multi-processor system, you may see this number go beyond 100%. It could potentially go to 100% per processor, so a two-processor system may show 200% utilization. This varies among UNIX variants.
STIME	Start time of the process.
TTY	The controlling terminal for the process.
TIME	The cumulative execution time for the process.
COMMAND	The command name and arguments.

ps gives a quick profile of the processes running on your system. To get more detailed information, you can include the "*l*" option, which includes a lot of useful additional information, as shown in the following example:

```
martyp $ ps -efl
 F S      UID    PID  PPID  C PRI NI    ADDR    SZ    WCHAN    STIME TTY       D
19 T     root      0     0  0   0 SY f026f7f0     0            Feb 18 ?        d
 8 S     root      1     0  0  41 20 f5b90808   175 f5b90a30   Feb 18 ?        -
19 S     root      2     0  0   0 SY f5b90108     0 f0283fd0   Feb 18 ?        t
19 S     root      3     0  0   0 SY f5b8fa08     0 f0287a44   Feb 18 ?        6h
 8 S     root   3065  3059  0  40 20 f626d040  1639 f62aab96   Feb 22 ?        c
 8 S     root     88     1  0  40 20 f5b8d708   377 f5b59df6   Feb 18 ?        q
 8 S     root    478     1  0  41 20 f5b8ec08   388 f5b51bb8   Feb 18 ?        0
 8 S     root     94     1  0  41 20 f5b8d008   527 f5b59e46   Feb 18 ?        d
 8 S     root    150     1  0  41 20 f5da1a10   808 f5b59806   Feb 18 ?        d
 8 S     root     96     1  0  67 20 f5da2810   535 f5b59ad6   Feb 18 ?        v
 8 S     root    144     1  0  41 20 f5da0c10  2694 ef69f61c   Feb 18 ?        5d
 8 S     root   1010     1  0   0 RT f61da330   496 f5dbec1c   Apr 12 ?        n
 8 S     root    106     1  0  41 20 f5da1310   485 f5b59e96   Feb 18 ?        s
 8 S     root    156     1  0  51 20 f5b8de08   446 f5b51eb8   Feb 18 ?        n
 8 S     root    176     1  0  53 20 f5da2110   740 f5b59036   Feb 18 ?        d
 8 S     root    129     1  0  56 20 f5d9fe10   447 f5b59cb6   Feb 18 ?        d
 8 S   daemon    130     1  0  41 20 f5d9f710   564 f5b59b76   Feb 18 ?        d
 8 S     root  14798     1  0  45 20 f5b8e508   616 f5b8e730   Mar 09 ?        3d
 8 S     root    133     1  0  51 20 f5e18818   507 f5b59c66   Feb 18 ?        s
 8 S     root    197     1  0  63 20 f5e15e18   284 f5e16040   Feb 18 ?        d
 8 S     root    196     1  0  41 20 f5da0510   429 f5c68f8e   Feb 18 ?        c
 8 S     root    213     1  0  41 20 f5e16518   586 f5c68b2e   Feb 18 ?        4d
 8 S     root    199   196  0  41 20 f5e16c18   451 f5b59f86   Feb 18 ?        i
 8 S     root    219     1  0  41 20 f5e17318   658 f5b59d06   Feb 18 ?        m
```

```
8 S    root     209     1   0  41 20 f5e18118    234 f5c68e4e  Feb 18 ?           d
8 S    root    2935   266   0  40 20 f61db130   2473 f62aaa56  Feb 22 ?           4
8 S    root   16800  3059   1  81 30 f626f340   1466 f61b345e  07:59:40 ?         k
8 S    root    2963  2954   0  40 20 f5f52028    513 f61b313e  Feb 22 ?           e
8 S    root     479     1   0  55 20 f5ee7120    407 f5fde2c6  Feb 18 console     g
8 S    root   10976     1   0  65 20 f5f55828    478 f5c6853e  Jun 01 ?           d
8 S    root    7468     1   0  46 20 f621da38   2851     8306c  Feb 24 ?          d
8 S    root     266     1   0  41 20 f5ee5520   1601 f5c6858e  Feb 18 ?           n
8 S    martyp 16763 16761   0  51 20 f6270140    429 f62701ac  07:46:46 pts/4     h
8 S    root   10995     1   0  41 20 f5b8f308   2350 f5fde5e6  Jun 01 ?           d
8 S    root     484   478   0  41 20 f5ee4e20    408 f5ee5048  Feb 18 ?           n
8 S    root     458     1   0  41 20 f5f54a28    504 f5fde906  Feb 18 ?          2m
8 O    root   16802 16763   1  61 20 f5ee7820    220            08:00:05 pts/4    l
8 S    root     471     1   0  41 20 f5f53c28    658 f5fde726  Feb 18 ?           d
8 S    root     474     1   0  51 20 f5f53528    804 f61a58b6  Feb 18 ?           g
8 S    root     485   458   0  40 20 f5f52e28    734 f607ecde  Feb 18 ?          74
8 S    root    2954  2936   0  40 20 f626e540    433 f626e5ac  Feb 22 ?           n
8 S    root    2936   266   0  66 20 f5ee4720   1637 f5ee478c  Feb 22 ?           n
8 S    root    3061  3059   0  40 20 f5e17a18   2041 f61b359e  Feb 22 ?           m
8 S    root    3058     1   0  40 20 f61daa30   1067 f62aadc6  Feb 22 pts/2       n
8 S    root     712   133   0  41 20 f61d8e30    798 f61b390e  Feb 18 ?           d
8 Z    root   11001 11000   0   0                                                 >
8 S    root    2938     1   0  60 20 f5ee6320    513 f601bfb6  Feb 22 ?           0
8 S    root    2999  2954   0  40 20 f621e138   1450 f61b33be  Feb 22 pts/2       t
8 S    root    3059  3002   1  51 20 f626de40   4010 f62aafa6  Feb 22 pts/2      2n
8 S    root    3063  3059   0  50 20 f621e838   1952 f62aa556  Feb 22 ?
8 S    root    3099  3062   0  40 20 f5f52728   2275 f60a1d18  Feb 22 ?           0
8 S    root   11000 10995   0  48 20 f626d740   2312     55694  Jun 01 ?          e
8 S    root    3002  2999   0  43 20 f61d8730    427 f61d879c  Feb 22 pts/2       =
8 S    root     730   133   0  40 20 f61d9530    422 f62aa9b6  Feb 18 ?           d
8 S    root    3062  3059   0  61 20 f621b738   2275 f62aa506  Feb 22 ?           0
8 S    root    3067     1   0  40 20 f5ee5c20    424 f5ee5c8c  Feb 22 ?           d
8 S    root    3000     1   0  40 20 f61d8030    518 f62aa8c6  Feb 22 ?           m
8 S    root    3078  3067   0  40 20 f61d9c30    211 f5b512b8  Feb 22 ?           0
8 S    root   10984     1   0  41 20 f5f54328   2484 eee46e84  Jun 01 ?          1b
8 S    root   16761   133   0  44 20 f5ee4020    411 f5c6894e  07:46:45 ?         d
martyp $
```

In this example, the first column is *F* for flags. *F* provides octal information about whether the process is swapped, in core, a system process, and so on. The octal value sometimes varies from system to system, so check the manual pages for your system to see the octal value of the flags.

S is for state. The state can be sleeping, as indicated by *S* for most of the processes shown in the example, waiting, running, intermediate, terminated, and so on. Again, some of these values may vary from system to system, so check your manual pages.

Some additional useful information in this output are: *NI* for the nice value, *ADDR* for the memory address of the process, *SZ* for the size of the process in physical pages, and *WCHAN*, which is the event for which the process is waiting.

Killing a Process

If you issue the **ps** command and find that one of your processes is hung, or
if you started a large job that you wish to stop, you can do so with the **kill**
command. **kill** is a utility that sends a signal to the process you identify. You
can **kill** any process that you own. In addition, the superuser can kill almost
any process on the system.

To kill a process that you own, simply issue the **kill** command and the
Process ID (PID). The following example shows issuing the **ps** command to
find all processes owned by *martyp*, killing a process, and checking to see
that it has disappeared:

```
martyp $ ps -ef | grep martyp
  martyp 19336 19334 0 05:24:32 pts/4  0:01 -ksh
  martyp 19426 19336 0 06:01:01 pts/4  0:00 grep martyp
  martyp 19424 19336 5 06:00:48 pts/4  0:01 find / -name .login
martyp $ kill 19424
martyp $ ps -ef | grep martyp
  martyp 19336 19334 0 05:24:32 pts/4  0:01 -ksh
  martyp 19428 19336 1 06:01:17 pts/4  0:00 grep martyp
[1] + Terminated              find / -name .login &
martyp $
```

The example shows killing process *19424,* which is owned by *martyp*.
We confirm that the process has indeed been killed by reissuing the **ps** command. You can also use the *-u* option to **ps** to list processes with the login
name you specify.

You can kill several processes on the command line by issuing **kill** followed by a space-separated list of all the process numbers you wish to kill.

Take special care when killing processes if you are logged in as superuser. You may adversely affect the way the system runs and have to manually restart processes or reboot the system.

Signals

When you issue the **kill** command and process number, you are also sending
a *signal* associated with the **kill**. We did not specify a *signal* in our **kill**

example; however, the default *signal* of 15, or *SIGTERM*, was used. These *signals* are used by the system to communicate with processes. The *signal* of 15 we used to terminate our process is a software termination *signal* that is usually enough to terminate a user process such as the **find** we had started. A process that is difficult to kill may require the *SIGKILL*, or 9 *signal*. This *signal* causes an immediate termination of the process. I use this only as a last resort because processes killed with *SIGKILL* do not always terminate smoothly. To kill such processes as the shell, you sometimes have to use *SIGKILL*.

You can use either the *signal* name or number. These signal numbers sometimes vary from system to system, so view the manual page for *signal*, usually in section 5, to see the list of *signals* on your system. A list of some of the most frequently used *signal* numbers and corresponding *signals* follows:

Signal Number	Signal
1	SIGHUP
2	SIGINT
3	SIGQUIT
9	SIGKILL
15	SIGTERM
24	SIGSTOP

To kill a process with id *234* with *SIGKILL*, you would issue the following command:

```
$ kill -9 234
     |    |   |
     |    |   |> process id (PID)
     |    |> signal number
     |> kill command to terminate the process
```

Showing Remote Mounts with showmount

showmount is used to show all remote systems (clients) that have mounted a local file system. **showmount** is useful for determining the file systems that are most often mounted by clients with NFS. The output of **showmount** is particularly easy to read because it lists the host name and directory that was mounted by the client.

NFS servers often end up serving many NFS clients that were not originally intended to be served. This situation ends up consuming additional UNIX system resources on the NFS server, as well as additional network bandwidth. Keep in mind that any data transferred from an NFS server to an NFS client consumes network bandwidth, and in some cases, may be a substantial amount of bandwith if large files or applications are being transferred from the NFS server to the client. The following example is a partial output of **showmount** taken from a system. **showmount** runs on the HP-UX, AIX, and Linux systems I have been using throughout this chapter, but not on the Solaris system:

```
# showmount -a

sys100.ct.mp.com:/applic

sys101.ct.mp.com:/applic

sys102.cal.mp.com:/applic

sys103.cal.mp.com:/applic

sys104.cal.mp.com:/applic

sys105.cal.mp.com:/applic

sys106.cal.mp.com:/applic

sys107.cal.mp.com:/applic

sys108.cal.mp.com:/applic

sys109.cal.mp.com:/applic

sys200.cal.mp.com:/usr/users

sys201.cal.mp.com:/usr/users

sys202.cal.mp.com:/usr/users
```

```
# showmount -a
```

sys203.cal.mp.com:/usr/users

sys204.cal.mp.com:/usr/users

sys205.cal.mp.com:/usr/users

sys206.cal.mp.com:/usr/users

sys207.cal.mp.com:/usr/users

sys208.cal.mp.com:/usr/users

sys209.cal.mp.com:/usr/users

The three following options are available for the **showmount** command:

-a prints output in the format "name:directory," as shown above.
-d lists all the local directories that have been remotely
    mounted by clients.
-e prints a list of exported file systems.

The following are examples of **showmount -d** and **showmount -e**:

```
# showmount -d
```

/applic

/usr/users

/usr/oracle

/usr/users/emp.data

/network/database

/network/users

/tmp/working

```
# showmount -e
```

export list for server101.cal.mp.com

```
# showmount -e
```

/applic

/usr/users

/cdrom

Showing System Swap

If your system has insufficient main memory for all the information it needs to work with, it will move pages of information to your swap area or swap entire processes to your swap area. Pages that were most recently used are kept in main memory, and those not recently used will be the first moved out of main memory.

System administrators spend a lot of time determining the right amount of swap space for their systems. Insufficient swap may prevent a system from starting additional processes, hang applications, or not permit additional users to get access to the system. Having sufficient swap prevents these problems from occurring. System administrators usually go about determining the right amount of swap by considering many important factors, including the following:

1. How much swap is recommended by the application(s) you run? Use the swap size recommended by your applications. Application vendors tend to be realistic when recommending swap space. There is sometimes competition among application vendors to claim the lowest memory and CPU requirements in order to keep the overall cost of solutions as low as possible, but swap space recommendations are usually realistic.

2. How many applications will you run simultaneously? If you are running several applications, sum the swap space recommended for each application you plan to run simultaneously. If you have a database application that recommends 200 MBytes of swap and a development tool that recommends 100 MBytes of swap, then configure your system with 300 MBytes of swap, minimum.

3. Will you be using substantial system resources on peripheral functionality such as NFS? The nature of NFS is to provide access to file systems, some of which may be very large, so this use may have an impact on your swap space requirements.

Swap is listed and manipulated on different UNIX variants with different commands. The following example shows listing the swap area on a Solaris system with **swap -l**:

```
# swap -l
swapfile               dev  swaplo blocks    free
/dev/dsk/c0t3d0s1     32,25       8 263080 209504
```

These values are all in 512 KByte blocks. In this case, the free blocks are *209504*, which is a significant amount of the overall swap allocated on the system.

You can view the amount of swap being consumed on your HP-UX system with **swapinfo**. The following is an example output of **swapinfo**:

```
# swapinfo

            Kb      Kb      Kb  PCT  START/      Kb
TYPE     AVAIL    USED    FREE USED  LIMIT RESERVE  PRI  NAME
dev      49152   10532   38620  21%      0       -    1  /dev/vg00/lvol2
dev     868352   10888  759160   1%      0       -    1  /dev/vg00/lvol8
reserve      -  532360 -532360
memory  816360  469784  346576  58%
```

Following is a brief overview of what **swapinfo** gives you.

In the preceding example, the "TYPE" field indicated whether the swap was "dev" for device, "reserve" for paging space on reserve, or "memory." Memory is a way to allow programs to reserve more virtual memory than you have hard disk paging space set up for on your system.

"Kb AVAIL" is the total swap space available in 1024-byte blocks. This includes both used and unused swap.

"Kb USED" is the current number of 1024-byte blocks in use.

"Kb FREE" is the difference between "Kb AVAIL" and "Kb USED."

"PCT USED" is "Kb USED" divided by "Kb AVAIL."

"START/LIMIT" is the block address of the start of the swap area.

"Kb RESERVE" is "-" for device swap or the number of 1024-byte blocks for file system swap.

"PRI" is the priority given to this swap area.

"NAME" is the device name of the swap device.

You can also issue the **swapinfo** command with a series of options. Here are some of the options you can include:

-m to display output of **swapinfo** in MBytes rather than in 1024-byte blocks.

-d prints information related to device swap areas only.

-f prints information about file system swap areas only.

sar: The System Activity Reporter

sar is another UNIX command for gathering information about activities on your system. You can gather data over an extended time period with **sar** and later produce reports based on the data. **sar** is similar among UNIX variants in that the options and outputs are similar. The Linux system I was using for the examples did not support **sar**, but the Solaris, HP-UX, and AIX systems had the same options and nearly identical outputs. The following are some useful options to **sar,** along with examples of reports produced with these options where applicable:

sar -o   Save data in a file specified by "o." After the file name, you would usually also enter the time interval for samples and the number of samples. The following example shows saving the binary data in file **/tmp/sar.data** at an interval of 60 seconds 300 times:

`sar -o /tmp/sar.data 60 300`

The data in **/tmp/sar.data** can later be extracted from the file.

sar -f	Specify a file from which you will extract data.
sar -u	Report CPU utilization with the headings %usr, %sys, %wio, %idle with some processes waiting for block I/O, %idle. This report is similar to the **iostat** and **vmstat** CPU reports. You extract the binary data saved in a file to get CPU information, as shown in the following example. The following is a **sar -u** example:

```
# sar -u -f /tmp/sar.data

Header Information for your system

12:52:04    %usr    %sys    %wio    %idle
12:53:04     62       4       5       29
12:54:04     88       5       3        4
12:55:04     94       5       1        0
12:56:04     67       4       4       25
12:57:04     59       4       4       32
12:58:04     61       4       3       32
12:59:04     65       4       3       28
13:00:04     62       5      16       17
13:01:04     59       5       9       27
13:02:04     71       4       3       22
13:03:04     60       4       4       32
13:04:04     71       5       4       20
13:05:04     80       6       8        7
13:06:04     56       3       3       37
13:07:04     57       4       4       36
13:08:04     66       4       4       26
13:09:04     80      10       2        8
13:10:04     73      10       2       15
13:11:04     64       6       3       28
13:12:04     56       4       3       38
13:13:04     55       3       3       38
13:14:04     57       4       3       36
13:15:04     70       4       5       21
13:16:04     65       5       9       21
13:17:04     62       6       2       30
```

```
13:18:04          60          5          3          33
13:19:04          77          3          4          16
13:20:04          76          5          3          15

                              .
                              .
                              .

14:30:04          50          6          6          38
14:31:04          57         12         19          12
14:32:04          51          8         20          21
14:33:04          41          4          9          46
14:34:04          43          4          9          45
14:35:04          38          4          6          53
14:36:04          38          9          7          46
14:37:04          46          3         11          40
14:38:04          43          4          7          46
14:39:04          37          4          5          54
14:40:04          33          4          5          58
14:41:04          40          3          3          53
14:42:04          44          3          3          50
14:43:04          27          3          7          64

Average           57          5          8          30
```

sar -b   Report buffer cache activity. A database application such as Oracle would recommend that you use this option to see the effectiveness of buffer cache use. You extract the binary data saved in a file to get CPU information, as shown in the following example:

```
# sar -b -f /tmp/sar.data

Header information for your system

12:52:04 bread/s lread/s %rcache bwrit/s lwrit/s %wcache pread/s pwrit/s
12:53:04       5     608      99       1      11      95       0       0
12:54:04       7     759      99       0      14      99       0       0
12:55:04       2    1733     100       4      24      83       0       0
12:56:04       1     836     100       1      18      96       0       0
12:57:04       0     623     100       2      21      92       0       0
12:58:04       0     779     100       1      16      96       0       0
12:59:04       0    1125     100       0      14      98       0       0
13:00:04       2    1144     100       9      89      89       0       0
13:01:04      10     898      99      11      76      86       0       0
13:02:04       0    1156     100       0      14      99       0       0
13:03:04       1     578     100       2      22      88       0       0
13:04:04       5    1251     100       0      12      99       0       0
```

13:05:04	3	1250	100	0	12	97	0	0
13:06:04	1	588	100	0	12	98	0	0
13:07:04	1	649	100	2	15	86	0	0
13:08:04	1	704	100	2	15	86	0	0
13:09:04	1	1068	100	0	18	100	0	0
13:10:04	0	737	100	1	44	99	0	0
13:11:04	0	735	100	1	13	95	0	0
13:12:04	0	589	100	1	15	93	0	0
13:13:04	0	573	100	0	16	99	0	0
13:14:04	1	756	100	1	16	91	0	0
13:15:04	1	1092	100	9	49	81	0	0
13:16:04	2	808	100	6	82	93	0	0
13:17:04	0	712	100	1	9	93	0	0
13:18:04	1	609	100	0	13	97	0	0
13:19:04	1	603	100	0	10	99	0	0
13:20:04	0	1127	100	0	14	98	0	0
		.						
		.						
14:30:04	2	542	100	1	22	94	0	0
14:31:04	10	852	99	12	137	92	0	0
14:32:04	2	730	100	10	190	95	0	0
14:33:04	4	568	99	2	26	91	0	0
14:34:04	4	603	99	1	13	91	0	0
14:35:04	1	458	100	1	13	89	0	0
14:36:04	13	640	98	1	24	98	0	0
14:37:04	21	882	98	1	18	95	0	0
14:38:04	7	954	99	0	19	98	0	0
14:39:04	3	620	100	1	11	94	0	0
14:40:04	3	480	99	2	15	85	0	0
14:41:04	1	507	100	0	9	98	0	0
14:42:04	1	1010	100	1	10	91	0	0
14:43:04	5	547	99	1	9	93	0	0
Average	3	782	100	3	37	91	0	0

sar -d   Report disk activity. You get the device name, percent that the device was busy, average number of requests outstanding for the device, number of data transfers per second for the device, and other information. You extract the binary data saved in a file to get CPU information, as shown in the following example:

```
# sar -d -f /tmp/sar.data

Header information for your system
```

12:52:04	device	%busy	avque	r+w/s	blks/s	avwait	avserv
12:53:04	c0t6d0	0.95	1.41	1	10	16.76	17.28
	c5t4d0	100.00	1.03	20	320	8.36	18.90
	c4t5d1	10.77	0.50	13	214	5.02	18.44
	c5t4d2	0.38	0.50	0	3	4.61	18.81
12:54:04	c0t6d0	0.97	1.08	1	11	10.75	14.82
	c5t4d0	100.00	1.28	54	862	9.31	20.06
	c4t5d1	12.43	0.50	15	241	5.21	16.97
	c5t4d2	0.37	0.50	0	3	3.91	18.20
12:55:04	c0t6d0	1.77	1.42	1	22	13.32	14.16
	c5t4d0	100.00	0.79	26	421	8.33	16.00
	c4t5d1	14.47	0.51	17	270	5.30	13.48

	c5t4d2	0.72	0.50	0	7	4.82	15.69
12:56:04	c0t6d0	1.07	21.57	1	22	72.94	19.58
	c5t4d0	100.00	0.60	16	251	6.80	13.45
	c4t5d1	8.75	0.50	11	177	5.05	10.61
	c5t4d2	0.62	0.50	0	6	4.79	15.43
12:57:04	c0t6d0	0.78	1.16	1	9	13.53	14.91
	c5t4d0	100.00	0.66	15	237	7.60	13.69
	c4t5d1	9.48	0.54	13	210	5.39	13.33
	c5t4d2	0.87	0.50	1	10	4.86	14.09
12:58:04	c0t6d0	1.12	8.29	1	17	54.96	14.35
	c5t4d0	100.00	0.60	11	176	7.91	14.65
	c4t5d1	5.35	0.50	7	111	5.23	10.35
	c5t4d2	0.92	0.50	1	10	4.63	16.08
12:59:04	c0t6d0	0.67	1.53	1	8	18.03	16.05
	c5t4d0	99.98	0.54	11	174	7.69	14.09
	c4t5d1	3.97	0.50	5	83	4.82	9.54
	c5t4d2	1.05	0.50	1	11	4.69	16.29
13:00:04	c0t6d0	3.22	0.67	3	39	8.49	16.53
	c5t4d0	100.00	0.60	65	1032	8.46	14.83
	c4t5d1	21.62	0.50	31	504	5.30	8.94
	c5t4d2	6.77	0.50	5	78	4.86	14.09
13:01:04	c0t6d0	4.45	3.08	5	59	25.83	11.49
	c5t4d0	100.00	0.65	42	676	7.85	14.52
	c4t5d1	21.34	0.55	30	476	5.87	18.49
	c5t4d2	4.37	0.50	3	51	5.32	13.50
		.					
		.					
		.					
14:42:04	c0t6d0	0.53	0.83	0	7	12.21	16.33
	c5t4d0	100.00	0.56	7	107	6.99	14.65
	c4t5d1	6.38	0.50	7	113	4.97	15.18
	c5t4d2	0.15	0.50	0	2	4.53	16.50
14:43:04	c0t6d0	0.52	0.92	0	7	11.50	15.86
	c5t4d0	99.98	0.92	17	270	8.28	18.64
	c4t5d1	10.26	0.50	9	150	5.35	16.41
	c5t4d2	0.12	0.50	0	1	5.25	14.45
Average	c0t6d0	1.43	108.80	2	26	0.00	14.71
Average	c5t4d0	100.00	0.74	25	398	7.83	-10.31
Average	c4t5d1	19.11	0.51	25	399	5.26	-13.75
Average	c5t4d2	1.71	0.53	1	21	5.29	13.46

sar -q   Report average queue length. You may have a problem any time the run queue length is greater than the number of processors on the system:

```
# sar -q -f /tmp/sar.data

Header information for your system

12:52:04 runq-sz %runocc swpq-sz %swpocc
12:53:04    1.1     20     0.0      0
12:54:04    1.4     51     0.0      0
12:55:04    1.3     71     0.0      0
12:56:04    1.1     22     0.0      0
12:57:04    1.3     16     0.0      0
12:58:04    1.1     14     0.0      0
12:59:04    1.2     12     0.0      0
13:00:04    1.2     21     0.0      0
13:01:04    1.1     18     0.0      0
13:02:04    1.3     20     0.0      0
```

```
13:03:04      1.2      15      0.0         0
13:04:04      1.2      20      0.0         0
13:05:04      1.2      43      0.0         0
13:06:04      1.1      14      0.0         0
13:07:04      1.2      15      0.0         0
13:08:04      1.2      26      0.0         0
13:09:04      1.5      38      0.0         0
13:10:04      1.5      30      0.0         0
13:11:04      1.2      23      0.0         0
13:12:04      1.3      11      0.0         0
13:13:04      1.3      12      0.0         0
13:14:04      1.4      16      0.0         0
13:15:04      1.4      27      0.0         0
13:16:04      1.5      20      0.0         0
13:17:04      1.3      21      0.0         0
13:18:04      1.1      15      0.0         0
13:19:04      1.2      19      0.0         0
13:20:04      1.4      22      0.0         0
                        .
                        .
                        .
14:30:04      1.5       5      0.0         0
14:31:04      1.6      12      0.0         0
14:32:04      1.4       9      0.0         0
14:33:04      1.1       6      0.0         0
14:34:04      1.3       3      0.0         0
14:35:04      1.1       4      0.0         0
14:36:04      1.2       6      0.0         0
14:37:04      1.4       5      0.0         0
14:38:04      1.2      10      0.0         0
14:39:04      1.3       4      0.0         0
14:40:04      1.1       3      0.0         0
14:41:04      1.6       3      0.0         0
14:42:04      1.1       4      0.0         0
14:43:04      1.3       1      0.0         0

Average       1.3      17      1.2         0
```

sar -w   Report system swapping activity.

```
# sar -w -f /tmp/sar.data

Header information for your system

12:52:04 swpin/s bswin/s swpot/s bswot/s pswch/s
12:53:04    1.00     0.0    1.00     0.0     231
12:54:04    1.00     0.0    1.00     0.0     354
12:55:04    1.00     0.0    1.00     0.0     348
12:56:04    1.00     0.0    1.00     0.0     200
12:57:04    1.00     0.0    1.00     0.0     277
12:58:04    1.00     0.0    1.00     0.0     235
```

12:59:04	1.02	0.0	1.02	0.0	199
13:00:04	0.78	0.0	0.78	0.0	456
13:01:04	1.00	0.0	1.00	0.0	435
13:02:04	1.02	0.0	1.02	0.0	216
13:03:04	0.98	0.0	0.98	0.0	204
13:04:04	1.02	0.0	1.02	0.0	239
13:05:04	1.00	0.0	1.00	0.0	248
13:06:04	0.97	0.0	0.97	0.0	170
13:07:04	1.00	0.0	1.00	0.0	166
13:08:04	1.02	0.0	1.02	0.0	209
13:09:04	0.98	0.0	0.98	0.0	377
13:10:04	1.00	0.0	1.00	0.0	200
13:11:04	1.00	0.0	1.00	0.0	192
13:12:04	0.87	0.0	0.87	0.0	187
13:13:04	0.93	0.0	0.93	0.0	172
13:14:04	1.00	0.0	1.00	0.0	170
13:15:04	1.00	0.0	1.00	0.0	382
13:16:04	1.00	0.0	1.00	0.0	513
13:17:04	1.00	0.0	1.00	0.0	332
13:18:04	1.00	0.0	1.00	0.0	265
13:19:04	1.02	0.0	1.02	0.0	184
13:20:04	0.98	0.0	0.98	0.0	212
.					
.					
.					
14:30:04	0.00	0.0	0.00	0.0	301
14:31:04	0.00	0.0	0.00	0.0	566
14:32:04	0.00	0.0	0.00	0.0	539
14:33:04	0.00	0.0	0.00	0.0	400
14:34:04	0.00	0.0	0.00	0.0	242
14:35:04	0.00	0.0	0.00	0.0	286
14:36:04	0.00	0.0	0.00	0.0	295
14:37:04	0.00	0.0	0.00	0.0	249
14:38:04	0.00	0.0	0.00	0.0	300
14:39:04	0.00	0.0	0.00	0.0	296
14:40:04	0.00	0.0	0.00	0.0	419
14:41:04	0.00	0.0	0.00	0.0	234
14:42:04	0.00	0.0	0.00	0.0	237
14:43:04	0.00	0.0	0.00	0.0	208
Average	0.70	0.0	0.70	0.0	346

Using timex to Analyze a Command

If you have a specific command you want to find out more about, you can use **timex**, which reports the elapsed time, user time, and system time spent in the execution of any command you specify.

     timex is a good command for users because it gives you an idea of the system resources you are consuming when issuing a command. The following two examples show issuing **timex** with no options to get a short output of the amount of *cpu* consumed; the second example shows issuing **timex -s** to report "total" system activity on a Solaris system:

```
martyp $ timex listing

real       0.02
user       0.00
sys        0.02


martyp $ timex -s listing

real       0.02
user       0.00
sys        0.01


SunOS 5.7 Generic sun4m     08/21

07:48:30   %usr    %sys     %wio     %idle
07:48:31     32      68        0         0

07:48:30  bread/s  lread/s  %rcache  bwrit/s  lwrit/s  %wcache  pread/s  pwrit/s
07:48:31        0        0      100        0        0      100        0        0

Average         0        0      100        0        0      100        0        0

07:48:30   device        %busy   avque   r+w/s   blks/s   avwait   avserv

07:48:31   fd0               0     0.0       0        0      0.0      0.0
           nfs1              0     0.0       0        0      0.0      0.0
           nfs219            0     0.0       0        0      0.0      0.0
           sd1               0     0.0       0        0      0.0      0.0
           sd1,a             0     0.0       0        0      0.0      0.0
           sd1,b             0     0.0       0        0      0.0      0.0
           sd1,c             0     0.0       0        0      0.0      0.0
           sd1,g             0     0.0       0        0      0.0      0.0
           sd3               0     0.0       0        0      0.0      0.0
           sd3,a             0     0.0       0        0      0.0      0.0
           sd3,b             0     0.0       0        0      0.0      0.0
           sd3,c             0     0.0       0        0      0.0      0.0
           sd6               0     0.0       0        0      0.0      0.0

Average    fd0               0     0.0       0        0      0.0      0.0
           nfs1              0     0.0       0        0      0.0      0.0
           nfs219            0     0.0       0        0      0.0      0.0
           sd1               0     0.0       0        0      0.0      0.0
           sd1,a             0     0.0       0        0      0.0      0.0
           sd1,b             0     0.0       0        0      0.0      0.0
           sd1,c             0     0.0       0        0      0.0      0.0
           sd1,g             0     0.0       0        0      0.0      0.0
           sd3               0     0.0       0        0      0.0      0.0
           sd3,a             0     0.0       0        0      0.0      0.0
           sd3,b             0     0.0       0        0      0.0      0.0
           sd3,c             0     0.0       0        0      0.0      0.0
           sd6               0     0.0       0        0      0.0      0.0

07:48:30  rawch/s  canch/s  outch/s  rcvin/s  xmtin/s  mdmin/s
07:48:31        0        0      147        0        0        0

Average         0        0      147        0        0        0

07:48:30  scall/s  sread/s  swrit/s  fork/s   exec/s  rchar/s  wchar/s
07:48:31     2637        0       95   15.79    15.79        0    19216

Average      2637        0       95   15.79    15.79        0    19216
```

```
07:48:30 swpin/s bswin/s swpot/s bswot/s pswch/s
07:48:31    0.00    0.0    0.00    0.0    116

Average     0.00    0.0    0.00    0.0    116

07:48:30 iget/s namei/s dirbk/s
07:48:31      0    195     121

Average      0    195     121

07:48:30 runq-sz %runocc swpq-sz %swpocc
07:48:31    2.0     526

Average     2.0     526

07:48:30  proc-sz    ov  inod-sz    ov  file-sz    ov  lock-sz
07:48:31   45/986     0  973/4508    0  357/357     0   0/0

07:48:30  msg/s  sema/s
07:48:31   0.00    0.00

Average    0.00    0.00

07:48:30 atch/s  pgin/s ppgin/s  pflt/s  vflt/s slock/s
07:48:31   0.00    0.00    0.00  505.26 1036.84    0.00

Average    0.00    0.00    0.00  505.26 1036.84    0.00

07:48:30  pgout/s ppgout/s pgfree/s pgscan/s %ufs_ipf
07:48:31    0.00     0.00     0.00     0.00     0.00

Average     0.00     0.00     0.00     0.00     0.00

07:48:30 freemem freeswap
07:48:31   15084  1224421

Average    15084  1224421

07:48:30 sml_mem    alloc  fail  lg_mem    alloc  fail ovsz_alloc  fail
07:48:31 2617344 1874368     0 17190912 10945416    0    3067904     0

Average   186953  133883     0 1227922   781815    0     219136     0
```

More Advanced and Graphical Performance Tools

The command line is a way of life when working with UNIX. UNIX grew out of the command line and is still primarily command line-based. Although you need to know a lot when issuing commands, especially when it comes to system performance, you can dig deeply very quickly with many of the commands I just covered.

You have the option with most UNIX variants to buy graphical performance tools. Some systems come with basic graphical performance tools, but will usually end up buying an advaced performance analysis tool if you want to perform advanced performance analysis. We'll take a quick look at a few performance tools in upcoming sections.

Figure 12-3 shows three performance tools that came with the Red Hat Linux system I used for many of the examples in this chapter:

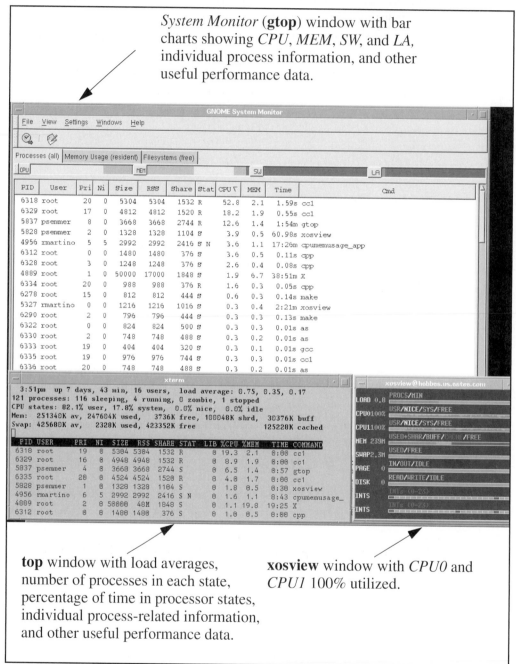

System Monitor (**gtop**) window with bar charts showing *CPU, MEM, SW,* and *LA,* individual process information, and other useful performance data.

top window with load averages, number of processes in each state, percentage of time in processor states, individual process-related information, and other useful performance data.

xosview window with *CPU0* and *CPU1* 100% utilized.

Figure 12-3 Red Hat Linux *Performance Tools* Screen Shot

The three performance tools shown in this diagram are **xosview** in the lower right, the *System Monitor* across the top of the screen, and **top** shown in the lower left. The *System Monitor* provides bar charts across the top of the screen that indicate the amount of CPU, Memory, Swap, and LAN utilization taking place. There is then tabular data supplied for every process on the system. The *System Monitor* is a graphical version of **top** that I invoked with the command **gtop** for **g**raphical **top**. **xosview** is a small load meter that you can keep running that provides bar charts of system activity shown in the bottom right window. This is the **X** Windows **o**perating **s**ystem **view** program, hence the name **xosview**. You can't see the bar charts clearly in this diagram, because this is a color-based application and the book is printed in only black and white. The bar charts are, however, clear on the computer screen. The final, and most often used, tool on UNIX systems is the character version of **top** that is running in the bottom left **xterm**. **top** is found on many UNIX variants and supplies a lot of useful system information.

Among the useful **top** system data displayed is the following:

- Load averages in the last one, five, and fifteen minutes.

- Number of existing processes and the number of processes in each state.

- Percentage of time spent in each of the processor states per processor on the system.

This same information is included in the bottom of the *System Monitor* window, which is covered by the **top** and **xosview** windows.

Next in the **top** window is memory data, including used, free, and shared.

Data is also provided for individual processes in a format similar to **ps**, including the following:

PID - Process ID number.

USER - Name of the owner of the process.

PRI - Current priority of the process.

NI - Nice value, ranging from -20 to +20.

SIZE - Total size of the process in kilobytes.

RSS - Resident size of the process in kilobytes.

STATE - Current state of the process.

TIME - Number of system and CPU seconds the process has consumed.

%CPU - CPU percentage.

%MEM - Memory percentage.

COMMAND - Name of the command the process is currently running.

As with most of the commands we have been covering, **top** is different among UNIX variants. You may see some different fields on the different UNIX variants. I am usually confident when I sit down at any UNIX system that I can run **top** and quickly see how the system is running. Most versions of **top** I have run are character-based applications, so you don't even need a graphics terminal to run them. I have run **top** in this example in character mode within an X terminal.

The system used in this example has two CPUs. If you look carefully in the **xosview** window, you'll see that both *CPU0* and *CPU1* are 100 percent used. At the time this screen shot was obtained, I was compiling the Linux kernel on this system, which consumed all the CPU resources on the system for a short period of time. You can see from both the **top** and *System Monitor* windows that the program **cc1**, used to compile the kernel, was consuming a substantial amount of the CPU resources on the system.

Figure 12-3 helps illustrate how different tools can help with viewing how system resources are consumed. **xosview** provides a quick reference, graphical overview of how many system resources are being consumed. **top** and *System Monitor* can then be used to determine the specific process consuming the most system resources.

HP GlancePlus/UX

Using UNIX commands to get a better understanding of what your system is doing requires you to do a lot of work. In the first case, issuing UNIX commands gives you the advantage of obtaining data about what is taking place on your system that very second. Unfortunately, you can't always issue additional commands to probe more deeply into an area, such as a process, about which you want to know more.

Now I'll describe another technique, a tool that can help get useful data in real time, allow you to investigate a specific process, and not bury you in reports. This tool is HP GlancePlus/UX (GlancePlus). This tool runs on several UNIX variants, including Solaris, HP-UX, and AIX.

GlancePlus can be run in character mode or in graphic mode. I chose to use the character-based version of GlancePlus, because this will run on any display, either graphics- or character-based, and the many colors used by the Motif version of GlancePlus do not show up well in a book. My examples are displayed much more clearly in the book when using the character mode. I recommend that you try both versions of GlancePlus to see which you prefer.

The system used in the examples has eight processors, 4 GBytes of RAM, and a substantial amount of EMC Symmetrix disk connected to it.

Figure 12-4 shows one of several interactive screens of GlancePlus. This one is the *Process List* screen, also referred to as the *Global* screen. This is the default screen when bringing up GlancePlus.

Two features of the screen shown in Figure 12-4 are worth noticing immediately:

1. Four histograms at the top of the screen give you a graphical representation of your CPU, Disk, Memory, and Swap Utilization in a format much easier to assimilate than a column of numbers.

2. The "Process Summary" has columns similar to **ps -ef**, with which many system administrators are familiar and comfortable. GlancePlus, however, gives you the additional capability of filtering out processes that are using very few resources by specifying thresholds.

Using GlancePlus, you can take a close look at your system in many areas, including the following:

- *Process List*
- *CPU Report*
- *Memory Report*
- *Swap Space*
- *Disk Report*
- *LAN Detail*
- *NFS by System*
- *PRM Summary (Process Resource Manager)*
- *I/O by File System*
- *I/O by Disk*
- *I/O by Logical Volume*
- *System Tables*

Figure 12-4 is a GlancePlus screen shot.

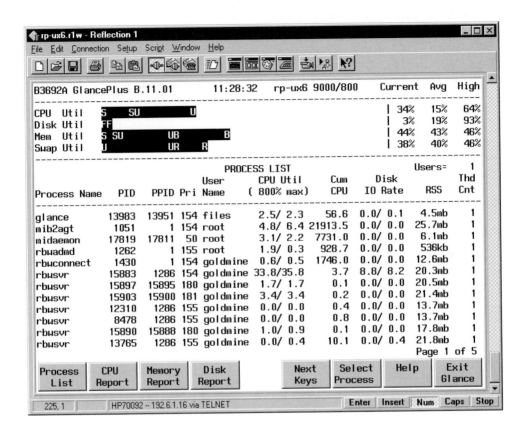

Figure 12-4 HP GlancePlus/UX *Process List* Screen Shot

Because the *Process List* shown in the example tells you where your system resources are going at the highest level, I'll start my description here. I am using a terminal emulator on my portable computer to display Glance-Plus. I find that many system administrators use a PC and a terminal emulator to perform UNIX management functions. Keep in mind that the information shown on this screen can be updated at any interval you choose. If your system is running in a steady-state mode, you may want to have a long interval because you don't expect things to much change. On the other hand, you may have a dynamic environment and want to see the histograms and other information updated every few seconds. In either case, you can change the update interval to suit your needs. You can use the function keys at the bottom of the screen to go into other functional areas.

Process List Description

The *Process List* screen provides an overview of the state of system resources and active processes.

The top section of the screen (the histogram section) is common to the many screens of GlancePlus. The bottom section of the screen displays a summary of active processes.

Line 1 provides the product and version number of GlancePlus, the time, name of your system, and system type. In this case, we are running version 11.01 of GlancePlus.

Line 3 provides information about the overall state of the CPU. This tends to be the single most important piece of information that administrators want to know about their system - Is my CPU overworked?

The CPU Utilization bar is divided into the following parts:

1. "S" indicates the amount of time spent on "system" activities such as context switching and system calls.

2. "N" indicates the amount of time spent running "nice" user processes (those run at a low priority).

3. "U" indicates the amount of time spent running user processes.

4. "R" indicates real-time processes.

5. "A" indicates the amount of time spent running processes at a negative "nice" priority.

The far right of line 3 shows the percentage of CPU utilization. If your system is "CPU-Bound," you will consistently see this number near 100 percent. You get statistics for Current, Average (since analysis was begun), and High.

Line 4 shows Disk Utilization for the busiest mounted disk. This bar indicates the percentage of File System and Virtual Memory disk I/O over the update interval. This bar is divided into two parts:

1. "F" indicates the amount of file system activity of user reads and writes and other non-paging activities.

2. "V" indicates the percentage of disk I/O devoted to paging virtual memory.

The Current, Avg, and High statistics have the same meaning as in the CPU Utilization description.

Line 5 shows the system memory utilization. This bar is divided into three parts:

1. "S" indicates the amount of memory devoted to system use.

2. "U" indicates the amount of memory devoted to user programs and data.

3. "B" indicates the amount of memory devoted to buffer cache.

The Current, Avg, and High statistics have the same meaning as in the CPU Utilization description.

Line 6 shows Swap Util information, which is divided into two parts:

1. "R" indicates reserved, but not in use.

2. "U" indicates swap space in use.

All three of these areas (CPU, Memory, and Disk) may be further analyzed by using the F2, F3, and F4 function keys, respectively. Again, you may see different function keys, depending on the version of GlancePlus you are running. When you select one of these keys, you move from the *Process List* screen to a screen that provides more in-depth functions in the selected area. In addition, more detailed screens are available for many other system areas. Because most investigation beyond the *Process List* screen takes place on the CPU, Memory, and Disk screens, I'll describe these in more detail shortly.

The bottom of the *Process List* screen shows the active processes running on your system. Because there are typically many processes running on a UNIX system, you may want to consider using the **o** command to set a threshold for CPU utilization. If you set a threshold of five percent, for instance, then only processes that exceed the average CPU utilization of five percent over the interval will be displayed. There are other types of thresholds that can be specified, such as the amount of RAM used (Resident Size). If you specify thresholds, you see only the processes you're most interested in, that is, those consuming the greatest system resources.

There is a line for each active process that meets the threshold requirements you defined. There may be more than one page of processes to display. The message in the bottom-right corner of the screen indicates which page you are on. You can scroll forward to view the next page with **f** and backward with **b**. Usually, only a few processes consume most of your system resources, so I recommend setting the thresholds so that only one page of processes is displayed. There are a whole series of commands you can issue in GlancePlus. The final figure in this section shows the commands recognized by GlancePlus.

Here is a brief summary of the process headings:

Process Name   The name or abbreviation used to load the executable program.

PID   The process identification number.

PPID   The PID of the parent process.

Pri   The priority of the process. The lower the number, the higher the priority. System-level processes usually run between 0 and 127. Other processes usually run between 128 and 255. "Nice" processes are those with the lowest priority and they have the largest number.

User Name   Name of the user who started the process.

CPU Util   The first number is the percentage of CPU utilization that this process consumed over the update interval. Note that this is 800% maximum for our eight-processor system. The second number is the percentage of CPU utilization that this process consumed since GlancePlus was invoked. Most system administrators leave GlancePlus running continuously on their systems with a low update interval. Since GlancePlus uses very little system overhead, there is virtually no penalty for this.

Cum CPU   The total CPU time used by the process. GlancePlus uses the "midaemon" to gather information. If the **midaemon** started before the process, you will get an accurate measure of cumulative CPU time used by the process.

Disk IO Rate   The first number is the average disk I/O rate per second over the last update interval. The second number is the average disk I/O rate since Glance-

Plus was started or since the process was started. Disk I/O can mean a lot of different things. Disk I/O could mean taking blocks of data off the disk for the first time and putting them in RAM, or it could be entirely paging and swapping. Some processes will simply require a lot more Disk I/O than others. When this number is very high, however, take a close look at whether or not you have enough RAM. Keep in mind that pageout activity, such as deactivation and swapping, are attributed to the *vhand* process.

RSS Size   The amount of RAM in KBytes that is consumed by the process. This is called the Resident Size. Everything related to the process that is in RAM is included in this column, such as the process's data, stack, text, and shared memory segments. This is a good column to inspect. Because slow systems are often erroneously assumed to be CPU-bound, I always make a point of looking at this column to identify the amount of RAM that the primary applications are using. This is often revealing. Some applications use a small amount of RAM but use large data sets, a point often overlooked when RAM calculations are made. This column shows all the RAM your process is currently using.

Block On   The reason the process was blocked (unable to run). If the process is currently blocked, you will see why. If the process is running, you will see why it was last blocked. There are many reasons a process could be blocked. After *Thd Cnt* is a list of the most common reasons for the process being blocked.

Thd Cnt   The total number of threads for this current process.

Abbreviation	**Reason for the Blocked Process**
CACHE	Waiting for a cache buffer to become available
DISK	Waiting for a disk operation to complete
INODE	Waiting for an inode operation to complete
IO	Waiting for a non-disk I/O to complete
IPC	Waiting for a shared memory operation to complete
LAN	Waiting for a LAN operation to complete
MESG	Waiting for a message queue operation to complete
NFS	Waiting for an NFS request to complete
PIPE	Waiting for data to or from a pipe
PRI	Waiting because a higher-priority process is running
RFA	Waiting for a Remote File Access to complete
SEM	Waiting for a semaphore to become available
SLEEP	Waiting because the process called **sleep** or **wait**
SOCKT	Waiting for a socket operation to complete
SYS	Waiting for system resources
TERM	Waiting for a terminal transfer
VM	Waiting for a virtual memory operation to complete
OTHER	Waiting for a reason GlancePlus can't determine

CPU Report **Screen Description**

If the *Process List* screen indicates that the CPU is overworked, you'll want
to refer to the *CPU Report* screen shown in Figure 12-5. It can provide useful information about the seven types of states on which GlancePlus reports.

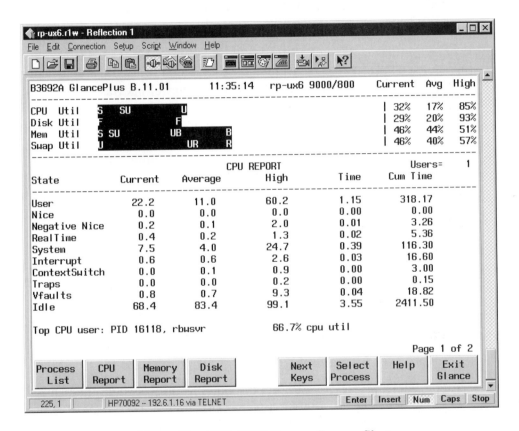

Figure 12-5 HP GlancePlus/UX *CPU Report* Screen Shot

For each of the seven types of states, there are columns that provide additional information. Following is a description of the columns:

Current   Displays the percentage of CPU time
                 devoted to this state over the last time inter-
                 val.

Average	Displays the average percentage of CPU time spent in this state since GlancePlus was started.
High	Displays the highest percentage of CPU time devoted to this state since GlancePlus was started.
Time	Displays the CPU time spent in this state over the last interval.
Cum Time	Displays the total amount of CPU time spent in this state since GlancePlus was started.

A description of the seven states follows:

User	CPU time spent executing user activities under normal priority.
Nice	CPU time spent running user code in nice mode.
Negative Nice	CPU time spent running code at a high priority.
Realtime	CPU time spent executing real-time processes that run at a high priority.
System	CPU time spent executing system calls and programs.
Interrupt	CPU time spent executing system interrupts. A high value here may indicate a lot of I/O, such as paging and swapping.
ContSwitch	CPU time spent context switching between processes.
Traps	CPU time spent handling traps.
Vfaults	CPU time spent handling page faults.
Idle	CPU time spent idle.

The *CPU Report* screen also shows your system's run queue length or load average. This is displayed on the second page of the *CPU Report* screen. The Current, Average, and High values for the number of runnable processes waiting for the CPU are shown. You may want to get a gauge of your system's run queue length when the system is mostly idle and compare these numbers with those you see when your system is in normal use.

The final area reported on the *CPU Report* screen is load average, system calls, interrupts, and context switches. I don't inspect these too closely, because if one of these is high, it is normally the symptom of a problem and not the cause of a problem. If you correct a problem, you will see these numbers reduced.

You can use GlancePlus to view all the CPUs in your system, as shown in Figure 12-6. This is an eight-processor system.

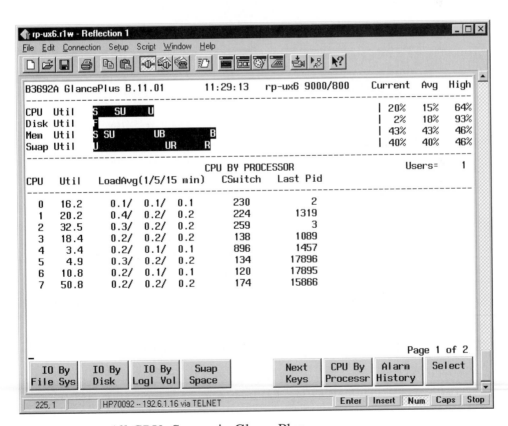

Figure 12-6 *All CPUs* Screen in GlancePlus

Memory Report Screen Description

The *Memory Report* Screen, shown in Figure 12-7, provides information on several types of memory management events. The statistics shown are in the form of counts, not percentages. You may want to look at these counts for a mostly idle system and then observe what takes place as the load on the system is incrementally increased. My experience has been that many more memory bottlenecks occur than CPU bottlenecks, so you may find this screen revealing.

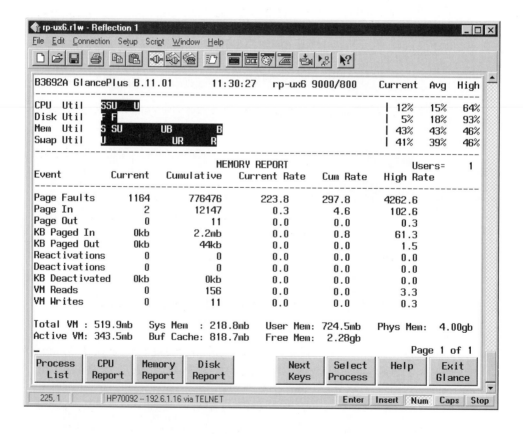

Figure 12-7 HP GlancePlus/UX *Memory Report* Screen Shot

The following five statistics are shown for each memory management event:

Current
: The number of times an event occurred in the last interval. The count changes if you update the interval, so you may want to select an interval you are comfortable with and stick with it.

Cumulative
: The sum of all counts for this event since GlancePlus was started.

Current Rate
: The number of events per second.

Cum Rate
: Average of the rate over the cummulative collection interval.

High Rate
: The highest rate recorded.

Following are brief descriptions of the memory management events for which statistics are provided:

Page Faults
: Any address translation fault, such as reclaims, pid faults, and so on.

Page In/Page Out
: Pages of data moved from virtual memory (disk) to physical memory (page in), or vice versa.

KB Paged In
: The amount of data paged in because of page faults.

KB Paged Out
: The amount of data paged out to disk.

Reactivations/Deactivations
: The number of processes swapped in and out of memory. A system low on RAM will spend a lot of time swapping processes in and out of RAM. If a lot of this type of swapping is taking place, you may see high CPU utilization and some other statistics may increase as well. These may only be symptoms that a lot of swapping is taking place.

KB Reactivated   The amount of information swapped into RAM as a result of processes having been swapped out earlier due to insufficient RAM.

KB Deactivated   The amount of information swapped out when processes are moved to disk.

VM Reads   The total count of the number of virtual memory reads to disk. The higher this number, the more often your system is going to disk.

VM Writes   The total count of memory management I/O.

The following values are also on the Memory screen:

Total VM   The amount of total virtual memory used by all processes.

Active VM   The amount of virtual memory used by all active processes.

Sys Mem   The amount of memory devoted to system use.

Buf Cache Size   The current size of buffer cache.

User Mem   The amount of memory devoted to user use.

Free Memory   The amount of RAM not currently allocated for use.

Phys Memory   The total RAM in your system.

This screen gives you a lot of information about how your memory subsystem is being used. You may want to view some statistics when your system is mostly idle and when it is heavily used and compare the two. Some good numbers to record are "Free Memory" (to see whether you have any free RAM under either condition) and "Total VM" (to see how much virtual memory has been allocated for all your processes). A system that is RAM-rich will have available memory; a system that is RAM-poor will allocate a lot of virtual memory.

Disk Report **Screen Description**

The *Disk Report* screen appears in Figure 12-8. You may see groupings of "local" and "remote" information.

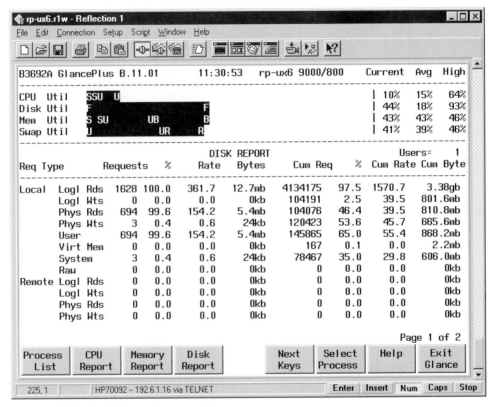

HP GlancePlus/UX *Disk Report* Screen Shot

There are eight disk statistics provided for eight events related to logical and physical accesses to all the disks mounted on the local system. These events represent all the disk activity taking place on the system.

Here are descriptions of the eight disk statistics provided:

Requests   The total number of requests of that type over the last interval.

%	The percentage of this type of disk event relative to other types.
Rate	The average number of requests of this type per second.
Bytes	The total number of bytes transferred for this event over the last interval.
Cum Req	The cumulative number of requests since GlancePlus started.
%	The relative percentage of this type of disk event since GlancePlus started.
Cum Rate	Average of the rate over the cumulative collection interval.
Cum Bytes	The total number of bytes transferred for this type of event since GlancePlus started.

Next are descriptions of the disk events for which these statistics are provided, which may be listed under "Local" on your system:

Logl Rds and Logl Wts

	The number of logical reads and writes to a disk. Because disks normally use memory buffer cache, a logical read may not require physical access to the disk.
Phys Rds	The number of physical reads to the disk. These physical reads may be due to either file system logical reads or to virtual memory management.
Phys Wts	The number of physical writes to the disk. This may be due to file system activity or virtual memory management.
User	The amount of physical disk I/O as a result of user file I/O operations.
Virtual Mem	The amount of physical disk I/O as a result of virtual memory management activity.

| System | Housekeeping I/O such as inode updates. |
| Raw | The amount of raw mode disk I/O. |

A lot of disk activity may also take place as a result of NFS mounted disks. Statistics are provided for "Remote" disks as well.

Disk access is required on all systems. The question to ask is: What disk activity is unnecessary and slowing down my system? A good place to start is to compare the amount of "User" disk I/O with "Virtual Mem" disk I/O. If your system is performing much more virtual memory I/O than user I/O, you may want to investigate your memory needs.

GlancePlus Summary

In addition to the Process List, or Global, screen and the CPU, Memory, and Disk screens described earlier, there are many other useful screens, including the following:

Swap Space	Shows details of all swap areas. May be called by another name in other releases.
Netwk By Intrface	Gives details about each LAN card configured on your system. This screen may have another name in other releases.
NFS Global	Provides details on inbound and outbound NFS-mounted file systems. May be called by another name in other releases.
Select Process	Allows you to select a single process to investigate. May be called by another name in other releases.
I/O By File Sys	Shows details of I/O for each mounted disk partition.
I/O By Disk	Shows details of I/O for each mounted disk.
I/O By Logl Vol	Shows details of I/O for each mounted logical volume.

System Tables   Shows details of internal system tables.

Process Threshold   Defines which processes will be displayed
                     on the Process List screen. May be called
                     by another name, such as the Global
                     screen, in other releases.

As you can see, although I described the four most commonly used screens in detail, you can use many others to investigate your system further.

There are also many commands that you can issue within GlancePlus. Figures 12-9 and 12-10 show the *Command List* screens in GlancePlus.

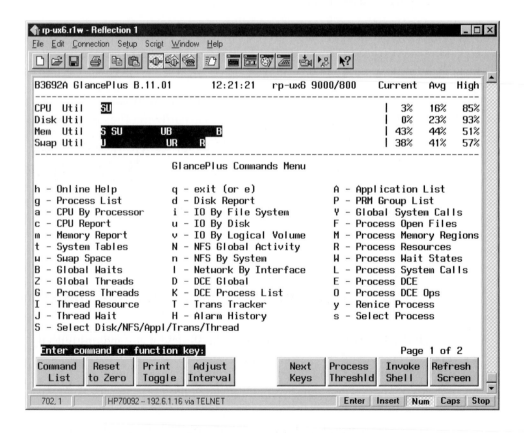

Figure 12-9 HP GlancePlus/UX *Command List* Screen 1

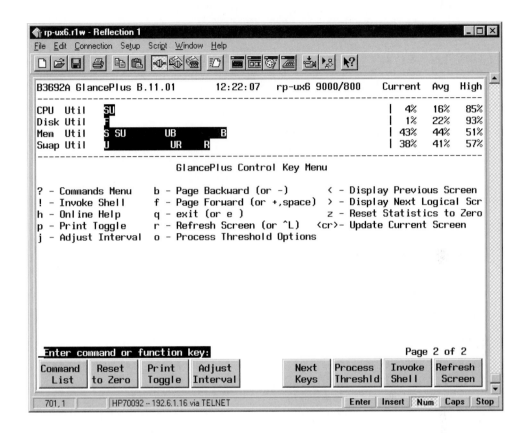

Figure 12-10 HP GlancePlus/UX *Command List* Screen 2

Using VantagePoint Performance Agent to Identify Bottlenecks

VantagePoint Performance Agent allows you to view many metrics related to system performance that can help you identify the source of bottlenecks in your system. You can use the graphical version of GlancePlus, called gpm, to specify the metrics you want to keep track of. You can then view them in the gpm interface and sort them a variety of different ways.

The following are the most important types of bottlenecks you can encounter on a system and the metrics associated with each type of bottleneck. This information was provided by Doug Grumann and Stephen Ciullo of Hewlett-Packard, who are two performance experts.

1. CPU bottleneck Using VantagePoint Performance Agent:

   - Consistent High global CPU utilization with *GBL_CPU_TOTAL_UTIL*>90% and next bullet.

   - Significant *Run Queue* or *Load Average* indicated by *GBL_PRI_QUEUE* or *GBL_RUN_QUEUE*>3.

   - Look for processes blocked on priority with *PROC_STOP_REASON=PRI*.

2. System CPU bottleneck using VantagePoint Performance Agent (same as 1 with addition of first bullet):

   - Most of the CPU time spent in kernel mode with *GBL_CPU_SYS_MODE_UTIL*>50%.

   - Consistent High global CPU utilization with *GBL_CPU_TOTAL_UTIL*>90% and next bullet.

   - Significant *Run Queue* or *Load Average* indicated by *GBL_PRI_QUEUE* or *GBL_RUN_QUEUE*>3.

   - Look for processes blocked on priority with *PROC_STOP_REASON=PRI*.

3. Context switching bottleneck using VantagePoint Performance Agent (same as 2 with addition of first bullet):

   - Significant CPU time spent switching with *GBL_CPU_CSWITCH*>30%.

   - Most of the CPU time spend in kernel mode with *GBL_CPU_SYS_MODE_UTIL*>50%.

   - Consistent High global CPU utilization with *GBL_CPU_TOTAL_UTIL*>90% and next bullet.

- Significant *Run Queue* or *Load Average* indicated by *GBL_PRI_QUEUE* or *GBL_RUN_QUEUE*>3.

- Look for processes blocked on priority with *PROC_STOP_REASON=PRI*.

4. User CPU bottleneck Using VantagePoint Performance Agent (same as 1 with addition of first bullet):

- Most of the CPU time spent in user mode with *GBL_CPU_USER_MODE_UTIL*>50%.

- Consistent High global CPU utilization with *GBL_CPU_TOTAL_UTIL*>90% and next bullet.

- Significant *Run Queue* or *Load Average* indicated by *GBL_PRI_QUEUE* or *GBL_RUN_QUEUE*>3.

- Look for processes blocked on priority with *PROC_STOP_REASON=PRI*.

5. Disk bottleneck Using VantagePoint Performance Agent:

- At least one disk device with consistently high utilization with *BYDSK_UTIL*>50%.

- Queue lengths greater than zero with *BYDSK_QUEUE*>0.

- Processes or threads blocked on I/O for a variety of reasons with *PROC_STOP_REASON=CACHE, DISK* or *IO*.

- Look for processes blocked on priority with *PROC_STOP_REASON=PRI*.

6. Buffer Cache bottleneck Using VantagePoint Performance Agent:

- Moderate utilization of at least one disk with *BYDSK_UTIL*>25%.

- Queue lengths greater than zero with *BYDSK_QUEUE*>0.

- Low Buffer cache read hit percentage with
  GBL_MEM_CACHE_HIT_PCT<90%.

- Processes or threads blocked on cache with
  PROC_STOP_REASON=CACHE.

7. Memory bottleneck Using VantagePoint Performance Agent:

- High physical memory utilization with
  GBL_MEM_UTIL>95%.

- Significant pageouts or any deactivations with
  GBL_MEM_PAGEOUT_RATE>1 or
  GBL_MEM_SWAPOUT_RATE>0.

- vhand processes consistently active with vhand's
  PROC_CPU_TOTAL_UTIL>5%.

- Processes or threads blocked on virtual memory with
  PROC_STOP_REASON=VM.

8. Networking bottleneck Using VantagePoint Performance Agent:

- High network packet rates with
  GBL_NET_PACKET_RATE>2 average. Keep in mind
  that this varies greatly depending on configuration.

- Any output queuing taking place with
  GBL_NET_OUTQUEUE>0.

- Higher than normal number of processes or threads
  blocked on networking with
  PROC_STOP_REASON=NFS, LAN, RPC or *SOCKET*
  *GBL_NETWORK_SUBSYSTEM_QUEUE>*average.

- One CPU with a high system mode CPU utilization while
  other CPUs are mostly idle with
  BYCPU_CPU_INTERRUPT_TIME>30.

- Using *lanadmin,* check for frequent incrementing of *Outbound Discards* or excessive *Collisions.*

In order to identify a problem on your system, you must first characterize your system when it is running smoothly and has no problems. Should your system start to perform poorly in some respect or another, you can compare the performance data of a smoothly running system to one with potential problems.

HP VantagePoint Performance Agent and HP VantagePoint Performance Analyzer/UX

There are performance tools that track and chart data over a long period of time. System administrators often call this exercise "capacity planning." The goal of capacity planning is to view what system resources have been consumed over a long period of time and determine what adjustments or additions can be made to the system to improve performance and plan for the future. We'll use HP VantagePoint Performance Agent (what used to be MeasureWare Agent) and HP VantagePoint Performance Analyzer/UX (what used to be PerfView Analyzer) together to take a look at the performance of a system. These tools run on HP-UX and are similar to many advanced tools that run on other UNIX variants.

The VantagePoint Performance Agent is installed on individual systems throughout a distributed environment. It collects resource and performance measurement data on the individual systems. The VantagePoint Performance Analyzer/UX management console, which you would typically install on a management system, is then used to display the historical VantagePoint Performance Agent data. You could also set alarms to be triggered off by exception conditions using the VantagePoint Performance agent. For instance, if the VantagePoint Performance agent detects an exception condition, such as CPU utilization greater than 90%, it produces an alarm message. The alarm messages are then displayed with VantagePoint Performance Analyzer/UX. We're going to use the VantagePoint Performance Analyzer/UX in our upcoming examples; however, there are really three VantagePoint Performance components:

Monitor   Provides alarm monitoring capability by accepting alarms from VantagePoint Performance and displays alarms.

Planner   Provides forecasting capability by extrapolating VantagePoint Performance data for forecasts.

Analyzer   Analyzes VantagePoint Performance data from multiple systems and displays data. You can view the data from multiple systems simultaneously.

In our example, we will be working with a single system. We'll take the VantagePoint Performance data, collected over roughly a one-week period, and display some of it. In this example, we won't take data from several distributed systems and we'll use only one server in the example.

HP VantagePoint Performance Agent produces log files that contain information about the system resource consumption. The longer HP VantagePoint Performance Agent runs, the longer it records data in the log files. I am often called to review systems that are running poorly to propose system upgrades. I usually run HP VantagePoint Performance Agent for a minimum of a week so that I obtain log information over a long enough period of time to obtain useful data. For some systems, this time period is months. For other systems with a regular load, a week may be enough time.

After having run VantagePoint Performance for a week, I invoked VantagePoint Performance Analyzer/UX to see the level of system resource utilization that took place over the week. The graphs we'll review are CPU, Memory, and Disk. Figure 12-11 shows *Global CPU Summary* for the week:

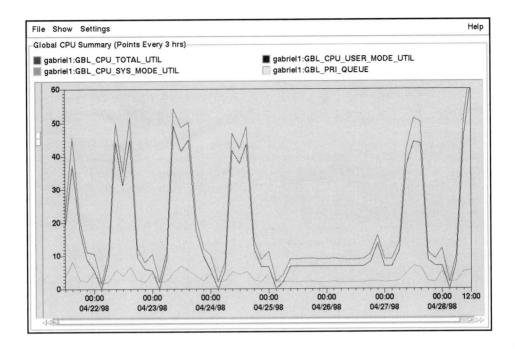

Figure 12-11 *Global CPU Summary* Screen

You can adjust every imaginable feature of this graph with Vantage-Point Performance Analyzer/UX. Unfortunately, the color in this graph is lost in the book. The colors used allow you to discern the parameters when viewing the graph on the computer screen. Total CPU utilization is always the top point in the graph and it is the sum of system and user mode utilization.

Figure 12-11 shows classic CPU utilization with prime hours reflecting high CPU utilization and non-prime hours reflecting low CPU utilization. In some respects, however, this graph can be deceiving. Because there is a data point occurs every three hours, hence the eight ticks per 24-hour period, you don't get a view of the actual CPU utilization during a much smaller window of time. We can't, for instance, see precisely what time in the morning the CPU becomes heavily used. We can see that it is between the second and third tick, but this is a long time period - between 6:00 and 9:00 am. The same lack of granularity is true at the end of the day. We see a clear fall-off in CPU utilization between the fifth and seventh ticks, but this does not give us a well defined view. Figure 12-12 shows CPU utilization during a much shorter time window.

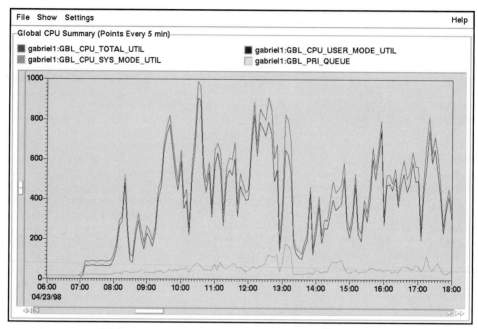

Figure 12-12 *Global CPU Summary* - Short Time Period

Figure 12-12 shows a finer granularity of CPU utilization during the shorter time window. The much finer granularity of this window makes clear the activity spikes that occur throughout the day. For instance, a clear login spike occurs at 8:30 am.

Memory utilization can also be graphed over the course of the week, as shown in Figure 12-13.

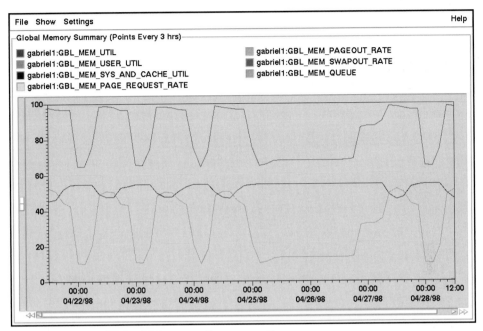

Figure 12-13 *Global Memory Summary* Screen

The user memory utilization is the bottom line of the graph, which roughly corresponds to the CPU utilization shown earlier. User memory utilization is low during non-prime hours and high during prime hours.

System memory utilization is the middle line of the graph, which remains fairly steady throughout the week.

Total memory utilization is always the top line of the graph, and it is the sum of system and user utilization. It rises and drops with user utilization, because system memory utilization remains roughly the same.

The three-hour interval between data points on this graph may not give us the granularity we require. Figure 12-14 shows memory utilization during a much shorter time window.

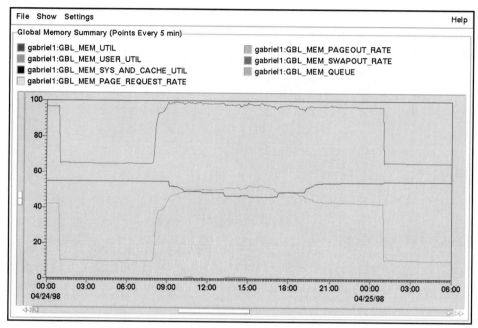

File Show Settings   Help

Global Memory Summary (Points Every 5 min)

■ gabriel1:GBL_MEM_UTIL   gabriel1:GBL_MEM_PAGEOUT_RATE
gabriel1:GBL_MEM_USER_UTIL   ■ gabriel1:GBL_MEM_SWAPOUT_RATE
■ gabriel1:GBL_MEM_SYS_AND_CACHE_UTIL   gabriel1:GBL_MEM_QUEUE
gabriel1:GBL_MEM_PAGE_REQUEST_RATE

Figure 12-14   *Global Memory Summary* - Short Time Period

Figure 12-14 shows a finer granularity of memory utilization during the shorter time window. You can now see precisely how memory utilization is changing over roughly one day.

Disk utilization can also be graphed over the course of the week, as shown in Figure 12-15.

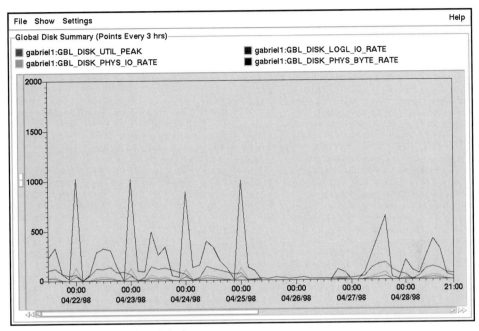

Figure 12-15 Global Disk Summary

Like the CPU and memory graph, this is an entire week of disk usage. Because many spikes occur on this graph, we would surely want to view and analyze much shorter time windows.

Figure 12-16 shows disk utilization during a much shorter time window.

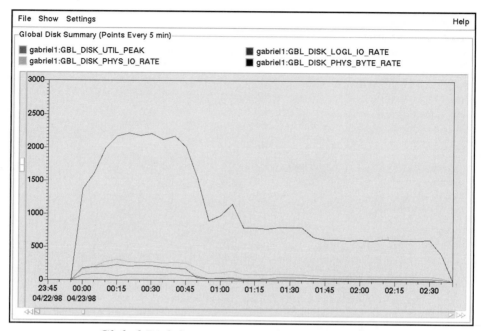

Figure 12-16 *Global Disk Summary* - Short Time Period

This much shorter time window, of roughly three hours, shows a lot more detail. There are tremendous spikes in disk activity occurring in the middle of the night. These could take place for a variety of reasons, including batch job processing or system backup.

You are not limited to viewing parameters related to only one system resource at a time. You can also view the way many system resources are used simultaneously, as shown in Figure 12-17.

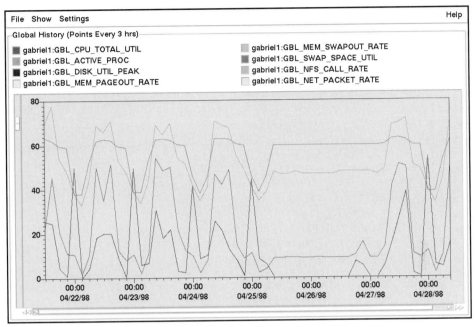

Figure 12-17 *Global Summary History* Screen

Many system resources are present on this graph, including CPU, disk, and memory. You would surely want to view a much shorter time period when displaying so many system resources simultaneously.

Figure 12-18 shows the same parameters during a much shorter time window.

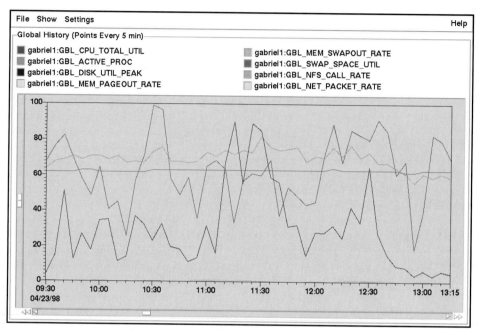

File Show Settings   Help

Global History (Points Every 5 min)

■ gabriel1:GBL_CPU_TOTAL_UTIL   ▨ gabriel1:GBL_MEM_SWAPOUT_RATE
▨ gabriel1:GBL_ACTIVE_PROC   ■ gabriel1:GBL_SWAP_SPACE_UTIL
■ gabriel1:GBL_DISK_UTIL_PEAK   ▨ gabriel1:GBL_NFS_CALL_RATE
▨ gabriel1:GBL_MEM_PAGEOUT_RATE   ▨ gabriel1:GBL_NET_PACKET_RATE

Figure 12-18 *Global Summary* - Short Time Period

Figure 12-18 shows a finer granularity of the utilization of many system resources during the shorter time window. You can now view the ways in which various system resources are related to other system resources.

You can find the status of VantagePoint Performance Analyzer/UX running on your system with a useful command called **perfstat**. The following example shows issuing the **perfstat** command with the -? option to see all **perfstat** options:

```
# perfstat -?

usage: perfstat [options]

Unix option   Function
-----------   --------
    -?        List all perfstat options.
    -c        Show system configuration information.
    -e        Search for warnings and errors from
                performance tool status files.
    -f        List size of performance tool status files.
    -p        List active performance tool processes.
    -t        Display last few lines of performance tool
```

```
                          status files.
     -v           List version strings for performance tool files.
     -z           Dump perfstat info to a file and tar tape.
```

Using the *-c* option, you get information about your system configuration, as shown in the following listing:

```
# perfstat -c

**********************************************************
** perfstat for rp-ux6 on Fri May 15 12:20:06 EDT
**********************************************************

system configuration information:

uname -a: HP-UX ux6 B.11.00 E 9000/800 71763 8-user license

mounted file systems with disk space shown:
Filesystem            kbytes      used   avail %used Mounted on
/dev/vg00/lvol3        86016     27675   54736  34% /
/dev/vg00/lvol1        67733     44928   16031  74% /stand
/dev/vg00/lvol8       163840     66995   90927  42% /var
/dev/vg00/lvol7       499712    358775  132155  73% /usr
/dev/rp06vgtmp/tmp   4319777   1099297 3134084  26% /tmp
/dev/vg00/lvol6       270336    188902   76405  71% /opt
/dev/vgroot1/var      640691     15636  605834   3% /newvar
/dev/vgroot1/usr      486677    356866  115210  76% /newusr
/dev/vgroot1/stand     67733     45109   15850  74% /newstand
/dev/vgroot1/root      83733     21181   54178  28% /newroot
/dev/vgroot1/opt      263253    188109   67246  74% /newopt
/dev/vg00/lvol5        20480      1109   18168   6% /home


LAN interfaces:
Name    Mtu     Network       Address      Ipkts      Opkts
lo0     4136    127.0.0.0     localhost    7442       7442
lan0    1500    192.60.11.0   rp-ux6       7847831    12939169


************* (end of perfstat -c output) ***************
```

Using the *-f* option shows the size of the performance tools status files, as shown in the following listing:

```
# perfstat -f

***********************************************************
** perfstat for ux6 on Fri May 15 12:20:08 EDT
***********************************************************

ls -l list of performance tool status files in /var/opt/perf:

-rw-rw-rw-   1 root    root     7812 May 10 19:35 status.alarmgen
-rw-r--r--   1 root    root        0 May 10 02:40 status.mi
-rw-rw-rw-   1 root    root     3100 May 10 02:40 status.perflbd
-rw-rw-rw-   1 root    root     3978 May 10 02:40 status.rep_server
-rw-r--r--   1 root    root     6079 May 11 23:30 status.scope
-rw-r--r--   1 root    root        0 Mar 31 07:26 status.ttd

************* (end of perfstat -f output) ****************
```

Using the *-v* option displays the version strings for the performance tools running, as shown in the following listing:

```
# perfstat -v

***********************************************************
** perfstat for ux6 on Fri May 15 12:20:08 EDT
***********************************************************

listing version strings for performance tool files:

NOTE:    The following software version information can be com-
pared
with the version information shown in the /opt/perf/ReleaseNotes
file(s).

MeasureWare executables in the directory /opt/perf/bin
        scopeux   C.01.00      12/17/97 HP-UX 11.0+
            ttd   A.11.00.15   12/15/97 HP-UX 11.00
        perflbd   C.01.00      12/17/97 HP-UX 11.0+
       alarmgen   C.01.00      12/17/97 HP-UX 11.0+
      agdbserver   C.01.00      12/17/97 HP-UX 11.0+
        agsysdb   C.01.00      12/17/97 HP-UX 11.0+
     rep_server   C.01.00      12/17/97 HP-UX 11.0+
        extract   C.01.00      12/17/97 HP-UX 11.0+
        utility   C.01.00      12/17/97 HP-UX 11.0+
            mwa   A.10.52      12/05/97
       perfstat   A.11.01      11/19/97
         dsilog   C.01.00      12/17/97 HP-UX 11.0+
        sdlcomp   C.01.00      12/17/97 HP-UX 11.0+
         sdlexpt   C.01.00      12/17/97 HP-UX 11.0+
      sdlgendata   C.01.00      12/17/97 HP-UX 11.0+
         sdlutil   C.01.00      12/17/97 HP-UX 11.0+

Measureware libraries in the directory /opt/perf/lib
       libmwa.sl   C.01.00      12/17/97 HP-UX 11.0+
        libarm.a   A.11.00.15   12/15/97 HP-UX 11.00
       libarm.sl   A.11.00.15   12/15/97 HP-UX 11.00
```

```
Measureware metric description file in the directory /var/opt/
perf
        metdesc  C.01.00     12/17/97

All critical MeasureWare files are accessible

    libnums.sl  B.11.00.15  12/15/97 HP-UX 11.00
    midaemon    B.11.00.15  12/15/97 HP-UX 11.00
      glance  B.11.01      12/16/97 HP-UX 11.00
        gpm  B.11.01      12/16/97 HP-UX 11.00

************* (end of perfstat -v output)  ****************
```

CHAPTER 13

Networking

Virtual Partitions and Networking

You should have a minimum of one networking card devoted to each Virtual Partition. vPars will communicate with other vPars and other systems over the networking card(s). Like all components, networking cards in different Virtual Partitions are managed independently of one another and from the Virtual Partition to which they are attached. In the upcoming sections we'll perform some basic work on networking cards and the networks of Virutual Partitions in general. We'll view the configuration of network cards and the way in which Virtual Partitions communicate with one another over the network - even when these vPars are running on the same system.

To perform basic tasks such as **telnet** or *file transfer protocol* between two Virtual Partitions running on the same system, you would use their network cards. There is no low-level vPar-specific functionality that allows communication over the backplane between vPars as opposed to through the respective network cards of the vPars.

Virtual Partition Host-Related Information

One aspect of Virtual Partitions that can be confusing is the host-related information associated with each Virtual Partition. Virtual Partitions are, for all intents and purposes, different hosts. This means that a system connecting to a Virtual Partition thinks it is an altogether separate host from any other Virtual Partition running on the same server. So for each Virtual Partition you have both information defining the Virtual Partition and information defining the host. From a networking standpoint, such as connecting to a Virtual partition using **telnet**, you would use the host name. From a Virtual Partition standpoint, such as issuing vPar commands such as **vparstatus**, you would use the vPar name. It is highly desirable for these two names to be the same so that you can issue any command using one name that defines both the vPar and hostname.

man page

vparstatus
appendix a

In our earlier example in Chapter 2 we loaded HP-UX 11i on two separate disks, each of which would be used for a separate Virtual Partition. When loading the operating systems for the respective Virtual Partitions, you can specify the host-related information when loading the operating systems. For instance, at the time you are loading HP-UX 11i, you can enter *hostname* and other system-related information. This information is different for each instance of HP-UX 11i because even though the Virtual Partitions are running on the same physical server, the instances of 11i are used for different Virtual Partitions. The Virtual Partitions are really different hosts and will, therefore, have different system-related parameters. The host-related information can be changed for each Virtual Partition using **set_parms** after the HP-UX 11i has been installed or after the Virtual Partition is up and running.

The concept of having multiple hosts on one physical computer can take a little getting used to for UNIX users who are accustomed to servers with only one instance of HP-UX and therefore only one set of host-related information.

man page

vparmodify
appendix a

The Virtual Partition-related information such as *name* can be modified with **vparmodify**. The host-related information is updated with **set_parms** (or manually by updating the appropriate files.) So for each Virtual Partition you have both information defining the Virtual Partition and information defining the host.

Let's take a look at two Virtual Partitions with **vparstatus** to view the I/O addresses corresponding to the LAN interfaces of the two vPars:

```
# vparstatus -v

[Virtual Partition Details]
Name:          cable1
State:         Up
Attributes:    Dynamic,Manual
Kernel Path:   /stand/vmunix
Boot Opts:

[CPU Details]
Min/Max:   2/3
Bound [Path]:    33
                 37
Unbound [Path]:

[IO Details]
    0.0.1.1.2.0  BOOT
    0.0.4.0  CONSOLE
    0.0.0.0                              <-- LAN for cable1
    0.0.1.0.3.0

[Memory Details]
Specified [Base  /Range]:
         (bytes) (MB)
Total Memory (MB):  2048

[Virtual Partition Details]
Name:          cable2
State:         Up
Attributes:    Dynamic,Manual
Kernel Path:   /stand/vmunix
Boot Opts:

[CPU Details]
Min/Max:   1/2
Bound [Path]:    97
Unbound [Path]:  101

[IO Details]
    0.8.0.0.8.0.5.0.0.0, BOOT
    0.10.0.0                             <-- LAN for cable2

[Memory Details]
Specified [Base  /Range]:
         (bytes) (MB)
Total Memory (MB):  1024
#
```

These two hardware paths correspond to different Local Bus Adapters (LBAs), which is a requirement at the time of this writing. The first vPar uses the Core I/O card at LBA 0, and the second vPars uses LBA 10. Let's now proceed to see the software configuration of these two cards.

We had been working with a vPar name *cable1* extensively with many of our examples in Chapter 2. The following shows the contents of the **/etc/hosts** file on for the vPar *cable1*:

```
# cat /etc/hosts
# @(#)B.11.11_LRhosts $Revision: 1.9.214.1 $ $Date: 96/10/08
13:20:01 $
#
# The form for each entry is:
# <internet address>    <official hostname> <aliases>
#
# For example:
# 192.1.2.34     hpfcrm   loghost
#
# See the hosts(4) manual page for more information.
# Note: The entries cannot be preceded by a space.
#     The format described in this file is the correct format.
#      The original Berkeley manual page contains an error in
#       the format description.
#

172.16.15.36     cvhdcon3
172.16.14.44     cvhdcon4
127.0.0.1        localhost        loopback
#
```

There is no mention of the vPar name *cable1* in this file. As far as HP-UX is concerned, the hostname of *cvhdcon3* is all that is required for this host and this Virtual Partition. The hostname for the second vPar running on this system is *cvhdcon4*. The communication between these two hosts is over the network cable using the two hostnames shown in **/etc/hosts**. The vPar names are not present in the **/etc/hosts** file. All of the vPar-related information is in **/etc/vpdb**. You may want to add an alias of the vPar name if indeed your *hostname* and Virtual Partition name are different. You could add an alias in the **/etc/hosts** file of *cable1* for *cvhdcon3* and an alias of *cable2* for *cvhdcon4*.

Let's now run **ifconfig** on both hosts to see how the network interfaces are set up:

```
# hostname
cvhdcon3
# ifconfig lan0
lan0: flags=843<UP,BROADCAST,RUNNING,MULTICAST>
         inet 172.16.15.36 netmask ffffff00 broadcast 172.16.15.255
#


-------------------------


#  hostname
cvhdcon4
# ifconfig lan1
lan1: flags=843<UP,BROADCAST,RUNNING,MULTICAST>
         inet 172.16.14.44 netmask ffffff00 broadcast 172.16.14.255
#
```

Note the LAN interface for the first vPar is *lan0* and the second is *lan1*. There are two LAN interfaces in this server, and even though they are separate vPars and instances of HP-UX, two different LAN interface names are required for the server to discern one interface from the other, as we'll see in the upcoming **netconf** files.

Host-related information is stored in **/etc/rc.config.d/netconf**. The following listing shows information related to *cvhdcon3* and again has no mention of the vPar name *cable1*:

netconf on host *cvhdcon3* (vPar *cable1*)

```
# cat /etc/rc.config.d/netconf
# netconf:  configuration values for core networking subsystems
#
# @(#)B.11.11_LR $Revision: 1.6.119.6 $ $Date: 97/09/10 15:56:01 $
#
# HOSTNAME:          Name of your system for uname -S and hostname
#
# OPERATING_SYSTEM:  Name of operating system returned by uname -s
#                    ---- DO NOT CHANGE THIS VALUE ----
#
# LOOPBACK_ADDRESS:  Loopback address
#                    ---- DO NOT CHANGE THIS VALUE ----
#
# IMPORTANT:  for 9.x-to-10.0 transition, do not put blank lines between
# the next set of statements

HOSTNAME="cvhdcon3"
OPERATING_SYSTEM=HP-UX
LOOPBACK_ADDRESS=127.0.0.1

# Internet configuration parameters.  See ifconfig(1m), autopush(1m)
#
# INTERFACE_NAME:    Network interface name (see lanscan(1m))
#
# IP_ADDRESS:        Hostname (in /etc/hosts) or IP address in decimal-dot
```

```
#                        notation (e.g., 192.1.2.3)
#
# SUBNET_MASK:          Subnetwork mask in decimal-dot notation, if different
#                        from default
#
# BROADCAST_ADDRESS:    Broadcast address in decimal-dot notation, if
#                        different from default
#
# INTERFACE_STATE:      Desired interface state at boot time.
#                        either up or down, default is up.
#
# DHCP_ENABLE           Determines whether or not DHCP client functionality
#                        will be enabled on the network interface (see
#                        auto_parms(1M), dhcpclient(1M)). DHCP clients get
#                        their IP address assignments from DHCP servers.
#                        1 enables DHCP client functionality; 0 disables it.
#
# For each additional network interfaces, add a set of variable assignments
# like the ones below, changing the index to "[1]", "[2]" et cetera.
#
# IMPORTANT:  for 9.x-to-10.0 transition, do not put blank lines between
# the next set of statements

INTERFACE_NAME[0]=lan0                         <-- lan0
IP_ADDRESS[0]=172.16.15.36
SUBNET_MASK[0]=255.255.255.0
BROADCAST_ADDRESS[0]=""
INTERFACE_STATE[0]=""
DHCP_ENABLE[0]=0

# Internet routing configuration.  See route(1m), routing(7)
#
# ROUTE_DESTINATION:    Destination hostname (in /etc/hosts) or host or network
#                        IP address in decimal-dot notation, preceded by the word
#                        "host" or "net"; or simply the word "default".
#
# ROUTE_MASK:           Subnetwork mask in decimal-dot notation, or C language
#                        hexadecimal notation.  This is an optional field.
#                        A IP address, subnet mask pair uniquely identifies
#                        a subnet to be reached. If a subnet mask is not given,
#                        then the system will assign the longest subnet mask
#                        of the configured network interfaces to this route.
#                        If there is no matching subnet mask, then the system
#                        will assign the default network mask as the route's
#                        subnet mask.
#
# ROUTE_GATEWAY:        Gateway hostname (in /etc/hosts) or IP address in
#                        decimal-dot notation.  If local interface, must use the
#                        same form as used for IP_ADDRESS above (hostname or
#                        decimal-dot notation). If loopback interface, i.e.,
#                        127.0.0.1, the ROUTE_COUNT must be set to zero.
#
# ROUTE_COUNT:          An integer that indicates whether the gateway is a
#                        remote interface (one) or the local interface (zero)
#                        or loopback interface (e.g., 127.*).
#
# ROUTE_ARGS:           Route command arguments and options.  This variable
#                        may contain a combination of the following arguments:
#                        "-f", "-n" and "-p pmtu".
#
# For each additional route, add a set of variable assignments like the ones
# below, changing the index to "[1]", "[2]" et cetera.
#
# IMPORTANT:  for 9.x-to-10.0 transition, do not put blank lines between
# the next set of statements

# ROUTE_DESTINATION[0]=default
# ROUTE_MASK[0]=""
# ROUTE_GATEWAY[0]=""
# ROUTE_COUNT[0]=""
# ROUTE_ARGS[0]=""

# Dynamic routing daemon configuration.  See gated(1m)
#
# GATED:        Set to 1 to start gated daemon.
```

```
# GATED_ARGS:    Arguments to the gated daemon.

GATED=0
GATED_ARGS=""

#
# Router Discover Protocol daemon configuration.  See rdpd(1m)
#
# RDPD:          Set to 1 to start rdpd daemon
#

RDPD=0

#
# Reverse ARP daemon configuration.  See rarpd(1m)
#
# RARP:          Set to 1 to start rarpd daemon
#

RARP=0

ROUTE_GATEWAY[0]=172.16.15.1
ROUTE_COUNT[0]=1
ROUTE_DESTINATION[0]=default
#
```

Although there is a substantial amount of information in this file such as hostname, IP address, subnet mask, and gateway, there is no entry for any vPar-specific information.

The **/etc/rc.config.d/netconf** for *cvhdcon4* specifies *lan1* as the networking interface for this vPar, as shown in the following listing. These are two separate hosts that must communicate over their respective networking interfaces. The system has in it one lan interface (*lan0*) devoted to *cvhdcon3* (vPar *cable1*) and a second lan interface (*lan1*) devoted to *cvhdcon4* (vPar *cable2*). The *lan0* and *lan1* references in the respective **netconf** files are required in order to devote the two lan cards to their respective vPars.

netconf on host *cvhdcon4* (vPar *cable2*)

```
# cat /etc/rc.config.d/netconf
# netconf:  configuration values for core networking subsystems
#
# @(#)B.11.11_LR $Revision: 1.6.119.6 $ $Date: 97/09/10 15:56:01 $
#
# HOSTNAME:          Name of your system for uname -S and hostname
#
# OPERATING_SYSTEM:  Name of operating system returned by uname -s
#                    ---- DO NOT CHANGE THIS VALUE ----
#
# LOOPBACK_ADDRESS:  Loopback address
#                    ---- DO NOT CHANGE THIS VALUE ----
#
# IMPORTANT:  for 9.x-to-10.0 transition, do not put blank lines between
# the next set of statements

HOSTNAME="cvhdcon4"
OPERATING_SYSTEM=HP-UX
LOOPBACK_ADDRESS=127.0.0.1
```

```
# Internet configuration parameters.  See ifconfig(1m), autopush(1m)
#
# INTERFACE_NAME:      Network interface name (see lanscan(1m))
#
# IP_ADDRESS:          Hostname (in /etc/hosts) or IP address in decimal-dot
#                      notation (e.g., 192.1.2.3)
#
# SUBNET_MASK:         Subnetwork mask in decimal-dot notation, if different
#                      from default
#
# BROADCAST_ADDRESS:   Broadcast address in decimal-dot notation, if
#                      different from default
#
# INTERFACE_STATE:     Desired interface state at boot time.
#                      either up or down, default is up.
#
# DHCP_ENABLE          Determines whether or not DHCP client functionality
#                      will be enabled on the network interface (see
#                      auto_parms(1M), dhcpclient(1M)). DHCP clients get
#                      their IP address assignments from DHCP servers.
#                      1 enables DHCP client functionality; 0 disables it.
#
# For each additional network interfaces, add a set of variable assignments
# like the ones below, changing the index to "[1]", "[2]" et cetera.
#
# IMPORTANT:  for 9.x-to-10.0 transition, do not put blank lines between
# the next set of statements

INTERFACE_NAME[0]=lan1                    <-- lan1
IP_ADDRESS[0]=172.16.14.44
SUBNET_MASK[0]=255.255.255.0
BROADCAST_ADDRESS[0]=""
INTERFACE_STATE[0]=""
DHCP_ENABLE[0]=0
```

```
# Internet routing configuration.  See route(1m), routing(7)
#
# ROUTE_DESTINATION:   Destination hostname (in /etc/hosts) or host or network
#                      IP address in decimal-dot notation, preceded by the word
#                      "host" or "net"; or simply the word "default".
#
# ROUTE_MASK:          Subnetwork mask in decimal-dot notation, or C language
#                      hexadecimal notation.  This is an optional field.
#                      A IP address, subnet mask pair uniquely identifies
#                      a subnet to be reached. If a subnet mask is not given,
#                      then the system will assign the longest subnet mask
#                      of the configured network interfaces to this route.
#                      If there is no matching subnet mask, then the system
#                      will assign the default network mask as the route's
#                      subnet mask.
#
# ROUTE_GATEWAY:       Gateway hostname (in /etc/hosts) or IP address in
#                      decimal-dot notation.  If local interface, must use the
#                      same form as used for IP_ADDRESS above (hostname or
#                      decimal-dot notation). If loopback interface, i.e.,
#                      127.0.0.1, the ROUTE_COUNT must be set to zero.
#
# ROUTE_COUNT:         An integer that indicates whether the gateway is a
#                      remote interface (one) or the local interface (zero)
#                      or loopback interface (e.g., 127.*).
#
# ROUTE_ARGS:          Route command arguments and options.  This variable
#                      may contain a combination of the following arguments:
#                      "-f", "-n" and "-p pmtu".
#
# For each additional route, add a set of variable assignments like the ones
# below, changing the index to "[1]", "[2]" et cetera.
#
# IMPORTANT:  for 9.x-to-10.0 transition, do not put blank lines between
# the next set of statements

# ROUTE_DESTINATION[0]=default
# ROUTE_MASK[0]=""
# ROUTE_GATEWAY[0]="172.16.14.1"
# ROUTE_COUNT[0]=""
```

```
# ROUTE_ARGS[0]=""


# Dynamic routing daemon configuration.  See gated(1m)
#
# GATED:        Set to 1 to start gated daemon.
# GATED_ARGS:   Arguments to the gated daemon.

GATED=0
GATED_ARGS=""


#
# Router Discover Protocol daemon configuration.  See rdpd(1m)
#
# RDPD:         Set to 1 to start rdpd daemon
#


RDPD=0


#
# Reverse ARP daemon configuration.  See rarpd(1m)
#
# RARP:         Set to 1 to start rarpd daemon
#


RARP=0


ROUTE_GATEWAY[0]=172.16.14.1
ROUTE_COUNT[0]=1
ROUTE_DESTINATION[0]=default
#
```

We can also view and configure networking-related in SAM. Figure 13-1 shows networking-related information for *lan1* on the second vPar (*cable2*) in SAM:

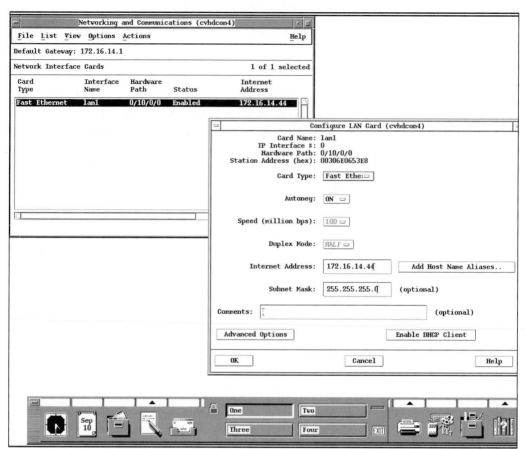

Figure 13-1 SAM LAN Card Configuration for Second vPar

These windows display the information that we viewed in various files and at the command line earlier. Some system administrators prefer modifying and viewing information in SAM and others at the command line.

Using the Two Networking Cards With Telnet

The LAN cards devoted to Virtual Partitions can be used for a variety of purposes just as they would on a non-vPar system. When users or applications in two different vPars communicate, it is over the LAN. There is not any special provision in vPars for communicating in normal operation. (There is, however, special system administration communication among vPars, such as synchronization of the Virtual Partition Database, that takes place in a special way.) When establishing a communication session between two vPars, even if they are on the same server, the LAN interfaces on both vPars are used. This includes **telnet**, **ftp**, and the Berkely "r" commands such as **rlogin**. The following example shows a **telnet** session among two vPars used in many examples throughout the book. vPar *cable1* (hostname *cvhdcon3*) initiates a **telnet** session with vPar *cable2* (hostname *cvhdcon4*) in this example:

```
# hostname
cvhdcon3                          <-- start on cable1
# telnet cvhdcon4                 <-- telnet to cable2
Trying...
Connected to cvhdcon4.
Escape character is '^]'.
Local flow control on
Telnet TERMINAL-SPEED option ON

HP-UX cvhdcon4 B.11.11 U 9000/800 (tc)

login: root
Password:
Please wait...checking for disk quotas
(c)Copyright 1983-2000 Hewlett-Packard Co.,  All Rights Reserved.
(c)Copyright 1979, 1980, 1983, 1985-1993 The Regents of the Univ. of Cal-
ifornia
(c)Copyright 1980, 1984, 1986 Novell, Inc.
(c)Copyright 1986-1992 Sun Microsystems, Inc.
(c)Copyright 1985, 1986, 1988 Massachusetts Institute of Technology
(c)Copyright 1989-1993  The Open Software Foundation, Inc.
(c)Copyright 1986 Digital Equipment Corp.
(c)Copyright 1990 Motorola, Inc.
(c)Copyright 1990, 1991, 1992 Cornell University
(c)Copyright 1989-1991 The University of Maryland
(c)Copyright 1988 Carnegie Mellon University
(c)Copyright 1991-2000 Mentat Inc.
(c)Copyright 1996 Morning Star Technologies, Inc.
(c)Copyright 1996 Progressive Systems, Inc.
(c)Copyright 1991-2000 Isogon Corporation, All Rights Reserved.
```

```
                    RESTRICTED RIGHTS LEGEND
Use, duplication, or disclosure by the U.S. Government is subject to
restrictions as set forth in sub-paragraph (c)(1)(ii) of the Rights in
Technical Data and Computer Software clause in DFARS 252.227-7013.

                    Hewlett-Packard Company
                    3000 Hanover Street
                    Palo Alto, CA 94304 U.S.A.

Rights for non-DOD U.S. Government Departments and Agencies are as set
forth in FAR 52.227-19(c)(1,2).

Value of TERM has been set to "hp".
WARNING:  YOU ARE SUPERUSER !!

# hostname
cvhdcon4                                      <-- connected to cable2
#
```

You can use **telnet**, **rlogin**, or other such connection methods only if you have two networking cards in your system - one for each vPar. This is true for other functionality as well, such as the backups from a vPar to another vPar or system with a local tape drive, which require a network card on both systems. I consider one networking card devoted to each vPar a necessity.

There is a substantial amount of networking background information in the remainder of the chapter.

Non-vPar-Specific Section of Chapter: Networking Background

Networking varies greatly from installation to installation. Some installations, such as highly centralized and isolated systems that have only ASCII terminals connected to the system, require the system administrator to pay very little attention to networking. Other installations, such as highly distributed environments in which thousands of systems are connected to a network that may span many geographic sites, may require the system administrator to pay a great deal of attention to networking. In this second scenario, the amount of time a system administrator devotes to networking may exceed the amount of time spent on all other system administration functions combined! Rather than ignoring networking altogether, as the first system administrator might, or covering all aspects of network administration, as the second system administrator may require, I cover in this chapter the aspects of networking that apply to most UNIX systems. This content is based on my experience of working in a variety of new UNIX installations. In the event that you require more networking background than I cover in this chapter, I recommend the following book as an excellent source of networking information - *UNIX Networks* by Bruce H. Hunter and Karen Bradford Hunter (Prentice Hall, ISBN 0-13-08987-1).

In this chapter, I provide primarily background rather than setup information on many networking topics, because setup is predominantly performed by system administrators. Most of what I cover is sometimes called "Internet Services." In general, I am going to cover the basics of networking in this chapter. This includes ARPA and Berkeley Services. Here is a list of topics I cover:

- General UNIX networking background

- Internet Protocol (IP) addressing (classes A, B, and C)

- Subnet mask

- ARPA Services

- Berkeley commands

- Host name mapping

- Network File System (NFS) background

- UNIX networking commands

I provide summaries and examples of many UNIX commands in this chapter. A great deal more detail can be found in the online manual pages for these commands on your HP-UX system.

Although vPars run on only HP-UX I use a variety of systems in the examples in this chapter, including Solaris, AIX, and HP-UX. HP-UX system administrators often manage many UNIX variants so I wanted to suppy as thorough a set of examples as possible.

UNIX Networking

Connecting to other machines is an important part of every UNIX network. This means connecting both to other UNIX machines as well as to non-UNIX machines. The machines must be physically connected to one another as well as functionally connected to one another, so that you can perform such tasks as transferring files and logging into other systems. Many commands exist on your UNIX system that provide you with the functionality to log in and transfer files between systems. These are known as the ARPA commands, **telnet** and **ftp**.

The **telnet** command allows remote logins in a heterogeneous environment. From your UNIX system, for instance, you can **telnet** to non-UNIX systems and log in. After login on the remote system, you need to have an understanding of the operating system running on that system. If you need to connect to a different computer only for the purpose of transferring files to and from the system, then you can use **ftp**. This command allows you to transfer files between any two systems without having an understanding of the operating system running on the remote system.

These commands are somewhat primitive compared to the commands that can be issued between UNIX systems. To UNIX systems, networking is not an afterthought that needs to be added on to the system. The **ftp** and **telnet** commands come with your UNIX system, as well as more advanced commands and functionality that you can use to communicate between your UNIX system and other UNIX systems. These more advanced commands, known as Berkeley commands, allow you to perform many commands remotely, such as copying files and directories and logging in. This functionality continues to increase to a point where you are working with files that can be stored on any system on the network, and your access to these files is transparent to you with the Network File System (NFS).

Let's take a look at some of the basics of UNIX networking.

An Overview of IEEE802.3, TCP/IP

In order to understand how the networking on your UNIX system works, you first need to understand the components of your network that exist on your UNIX system. Seven layers of network functionality exist on your UNIX system, as shown in Figure 13-2. I cover the bottom four layers at a cursory level so that you can see how each plays a part in the operation of your network and, therefore, be more informed when you configure and troubleshoot networking on your UNIX system. The top layers are the ones that most UNIX system administrators spend time working with because those layers are closest to the functionality to which you can relate. The bottom layers are, however, also important to understand at some level, so that you can perform any configuration necessary to improve the network performance of your system, which has a major impact on the overall performance of your system.

Layer Number	Layer Name	Data Form	Comments
7	Application		User applications here.
6	Presentation		Applications prepared.
5	Session		Applications prepared.
4	Transport	Packet	Port-to-port transportation handled by TCP.
3	Network	Datagram	Internet Protocol (IP) handles routing by going directly to either the destination or default router.
2	Link	Frame	Data encapsulated in Ethernet or IEEE 802.3 with source and destination addresses.

Layer Number	Layer Name	Data Form	Comments
1	Physical		Physical connection between systems. Usually thinnet or twisted pair.

Figure 13-2 ISO/OSI Network Layer Functions

I start reviewing Figure 13-2 at the bottom with layer 1 and then describe each of the four bottom layers. This is the International Standards Organization Open Systems Interconnection (ISO/OSI) model. It is helpful to visualize the way in which networking layers interact.

Physical Layer

The beginning is the physical interconnection between the systems on your network. Without the **physical layer,** you can't communicate between systems, and all the great functionality you would like to implement is not possible. The physical layer converts the data you would like to transmit to the analog signals that travel along the wire (I'll assume for now that whatever physical layer you have in place uses wires). The information traveling into a network interface is taken off the wire and prepared for use by the next layer.

Link Layer

In order to connect to other systems local to your system, you use the link layer that is able to establish a connection to all the other systems on your local segment. This is the layer where you have either IEEE 802.3 or Ethernet. Your UNIX system supports both of these "encapsulation" methods. This is called encapsulation because your data is put in one of these two forms (either IEEE 802.3 or Ethernet). Data is transferred at the link layer in frames (just another name for data), with the source and destination addresses and some other information attached. You might think that because two different encapsulation methods exist, they must be very different. This assumption, however, is not the case. IEEE 802.3 and Ethernet are nearly identical. For this reason, many UNIX systems can handle both types of encapsulation. So with the bottom two layers, you have a physical connection between your systems and data that is encapsulated into one of two formats with a source and destination address attached. Figure 13-3 lists the components of an **Ethernet** encapsulation and makes comments about IEEE802.3 encapsulation where appropriate:

destination address	6 bytes	address data is sent to
source address	6 bytes	address data is sent from
type	2 bytes	this is the "length count" in 802.3
data	46-1500 bytes	38-1492 bytes for 802.3; the difference in these two data sizes (MTU) can be seen with the **ifconfig** command
crc	4 bytes	checksum to detect errors

Figure 13-3 Ethernet Encapsulation

One interesting item to note is the difference in the maximum data size between IEEE 802.3 and Ethernet of 1492 and 1500 bytes, respectively. This is the Maximum Transfer Unit (MTU). The **ifconfig** command covered shortly displays the MTU for your interface. The data in Ethernet is called a *frame* (the re-encapsulation of data at the next layer up is called a *datagram* in IP, and encapsulation at two levels up is called a *packet* for TCP).

Keep in mind that Ethernet and IEEE 802.3 will run on the same physical connection, but there are indeed differences between the two encapsulation methods. With your UNIX systems, you don't have to spend much, if any, time setting up your network interface for encapsulation.

Network Layer

Next we work up to the third layer, which is the network layer. This layer on UNIX systems is synonymous with the Internet Protocol (IP). Data at this layer is transported as *datagrams*. This is the layer that handles the routing of data around the network. Data that gets routed with IP sometimes encounters an error of some type, which is reported back to the source system with an Internet Control Message Protocol (ICMP) message. We will see some

ICMP messages shortly. **ifconfig** and **netstat** are two UNIX commands that are commonly used to configure this routing.

Unfortunately, the information that IP uses does not conveniently fit inside an Ethernet frame, so you end up with fragmented data. This is really re-encapsulation of the data, so you end up with a lot of inefficiency as you work your way up the layers.

IP handles routing in a simple fashion. If data is sent to a destination connected directly to your system, then the data is sent directly to that system. If, on the other hand, the destination is not connected directly to your system, the data is sent to the default router. The default router then has the responsibility of getting the data to its destination. This routing can be a little tricky to understand, so I'll cover it in detail shortly.

Transport Layer

The *trasport level* is the next level up from the network layer. It communicates with *ports*. TCP is the most common protocol found at this level, and it forms packets that are sent from port to port. The port used by a program is usually defined in **/etc/services**, along with the protocol (such as TCP). These ports are used by network programs such as **telnet**, **rlogin**, **ftp**, and so on. You can see that these programs, associated with ports, are the highest level we have covered while analyzing the layer diagram.

Internet Protocol (IP) Addressing

The Internet Protocol address (IP address) is either a class "A," "B," or "C" address (there are also class "D" and "E" addresses I will not cover). A class "A" network supports many more nodes per network than either a class "B" or "C" network. IP addresses consist of four fields. The purpose of breaking down the IP address into four fields is to define a node (or host) address and a network address. Figure 13-4 summarizes the relationships between the classes and addresses.

Address Class	Networks	Nodes per Network	Bits Defining Network	Bits Defining Nodes per Network
A	a few	the most	8 bits	24 bits
B	many	many	16 bits	16 bits
C	the most	a few	24 bits	8 bits
Reserved	-	-	-	-

Figure 13-4 Comparison of Internet Protocol (IP) Addresses

These bit patterns are significant in that the number of bits defines the ranges of networks and nodes in each class. For instance, a class A address uses 8 bits to define networks, and a class C address uses 24 bits to define networks. A class A address therefore supports fewer networks than a class C address. A class A address, however, supports many more nodes per network than a class C address. Taking these relationships one step further, we can now view the specific parameters associated with these address classes in Figure 13-5.

Figure 13-5 Address Classes

Address Class	Networks Supported	Nodes per Network	Address Range		
A	127	16777215	0.0.0.1	-	127.255.255.254
B	16383	65535	128.0.0.1	-	191.255.255.254
C	2097157	255	192.0.0.1	-	223.255.254.254
Reserved	-	-	224.0.0.0	-	255.255.255.255
Looking at the 32-bit address in binary form, you can see how to determine the class of an address:					

Figure 13-5   Address Classes (Continued)

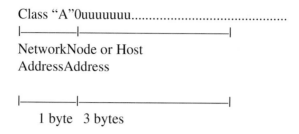

Class "A"0uuuuuuu..
|————|——————————|
NetworkNode or Host
AddressAddress

|————|——————————————|
1 byte   3 bytes

net.host.host.host

A class "A" address has the first bit set to 0. You can see how so many nodes per network can be supported with all the bits devoted to the node or host address. The first bit of a class A address is 0, and the remaining 7 bits of the network portion are used to define the network. Then a total of 3 bytes are devoted to defining the nodes with a network.

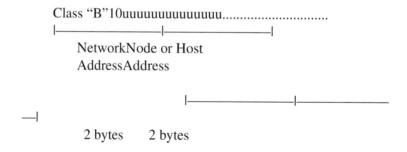

Class "B"10uuuuuuuuuuuuuuu............................
|——————————|——————————|
NetworkNode or Host
AddressAddress

|———————————|——————————
—|
2 bytes   2 bytes

net.net.host.host

A class "B" address has the first bit set to a 1 and the second bit to a 0. More networks are supported here than with a class A address, but fewer nodes per network. With a class B address, 2 bytes are devoted to the network portion of the address and 2 bytes devoted to the node portion of the address.

Figure 13-5   Address Classes (Continued)

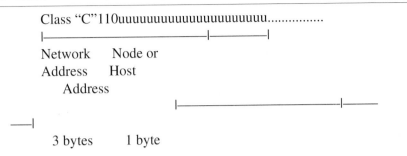

Class "C"110uuuuuuuuuuuuuuuuuuuuuu................

|————————————————|————|

Network   Node or
Address   Host
      Address

            |————————————————|————

——|

3 bytes   1 byte

net.net.net.host

A class "C" address has the first bit and second bit set to 1, and the third bit is 0. The greatest number of networks and fewest number of nodes per network are associated with a class C address. With a class C address, 3 bytes are devoted to the network and 1 byte is devoted to the nodes within a network.

These addresses are used in various setup files that are covered later when the **/etc/hosts** file is described. Every interface on your network must have a unique IP address. Systems that have two network interfaces must have two unique IP addresses.

Subnet Mask

Your UNIX system uses the subnet mask to determine whether an IP datagram is for a host on its own subnet, a host on a different subnet but the same network, or a host on a different network. Using subnets, you can have some hosts on one subnet and other hosts on a different subnet. The subnets can be separated by routers or other networking electronics that connect the subnets.

To perform routing, the only aspects of an address that your router uses are the net and subnet. The subnet mask is used to mask the host part of the address. Because you can set up network addresses in such a way that you are the only one who knows which part of the address is the host, subnet, and network, you use the subnet mask to make your system aware of the bits of your IP address that are for the host and which are for the subnet.

In its simplest form, what you are really doing with subnet masking is specifying which portion of your IP address defines the host, and which part defines the network. One of the most confusing aspects of working with subnet masks is that most books show the subnet masks in Figure 13-6 as the most common.

Address Class	Decimal	Hex
A	255.0.0.0	0xff000000
B	255.255.0.0	0xffff0000
C	255.255.255.0	0xffffff00

Figure 13-6 Subnet Mask

This way of thinking, however, assumes that you are devoting as many bits as possible to the network and as many bits as possible to the host, and that no subnets are used. Figure 13-7 shows an example of using subnetting with a class B address.

Address Class	Class B		
host IP address	152.128.	12.	1
breakdown	network	subnet	hostid
number of bits	16 bits	8 bits	8 bits
subnet mask in decimal	255.255.	255.	0
subnet mask in hexadecimal	0xffffff00		
Example of different host on same subnet	152.128.	12.	2
Example of host on different subnet	152.128.	13.	1

Figure 13-7 Class B IP Address and Subnet Mask Example

In Figure 13-7, the first two bytes of the subnet mask (255.255) define the network, the third byte (255) defines the subnet, and the fourth byte (0) is devoted to the host ID. Although this subnet mask for a class B address did not appear in the earlier default subnet mask figure, the subnet mask of 255.255.255.0 is widely used in class B networks to support subnetting.

How does your UNIX system perform the comparison using the subnet mask of 255.255.255.0 to determine that 152.128.12.1 and 152.128.13.1 are on different subnets? Figure 13-8 shows this comparison.

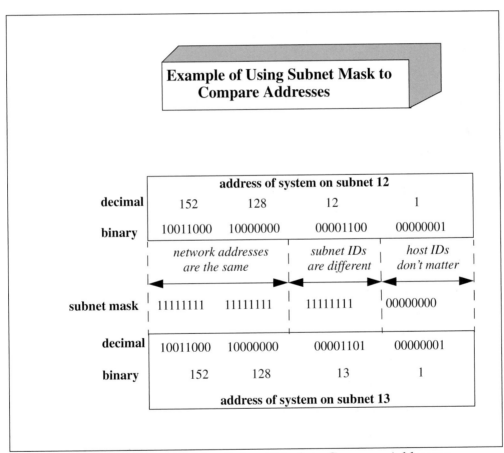

Figure 13-8 Example of Using Subnet Mask to Compare Addresses

Figure 13-9 shows these two systems on the different subnets:

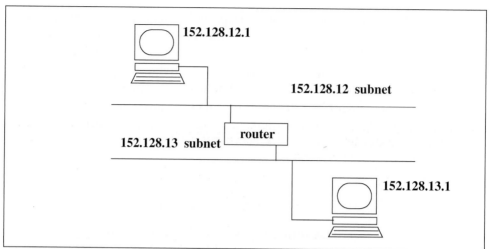

Figure 13-9 Class B Systems on Different Subnets

You don't have to use the 8-bit boundaries to delineate the network, subnet, and host ID fields. If, for instance, you want to use part of the subnet field for the host ID, you can do so. A good reason for this approach would be to accommodate future expandability. You might want subnets 12, 13, 14, and 15 to be part of the same subnet today and make these into separate subnets in the future. Figure 13-10 shows this setup:

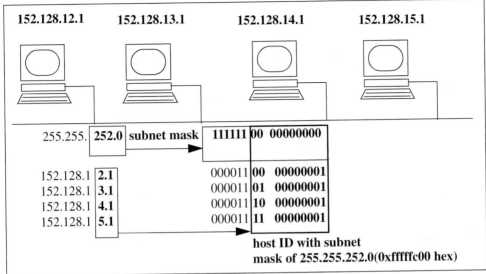

Figure 13-10 Future Expandability Using Subnet Mask

These systems are connected to the same subnet, even though part of the third byte, normally associated with the subnet, is used for the host ID. In the future, the subnet mask could be changed to 255.255.252.0 and have four separate subnets of 12, 13, 14, and 15. This arrangement would require putting routers in place to route to these separate subnets.

Let's now switch to a higher levels of the ISO/OSI model and look at some networking functionality.

Using Networking

The ISO/OSI model is helpful for visualizing the way in which the networking layers interact. The model does not, however, tell you how to use the networking. Two widely used networking services that may be running on your system(s) and are worth taking a look at are ARPA and NFS.

The first networking product to try on your system is what is sometimes called ARPA Services - what I have been calling ARPA. ARPA is a combination of "ARPA Services" and "Berkeley Services." ARPA Services supports communications among systems running different operating systems, and Berkeley Services supports UNIX systems. The following sections are a list of the most common ARPA and Berkeley commands. Although many programs can be run under each of these services, the following are the most commonly used ones in the UNIX world. In some cases, there are examples that show how these commands are used. For most of the examples, the local host is **system1** and the remote host is **system2**.

ARPA Services (Communication among Systems w/ Different OS)

File Transfer Protocol (ftp) Transfer a file, or multiple files, from one system to another. This is often used when transferring files between a UNIX workstation and a Windows PC, VAX, etc. The following example shows copying the file **/tmp/krsort.c** from system2 (remote host) to the local directory on system1 (local host):

	Comments
$ ftp system2	Issue ftp command
Connected to system2.	
system2 FTP server (Version 4.1) ready.	
Name (system2:root): root	Log in to system2
Password required for root.	
Password:	Enter password
User root logged in.	
Remote system type is UNIX.	
Using binary mode to transfer files.	
ftp> **cd /tmp**	**cd** to **/tmp** on system2
CWD command successful	
ftp> **get krsort.c**	Get krsort.c file
PORT command successful	
Opening BINARY mode data connection for **krsort.c**	
Transfer complete.	
2896 bytes received in 0.08 seconds	
ftp> **bye**	Exit ftp
Goodbye.	
$	

In this example, both systems are running UNIX; however, the commands you issue through **ftp** are operating system-independent. The **cd** for change directory and **get** commands used above work for any operating system on which **ftp** is running. If you become familiar with just a few **ftp** commands, you may find that transferring information in a heterogeneous networking environment is not difficult.

Chances are that you are using your UNIX system(s) in a heterogeneous environment and may therefore use **ftp** to copy files and directories from one system to another. Because **ftp** is so widely used, I describe some of the more commonly used **ftp** commands:

ascii	Set the type of file transferred to ASCII. This means that you are transferring an ASCII file from one system to another. This is usually the default, so you don't have to set it.
	Example: **ascii**
binary	Set the type of file transferred to binary. This means that you are transferring a binary file from one system to another. If, for instance, you want to have a directory on your UNIX system that holds applications that you copy to non-UNIX systems, then you want to use binary transfer.
	Example: **binary**
cd	Change to the specified directory on the remote host.
	Example: **cd /tmp**

dir	List the contents of a directory on the remote system to the screen or to a file on the local system, if you specify a local file name.
get	Copy the specified remote file to the specified local file. If you don't specify a local file name, then the remote file name will be used.
lcd	Change to the specified directory on the local host. Example: **lcd /tmp**
ls	List the contents of a directory on the remote system to the screen or to a file on the local system, if you specify a local file name.
mget	Copy multiple files from the remote host to the local host. Example: **mget *.c**
put	Copy the specified local file to the specified remote file. If you don't specify a remote file name, then the local file name will be used. Example: **put test.c**
mput	Copy multiple files from the local host to the remote host. Example: **mput *.c**

bye/quit	Close the connection to the remote host.
	Example: **bye**

Other **ftp** commands are available in addition to those I have covered here. If you need more information on these commands or wish to review additional **ftp** commands, the UNIX manual pages for **ftp** are helpful.

telnet	Used for communication with another host using the telnet protocol. Telnet is an alternative to using **rlogin**, described later. The following example shows how to establish a telnet connection with the remote host, system2:

	Comments
$ telnet system2 Connected to system2. AIX version 4 system2	Telnet to system2
login: **root** password:	Log in as root on system2 Enter password
Welcome to system2. - rs6000 aix 4.3.1.0	
$	AIX prompt on system2

Berkeley Commands (Communication between UNIX Systems)

Remote Copy (rcp)

This program is used to copy files and directories from one UNIX system to another. To copy **/tmp/krsort.c** from system1 to system2, you could do the following:

$ **rcp   system2:/tmp/krsort.c   /tmp/krsort.c**

Some networking configuration needs to be made to files to get this level of functionality. In this example, the user who issues the command is considered "equivalent" on both systems and has permission to copy files from one system to the other with **rcp** (These terms are described shortly).

Remote login (rlogin)

Supports login to a remote UNIX system. To remotely log in to system2 from system1, you would do the following:

$ **rlogin system2**

password:

Welcome to system2

$

If a password is requested when the user issues the **rlogin** command, the users are not equivalent on the two systems. If no password is requested, then the users are indeed equivalent. You can also issue **rlogin** *system* **-l** *user* to specify the *system* and *user* as part of the command.

Remote shell (remsh)

With the **remsh** command, you can sit on one UNIX system and issue a command to be run remotely on a different UNIX system and have the results displayed locally. In this case, a **remsh** is issued to show a long listing of **/tmp/krsort.c**. The command is run on system2, but the result is displayed on system1, where the command was typed:

$ **remsh system2 ll /tmp/krsort.c**

-rwxrwxrwx 1 root sys 2896 Sept 1 10:54 /tmp/krsort.c

$

In this case, the users on system1 and system2 must be equivalent, or else permission is denied to issue this command.

Remote who (rwho)

Find out who is logged in on a remote UNIX system. Here is the output of issuing **rwho**:

$ **rwho**
```
root       system1:ttyu0     Sept 1 19:21
root       system2:console   Sept 1 13:17
tomd       system2:ttyp2     Sept 1 13:05
 |           |        |             |      |> time of login
 |           |        |             |> day of login
 |           |        |
 |           |        |> terminal line
 |           |> machine name
 |
 |> user name
```

For **rwho** to work, the **rwho** daemon (**rwhod**) must be running.

Other "r" commands, in addition to those covered are available. Also, variations of these commands occur going from one UNIX variant to another, so you may not run exactly the same "r" command on your UNIX system.

Host Name Mapping

The most important decision related to networking is how host name mapping is implemented on your system in ARPA. Three techniques are available for host name mapping:

- Berkeley Internet Named Domain (BIND)

- Network Information Service (NIS)

- UNIX file **/etc/hosts**

The most common and simplest way to implement host name mapping is with **/etc/hosts**, so I cover this technique in the next section. Keep in mind that there are probably networking manuals for your UNIX variant devoted to many networking topics including NFS, ARPA, and others. These manuals serve as good reference material if you need to know more about networking than is covered here.

Using the **/etc/hosts** file, as you are about to see, becomes very difficult for environments where there are many systems deployed. With this solution there is one **/etc/hosts** file that must be kept up-to-date and propagated to all other systems.

The Domain Name System (DNS) is widely used in large environments. DNS uses Berkeley Internet Name Domain Service (BIND) to resolve names to addresses. There are name servers that fill a request for name data. This is the server side to BIND. There is a client side to BIND, called the resolver, that accesses the name server(s) to resolve names. Using this client/server model, it is much easier to maintain naming information, because it only needs to be kept in a few places as opposed to on each system.

Clients use a file called **/etc/resolv.conf** to configure the resolver. The name server and its corresponding address are the keys to resolving information.

This solution makes it much easier to maintain system names and addresses in large environments. DNS and BIND are primarily a system administration exercise to setup. From a user standpoint, you don't need to know much about them. What I will instead focus on in the upcoming sections are some of the programs in which users are more interested. I will supply some background so that the way in which the programs are used has more meaning. In general, though, I'll concentrate on the user aspect of these networking topics, as opposed to the system administration aspect of them.

/etc/hosts

This file contains information about the other systems to which you are connected. It contains the Internet address of each system, the system name, and any aliases for the system name. If the **/etc/hosts** file is modified to contain the names of the systems on your network, they have provided the basis for **rlogin** to another system. Although you can now **rlogin** to other UNIX systems, you cannot yet **rcp** or **remsh** to another system. Although adding **remsh** and **rcp** functionality is easy, it does indeed compromise security, so it is not always set up on all systems. Here is an example **/etc/hosts** file:

```
127.0.0.1localhostloopback
15.32.199.42a4410827
15.32.199.28a4410tu8
15.32.199.7a4410922
15.32.199.21a4410tu1
15.32.199.22a4410tu2
15.32.199.62a4410730
15.32.199.63hpxterm1
15.32.199.64a4410rd1
15.32.199.62a4410750hp1
```

This file is in the following format:

\<internet_address\>   \<official_hostname\>   \<alias\>

The Internet Protocol address (IP address) is a class "A," "B," or "C" address. A class "A" network supports many more nodes per network than either a class "B" or "C" network. The purpose of breaking down the IP address into four fields is to define a node (or host) address and a network address. Figures 9-3 through 9-6 described these classes in detail.

Assuming that the above **/etc/hosts** file contains class "C" addresses, the rightmost field is the host or node address, and the other three fields comprise the network address.

You could use either the official_hostname or alias from the **/etc/hosts** file when issuing one of the ARPA or Berkeley commands described earlier. For instance, either of the following ARPA commands work:

$ **telnet a4410750**

or

$ **telnet hp1**

Similarly, either of the following Berkeley commands works:

$ **rlogin a4410750**

or

$ **rlogin hp1**

/etc/hosts.equiv

Your system may be setup so user's don't have to issue a password when they **rlogin** to a remote system, they can set up equivalent hosts by editing this file. As I mentioned earlier, this is technique sometimes considered a security risk, so it is not always employed. The login names must be the same on both the local and remote systems for **/etc/hosts.equiv** to allow the user to bypass entering a password. You can either list all the equivalent hosts in **/etc/hosts.equiv** or list the host and user name you wish to be equivalent. Users can now use **rcp** and **remsh**, because they are equivalent users on these systems. I usually just enter all the host names on the network. Here is an example of **/etc/hosts.equiv**:

```
a4410730
a4410tu1
a4410tu2
hpxterm1
a4410827
a4410750
```

Keep in mind the potential security risks of using **/etc/hosts.equiv**. If a user can log into a remote system without a password, you have reduced the overall level of security on your network. Even though users may find it convenient to not have to enter a password when logging into a remote system, you have given every user in **/etc/ hosts.equiv** access to the entire network. If you could ensure that all the permissions on all the files and directories on all systems were properly set up, then you wouldn't care who had access to what system. In the real UNIX world, however, permissions are sometimes not what they are supposed to be. Users have a strong tendency to "browse around," invariably stumbling upon a file they want to copy to which they really shouldn't have access.

/.rhosts

This file is the **/etc/hosts.equiv** for superuser. If you log in as root, you want to have this file configured with exactly the same information as **/etc/ hosts.equiv**. If you do, however, you have compounded your network security risk by allowing superuser on any system to log in to a remote system without a root password. If you are the undisputed ruler of your network and you're 100 percent certain that no security holes exist, then you may want to set up **/.rhosts** so that you don't have to issue a password when you log in remotely to a system as superuser. From a security standpoint, however, you should know that this setup is frowned upon.

If the appropriate changes have been made to the appropriate entries in **/etc/hosts**, **/etc/hosts.equiv**, and **/.rhosts**, you can use the ARPA Services commands **ftp** and **telnet**, as well as the Berkeley commands **rcp**, **rlogin**, **remsh**, and **rwho**.

I have described the process of setting up the appropriate files to get the most commonly used ARPA Services up and running. There is sometimes even more advanced functionality, such as DNS/BIND, required. Your system may have DNS/BIND or similar functionality set up that gives you access to some or all of the commands covered throughout this section.

Network File System (NFS)

NFS allows you to mount disks on remote systems so that they appear as though they are local to your system. Similarly, NFS allows remote systems to mount your local disk so that it looks as though it is local to the remote system. Configuring NFS to achieve this functionality is simple. Here are the steps to go through in order to configure NFS:

1. Start NFS.

2. Specify whether your system will be an NFS Client, NFS Server, or both.

3. Specify which of your local file systems can be mounted by remote systems.

4. Specify the remote disks that you want to mount and view as if they were local to your system.

As with ARPA, you could enable other aspects to NFS, but again, I cover what I know to be the NFS functionality that nearly every UNIX installation uses.

Because NFS may be setup on your system to meet the needs of many users, you may want to understand the terminology associated with NFS. The following are commonly used NFS terms:

Node   A computer system that is attached to or is part of a computer network.

Client   A node that requests data or services from other nodes (servers).

Server   A node that provides data or services to other nodes (clients) on the network.

File System   A disk partition or logical volume.

Export   Makes a file system available for mounting on remote nodes using NFS.

Mount	Accesses a remote file system using NFS.
Mount Point	The name of a directory on which the NFS file system is mounted.
Import	Mounts a remote file system.

Some of the specific configuration tasks and related files are different among UNIX variants. The following are some general tasks and examples related to configuring NFS. Your system administrator, of course, has to deal with the specifics of configuration on the UNIX variants.

Your system must be an NFS client, NFS server, or both. There are also daemons which must be running to support NFS. Both of these tasks are performed somewhat differently among the UNIX variants.

Your system then imports remote file systems to which you have local access and exports local file systems that are accessed by other systems.

A remote file system that you are mounting locally has an entry similar to the one that follows in **/etc/fstab, /etc/vfstab, /etc/filesystems**, or whatever file is used to mount file systems:

```
system2:/opt/app3    /opt/app3    nfs  rw,suid   0 0
```

In this case, we are mounting **/opt/app3** on *system2* locally as **/opt/app3**. This is an NFS mount with the permissions shown.

You can use the **showmount** command to show all remote systems (clients) that have mounted a local file system. This command is supported on most UNIX variants. **showmount** is useful for determining the file systems that are most often mounted by clients with NFS. The output of **showmount** is particularly easy to read, because it lists the host name and the directory that was mounted by the client. You have the three following options to the **showmount** command:

-a prints output in the format "name:directory"
-d lists all the local directories that have been remotely mounted by clients
-e prints a list of exported file systems

Set Up DNS Servers Using BIND 8.1.2 on HP-UX 11.0 and 11i

This procedure documents how to setup a Master (primary), a Slave (secondary), and a Caching-only DNS server on HP-UX 11.0/11i platforms with the latest supported BIND version 8.1.2 release for HP-UX. BIND 8.1.2 is loaded on 11.0 via a patch from *http://software.hp.com* and is provided on the 11i release media. For a more detailed discussion on BIND 8.1.2, please refer to the O'Reilly and Associates 3rd Edition book DNS and BIND, by Albitz and Liu. BIND 8.1.2 is available on the 11.0/11i platforms only and not on 10.20. 10.20 uses the older 4.9.7 version. It is important to be aware that the older 4.9.X versions of BIND have a different configuration file (boot file) format. There are also some terminology differences. The "boot" file is now called a "config" or "conf" file. HP Primary nameservers are now called Master nameservers; Secondary name servers are now called Slaves.

In most cases, DNS implementation is fairly straightforward, i.e., resource records and database files, etc. The real test comes in planning. Considerations such as whether the DNS system will be protected behind a firewall, whether or not you wish your resolvers to "peer" out on the Internet, and nslookup remote domains and addresses must be considered. Some administrators choose to turn off looking out on the internet to reduce the network traffic it creates. If you are directly attached to the Internet, you will need to register at least two nameservers with an authorized Internet Domain Name provider. A list of these providers can be found at http://www.icann.org/registrars/accredited-list.html. If you are not directly attached, i.e., sitting behind a firewall, an ISP is a good choice for DNS services and will do most of the work for you.

When you have completed your planning you need to configure your DNS server. What names should you use? Some people use planets, locational references, and sometimes people use names for their network computers and printers. The decision is up to you, but do not use underscores in your hostnames (see "check-names" boot file options), and make the names easy to remember.. Here are the steps to creating a Master (Primary) DNS server for your network:

1. Populate **/etc/hosts** with all of the hosts that you want to administer, separated by network segment and domains, and keep everything in an orderly

fashion so that a tool such as hosts_to_named can safely and efficiently administer database files for you as in the following example:

```
/etc/hosts
15.17.186.159 wtec712-rtr

127.0.0.1 localhost loopback
# 812 Bogus Domain BASEBALL.HP.COM

# NL - EAST DIVISION
10.1.1.1 atlantabraves atlantabraves.baseball.hp.com

10.1.1.2 newyork newyorkmets.baseball.hp.com
# NL - CENTRAL DIVISION

10.1.2.1 houstonastros houstonastros.baseball.hp.com

10.1.2.2 chicagocubs chicagocubs.baseball.hp.com

10.1.2.3 stlouiscardinals stlouscardinals.baseball.hp.com
```

2. Create a *param* file with the parameters for your domain as shown in the following example for **/tmp/parm**:

/tmp/param

```
-d baseball.hp.com    <--------- Your domain.
-n 10.1.1             <--------- Your subnet(s).
-n 10.1.2
-n 10.1.3
-n 15.17.186
-H /etc/hosts.dnstest <--------- hosts file you will use.
-r                    <--------- If this nameserver is a
                                 root NS. Our examples
                                 below are NOT for root NS.
```

3. Run **hosts_to_named** with your newly created **param** file from the directory in which you want to place the database. Note that the **param** file is not necessary, but, it is a good idea; the options can be run from the command line instead of including a file. Another common error with **hosts_to_named** is not running it in a "clean" directory. If you need to preserve results before you run it, **mkdir /etc/named.data.old**; **mv /etc/named.data/* /etc/named.data.old** to preserve the prior configuration.

```
# cd /etc/named.data

# hosts_to_named -f /tmp/param
```

```
Translating /tmp/hosts.dns to lower case ...

Collecting network data ...

10.1.1
10.1.2
10.1.3
15.17.186

Creating list of multi-homed hosts ...
Creating "A" data (name to address mapping) for net 10.1.1 ...
Creating "PTR" data (address to name mapping) for net 10.1.1 ...
Creating "A" data (name to address mapping) for net 10.1.2 ...
Creating "PTR" data (address to name mapping) for net 10.1.2 ...
Creating "A" data (name to address mapping) for net 10.1.3 ...
Creating "PTR" data (address to name mapping) for net 10.1.3 ...
Creating "A" data (name to address mapping) for net 15.17.186 ...
Creating "PTR" data (address to name mapping) for net 15.17.168 ...
Creating "MX" (mail exchanger) data ...
Building default named.boot file …

Building default db.cache file ...
WARNING: db.cache must be filled in withthe name(s) and address(es)
of the rootserver(s)
Building default boot.cacheonly for caching only servers ...
done
```

4. **hosts_to_named** will produce both a BIND 4.X **named.boot** file and a
BIND 8.X **named.conf** file. Match the db files created in **/etc/named.data**
with those found in **/etc/named.data/named.conf.** Here is an example for a
non-root name server:

```
// generated by named-bootconf.pl

options {
check-names response fail;    // do not change this
check-names slave warn;
directory "/etc/named.data"; // running directory for named
/*
* If there is a firewall between you and nameservers you want
* to talk to, you might need to uncomment the query-source
* directive below. Previous versions of BIND always asked
* questions using port 53, but BIND 8.1 uses an unprivileged
* port by default.
*/
// query-source address * port 53;
};

//
// type domain source file
//

zone "0.0.127.IN-ADDR.ARPA" {
type master;
```

```
file "db.127.0.0";
};

zone "baseball.hp.com" {
type master;
file "db.baseball";
};

zone "1.1.10.IN-ADDR.ARPA" {
type master;
file "db.10.1.1";
};

zone "2.1.10.IN-ADDR.ARPA" {
type master;
file "db.10.1.2";
};

zone "3.1.10.IN-ADDR.ARPA" {
type master;
file "db.10.1.3";
};

zone "186.17.15.IN-ADDR.ARPA" {
type master;
file "db.15.17.186";
};

zone "." {
type hint;
file "db.cache";
};

(wtec712-rtr)named.data- ls

boot.cacheonly db.10.1.2 db.15.17.186 named.boot
conf.cacheonly db.10.1.3 db.baseball named.conf
db.10.1.1 db.127.0.0 db.cache params-file
```

As you can see, **hosts_to_named** created reverse lookup (IP addresses to names) db files with one parent domain, **baseball.hp.com**. Each of the nodes in our network will have the fully-qualified name **shortname.baseball.hp.com**.

5. Since many installations still use underscores in hostnames, we highly recommend you allow for this by modifying the *check-names* options lists in the **named.conf** file that **hosts_to_named** generates. For example, you may want to change these lines:

```
options {
check-names response fail            // do not change this
check-names slave warn
.
.
.

to:

options {
check-names response ignore    //change "fail" to "ignore"
check-names slave ignore       //change "warn" to "ignore"
check-names master ignore      //add this whole new line
.
.
.
```

6. Fill in **db.cache** with the addresses of the root name servers. If you are directly connected to the Internet and will be querying the root nameservers at the NIC, obtain an updated list from the site ftp://internic.net/domain/named.cache.

Next, copy the file to **db.cache** after you have downloaded. If you are not directly connected to the Internet and have to go through a firewall to query the root name servers, make the firewall your root name server and point your **db.cache** entry at the firewall in the same fashion that you would specify the root name servers. It is very important to configure **db.cache** correctly or services such as mail and name resolution will be affected. Here is an example of this:

```
; FILL IN THE NAMES AND ADDRESSES OF THE ROOT SERVERS

;

;  . 99999999 IN NS root.server.

; root.server. 99999999 IN A ??.??.??.??

;
. 99999999 IN NS firewall.baseball.hp.com.

firewall.baseball.hp.com. 99999999 IN A 15.17.186.99
```

In this case, **firewall.baseball.hp.com.** is my firewall and since my name server cannot directly query the root nameservers, **db.cache** is directed to my firewall.

7. If you are going to have a Master (primary) name server which will not talk to the internet in any way, shape, or form, then you need to setup your name server as a root name server by doing a couple of things. Either use the *-r* option in your **params** file to **hosts_to_named** or make the following changes:

In your **named.conf** file, change:

```
zone "." {

type hint;

file "db.cache";
```

to:

```
zone "." {

type master;

file "db.root";
```

The root name server database file **db.root** would contain:

```
.   IN   SOA   m3107ced.baseball.hp.com.   root.m3107ced.base-
ball.hp.com.

(

            1          ; Serial
            10800      ; Refresh every 3 hours
            3600       ; Retry every hour
            604800     ; Expire after a week
            86400 )    ; Minimum ttl of 1 day

     IN NS m3107ced.baseball.hp.com.
m3107ced.baseball.hp.com. IN A 15.50.73.92
```

What we have done is set up an internal root name server, **db.root**, with one record, **m3107ced.baseball.hp.com.**

8. The next consideration is where to send queries for domains that you are not authoritative for. If your domain is **baseball.hp.com** and someone asks for **jughead.ibm.com**, what happens to the request? Well, if you've configured a root nameserver with no forwarder statements, the answer is nothing. The query will fail with host not found. This might be a good thing if you do not want your internal systems querying internet domains. Security and network congestion are usually the reason. What if you want to resolve Internet names and addresses, however? Easy, configure a forwarders statement in your **/etc/named.conf** to point to the firewall or whichever system is talking directly to the root name servers as shown in the following example:

```
options {
check-names response ignore ;    // change fail to ignore

check-names slave ignore          // change warn to ignore

check-names master ignore        // add this line


forwards 15.253.24.10 15.253.32.10 15.253.24.10 15.253.32.10

directory "/etc/named.data"; // running directory for named

/*
* If there is a firewall between you and nameservers you want
* to talk to, you might need to uncomment the query-source
* directive below. Previous versions of BIND always asked
* questions using port 53, but BIND 8.1 uses an unprivileged
* port by default.
*/
// query-source address * port 53;
};
```

What's happening here is that queries for domains that we are not authoritative for, basically anything outside **baseball.hp.com**, we are sending to the forwarders to let them handle it. As you can see, there are two forwarders, each listed twice. The reason for this is that forwarders tend to be quite busy and by specifying two of them, you prevent the query from timing out. Be sure to copy **/etc/named.data/named.conf** to **/etc/named.conf**. All versions of BIND will look for the boot file in **/etc/** by default, so don't forget to copy it to **/etc** when you are ready.

9. Configure **/etc/resolv.conf** and **/etc/nsswitch.conf** on your name server and all clients that will be pointed at the name server:

/etc/resolv.conf

```
domain baseball.hp.com
search baseball.hp.com atl.hp.com hp.com rose.hp.com cup.hp.com
external.hp.com

nameserver 15.50.73.92 # authoritative name server 4 atl.hp.com
nameserver 15.51.240.8 # non-authoritate cache only servers
```

/etc/resolv.conf is pretty simple: the domain statement identifies which domain the system is part of; the search statements are used to simplify typing when ther is more than one domain. When you issue a query for say, *jughead*, it will search for *jughead* first in **baseball.hp.com**, then **atl.hp.com**, **rose.hp.com**, and finally, **cup.hp.com**. **/etc/nsswitch.conf** modifies the switch order you will use to look up hosts and IP addresses. There are four possible sources for this information: 1) **/etc/hosts**, 2) **nis**, 3) **nis-plus**, 4) and **dns** By default, the hard coded order is **dns nis** files. To modify the switch order, you need to copy in a fresh **/etc/nsswitch.conf** file from **/usr/newconfig/etc/nsswitch.hp_defaults** and modify the *hosts* entry:

```
# /etc/nsswitch.hp_defaults:

#

# An example file that could be copied over to /etc/nss-
witch.conf; it

# uses NIS (YP) in conjunction with files.

#

passwd: compat

group: compat

hosts: files [NOTFOUND=return] dns

networks: nis [NOTFOUND=return] files

protocols: nis [NOTFOUND=return] files

rpc: nis [NOTFOUND=return] files

publickey: nis [NOTFOUND=return] files

netgroup: nis [NOTFOUND=return] files

automount: files nis
```

```
aliases: files nis

services: nis [NOTFOUND=return] files
```

As you can see, the *hosts* line has been modified so that we consult the **/etc/ hosts** file first then continue on to *dns* if the query is unsuccessful. There are many ways to modify the switch order and many ways to mess things up. Use discretion when changing the switch order and consult the man pages on *switch* for more information.

10. Start up the DNS name server process as follows:

```
# /usr/sbin/named.
# ps -eaf|grep named

root 8074 1 0 08:42:08 ? 0:00 /usr/sbin/named <--- check to make
                                           sure it is running..

root 8077 8072 2 08:42:13 ttyp7 0:00 grep named
```

After the name server is started, you use can **sig_named** to perform various functions. After you modify any of the *db* files or **/etc/named.boot**, you need to tell named to refresh its databases. You can accomplish this using either of the two following commands:

```
 # sig_named restart

 # kill -HUP `/var/run/named.pid`
```

This will reload the databases, which you can verify by viewing the end of file **/var/adm/syslog/syslog.log** as shown below:

```
Oct 12 08:49:13 m3107ced named[8074]: primary zone "0.0.127.IN-AD-
DR.ARPA" loaded (serial 1)

Oct 12 08:49:13 m3107ced named[8074]: primary zone "baseball.hp.com"
loaded (serial 1)

Oct 12 08:49:13 m3107ced named[8074]: primary zone "1.1.10.IN-AD-
DR.ARPA" loaded(serial 1)

Oct 12 08:49:13 m3107ced named[8074]: primary zone "2.1.10.IN-AD-
DR.ARPA" loaded(serial 1)

Oct 12 08:49:13 m3107ced named[8074]: primary zone "3.1.10.IN-AD-
```

```
DR.ARPA" loaded(serial 1)

Oct 12 08:49:13 m3107ced named[8074]: primary zone "1.168.192.IN-AD-
DR.ARPA" loaded (serial 1)

Oct 12 08:49:13 m3107ced named[8074]: primary zone "2.168.192.IN-AD-
DR.ARPA" loaded (serial 1)

Oct 12 08:49:13 m3107ced named[8074]: primary zone "3.168.192.IN-AD-
DR.ARPA" loaded (serial 1)

Oct 12 08:49:13 m3107ced named[8074]: Ready to answer queries.
```

As you can see, **named** loaded each of our databases, or zones, and is ready to answer queries.

11. Test queries both by name and IP address.

```
# nslookup atlantabraves
Using /etc/hosts on: wtec712-rtr
looking up FILES
Trying DNS

Name: atlantabraves.baseball.hp.com

Address: 10.1.1.1

# nslookup 10.1.1.1

Using /etc/hosts on: wtec712-rtr
looking up FILES
Trying DNS
Trying DNS
Name: atlantabraves.baseball.hp.com
Address: 10.1.1.1
```

Looking up *atlantabraves* by name and IP address worked and generally we are done.

We always check **/var/adm/syslog/syslog.log** for messages from **named**. **named** logs a lot of seemingly unimportant chatter, but it always deserves at least a short look.

A Word on Slave (Secondary) Name Servers

Once you have created a Master (primary) DNS server, you have completed all the hard work. Creating Slaves and cache-only servers is simple. Let's walk through this process step-by-step:

1. Use **ftp** to copy the **named.conf** file and **db.cache** from the Master (primary).

2. Edit the **named.conf** file as follows:

- Change each instance of "master" to "slave", except for the loopback domain db.127.0.0 and the cache entry.
- Add a "masters" entry for each zone with the IP address of the Master DNS server.

We'll use our example from above:

```
# cat /etc/named.conf

// generated by named-bootconf.pl

options {

check-names response fail; // do not change this
check-names slave warn;
directory "/etc/named.data"; // running directory for named

/*
 * If there is a firewall between you and nameservers you want
 * to talk to, you might need to uncomment the query-source
 * directive below. Previous versions of BIND always asked
 * questions using port 53, but BIND 8.1 uses an unprivileged
 * port by default.
 */
// query-source address * port 53;
};

//
// type domain source file
//
zone "0.0.127.IN-ADDR.ARPA" {
type master;
file "db.127.0.0";
};

zone "baseball.hp.com" {
type slave;
file "db.baseball";
masters ( 15.17.186.159);
};
```

```
zone "1.1.10.IN-ADDR.ARPA" {
type slave;
file "db.10.1.1";
masters ( 15.17.186.159);
};

zone "2.1.10.IN-ADDR.ARPA" {
type slave;
file "db.10.1.2";
masters ( 15.17.186.159);
};

zone "3.1.10.IN-ADDR.ARPA" {
type slave;
file "db.10.1.3";
masters ( 15.17.186.159);
};

zone "186.17.15.IN-ADDR.ARPA" {
type slave;
file "db.15.17.186";
masters ( 15.17.186.159);
};

zone "." {
type hint;
file "db.cache";
};
```

2. Now, all you need to do, once your **named.boot** has been copied to **/etc/named.boot** and your **/etc/named.data** directory has been created, is kick off a zone transfer.

To kick off a zone transfer, all you need to do is **kill named** with

sig_named restart

or

kill -HUP `/var/run/named.pid`

to start the transfer.

Take a look at **/etc/named.data** and you should see all the database files there now. Also, check **/var/adm/syslog/sylog.log** to make sure the zones were loaded properly as shown in the following example:

```
Oct 12 09:21:34 stimpy named[1893]: secondary zone "1.1.10.IN-AD-
DR.ARPA" loaded (serial 1)

Oct 12 09:21:35 stimpy named[1893]: secondary zone "baseball.hp.com"
loaded (ser ial 1)

Oct 12 09:21:35 stimpy named[1893]: secondary zone "2.1.10.IN-AD-
DR.ARPA" loaded (serial 1)

Oct 12 09:21:35 stimpy named[1893]: secondary zone "1.168.192.IN-AD-
DR.ARPA" loaded (serial 1)

Oct 12 09:21:35 stimpy named[1893]: secondary zone "3.1.10.IN-AD-
DR.ARPA" loaded (serial 1)

Oct 12 09:21:36 stimpy named[1893]: secondary zone "2.168.192.IN-AD-
DR.ARPA" loaded (serial 1)

Oct 12 09:21:36 stimpy named[1893]: secondary zone "3.168.192.IN-AD-
DR.ARPA" loaded (serial 1)
```

Notice the serial number entries. They should match on the Master (primary)
and Slaves (secondaries).

A Word on Cache-Only Name Servers

Why in the world would you want a cache-only name server? In a word, performance. If you want to maintain a local cache but do not want to manage
database files, this is the way to go. It will act as any other name server,
responding to queries in the same fashion, except queries that are built in the
cache will be non-authoritative. Any query that comes back with a non-
authoritative reply is a query received from cache. Is that a bad thing? No,
but be aware that the data may have changed on the Master (primary) and
the cache replies may be outdated. The Time To Live (TTL) flag for each
query is a way to manipulate the time, in seconds, that a name server may
cache the answer to a query, versus having to contact an authoritative name
server. The default TTL for records is usually 86400 seconds, or 24 hours.
You may want to play with this value, depending on how frequently or infrequently the records are updated. A good rule of thumb is to have at least one
name server per subnet, and cache-only name servers are an excellent
choice.

To configure a cache-only name server, copy down the **conf.cacheonly** file and db.cache from the Master (primary) nameserver .

```
// generated by named-bootconf.pl

options {
check-names response fail; // do not change this
check-names slave warn;
directory "/tmp/testhack"; // running directory for named
/*
* If there is a firewall between you and nameservers you want
* to talk to, you might need to uncomment the query-source
* directive below. Previous versions of BIND always asked
* questions using port 53, but BIND 8.1 uses an unprivileged
* port by default.
*/
// query-source address * port 53;
};

//
// type domain source file
//
zone "0.0.127.IN-ADDR.ARPA" {
type master;
file "db.127.0.0";
};

zone "." {
type hint;
file "db.cache";
};
```

Please don't forget to fill in **db.cache** with the name server(s) that you will be caching data for.

A Final Word on Name Server Setup

This section in no way offers a comprehensive discussion on setting up DNS. It is only intended to act as a cookbook after all your planning has been completed. Please refer to the book <u>HP Installing and Administering Internet Services</u> at *http://docs.hp.com*. DNS is pretty straightforward, but any syntax errors or problems with **/etc/named.boot** can have dramatic consequences. The **syslog** can be your best friend when zones are not transferring or there are problems with the data.

Other Networking Commands and Setup

Setting up a network is an intensive planning exercise for both network and system administrators. No two networking environments are alike. There is typically a lot of networking electronics to which your system is connected. There are many useful commands related to testing connectivity to other systems and networking configuration. Should you encounter a problem, you want to have an understanding of some networking commands that can be lifesavers. In addition, you can encounter some tricky aspects to networking setup if you have some networking hardware that your UNIX systems must interface to, such as routers, gateways, bridges, etc. I give an example of one such case: connecting a UNIX system to a router. At the same time, I cover some of the most handy networking commands as part of this description.

Consider Figure 13-11, in which a UNIX system is connected directly to a router.

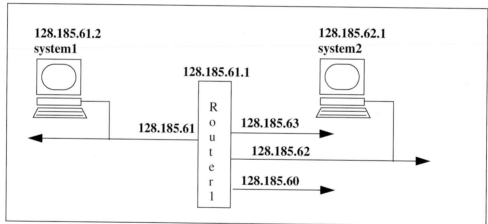

128.185.61.2
system1

128.185.62.1
system2

128.185.61.1

R
o   128.185.61   128.185.63
u
t   128.185.62
e
r   128.185.60
1

Figure 13-11   UNIX System and Router Example

Here we have a UNIX system connected to segment 128.185.61. This is a class "B" Internet address with subnetting enabled.

The **/etc/hosts** file needs to have in it the UNIX system with node ID 2, the router, and any other systems on this segment or segments on the other side of the router.

If the router is properly configured, we should be able to seamlessly connect from 61 to systems on segments 60, 62, and 63. The router should be configured to allow our system to connect to systems on other segments (60, 62, and 63) by going through the router. Some unforeseen configuration was required to make this simple network operate seamlessly. In this case, a problem occurred getting system1 to connect to systems on the other side of the router on 60, 62, and 63. Before discussing the additional configuration that needed to be done, I first show the **/etc/hosts** file and then use some very useful UNIX commands that show the state of the network. Here is the **/etc/hosts** file showing just the UNIX system and router:

$ cat /etc/hosts

127.0.0.1   localhosts loopback
128.185.61.1   router1# router
128.185.61.2   system1# UNIX system on 61
128.185.62.1   system2# UNIX system on 62

This host file is simple and allows system1 to connect to router1 and system2. The connection from system1 to system2 is accomplished by going through the router.

ping

Let's look at one of the most commonly used networking commands - **ping**. This command is used to determine whether or not a connection exists between two networking components. **ping** is a simple command that sends an ICMP echo packet to the host you specify once per second. You may recall that ICMP was covered earlier under the network, or third layer. **ping** stands for Packet InterNet Groper. **ping** differs somewhat among UNIX variants, mostly in the reporting that **ping** produces when no options are provided.

Some systems provide performance information when **ping** is issued with no options; others report that the system "is alive". The following is an example of checking the connection between the local system and another system on the network called *austin*:

```
martyp $ ping austin
austin is alive
martyp $
```

You can adjust the packet size and number of iterations on most UNIX variants as in the HP-UX example shown below specifying a packet size of *4096* and interval of *5*:

```
# ping 12 4096 5
PING 12: 4096 byte packets
4096 bytes from 10.1.1.12: icmp_seq=0. time=2. ms
4096 bytes from 10.1.1.12: icmp_seq=1. time=2. ms
4096 bytes from 10.1.1.12: icmp_seq=2. time=2. ms
4096 bytes from 10.1.1.12: icmp_seq=3. time=2. ms
4096 bytes from 10.1.1.12: icmp_seq=4. time=2. ms

----12 PING Statistics----
5 packets transmitted, 5 packets received, 0% packet loss
round-trip (ms)  min/avg/max = 2/2/2
#
```

AIX allows you to specify the interval with *-I* as well as other options, including packet size, and number of iterations. These options are shown for an AIX system in the following example:

```
martyp $ ping -I 5 austin 4096 10
PING austin: 4096 data bytes
4104 bytes from austin (128.185.61.5): icmp_seq=0. time=8. ms
4104 bytes from austin (128.185.61.5): icmp_seq=1. time=9. ms
4104 bytes from austin (128.15.61.5): icmp_seq=2. time=9. ms
4104 bytes from austin (128.15.61.5): icmp_seq=3. time=9. ms
4104 bytes from austin (128.15.61.5): icmp_seq=4. time=8. ms
4104 bytes from austin (128.15.61.5): icmp_seq=5. time=9. ms
4104 bytes from austin (128.15.61.5): icmp_seq=6. time=9. ms
4104 bytes from austin (128.15.61.5): icmp_seq=7. time=9. ms
4104 bytes from austin (128.15.61.5): icmp_seq=8. time=9. ms
4104 bytes from austin (128.15.61.5): icmp_seq=9. time=9. ms

----austin PING Statistics----

10 packets transmitted, 10 packets received, 0% packet loss
round-trip (ms)  min/avg/max = 9/9/15
martyp $
```

In this example, we **ping** *austin* every five seconds, with a packet size of *4096* bytes for a total of ten times.

Let's now get back to our example.

How do I know that I have a connection between system1 and the router and the other systems on the other side of the router? I use the **ping** command. Here is how I know that system1 is connected to router1:

```
$ ping router1
PING router1: 64 byte packets
64 bytes from 128.185.61.2: icmp_seq=0. time=0. ms
64 bytes from 128.185.61.2: icmp_seq=1. time=0. ms
64 bytes from 128.185.61.2: icmp_seq=2. time=0. ms
```

Each line of output here represents a response that was returned from the device that was pinged. This means that the device responded. You continue to get this response indefinitely and have to type **^c** (control c) to terminate the **ping**. If no output is produced, as shown below, then no response occurred and you may have a problem between your system and the device to which you are checking the connection:

```
$ ping system2
PING router1: 64 byte packets
```

In this scenario, you would see this message and that is as far as you would get. A **^c** will kill the **ping**, and you see that some number of packets were sent and none were received. I did indeed get this response when issuing the **ping** command, so I know that a problem exists with the connection between system1 and router1.

ping should be used only for testing purposes such as manual fault isolation, because it generates a substantial amount of network traffic. You do not want to use ping on an ongoing basis, such as in a script that is running continuously.

A nice variation of **ping** that I use is to specify a packet size of 4096 bytes, rather than the default of 64 bytes shown in the previous examples, and count the number of times **ping** transmits before terminating, rather than having to type **^c** to terminate **ping**. The following example shows this:

```
$ ping router1 4096 5

PING router1: 64 byte packets
4096 bytes from 128.185.51.2: icmp_seq=0. time=8. ms
4096 bytes from 128.185.51.2: icmp_seq=1. time=8. ms
4096 bytes from 128.185.51.2: icmp_seq=2. time=9. ms
4096 bytes from 128.185.51.2: icmp_seq=3. time=8. ms
4096 bytes from 128.185.51.2: icmp_seq=4. time=8. ms
```

Notice that the time required to transmit and receive a response, the round-trip time, is substantially longer than with only 64 bytes transmitted. I usually find that the round-trip time for 64 bytes is 0 ms, although this depends on a number of factors, including network topology and network traffic.

netstat

From the earlier description of the subnet mask, you can see that routing from one host to another can be configured in a variety of ways. The path that information takes in getting from one host to another depends on routing.

You can obtain information related to routing with the **netstat** command. The *-r* option to **netstat** shows the routing tables, which you usually want to know, and the *-n* option can be used to print network addresses as numbers rather than as names. With the *-v* option, you get additional information related to routing, such as the subnet mask. In the following examples, **netstat** is issued with the *-r* option (this is used when describing the **netstat** output), the *-rn* options, and the *-rnv* options, so you can compare the outputs:

```
# netstat -r
Routing tables
Dest/Netmask         Gateway        Flags  Refs       Use  Interface  Pmtu
o2                   o2             UH        0   1890905  lo0        4136
o2                   o2             UH        0       343  lan1       4136
o2                   o2             UH        0         0  lan0       4136
10.1.1.0             o2             U         2         0  lan0       1500
10.1.1.0             o2             U         2         0  lan1       1500
127.0.0.0            o2             U         0         0  lo0        4136
default              10.1.1.1       UG        0         0  lan1       1500
#
```

```
# netstat -rn
Routing tables
Dest/Netmask         Gateway        Flags  Refs       Use  Interface  Pmtu
127.0.0.1            127.0.0.1      UH        0   1891016  lo0        4136
10.1.1.10            10.1.1.10      UH        0       343  lan1       4136
10.1.1.110           10.1.1.110     UH        0         0  lan0       4136
10.1.1.0             10.1.1.110     U         2         0  lan0       1500
10.1.1.0             10.1.1.10      U         2         0  lan1       1500
127.0.0.0            127.0.0.1      U         0         0  lo0        4136
default              10.1.1.1       UG        0         0  lan1       1500
#
```

```
# netstat -rnv
Routing tables
Dest/Netmask                   Gateway        Flags  Refs       Use  Interface  Pmtu
127.0.0.1/255.255.255.255      127.0.0.1      UH        0   1891036  lo0        4136
10.1.1.10/255.255.255.255      10.1.1.10      UH        0       343  lan1       4136
```

```
10.1.1.110/255.255.255.255    10.1.1.110      UH      0       0  lan0      4136
10.1.1.0/255.255.255.0        10.1.1.110      U       2       0  lan0      1500
10.1.1.0/255.255.255.0        10.1.1.10       U       2       0  lan1      1500
127.0.0.0/255.0.0.0           127.0.0.1       U       0       0  lo0       4136
default/0.0.0.0               10.1.1.1        UG      0       0  lan1      1500
#
```

The first and second outputs show that our system, *o2*, has three interfaces: The first is the loopback interface called *lo0*. The second. is at *.10*, and the third is at *.110* (which we can see from the *-rn* output). The next two lines show that our destination of *10.1.1.0*, which is a network, can be accessed through either the card at *.10* or *.110*. The third output provides verbose information. The last line is for the default route. This entry says to send packets to *10.1.1.1* if a more direct route can't be found.

With **netstat**, some information is provided about the router. The *-r* option shows information about routing, but many other useful options to this command are also available. Of particular interest in this output is "Flags," which defines the type of routing that takes place. Here are descriptions of the most common flags from the UNIX manual pages:

1=U   Route to a *network* via a gateway that is the local host itself.

3=UG   Route to a *network* via a gateway that is the remote host.

5=UH   Route to a *host* via a gateway that is the local host itself.

7=UGH   Route to a *host* via a remote gateway that is a host.

Also, I use two forms of **netstat** to obtain network statistics, as opposed to routing information. The first is **netstat -i**, which shows the state of interfaces that are autoconfigured. Because I am most often interested in getting a summary of **lan0**, I issue this command. **netstat -i** gives a good rundown of *lan0*, such as the network it is on, its name, and so on.

The following example shows the output of **netstat -i** on a Solaris and HP-UX system, respectively:

```
# netstat -i

Name  Mtu   Network      Address            Ipkts Ierrs   Opkts Oerrs  Coll
ni0*  0     none         none                   0     0       0     0     0
ni1*  0     none         none                   0     0       0     0     0
lo0   4608  loopback     127.0.0.1            232     0     232     0     0
lan0  1500  169.200.112  169.200.112.2    3589746     2   45630     0   104


# netstat -i
Name          Mtu Network      Address            Ipkts       Opkts
lan1         1500 10.1.1.0     o2              59935480   163641547
lan0         1500 10.1.1.0     o2                139173    12839358
lo0          4136 127.0.0.0    o2               1892333     1892345
#
```

Here is a description of the fields in the **netstat** example:

Name	The name of your network interface (Name), in this case, *lan0*.
MTU	The "maximum transmission unit," which is the maximum packet size sent by the interface card.
Network	The network address of the LAN to which the interface card is connected (169.200).
Address	The host name of your system. This is the symbolic name of your system as it appears in the file **/etc/hosts**.

The statistical information includes:

Ipkts	The number of packets received by the interface card, in this case **lan0**.
Ierrs	The number of errors detected on incoming packets by the interface card (on some UNIX variants).
Opkts	The number of packets transmitted by the interface card.

      Oerrs   The number of errors detected during the transmission of packets by the interface card (on some UNIX variants.)

      Collis   The number of collisions that resulted from packet traffic (on some UNIX variants.)

netstat provides cumulative data since the node was last powered up; you might have a long elapsed time over which data was accumulated. If you are interested in seeing useful statistical information, you can use **netstat** with different options. You can also specify an interval over which to report statistics. I usually ignore the first entry, because it shows all data since the system was last powered up. Therefore, the data includes non-prime hours when the system was idle. I prefer to view data at the time the system is working its hardest. The following **netstat** example provides network interface information every five seconds on a Solaris system:

```
# netstat -I lan0 5

(lan0)-> input              output             (Total)-> input              output
    packets  errs  packets  errs colls        packets  errs  packets  errs colls
    3590505     2    45714     0   104         3590737     2    45946     0   104
        134     0        5     0     0             134     0        5     0     0
        174     0        0     0     0             174     0        0     0     0
        210     0       13     0     0             210     0       13     0     0
        165     0        0     0     0             165     0        0     0     0
        169     0        0     0     0             169     0        0     0     0
        193     0        0     0     0             193     0        0     0     0
        261     0        7     0     0             261     0        7     0     0
        142     0        8     0     0             142     0        8     0     0
        118     0        0     0     0             118     0        0     0     0
        143     0        0     0     0             143     0        0     0     0
        149     0        0     0     0             149     0        0     0     0
```

With this example, you get multiple outputs of what is taking place on the LAN interface. As I mentioned earlier, you may want to ignore the first output, because it includes information over a long time period. This may include a time when your network was idle, and therefore the data is not important to you.

The following **netstat** example provides network interface information every five seconds on an HP-UX 11i system:

```
# netstat -I lan0 5
(lan0)-> input       output        (Total)-> input       output
         packets      packets                 packets      packets
          139185     12841621                61968131    178375605
```

```
     139185      12841714
     139185      12841810          61968172    178375698
     139185      12841877          61968213    178375794
     139185      12841912          61968247    178375861
     139185      12842095          61968265    178375896
     139187      12842244          61968358    178376079
     139189      12842352          61968413    178376240
     139189      12842453          61968470    178376360
     139190      12842482          61968525    178376461
     139190      12842539          61968565    178376498
     139190      12842671          61968594    178376555
                                   61968667    178376699
```

You can specify the network interface on which you want statistics reported by using **-I interface**; in the case of the example, it was *-I lan0*. An interval of five seconds was also used in this example.

Yet another use of **netstat** is to show the state of network sockets. **netstat -a** produces a list of protocols, queues, local and remote addresses, and protocol states. All this information is useful for showing active communications, as shown in the following example:

```
# netstat -a
Active Internet connections (including servers)
Proto Recv-Q Send-Q Local Address       Foreign Address           (state)
tcp      0      2    system1.telnet      atlm0081.atl.hp..1319   ESTABLISHED
tcp      0      0    *.1095              *.*                     LISTEN
tcp      0      0    *.psmond            *.*                     LISTEN
tcp      0      0    *.mcsemon           *.*                     LISTEN
tcp      0      0    localhost.8886      localhost.1062          ESTABLISHED
tcp      0      0    localhost.1062      localhost.8886          ESTABLISHED
tcp      0      0    *.8886              *.*                     LISTEN
tcp      0      0    *.8887              *.*                     LISTEN
tcp      0      0    *.1006              *.*                     LISTEN
tcp      0      0    *.978               *.*                     LISTEN
tcp      0      0    *.22370             *.*                     LISTEN
tcp      0      0    *.389               *.*                     LISTEN
tcp      0      0    *.8181              *.*                     LISTEN
tcp      0      0    *.1054              *.*                     LISTEN
tcp      0      0    *.1053              *.*                     LISTEN
tcp      0      0    *.diagmond          *.*                     LISTEN
tcp      0      0    *.1045              *.*                     LISTEN
tcp      0      0    *.1038              *.*                     LISTEN
tcp      0      0    *.135               *.*                     LISTEN
tcp      0      0    *.smtp              *.*                     LISTEN
tcp      0      0    *.1036              *.*                     LISTEN
tcp      0      0    *.appconn           *.*                     LISTEN
tcp      0      0    *.spc               *.*                     LISTEN
tcp      0      0    *.dtspc             *.*                     LISTEN
tcp      0      0    *.recserv           *.*                     LISTEN
tcp      0      0    *.klogin            *.*                     LISTEN
tcp      0      0    *.kshell            *.*                     LISTEN
tcp      0      0    *.chargen           *.*                     LISTEN
tcp      0      0    *.discard           *.*                     LISTEN
tcp      0      0    *.echo              *.*                     LISTEN
tcp      0      0    *.time              *.*                     LISTEN
tcp      0      0    *.daytime           *.*                     LISTEN
tcp      0      0    *.printer           *.*                     LISTEN
tcp      0      0    *.auth              *.*                     LISTEN
tcp      0      0    *.exec              *.*                     LISTEN
tcp      0      0    *.shell             *.*                     LISTEN
tcp      0      0    *.login             *.*                     LISTEN
tcp      0      0    *.telnet            *.*                     LISTEN
tcp      0      0    *.ftp               *.*                     LISTEN
tcp      0      0    *.795               *.*                     LISTEN
```

```
tcp      0      0   *.792                 *.*                    LISTEN
tcp      0      0   *.*                   *.*                    CLOSED
tcp      0      0   *.787                 *.*                    LISTEN
tcp      0      0   *.783                 *.*                    LISTEN
tcp      0      0   *.779                 *.*                    LISTEN
tcp      0      0   *.portmap             *.*                    LISTEN
tcp      0      0   *.2121                *.*                    LISTEN
udp      0      0   *.1127                *.*
udp      0      0   *.177                 *.*
udp      0      0   *.1003                *.*
udp      0      0   *.*                   *.*
udp      0      0   *.*                   *.*
udp      0      0   *.*                   *.*
udp      0      0   *.*                   *.*
udp      0      0   *.nfsd                *.*
udp      0      0   *.976                 *.*
udp      0      0   *.22370               *.*
udp      0      0   *.1097                *.*
udp      0      0   *.1095                *.*
udp      0      0   *.1079                *.*
udp      0      0   *.135                 *.*
udp      0      0   *.*                   *.*
udp      0      0   *.1045                *.*
udp      0      0   *.snmp                *.*
udp      0      0   *.1040                *.*
udp      0      0   *.tftp                *.*
udp      0      0   *.chargen             *.*
udp      0      0   *.discard             *.*
udp      0      0   *.echo                *.*
udp      0      0   *.time                *.*
udp      0      0   *.daytime             *.*
udp      0      0   *.ntalk               *.*
udp      0      0   *.bootps              *.*
udp      0      0   *.1023                *.*
udp      0      0   *.787                 *.*
udp      0      0   *.798                 *.*
udp      0      0   *.797                 *.*
udp      0      0   *.1037                *.*
udp      0      0   *.*                   *.*
udp      0      0   *.1036                *.*
udp      0      0   *.1035                *.*
udp      0      0   *.777                 *.*
udp      0      0   *.portmap             *.*
udp      0      0   *.1034                *.*
udp      0      0   *.syslog              *.*
udp      0      0   *.2121                *.*
Active UNIX domain sockets
Address  Type    Recv-Q Send-Q   Inode    Conn    Refs   Nextref Addr
  bb9c00 stream      0      0   af9000      0        0        0 /tmp/.AgentSoA
  ced700 dgram       0      0   c99400      0        0        0 /opt/dcelocalr
  ce9e00 dgram       0      0   d23000      0        0        0 /opt/dcelocalr
  b0d200 dgram       0      0   b87000      0        0        0 /opt/dcelocal1
  997a00 stream      0      0   b84800      0        0        0 /opt/dcelocal1
  b24e00 dgram       0      0   b84000      0        0        0 /var/tmp/psb_t
  d59400 dgram       0      0   b66400      0        0        0 /var/tmp/psb_t
  d85c00 dgram       0      0   b67000      0        0        0 /opt/dcelocalr
  c8b200 dgram       0      0   b12000      0        0        0 /opt/dcelocal5
  c8b400 stream      0      0   b78400      0        0        0 /opt/dcelocal5
  c8b300 dgram       0      0   b78000      0        0        0 /opt/dcelocalr
  c90900 dgram       0      0   d22400      0        0        0 /opt/dcelocal0
  c78c00 dgram       0      0   ba1000   c4a180      0        0 /opt/dcelocald
  b1e900 dgram       0      0   9a4400      0     c32e80      0 /opt/dcelocal5
  d64100 stream      0      0   d24c00      0        0        0 /opt/dcelocal2
  9e1600 dgram       0      0   9a4000   d4d940      0        0 /opt/dcelocal9
  d64200 dgram       0      0   cfc800      0     c32c80      0 /opt/dcelocal1
  d12d00 dgram       0      0   cfc000   c32c00      0        0 /opt/dcelocal4
  c5ee00 stream      0      0   b1c000      0        0        0 /opt/dcelocald
  d19d00 dgram       0      0   ce4800      0     af15c0      0 /opt/dcelocal7
  cf0c00 dgram       0      0   a92800      0     af15c0      0 /opt/dcelocal0
  d2d600 dgram       0      0   a93800   c32c00      0   d4db80 /opt/dcelocald
  c9b900 dgram       0      0   a93c00      0        0        0 /var/opt/OV/sT
  d6c800 stream      0      0   ba3000      0        0        0
#
```

A lot of information is in this output. You can refer to the online manual pages on your HP-UX system.

The first line shows the *Proto tcp* to the *Local Address system1.telnet* as having a *(state)* of *ESTABLISHED*. This is the connection we have initiated to this system. We are sitting on *system1* with a telnet session open to the system on which we ran **netstat**.

Most of the remaining *tcp* protocol entries are listening. This means that they are listening for incoming connections, as indicated by the *LISTEN*. They have a wildcard in the *Foreign Address* field, which will contain the address when a connection has been established. We are one of the few connections that has been made, as indicated by the *ESTABLISHED*.

All the send and receive queues, shown as *Recv-Q* and *Send-Q*, are empty as indicated by *0*.

The UNIX domain sockets at the end of the output are stream and datagram connections for a variety of services such as NFS.

This output gives you an appreciation of the immense amount of activity taking place from a networking perspective on your UNIX system. Networking and connectivity have been among the most advanced aspects of UNIX since its inception.

route

The information displayed with **netstat** is the routing tables for your system. Some are automatically created with the **ifconfig** command when your system is booted or when the network interface is initialized. Routes to networks and hosts that are not directly connected to your system are entered with the **route** command.

Routing changes can be made on the fly, as I did to change the *Flags* from *U* to *UG*:

```
$ /usr/sbin/route add default 128.185.61.1 3
```

First is the **route** command. Second, we specify that we wish to add a route; the other option is to delete a route. Third, we specify the destination, in this case, the default. This could be a specific host name, a network name, an IP address, or default that signifies the wildcard gateway route that is shown in our example. Fourth is the gateway through which the destination is reached. In the above example, the IP address was used, but this could also be a host name. The 3 corresponds to the count that is used to specify whether the gateway is the local host or a remote gateway. If the gateway is the local host, then a count of 0 is used. If the gateway is a remote host, which is the case in the example, a count of >0 is used. This corresponds to *UG* for *Flags*. This manually changed the network routing table by adding a default route with the appropriate *Flags*. Issuing this command fixed the problem I encountered trying to get system1 to talk to the systems on the other side of the router (remember Figure 13-11).

Before issuing **/usr/sbin/route** with the **add** option, you can first use the **delete** option to remove the existing default route, which is not working.

route commands usually appear in one of the system's startup files so that every time the system boots, **route** commands are issued. This ensures that the right connectivity information is in place every time the system starts.

ifconfig

The **ifconfig** command provides additional information on a LAN interface. The following example provides the configuration of a network interface:

```
$ /etc/ifconfig lan0
lan0:   flags=863<UP,BROADCAST,NOTRAILERS,RUNNING>
        inet 128.185.61.2 netmask ffff0000 broadcast 128.185.61.255
```

From this example, we can quickly see that the interface is up, it has an address of 128.185.61.2, and it has a netmask of *ffff0000*. Again, keep in mind that your network interface may have a different name, such as *le0*.

You can use **ifconfig** to get the status of a network interface as I have done here to assign an address to a network interface, or to configure network interface parameters. The network address you have falls into classes such as "A," "B," or "C," as mentioned earlier. You want to be sure that you know the class of your network before you start configuring your LAN interface. This example is a class "B" network, so the netmask is defined as ffff0000 (typical for a class "B" address), as opposed to ffffff00, which is typical for a class "C" network. The netmask is used to determine how much of the address to reserve for subdividing the network into smaller networks. The netmask can be represented in hex, as shown above, or in decimal format, as in the **/etc/hosts** file. Here is the **ifconfig** command I issued to configure the interface:

```
$ /etc/ifconfig lan0 inet 128.185.61.2 netmask 255.255.0.0
```

- The *255.255.0.0* corresponds to the hex *ffff000* shown earlier for the class "B" subnet mask.

- *lan0* is the interface being configured.

- *inet* is the address family, which is currently the only one supported for this system.

- *128.185.61.2* is the address of the LAN interface for system1.

- **netmask** shows how to subdivide the network.

- *255.255.0.0* is the same as *ffff0000*, which is the netmask for a class "B" address.

I have made good use of **netstat**, **ping**, and **ifconfig** to help get the status of the network. **ifconfig**, **route**, and **/etc/hosts** are used to configure the network, should you identify any changes you need to make. The subnet examples show how flexible you can be when configuring your network for both your current and future needs. In simple networks, you may not need to use many of these commands or complex subnetting. In complex networks, or at times when you encounter configuration difficulties, you may have to make extensive use of these commands. In either case, network planning is an important part of setting up UNIX systems.

Most of the commands used throughout this chapter are a part of every system administrator's tool box. Networking is so vital to the use of UNIX systems, however, that having background in this area can help with your overall understanding of the system and how to use it more effectively.

rpcinfo

As a user, you may have a need to NFS mount a directory on another system or perform some other function that you haven't before used on your system. You can determine whether various pieces of functionality have been enabled by evaluating the daemons running on your system. **rpcinfo** allows you to generate a Remote Procedure Call (RPC) on a system, including your local system, by issuing the command **rpc -p** *system_name*.

The following example shows issuing **rpcinfo -p** on our local system:

```
# rpcinfo -p
   program vers proto   port  service
   100000   2    tcp    111   portmapper
   100000   2    udp    111   portmapper
   100024   1    udp    777   status
   100024   1    tcp    779   status
   100021   1    tcp    783   nlockmgr
   100021   1    udp    1035  nlockmgr
   100021   3    tcp    787   nlockmgr
   100021   3    udp    1036  nlockmgr
   100020   1    udp    1037  llockmgr
   100020   1    tcp    792   llockmgr
   100021   2    tcp    795   nlockmgr
   100068   2    udp    1040  cmsd
   100068   3    udp    1040  cmsd
   100068   4    udp    1040  cmsd
   100068   5    udp    1040  cmsd
   100083   1    tcp    1036  ttdbserver
   100005   1    udp    976   mountd
   100005   1    tcp    978   mountd
   100003   2    udp    2049  nfs
   150001   1    udp    1003  pcnfsd
   150001   2    udp    1003  pcnfsd
   150001   1    tcp    1006  pcnfsd
   150001   2    tcp    1006  pcnfsd
#
```

Many daemons are running on the system that are important to the functionality I like to use. **mountd** is running, which indicates that a server could NFS mount file systems on this computer. There is other setup required for the mount to take place, but at least the daemon is running to support this functionality. In addition, **pcnfsd** is running, meaning that we have support for Windows-based NFS access.

arp

The mechanism used to maintain a list of IP addresses and their corresponding MAC addresses is the *ARP cache*. The mapped addresses are only held in the cache for minutes, so if you want to see what addresses have been mapped recently, you can use the **arp** command as shown in the following example:

```
# arp -a
o2 (10.1.1.10) at 0:10:83:f7:a2:f8 ether
l1 (10.1.1.11) at 0:10:83:f7:2e:d0 ether
63.88.85.1 (63.88.85.1) at 0:30:94:b0:b8:a0 ether
l3 (10.1.1.200) at 0:10:83:fc:92:88 ether
tape1 (10.1.1.14) at 0:10:83:f7:e:32 ether
tape1 (10.1.1.14) at 0:10:83:f7:e:32 ether
tape1 (10.1.1.14) at 0:10:83:f7:e:32 ether
tape1 (10.1.1.14) at 0:10:83:f7:e:32 ether
63.88.85.18 (63.88.85.18) -- no entry
```

Current *arp* entries are displayed with the *-a* command. You can create an entry with the *-s* option.

lanadmin

lanadmin is used to view and perform administration on network cards. Issuing **lanadmin** with no options brings you into the interactive interface as shown in the following example:

```
# lanadmin

        LOCAL AREA NETWORK ONLINE ADMINISTRATION, Version 1.0

           Copyright 1994 Hewlett Packard Company.
                 All rights are reserved.
Test Selection mode.
```

```
           lan    = LAN Interface Administration
           menu   = Display this menu
           quit   = Terminate the Administration
           terse  = Do not display command menu
           verbose = Display command menu

Enter command: lan

LAN Interface test mode. LAN Interface PPA Number = 0

           clear   = Clear statistics registers
           display = Display LAN Interface status and statistics registers
           end     = End LAN Interface Administration, return to Test Selection
           menu    = Display this menu
           ppa     = PPA Number of the LAN Interface
           quit    = Terminate the Administration, return to shell
           reset   = Reset LAN Interface to execute its selftest
           specific = Go to Driver specific menu

Enter command: d
                    LAN INTERFACE STATUS DISPLAY


PPA Number                        = 0
Description                       = lan0 Hewlett-Packard 10/100 TX Half-Duplex  TT = 1500
Type (value)                      = ethernet-csmacd(6)
MTU Size                          = 1500
Speed                             = 100000000
Station Address                   = 0x1083ffcaae
Administration Status (value)     = up(1)
Operation Status (value)          = down(2)
Last Change                       = 237321866
Inbound Octets                    = 0
Inbound Unicast Packets           = 0
Inbound Non-Unicast Packets       = 0
Inbound Discards                  = 0
Inbound Errors                    = 0
Inbound Unknown Protocols         = 0
Outbound Octets                   = 820
Outbound Unicast Packets          = 20
Outbound Non-Unicast Packets      = 0
Outbound Discards                 = 1
Outbound Errors                   = 0
Outbound Queue Length             = 0
Specific                          = 655367

Press <Return> to continue
```

In this example, we issued **lanadmin** and specified that we wanted to go into the *lan* interface administration and that we wanted to *d*isplay information about the interface.

lanadmin can also be used to perform such tasks as to change the MTU or speed of a lan interface with the *-M* and *-s* options, respectively.

ndd

ndd is used to perform network tuning and view information about network parameters. To view information about all supported tunable parameters with **ndd**, you would issue **ndd -h supported**. You can get the value of a parameter using the *-get* option you can set the value of a parameter with the *-set* option.

nslookup

nslookup is used to resolve a host name into an IP address. You issue **nslookup** *hostname* and **nslookup** will access either the **/etc/resolv.conf** file or **/etc/hosts** to resolve the host name. The following example shows a system using **/etc/hosts** to produce the IP address of system *l2*:

```
# nslookup l2
Using /etc/hosts on:   l3

looking up FILES
Name:     l2
Address:  10.1.1.12

#
```

You can also run **nslookup** in interactive mode by issuing the command with no command-line arguments. The following example shows issuing the command with no command line arguments to get into interactive mode and then typing help to get information on commands you can issue:

```
# nslookup l2
> help
NAME              - print address information about NAME
IP-ADDRESS        - print hostname information about IP-ADDRESS
policy            - print switch policy information
server NAME       - set default server to NAME, using current de-
fault server
lserver NAME      - set default server to NAME, using initial serv-
er
```

```
set OPTION       - sets the OPTION
    all          -  print options, current server and host
    [no]swtrace -  print lookup result and lookup switch messages
>
```

CHAPTER 14

Common Desktop Environment

CDE and Virtual Partitions

Running multiple instances of HP-UX on the same computer is just like having multiple systems. This means that your Common Desktop Environment (CDE) configuration for users in different vPars is done just as it would be on different systems. There are configuration files that affect CDE on a system-wide basis. You'll need to set up these system-wide configuration files on each vPar to meet the specific needs of the individuals working in the respective vPars.

In the upcoming sections we'll modify CDE in a Virtual Partition to include a custom CDE Greeting at the login screen and customize the menu to include some Virtual Partition-specific commands.

Custom Greeting for Different Virtual Partitions

The first encounter users have with CDE on the vPars system is the login screen. Let's customize the login screen so it shows the hostname, which is probably already configured on your CDE login screen, as well as the vPar name as part of the greeting. If your hostname and vPar name are the same then you don't need to supply the vPar name on the login screen. This is an interesting customization to CDE so I'll provide the login screen changes as an example customization.

The default information for the login screen is contained in **/usr/dt/ config/C/Xresources**. We'll copy this file to **/etc/dt/config/C/Xresrouces** and then add the vPar name to the file. The portion of the file that includes the *GREETING* is shown below:

```
!!######################################################################
!!
!!   GREETING
!!

!! Dtlogin*greeting.foreground:          black
!! Dtlogin*greeting.background:          #a8a8a8
!! Dtlogin*greeting.labelString:         Welcome to %LocalHost%
!! Dtlogin*greeting.persLabelString:     Welcome %s
!! Dtlogin*greeting.alignment:           ALIGNMENT_CENTER

!!######################################################################
!!
```

The *!!* in this file indicates a comment (unlike the # that we are accustomed to using in shell programs.) We could uncomment the line that shows *%LocalHost%* and add to it the Virtual Partition name as shown below:

From:

```
!! Dtlogin*greeting.labelString:    Welcome to %LocalHost%
```

To:

```
Dtlogin*greeting.labelString:         Welcome to %LocalHost% \n\
```

This is Virtual Partition vPar Name

You would substitute the name of your Virtual Partition for *vPar Name* if indeed the vPar name and hostname are different. Figure 14-1 shows the modified greeting we created:

Figure 14-1 Login Screen with Update Greeting

This screen shows our updated greeting at the login screen with the hostname of *actappd1* as well as the line on which we would place the vPar name.

Menu Picks for Virtual Partitions

In this section we'll add some Virtual Partition-related commands to our CDE menu. Since most Virtual Partition work is performed by the system administrator, we'll update the menu picks for *root* only in the upcoming example. The default information for the login screen is contained in **/usr/ dt/config/C/Xresources**. We'll copy this file to the home directory and **.dt** directory for root, which, on this vPar, is **/.root/.dt**. We'll rename the file **dtwmrc** after copying it. The menu portion of **/.root/.dt/dtwmrc** looks like the following before it is updated:

```
Menu DtRootMenu
{
    "Workspace Menu"                        f.title
    "Shuffle Up"                            f.circle_up
    "Shuffle Down"                          f.circle_down
    "Refresh"                               f.refresh
    "Minimize/Restore Front Panel"          f.toggle_frontpanel
     no-label                               f.separator
    "Restart Workspace Manager..."          f.restart
     no-label                               f.separator
    "Log out..."                            f.action ExitSession

}
```

We're going to add our new menu pick just after the *DtRootMenu* entry, which we see on our system as the left mouse button's "Workspace Menu." After adding our menu picks the file now looks like the following:

```
Menu DtRootMenu
{
    "Workspace Menu"                    f.title
    "Shuffle Up"                        f.circle_up
    "Shuffle Down"                      f.circle_down
    "Refresh"                           f.refresh
    "Minimize/Restore Front Panel"      f.toggle_frontpanel
     no-label                           f.separator
    "Restart Workspace Manager..."      f.restart
     no-label                           f.separator
    "Log out..."                        f.action ExitSession

Menu vParMenu
    "vPar Menu"                 f.title
    "vparstatus"               f.exec "xterm -T vparstatus -e
                                    /usr/bin/sh -c 'vparstatus; read xxx'"
    "vparstatus -v"            f.exec "xterm -geometry 80x50+830+0
                                    -sl 200 -bg white -T vparstatus_verbose
                                    -e /usr/bin/sh -c 'vparstatus -v|more; read xxx'"
    "Login vPar2"                f.exec "xterm -geometry 80x50+830+0 -sl 200 -bg white
                                    -T vPar2 -e remsh ecvpard2 &"

}
```

The **f.title** function shows that this is the menu title. **f.exec** means to execute the following string. In the first menu pick, *vparstatus*, we simply open an *xterm* window, run the **vparstatus** command, and wait for user input before we close the window with **read**. The next command uses **vparstatus -v** which has a more extensive output. For this command I open a much bigger *xterm* window and run **vparstatus -v|more** so the user can hit the space-bar if the command results in more than one window of output. (There is a single quote around the **vparstatus** and **read** commands.) I included yet more options on the **xterm** for the remote login to the second vPar, making the terminal window very large, with lots of terminal memory and using specific colors. Our new menu now looks like that shown in Figure 14-2:

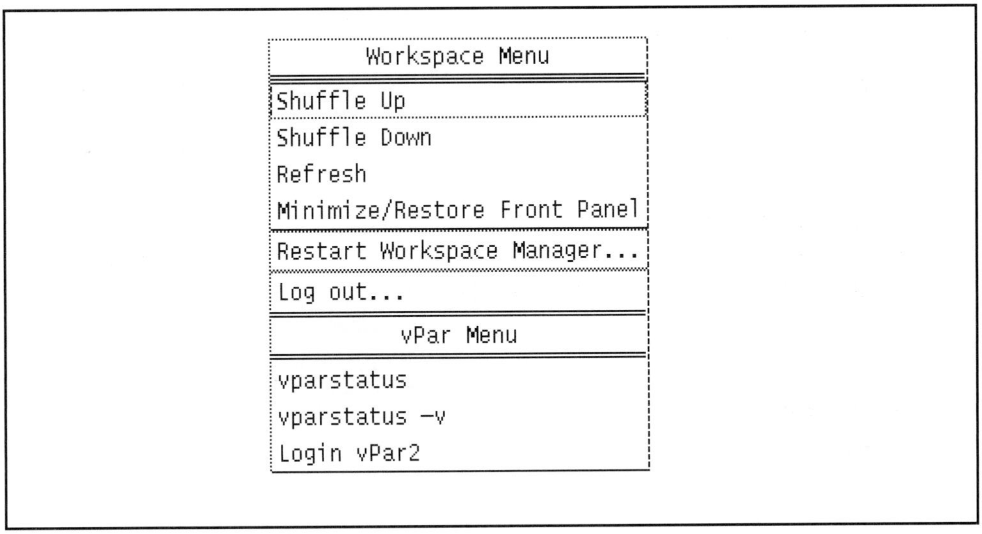

```
            Workspace Menu
Shuffle Up
Shuffle Down
Refresh
Minimize/Restore Front Panel
Restart Workspace Manager...
Log out...
              vPar Menu
vparstatus
vparstatus -v
Login vPar2
```

Figure 14-2 vPars Menu Picks

These menu picks give us vPar status, status with verbose output, and a remote login to our second vPar. Issuing these commands open up windows and execute the commands shown in our menu picks.

Figure 14-3 shows a screen shot with the two **vparstatus** windows open from having selected the two **vparstatus** commands from the menu:

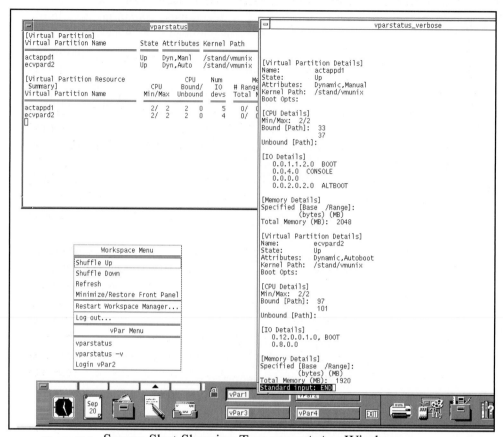

Figure 14-3 Screen Shot Showing Two **vparstatus** Windows

The upper left-hand window contains the output of **vparstatus** and the right-hand window contains the output of **vparstatus -v**. The updated menu is shown in the lower left of the screen.

We can perform additional CDE customization, such as create workspaces for our vPars so that when we select a workspace we have windows open to the vPar for which the workspace is named.

The remainder of this chapter provides CDE backgound. We performed only basic customization to CDE for our vPars environment. You can perform extensive customization in CDE. The background provided in the remainder of this chapter provides information that can help you with additional customization.

Non-vPars-Specific Part of Chapter: Introduction

The Common Desktop Environment (CDE) represents the effort of major UNIX vendors to unify UNIX at the desktop level. CDE is widely used by X terminal and workstation users on many UNIX systems. Because you may be managing many UNIX variants that run CDE, I'll cover CDE on IBM's AIX systems, Hewlett Packard's HP-UX systems, and Sun Microsystems' Solaris systems. This chapter provides an introduction to CDE: it touches on the basics of CDE's look and feel, describes making changes to the CDE environment, and includes a bit of background about the X, Motif, and CDE relationships. CDE versions used to write this chapter are: AIX CDE 1.0, HP-UX CDE 2.1.0, and Solaris CDE 1.3. Newer releases will have enhanced features, but in general, they should still work the same.

Several features make it easy to customize CDE. The Style Manager, which every user has access to, makes it easy to customize CDE on an individual user basis. Sooner or later, however, you may want to provide some common denominator of CDE functionality for your users. If, for instance, you have an application that most users will run, you can set up environment variables, prepare pull-down menus, provide suitable fonts, etc., that will make your users more productive. Users can then perform additional customizations such as defining File Manager characteristics and selecting backgrounds.

To help you thoroughly understand CDE, I'll cover the following topics:

1. Why a Graphical User Interface (GUI)?

2. CDE Basics

3. Customizing CDE

4. CDE: Advanced Topics

   •The Relationship Among X, Motif, and CDE

   •X, Motif, and CDE Configuration Files

   •The Sequence of Events When CDE Starts

   •CDE and Performance

First, I'll provide you with the reasoning behind providing a graphical interface rather than the more common, but also more cumbersome, line-by-line terminal interface. An overview of the CDE desktop workspaces follows. This is divided into two sections: AIX and HP-UX (because they are so similar) and Solaris. Each will give an overview of the front panel features. Next I'll guide you through making some CDE customizations. These customizations will give you a working basis for making more advanced changes on your own. I'll show you how to make some basic, simple changes, and then more complex changes, ending with modifying the login screen with a new logo and new welcome messages. Last, I'll delve into the more advanced topics of X, Motif, and CDE relationships, configuration file usage and location, what happens internally when CDE starts up, and some CDE performance tips.

Why a Graphical User Interface (GUI)?

For computers to be used on every desktop, they had to be made easier to use. A new method of accessing computer power was required, one that avoided the command-line prompt, didn't require users to memorize complex commands, and didn't require a working knowledge of technological infrastructures such as networking. Not that this information was unimportant; far from it. The information was both too important and too specialized to be of use to the average worker-bee computer user. A knowledge of their applications was all that was important for these users. After all, so the reasoning goes, to drive a car one doesn't have to be a mechanic, so why should a computer user have to understand computer technology? The graphical user interface (GUI) makes computers accessible to the application end-user.

Figure 14-4 illustrates the relationship among the computer hardware, the operating system, and the graphical user interface. The computer is the hardware platform on the bottom. The operating system, the next layer up, represents a character-based user interface. To control the computer at this level, users must type commands at the keyboard. The next several layers, beginning with the X Window System, represent the graphical user interface. To control the computer at these levels, users manipulate graphical controls with a mouse.

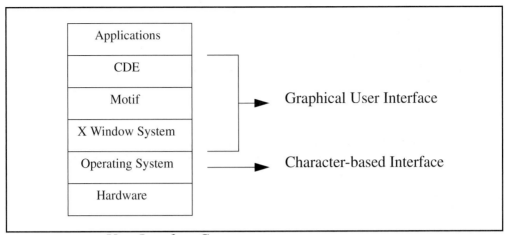

Figure 14-4 User Interface Components

GUIs replaced memorization with exploration. A user could now use pull-down menus, push buttons, sliding scroll bars, and other direct manipulation to use a computer. Typing operating system commands to perform a function is greatly reduced. With a GUI, to use a computer is both easier to learn and easier to use.

While fairly inexpensive in terms of dollars (CDE is bundled "free" with the operating system), GUIs are not without cost in terms of RAM usage and performance. Despite this performance expense, GUIs have become a permanent part of the computing environment. The benefits of their utility are worth the cost.

Beyond the graphical controls that reduce training, make mundane tasks simpler to do, and generally ease the stress of using a computer, two other benefits of GUIs are worth mentioning: multiple windows per display and client-server topology.

The benefit of multiple windows that GUIs provide is that each window (literally a rectangular area surrounded by a window frame) contains a separate application. The user can work with multiple windows open. CDE goes one step further: its multiple workspaces allow users to separate application windows by task into specific workspaces. For instance, in a workspace named "Mail," users may have application windows showing the list of incoming electronic mail, a mail message they are currently reading, and a message they are composing for later transmission. In another workspace called "Financials," they could be working on several spreadsheets, each in its own window.

Client-server topology enables the computing resources spread around a network to be accessed efficiently to meet computing needs. In a client-server topology, powerful computers on the network are dedicated to a specific purpose (file management on a file server and running applications on an application server). Users working on less powerful client computers elsewhere on the network access the files or applications remotely. A file server reduces system administration by centralizing file backup, enabling the system administrator to back up only the file server, not each individual client computer. This setup also ensures that files will be backed up at regular intervals. An application server reduces operating costs by reducing the number and size of storage disks required and the size of RAM required on each client computer. A single version of an application resides and runs on the application server and is accessed by multiple users throughout the network.

Although this topology sounds complicated, the CDE GUI makes it easy. To access a file, users "drag and drop" a file icon from the file manager window. To start an application, users double-click the application icon. To print a file, users drag the file to the icon of the appropriate printer in the front panel and drop it there. Users don't have to know where these files and applications are, what directories they are in, what computers they are on, or how they are accessed. The underlying infrastructure and control you have put in place, along with the power of the GUI, allow users to concentrate on their work and not on the mechanics of their computer.

CDE Basics

Because most systems come with a set of CDE user guides, I'm only going to give an overview of what CDE looks like and the main areas we will be working with when we do some customizations. Along the way, I'll point out similarities and differences among the different flavors of CDE.

The CDE login screen presents you with several choices before you even log in. Under the area where you enter your user name are four buttons: **OK**, **Start Over**, **Options**, and **Help**. **OK** is just the same as pressing *Enter* when you enter your login and then password. The **Start Over** button clears your user login and allows you to start over. **Options** provides you with some initial session configuration that would need to be made before you log in. **Language** allows you to change your default language. Suppose that you need to test your company's software in another language. Assuming that the proper language is preloaded on your system, you can swap between the languages for testing by simply choosing CDE to come up in a different language. **Session** allows you to choose to come up in the CDE desktop session or into a **Failsafe** session, which is an X session but without the CDE desktop. Solaris also has options to log in to their **OpenWindow Desktop** or into the **User's Last Desktop**. **Command Line Login** allows you to log in without CDE being invoked. This would be just a regular terminal mode session. **Reset Login Screen** does just what its name suggests. And finally, **Help** lists all these features with a brief description of each.

The login screen itself displays a CDE logo, an operating system logo such as AIX, or possibly your company's logo. A welcome message appears along with a place to enter your user login. After entering your user name, you are prompted for your password. Once entered and verified as correct, CDE is started and the desktop is displayed. On Solaris systems, the first time you log in, you are presented with a choice as to whether you want to log into CDE or OpenWindows Desktop.

The CDE desktop is comprised of four desktop workspaces and a front panel shared by each. The front panel is an easy-to-use interface to various applications, commands, and tools. The various components are easily accessed by the simple point-and-click method. Front panel components are a collection of objects, subpanels, and access to desktop workspaces. Some objects are used only to display items such as the clock, whereas others, when clicked, either bring up an application, such as the calendar or dtmail, or perform an action, such as the lock or the exit action icons. Subpanels pop up a menu of objects that can be accessed. These objects can also simply display items or bring up applications. By default, on AIX and HP-UX, you see Personal Printer subpanels, Personal Applications subpanels, and Help subpanels. On Solaris, all panels contain subpanels. Subpanels can be added to the other panels on AIX and HP-UX as you will see in the next section "Customizing CDE." You can tell that these have subpanels, because they each have a little arrow above the panel where you click to pop it up. In the center of the front panel are four workspaces. These provide areas in which to perform related tasks, enabling the user to separate work and not clutter up the desktop.

CDE on AIX and HP-UX is very similar and, in general, what is displayed on the front panel on one is the same as on the other. Solaris, however, while retaining the basic CDE look and feel, has greatly expanded what is included on the default front panel and the subpanels behind it. I'm going to give an overview of CDE as found on HP-UX and AIX first. Then I'll point out the Solaris enhancements to CDE.

CDE on AIX and HP-UX

The front panel is divided into 11 main areas: 5 panels, 1 workspaces area, and 5 more panels. I'll give an overview of each area from left to right, beginning with the Clock and ending with the Trash Can, as shown in Figure 14-5.

Figure 14-5 Front Panel

Clock - As you would expect, this displays the current time.

Calendar - The Calendar icon displays the current date, and when clicked, brings up an appointment calendar. The calendar allows you to set appointments and reminders and to create a task list. Appointments can be set as a one-time-only events or as recurring. You can be notified of an appointment by a beep, a pop-up message, or an e-mail. The calendar and associated appointments can be displayed by the day, the week, or the month. A yearly calendar can also be displayed, but without appointments.

File Manager - The File Manager opens a window that displays your home directory and associated files. From here, you can do any number of basic file manipulations, such as copy a file, move a file, delete a file, or execute a program or script. More infrequently used operations, such as creating a symbolic link or changing file permissions or ownership, can also be done here. Removing a file from within File Manager moves it to the Trash Can rather than permanently deleting the file. This way, if you decide that you need it back, you can simply retrieve it from the Trash Can rather than having it restored from a backup - a more time-consuming operating. However, note that the Trash Can is automatically "emptied" at the end of every session. So when you log off, the files are permanently removed.

Personal Application - The Personal Application subpanel contains the CDE's text editor, **dtpad,** and terminal emulator, **dtterm**. It also contains the Icon Editor. The **dtpad** is an easy-to-use, full-screen text editor. As in a PC-based word processor, **dtpad** allows you to move the cursor anywhere to add, change, and delete text, unlike the popular **vi**, which is a line-by-line text editor. CDE's dtterm is a good basic terminal emulator. The Icon Editor opens bitmap (.bm) or pixmap (.pm) files and allows you to edit them.

The Personal Applications subpanel is the first place we find the Install Icon application. This is where new icons are added to the subpanel. This allows the application associated with the icon to be executed when the icon is double clicked. We'll be using this when we modify the desktop in "Customizing CDE."

Mail - The CDE mailer, **dtmail**, is invoked when this icon is clicked. From here, mail messages can be composed, messages replied to, and messages forwarded. Most advanced mail features that you've come to think of as basic features are included: items such as adding attachments to messages, replying to just the sender or all recipients, and setting automatic messages saying that you're on vacation. Another feature is when a new message arrives, the **dtmail** icon changes to show a letter popping into the mailbox.

Workspace Area - The next four items comprise the workspace area.

Lock Button - The Lock button allows you to lock your session while you're away from your desk. This security feature keeps others from viewing or accessing your work when you're not there. It saves you from logging off and on every time you need to step away. Your login password, or root's password, must be entered to unlock it again.

Workspace Switch - Four in number, these are the separate workspaces created by default. These allow you to organize your work so that your workspace doesn't get cluttered up. By using the workspaces, you can keep work on different tasks, applications, or systems separated from each other. You change from one workspace to another simply by clicking on the workspace number: One, Two, Three, or Four. You'll notice that no matter what workspace you are in, the Front Panel follows you. In "Customizing CDE," you'll see how easy you can increase the number of workspaces and to change the names.

Activity Light - The Activity light, quite simply, blinks when the system is busy doing work.

Exit button - The Exit button is where you log out of CDE, terminating your CDE session. Upon exiting, depending on how you have CDE configured, you are prompted to resume your current session or return to your home session. If you choose to resume your current session, the next time you login, the desktop looks exactly the same as it does when you log out - as closely as possible. Some things, such as remote logins, are not possible, but others are, such as having an application automatically executed. If you choose to return to your home session, the next time you log in, you are returned to a known, preset configuration. This configuration is set in the Style Manager panel, discussed shortly.

Personal Printers - This subpanel contains printers that you have configured on your system, including the default printer designated as such and the Print Manager. The front panel icon is that of the default printer. To print one of your documents, simply drag it from the File Manager and drop it on the printer icon. The Print Manager allows you to view queued print files and remove them before they print. However, this works only with printers directly managed by your system. In today's networked offices, printers are usually shared and the print manager function is on a server, probably in the next building.

Style Manager - The Style Manager is one of those places where you can either get really creative getting your desktop to look just like you want or waste a lot of time - depending on your point of view. Here is where you personalize your login to the system to your own preferences. You can change your font size, your background, your mouse speed, and whether or not your session automatically locks after a certain amount of non-activity, or idle time. This is where you can set your home session, as referred to earlier, to come back to every time you log in or set your system to return to the current session or choose the option of being asked every time you log out. One other configuration you can make here is whether your window focus follows your mouse or whether you have to click on a window before it is the active window. On AIX systems, you can toggle on or off whether the workspaces are displayed on the front panel.

Application Manager - When opened, the Application Manager displays folders with useful applications and actions. Although they differ among manufacturers and even operating systems for that matter, AIX, HP-UX, and Solaris all have some basic features: Desktop Applications, Desktop Tools, Information, and System Administration. Desktop Applications contains such applications and tools as Calculator, Man Page Viewer, Icon Editor, and Create Action. Desktop Tools includes tools like **xterm**, **xwd** capture, compress files, and reload resources. System Administration contains operating system-specific applications such as SAM in HP-UX, SMIT in AIX, and Admintool in Solaris, besides more generic actions such as change password. Take the time to look around here. You'll find many items you may want to incorporate on your customized CDE front panel. I, for one, have found the Man Page Viewer to be an invaluable resource and moved it to my front panel, where it can be readily accessed.

Help - The Help subpanel is a compilation of the Help Manager, a Desktop Introduction, Front Panel help, and an On-Item Front Panel help mechanism. The Help Manager is the main online help facility for CDE. This is a comprehensive help system with topic trees and the ability to search the index using keywords or pattern matching, backtrack where you've been in the help manager, and view the history of items for which you requested help. The Desktop Introduction is an overview of CDE and how it works. The Front Panel help facility gives information about how to use the front panel icons, subpanels, and workspaces. The On-Item Front Panel help mechanism allows you to click on the front panel item about which you wish assistance. Along with the Help Subpanel, Help can also be requested by pressing the F1 function key. If installed on your system, AIX may also include Basic Desktop Customization help and Base Library.

Trash Can - The Trash Can, used with the File Manager, holds files and folders that you have deleted during the current session. Using the facility allows you to quickly retrieve files that you should not have removed. The Trash Can can be "emptied" at any time to permanently remove items. Also, the Trash Can is "emptied" when you log out of your session.

CDE on Solaris

As mentioned earlier, Solaris has embellished CDE, adding many more subpanels and items to the subpanels, as shown in Figure 14-6. Where

Solaris has greatly changed the panel and subpanels, I'll give an overview of what you'll find, as I did in the preceding section on AIX and HP-UX. Where they are the same, I'll simply note that they are the same.

Figure 14-6 Front Panel

Like AIX and HP-UX, Solaris' front panel is divided into 11 main areas: 5 panels, 1 workspaces area, and 5 more panels. I'll give an overview of each area from left to right, beginning with the World and ending with the Trash Can.

Links - As you might guess by the World icon, this is where you access the world. Solaris' Web browser, HotJava, lives here. There are also actions included to access Personal Bookmarks for the web browser, and a Find Web Page search engine. As indicated on the front panel icon, the world has a clock on it, too.

Cards - The calendar is the same as on AIX and HP-UX. However, included in the subpanel is Find Card, which is a Rolodex-type address manager.

Files - Although the title is slightly different, this is where the File Manager resides. In the subpanel are special icons to perform file actions associated with: Properties, Encryption, Compress File, Archive, and Find File. Solaris has also included actions to manage your floppy disk drive and CD-ROM.

Applications - Renamed simply Applications, here is where you'll not only find the Text Editor, but also Text Note and Voice Note. For the audio enabled, Voice Note allows you to play, record, or save audio files with WAV, AU, and AIFF formats. On this subpanel, you'll also find the Applications subpanel found under Application Manager on the AIX and HP-UX systems. As on the others, this includes Desktop Applications, Desktop

Tools, Information, and System Administration. These are basically the same on all systems.

Mail - This subpanel, in addition to **dtmail**, has been enhanced to include a Suggestion Box. A very clever idea, this automatically opens up a message, pre-addressed to Sun Microsystems, Inc., so that you can send them your suggestions.

Workspace Area - The next five items comprise the workspace area:

•*Lock button* - This is the same as on AIX and HP-UX.

•

•*Workspace switch* - Same as on AIX and HP-UX.

•

•*Progress Indicator* - This is the same as the Busy Indicator on AIX and HP-UX.

•

•*Exit button* - Same as on AIX and HP-UX.

•

•*Personal Printers* - Same as on AIX and HP-UX.

Tools - The Style Manager is located here and is displayed on the front panel. You'll also find easy access to the CDE error log, and Find Process allows you to view all processes running on your system and kill selected ones. The Customized Workspace Menu and Add Item to Menu actions allow you to easily modify the Workspace Menu. The Workspace Menu is accessed by placing the mouse over a blank area of the desktop and pressing the right mouse key. Whereas AIX and HP-UX come with a generic menu, Solaris has incorporated the front panel and subpanel actions into the Workspace Menu as another way to access these actions.

Hosts - Here, Solaris differs greatly from AIX and HP-UX. The Hosts subpanel contains system-related actions. On the front panel, you'll find the Performance Monitor icons indicating how busy your CPU and disk drives are. From the subpanel, this Host opens up the *dtterm* terminal emulator, and Console opens up a *dtterm* specifically for displaying console messages. System Information provides system information, including system name, hardware model, network IP address and domain, physical and virtual memory, operating system version, and date and time last rebooted. Find Host is the same as Find Card in the Cards subpanel.

Help - This is the same as on AIX and HP-UX.

Trash - The Trash Can is the same, with the addition of a subpanel icon to "empty" the Trash Can.

This concludes the overview of the look and feel of CDE. Armed with this knowledge, you can easily navigate around your desktop environment with confidence and ease. Next, you'll learn how to change that look and feel to conform to your work environment.

Customizing CDE

Before you modify any CDE configuration files, first develop a strategy. I know that I've mentioned this before, but it's important enough to mention again.

The following questions should get you started:

1. What are your users' needs?

2. Which of those needs can be met by reconfiguring CDE?

3. At what level should these changes be made (system-wide, groups of users, individual users only)?

4. Which CDE files do you need to modify (names and locations)?

5. What are the changes, and what is their order within the file?

It's also a good idea to have handy a binder containing man pages for each of the CDE components (for looking up resources and their values) and a copy of each of the CDE configuration files.

Now that you have a good understanding as to how CDE works, I'll lead you through making changes and customizing the system for either the entire user community or each individual user.

I'll precede each change with a discussion of what is involved in making the change. I'll be making some basic, simple changes as well as some more advanced changes to show you how versatile CDE can be.

One thing I need to mention is that all these changes can be made on any system. And knowing how to do these tasks "the hard way" increases your understanding of what these tools are doing for you in the background. So be sure to give each one a try.

Making Changes Using Style Manager

Font Size

When we first log in to CDE and the workspace comes up, as shown in Figure 14-7, one of the first things many users change is the size of the font. Initially set to 4, most users want a bigger font. This change is easy.

Figure 14-7 Style Manager

1. **Click on the Style Manager icon** on the front panel. This action brings up the Style Manager.

2. **Click on Font.**

3. **Highlight 5**.

4. **Click on OK**.

Backdrop and Colors

The Style Manager is also where we can change the backdrop and colors:

1. **Click on Backdrop** and we are presented with a variety of backdrop choices.

2. After we see one we like, such as Pebbles, we can **click on apply** and then **click on close** to change our backdrop. Notice, however, that this action changes the backdrop only for the workspace that we are in.

To change the other workspaces, we can either go to them and bring up the Style Manager in that workspace or, because we already have Style Manager up, we can click in the top-right corner on the little "-" on the window itself, above "File," and access the pull-down menu. From here, we can choose Occupy All Workspaces. Then we can simply go to the other workspaces, and Style Manager is already up and ready for us there. The Backdrop area is the only place we have to worry about moving to other workspaces.

3. To change colors, **click on the Color icon**. We are given a list of different color schemes from which to choose. And if one isn't quite to our liking, we can easily modify the color, hue, brightness, and contrast. We can even grab a color from somewhere else, such as an image off the Internet, to include in the color scheme. Once we have the colors we like, we can save the scheme with its own name.

Adding Objects to or Removing Objects from the Front Panel

The front panel can make life just a little easier for us by including frequently used items on it. One of the most frequent actions is opening up a terminal window. And although CDE comes with dtterm as the default terminal window, we sometimes might want to use an xterm window. We'll add it to the Personal Applications subpanel, where dtterm lives on AIX and HP-UX systems. Solaris users can do the same by putting the **xterm** on the Hosts subpanel, where the This Host terminal emulator lives.

You have two ways to add objects to the CDE front panel:

- Drag and drop them into a slideup subpanel and then make them the default for that subpanel.

- Modify the **/etc/dt/appconfig/types/C/dtwm.fp** configuration file. This approach will be used later when we create actions and file types.

The basic actions to add a control button through drag and drop are as follows:

- Drag the application icon you want as a front panel button from an application manager view and drop the icon onto the installation section (the top section) of the appropriate subpanel.

- Place the mouse pointer over the icon and press mouse button 3 to display the subpanel menu.

- Select *Copy to Main Panel.*

1. **Click on the up arrow** of the Personal Applications subpanel on AIX or HP-UX or on the Hosts subpanel on Solaris so that it pops up.

2. **Click on the Application Manage**r icon, where Desktop Applications and Desktop Tools live.

3. **Double-click on Desktop_Tools**. Here you'll find **Xterm**.

4. **Drag and drop the Xterm** icon from Desktop_Tools to the Install Icon box at the top of the Personal Applications subpanel on HP-UX and AIX, or Hosts on Solaris.

Now if we want to include **xterm** on the front panel:

1. **Right-click on the Xterm** icon in the Personal Applications or Hosts subpanel.

2. **Select Copy to Main Panel** or **Promote to Front Panel**, depending on which CDE you are using.

Adding Another Workspace

Another easy change to the front panel is to add another workspace. CDE comes with a default of four workspaces, but this is easy to change. We'll add one more and call it "Web View." This can be the window where we'll access the Internet.

1. **Place the mouse in the Workspace area of the front panel** and **press the right mouse button**.

2. **Select Add Workspace** from the pull-down menu. The workspace "New" has been added.

3. **Right-click on the new workspace labeled "New"** and select **Rename**. **Type Web View** and **press Return**.

If we want to delete a Workspace, simply right-click on the Workspace to be removed and then select delete.

Making these kinds of changes is easy, and they help personalize the workspace for the individual user.

Changing the Front Panel in Other Ways

In addition to adding and removing buttons, you can shape the front panel in other ways. These other ways use Workspace Manager resources to modify default values. The following resources relate to the front panel:

- **clientTimeoutInterval** - Length of time the Busy light blinks and the pointer remains an hourglass when a client is started from the front panel.

- **geometry** - x and y coordinate location of the front panel.

- **highResFontList** - Font to use on a high-resolution display.

- **lowResFontList** - Font to use on a low-resolution display.

- **mediumResFontList** - Font to use on a medium-resolution display.

- **name** - Name of the front panel to use when multiple front panels are in **dtwm.fp**.

- **pushButtonClickTime** - Time interval distinguishing two single mouse clicks from a double click (to avoid double launching an application accidentally).

- **waitingBlinkRate** - Blink rate of the front panel Busy light.

- **workspaceList** - List of workspace names.

- **title** - Title to appear on a workspace button.

Like all other workspace manager resources, these front-panel resources have the following syntax:

```
Dtwm*screen*resource: value
```

For example, suppose that instead of the default four workspaces, all that your users need is a front panel with six workspaces named Mail, Reports, Travel, Financials, Projects, and Studio. Further, they prefer a large font and have decided upon New Century Schoolbook 10-point bold. As system administrator, you'd make everyone happy with the following resource specifications:

```
Dtwm*0*workspaceList: One Two Three Four Five Six
Dtwm*0*One*title: Mail
Dtwm*0*Two*title: Reports
Dtwm*0*Three*title: Travel
Dtwm*0*Four*title: Financials
Dtwm*0*Five*title: Projects
Dtwm*0*Six*title: Studio
Dtwm*0*highResFontList:
          -adobe-new century schoolbook-bold-r-normal\
          --10-100-75-75-p-66-iso8859-1
```

The screen designation is usually *0*, except for displays capable of both image and overlay planes. The order of screens in the **X*screens** file is what determines the screen number; the first screen, typically the image plane, is designated as 0. Note also the inclusion of workspace names (One, Two, Three, Four, Five, and Six) in the six title resource specifications.

These changes can be added to the **sys.resources** file, which is discussed in detail in "Advanced CDE Topics" later in this chapter. These changes can also be made by use of the **EditResources** action to insert the new resource lines into each user's **RESOURCE_MANAGER** property and then restart the Workspace Manager.

The obvious disadvantage is that you have to physically go to each user's work area and take over the machine for a few minutes. However, on the plus side, the changes are immediate and are automatically saved in the

correct **dt.resources** for users who restore their current session. You also
avoid having your changes overwritten, which could happen if you modify
the right **dt.resources** file at the wrong time, while the user is still logged in.

Modifying Things in Slide-up Subpanels

Subpanels are defined in **dtwm.fp** after the front panel and front-panel control definitions. To associate a subpanel with a front panel control button, the
front-panel control name is listed as the container name in the subpanel definition.

Note: **/etc/dt** is where global changes are made. **$HOME/.dt** is where local
or individual user changes are made.

To add a slideup subpanel to the front panel, follow these steps:

1. Copy the file **/usr/dt/appconfig/types/C/dtwm.fp** to either
   /etc/dt/appconfig/types/C/dtwm.fp or **$HOME/.dt/types/
   dtwm.fp**.

2. Decide which control button with which the slide-up is to be
   associated.

3. Create the subpanel definition file in **dtwm.fp**. This will take
   the following form:

```
SUBPANEL     SubPanelName
{
CONTAINER_NAME  AssociatedFrontPanelControlButton
TITLE   SubPanelTitle
}
```

4. Create subpanel control definitions for the subpanel. These
   will take the following form:

```
CONTROL   ControlName
{
TYPE   icon
CONTAINER_NAME    SubPanelName
CONTAINER_TYPE    SUBPANEL
ICON   BitmapName
PUSH_ACTION    ActionName
}
```

As with front panel control buttons, it's easier to copy and modify an existing subpanel file than to start from scratch.

Changing the Default Printer Name Display

We'll now make an easy change to one of the slide-up subpanels. If we pop up the Personal Printers subpanel, it shows that we have a default printer configured, but not the name of it. Let's go back into the front panel file, **dtwm.fp**, and change that:

1. Bring up your favorite editor, such as **dtpad** or **vi**, and edit the file **/$HOME/.dt/types/dtwm.fp**.

2. Scroll down to CONTROL Printer. You'll see that the LABEL is Default. Change or add to that the name of your default printer. My printer is called *a464*.

LABEL   Default - a464

3. **Save the file** and **restart the Workspace Manager**. Position the mouse over a blank area on your workspace and press the right mouse button. Select Restart Workspace Manager. On Solaris, press the right mouse button to bring up the Customized Workspace Menu. From here, select Windows, where you'll find the Restart Workspace Manager key.

Pop up the Personal Printers subpanel to see what the default printer really is. Of course, if we change the default, we'll have to change the front panel again. But we know how to do that now, don't we! Figure 14-8 shows the Front Panel.

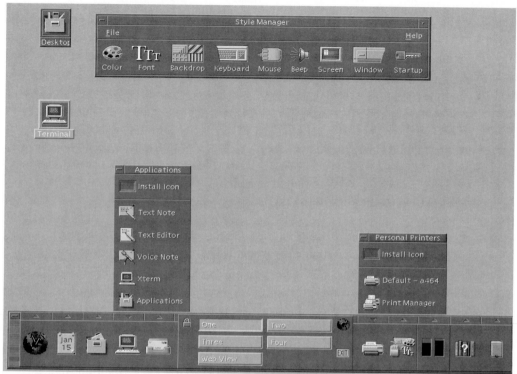

Figure 14-8 Front Panel with Changes

Front Panel Animation

Animation for front panel or slide-up subpanel drop zones is created by displaying a progressive series of bitmaps. By convention, the bitmaps are in **/usr/dt/appconfig/icons**. The list of bitmaps to display is contained in animation definitions at the end of **dtwm.fp**.

To create an animation sequence for a drop zone:

1. Create a progressive series of bitmaps.

2. Add a list of these bitmap files to the appropriate configuration file using the following syntax:

```
ANIMATION AnimationName
{
 bitmap0
 bitmap1
 bitmap2
 bitmap3
 bitmap4
 bitmap5
}
```

3. Add a line to the appropriate control definition using the syntax:

```
DROP_ANIMATION AnimationName
```

Adding Items to the Workspace Menu

The workspace menu is defined in the **sys.dtwmrc** file. As mentioned in the overview of the front panel for Solaris, the Workspace Menu is accessed by placing the mouse over a blank area of the desktop and pressing the right mouse key. Where AIX and HP-UX come with a generic menu, Solaris has incorporated the front panel and subpanel actions into the Workspace Menu as another way to access these actions. However, we can create customized Workspace Menu for all three systems using the left mouse key to access it. We'll be doing this task next.

A customized Workspace menu can contain frequently used commands and applications. The customized menu is usually accessed by pressing the left mouse button, which pops up the menu for viewing and selection. A Workspace menu comes in handy for those who have a set number of things they do regularly. For instance, a programmer who uses **C++**, **vi**, and **isql** may have a menu with those items, or a system administrator may have a menu with **df**, **ps -ef**, and **netstat** on it. Or those on an expansive network may want a menu of system logins.

For one or two changes, you can modify the existing Workspace menu. For major changes, it's probably easier to insert an entirely new menu definition in **sys.dtwmrc**.

A menu definition has the following syntax:

```
Menu MenuName
{
  "Menu Name"          f.title
  "Frame"              f.exec /nfs/system1/usr/frame/bin/maker
  "Second Item"        action
  "Third Item"         action
}
```

The first line specifies the menu name, following the keyword **Menu**. The lines between the curly braces list the items that appear in the menu in their order of appearance; thus the first line is the title as designated by the function **f.title**. The second line is an example of a definition that would start **FrameMaker** from a remote application server in a distributed environment. Numerous other functions exist, approximately 45 in all. For a complete list, see the **dtwmrc** (4) man page.

For users to display the menu, you need to bind the menu definition to a mouse button and a screen location using the action **f.menu MenuName**. For example, if your users want to post the menu by pressing mouse button 3 when the pointer is on the workspace background, you would insert the following line in the Mouse Button Bindings Description section at the end of **sys.dtwmrc**:

```
<Btn3Down> root f.menu MenuName
```

(Actually, it would be easier to modify the line that's already there by exchanging **MenuName** for **DtRootMenu** on the second line.)

Now we'll create a simple menu. Our menu is going to include running FrameMaker, running the **vi** editor, and logging into a remote system.

1. First we need a copy of the **/usr/dt/config/C/sys.dtwmrc** file to **/etc/dt/config/C**:

cp /usr/dt/config/C/sys.dtwmrc /etc/dt/config/C/sys.dtwmrc

If we were going to make this a local change for one user only, it would be copied to **/$HOME/.dt** and renamed **dtwmrc**. For the admin1 user, that would be **/home/admin1/.dt/dtwmrc** or on Solaris in **/home/admin1/.dt/C/dtwmrc**.

2. Go into our favorite editor and **modify the file**. We're going to add our new menu just after the DtRootMenu entry, which we see on our system as the left mouse button's "Workspace Menu." Add the following:

```
Menu AdminMenu
{
  "Admin1's Menu"          f.title
  "Frame Maker"            f.exec "/nfs/system1/usr/frame/bin/maker"
  "VI Editor"              f.exec "xterm -e /usr/bin/vi"
  "Login systemA"          f.exec "xterm -geometry 80x50+830+0 -sl 200
-bg DarkOrchid4 -fg white -n SYSTEMA -T SYSTEMA -e remsh systemA
&"
}
```

The **f.title** function shows that this is the menu title. **f.exec** means to execute the following string. Notice that FrameMaker does not need a terminal window because it uses its own, whereas **vi** and the login both need a terminal window in which to run. Also, I embellished on the **xterm** for the login, making the terminal window very large, with lots of terminal memory and using specific colors.

Now, let's restart the Workspace Manager and try out our new menu:

3. Position the mouse over a blank area on the workspace and press the left mouse button. Select **Restart Workspace Manager**.

Creating pull-down menus is easy and can easily be expanded by adding submenus to the menu. Just use the function **f.menu** followed by the menu name. Add the following just after "Admin1's Menu":

```
"Work Menu"       f.menu   WorkMenu"
```

And then after the } from the Menu AdminMenu section, add:
```
Menu WorkMenu
{
  .
}
```

Performing these advanced functions really isn't so hard. The hardest part is remembering which directories to put the files in: **/etc/dt** for global changes or **$HOME/.dt** for individual changes.

Creating Control Buttons, Actions, and File Types

An action starts a process such as a shell script or an application. An action can be connected to a front-panel button to start when the button is clicked. An action can be connected to a front panel drop zone to be performed when a data file is dropped on the drop zone. An action can be associated with an icon in a file manager window so that the action can be started by double clicking the icon. An action can be associated with a particular data type so that double-clicking the data file icon starts the action and opens the data file.

In addition to setting up a front panel and default session to meet your user's needs, the single most important thing you can do to make computing life easier for the people who depend on you is to create actions and data types.

CDE actions and data types are defined in files that end in **.dt**. Similar to most other CDE configuration files, ***.dt** files have a system-wide version that can be copied into a user's personal directory and customized for personal use. Most system-wide ***.dt** files are found in **/usr/dt/appconfig/ types/C**; personal ***.dt** files are created by copying **user-prefs.dt** from **/usr/ dt/appconfig/types/C** to **$HOME/.dt/types**.

The default search path that CDE uses to look for actions and file types includes the following main directories in the order listed:

- $HOME/.dt/types

- /etc/dt/appconfig/types

- /usr/dt/appconfig/types

You can add more directories to the search path using the **DTDATA-BASESEARCHPATH** environment variable. Insert this environment variable and the new search path into **/etc/dt/config/Xsession** for a system-wide influence. Insert the environment variable and search path into **$HOME/ .dtprofile** for individual users.

The basic control definition has six parts:

- **CONTROL name** - The definition name. This is the only part of the definition outside the curly braces.

- **TYPE** - The type of control. Several types exist. The most useful for customizing the front panel are probably blank and icon. A blank is useful as a space holder. An icon can start an action or application or be a drop zone.

- **ICON** - The bitmap to display on the front panel. Front-panel bitmaps are located in the **/usr/dt/appconfig/icons** directory.

- **CONTAINER_NAME** - The name of the container that holds the control. This must correspond to the name of an actual container listed in **dtwm.fp**.

- **CONTAINER_TYPE** - The type of container that holds the control. This can be **BOX**, **SWITCH**, or **SUBPANEL**, but it must agree with the type of the container name.

- **PUSH_ACTION** - This is what happens when the control button is pushed. **PUSH_ACTION** is just one of several possible actions. For more information, see the **dtwm** man page.

To remove a control button from the front panel, type a pound sign (#) in the left-most column of the **CONTROL** definition line. The (#) turns the control specification into a comment line.

Add a control button by editing the **dtwm.fp** file:

1. Copy **dtwm.fp** from **/usr/dt/appconfig/types/C** to **/etc/dt/appconfig/types/C**.

2. Add the new control definition using the following format:

```
CONTROL NewControl
{
TYPE            icon
CONTAINER_NAME  Top
CONTAINER_TYPE  BOX
ICON            NewControlBitmap
PUSH_ACTION     NewControlExecutable
}
```

Action and File Types have their own peculiarities in that each has a couple of parts, and each must live in its own directory location. These peculiarities will become clear as we create an action on the subpanel. The following are the recommended locations in which to create an action or file type definition:

- Create a completely new file in the **/etc/dt/appconfig/types** directory. This file has a system-wide influence. Remember, the file must end with the **.dt** extension.

- Copy **user-prefs.dt** from **/usr/dt/appconfig/types** to the **/etc/dt/appconfig/types** directory and insert the definition there for system-wide use.

- Copy **user-prefs.vf** to **$HOME/.dt/types** and insert the definition there for individual users.

A typical action has the following syntax:

```
ACTION      ActionName
{
 TYPE        type
 keyword     value
 keyword     value
}
```

For example, here's a FrameMaker action:

```
ACTION      FRAME
{
  TYPE        COMMAND
  WINDOW-TYPE NO-STDIO
  EXEC-STRING /nfs/hpcvxmk6/usr/frame/bin/maker
}
```

A typical data type has the following syntax:

```
DATA_ATTRIBUTES           AttributesName
{
  keyword         value
  keyword         value
  ACTIONS         action, action
}
DATA_CRITERIA
{
 DATA_ATTRIBUTES AttributesName
 keyword          value
```

```
 keyword          value
}
```

Note that all definitions have the following general syntax:

```
KEYWORD value
```

Notice that a data type definition is actually in two parts: an attribute part and a criteria part. The attribute portion of the data type definition specifies the look of the datatype; the criteria portion specifies the behavior of the data type.

For example, here's a file type for FrameMaker files that uses the FRAME action:

```
DATA_ATTRIBUTES      FRAME_Docs
{
  DESCRIPTION        This file type is for FrameMaker documents.
  ICON               makerIcon
  ACTIONS            FRAME
}
DATA_CRITERIA
{
DATA_ATTRIBUTES_NAME  FRAME_Docs
NAME_PATTERN  *.fm
MODE    f
}
```

You can create actions and file types from scratch using these formats. However, the easiest way to create an action is to use the **CreateAction** tool. **CreateAction** is located in the Desktop Applications folder of the Applications Manager and presents you with a fill-in-the-blank dialog box that guides you through creating an **action.dt** file containing the action definition. You can then move this file to the appropriate directory for the range of influence you want the action to have: **/etc/dt/appconfig/types** for a system-wide influence; **$HOME/.dt/types** for individual users.

Creating a New Icon and Action

Creating an icon is a challenging task. We could use the Icon Editor found in Desktop_Apps to create a new icon, or we could find a picture we like and use it. One thing to be careful of when pulling in a picture, in order for it to be seen correctly on the front panel, is that it has to be no larger than 32x32 pixels or only a portion of the icon will be displayed. Viewing the picture in the Icon Editor shows you the size of the picture. You may want to search through the application directories for useful icons or pull one down from the Internet.

For this entire example, I'm going to use the Instant Information software that comes with HP-UX. This is the manual set on the CD. Other application software will work just as well; just make sure that your paths correspond with the software you are using. Also, I'm going to use a fictitious user's home directory: **/home/admin1**.

1. **Bring up the Icon Editor** from the Desktop_Apps (HP-UX), Desktoptools (AIX), or from the Desktop_Tools, on Solaris all in the Application Manager.

2. Choose **File -> Open**.

3. Enter a path or folder name: **/opt/dynatext/data/bitmaps**.

4. Enter the file name: **logoicon.bm**

5. Choose **Open**.

We'll see the icon and that it is indeed 32x32. Now we need to save the icon to our own **.dt** directory.

6. Choose **File -> Save As**.

7. Enter path or folder name: **/$HOME/.dt/icons**. For the admin1 user, that would be in **/home/admin1/.dt/icons**.

If we were going to do this task globally, we'd put this in **/etc/dt/app-config/types/C**.

8. Leave the file name as is.

9. **Save**.

Now that we have the icon, we need to create an action file and a description file to go with it.

1. **Using your favorite Text Edito**r, enter the following:

```
ACTION instinfo
{
LABEL              instinfo
TYPE               COMMAND
WINDOW_TYPE        NO_STDIO
EXEC_STRING        /opt/dynatext/bin/dynatext
DESCRIPTION        This action starts Instant Information
}
```

The LABEL is the name of the action, the TYPE is a command, the WINDOW_TYPE is none (no standard I/O or NO_STDIO) because the application has its own window, EXEC_STRING is the command to be executed, and the DESCRIPTION is just a description of what this action does. Make sure that the NO_STDIO has an underscore and not a dash, and don't forget the last }. I've done both of these and then had fun trying to figure out why the action either didn't appear to exist or, if it did appear, why it wouldn't work.

2. **Save this file as /$HOME/.dt/types/instinfo.dt**. For the admin1 user, that would be **/home/admin1/.dt/types/instinfo.dt**. If this were a global configuration, we'd save the file as **/etc/dt/appconfig/types/C/ instinfo.dt**.

Now that we have an action, we need to create a description file. Note that this is a new file with just these two lines in it. The contents of this file are irrelevant, but the permissions *must* include executable.

3. Again, **using your favorite editor**, enter:

```
ACTION instinfo
DESCRIPTION  This action starts Instant Information
```

4. **Save this file as /$HOME/.dt/appmanager/instinfo**. For the admin1 user, that would be **/home/admin1/.dt/appmanager/instinfo**. If this

were a global configuration, we'd save the file as **/etc/dt/appconfig/app-manager/instinfo**.

5. Change the permissions to include execute as follows:

chmod 555 /$HOME/.dt/appmanager/instinfo

Now it's time to modify the front panel to include the icon and action we just created. The front panel file, **dtwm.fp**, is located in the **/usr/dt/app-config/types/C** directory. Because we don't want to overwrite the system file, we need to copy it locally and then modify it for our use.

1. Copy this to **/$HOME/.dt/types/dtwm.fp** for AIX and HP-UX and to **/$HOME/.dt/types/fp-dynamic/dtwm.fp** for Solaris. For the admin1 user, that would be:
     cp /usr/dt/appconfig/types/C/dtwm.fp   /home/admin1/.dt/types/dtwm.fp

or for Solaris:

     cp   /usr/dt/appconfig/types/C/dtwm.fp   /home/admin1/.dt/types/fp-dynamic/dtwm.fp

2. **Using your favorite edito**r, modify the local **dtwm.fp** file.

As we look at the file, we notice that it is in the same order as the front panel is displayed. The clock is the first CONTROL in the file and the first item on the front panel. Also notice that the POSITION_HINTS is 1. Date is next and so is POSITION_HINTS 2. What we want to do is put our new icon and action after POSITION_HINTS 4, the TextEditor CONTROL.

3. Go down just past the } ending CONTROL TextEditor and before CONTROL Mail. At this point, **insert the following exactly as shown below**. Make sure that the uppercase letters are capitalized and the lowercase letters aren't.

```
CONTROL  Info
{
  TYPE                icon
  CONTAINER_NAME    Top
  CONTAINER_TYPE     BOX
```

```
            POSITION_HINTS        5
            ICON                  logoicon.bm
            LABEL                 Instant Info
            PUSH_ACTION           instinfo
        }
```

4. Now be careful; this part is tricky. The next items have to have their POSITION_HINTS renumbered. But we are going to **renumber only the next eight items, beginning with Mail and ending with Trash**. Instead of 5 through 12, these are going to become 6 through 13.

5. **Save** the file.

Now, let's restart the Workspace Manager. If we did everything right, we'll have a new icon, which, when clicked, will bring up Instant Information, shown in Figure 14-9.

6. Position the mouse over a blank area on the workspace and press the right mouse button. Select **Restart Workspace Manager**.

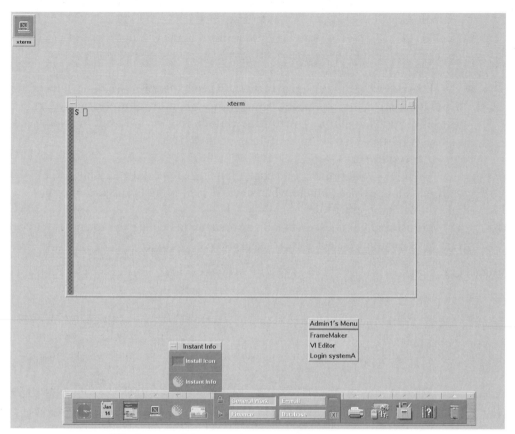

Figure 14-9 Workspace Menu and New Subpanel and Action

A couple of things to remember when creating actions: first and foremost, make sure that the PUSH_ACTION and the file names are the same. That similarity is how they find each other. Make sure the that action file ends with **.dt** and make sure that the description file is executable. If any of these are wrong, the action either won't work or won't appear.

To avoid a lot of typing, sometimes the easiest approach is just to copy an existing definition and insert it where you want your new control to be and then modify it. As you move down the list of control definitions, you're moving from left to right across the front panel (notice that the POSITION_HINTS value increases in each definition). So if you want your new control to be to the right of the date on the front panel, you insert the control on the line below "date" and add a POSITION_HINTS 3 line to your definition; if you wanted your new control to be to the left of "date," insert the control on the line above "date" with a POSITION_HINTS of 1.

The new control definition can be located anywhere in the list of control definitions. The POSITION_HINTS line keeps it from getting inadvertently bumped to a new position. It's still a good idea to copy an existing definition and avoid extra typing; it reduces the chance of typing mistakes. And don't forget to include the curly braces.

Using Different Fonts

Although CDE fonts have been carefully selected for readability, you may have valid reasons to prefer other fonts. To make your fonts available system-wide throughout the CDE environment, put them in **/etc/dt/app-defaults/Dtstyle** so that they will appear in the style manager's font dialog box. To make fonts available only for a particular X client application, specify the font in the **app-defaults** file for the application. Just remember, this overrides the fonts in the style manager.

The font dialog box can contain a maximum of seven font sizes. You can adjust this number downward by resetting the value of **Dtstyle*NumFonts** in **/etc/dt/app-defaults/Dtstyle**; however, you can't increase the number higher than seven.

The Font Dialog section of the **Dtstyle** configuration file has seven **SystemFont** resources and seven **UserFont** resources. Again, you can have fewer than seven system and seven user fonts, but you can't have more.

To specify fonts for a particular application, use the ***FontList** resource in the **app-defaults** file for the application.

To modify font resources on an individual user basis, you can use the **EditResources** action as described in the earlier section "Changing the Front Panel in Other Ways."

Changing the Login Messages

One of the nice things about CDE is the ability to modify so many parts. You can customize individual login accounts or the entire system. By customizing the login screen, you can show those about to log in the name of the system they are accessing, the company logo, and a personalized greeting. These modifications take place in the **Xresources** file:

1. As we've done already with the **dtwm.fp** and **dtwmrc** files, we will need to copy the system file from **/usr/dt/config/C** to **/etc/dt/config/C** as follows:

cp /usr/dt/config/C/Xresources   /etc/dt/config/C/Xresources

2. **Go into your favorite editor** and bring up the **Xresources** file so that it can be edited.

3. **Go to the GREETING area**. Here we'll find the following lines:

!!Dtlogin*greeting.labelString: Welcome to %LocalHost%
!!Dtlogin*greetingpersLabelString: Welcome %s

The first line is the message on the initial login screen. Let's change that so that it welcomes us to our company, ABC, Inc.:

1. **Remove the comment notations**. Unlike shell scripts that most of us are used to, the Xresources file uses two exclamation points as comment notation. Remove the !!.

2. Next, **modify "Welcome to %LocalHost%"**. The %LocalHost% variable is replaced with our system name in the login screen. The line should look like this:

Dtlogin*greeting.labelString: ABC, Inc, Welcomes You to %LocalHost%

3. Next let's **change the second line** to include the department that this system is dedicated to: finance. This second line shows what is displayed when we are prompted for our password. The %s variable is our user name. The line should now look like this:

Dtlogin*greetingpersLabelString: The Finance Department Welcomes %s

4. **Save the file**.

5. **Now log out and back in**. We should see the changes in the login screen. We didn't need to "reload" the file, because the act of logging out and back in does that action.

Changing the Login Picture

Adding a new picture to the login screen is easy if you know one thing. The file has to be a bitmap (.bm) or pixmap (.pm) file. A bitmap file is black and white, and the pixmap file is color. I've tried using other kinds of pictures (.gif and .jpg formats), but they just don't display. The good news is that these can be imported from other systems or the Internet for our use. To make things simple, we're going to use one already on the system. A bitmap showing a birthday cake was found in **/usr/lib/X11/bitmaps** on an HP-UX workstation. However, I have also successfully pulled down pictures of flowers, the Grand Canyon, and country music singers (note: Donna wrote this chapter, not Marty) from the Internet and put them on my system login screen.

1. Once more, let's go into our favorite editor and modify **/etc/dt/config/C/Xresources**.

2. **Go to the MISC area**. Here we'll find the following lines:

!!Dtlogin*logo*bitmapFile: < bitmap or pixmap file >

3. **Delete the leading !!**, which are the comment designators.

4. **Replace < bitmap or pixmap file >** with the name of the bitmap file using the entire path location. The line should look as follows:

Dtlogin*logo*bitmapFile: /usr/lib/X11/bitmap/cake.bm

5. **Save the file**.

6. **Now log out and back in**. We should see the birthday cake in the login screen. Again, we didn't need to "reload" the file, because the act of logging out and back in does that task.

Now that we've seen how easily we can make some simple customizations in CDE for our end-users, we should be able to take this knowledge and really make their CDE environments a productive and friendly place to work.

CDE - Advanced Topics

The Relationship among X, Motif, and CDE
X, OSF/Motif, and CDE are enabling framework technologies. Taken together, X, Motif, and CDE make up the three graphical layers on top of the operating system and hardware platform.

The GUI layers provide increasingly richer ease-of-use functions in a progressive series of layers that buffer the end user from the "user-hostile," character-based interface of the operating system layer.

The X Window System

The X Window System consists of the following:

- Xlib - Low-level library for programming window manipulation; graphics capabilities such as line drawing and text placement; controlling display output, mouse, and keyboard input; and application network transparency.

- Xt Intrinsics - Higher-level library for programming widgets and gadgets (graphical controls components like menus, scrollbars, and push buttons).

- Display servers - Hardware-specific programs, one per display, that manage the graphical input and output.

- Interclient communication conventions (ICCC) - A manual specifying standards for how X client programs should communicate with each other.

- Configuration files - One configuration file that specifies the default session to start (**sys.x11start**) and another specifying values for resources used to shape the X environment (**sys.Xdefaults**).

Through these mechanisms, X provides the standard upon which the graphical part of the network-oriented, client/server, distributed computing paradigm is based. A knowledge of **Xlib** and the **Xt** Intrinsics is important for programming in X and for programming at the Motif level. For system administrators, however, as long as the display servers work and X client applications are ICCC-compliant, you shouldn't need to delve into the X layer. CDE enables you to view X pretty much as part of "all that underlying technological infrastructure stuff" and focus on developing appropriate configurations of CDE to meet your users' work contexts.

Motif

Motif consists of the following:

- mwm window manager - Executable program that provides Motif-based window frames, window management, and a workspace menu in the X environment.

- Motif widget toolkit - Higher-level library of widgets and gadgets, the graphical components used to control the user environment.

- Motif style guide - A manual defining the Motif appearance and behavior for programmers.

- Configuration files - The **system.mwmrc** file containing configuration information for the workspace menu and key and button bindings. Resources for the window manager are in **mwm** in the **/usr/lib/X11/app-defaults** directory.

Motif provides the window manager for the end-user, the widget toolkit for application developers, and the style guide to help developers design and build proper Motif-conformant applications. As with X, system administrators can view Motif mostly as "programmer's stuff," part of the underlying infrastructure, and focus on developing appropriate CDE configuration files.

CDE

As we have already seen, CDE consists of the following:

- Workspace Manager - Executable program that provides Motif-based window frames, window management, a workspace menu, and the front panel.

- File Manager - Program that iconically manages files and directories through direct manipulation.

- Style Manager - Container of dialog boxes that control elements of the CDE environment, like workspace color and fonts.

- Help Manager - This program provides context-sensitive help text on CDE components.

- Login Manager - Daemon-like application that handles login and password verification.

- Session Manager - Manager that handles saving and restoring user sessions.

- Application Manager - Manager that registers and keeps track of applications in the CDE environment.

- Configuration Files - A big bunch, most of which you can avoid dealing with (see the next section).

CDE also provides a number of basic, end-user productivity-enhancing applications. In general, CDE provides a graphical environment into which users, or you, their system administrator, can incorporate the software tools needed to do their work.

X, Motif, and CDE Configuration Files

X, Motif, and CDE all use configuration files to shape their appearance and behavior. Elements of appearance and behavior such as foreground color, keyboard focus policy, and client decoration are resources that can be controlled by values in the appropriate configuration file. In X, Motif, and CDE, the word "resource" has a special meaning. It doesn't refer to vague natural resources or generic system resources, but to rather specific elements of appearance and behavior. Some examples are the **foreground** resource, the **keyboardFocusPolicy** resource, and the **clientDecoration** resource. For example, the foreground color could be black, keyboard focus policy could be explicit, and client decoration could be plus-title (title bar only). These would appear in some appropriate configuration file as the following:

    *foreground: black

    *keyboardFocusPolicy:explicit

*clientDecoration: +title

Which configuration file these resources appear in depends on the scope of the effect desired (system-wide or individual user) and the graphical interface level being used (X, Motif, or CDE).

X Configuration Files

The X Window System has the following configuration files:

sys.x11start

sys.Xdefaults

system.mwmrc

X*screens

X*devices

X*pointerkey

By convention, these files are located in the **/usr/lib/X11** directory; however, I have noticed that many systems have eliminated this directory and moved many of the X-related files elsewhere in the system. In addition, each X client application has its own app-defaults configuration file located, also by convention, in the **/usr/lib/X11/app-defaults** directory. Although six files are listed above, unless you're configuring a workstation for multiple-display screens (X*screens), multiple-input devices (X*devices), or keyboard-only pointer navigation (X*pointerkey), you'll typically need to work with only **sys.x11start**, **sys.Xdefaults**, and **system.mwmrc**.

The **sys.x11start** file was a script used to start X and X clients before the advent of CDE. System administrators or knowledgeable users modified **sys.x11start** so that the appropriate mix of X clients started "automatically." The **sys.Xdefaults** file was read as X started to obtain values for various appearance and behavior resources. Modifications to **sys.Xdefaults** ensured that the X environment and clients had the proper appearance and behavior. **system.mwmrc** contained the configuration of the Workspace menu and button and key bindings. **system.mwmrc** has been replaced by the Motif version also, **system.mwmrc**.

Motif Configuration Files

Motif added only one new configuration file to the X list: **system.mwmrc**.

By convention, this file is kept with the X configuration files in   /
usr/lib/X11. Actually, this file isn't new; it is the Motif version of   **sys-
tem.mwmrc,** which simply replaced **system.mwmrc** in Motif environments.

Whereas X brought network and interclient communication standards to the
graphical user interface, Motif brought a standard for appearance and behavior, the standard originally defined in IBM's System Application Architecture Common User Access (SAACUA), which forms the basis of most PC-
based GUIs. Thus, push buttons and scroll bars have a defined look and a
defined behavior, and double-clicking always causes the default action to
happen.

From a programmer's point of view, the Motif Widget Toolkit represents quite an advance over programming in "raw" X. From a user's or system administrator's point of view, the Motif user environment is about the
same as the X environment, except that the **mwm** Window Manager is
replaced with the Motif window manager.

CDE Configuration Files

It is possible to point to over 80 files that, in one way or another, con-
tribute to configuring some aspect of CDE. By convention, these files reside
in the **/usr/dt** directory. However, if you remove from this list such files as
those that:

- Configure CDE applications as opposed to the environment
  itself

- Establish default actions and datatype definitions that, although
  you create your own definitions in separate files, you never
  modify

- Are CDE working files and should not be customized

- Are more appropriately associated with configuring the UNIX,
  X, and Motif environments underlying CDE, including the
  various shell environments, then CDE has approximately 19
  configuration files, as shown in Table 14-1

Table 14-1   CDE Configuration Files

* .Xauthority	* sys.font	* Xresources
* .Xdefaults	* sys.resources	* Xservers
* .dtprofile	* sys.sessions	* Xsession
* dtwm.fp	* Xaccess	* Xsetup
* dt.wmrc	* Xconfig	* Xstartup
* sys.dtprofile	* Xfailsafe	
* sys.dtwmrc	* Xreset	

Although 19 configuration files are still a lot, don't be alarmed by the number. You won't need to modify many of them, and can ignore a couple that you modify once and then forget. You need to understand in depth for periodic modification only one or two, perhaps a system-wide *.**dt** file for custom actions and datatypes or maybe **dtwm.fp**, if you are required to modify the front panel on a regular basis for some reason.

Still, configuring CDE is not something you want to start hacking at without a little preparation and a good idea of what you want to accomplish. All CDE configuration files are pretty well commented, so a good first step is to print the ones you want to modify.

Table 14-2 organizes CDE configuration files according to their content and the breadth of their influence:

.

Table 14-2   CDE Configuration File Influence

Nature of Configuration File	System-Wide Influence	User's Personal Influence
Environment Variables	sys.dtprofile Xconfig Xsession	.dtprofile
Appearance & Behavior Resources	sys.resources Xconfig Xresources sys.fonts	.Xdefaults

Table 14-2   CDE Configuration File Influence (Continued)

Nature of Configuration File	System-Wide Influence	User's Personal Influence
File Types & Action Definitions	misc *.dt files	user-prefs.dt
Client Startup at Login	sys.sessions Xstartup Xsession Xreset Xfailsafe	.xsession sessionetc
Workspace Manager & Front Panel	sys.dtwmrc dtwm.fp	dtwmrc user-prefs.fp
Clients/Servers & Access	Xaccess Xservers	.Xauthority

The file **sys.dtwmrc** controls the configuration of the Workspace Manager at the system level. This includes all of the following:

Workspace Menu A menu that displays when mouse button 3 is pressed while the mouse pointer is over the workspace backdrop.

Button Bindings Definitions of what action happens when a particular mouse button is pressed or released while the mouse pointer is over a particular area (frame, icon, window, or root).

Key Bindings   Definitions of what action happens when a particular key or key sequence is pressed while the mouse pointer is over a particular area (frame, icon, window, or root).

Unlike configuration files for X or Motif, **sys.dtwmrc** does not control the following configuration elements:

Front Panel   The box, usually at the bottom of the work-space, that contains commonly referenced indicators and frequently used graphical controls, including a six-button workspace switch.

Slideup Subpanels Menus that slide up from the front panel at various locations to provide more functionality without consuming more screen space.

Instead, to avoid a massively large and overly complex configuration file, these elements were separated into their own configuration file in CDE, **dtwm.fp**.

Some front panel configuration elements, like the number of workspaces and their arrangement in the workspace switch, are controlled through resources in a **sys.resources**, **dt.resources**, or **.Xdefaults** file. Like other Workspace Manager configuration files, **sys.dtwmrc** can be copied to a user's home directory, actually to **$HOME/.dt/** as **dtwmrc**, and modified to personalize the user's environment beyond the system-wide configuration of **sys.dtwmrc**.

The **sys.resources** file is one of those files you might modify once, and then never again. The **dt.resources** file is one of those files you won't ever need to modify and can ignore. The **.Xdefaults** file is one you or your users may modify on occasion.

The **sys.resources** file is where you put any non-default resources that you want in effect when a brand new user logs into CDE for the very first time. For example, as system administrator, you may want your users to have a CDE front panel with prenamed workspaces, special colors, particular fonts, or application windows in certain locations. After the first-time login, **sys.resources** is ignored in favor of **dt.resources**. This file, **dt.resources**, resides in **$HOME/.dt/sessions/current** (or **$HOME/.dt/sessions/home** when the home session is restored) and is created automatically by CDE. You can consider it a CDE working file and forget about it. The **.Xdefaults** file is where you or an end-user would list X resources specific to the user's personal CDE environment. **sys.resources**, **dt.resources**, and **.Xdefaults** contain a list of resources and their values.

The **sys.sessions** file controls which clients start the very first time a new user logs into CDE. The **dt.sessions** file is to **sys.sessions** as **dt.resources** is to **sys.resources**.

It may be efficient to configure CDE to start particular applications for your users. You would specify these applications in **sys.sessions**. When a new user logs in for the first time, the CDE environment includes the specified clients. At the end of this first session by logging out, the remaining clients would be recorded in **$HOME/.dt/sessions/current** for CDE (**$HOME/.dt/sessions/home** when the home session is restored).

The **sys.dtprofile** file is a template that is automatically copied at first login into each new user's home directory as **.dtprofile. sys.dtprofile** replaces **.profile** or **.login** in the CDE environment (although either **.profile** or **.login** can be sourced in **.dtprofile** by removing the # comment symbol in front of **DTSOURCEPROFILE=true**). The **.dtprofile** file holds the personal environment variables that would, in a character-based environment, be found in **.profile** or **.login**. Use **.dtprofile** to avoid the interference that terminal I/O commands cause to CDE's graphical environment.

The CDE login manager, **dtlogin**, presets the following environment variables to default values:

DISPLAY	The name of the local display
EDITOR	The default text editor
HOME	The user's home directory as specified in **/etc/passwd**
KBD_LANG	The current language of the keyboard
LANG	The current NLS language
LC_ALL	The value of LANG
LC_MESSAGES	The value of LANG
LOGNAME	The user's login name as specified in **/etc/passwd**
MAIL	The default file for mail (usually **/var/mail/$USER**)
PATH	The default directories to search for files and applications
USER	The user name
SHELL	The default shell as specified in **/etc/passwd**
TERM	The default terminal emulation
TZ	The time zone in effect

Variations to these default values belong in each user's **.dtprofile**. Additional environment variables can be added as needed to shape the user's environment to the needs of the work context. Just beware of using commands that cause any terminal I/O.

Like **.dtprofile**, **Xsession** is a shell script that sets user environment variables. The environment variables in **Xsession** apply system-wide. The environment variables in **.dtprofile** apply only to a user's personal environment. Furthermore, Because the login manager runs **Xsession** after the X server has started, the variables in **Xsession** are not available to the X server. Variables typically set in **Xsession** include the following:

EDITOR	The default text editor.
KBD_LANG	The language of the keyboard (usually, set to the value of $LANG).
TERM	The default terminal emulation.
MAIL	The default file for mail, which is usually **/var/mail/$USER**.
DTHELPSEARCHPATH	The locations to search for CDE help files.
DTAPPSEARCHPATH	The locations to search for applications registered with the CDE application manager.
DTDATABASESEARCHPATH	The locations to search for additional action and datatype definitions.
XMICONSEARCHPATH	The locations to search for additional icons.
XMICONBMSEARCHPATH	Same as above.

As an example, suppose that you are the system administrator for several mixed workstation and X terminal clusters located at a single site. As usually happens, most users have grown accustomed to certain text editors. Some like **vi**, others prefer **emacs**, and a couple wouldn't be caught dead without **dmx**. An easy way to provide each user with his or her favored text editor would be to reset their EDITOR variable to the appropriate value in the individual **.dtprofile** files.

Xconfig contains resources that control the behavior of **dtlogin** and it also provides a place to specify the locations for any other **dtlogin** configuration files you create. The **Xconfig** file works on a system-wide basis, so it's one of those files that you modify only once and then forget about. When, during login, **Xconfig** is run, several CDE configuration files get referenced: **Xaccess**, **Xservers**, **Xresources**, **Xstartup**, **Xsession**, **Xreset**, and **Xfailsafe**. Like **Xconfig** itself, most of these files are the type that you modify once when installing CDE and then, unless the network topology changes, you never deal with again.

Xaccess, as the name implies, is a remote display access control file. **Xaccess** contains a list of the host names allowed or denied XDMCP connection access to the local computer. For example, when an X terminal requests login service, **dtlogin** consults the **Xaccess** file to determine whether service should be granted.

The primary use of the **Xservers** file is to list the display screens on the local system that **dtlogin** is responsible for managing. **dtlogin** reads the **Xservers** file and starts an X server for each display listed there. It then starts a child **dtlogin** process to manage the server and display the login screen. Note that **dtlogin** works only locally; **dtlogin** can't start an X server on a remote system or X terminal. For remote display servers, some other mechanism must be used to start the server, which then uses the X Display Management Control Protocol (XDMCP) to request a login screen from **dtlogin**.

The **Xservers** file is another of those files that you may spend some time with initially and then, unless the topology of your network changes, never deal with again. When do you use **Xservers**? When a display doesn't match the default configuration. The default configuration assumes that each system has a single bitmap display and is the system console. X terminals, multiple displays (heads), multiple screens, and Starbase applications all require configuration lines in the **Xservers** file.

The **Xresources** file contains the list of resources that control the appearance and behavior of the login screen. After you substitute your company's logo for the CDE logo and change the fonts and colors, you'll probably never have to deal with **Xresources** again (unless your company changes its logo).

Xstartup is a system-wide configuration file executed by the login manager, from which it receives several environment variables:

DISPLAY	The name of the local display.
USER	The login name of the user.
HOME	The user's home directory.
PATH	The value of the **systemPath** resource in **Xconfig**.
SHELL	The value of the **systemShell** resource in **Xconfig**.
XAUTHORITY	The file to access for authority permissions.
TZ	The local time zone.

Because it can execute scripts and start clients on a system-wide basis, **Xstartup** is similar to **sys.sessions**. The difference is that **Xstartup** runs as root. Thus, modifications to **Xstartup** should be reserved for actions like mounting file systems.

Xreset is a system-wide companion script to **Xstartup**. It runs as root and essentially undoes what **Xstartup** put in motion.

The **Xfailsafe** file contains customizations to the standard failsafe session. The failsafe session provides a way to correct improper CDE sessions caused by errors in the login and session configuration files. As such, **Xfailsafe** is something that your users are not ever going to use, but you can make your life a little easier with a few judicious customizations.

The **sessionetc** file resides in a user's **.dt/sessions** directory and personalizes that user's CDE session. **sessionetc** handles the starting of additional X clients like **sys.session**, but on a per-user basis, as opposed to system-wide. Although **dt.session** also starts clients on a per-user basis, the clients are those of the default or current session. **dt.session** resides in **.dt/ session/current**. **sessionetc**, which resides in **.dt/session**, and should contain only those clients that are not automatically restored. Typically, these are clients that do not set the **WM_COMMAND** properly, so the session manager can't save or restore them; thus, they need to be restarted in **sessionetc**.

The **sys.font** file contains the system-wide, default session font configuration. These default fonts were based on usability studies, so **sys.font** is a file you may never change. However, should you encounter a situation that requires a different mix of fonts on a system-wide basis, this is where you'd change them. Note that the font resources and values mentioned in **sys.font** must match exactly the default font resources specified in the **/usr/dt/app-defaults/C/Dtstyle** file.

CDE has a bunch of files that specify CDE action and data type definitions. All these files end with the file extension ***.dt**. A ***.dt** ("dt" for "desk top") contains both data type and action definitions. The default ***.dt** files are in **/usr/dt/appconfig/types/C** and act on a system-wide basis. Similarly, **user-prefs.dt**, the master copy of which is also located in **/usr/dt/appconfig/ types/C**, is used at the personal user level.

The **.Xauthority** file is a user-specific configuration file containing authorization information needed by clients that require an authorization mechanism to connect to the server.

CDE Configuration File Locations

Where CDE looks for particular configuration files depends on the nature of the configuration files, principally what the files configure and how wide their influence is. Table 13-3 shows the location of system and user configuration files based on the nature of the file content.

For each of the default system-wide file locations listed in Table 14-3, a corresponding location exists for custom system-wide configuration files. These custom files should be located in the appropriate subdirectory under **/etc/dt**. The basic procedure is to copy the file you need to customize from **/usr/dt/something** to **/etc/dt/something** and then do your modifications there. For example, to change the default logo in **Xresources**, copy **/usr/dt/config/C/Xresources** to **/etc/dt/config/C/Xresources**, open **/etc/dt/config/C/Xresources**, and make your changes.

Table 14-3   CDE System and User Configuration Files

Nature of Configuration File	System-Wide Influence	User's Personal Influence
Environment Variables	/usr/dt/config/	$HOME/
Appearance & Behavior Resources	/usr/dt/config/C /usr/dt/app-defaults/C	$HOME/.dt/ $HOME/.dt/sessions/current/ $HOME/.dt/sessions/home/
File Types & Action Definitions	/usr/dt/appconfig/ types/C	$HOME/.dt/types
Client Startup at Login	/usr/dt/config/ /usr/dt/config/C	$HOME/.dt/session/ $HOME/.dt/session/current/ $HOME/.dt/session/home/
Workspace Manager	/usr/dt/config	$HOME/.dt/

This is an important point. Files located under **/usr/dt** are considered CDE system files and will be overwritten during updates. Thus, any customizations you do there will be lost. Make all modifications to system-wide configuration files in **/etc/dt** and its subdirectories.

How Configuration Files Play Together

From the material covered so far, you've probably concluded correctly that CDE configuration files aren't something to go hacking at without a plan - a well-thought-out plan. You've probably figured out that the element you want to configure and the breadth of influence you want it to have determine which configuration file you modify.

For instance, if you wanted to set an environment variable, you have a choice of four configuration files: **sys.dtprofile**, **Xconfig**, **Xsession**, and **.dtprofile**. But if you want to set environment variables that affect only a particular user, your choice immediately narrows to a single file, **.dtprofile**.

Now the only remaining piece of the puzzle is to understand the order in which CDE reads its configuration files. When a configuration element (an environment variable, resource, action, or data type) is specified twice but with different values, you obviously want the correct value used and the incorrect value ignored.

The following rules apply:

- For environment variables, the last specified value is used.

- For resources, the last specified value is used. However, this is influenced by specificity. Thus, **emacs*foreground** takes precedence over just ***foreground** for *emacs* clients, regardless of the order in which the resources were encountered.

- For actions, the first specified is used.

- For data types, the first specified is used.

Table 14-4 illustrates which specification is used when CDE reads multiple specifications of configuration elements in its configuration files:

Table 14-4 What CDE Uses for Configuration

Configuration Element	Element Used
resource	last encountered or most specific
environment	last encountered
action	first encountered
file type	first encountered

Put in terms of scope, a user configuration file overrides a system-wide configuration file. Looking at the order of precedence of just system-wide configuration files, the files in **/etc/dt** have precedence over those in **/usr/dt**, so global custom configurations have precedence over the CDE default configuration. And **$HOME/.dt** files take precedence over those in **/etc/dt.**

For resources, the elements used to specify a GUI's appearance and behavior, CDE sets values according to the following priorities:

1. **Command line** -   When you start a client from the command line, options listed on the command line have top priority.

2. **Xresources, .Xdefaults, dt.resources, sys.resources,** -   When CDE starts, it reads these resource configuration files to determine the value of X resources to use for the session.

3. **RESOURCE MANAGER** - Resources already in the property **RESOURCE_MANAGER** may affect an application that is just starting.

4. **app-defaults** - Specifies "default" resource values that differ from built-in resource values.

5. **built-in defaults** - Default resources that are "hard-coded" have the lowest priority.

Specific resource specifications take precedence over general resource specifications. For example, suppose that you want a certain font in your text entry areas. You could correctly specify a ***FontList** resource in your personal **.Xdefaults** file, only to have it overwritten by an ***XmText*FontList** in an **app-defaults** file. Although **app-defaults** is of lower priority than **.Xdefaults**, the resource specification set there is more specific, so it takes precedence.

For environment variables, CDE sets values according to the following priorities:

1. **$HOME/.dtprofile** - User-specific variables have top priority.

2. **/etc/dt/config/C/Xsession -** Custom system-wide variables not read by X server.

3. **/etc/dt/config/C/Xconfig** - Custom system-wide variables read by X server.

4. **/usr/dt/config/C/Xsession** - Default system-wide variables not read by X server.

5. **/usr/dt/config/C/Xconfig** - Default system-wide variables read by X server.

6. **/usr/dt/bin/dtlogin** - Built-in default variables have the lowest priority.

For data type and action definitions, CDE looks for **.dt** files according to the following priority:

1. $HOME/.dt/types

2. /etc/dt/appconfig/types/C

3. /usr/dt/appconfig/types/C

Remember that for data types or actions, the first value that it finds is the one it uses. So if you just can't get a file type or action to work, check for a duplicate entry earlier in the file or for an entry in a file with higher priority. Note also that the environment variable DTDATABASESEARCHPATH can be set either in **/etc/dt/config/Xsession** or **$HOME/.dtprofile**, to add directories where CDE can search for file type and action definition information.

Specifying Appearance and Behavior

You need to know only two tricks to specifying appearance and behavior resources in configuration files. The first is to specify the resource and its value correctly. The second is to specify the resource and value in the correct configuration file.

Two caveats involve colors and fonts. The CDE style manager provides a graphical interface for modifying colors and fonts. However, if you specify an application's color or font directly, this specification will override the ability of the style manager to manage that resource for the application.

Typical ways to specify a color or font directly include the following:

- Type the specification on the command line as a startup option.

- Include the specification in the application's **app-defaults** file.

- Use the **xrdb** utility to add resources for the application to the resource database.

The Sequence of Events When CDE Starts

The following section is a blow-by-blow account of what happens when a user logs into CDE. In this particular account, assume a distributed topology like a diskless cluster. The account begins with the boot of the hub system and nodes in step 1. By step 4, X servers are running on each node and login screens are being displayed. By step 6, the user is logged in. By step 11, the session manager is busy re-creating the user's session.

1. The **dtlogin** executable is started as part of the **init** process that occurs during the system boot sequence on the hub machine and each cluster node.

2. **dtlogin** reads **/usr/dt/config/Xconfig** to get a list of resources with which to configure the login process. This is where **dtlogin** first learns about files like **Xaccess**, **Xservers**, **Xresources**, **Xstartup**, **Xsession**, and **Xreset** and gets the values of a number of appearance and behavior resources.

3. **dtlogin** reads two files in **/usr/dt/config**:

   - **Xservers** or the file identified by the **Dtlogin*servers** resource setting in **Xconfig**.

   - **Xresources** or the file identified by the **Dtlogin*resources** resource setting in **Xconfig**.

4. **dtlogin** starts an X server and a child **dtlogin** for each local display.

5. Each child **dtlogin** invokes **dtgreet**, the login screen.

6. When a login and password are validated, a child **dtlogin** sets certain environment variables to default values.

7. The child **dtlogin** runs **/usr/dt/config/Xstartup**.

8. The child **dtlogin** runs **/usr/dt/config/Xsession**.

9. **Xsession** runs **dthello**, the copyright screen.

10. **Xsession** reads **$HOME/.dtprofile**, setting any additional environment variables or overwriting those set previously by **dtlogin**.

11. The child **dtlogin** invokes the session manager, **dtsession**.

12. **dtsession** restores the appropriate session. For example, to restore the current session, **dtsession** reads **dt.resources** and **dt.session** in **$HOME/.dt/sessions/current**.

At logout, the reverse happens. The session is saved and **dtlogin** runs **/usr/dt/config/Xreset**. After **Xreset** completes, **dtlogin** again displays the login screen, as in step 4.

CDE and Performance

CDE isn't a monolithic application; it's a set of components layered on top of the operating system, the X Window System, and Motif. Each underlying layer takes its share of RAM before CDE or any other client even starts. Because of the low-level nature of these layers, the RAM they use is hardly ever regained through swapping to disk.

In some cases, operating system overhead and user application requirements restrict the amount of RAM available for a graphical user interface to little more than enough to run a window manager such as Motif. Because the CDE workspace manager and the Motif window manager take roughly the same amount of RAM, users can enjoy an enriched graphical environment with the added value of CDE's multiple workspaces at essentially no extra RAM cost over running the Motif window manager.

Tactics for Better Performance

Unless all your users have RAM-loaded powerhouses for systems, you will need to spend some time developing a performance strategy. If you conceive of performance as a bell-shaped curve, satisfaction lies on the leading edge. Your performance strategy should do everything it can to keep your users on the leading edge.

Probably the most logical approach is to start small and grow. In other words, start out with minimal user environments on all the systems on your network. Gradually add software components until you or your users begin to notice performance degradation. Then back off a little. Such an approach might take several weeks or more to evaluate, as you add components and as your users spend several days actually working in the environment to determine the effect of your changes on system performance and their frustration levels.

The most RAM-expensive pieces of CDE are the workspace manager, the session manager, and the file manager. The workspace manager is expensive because portions of it are always in RAM (assuming that you are moving windows around and switching workspaces). The CDE workspace manager is no more expensive than the Motif window manager; if you want a GUI, it's just a price you have to pay. The session manager is expensive only during logout and login, as it saves and restores sessions. The rest of the time, the session manager is dormant and gets swapped out of RAM. Saving your current work session is nice at the end of the day, but it's something to consider giving up if you want to improve your login and logout performance. The file manager is expensive because it wakes up periodically and jumps into RAM to check the status of the file system and update its file manager windows. When it jumps into RAM, it pushes something else out, for example, maybe the desktop publishing program you're using.

Here are some other ideas that you may find useful:

Terminal Emulators	**xterms** are a little less RAM-expensive than **dtterms**. Unless you need the block mode functionality of a **dtterm**, **xterm** might be a better choice for terminal emulation.
Automatic Saves	Some applications automatically save data at periodic intervals. Although this feature can be beneficial, you need to evaluate its effect in light of performance. If the application is central to your users' work, fine, but if not, you might want to disable the automatic save feature.

Scroll Buffers	Large scroll buffers in terminal emulators can be a real convenience, but they can also take up a lot of RAM. Even modestly sized scroll buffers, when multiplied by three or four terminal emulators, consume a lot of RAM.
Background Bitmaps	Avoid large bitmaps; they increase the X server size. Especially avoid switching large bitmaps frequently within a session. If you are hunting for a new background, be sure to restart the X server after you've found the one you want and have included it in the proper **sessionetc** file. The most efficient bitmaps are small ones that can be repeated to tile the background.
Front Panel	Reconfigure the front panel to minimize the number of buttons. Keep just enough to meet user needs. This tactic decreases the workspace manager size in RAM and speeds login and logout.
Pathnames	Whenever possible, use absolute pathnames for bitmap specifications. Although this approach decreases the flexibility of the system, it speeds access time.

Conclusion

The default CDE is ready to use, but given its power and flexibility, you will inevitably want to customize the CDE environment for your users' work context and optimum performance. Take the time to develop a good idea of what changes you need to make, the order in which to make them, and exactly where to make them. In so doing, all the power and flexibility of CDE will be open to you.

Appendix A

Virtual Partitions Online Manual Pages

Man Pages

The commands for working with Virtual Partitions appear in every chapter in this book. Many examples are provided in the chapters. In addition, the Quick Reference Tear Out card has on it summaries and examples of all of the commands. There is, however, nothing like the command detail that appears in the man pages for a command. The man pages for Virtual Partitions commands are well written and thorough. This appendix consists of the manual pages for Virtual Partitions commands only. The following is a list of the commands:

vparboot - Boots (starts) a virtual partition.
vparcreate - Creates a new virtual partition.
vparmodify - Modifies an existing virtual partition.
vparremove - Removes (deletes) an existing virtual partition.
vparreset - Sends a TOC or hard reset to a virtual partition.
vparresources - Provides description of Virtual Partitions and their resources.
vparstatus - Displays virtual partition and available resources information.
vpartition - Displays information about the vPars Command Line Interface.
vparutil - Works with SCSI information of disks in vPar.

vparboot - Boots (starts) a virtual partition.

vparboot(1M)   vparboot(1M)

NAME
     vparboot - boot a virtual partition

SYNOPSIS
     vparboot -p vp_name [-b kernel_path] [-o boot_opts] [-B boot_addr]

     vparboot -p vp_name -I ignite_kernel

DESCRIPTION
     The vparboot command causes the virtual partition monitor to boot the
     specified virtual partition. The monitor must be running. The
     virtual partition must exist in the monitor configuration and be in
     the Down state. For example, not running. For this reason, it is not
     possible to boot the current partition using this command. The
     partition in which the command is executing is called the current
     partition.

     Only a superuser can execute the vparboot command.

  Options
     vparboot recognizes the following command line options and arguments:

        -p vp_name   Specifies the unique name of the virtual partition
                        which is to be booted. The virtual partition must
                        exist in the monitor's database, must be in the
                        Down state, and must have a configured boot
                        device. Required.

        -b kernel_path Specifies the absolute path to a bootable kernel
                        for the virtual partition. For example, if a
                        non-partitioned system start string at the ISL
                        prompt is:

ISL> hpux -iS /stand/vmunix

the kernel-path is the /stand/vmunix portion of
this string.

If this option is omitted, the value is taken from
any -b kernel_path specified during virtual
partition creation or its most recent
modification, or /stand/vmunix if -b kernel_path
has never been specified.

        -o boot_opts   Specifies the command-line options applied when
                        the virtual partition is booted. For example, if
                        a non-partitioned system start string at the ISL
                        prompt is:

```
ISL> hpux -iS /stand/vmunix
```

the boot_opts string in this case will be -iS.
Note that if any whitespace is included in the
string, the string must be quoted.

Refer to the virtual partitions administration
guide and the chapter titled "Monitor and Shell
Commands" for a full list of supported boot option
strings.

If the -o option is omitted, the value is taken
from any -o boot_opts specified during virtual
partition creation or its most recent
modification, or the empty string if -o boot_opts
has never been specified.

-B boot_addr   Specifies the device from which the virtual
                partition kernel image is read. It must be one of
                the following three forms:

                bo[ot] | pri[mary]
                    (case-insensitive). This is the default if
                    the -B option is omitted. vparboot attempts
                    to boot vp_name from the device previously
                    configured with the BOOT attribute. It is an
                    error if no device has been so configured.

                alt[ernate|boot]
                    (case-insensitive). vparboot attempts to
                    boot vp_name from the device previously
                    configured with the ALTBOOT attribute. It is
                    an error if no device has been so configured.

                Boot From Hardware Path:
                    Any other string is assumed to be the
                    hardware path (for example, 10/6.0) to the
                    desired boot device. vparboot does not check
                    any part of such a specification. If it is
                    not a proper path, the path does not exist,
                    the virtual partition does not own the device
                    at that path, or there is no bootable device
                    at that path, the command either fails with
                    an error, or the boot attempt fails with no
                    error indication.

-I ignite_kernel Specifies a path to a cold-install kernel such as
                 /opt/ignite/boot/WINSTALL. This form of the
                 command is used to cold-install an instance of
                 HP-UX on a virtual partition. Most often, this is
                 done on a newly-created virtual partition, one
                 that has a completely unwritten disk. However, it

can be used to cold-install HP-UX over an existing
instance.

ignite_kernel can reside either on the current
virtual partition (the one on which vparboot is
run) or on any other networked system or virtual
partition accessible from that partition. The
syntax for ignite_kernel is:

[Server name or IP addr,]cold-install_kernel

If cold-install_kernel begins with a slash, "/",
you are specifying an absolute path and vparboot
looks for it at that location. If cold-
install_kernel does not begin with "/", the
default path /opt/ignite/boot/ is prepended to
cold-install_kernel.

If the Server name or IP address, is not specified, vparboot loads the
cold-install kernel from the filespace of the current virtual
partition. Otherwise the command loads it from the filespace of the
specified server. The comma is a required part of the server name
syntax.

RETURN VALUE
    The vparboot command exits with one of the following values:

    0   Successful completion.
    1   One or more error conditions occurred.

EXAMPLES
    Boot the virtual partition called Oslo

  vparboot -p Oslo

    Boot the virtual partition Bergen specifying an alternate kernel

  vparboot -p Bergen -b /stand/vmunix_debug

    Cold-install the virtual partition Trondheim from a file on a remote
    server

  vparboot -p Trondheim -I mysys.myserver.mydomain.com,/mypath/myinst

    Cold-install the virtual partition Sandefjord from a file at the
    default path /opt/ignite/boot on the current virtual partition

  vparboot -p Sandefjord -I WINSTALL

ERRORS
    vparboot displays error messages on stderr for any of the following
    conditions:

  vp_name does not exist in the monitor.

  vp_name is in some state other than Down, and so cannot be
  booted. Use the vparreset(1M) command instead.

An error occurs while trying to access an Ignite server or cold-install file.

You have specified the BOOT or ALTBOOT device, but the corresponding device has not been configured in vp_name.

NOTE: If the boot device has not been configured properly the vparboot command will complete without error, but the virtual partition will not boot. Two possible reasons for this could be:

+ The BOOT or ALTBOOT attribute was assigned to a device other than a disc or tape.

+ The file at the default or configured kernel path does not exist or is not a bootable image.

AUTHOR
    vparboot was developed by the Hewlett-Packard Company.

SEE ALSO
    vparcreate(1M), vparmodify(1M), vparremove(1M), vparreset(1M), vparstatus(1M), vparresources(5), vpartition(5).

man page

vparcreate
appendix a

vparcreate - Creates a new virtual partition.

vparcreate(1M)   vparcreate(1M)

NAME
    vparcreate - create a virtual partition

SYNOPSIS
    vparcreate -p vp_name [-B boot_attr] [-D db_file] [-S static_attr]
    [-b kernel_path] [-o boot_opts] [-a rsrc]...

DESCRIPTION
    The vparcreate command creates a new virtual partition (vPar) using
    the specified hardware resources. vp_name is a symbolic name for the
    virtual partition and must be used in all references to it. If the -D
    option is specified, the virtual partition is created in db_file.
    Otherwise it is created in the virtual partition monitor database. In
    either case, a virtual partition named vp_name must not already exist
    in the database.Any error terminates the command without creating a
    virtual partition.

    Only a superuser can execute the vparcreate command.

  Options
    No option except -a (add resource) may be specified more than once.
    Resources allocated with the -a option must be available, that is, not
    already allocated to a virtual partition, nor exceeding the overall
    limits of the resources.Resources assigned with multiple -a options
    must not conflict. Violation of any condition is a command error.

    The vparcreate command recognizes the following command line options
    and arguments:

        -p vp_name   Specifies the symbolic name of the virtual
                        partition. The name can consist of alpha-numeric
                        characters A-Z, a-z, 0-9, the underbar character
                        (_), and the period (.). The maximum length of
                        the name is 239 characters. Required.

        -B boot_attr   Specifies the autoboot attribute of the virtual
                        partition. boot_attr can have the following
                        (case-insensitive) values:

    auto   sets the autoboot attribute.

    manual   clears the autoboot attribute.

                        If the autoboot attribute is set to auto, the
                        virtual partition is rebooted after a successful
                        vparreset command or when the virtual partition
                        monitor is first loaded, if appropriate monitor
                        options have been specified.

If the attribute is set to manual, the virtual
partition halts after a vparreset, and does not
boot when the monitor is loaded. It must then be
booted manually with the vparboot command.

If the -B option is omitted, the attribute
defaults to auto.

-D db_file   Create the virtual partition in the virtual
                  partition database contained in db_file. If
                  db_file does not exist, it is created by this
                  command. This option should be used when creating
                  a new virtual partition database.

                  The virtual partition monitor need not be running.
                  If it is, it is not notified of the new virtual
                  partition.

                  Although db_file can reside in any path when
                  accessed as an alternate database, it must be
                  placed in the /stand directory before it can be
                  loaded by the virtual partition monitor as its
                  live database.

                  If the -D option is omitted and the virtual
                  partition monitor is running, the virtual
                  partition is created in the virtual partition
                  monitor's live database. If the monitor is not
                  running, the virtual partition is created in the
                  default database file /stand/vpdb, which is itself
                  created if it does not exist.

-S static_attr Specifies the static vPar attribute. static_attr
               can have the following (case-insensitive) values:

static   sets the static attribute.

dynamic   resets the static attribute.

                  virtual partitions set to static do not support
                  any dynamic resource migration, nor can resource
                  attributes be added/deleted/modified with
                  vparmodify. This attribute becomes effective
                  after any initial resource allocation, so it is
                  possible to assign resources when creating a new
                  virtual partition and still specify that the
                  resulting virtual partition be static.

                  If the -S option is omitted, the attribute

defaults to dynamic.

-b kernel_path   Specifies the absolute path to a bootable kernel
                  for the partition. For example, if a non-
                  partitioned system start string at the ISL prompt
                  is:

ISL> hpux -iS /stand/vmunix

                  the kernel_path is the /stand/vmunix portion of
                  this string.If this option is omitted, the
                  virtual partition is created with a default kernel
                  path of /stand/vmunix.

-o boot_opts   Specifies the command-line string, except for the
                  kernel path, applied when the virtual partition is
                  booted. For example, if a non-partitioned system
                  start string at the ISL prompt is:

ISL> hpux -iS /stand/vmunix

                  the boot_opts string is the -iS portion of this
                  string. Note that if the string includes any
                  whitespace, the string must be quoted.

                  Refer to the virtual partitions administration
                  guide and the chapter titled "Monitor and Shell
                  Commands" for a full list of supported boot option
                  strings.

                  The default is the empty string.

-a rsrc   Adds resources to a virtual partition. rsrc is a
                  hardware resource specification, as described in
                  detail in the vparresources(5) manpage. A summary
                  of resource syntax forms is shown in Table 1
                  below. Multiple -a rsrc specifications in the
                  same command are allowed, but some syntax forms
                  are only allowed once. This in indicated in Table
                  1. In all cases, resources in multiple
                  specifications must not repeat or conflict with
                  each other.

Table 1. Resource syntax summary

Resource	Forms	# times/command
CPU	cpu:path	Multiple
	cpu::num	Once
	cpu:::[min][:[max]]	Once
I/O	io:path[:attr1[,attr2]]	Multiple
Memory	mem::size	Once
	mem:::base:range	Multiple

Certain tasks can affect the outcome of others. To avoid errors, see the detailed description of the dependencies in the vparresources(5) manpage.

RETURN VALUE
       The vparcreate command exits with one of the following values:

       0   Successful completion.
       1   One or more error conditions occurred.

EXAMPLES
       Create the virtual partition called Oslo in the virtual partition monitor database, but do not assign any resources:

   vparcreate -p Oslo

       Create the virtual partition Bergen in the virtual partition monitor database, setting the autoboot attribute and specifying five processors, two of which are bound, 2 Gb of physical memory, and a boot disk:

   vparcreate -p Bergen -a cpu::5 -a cpu:::2:6 \
      -a mem::2048 -a io:1/0/2/0.6.0:boot -B auto

       Since the -b option was not specified, the default kernel path /stand/vmunix will be used at boot time.

ERRORS
       vparcreate displays error messages on stderr for any of the following conditions:

   An invalid option is specified.

   An invalid value is specified for an option or a value is omitted.

   vp_name already exists in the monitor database or specified db_file. Use the vparmodify command instead.

   One or more options other than -a has been specified more than once or the same resource was allocated more than once.

   An unavailable resource (allocated to another virtual partition or exceeding the available resource limit) was specified.

   A value was omitted for an argument that requires one, or a value was supplied for an argument which does not take one.

AUTHOR
       vparcreate was developed by the Hewlett-Packard Company.

SEE ALSO
    vparboot(1M), vparmodify(1M), vparremove(1M), vparreset(1M), vparstatus(1M), vparresources(5), vpartition(5).

vparmodify - Modifies an existing virtual partition.

man page

vparmodify
appendix a

NAME
     vparmodify - modify the attributes of a virtual partition

SYNOPSIS
     vparmodify -p vp_name [-B boot_attr] [-D db_file] [-S static_attr]
     [-b kernel_path] [-o boot_opts] [-P new_vp_name] [-a rsrc]...
     [-m rsrc]... [-d rsrc]...

DESCRIPTION
     The vparmodify command modifies attributes and resources of the
     specified virtual partition. The command can also rename the virtual
     partition. vp_name is a symbolic name for an existing virtual
     partition and must be used in all references to it. vparmodify cannot
     create a virtual partition. Use the vparcreate command for that
     purpose.

     Only a superuser can execute the vparmodify command.

     If the -D option is specified, vp_name in db_file is modified;
     otherwise vp_name in the virtual partition monitor database is
     modified.

     If the static attribute has been configured in vp_name, none of its
     resources may be added, modified, or deleted. Attributes (all options
     except -a, -m, and -d) may be modified. Refer to the -S option
     description.

   Options
     Only the -S, -a, -m, and/or -d options may be specified more than once
     in a command. Resources allocated with the -a option must be
     available, that is, not already allocated to a virtual partition.
     They must also not exceed the overall limits of the resources.
     Resources to be modified (-m) or deleted (-d) must be owned by
     vp_name.Violation of any condition is a command error.

     vparmodify recognizes the following command line options and
     arguments. The options are processed from left to right.

        -p vp_name   Specifies the symbolic name of the existing
                        virtual partition which is to be modified.
                        Required.

        -B boot_attr   Specifies the autoboot attribute of the virtual
                        partition. boot_attr can have the following
                        case-insensitive values:

     auto   sets the autoboot attribute.

     manual   clears the autoboot attribute.

                        If the autoboot attribute is set to auto, the
                        virtual partition is rebooted after a successful

vparreset command or when the virtual partition
monitor is first loaded, if appropriate monitor
options have been specified.

If the attribute is set to manual, the virtual
partition halts after a vparreset and does not
boot when the monitor is loaded. It must then be
booted manually with the vparboot command.

If the -B option is omitted, the attribute is not
changed.

-D db_file   Apply changes to the vp_name contained in db_file.
                  The virtual partition monitor need not be running.
                  If it is, it is not notified of the modification.

                  Although db_file can reside in any path when
                  accessed as an alternate database, it must be
                  placed in the /stand directory before it can be
                  loaded by the virtual partition monitor as its
                  live database.

                  If the -D option is omitted, the virtual partition
                  monitor must be running. Changes are applied to
                  vp_name in the monitor's database. A vp_name in
                  the monitor database must be in the Down state,
                  with one exception: Unbound cpu resources can be
                  added to or deleted from a running virtual
                  partition. This restriction may be relaxed for
                  other types of resource management in a future
                  release.

-S static_attr Specifies the static virtual partition attribute.
                static_attr can have the following values:

static   sets the static attribute.

dynamic   resets the static attribute.

                  If the -S option is omitted, the attribute is not
                  changed.

                  No hardware resource changes can be made to a
                  static virtual partition, that is, the -a, -m, and
                  -d options are not allowed. This restriction
                  applies to all virtual partitions, whether in an
                  alternate database file, or in the monitor's
                  database.

Since command line options are processed left-to-right, you can modify resources in a static partition by specifying -S dynamic on the command line before any resource options, then specifying -S static after all resource options to prevent further resource modifications.

-b kernel_path   Specifies the absolute path to a bootable kernel for the partition. If the option is omitted, the kernel_path is not changed.

-o boot_opts   Specifies the command-line string, except for the kernel path, applied when the virtual partition is booted. For example, if a non-partitioned system start string at the ISL prompt is:

ISL> hpux -iS /stand/vmunix

the boot_opts string is the -iS portion of this string. Note that if the string includes any whitespace, the string must be quoted.

Refer to the virtual partitions administration guide and the chapter titled "Monitor and Shell Commands" for a full list of supported boot option strings.

If the -o option is omitted, the boot_opts is not changed.

-P new_vp_name   Specifies the new name for the virtual partition being modified, that is, after all modifications are successfully applied to vp_name, it is renamed to new_vp_name, assuming no virtual partition with that name already exists in the monitor database or specified alternate database file. The name can consist of alpha-numeric characters A-Z, a-z, 0-9, the underbar character (_), and period (.). The maximum length of the name is 239 characters.

-a rsrc   -a adds resources to a virtual partition.
-d rsrc   -d deletes resources from a virtual partition.
-m rsrc   -m modifies existing resources in a virtual partition. rsrc is a hardware resource specification, as described in detail in the vparresources(5) manpage. A summary of resource syntax forms is shown in Table 1 below. Multiple resource specifications in the same command are

allowed, but some syntax forms are restricted to
specific options, and some are only allowed once.
Both are indicated in Table 1. In any case,
resources in multiple specifications must not
repeat or conflict with each other.

Table 1. Resource syntax summary

Resource	Forms	Options	# times/command
CPU	cpu:path	-a, -d	Multiple
	cpu::num	-a, -m, -d	Once
	cpu:::[min]:[max]	-m	Once
I/O	io:path[:attr1[,attr2]]	-a, -m, -d	Multiple
Memory	mem::size	-a, -m, -d	Once
	mem:::base:range	-a, -d	Multiple

Certain tasks can affect the outcome of others. To avoid errors, see
the detailed description of the dependencies in the vparresources(5)
manpage.

RETURN VALUE
     The vparmodify command exits with one of the following values:

     0   Successful completion.
     1   One or more error conditions occurred.

EXAMPLES
     Change the name of the virtual partition called Oslo to Bergen

   vparmodify -p Oslo -P Bergen

     Turn off the autoboot attribute for the virtual partition Oslo

   vparmodify -p Oslo -B manual

     Add two processors to the virtual partition Bergen in alternate
     database file /stand/Norway

   vparmodify -p Bergen -D /stand/Norway -a cpu::2

ERRORS
     vparmodify displays error messages on stderr for any of the following
     conditions:

   An invalid option is specified.

   An invalid value is specified for an option or a value is
   omitted.

   The specified db_file does not exist, cannot be accessed, or has
   been corrupted.

   vp_name does not exist in the specified db_file or in the monitor
   database.

   new_vp_name already exists in the monitor database or specified
   db_file.

   vp_name is static and you have attempted to change a resource.

One or more options other than -S, -a, -m, -d is specified more than once.

For the -a or -m option, an unavailable resource (allocated to another virtual partition or exceeding the available resource limit) is specified.

For the -m or -d option, the specified resource is not presently assigned to vp_name.

The state of the modified vPar following an error depends on the following factors:

+   If the error is detected during syntax and semantic checks of the

command line, the vPar is not changed.

+   If the error is detected while actually modifying the vPar, AND you

are modifying an alternate database, the vPar is not changed. This

is because changes are not committed until the end of the command.

+   If the error is detected while modifying the vPar, AND you are

modifying the database currently loaded into the monitor, then any

changes made to the point of the error (working left-to-right on

the command line) will remain. This is because changes to the live

database are made incrementally, as they are requested.

AUTHOR
    vparmodify was developed by the Hewlett-Packard Company.

SEE ALSO
    vparboot(1M), vparcreate(1M), vparremove(1M), vparreset(1M),
    vparstatus(1M), vparresources(5), vpartition(5).

vparremove - Removes (deletes) an existing virtual partition.

vparremove(1M)   vparremove(1M)

NAME
     vparremove - remove a virtual partition

SYNOPSIS
     vparremove -p vp_name [-D db_file] [-f]

DESCRIPTION
     The vparremove command deletes a virtual partition previously created
     using the vparcreate(1M) command. All resources associated with the
     virtual partition are made available for allocation to other
     partitions.

     Only a superuser can execute the vparremove command.

     Unintentional use of this command has serious consequences; therefore
     the user is prompted to confirm the operation unless the -f (force)
     option is specified.

   Options
     vparremove recognizes the following command line options and
     arguments:

        -p vp_name   Specifies the unique name of the virtual partition
                       which is to be removed. Required.

        -D db_file   Removes a virtual partition from the partition
                       database contained in db_file. If this option is
                       omitted, the virtual partition is removed from the
                       monitor's database. In this case, the partition
                       must be in the Down state to be removed. Thus it
                       is an error to try to remove the current virtual
                       partition, the one in which the command is
                       executing.

        -f   Specifies the force option. Omits the
                       confirmation dialog before removing the virtual
                       partition. This option is intended for use by
                       scripts and other non-interactive applications.

RETURN VALUE
     The vparremove command exits with one of the following values:

     0   Successful completion.
     1   One or more error conditions occurred.

EXAMPLES
     Destroy the virtual partition Oslo in the partition database currently
     running in the monitor:

     vparremove -p Oslo

Remove virtual partition Oslo? [n]: y

Destroy the virtual partition Oslo in the partition database currently running in the monitor using the force option:

vparremove -f -p Oslo

Delete partition Bergen in partition database file Norway

vparremove -f -D /stand/Norway -p Bergen

ERRORS
vparremove displays error messages on stderr for any of the following conditions:

+ db_file does not exist, cannot be accessed, is not a virtual partition database file, or is corrupt.

+ vp_name does not exist in the monitor's database or in db_file.

+ vp_name in the monitor's database is in some state other than Down.

AUTHOR
vparremove was developed by the Hewlett-Packard Company.

SEE ALSO
vparboot(1M), vparcreate(1M), vparmodify(1M), vparreset(1M), vparstatus(1M), vparresources(5), vpartition(5).

vparreset - Sends a TOC or hard reset to a virtual partition.

vparreset(1M)   vparreset(1M)

NAME
     vparreset - reset a virtual partition

SYNOPSIS
     vparreset -p vp_name [-h|-t] [-q] [-f]

DESCRIPTION
     The vparreset command simulates, at the virtual partition level, the
     RS and TOC operations at a Control-B prompt on the system console.

     Only a superuser can execute the vparreset command.

     vparreset causes the virtual partition monitor to simulate a hard (RS)
     reset or soft (TOC) reset of the specified virtual partition. Either
     operation gathers new Processor Information Module (PIM) data, which
     is displayed unless the -q (quiet) option is also specified.

     Unintentional use of the vparreset command has serious consequences;
     therefore the user is prompted to confirm the operation unless the -f
     (force) option is specified.

   Options
     vparreset recognizes the following command line options and arguments:

       -p vp_name   Specifies the unique name of the virtual partition
                           to be reset.The virtual partition must be in a
                           state other than Down or Crashing. Required.

       -t   Simulates a TOC reset. Displays current PIM data
                           before resetting unless the -q option is also
                           specified.

                           The TOC reset is also the default operation of the
                           command, applied if neither the -h nor -t option
                           is specified.

                           The -t and -h options cannot both be specified in
                           the same command.

       -h   Simulates a hard (RS) reset instead of a TOC.
                           Displays current PIM data before resetting unless
                           the -q option is also specified.

       -q   Bypasses the display of current PIM data when
                           resetting the virtual partition.

       -f   The force option. Omits the confirmation dialog

before resetting the virtual partition. This
option is intended for use by scripts and other
non-interactive applications.

RETURN VALUE
   The vparreset command exits with one of the following values:

   0   Successful completion.
   1   One or more error conditions occurred.

EXAMPLES
   Perform a TOC reset on the virtual partition called Oslo, dumping the
   PIM data:

   vparreset -p Oslo -t
   Reset virtual partition Oslo? [n] y

   Perform a hard reset on virtual partition Bergen skipping the
   confirmation dialog:

   vparreset -p Bergen -h -f

ERRORS
   vparreset displays error messages on stderr for any of the following
   conditions:

   + A required option is omitted.

   + An unknown option is specified.

   + A value is omitted for an argument that requires one, or a value is
   specified for an argument which does not take one.

   + vp_name does not exist in the monitor database, or is in the wrong
   state.

   + Both the -h and -t options are specified.

AUTHOR
   vparreset was developed by the Hewlett-Packard Company.

SEE ALSO
   vparboot(1M), vparcreate(1M), vparmodify(1M), vparremove(1M),
   vparstatus(1M), vparresources(5), vpartition(5).

vparresources - Sends a TOC or hard reset to a virtual partition.

vparresources(5)   vparresources(5)

NAME
     vparresources - description of virtual partition resources and their
     requirements

DESCRIPTION
     Hardware resources are the most important property of a virtual
     partition (vPar). These resources are divided into three major
     categories:

     + CPUs, or processors

     + Memory

     + I/O devices, such as disks, terminals, and printers.

     CPUs are further subdivided into bound and unbound processors. A
     bound processor is interrupt-enabled and, at initial release, cannot
     be de-configured while the vPar is running. An unbound, or floating,
     processor cannot process interrupts, but can be de-configured from a
     running vPar, and assigned to another running vPar.

     Each vPar can configure a subset of total system hardware resources
     such that a given physical resource is assigned to at most one vPar.
     This job is managed by two of the six virtual partition commands:

     + vparcreate(1M), used when creating a new vPar. Resources can only
     be added.

     + vparmodify(1M), used when modifying an existing vPar configuration.
     Resources can be added, modified, or deleted.

     Each command has specific resource syntax and semantic requirements.
     For example, some resource changes can only be made if the target vPar
     is not running. Some syntax forms can be specified multiple times in
     one command. Others can only be specified once.All of these
     conditions are described in the tables below.

     The general form of a resource specification is up to five positional
     fields delimited by colons (":"). No whitespace is allowed within any
     field.

     Table I summarizes the three categories and all the allowable
     forms for each.

     Table II specifies which forms are allowed for each of the three
     tasks (add, modify, or delete).

     Table III is a detailed description of each syntax form and the
     conditions required for its use.

Table I. Resource syntax summary

Resource	Form	# times/command
CPU	cpu:path cpu::num cpu:::[min][:[max]]	Multiple Once Once
I/O	io:path[:attr1[,attr2]]	Multiple
Memory	mem::size mem:::base:range	Once Multiple

The first field is always one of the (case-insensitive) strings cpu, io, or mem.

The second field, when used, is a hardware path, for example, 10/12/6.

num, min, and max are all positive integers.

size and range are positive 64-bit integers in units of megabytes. base is an unsigned 64-bit integer in units of bytes. The commands round each of them upward as required to 64 megabyte boundaries. size, range, and base may each be specified in decimal or in hexadecimal. A hex specification should be preceded by 0x, as in 0x8000000.

The attributes for the I/O specification are zero, one, or both of the following (case-insensitive) strings: ALTBOOT and BOOT. If both are specified, separate them with a comma.

Each of the attributes can be assigned to no more than one I/O device. If it is already assigned to a device, a new assignment silently de-assigns it from its present device. However, one device can associate both attributes.This means it is possible for one device to own both the ALTBOOT and BOOT attributes, but it is not possible for two or more devices to own BOOT.

Users must guard against assigning an attribute to an inappropriate device, for example, assigning BOOT to a tty. The commands do not check for this, nor do they prevent it.

Table II. Allowed forms for each task

Task	Form	Allowed with vPar running
-a (add)	cpu:path cpu::num cpu:::[min][:[max]] (vparcreate only) io:path[:attr1[,attr2]] mem::size mem:::base:range	No Yes N/A No No No
-m (modify)	cpu::num cpu:::[min][:[max]] io:path[:attr1[,attr2]] mem::size	Yes No No No

-d (delete)	cpu:path	No
	cpu::num	Yes
	io:path[:attr1[,attr2]]	No
	mem::size	No
	mem:::base:range	No

The forms above are subject to the following semantic rules enforced by the commands.Note that according to Table II, except for the cpu::num form, a vPar must be in the Down state (or in an alternate database) to apply any of the changes described below. This requirement may be relaxed or removed in a future release.

+ CPUs

+   The total number of CPUs assigned to a vPar, specified by cpu::num, must always be within the range specified by the cpu:::min:max specification. min of these are bound; (num-min) are unbound.

+   Any or all bound CPUs can be specified by explicit path, the cpu:path form. Any that are not so specified are allocated from the available pool and bound by the vPar monitor.

    A corollary to this is that you cannot specify more than the min CPUs by explicit path. If you wish to specify more, you must first increase the min, which in turn may require you to increase the max, num, or both.

    When you use -a cpu:path or -d cpu:path you do not change the total number of CPUs in your vPar.Instead, you replace a monitor-assigned bound CPU with one that you specify (-a) or replace a CPU that you specified with a monitor-assigned CPU (-d).

    Hewlett-Packard recommends that users configure specific CPUs only when required for performance reasons. In other situations, specify only the total number of CPUs (num) and how many of these should be bound (min), and allow the monitor to manage the actual CPUs allocated.

+   Since the monitor is not consulted when you are configuring a vPar in an alternate database (it need not even be running), you can specify any value for min (but <= max) in this case. When this database is loaded into the monitor, the monitor adjusts min downward as required if the specified number of CPUs is not available.

+   Defaults: When a vPar is created, the following defaults are in effect:

    +   min: Platform dependent, usually 1

    +   num: 1

    +   max: If the vPar is created in an alternate database, 32767. If it is created in the live monitor database, max is equal to the total number of CPUs on the entire hardware system.

        You can modify these defaults with command line options to the vparcreate or vparmodify command.

+   Memory

    +   The total amount of memory specified in explicit memory

ranges, using the mem:::base:range specification, must be
less than or equal to the total memory assigned to the vPar
using the mem::size specification.

When you specify a specific range of memory (whether adding
or deleting), you do not change the total amount of memory
assigned to the vPar. When adding, you merely specify that
the particular range you specify be one part of the total
amount assigned to your vPar. When deleting, the specific
range is returned to the pool of unspecified total memory
assigned to the vPar.

Hewlett-Packard recommends that users configure specific
memory ranges only when required for performance reasons. In
other situations, specify only total memory and allow the
monitor to manage the actual ranges allocated.

EXAMPLES
If more than one task is specified in a command, they are processed in
the order (left-to-right) in which they are encountered on the command
line. Some tasks will affect the outcome of others. Here is an
example of correct usage, as well as counterexamples within the
description.

vparcreate -p winona2 -a cpu::2 -a cpu:::2:4 -a cpu:41 -a cpu:45

-a mem::1280 -a mem:::0x40000000:128 -a io:0/8 -a io:1/10

-a 0/8/0/0.5.0:boot

At creation time, before any options are processed, min is equal to 1,
as does num. Assume that the default max is sufficiently high, and
that the specified resources are available for allocation.

+ -a cpu::2 succeeds because num(2) is within the range of the min
and the max.

+ -a cpu:::2:4 then succeeds because num(2) is still within the
required range. Note that if the two options were reversed the
command would return an error due to left-to-right option
processing, and the desired min would exceed the default num.

+ Finally, the specification of the two CPUs at explicit paths 41
and 45 succeeds because such assignments create bound CPUs.
Since we have set min equal to 2, they can be accommodated.
Note that without the first two -a options, the -a cpu:45 option
would fail, because there would only be room for one (the
default) bound CPU.

+ The allocation of 128 MB of specific memory at address
0x40000000 succeeds only because the total allocated memory was
first set to 1280 MB. The 128 MB is taken from that 1280 MB; no
new memory is added as a result of the -a mem:::0x40000000:128
option.

The following vparmodify(1M) command adds two floating (unbound) CPUs
to a vPar that has the Static attribute set. The Static attribute is
then restored.

vparmodify -p winona3 -S dynamic -a cpu::2 -S static

Table III. Detailed resource specifications
    Task: -a cpu:path

Explanation	Assigns a CPU resource at a specific path (bound CPU) to the vPar's configuration. The CPU replaces a monitor-assigned bound CPU. Bound CPUs are able to process interrupts.
Value	A text string of the form returned by the ioscan(1M) command, such as "10/12/6"
Usage Restrictions	The vPar must not be running. This restriction may be removed in a future release. The total number of CPUs at a specific path must be <= min In addition, if the vPar is in the monitor database: o A CPU must exist at path, o It must be available (not assigned to a vPar, including the target vPar).
Usage Guidelines	The addition does not increase either the number of total CPUs or bound CPUs allocated to the vPar. Instead, it replaces a previously bound CPU whose path had been selected by the monitor. To increase total CPU allocation, specify an appropriate new num. To increase the number of bound CPUs, specify a new min. Hewlett-Packard recommends that users configure specific CPUs only when required for performance reasons.In other situations, specify only the total number of CPUs (num) and how many of these should be bound (min), and allow the monitor to manage the actual CPUs allocated.

    Task: -a cpu::num

Explanation	Adds num unbound CPUs to the vPar's configuration. The CPUs are drawn from a systemwide pool of available CPUs.
Value	A positive integer
Usage Restrictions	If the vPar is in an alternate database file or is in the live monitor database but not running: o Total number of CPUs <= max In addition, if the vPar is running: o num CPUs must exist on the system, o They must have been available (not bound to any vPar) at the time the vPar was booted. If another vPar is deleted with the vparremove command, its bound CPUs cannot be added as floaters to a running vPar.

Task: -a cpu:::[min][:[max]]

Explanation	Specifies the minimum and maximum number of CPUs allowed for the vPar. This operation does not allocate any CPUs, but specifies the limits of other allocation tasks. Both min and max are optional. The default min is platform-dependent but is currently = 1. The default max is 32767 if creating a vPar in an alternate database. If creating a vPar in the monitor database, the default max is the total number of CPUs on the entire hardware system.
Value	If specified, min and max must be positive integers such that min <= max.
Usage Restrictions	This option is allowed only in the vparcreate command. min cannot exceed the total number of CPUs. The default total when the vPar is created is 1. Use the -a cpu::num option to change the total before setting a min other than 1. max cannot be less than the total. min cannot be less than the total number of CPUs configured by explicit path.

Task: -a io:path[:attr1[,attr2]]

Explanation	Adds the I/O resource at path to the vPar. If attributes are specified, they are associated with the resource. If the vPar already owns the resource, any specified attributes are added to its configuration. This option only adds specified attributes. The state of unspecified attributes is not changed.
Value	path: A text string of the form returned by the ioscan(1M) command, such as "10/12/6" attr: One or both of the case-insensitive attribute strings ALTBOOT and BOOT. If both are specified, they are separated by a comma (",").
Usage Restrictions	The vPar must not be running. The I/O resource must either be unassigned or (when adding attributes to an already assigned resource) be assigned to the target vPar.
Usage Guidelines	At most one device can be assigned the ALTBOOT and BOOT attributes. Assigning one of these attributes to a device silently deletes it from its former device, if any. Caution:You should assign attributes to appropriate

```
|              |  devices, but this is not checked. For example,  |
|              |  ALTBOOT and BOOT should be assigned to a disk or |
|              |  tape.  Failure to do this may result in an unbootable |
|              |  partition.                                        |
|_____|_____|
```

Task: -a mem::size

Explanation	Specifies the increase, in megabytes rounded upward to a 64 megabyte boundary, in the total amount of memory to be allocated to the vPar. This memory is taken from unspecified ranges of memory available to the system when the partition boots.
Value	A positive 64-bit integer <= 17592186044352
Usage Restrictions	The vPar must not be running. If the vPar is in the monitor database, this memory must physically exist and be available after the memory requirements of all other vPars have been satisfied. If the vPar is in an alternate database file, the assignment always succeeds. The amount of memory actually allocated if the database is loaded into the monitor may be less if some or all of it is needed in other vPars.

Task: -a mem:::base:range

Explanation	Specifies an explicit address space of memory starting at base bytes and extending for range megabytes.Both quantities are rounded upward as required to be aligned on 64 megabyte boundaries.
Values	Base: An unsigned 64-bit integer <= 0xfffffffffc000000 Range: A positive 64-bit integer <= 17592186044352
Usage Restrictions	The vPar must not be running. No part of the range may be already owned by this or another vPar. If the vPar is in the monitor database, the entire range must exist in the system. The total memory allocated in specific ranges must not exceed the vPar's memory size specification.
Usage Guidelines	Addition of specific memory ranges does not increase the total amount of memory allocated to the vPar. Any such memory is a part of that total amount. Caution:It is possible to specify memory ranges and sizes such that none of the vPars will launch. Hewlett-Packard recommends that users configure specific memory ranges only when required for performance reasons. In other situations, specify only total memory and allow the monitor to manage the actual ranges allocated.

|_____|_____|

Task: -m cpu::num

Explanation	Sets the total number of CPUs (bound and unbound) to num.
Value	A positive integer
Usage Restrictions	If the vPar is in an alternate database file or is in the live monitor database but not running: o num must be between min and max. In addition, if the vPar is in the live monitor database and num increases the total: o num CPUs must exist on the system, o They must have been available (not bound to any vPar) at the time the vPar was booted. If another vPar is deleted with the vparremove command, its bound CPUs cannot be added as floaters to a running vPar.

Task: -m cpu:::[min][:[max]]

Explanation	Specifies the minimum and maximum number of CPUs allowed for the vPar. This operation does not allocate any CPUs, but specifies the limits of other allocation tasks. You can change only min or max by not specifying the other field.
Value	If specified, min and max must be positive integers such that min <= max.
Usage Restrictions	The vPar must not be running. min cannot exceed the total number of CPUs. max cannot be less than the total. min cannot be less than the total number of CPUs configured by explicit path.

Task: -m io:path[:attr1[,attr2]]

Explanation	Changes the attributes of the resource to those specified in the option. Omitted attributes are removed from the attribute set. To retain an attribute, it must be specified.
Value	path: A text string of the form returned by the ioscan(1M) command, such as "10/12/6" attr: One or both of the case-insensitive attribute strings ALTBOOT and BOOT. If both are specified, they are separated by a comma (",").

Usage Restrictions	The vPar must not be running. The I/O resource must be assigned to the target vPar. Only attributes may be modified.
Usage Guidelines	At most one device can be assigned the ALTBOOT and BOOT attributes. Assigning one of these attributes to a device silently deletes it from its former device, if any. Caution:You should assign attributes to appropriate devices, but this is not checked. For example, ALTBOOT and BOOT should be assigned to a disk or tape. Failure to do this may result in an unbootable partition.

Task: -m mem::size

Explanation	Specifies the total amount of memory, in megabytes rounded upward to a 64 megabyte boundary, to be allocated to the vPar. Any memory in excess of that specifically allocated by base and range is taken from unspecified ranges of memory available to the system when the partition boots.
Value	A positive 64-bit integer <= 17592186044352
Usage Restrictions	The vPar must not be running. A decrease in total memory allocation must not result in a total less than that of all memory allocated in specific memory ranges. If the vPar is in the monitor database and the specification results in an increased memory allocation, the memory must physically exist and be available after the memory requirements of all other vPars have been satisfied. If the vPar is in an alternate database file and total memory is increased, the assignment always succeeds.The amount of memory actually allocated if the database is loaded into the monitor may be less if some or all of it is needed in other vPars.

Task: -d cpu:path

Explanation	De-assigns the bound CPU at the specified hardware path from the vPar and replaces it with a bound CPU of the monitor's choice. Depending on availability, this may be the same CPU that was de-assigned.
Value	A text string of the form returned by the ioscan(1M) command, such as "10/12/6"
Usage Restrictions	The vPar must not be running. The resource at the specified path must be a CPU resource.

```
|               |   The vPar must own the resource.                |
|_____|_____|
|Usage          | The deletion does not reduce either the number   |
|Guidelines     | of total CPUs or bound CPUs allocated to         |
|               | the vPar. Instead, it replaces the explicitly    |
|               | specified CPU with a bound CPU selected by the   |
|               | monitor.To reduce total CPU allocation,          |
|               | specify an appropriate new num.  To reduce       |
|               | the number of bound CPUs, specify a new min.     |
|               |                                                  |
|               | Hewlett-Packard recommends that users configure  |
|               | specific CPUs only when required for performance |
|               | reasons.In other situations, specify only the    |
|               | total number of CPUs (num) and how many of these |
|               | should be bound (min), and allow the monitor     |
|               | to manage the actual CPUs allocated.             |
|_____|_____|
```

Task: -d cpu::num

```
|Explanation    | Deletes num CPUs from the vPar's total   |
|               | configuration.                           |
|_____|_____|
|Value          | A positive integer                       |
|_____|_____|
|Usage          | The vPar must own at least num CPUs.      |
|Restrictions   |                                          |
|               | The new total number of CPUs >= min      |
|_____|_____|
```

Task: -d io:path[:attr1[,attr2]]

```
|Explanation    | Removes the specified attributes of the      |
|               | resource leaving any previously assigned     |
|               | attributes unchanged and the resource itself |
|               | assigned to the vPar.  If no attribute is    |
|               | specified, removes the resource and all its  |
|               | attributes.                                  |
|_____|_____|
|Value          | path:  A text string of the form returned    |
|               |        by the ioscan(1M) command,            |
|               |        such as "10/12/6"                      |
|               |                                              |
|               | attr:  One or both of the case-insensitive   |
|               |        attribute strings ALTBOOT and BOOT.  If|
|               |        both are specified, they are separated |
|               |        by a comma (",").                      |
|_____|_____|
|Usage          | The vPar must not be running.                |
|Restrictions   |                                              |
|               | The I/O resource must be assigned to the     |
|               | target vPar.                                 |
|_____|_____|
|Usage          | Deleting an attribute from an I/O device does |
|Guidelines     | not cause it to be assigned to another.  You  |
|               | must do that in a separate option or command. |
|               |                                              |
|               | At most one device can be assigned the ALTBOOT and |
|               | BOOT attributes.                             |
|               |                                              |
|               | Caution:You should assign attributes to appropriate |
|               | devices, but this is not checked. For example, |
|               | ALTBOOT and BOOT should be assigned to a disk or |
```

```
    |               |  tape.  Failure to do this may result in an unbootable |
    |               |  partition.                                            |
    |_____|_____|
```

Task: -d mem::size

```
|Explanation    |  Specifies the decrease, in megabytes rounded    |
|       |  upward to a 64 megabyte boundary, in the        |
|       |  amount of total memory allocated to the vPar        . |
|_____|_____|
|Value          |  A positive 64-bit integer <= 17592186044352         |
|_____|_____|
|Usage          |  The vPar must not be running.                       |
|Restrictions   |                                                      |
|               |  The vPar must own at least the specified            |
|               |  amount (after rounding) of non-specific             |
|               |  memory.                                             |
|               |                                                      |
|               |  The decrease must not result in a total less        |
|               |  than that of all memory allocated in specific       |
|               |  memory ranges.                                      |
|_____|_____|
```

Task: -d mem:::base:range

```
|Explanation    |  De-assigns an explicit address space of memory    |
|               |  starting at base bytes and extending for          |
|               |  range megabytes.Both quantities are rounded       |
|               |  upward as required to be aligned on 64 megabyte   |
|               |  boundaries.                                       |
|_____|_____|
|Values         |  Base:   An unsigned 64-bit integer <= 0xfffffffffc000000 |
|               |  Range:  A positive 64-bit integer <= 17592186044352 |
|_____|_____|
|Usage          |  The vPar must not be running.                     |
|Restrictions   |                                                    |
|               |  The vPar must own the entire range.               |
|               |                                                    |
|               |  Either the start or end point of the              |
|               |  specified range must match the start or end       |
|               |  point of an existing range.                       |
|_____|_____|
|Usage          |  De-assigning specific memory ranges does not decrease |
|Guidelines     |  the total amount of memory allocated to the vPar. |
|               |                                                    |
|               |  Caution:It is possible to specify memory ranges   |
|               |  and sizes such that none of the vPars will launch.|
|               |  Hewlett-Packard recommends that users configure   |
|               |  specific memory ranges only when required for     |
|               |  performance reasons.  In other situations, specify|
|               |  only total memory and allow the monitor to manage |
|               |  the actual ranges allocated.                      |
|_____|_____|
```

SEE ALSO
     vparboot(1M), vparcreate(1M), vparmodify(1M), vparremove(1M),
     vparreset(1M), vparstatus(1M), vpartition(5).

vparstatus - Displays virtual partition and available resources information.

man page

vparstatus
appendix a

vparstatus(1M)   vparstatus(1M)

NAME
     vparstatus - display information about one or more virtual partitions

SYNOPSIS
     vparstatus [-v | -M] [-p vp_name]... [-D db_file]

     vparstatus -A [-M]

     vparstatus -w

     vparstatus -e

     vparstatus -R [-p vp_name]

DESCRIPTION
     The various forms of the vparstatus command display:

     + The attributes and hardware resources associated with one or more
     virtual partitions (vPars) in either summary (the default) or
     detailed format. The -M option presents the same data in machine-
     readable format.

     + Resources currently available, that is, not assigned to any virtual
     partition. The -M option presents the same data in machine-
     readable format.

     + The name of the current virtual partition, that is, the virtual
     partition from which the command is run.

     + The virtual partition monitor's event log.

     + Processor Information Module (PIM) data from the most recent
     resetting of a virtual partition.

     Only a superuser can execute the vparstatus command.

     If no arguments are supplied, vparstatus displays a summary format of
     all attributes and resources of all virtual partitions in the monitor
     database. One or more virtual partitions may be specified explicitly
     in order to restrict the output to information about the selected
     virtual partitions. The -D option lists similar information from an
     alternate database file, but with a major difference. See the
     description of the -D option for further details.

     There are three major listing formats. The format chosen depends on
     command options and forms:

     + The summary format lists name, attributes, and resource totals. It
     is displayed if neither the -v nor -M option is used.

     + The detailed format lists name, attributes, and detailed resource
     assignments, one per line with annotative headings. The -v option
     produces this format.

+ The machine readable format displays the same information as the detailed format, except that field descriptive headers are omitted, and the information is all on one line. Individual fields are separated from each other by four delimiters. These are all described below.

Three additional formats are provided for the -w, -e and -R options.

Information displayed by vparstatus includes the following:

+ The name of the virtual partition (limited to 30 characters in summary format)

+ The state of the virtual partition, from the list below:

Up: The virtual partition has notified the monitor that it is up. This is the normal state of a running virtual partition, however it does not necessarily mean that the virtual partition has completed its initialization and is fully operational.

Down: The virtual partition is fully halted. This could be the result of a normal /etc/shutdown -h command, or a vparreset of a partition with its autoboot attribute set to manual. It is also the initial state of a virtual partition immediately after the virtual partition monitor is started.

Load: The monitor is loading the kernel image of the virtual partition. This state precedes the Boot state.

Boot: The virtual partition has been launched, but has not completely booted.

Crash: The virtual partition is shutting down ungracefully (either a panic or a reset)

Shut: The virtual partition is shutting down gracefully

Hung: The virtual partition has stopped sending heartbeat messages to the monitor.

N/A: The virtual partition is in an alternate database file, and so has no state.

+ The static/dynamic resource attribute

+ The auto/manual boot attribute

+ The path to the kernel (limited to 25 characters in summary format)

+ The boot options (limited to 5 characters in summary format)

+ Summary or detailed CPU, I/O, and memory resource allocations

Options
   vparstatus recognizes the following command line options and arguments:

   -p vp_name   Restricts the command display to information about vp_name. By default, information about all virtual partitions in the monitor database or specified alternate partition database is displayed. Multiple vp_names may be specified, except when used to display PIM data.

   -D db_file   Displays information from the alternate partition database file db_file rather than from the monitor database.

The attributes and resources of a vPar in an alternate
database file were specified in either the vparcreate
or vparmodify command, but have not necessarily been
checked for existence on a running system. They are
referred to as "requested" information. Existence of
the attributes and resources of a vPar in the live
monitor database have been verified; they are referred
to as "effective" information.

-v   Presents a detailed display, one attribute or resource
per line. Each attribute and resource type is
identified.

CPU resources are identified by path when path
information is available. Some CPU resources may not
be known when displaying the status of alternate
database vPars or vPars in the Down state. In this
case, "<no path>" is displayed.

-A   Displays information about available resources (that
is, those not assigned to any virtual partition) in
the virtual partition monitor's database. The monitor
must be running.Resources are displayed one per
line.

-M   Displays information in a machine readable format.
Individual fields are separated by one of four
delimiters:

+ The colon (:) separates each field and resource
type.For example, the state, attribute
information, and kernel path would be displayed as:

Up:Static,Autoboot:/stand/vmunix

+ The semicolon (;) separates subfields of a resource
type.For example, CPU resources are shown as:

5/10;33,37;51,53,55;<>,<>,<>

where the first subfield shows the minimum and
maximum CPUs configured for the virtual partition;
the second subfield lists the bound, or specified
path, CPUs specifically configured by the user; the
third subfield lists the remaining bound CPUs,
which are assigned by the monitor; and the final
subfield lists the unbound, or floating, CPUs.

In the example above, the paths of the unbound CPUs
are not known. This could be the case because the
example vPar is in an alternate database, or the
vPar is in a Down state for which unbound CPUs are
not assigned.In this case, "<>" is displayed in
place of the path.

+ The comma (,) separates individual items in a list
of similar items, such as the fixed path CPUs in
the previous example.

+ The slash (/) separates all other related items,
such as the CPU minimum and maximum in the same
example.

Elements in the display are in the same order as the

corresponding non-machine-readable display (-v or -A).

-w   Displays the name of the current virtual partition
(the one in which the command is executed). The
monitor must be running.

-e   Displays the monitor's event log, a circular file
roughly 4K bytes long. Once the file is full, new
entries overlay old ones to the nearest character. As
a result, the first entry displayed may be missing
some leading characters.The monitor must be running.

-R   Displays Processor Information Module (PIM) data from
the most recent reset of the specified virtual
partition. If a virtual partition is not specified,
PIM data from the current virtual partition, that is,
the one in which the command is executed, is
displayed.

If the virtual partition has not been reset, or if PIM
data has been cleared since then, no PIM data is
available so a message to that effect is displayed.

The monitor must be running.

RETURN VALUE
     The vparstatus command exits with one of the following values:

     0   Successful completion.
     1   Syntax error or invalid option.

EXAMPLES
     These examples assume the existence of an N-class hardware system,
     Europe, on which the virtual partition database Norway is currently
     loaded in the virtual partition monitor.Norway has two configured
     virtual partitions: Oslo, and Bergen. The vparstatus command is run
     from Oslo.

     Europe has eight CPUs, two System Bus Adapters (SBAs), each with six
     Local Bus Adapters (LBAs), and 2 Gbytes of main memory. These
     resources are allocated among Oslo and Bergen as follows:

     Oslo:

+ Two bound CPUs at hardware paths 33 and 37. The CPU at 33 was
   specified by the user with the -a cpu:path resource
   specification. The CPU at 37 was assigned by the monitor from
   the pool of CPUs available when Oslo was booted.
+ One floating (unbound) CPU at hardware path 41.
+ One SCSI boot disk at SBA/LBA/path 0/0/2/0.6.0.
+ One terminal at 0/0/4/0.
+ One LBA (0/4) to which are attached several LAN adapters.
+ Specific memory addresses 0x4000000 to 0xc000000 (Range = 64 MB)
   and 0x20000000 to 0x40000000 (Range = 128 MB). These specific
   ranges are part of a total memory allocation of 704 MB.

     Bergen:

+ Two bound CPUs at hardware path 97 and 101, both assigned by the
   monitor.
+ Two unbound CPUs at hardware paths 93 and 99.
+ One SCSI boot disk at 1/4/0/0.5.0.
+ One LBA (1/10) to which are attached several LAN adapters
+ Specific memory 0x44000000 to 0x50000000 (Range = 192 MB) and
   0x60000000 to 0x80000000 (Range = 512 MB).These specific
   ranges are part of a total memory allocation of 768 MB.

Display a summary format of all attributes and resources in all
virtual partitions:

```
# vparstatus
[Virtual Partition]
  Boot
Virtual Partition NameState Attributes Kernel Path   Opts
============================== ===== ========== ========================== =====
OsloUp    Stat,Auto /stand/vmunix
BergenUp    Dyn,Manl /stand/vmunix

[Virtual Partition Resource Summary]
   CPU    Num      Memory (MB)
   CPU   Bound/   IO # Ranges/
Virtual Partition Name Min/Max  Unbound  devs Total MB    Total MB
============================== ================  ==== ====================
Oslo   2/  4    21    3   2/640  704
Bergen   2/  4    22    2   2/704  768
```

Display detailed attributes and resources of partition Oslo:

```
# vparstatus -p Oslo -v
[Virtual Partition Details]
Name:       Oslo
State:      Up
Attributes:   Static,Autoboot
Kernel Path:  /stand/vmunix
Boot Opts:

[CPU Details]
Min/Max:  2/4
Bound by User [Path]:33
Bound by Monitor [Path]:  37
Unbound [Path]:  41

[IO Details]
   0.0.2.0.6.0 BOOT
   0.0.4.0
   0.4

[Memory Details]
Specified [Base  /Range]:  0x4000000/64
  (bytes) (MB)    0x20000000/128
Total Memory (MB):  704
```

Display Bergen's CPU resources in machine-readable format:

```
# vparstatus -p Bergen -M
Bergen:Up:Dynamic,Manual:/stand/vmunix::2/4;;97,101;93,99:1.4.0.0.5.0 BOOT,1.10
:0x44000000/192,0x60000000/512;768
```

Display the name of the current virtual partition:

```
# vparstatus -w
The current virtual partition is Oslo.
```

AUTHOR
      vparstatus was developed by the Hewlett-Packard Company.

SEE ALSO
      vparboot(1M), vparcreate(1M), vparmodify(1M), vparremove(1M),
      vparreset(1M), vparresources(5), vpartition(5).

vpartition - Displays information about the vPars Command Line Interface.

```
vpartition(5)          vpartition(5)
```

NAME
     vpartition - display information about the Virtual Partition Command
     Line Interface

SYNOPSIS
     vpartition

DESCRIPTION
     This manpage gives a listing and brief description of the commands
     which are used to manage virtual partitions.

Command	Description
vparboot	Boot (start) a virtual partition.
vparcreate	Create a new virtual partition.
vpardump	Manage monitor dump files.
vparextract	Extract memory images from a running virtual partition system.
vparmodify	Modify an existing virtual partition.
vparreloc	Relocate the load address of a vmunix file, determine if a vmunix file is relocatable, or promote the scope of symbols in a relocatable vmunix file.
vparremove	Remove (delete) an existing virtual partition.
vparreset	Send a TOC or hard reset to a virtual partition.
vparresources	Description of virtual partition resourcs and their requirements.
vparstatus	Display virtual partition and available resources information.
vparutil	Get and set SCSI parameters for disk devices from a virtual partition.

AUTHOR
     vpartition was developed by the Hewlett-Packard Company.

SEE ALSO
     vparboot(1M), vparcreate(1M), vpardump(1M), vparextract(1M),
     vparmodify(1M), vparreloc(1M), vparremove(1M), vparreset(1M),
     vparstatus(1M), vparutil(1M), vparresources(5).

vparutil - Works with SCSI-related information of disks in a vPar.

man page

vparutil
appendix a

vparutil(1M)   vparutil(1M)

NAME
      vparutil - get and set SCSI parameters for disk devices from a virtual
      partition

SYNOPSIS
      vparutil -g dev_path

      vparutil -s dev_path [id] [rate]

DESCRIPTION
      The vparutil command gets and sets SCSI paramaters for a specified
      SCSI device from a running virtual partition system.

      Only a superuser can execute the vparutil command.

   Options
      vparutil recognizes the following command-line options:

          -g   Gets the SCSI parameters for the specified SCSI disk device,
                dev_path.

          -s   Sets the SCSI parameters for the specified SCSI disk device,
                dev_path.

          vparutil recognizes the following command-line operands:

          dev_path   The device path of the SCSI disk device.

          id   The SCSI ID for the specified disk device.

          rate   The SCSI rate for the specified disk device.

EXAMPLES
      Set the SCSI ID for disk at 0/0/2/0.6.0 to 3:

      # vparutil -s 0/0/2/0.6.0 3

RETURN VALUE
      0 Successful.
      1 Could not communicate with virtual partition monitor.
      >1 Other error.

AUTHOR
      vparutil was developed by the Hewlett-Packard Company.

Appendix B

Superdome Virtual Partitions

Superdome vPars

At the time this book is going to press I have been working with the very first prerelease vPars software for Superdome. This appendix contains salient information related to vPars on Superdome based on my preliminary work. All of the material covered throughout this book applies to vPars on Superdome. The hardware paths of Superdome are substantially different from those on the L-Class and N-Class systems used in the examples throughout this book. I will, therefore, cover some brief examples of vPars on Superdome that include path-related information.

Each Superdome hard partition (nPartition) is the equivalent of a separate server. The examples of L-Class and N-Class systems that are used throughout this book are like a Superdome nPartition. We can, therefore, load several vPars on each nPartition provided that we meet all the requirement for vPars at the time of this writing, such as: a separate boot device for each vPar; each Local Bus Adapter (LBA) assigned to only one vPar; a minimum of one CPU per vPar; and so on. For the upcoming example we have indeed met these requirements.

The Guardian Service Processor (GSP) on the Superdome is used to supply console control for the Superdome complex. By connecting to the GSP you can select the nPartition that will have console control. You can switch the console control to any of the nPartitions in the Superdome complex. This is different from the Ctrl-A function we use to switch the console between vPars. When we connect to our nPartition using the console through the GSP, we are connected to the nPartition, not to one of the vPars within the nPartition. As part of the configuration of vPars in an nPartition, we will assign the core I/O card to one of the four vPars in our nPartition.

Let's begin our Superdome vPar work by viewing a complete Superdome complex and then focusing on one nPartition that will be used to support multiple vPars.

The Hierarchy of Partitions

Figure B-1 shows the hierarchy of partitions on our Superdome complex:

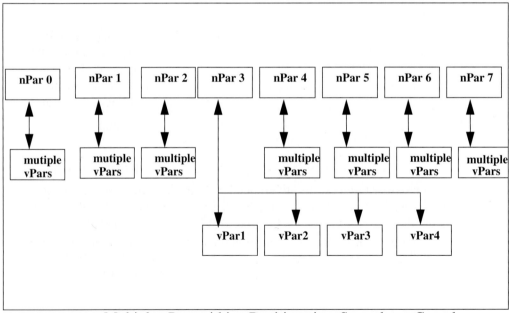

Figure B-1   Multiple vPars within nPartitions in a Superdome Complex

Each nPartition can contain multiple vPars. *nPar3* of the nPartitions in Figure B-1 is expanded to show that it will run four Virtual Partitions in our upcoming example.

Let's now move on to view the hardware in the nPartition in which we'll create our vPars.

nPartition and Superdome Background

nPartitions are hard partitions within a Superdome platform. A Superdome server can support anywhere from one to 16 nPartitions, each supporting its own operating system, applications, peripherals, and networks. Currently, each nPartition can host HP-UX operating environments. When the Intel IPF versions of Superdome are available, nPartions will support Linux and Windows environments as well. There are currently two nPartitions supported on an rp8400.

Superdome is based on a modular set of components. The system is built on a cell-based hierarchical crossbar architecture that can be configured as one large symmetric multiprocessor or as several independent partitions. A cell, or cell board, is the basic building block of the Superdome system; it is a symmetric multiprocessor (SMP), containing up to four processors and up to 16 GBytes of main memory.

At their core, nPartitions support a user-defined partitioning of resources and isolate hardware and software errors. A Superdome nPartition consists of one or more cells that communicate over a high-bandwidth, low-latency crossbar fabric. Cells are grouped into physical structures called *cabinets* or *nodes*. Special programmable hardware in the cells defines the boundaries of a partition in such a way that isolation is enforced from the actions of other partitions. Each partition runs its own independent operating system. Different partitions may be executing different versions of the operating system. In the future, when Itanium Processor Family (IPF) CPUs are supported, different operating systems, such as HP-UX, Linux, and Windows, will be supported simultaneously in different partitions.

Each partition has its own CPUs, memory, and I/O resources, consisting of the resources of the cells that make up the partition. Resources may be removed from one partition and added to another without having to physically manipulate the hardware, just by using commands that are part of the systems management interface. Additionally, dynamic additions of new nPartitions are supported. Adding or removing cell boards to or from existing nPartitions does not affect other partitions.

Working with nPartitions and vPars

To assign the components that will be assigned to the vPars within an nPartition, you must run **ioscan** in the nPartition in which the vPars will be created. This provides a list of all I/O components, CPUs, and so on, available in the nPartition to be used in the vPars. The **ioscan** does not show components in the other nPartitions. The following full **ioscan** listing shows all the components in the nPartition in which we'll create our four vPars:

```
# ioscan -f

Class       I  H/W Path         Driver     S/W State  H/W Type     Description
===============================================================================
root        0                   root       CLAIMED    BUS_NEXUS
cell        0  5                cell       CLAIMED    BUS_NEXUS
ioa         0  5/0              sba        CLAIMED    BUS_NEXUS    System
Bus Adapter (804)
ba          0  5/0/0            lba        CLAIMED    BUS_NEXUS    Local PCI
Bus Adapter (782)
tty         0  5/0/0/0/0        asio0      CLAIMED    INTERFACE    PCI
Serial (103c1048)
lan         0  5/0/0/1/0        btlan      CLAIMED    INTERFACE    HP PCI
10/100Base-TX Core
ba          1  5/0/1            lba        CLAIMED    BUS_NEXUS    Local PCI
Bus Adapter (782)
ext_bus     0  5/0/1/0/0        c720       CLAIMED    INTERFACE    SCSI C895
Fast Wide LVD
target      0  5/0/1/0/0.0      tgt        CLAIMED    DEVICE
disk        0  5/0/1/0/0.0.0    sdisk      CLAIMED    DEVICE       SEAGATE
ST318404LC
target      1  5/0/1/0/0.1      tgt        CLAIMED    DEVICE
disk        1  5/0/1/0/0.1.0    sdisk      CLAIMED    DEVICE       HP
73.4GST373405LC
target      2  5/0/1/0/0.7      tgt        CLAIMED    DEVICE
ctl         0  5/0/1/0/0.7.0    sctl       CLAIMED    DEVICE       Initiator
target      3  5/0/1/0/0.15     tgt        CLAIMED    DEVICE
ctl         1  5/0/1/0/0.15.0   sctl       CLAIMED    DEVICE       HP
A5272A
ba          2  5/0/2            lba        CLAIMED    BUS_NEXUS    Local PCI
Bus Adapter (782)
ba          3  5/0/2/0/0        PCItoPCI   CLAIMED    BUS_NEXUS    PCItoPCI
Bridge
lan         1  5/0/2/0/0/4/0    btlan      CLAIMED    INTERFACE    HP A5506B
```

```
PCI 10/100Base-TX 4 Port
lan         2   5/0/2/0/0/5/0   btlan    CLAIMED    INTERFACE    HP A5506B
PCI 10/100Base-TX 4 Port
lan         3   5/0/2/0/0/6/0   btlan    CLAIMED    INTERFACE    HP A5506B
PCI 10/100Base-TX 4 Port
lan         4   5/0/2/0/0/7/0   btlan    CLAIMED    INTERFACE    HP A5506B
PCI 10/100Base-TX 4 Port
ba          4   5/0/3           lba      CLAIMED    BUS_NEXUS    Local PCI
Bus Adapter (782)
ba          5   5/0/3/0/0       PCItoPCI CLAIMED    BUS_NEXUS    PCItoPCI
Bridge
lan         5   5/0/3/0/0/4/0   btlan    CLAIMED    INTERFACE    HP A5506B
PCI 10/100Base-TX 4 Port
lan         6   5/0/3/0/0/5/0   btlan    CLAIMED    INTERFACE    HP A5506B
PCI 10/100Base-TX 4 Port
lan         7   5/0/3/0/0/6/0   btlan    CLAIMED    INTERFACE    HP A5506B
PCI 10/100Base-TX 4 Port
lan         8   5/0/3/0/0/7/0   btlan    CLAIMED    INTERFACE    HP A5506B
PCI 10/100Base-TX 4 Port
ba          6   5/0/4           lba      CLAIMED    BUS_NEXUS    Local PCI
Bus Adapter (782)
ext_bus     1   5/0/4/0/0       c720     CLAIMED    INTERFACE    SCSI C895
Fast Wide LVD
target      4   5/0/4/0/0.0     tgt      CLAIMED    DEVICE
disk        2   5/0/4/0/0.0.0   sdisk    CLAIMED    DEVICE       SEAGATE
ST318404LC
target      5   5/0/4/0/0.1     tgt      CLAIMED    DEVICE
disk        3   5/0/4/0/0.1.0   sdisk    CLAIMED    DEVICE       HP
73.4GST373405LC
target      6   5/0/4/0/0.7     tgt      CLAIMED    DEVICE
ctl         2   5/0/4/0/0.7.0   sctl     CLAIMED    DEVICE       Initiator
target      7   5/0/4/0/0.15    tgt      CLAIMED    DEVICE
ctl         3   5/0/4/0/0.15.0  sctl     CLAIMED    DEVICE       HP
A5272A
ba          7   5/0/6           lba      CLAIMED    BUS_NEXUS    Local PCI
Bus Adapter (782)
ext_bus     2   5/0/6/0/0       c720     CLAIMED    INTERFACE    SCSI C895
Fast Wide LVD
target      8   5/0/6/0/0.0     tgt      CLAIMED    DEVICE
disk        4   5/0/6/0/0.0.0   sdisk    CLAIMED    DEVICE       SEAGATE
ST318404LC
target      9   5/0/6/0/0.1     tgt      CLAIMED    DEVICE
disk        5   5/0/6/0/0.1.0   sdisk    CLAIMED    DEVICE       HP
73.4GST373405LC
target     10   5/0/6/0/0.2     tgt      CLAIMED    DEVICE
disk        6   5/0/6/0/0.2.0   sdisk    CLAIMED    DEVICE       HP
73.4GST373405LC
target     11   5/0/6/0/0.7     tgt      CLAIMED    DEVICE
ctl         4   5/0/6/0/0.7.0   sctl     CLAIMED    DEVICE       Initiator
target     12   5/0/6/0/0.15    tgt      CLAIMED    DEVICE
ctl         5   5/0/6/0/0.15.0  sctl     CLAIMED    DEVICE       HP
A5272A
ba          8   5/0/8           lba      CLAIMED    BUS_NEXUS    Local PCI
Bus Adapter (782)
fc          0   5/0/8/0/0       td       CLAIMED    INTERFACE    HP
Tachyon TL/TS Fibre Channel Mass Storage Adapter
fcp         0   5/0/8/0/0.8     fcp      CLAIMED    INTERFACE    FCP
Protocol Adapter
ba          9   5/0/9           lba      CLAIMED    BUS_NEXUS    Local PCI
Bus Adapter (782)
ba         10   5/0/9/0/0       PCItoPCI CLAIMED    BUS_NEXUS    PCItoPCI
Bridge
lan         9   5/0/9/0/0/4/0   btlan    CLAIMED    INTERFACE    HP A5506B
PCI 10/100Base-TX 4 Port
lan        10   5/0/9/0/0/5/0   btlan    CLAIMED    INTERFACE    HP A5506B
PCI 10/100Base-TX 4 Port
lan        11   5/0/9/0/0/6/0   btlan    CLAIMED    INTERFACE    HP A5506B
PCI 10/100Base-TX 4 Port
lan        12   5/0/9/0/0/7/0   btlan    CLAIMED    INTERFACE    HP A5506B
PCI 10/100Base-TX 4 Port
ba         11   5/0/10          lba      CLAIMED    BUS_NEXUS    Local PCI
Bus Adapter (782)
fc          1   5/0/10/0/0      td       CLAIMED    INTERFACE    HP
Tachyon TL/TS Fibre Channel Mass Storage Adapter
fcp         1   5/0/10/0/0.8    fcp      CLAIMED    INTERFACE    FCP
```

```
Protocol Adapter
ba          12  5/0/11              lba      CLAIMED     BUS_NEXUS    Local PCI
Bus Adapter (782)
ext_bus      3  5/0/11/0/0          c720     CLAIMED     INTERFACE    SCSI C87x
Fast Wide Differential
target      13  5/0/11/0/0.1        tgt      CLAIMED     DEVICE
disk         7  5/0/11/0/0.1.0      sdisk    CLAIMED     DEVICE       HP DVD-ROM 304
target      14  5/0/11/0/0.3        tgt      CLAIMED     DEVICE
tape         0  5/0/11/0/0.3.0      stape    CLAIMED     DEVICE       HP C1537A
target      15  5/0/11/0/0.7        tgt      CLAIMED     DEVICE
ctl          6  5/0/11/0/0.7.0      sctl     CLAIMED     DEVICE       Initiator
ba          13  5/0/12              lba      CLAIMED     BUS_NEXUS    Local PCI
Bus Adapter (782)
ext_bus      4  5/0/12/0/0          c720     CLAIMED     INTERFACE    SCSI C895
Fast Wide LVD
target      16  5/0/12/0/0.0        tgt      CLAIMED     DEVICE
disk         8  5/0/12/0/0.0.0      sdisk    CLAIMED     DEVICE       SEAGATE
ST318404LC
target      17  5/0/12/0/0.1        tgt      CLAIMED     DEVICE
disk         9  5/0/12/0/0.1.0      sdisk    CLAIMED     DEVICE       HP 73.4GST373405LC
target      18  5/0/12/0/0.2        tgt      CLAIMED     DEVICE
disk        10  5/0/12/0/0.2.0      sdisk    CLAIMED     DEVICE       HP 73.4GST373405LC
target      19  5/0/12/0/0.7        tgt      CLAIMED     DEVICE
ctl          7  5/0/12/0/0.7.0      sctl     CLAIMED     DEVICE       Initiator
target      20  5/0/12/0/0.15       tgt      CLAIMED     DEVICE
ctl          8  5/0/12/0/0.15.0     sctl     CLAIMED     DEVICE       HP
A5272A
ba          14  5/0/14          lba      CLAIMED   BUS_NEXUS   Local PCI Bus Adapter (782)
ba          15  5/0/14/0/0      PCItoPCI CLAIMED   BUS_NEXUS   PCItoPCI Bridge
lan         13  5/0/14/0/0/4/0  btlan    CLAIMED   INTERFACE   HP A5506B
PCI 10/100Base-TX 4 Port
lan         14  5/0/14/0/0/5/0  btlan    CLAIMED   INTERFACE   HP A5506B
PCI 10/100Base-TX 4 Port
lan         15  5/0/14/0/0/6/0  btlan    CLAIMED   INTERFACE   HP A5506B
PCI 10/100Base-TX 4 Port
lan         16  5/0/14/0/0/7/0  btlan    CLAIMED   INTERFACE   HP A5506B
PCI 10/100Base-TX 4 Port
memory       0  5/5                 memory   CLAIMED   MEMORY      Memory
processor    0  5/10           processor CLAIMED  PROCESSOR   Processor
processor    1  5/11           processor CLAIMED  PROCESSOR   Processor
processor    2  5/12           processor CLAIMED  PROCESSOR   Processor
processor    3  5/13           processor CLAIMED  PROCESSOR   Processor
```

Note that the cell itself, which is for all intents and purposes a separate server, is at address *5*. There are four processors, shown at the end of the listing, at *5/10, 5/11, 5/12,* and *5/13*. We're going to assign many of the I/O components in this listing to our four vPars, so you may end up referring back to the diagram.

Defining and Configuring the Four vPars

After having run the **ioscan** in the nPartition on our Superdome, we have determined that the following configurations will exist in our four vPars:

vPar *bvvpard1*

```
name          bvvpard1
processors    min of one (bound) max of three (two unbound)
memory        2048 MB
LBA Core I/O  5/0/0 (all components on 0/0 are implied)
LAN           5/0/9
boot disk     5/0/12/0/0.0.0
kernel        /stand/vmunix (this is default)
autoboot      off (manual)
console       on core I/O at 5/0/0
```

vPar *bvvpard2*

```
name          bvvpard2
processors    min of one (bound) max of four (two unbound)
memory        2048 MB
LAN           5/0/14
boot disk     5/0/6/0/0.0.0
kernel        /stand/vmunix (this is default)
autoboot      off (manual)
console       virtual
```

vPar *extappd2*

```
name          extappd2
processors    min of one (bound) max of four (two unbound)
memory        2048 MB
LAN           5/0/3
boot disk     5/0/4/0/0.0.0
kernel        /stand/vmunix (this is default)
autoboot      off (manual)
console       virtual
```

vPar *intappd2*

```
name          intappd2
processors    min of one (bound) max of four (two unbound)
memory        2048 MB
```

```
LAN           5/0/2
boot disk     5/0/1/0/0.0.0
kernel        /stand/vmunix (this is default)
autoboot      off (manual)
console       virtual
```

We have all the software we need on our vPars disks, including HP-UX, vPars software, patches, and so on.

Now that we have the full **ioscan** of all the components in the nPartition and have mapped out the components we'd like to have in our four vPars, we can issue the **vparcreate** commands to create the four vPars.

man page

vparcreate appendix a

```
vparcreate -p bvvpard1 -B manual -b /stand/vmunix -a cpu:::1:3
-a mem::2048 -a io:5/0/9 -a io:5/0/12 -a io:5/0/12/0/0.0.0:boot
-a io:5/0/0 -a io:5/0/11

vparcreate -p bvvpard2 -B manual -b /stand/vmunix -a cpu:::1:4
-a mem::2048 -a io:5/0/6 -a io:5/0/14 -a io:5/0/6/0/0.0.0:boot

vparcreate -p extappd2 -B manual -b /stand/vmunix -a cpu:::1:4
-a mem::2048 -a io:5/0/4 -a io:5/0/3 -a io:5/0/4/0/0.0.0:boot

vparcreate -p intappd2 -B manual -b /stand/vmunix -a cpu:::1:4
-a mem::2048 -a io:5/0/1 -a io:5/0/2 -a io:5/0/1/0/0.0.0:boot
```

These commands use the same form covered in chapters earlier in the book. Chapter 2 covered several examples of using **vparcreate** its options.

Notice that vPar *bvvpard1* has in it the core I/O card at *5/0/0*, which give it console access, and the tape and DVD-ROM interface at *5/0/11*, because this vPar will be used as an Ignite-UX server

After having created and booted all four vPars, we can check the status of each and view their respective components with **vparstatus -v** as shown in the following listing:

man page

vparstatus appendix a

```
# vparstatus -v
[Virtual Partition Details]
Name:         bvvpard2                    <-- vPar bvvpard2
State:        Up
Attributes:   Dynamic,Manual
Kernel Path:  /stand/vmunix
Boot Opts:
```

```
[CPU Details]
Min/Max:  1/4
Bound by User [Path]:
Bound by Monitor [Path]:  5.10
Unbound [Path]:

[IO Details]
   5.0.6
   5.0.14
   5.0.6.0.0.0.0  BOOT

[Memory Details]
Specified [Base  /Range]:
        (bytes) (MB)
Total Memory (MB):  2048

[Virtual Partition Details]                    <-- vPar bvvpard1
Name:          bvvpard1
State:         Up
Attributes:    Dynamic,Manual
Kernel Path:   /stand/vmunix
Boot Opts:

[CPU Details]
Min/Max:  1/3
Bound by User [Path]:
Bound by Monitor [Path]:  5.11
Unbound [Path]:

[IO Details]
   5.0.9
   5.0.12
   5.0.12.0.0.0.0  BOOT
   5.0.0

[Memory Details]
Specified [Base  /Range]:
        (bytes) (MB)
Total Memory (MB):  2048

[Virtual Partition Details]                    <-- vPar extappd2
Name:          extappd2
State:         Up
Attributes:    Dynamic,Manual
Kernel Path:   /stand/vmunix
Boot Opts:

[CPU Details]
Min/Max:  1/4
Bound by User [Path]:
Bound by Monitor [Path]:  5.12
Unbound [Path]:

[IO Details]
   5.0.4
   5.0.3
   5.0.4.0.0.0.0  BOOT
```

```
[Memory Details]
Specified [Base  /Range]:
         (bytes) (MB)
Total Memory (MB):  2048

[Virtual Partition Details]
Name:          intappd2                        <-- vPar intappd2
State:         Up
Attributes:    Dynamic,Manual
Kernel Path:   /stand/vmunix
Boot Opts:

[CPU Details]
Min/Max:  1/4
Bound by User [Path]:
Bound by Monitor [Path]:  5.13
Unbound [Path]:

[IO Details]
   5.0.1
   5.0.2
   5.0.1.0.0.0.0  BOOT

[Memory Details]
Specified [Base  /Range]:
         (bytes) (MB)
Total Memory (MB):  2048
#
```

man page

vparstatus appendix a

We now have four vPars set up with the components that we have spec-ified. The output of this **vparstatus** command is identical to that we viewed in the earlier L-Class and N-Class examples in the book except that the paths employed are those from a Superdome.

The Console

We can use *Ctrl-A* to toggle between the four vPars on the console in the nPartition in which we're working. The console on the core I/O card at *5/0/0* in our nPartition is configured as part of vPar *bvvpard2*. Figure B-2 shows using *Ctrl-A* to toggle between the vPars using the console:

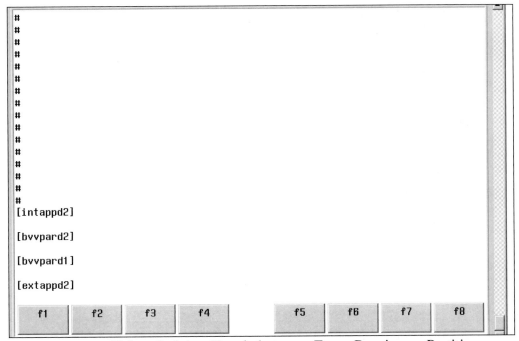

Figure B-2 Using *Ctrl-A* to Toggle between Four vPars in an nPartition

Figure B-2 shows hitting *Ctrl-A* four consecutive times in order to switch the vPars virtual console between our four vPars, named *intappd2*, *bvvpard2*, *bvvpard1*, and *extappd2*. As covered earlier in the book, when you switch between vPars with *Ctrl-A* you are supplied with the name of the console-connected vPar in brackets.

Since each of the vPars has a LAN card associated with it, we can connect with *Telnet* to any of the vPars over the network as well as using the console in Figure B-2.

Keep in mind that the console we're using is for the entire Superdome complex. We selected the nPartition in which our four vPars are configured and then switched between the vPars with *Ctrl-A*.

We connect to the GSP of the Superdome complex using the IP address of the GSP. When we log in to the GSP, the top screen in Figure B-3 appears. We then issue *CO*, which produces a list of consoles for the nPartitions in the Superdome as shown on the bottom of Figure B-3:

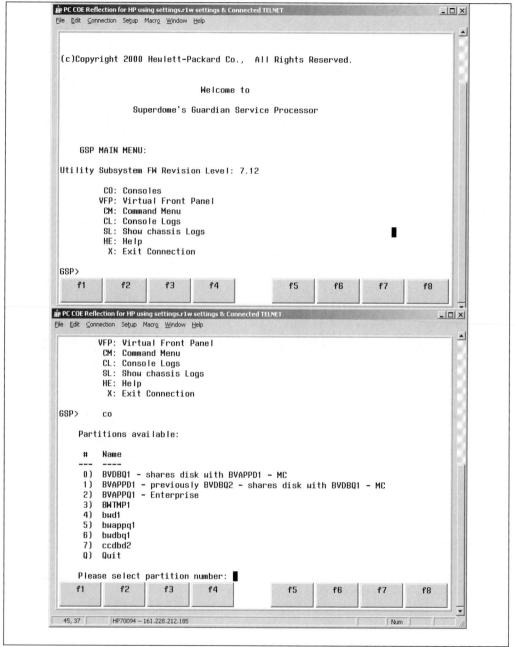

Figure B-3 Using *Ctrl-A* to Toggle between Four vPars in an nPartition

When we select the nPartition in which our vPars are configured, we are given console access to the nPartition and we can switch between the vPars as we did in Figure B-2. The console-related work in Superdome requires you to first select the nPartition in which you want to work and then issue *Ctrl-A* to switch between vPars. When working with the console, *Ctrl-B* brings you to the GSP main menu.

The environment we ended up with after configuring the four vPars looks like that shown in Figure B-4:

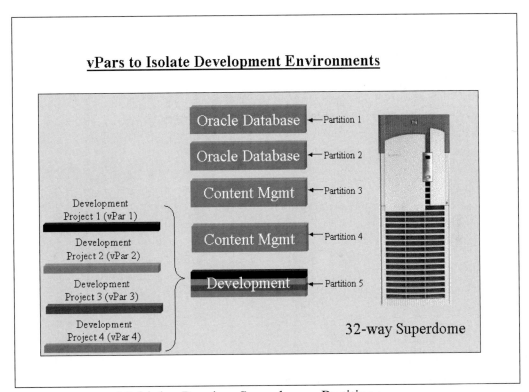

Figure B-4 Multiple vPars in a Superdome nPartition

Although the Superdome vPars software used in this appendix is new, prerelease software, it operates in the Superdome environment in the same way it operates on other systems. The commands work in the same manner on all systems, and the vPars operation is consistent.

INDEX

fulfill your needs

Want to know about new products, services and solutions from Hewlett-Packard Company — as soon as they're invented?

Need information about new HP services to help you implement new or existing products?

Looking for HP's newest solution to a specific challenge in your business?

HP Computer News features the latest from HP!

4 easy ways to subscribe, and it's FREE:

- **fax** complete and fax the form below to (651) 430-3388, or

- **online** sign up online at www.hp.com/go/compnews, or

- **email** complete the information below and send to hporders@earthlink.net, or

- **mail** complete and mail the form below to:

Twin Cities Fulfillment Center
Hewlett-Packard Company
P.O. Box 408
Stillwater, MN 55082

reply now to receive the first year FREE!

name _____ title _____

company _____ dept./mail stop _____

address _____

city _____ state _____ zip _____

email _____ signature _____ date _____

please indicate your industry below:

- ☐ accounting
- ☐ education
- ☐ financial services
- ☐ government
- ☐ healthcare/medical
- ☐ legal
- ☐ manufacturing
- ☐ publishing/printing
- ☐ online services
- ☐ real estate
- ☐ retail/wholesale distrib
- ☐ technical
- ☐ telecommunications
- ☐ transport and travel
- ☐ utilities
- ☐ other: _____

HP's world-class education and training offers hands on education solutions including:

- Linux
- HP-UX System and Network Administration
- Advanced HP-UX System Administration
- IT Service Management using advanced Internet technologies
- Microsoft Windows NT/2000
- Internet/Intranet
- MPE/iX
- Database Administration
- Software Development

HP's new IT Professional Certification program provides rigorous technical qualification for specific IT job roles including HP-UX System Administration, Network Management, Unix/NT Servers and Applications Management, and IT Service Management.

 become hp certified

http://education.hp.com

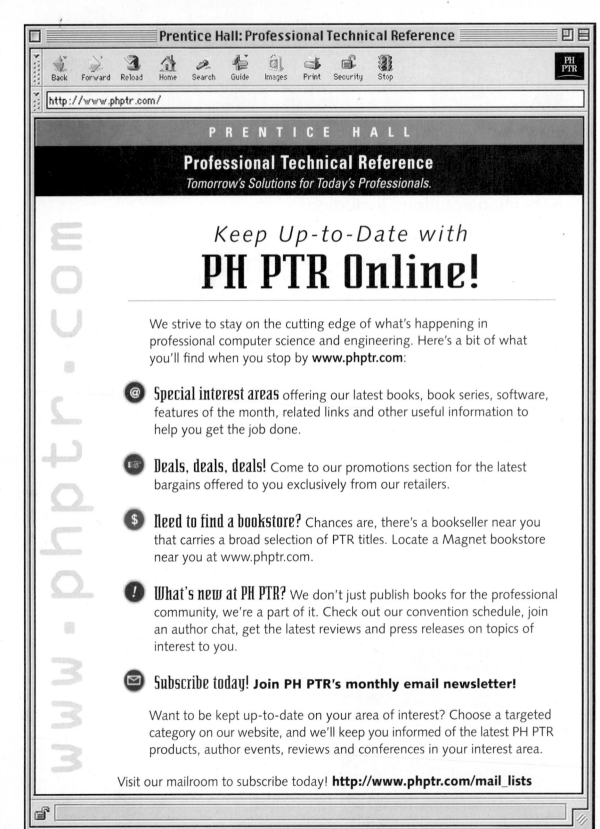